# INTRODUCTION TO INDUSTRIAL ORGANIZATION

SECOND EDITION

# INTRODUCTION TO INDUSTRIAL ORGANIZATION

SECOND EDITION

# LUÍS M. B. CABRAL

THE MIT PRESS

CAMBRIDGE, MASSACHUSETTS · LONDON, ENGLAND

© 2017 Massachusetts Institute of Technology

All rights reserved. No part of this book may be reproduced in any form by any electronic or mechanical means (including photocopying, recording, or information storage and retrieval) without permission in writing from the publisher.

This book was set in Melior by diacriTech, Chennai. Printed and bound in the United States of America.

Library of Congress Cataloging-in-Publication Data

Names: Cabral, Luis M. B., author.
Title: Introduction to industrial organization / Luis M.B. Cabral.
Description: Second edition. | Cambridge, MA : MIT Press, [2017] | Includes
    bibliographical references and index.
Identifiers: LCCN 2016045858 | ISBN 9780262035941 (hardcover : alk. paper)
Subjects: LCSH: Industrial organization (Economic theory)
Classification: LCC HD2326 .C33 2017 | DDC 338.6—dc21 LC record available
at https://lccn.loc.gov/2016045858

10  9  8  7  6  5  4  3  2  1

# Contents

# PREFACE

Sixteen years have passed since the first edition of *Introduction to Industrial Organization* (IIO). Meanwhile, a lot has happened in the world and in the field of industrial organization (IO). A second edition of IIO was thus long overdue.

There are many things new in the new edition. It has been my experience that IIO can be used as a text both in undergraduate economics and business courses; and in various non-economics masters programs. With that in mind, Part I now includes a more comprehensive overview of the basic microeconomics required for the understanding of IO: consumer utility and demand, firm costs and pricing (including price discrimination), competitive markets, market failure.

IO has witnessed a tremendous boost in terms of empirical analysis; however, most textbooks provide little guidance in this area. The present edition provides an introduction to statistical methods in three important areas: demand identification (Section 2.3); analysis of cartels and collusion (Section 9.4); and modeling product differentiation (Section 14.1).

In response to many requests, I added selected advanced materials. First, several chapters now include advanced sections (in smaller type) that provide an analytical treatment of ideas previously presented verbally. End-of-chapter exercises help the reader push the boundary, (a) formalizing ideas that are only briefly touched upon in the text; (b) generalizing results that are presented in simple form; or (c) applying conceptual results to the empirical analysis of particular industries (I included a new section at the end of each chapter: "applied exercises").

Finally, much of what is new in this edition corresponds to new and updated examples, both in the main text and as separate "boxes."

Despite all of these innovations and additions, *IIO 2nd Edition* retains the basic spirit of *IIO 1st Edition*: a book that is *issue* driven rather than *methodology* driven. Although I make extensive use of models (because I think they are very useful ways of understanding reality), I only introduce a new model when this is justified in terms of the marginal benefit in understanding some issue.[a] The focus on issues is also reflected on the focus on policy implications. While this was already the case in *IIO 1st Edition*, *IIO 2nd Edition* includes a policy section at the end of most chapters.

a. In particular, I should emphasize that the list of references in the book does *not* reflect a balanced survey of the IO literature. To stress this point, I have chosen not to make direct reference to sources in the text, leaving bibliographic references to notes at the end of the text. (These are the notes marked with numbers, as opposed to footnotes as this one, which are marked with letters.)

## ACKNOWLEDGMENTS

*IIO 1st Edition* included a long lists of acknowledgements. Since 2000, the number of teachers, students and other readers who provided suggestions, corrections — or simply encouragement — has enlarged my debt roll considerably. I apologize for possible omissions in what is now a long list:[b] Dan Ackerberg, Mark Armstrong, Helmut Bester, Bruno Cassiman, Allan Collard-Wexler, Pascal Courty, Greg Crawford, Leemore Dafny, Jan De Loecker, Kenneth Elzinga, Joe Farrell, Alfonso Gambardella, Joshua Gans, David Genesove, Ben Hermalin, Mitsuru Igami, Jos Jansen, Przemyslaw Jeziorski, Chris Knittel, Tobias Kretschmer, Francine LaFontaine, Ramiro Tovar Landa, Robin Lee, Frank Mathewson, David Mills, GianCarlo Moschini, Petra Moser, Hiroshi Ohashi, Ariel Pakes, Michael Peitz, Rob Porter, Michael Riordan, Daniil Shebyakin, John Small, Adriaan Soetevent, Scott Stern, John Sutton, Frank Verboven, Reinhilde Veugelers, Len Waverman, Matthew Weinberg, Ali Yurukoglu, Peter Zemsky, Christine Zulehner, and various anonymous reviewers who took their time to read previous drafts. Claire Finnigan, Mike Cheely and John Kim provided excellent research assistance. Finally, I thank various classes at London Business School, London School of Economics, Berkeley, Yale, and New York University, whom I taught based on previous versions of this book and from whom I received useful feedback. Unfortunately, I alone remain responsible for remaining errors and omissions.

b. Since much of what was in the first edition is also present in the second edition, the following lists includes acknowledgements included in the first edition as well.

# WHAT IS INDUSTRIAL ORGANIZATION?

What is industrial organization? It might help to start by clarifying the meaning of "industrial." According to Webster's *New World Dictionary*, "industry" refers to "manufacturing productive enterprises collectively, especially as distinguished from agriculture" (definition 5 a). "Industry" also means "any large-scale business activity," as in the tourism industry, for example (definition 4 b).

This double meaning is a frequent source of confusion regarding the object of industrial organization. For our purpose, "industrial" should be interpreted in the sense of Webster's definition 4 b. That is, industrial organization applies equally well to the steel industry and to the tourism industry; as far as industrial organization is concerned, there is nothing special about manufacturing.

Industrial organization is concerned with the *workings of markets and industries, in particular the way firms compete with each other.* The study of how markets operate, however, is the object of microeconomics; as a Nobel prize winner put it, "there is no such subject as industrial organization," meaning that industrial organization is nothing but a chapter of microeconomics.[1] The main reason for considering industrial organization as a separate subject is its emphasis on the study of a firm's strategies that are characteristic of market interaction: price competition, product positioning, advertising, research and development, and so forth. Moreover, whereas microeconomics typically focuses on the extreme cases of monopoly and perfect competition, industrial organization is primarily concerned with the intermediate case of oligopoly, that is, competition between a few firms (more than one, as in monopoly, but not as many as in competitive markets).

For the above reasons, a more appropriate definition of the field would be something like "economics of imperfect competition." But the term "industrial organization" was adopted, and I am not the one to change it.

> Industrial organization is concerned with the workings of markets and industries, in particular the way firms compete with each other.

## 1.1 AN EXAMPLE

Examples are often better than definitions. In this section, I look into the market for anti-ulcer, anti-heartburn drugs, a case that touches on a number of issues of interest to industrial organization. The case thus provides a useful introduction to the next section, where I look more systematically at the central questions addressed by industrial organization.

Until the late 1970s, there was no effective drug to treat ulcers; severe cases required surgery. Then a research project at Smith, Kline & French (which is now part of GlaxoSmithKline) culminated with the discovery of cimetidine, a wonder drug sold under the brand name Tagamet. The production cost of Tagamet was rather small compared to the price for which it was sold. In cases like this, the huge gap between price and cost is bound to raise a variety of issues. For example, it may seem unfair that many suffering patients be deprived of a cheap-to-produce drug simply because price is so high. Then again, without revenues from drugs such as Tagamet it seems impossible for firms like Smith, Kline & French to continue churning out blockbuster drugs.

The fact is that the market for anti-ulcer drugs was enormous. Although Smith, Kline & French had a patent for cimetidine (valid until 1997), this did not stop other pharmaceutical giants from coming up with alternative products: Zantac, introduced by Glaxo in 1983; Pepcid, introduced by Merck in 1986; and Axid, introduced by Eli Lilly in 1988.

For many industry experts, Zantac, Pepcid, and Axid were little more than a copycats (also known as "me too" drugs). In fact, reviews of clinical trials indicated that there was little difference in the success rates of the various drugs; in other words, one drug could easily substitute for any of the other ones. Why wasn't then price competition more intense? The answer is: advertising.

> BELLYACHE BATTLES. We knew that the battle for your bellyaches would be big, but we had no idea it would be so bloody. Hundreds of millions of dollars are being poured into advertising designed to establish brand loyalty for either Tagamet HB or Pepcid AC. Zantac 75 will join the fray shortly.
>
> These drugs were blockbusters as prescription ulcer treatments; now that they are available over the counter for heartburn their manufacturers have really taken off the gloves.[2]

Nor is this specific to anti-ulcer and heartburn drugs. Overall, the advertising budgets of large pharmaceutical companies are of the same order of magnitude as their research budgets. What matters is not just the product's worth, but also what consumers — and doctors, who frequently act as agents for the final consumer — think the product is worth.

Glaxo emerged as the winner of this advertising battle. It "set out to make heartburn into an acute and chronic 'disorder' that came with serious consequences if not treated twice daily with the company's two-dollar pill."[3] By 1988, Zantac had overtaken Tagamet as the world's best-selling drug.

Zantac's patent expired in the late 1990s, paving the way for competition by generics. A generic is a chemically equivalent drug that is mainly sold under the chemical name (Ranitidine, in the case of Zantac) rather than under the brand name. Notwithstanding numerous claims that generic Zantac has the same effect as branded Zantac, the latter still manages to command a large market share while selling at a much higher price. In July 1999, shortly after patent expiry, discount drug seller RxUSA was quoting a 30-tablet box of 300 mg Zantac at $85.95. For a little more than that, $95, one could buy a 250-tablet box of 300 mg generic Zantac Ranitidine — that is, for 7.5 times less per tablet. More than a decade after patent expiry, price differences remain significant: in January 2014, 150 mg Zantac cost almost 40 cents per tablet, whereas the corresponding generic sold for about 8 cents. Another testament to the enduring value of a strong brand is that, in 2006, Boehringer Ingelheim paid more than $500 million dollars for the US rights to Zantac.

At the time of Zantac's launch, Glaxo was an independent company. Since then, it first merged with Wellcome to form GlaxoWellcome, then with SmithKline (which in turn resulted from a then recent merger) to form GlaxoSmithKline.[a] Frequently, these mergers are heralded as the sources of important synergies. For example, when GlaxoWellcome was formed, the merging parties argued that the combination of Wellcome's AZT and Glaxo's 3TC worked better against AIDS than either drug alone.[4] Critics, however, see it primarily as a source of greater market power: if you cannot beat the competitor, then buy it.

## 1.2 CENTRAL QUESTIONS

The example in the previous section illustrates several issues that industrial organization is concerned with (see below, in italics): for decades, GlaxoWellcome was a firm that commanded a significant degree of *market power* in the anti-ulcer and heartburn therapeutical segment (the relevant *market definition*). GlaxoWellcome, which resulted from the *merger* of Glaxo and Wellcome, established its position by means of a clever *R&D strategy* that allowed it to enter an industry already dominated by SmithKline; and by means of an aggressive *marketing strategy* that increased its market share. For a period of time, Zantac's position was protected by *patent rights*. This is no longer the case, meaning that *differentiating the product* with respect to the incoming rivals (generics producers) is now a priority.

In this section, I attempt to formulate the object of industrial organization in a more systematic way. One can say that the goal of industrial organization is to address

a. It's a good thing the merged firms did not keep all of their names, else we would have to spell GlaxoWellcomeSmith-KlineFrench. An even more impressive example is given by Sanofi: if every one of its predecessor firms kept its name, the company would be called — take a deep breath — Sanofi Synthelabo Hoechst Marion Roussel Rhone Poulenc Rohrer Marion Merril Dow! (exclamation mark added).

the following four questions: (a) Do firms have market power? (b) How do firms acquire and maintain market power? (c) What are the implications of market power? (d) What role is there for public policy with regard to market power?

Since all of these questions revolve around the notion of market power, it may be useful to make this notion more precise. **Market power** may be defined as the ability to set prices above cost, specifically above incremental or marginal cost, that is, the cost of producing one extra unit.[b] So, for example, if GlaxoWellcome spends $10 to produce a box of Zantac and sells it for $50, then we say that it commands a substantial degree of market power.

Now for the questions.

■ **IS THERE MARKET POWER?** Understandably, this is an important question, in fact, a crucial one. If there is no market power, then there is little point in the study of industrial organization.

Over the years, many empirical studies have attempted to measure the extent of market power. Assuming that costs are proportional to output, a good approximation to the extent of market power can be obtained from data on prices, output and profit rates.[c] One study along these lines found that the extent of market power in the American economy is very low, a conclusion that follows from observing relatively low profit rates.[5] This finding is consistent with one of the central tenets of the so-called Chicago school of economics: as long as there is free entry into each industry, the extent of market power is never significant. If a firm were to persistently set prices above cost, a new firm would find it profitable to enter the market and undercut the incumbent. Therefore, market power cannot persist, the argument goes.[d]

Not every economist agrees with this view, either at a theoretical or at an empirical level. From an empirical point of view, an alternative approximation to the value of marginal cost is obtained by dividing the increase in cost from year $t$ to year $t + 1$ by the increase in output in the same period. Based on this approach, a study estimates that prices may be as much as three times larger than marginal cost.[7]

Evidence from particular industries also suggests that the extent of market power may be significant. Take, for example, the US airline industry. A 1996 US government report analyzed average fares in 43 large airports. In 10 of these airports, one or a few airlines held a tight control over takeoff and landing slots. The report found that, on average, fliers were paying 31% more at these airports than at the remaining 33 airports.[8] In other words, the report suggests that airlines which manage to control the critical asset of airport access hold a significant degree of market power.

Further examples could be supplied. These would not necessarily be representative of what takes place in every market. To be sure, there are a large number of industries where firms hold little or no market power (cf Section 4.1). The point is that there are *some* industries where market power exists to a significant extent.

b. A rigorous definition of marginal cost and other cost concepts is given in Section 3.1. If costs are proportional to output, then marginal cost is equal to unit cost.

c. The profit rate, $r$, is given by revenues minus cost divided by costs: $r = (R - C)/C$, where $R$ is revenues and $C$ is costs. If costs are proportional to output, then costs are given by unit cost times output: $UC \times Q$, where $UC$ is unit cost and $Q$ is output. Revenues, in turn, are given by price times quantity: $R = P \times Q$, where $P$ is price. It follows that $r = (P - UC)/UC$, so $r$ is a good measure of the gap between price and unit cost (which in this case is also equal to marginal cost).

d. The theory of **contestable markets** formalizes this argument.[6]

■ **HOW DO FIRMS ACQUIRE AND MAINTAIN MARKET POWER?** Market power translates into higher profits. Creating and maintaining market power is therefore an important part of a firm's value-maximization strategy.

How do firms acquire market power? One possibility is to be legally protected from competition, so that high prices can be set without new competitors entering the market. For example, in the 1940s and 1950s Xerox developed the technology of plain-paper photocopying, and patented it. Given the legal protection provided by Xerox's patents, it could raise prices to a significant level without attracting competition (cf Box 15.1).

Firm strategy may also play an important role in establishing market power. Take, for example, the case of the British Sky Broadcasting Group (BSkyB), a leading firm in the British digital TV market (formed in 1990 by the merger of Sky Television and British Satellite Broadcasting). Attempting to preempt the competition, in 1999 BSkyB introduced an aggressive package that included a free set-top decoder box, free Internet access, and a 40% discount on telephone charges.[9] The plan, which was largely successful, was to create an early lead in installed base of subscribers, an early lead that would hopefully become permanent. A more recent example is given by Samsung Electronics. Attempting to break into the lucrative smartphone market, Samsung sold their iPhone-like handsets at significantly lower prices than Apple's; and took a bet by being among the first to use Google's new Android operating system. By 2012, Samsung had already captured a third of the smartphone market.[10]

Creating market power is only one part of the story. A successful firm must also be able to maintain market power. Patents expire. Imitation takes place. Protected industries are deregulated. What can incumbents do in order to maintain their position? The airline industry provides an example. American Airlines managed to drive out various competitors who attempted to enter into its Dallas/Forth Worth hub: Vanguard, Sun Jet, Western Pacific. Fares on the route between Dallas and Kansas City, for example, fell from $108 to $80 when Vanguard entered the market. After Vanguard exited, American gradually raised fares up to $147. Joel Klein, then head of the Antitrust Division at the Justice Department, said that American's strategy achieved more than just driving current rivals out of the market — it also sent a clear signal to potential future entrants: "A sophisticated economist compared it to choosing between two fields with 'no trespassing' signs. One has two dead bodies in it, the other has no dead bodies in it. Which field would you feel ready to trespass?"[11] Reputation for toughness is a reliable means of maintaining a position of market power.

A more recent example from the high-tech world is given by Apple Computer. By a combination of constant innovation and clever marketing, the Cupertino giant has managed to maintain a strong market position for a long time. Particularly important is Apple's "ecosystem" of devices and software: "its phones, tablets, computers, and the mobile and desktop operating systems that run them are blending into a single, inseparable whole."[12]

In different chapters of this text, especially in Chapters 11–16, I will examine a large set of strategies that firms may deploy in order to create and maintain their market power.

■ **WHAT ARE THE IMPLICATIONS OF MARKET POWER?** From the firm's point of view, market power implies greater profits and greater firm value. From a social welfare point of view — or from a policymaker point of view, if we believe policymakers pursue the collective good — the implications are more complicated.

The first-order effect of a high price is a transfer from consumers to firms:[e] for each extra dollar in price, each buyer is transferring one extra dollar to the seller. If regulators put a greater weight on consumer welfare than on profits, then this transfer should be seen as a negative outcome. In fact, antitrust and competition policies are to a great extent motivated by the goal of protecting consumers from these transfers (see the next question).[f]

But, in addition to a transfer effect, a high price also implies an inefficient allocation of resources. High airfares, for example, mean that there are potential fliers who refrain from buying tickets even though the cost of carrying them as passengers would be very low. From a social point of view, it would be efficient to fly many of these potential travelers: although the value they derive from flying is lower than the price (hence they don't fly), that value is greater than the cost of flying (which is much lower than price). The loss that results from the absence of these sales is the **allocative inefficiency** implied by market power.[g]

"The best of all monopoly profits is the quiet life:"[13] A monopolist does not need to be bothered with competition. More generally, firms with greater market power have less incentives to be cost efficient, one may argue. For example, for many years European airlines were known to be less efficient than North-American airlines. To a great extent, this efficiency gap resulted from the more intense competition in the North-American market.[h] In other words, market power implies a second type of inefficiency: **productive inefficiency**, which we define as the increase in cost that results from market power.[i]

When market power is artificially maintained by government intervention, a third type of inefficiency may result: rent seeking. By **rent seeking** I mean unproductive resources spent by firms in an attempt to influence policymakers. Consider, for example, the following news article regarding AT&T's effort to maintain its position in the cable television market:

> This summer, AT&T Corp. faced the specter of cities around the country requiring it to open its cable television lines to rival Internet companies ... The threat never really materialized. Why not? It depends on whom you ask.
>
> AT&T attributes its success to its ability to explain the issues to local officials ... [Others have a different opinion:] "It comes down to bribery or threats," says Greg Simon, co-director of Opennet Coalition, a group of companies that has launched its own lobbying effort to promote open access.[14]

Another example of large amounts of resources spent in an attempt to influence decisionmakers is the 1998 US v. Microsoft case. Netscape, Sun Microsystems, and Microsoft

e. By "first-order" I mean the effect that is quantitatively most significant.

f. An alternative perspective on antitrust and competition policy is that it serves to protect the interests of firms. See Section 5.4.

g. A rigorous definition of this concept is given in Section 4.4.

h. Since European airline deregulation in the 1990s the situation has changed considerably.

i. Again, we defer the more precise definition to a later chapter. The discussion of the above hypothesis (market power leads to productive inefficiency) can be found in Chapter 5.

itself would not have spent the vast amounts they did spend if the operating system industry were not as profitable as it is; thus the idea that rent seeking is a consequence of market power.

Along similar lines, a more recent example is provided by Amazon's effort to maintain its dominance in the e-book retail market. When its business strategy was challenged by Apple's "agency model," Amazon approached the US Department of Justice (DOJ) with extensive legal arguments that the DOJ later used to sue Apple for anticompetitive practices.[15,j]

To summarize, the above paragraphs support the view that market power, good as it might be for firms, is bad for society. First, it makes the owners of firms richer at the expense of consumers. Second, it decreases economic efficiency (allocative and productive efficiency). Third, it induces firms to waste resources in order to achieve and maintain market power. However, from a *dynamic* point of view, an argument can be made in favor of market power:

> As soon as we go into the details and inquire into the individual items in which progress was most conspicuous, the trail leads not to the doors of those firms that work under conditions of comparatively free competition but precisely to the doors of the large concerns.[16]

This argument is one of the central points of the Austrian school, led by its greatest exponent, J. Schumpeter, author of the above quotation. I will examine it in greater detail in Section 15.1. Like the Chicago school, the Austrian school has a very clear position when it comes to market power. However, whereas a Chicago economist would argue that market power does not exist, a Schumpeterian would rather say that market power exists — and it's a good thing that it does, for market power is a precondition for innovation and progress.

■ **IS THERE A ROLE FOR PUBLIC POLICY AS REGARDS MARKET POWER?** In the context of industrial organization, the primary role of public policy is to avoid the negative consequences of market power. Public policy in this area can be broadly divided into two categories: regulation and antitrust (or competition policy).[k] Regulation (economic regulation) refers to the case when a firm retains monopoly or near-monopoly power and its actions (e.g., the price it sets) are directly under a regulator's oversight. For example, ConEdison, a US electricity and gas supplier, needs regulatory approval in order to change its rates.

Antitrust policy (or competition policy) is a much broader field. The idea is to prevent firms from taking actions that increase market power in a detrimental way. A couple of examples may help.

- For the past two decades, Mars and Unilever have engaged in a series of legal cases in European courts. The issue is the legality of Unilever's exclusivity policies regarding retail ice cream sales. In many European countries, Unilever imposes fridge exclusivity: if a store accepts a fridge paid by Unilever, then

j. I will return to this case in Section 9.5.

k. The terminology "antitrust" is more common in the US, whereas "competition policy" is the corresponding European term; see Section 5.5.

the store can only use the fridge to stock Unilever products. Mars claims that exclusivity effectively makes it impossible for Mars to sell Snickers ice cream and related products as most stores have no space for more than one fridge. Unilever responds that it's their fridges and that they require return on an expensive investment. Different but similar cases in various European countries have come to different conclusions, sometimes favorable to Unilever, sometimes favorable to Mars (see also Section 12.1).

- In March 2011, AT&T announced that it planned to purchase T-Mobile USA, a smaller wireless operator. Five months later, the US Department of Justice (DOJ) formally announced that it would seek to block the takeover, arguing that it would increase market power substantially. At first AT&T gave signs that it would defy DOJ's decision, but eventually the bid was abandoned. Although the merger might have brought some benefits to consumers, competition between the would-be merging parties has also been a positive force. For example, in 2013 T-Mobile USA announced that it would pay contract cancellation fees of AT&T subscribers who wanted to switch to T-Mobile.

The above two examples provide an idea of the variety of situations that may fall under the scope of public policy. The overall rationale is to prevent and remedy situations where market power may reach unreasonable levels, to the detriment of society — consumers in particular. Over the course of the next chapters, we will examine several other areas for policy intervention motivated by the goal of curbing market power.

As was stated earlier, the Chicago school takes a very different approach. The claim is that, in a world of free competition, market power is never very significant. In fact, the few situations where market power does exist result precisely from government intervention. In other words, the Chicago school reverses the order of causation: it's not that market power prompts government intervention but the exact opposite — government intervention creates market power, protecting the interests of firms and not those of consumers. As Milton Friedman, a leader of the Chicago school, put it in the late 1990s:

> Because we all believed in competition 50 years ago, we were generally in favor of antitrust. We've gradually come to the conclusion that, on the whole, it does more harm than good. [Antitrust laws] tend to become prey to the special interests. Right now, who is promoting the Microsoft case? It is their competitors, Sun Microsystems and Netscape.[17]

To summarize,

The central questions addressed by industrial organization are: (i) Is there market power? (ii) How do firms acquire and maintain market power? (iii) What are the implications of market power? (iv) Is there a role for public policy with regard to market power?

■ **INDUSTRIAL POLICY.** In addition to regulation and antitrust (or competition policy), some countries have followed policies that are intended to promote particular firms or groups of firms. Of particular importance is **industrial policy**. The goal of industrial policy is very different from regulation and antitrust. Whereas the latter attempt to promote competition, the former is geared towards strengthening the market position of a firm or industry, namely with respect to foreign firms. For example, much of the success of Airbus Industrie, a consortium backed by four European countries, is the result of the support it has received from the respective governments over the past three or four decades. Starting from a market share of less than 10% in the 1970s, Airbus is now fighting head to head with Boeing, the industry's main competitor.

Industrial policy is generally not favored by economists. In practice, it amounts to governments picking winners among a number of potential firms and industries. But why should governments know better than the market who the promising firms and industries are? A frequent argument in support of industrial policy is the example of MITI, the Japanese Ministry of Industry and Foreign Trade. True, the prowess of the Japanese export sector is a success story and owes a great deal to the role played by MITI. For example, MITI's support was an important factor in the emergence of Japan as a leader in semiconductors. But together with the success stories there are also a fair number of flops: for example, the 1980s project to develop a "fifth generation computer," which would leapfrog the American counterparts, lead to very poor results.[18]

Even in the US — the most pro-market western economy — we find examples of failed industrial policy. Recently, the state of Rhode Island approved $75 million in loans for a fledgling video game company led by a former Major League Baseball star pitcher. The ill-fated company went bankrupt two years later and managed to rack up $150 million in debt in the process.[19]

In sum, although there are success stories (Airbus?), the overall record of governments meddling in business strategy is at best poor. For these reasons, and as a matter of consistency, when talking about public policy I will restrict attention to regulation and antitrust (or competition policy).

## 1.3 COMING NEXT...

There are 15 chapters to come, divided into four different parts. Part I is introductory in nature. It provides basic tools required for the study of IO (consumer behavior in Chapter 2, firm behavior in Chapter 3); and covers the extreme situations when markets are efficient (Chapter 4) and when they are not (Chapter 5). I conclude Part I by discussing advanced pricing strategies, though still in a context where strategic interaction is absent (Chapter 6). For readers with a background in the field of microeconomics, some of the material treated in Chapters 2–5 may be familiar and can be skipped without much loss.

Insofar as industrial organization is the study of imperfect competition, Parts II through IV make up the core of the text. Within these, Part II plays a central role, as it introduces the basic theory of oligopoly competition. I begin with an introduction to game theory (Chapter 7), an essential tool for studying strategic behavior; and then cover static models (Chapter 8) and dynamic models (Chapter 9) of oligopoly interaction.

Throughout most of the text, I assume a *given* industry structure. Part III takes one step back and examines the endogenous determinants of industry structure. I begin by looking at how technology and demand conditions influence market structure (Chapter 10), and then move on to examine the role played by mergers and acquisitions (Chapter 11) and firm strategy (Chapter 12).

Part IV extends the analysis by considering firm strategies beyond the simple pricing and output decisions examined in Parts II and III. These include vertical relations (Chapter 13); product differentiation and advertising (Chapter 14); and innovation (Chapter 15). I conclude with a chapter on networks, a phenomenon of increasing importance in the "new economy" (Chapter 16).

■ **A NOTE ON METHODOLOGY.** Many economists analyze industries with reference to a framework known as the **structure-conduct-performance (SCP) paradigm**.[20] First, one looks at the aspects that characterize market structure: the number of buyers and sellers, the degree of product differentiation, and so forth. Second, one pays attention to the typical conduct of firms in the industry: pricing, product positioning and advertising, and so forth. Finally, one attempts to estimate how competitive and efficient the industry is.

Underlying this system is the belief that there is a causal chain linking the above components: market structure determines firm conduct, which in turn determines industry and firm performance. For example, in an industry with very few competitors, each firm is more likely to increase prices or collude with its rivals. And higher prices have the performance implications we saw in the previous section.

Causality also works in the reverse direction. For example, a firm that does not perform well exits the market, so performance influences market structure. Likewise, a firm may price very low in order to drive a rival out of the market, an instance where conduct influences structure. Finally, government intervention and basic demand and supply conditions also influence the different components of the SCP paradigm.

In Chapter 10 I examine the relation between the different components in the structure-conduct-performance paradigm. However, most of the text centers on the analysis of firm conduct and how it influences firm and industry performance as well as market structure.[1]

## SUMMARY

• Industrial organization is concerned with the workings of markets and industries, in particular the way firms compete with each other. • The central questions addressed by industrial organization are: (i) Is there market power? (ii) How do firms acquire and

l. It should be clear that the SCP paradigm is not a model that directly provides answers to the questions listed in the previous section. It is best thought of as a guide that allows one to analyze and understand the workings of different industries. Alternative frameworks have been proposed for the same or similar purposes. Examples include Michael Porter's **five-forces framework** for the analysis of industry competition. The five forces are: suppliers, buyers, substitute products, potential entrants, and competition between incumbent firms.[21]

maintain market power? (iii) What are the implications of market power? (iv) Is there a role for public policy with regard to market power?

## KEY CONCEPTS

• **market power**  • **contestable markets**  • **allocative inefficiency**  • **productive inefficiency**  • **rent seeking**  • **industrial policy**  • **structure-conduct-performance (SCP) paradigm**  • **five-forces framework**

## REVIEW AND PRACTICE EXERCISES

■ **1.1. COMPETITION AND PERFORMANCE.** Empirical evidence from a sample of more than 600 UK firms indicates that, controlling for the quantity of inputs (that is, taking into account the quantity of inputs), firm output is increasing in the number of competitors and decreasing in market share and industry concentration.[22] How do these results relate to the ideas presented in this chapter?

## NOTES

1. Stigler, George J. (1969), *The Organization of Industry*, Homewood, Illinois: R D Irwin, p. 1.

2. *The People's Pharmacy* (http://homearts.com/depts/health/kfpeop18.htm).

3. Petersen, Melody (2008), *Our Daily Meds: How the Pharmaceutical Companies Transformed Themselves into Slick Marketing Machines and Hooked the Nation on Prescription Drugs*, New York: Sarah Crichton Books.

4. *The Scientist,* Vol. 9, No. 14, p. 3, July 10, 1995.

5. Harberger, Arnold C. (1954), "Monopoly and Resource Allocation," *American Economic Review* **44**, 77–87.

6. Baumol, William, John Panzar, and Robert Willig (1982), *Contestable Markets and the Theory of Industry Structure*, New York: Harcourt Brace Jovanovich.

7. Hall, Robert E. (1988), "The Relationship Between Price and Marginal Cost in US Industry," *Journal of Political Economy* **96**, 921–947.

8. *The Wall Street Journal Europe*, November 14, 1996.

9. *The Wall Street Journal Europe*, May 6, 1999.

10. *The Economist*, September 17, 2014.

11. *Financial Times*, 24 May 1999.

12. "Apple Strengthens the Pull of Its Orbit With Each Device," *The New York Times,* October 23, 2014.

13. Hicks, John (1935), "Annual Survey of Economic Theory: The Theory of Monopoly," *Econometrica* **3**, 1–20.

14. *The Wall Street Journal*, November 24, 1999.

15. *The Wall Street Journal*, September 11, 2014.

16. Schumpeter, Joseph (1950), *Capitalism, Socialism, and Democracy,* 2nd Ed. (New York), pp. 82 and 106.

17. *The Wall Street Journal Europe,* June 10, 1998.

18. *The Economist,* August 31st, 1996.

19. *The New York Times,* April 20, 2013.

20. This framework is based on the seminal work by Mason and Bain. See Mason, Edward S. (1939), "Price and Production Policies of Large-Scale Enterprise," *American Economic Review* **29**, 61–74. Mason, Edward S. (1949), "The Current State of the Monopoly Problem in the United States," *Harvard Law Review* **62**, 1265–1285. Bain, Joe S. (1956), *Barriers to New Competition*, Cambridge, Mass.: Harvard University Press. Bain, Joe S. (1959), *Industrial Organization*, New York: John Wiley & Sons.

21. Porter, Michael E. (1980), *Competitive Strategy*, New York, NY: The Free Press.

22. Nickell, Stephen J. (1996), "Competition and Corporate Performance," *Journal of Political Economy* **104**, 724–746.

**MICROECONOMICS FOUNDATIONS**

# CONSUMERS

Markets are made of buyers and sellers. In many cases, buyers are consumers and sellers are firms. In this and in the next chapter I lay the behavioral foundations of consumers and firms, respectively.

## 2.1  CONSUMER PREFERENCES AND DEMAND

*Creating Demand: Move the Masses to Buy Your Product, Service, or Idea.* You will find this and many other such titles at your local bookstore (if it still exists, which is an interesting demand-related question). If there is no demand there is no business. Therefore, before deciding what to do in business it's important to have some knowledge of what the demand for your product is. The economist's answer to this is to think of consumers as having preferences; and from this to derive their demand function: how much they want to buy of a certain product as a function of a variety of factors, including price.

■ **CONSUMER TASTES.**  The traditional theoretical setup for thinking about demand starts with the tastes or preferences of an individual consumer. To see how this works, suppose there are two products, $A$ and $B$. We might express different combinations of purchases in a diagram with quantities of product $A$ on the vertical axis and quantities of product $B$ on the horizontal axis. The top left panel in Figure 2.1, for example, shows four possible combinations, from $E_1$ to $E_4$. A consumer's **preferences** can be described by a ranking over all possible combinations of $A$ and $B$. For example, a consumer might like the bundle $E_2$ best among the four possibilities; be indifferent between $E_1$ and $E_4$; and like $E_3$ the least.

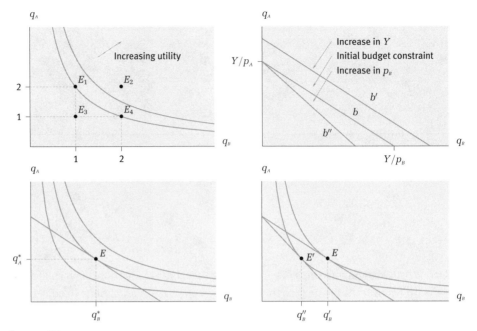

**FIGURE 2.1**
From consumer preferences to consumer demand

We can represent these preference orderings (that is, tastes) by drawing the consumer's indifference curves, as shown on the top left panel in Figure 2.1. For example, we might think of two units of product $A$ and one of product $B$ (point $E_1$) as equally desirable as the reverse (one unit of product $A$ and two units of product $B$, point $E_4$). A line connecting all such points about which we are indifferent (i.e., like equally well) is called an **indifference curve.** Generally, indifference curves are downward-sloping, since we need more of a product to compensate us for less of the other. (We call this the "no satiation" principle, which really means that "more is better.") We also assume they are curved away from the origin, since as we consider combinations with more and more of one product, we need increasing amounts of it to keep us equally satisfied.

If we put lots of indifference curves on our graph, we can get a complete description of our tastes. Since "more is better," indifference curves that are up and to the right (farther from the origin) represent higher levels of satisfaction.

■ **CONSUMER BUDGETS.** The other ingredient in our analysis is what the consumer can afford: the **budget set.** With two products, the budget might be expressed by the inequality:

$$p_A q_A + p_B q_B \le Y$$

where $p_i$ is the price of product $i$, $q_i$ the quantity purchased of product $i$ ($i = A, B$), and $Y$ the available income. If we solve for $q_A$ we see the budget set corresponds to the area below the following downward-sloping line:

$$q_A = \frac{Y}{p_A} - \frac{p_B}{p_A} q_B$$

which is line $b$ on the top right panel in Figure 2.1. This is a straight line whose position and slope depend on income and prices. If you increase income, for example, the budget line shifts out. This is illustrated by line $b'$ in the top right panel of Figure 2.1. If you increase $p_B$, the line rotates clockwise (around the vertical intercept, $Y/p_A$). This is illustrated by line $b''$ in the top right panel of Figure 2.1. And if you increase $p_A$, the line rotates counterclockwise (around the fixed horizontal intercept, $Y/p_B$).

■ **DEMAND.** Putting together tastes (represented by indifference curves) and possibilities (represented by the budget line) we can find out what our hypothetical consumer should do. Suppose that the consumer's goal is to **maximize utility**. Then the consumer's best choice corresponds to the point where the highest indifference curve has a common point with the budget line. This is illustrated in the bottom left panel in Figure 2.1, where $E$ is the best combination of $A$ and $B$ that the consumer can afford with a budget represented by the budget line $b$ (that is, the area under $b$).

The optimal point, $E$, corresponds to quantities $q_A^*$ and $q_B^*$. These are the quantities demanded by the consumer. Implicitly, these demands depend on tastes (which are built into the indifference curves); they also depend on income (since a change in income shifts the budget line and therefore leads to a change in demand) and prices (for the same reason).

We can summarize and abstract from the underlying indifference curves and budget sets by writing down a **demand function,** $q_i(p_i, \mathbf{z})$, denoting the quantity demanded, $q_i$, for a given price of the good, $p_i$, and for given values of other variables, $\mathbf{z}$, which might include income, the prices of all other goods, and any other relevant factors that affect the demand of good $i$. For example, if $i$ is "gasoline consumption" then $\mathbf{z}$ might include variables such as consumer income and the price of cars. (Can you think of other ones?)

> The demand curve gives the quantity demanded of a given good as a function of its price and of other factors; it can be derived from consumer preferences.

Instead of $q_i(p_i, \mathbf{z})$, we can equivalently write an **inverse demand function,** $p_i(q_i, \mathbf{z})$, which denotes what the price must be if the quantity demanded is to be equal to $q_i$.

To summarize, the quantity of a product demanded by an individual consumer depends on:

- The individual's tastes, expressed by indifference curves.

- The price of the product. Generally, the lower the price the higher the quantity demanded. Depending on the curvature of the indifference curves, a change in price might have a small or a¡ large impact on the quantity demanded.

- The price of other products. Decisions are not made in isolation: if we spend less on one product, that necessarily leaves more to spend on others.

- Income. At higher levels of income, we can buy more of everything (and generally do).

Frequently, we graph $q_i$ as a function of $p_i$ only.[a] We refer to the curve that shows $q_i$ as a function of $p_i$ as the **demand curve.** Basically, it corresponds to the demand function under the assumption that all variables other than $p_i$ are constant (that is, **z** is constant).

The bottom right panel of Figure 2.1 illustrates the process of deriving the demand curve. Keeping $Y$ and $p_A$ fixed, we change the value of $p_B$. For example, we increase the value of $p_B$ from $p_B'$ to $p_B''$. This implies a clockwise rotation of the budget line around the $q_A$ axis intercept. The consumer's optimal point is now given by $E'$. In other words, by increasing the value of $p_B$ from $p_B'$ to $p_B''$, the quantity of $q_B$ demanded decreases from $q_B'$ to $q_B''$. Repeating this exercise for all possible values of $p_B$, we get the demand curve for product $B$.

It is important to distinguish between movements along the demand curve and shifts in the demand curve itself. If $p_i$ changes, then the quantity demanded of product $i$ changes as we move *along* the demand curve. If however some other variable such as $p_j$ (the price of another good) changes, than $q_i$ changes because of a *shift* of the demand curve.

> A change in price leads to a movement along the demand curve; a change in other factors leads to a shift in the demand curve itself.

■ **Consumer surplus.** Suppose that before going to watch a movie you stop at a pizzeria and place your order. Pizza comes at $1 a slice. Imagine what would be the maximum price you would pay for one pizza slice. Perhaps $3, especially if you are very hungry and there is no alternative restaurant in the neighborhood. Consumers don't usually think about this; all they need to know is that they are willing to pay *at least* $1 for that pizza slice. But, for the sake of argument, let us suppose that the maximum you would be willing to pay is $3.

How about a second slice of pizza? While one slice is the minimum necessary to survive through a movie, a second slice is an option. It makes sense to assume you would be willing to pay less for a second slice than for the first slice; say, $1.50. How about a third slice? For most consumers, a third slice would be superfluous. If you are going to watch a movie, you might not have the time to eat it, anyway. If you were to buy a third slice, you would probably only eat the toppings and little else. You wouldn't be willing to pay more than, say, 20 cents.

Putting all of this information together, we have your demand curve for pizza. The left panel in Figure 2.2 illustrates this. On the horizontal axis, we have the number of pizza slices you buy. On the vertical axis, we measure the **willingness to pay,** that is, the maximum price (in dollars) at which you would still want to buy.

There are two things we can do with a demand curve. First, knowing what the price is ($1 per slice), we can predict the number of slices bought. This is the number of slices such that willingness to pay is greater or equal to price. Or, to use the demand curve, the quantity demanded is given by the point where the demand curve crosses the line $p = 1$: two slices.

a. Although we think of $q_i$ as a function of $p_i$, we normally measure price on the vertical axis. British economist Alfred Marshall started doing it this way back in the nineteenth century and things haven't changed ever since.

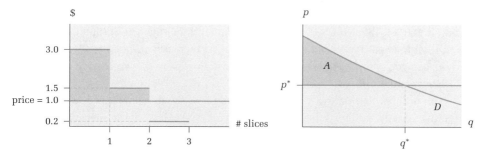

**FIGURE 2.2**
Consumer surplus: (a) demand for pizza slices and (b) general case.

A second important use of the demand curve is to measure the consumer's surplus. You would be willing to pay up to $3 for one slice of pizza. That is, had the price been $3, you would have bought one slice of pizza anyway. In fact, you only paid $1 for that first slice. Since the pizza is the same in both cases, you are $3−$1 = $2 better off than you would be had you bought the slice under the worst possible circumstances (or not bought it at all). Likewise, you paid 50 cents less for the second slice than the maximum you would have been willing to pay. Your total surplus as a consumer is thus $2+50cents = $2.50.

Consumer surplus is the difference between willingness to pay and price.

More generally, **consumer surplus** is given by the area under the demand curve and above the price paid by the consumer. This is illustrated in the right panel in Figure 2.2. If price is $p^*$, then quantity demanded is $q^*$ and consumer surplus is given by the shaded area $A$.

## 2.2   DEMAND ELASTICITY

Having established the foundations of the demand curve, I am now interested in characterizing its shape, that is, understanding how it depends on a variety of factors: how it depends on the price of the product in question, but also on the prices of other goods, as well as on the consumer's income. For this purpose, economists use the concept of demand elasticity.

■ **PRICE ELASTICITY OF DEMAND.** We presume (based on lots of evidence) that the demand for a product increases if we lower its price. This doesn't have to be the case, but it invariably is. The question is how sensitive demand is to price. If I were to tell you that the world oil demand decreases by 1.3 million barrels a day when price increases from $50 to $60 per barrel, would you consider the demand for oil very sensitive or not very sensitive to price? It's hard to tell, unless you have a very good idea of the size of the world oil market. What if I told you that the demand for sugar in Europe decreases by one million tons per day when average retail price increases from 80 to 90 euros cents per kilo: can you compare the demand for sugar in Europe to the worldwide demand for oil? It's even more difficult.

The problem is that, by measuring the slope of the demand curve, we are stuck with units: barrels, dollars, kilos, euros, and so on. The solution is to measure things in relative terms, that is, in terms of percent changes. Specifically, we measure the sensitivity of demand to changes in price by the **price elasticity of demand:**

$$\epsilon = \frac{\frac{dq}{q}}{\frac{dp}{p}} = \frac{dq}{dp}\frac{p}{q}$$

where $dq$ represents a differential variation of $q$ and $dq/dp$ stands for the derivative of $q$ with respect to $p$ (sometimes denoted $q'(p)$). In words:

> The price elasticity of demand is the ratio between the percentage change in quantity and the percentage change in price, for a small change in price.

A note on terminology: as I will show later, there are many elasticity concepts, including but not limited to the concept of price elasticity of demand. When economists simply refer to "demand elasticity" they really mean "price elasticity of demand." In the rest of the chapter (and in the rest of the book) I may fall in the same abuse of language.

In the above definition, by "small" change in price we mean, strictly speaking, an infinitesimally small change in price, something we represent by $dp$. In practice, we observe small but not infinitesimal changes in $p$, which we denote by $\Delta p$. We thus have:

$$\epsilon \approx \frac{\Delta q}{\Delta p}\frac{p}{q}$$

where the $\approx$ sign stands for "approximately equal to."

Note that elasticities are generally negative, since quantity demanded declines when price increases. The question is how negative. We say that products for which $|\epsilon| > 1$ have an "elastic" demand, meaning the quantity demanded is very sensitive to price; the higher $|\epsilon|$ is, the more sensitive to price. Conversely, if $0 < |\epsilon| < 1$ (elasticity is "small"), we say that demand is "inelastic," meaning that quantity demanded is relatively insensitive to price; the closer $\epsilon$ is to zero, the less sensitive demand is to price. Later we will see why the value 1 (the threshold between inelastic and elastic demand) is so important when classifying demand elasticity.[b]

Table 2.1 presents the values of the demand elasticity for selected products. Would you expect the demand for coffee to be inelastic? Would you expect the long-run demand elasticity for natural gas to be greater than the short-run elasticity? Would you expect the demand for foreign luxury cars in the US to be elastic? Why? I will return to some of these questions in Section 2.3.

b. Frequently, if product 1 has $\epsilon_1 = -3$ and product 2 has $\epsilon_2 = -2$ we say, with some abuse of language, that the demand for product 1 is more elastic. Strictly speaking, $\epsilon_1$ is smaller than $\epsilon_2$, but in absolute value the opposite is true.

Note that the elasticity is defined at a point: generally speaking, its value varies along a demand curve. The left panel in Figure 2.3 considers the case of a linear demand curve. As we go from the extreme when $p$ is equal to 0 to the extreme when $q$ is equal to zero, the value of $\epsilon$ varies from 0 to $-\infty$. (You can check this by looking at the definition of elasticity.) At some intermediate point (the midpoint, if the demand curve is linear), we have $|\epsilon| = 1$.

Although the value of demand elasticity varies from point to point, there is such a thing as a demand curve with constant elasticity, that is, with the same value of demand elasticity at every point. The right panel in Figure 2.3 depicts several examples. There are two extreme cases: a vertical demand curve ($\epsilon = 0$), such that for any price the quantity demanded is always the same; and a horizontal curve ($\epsilon = -\infty$), the extreme case such that even a very small change in price leads to an infinite increase in quantity demanded. These extreme examples are not found in any real-world situation, though some market demands may be close to it. (Can you think of examples?) For the majority of real-world markets, demand elasticity lies somewhere between the two extremes. Table 2.1 provides a few examples.

**TABLE 2.1** Price elasticity of demand for selected products and services.[2]

| Product and market | Elasticity |
|---|---|
| Norwegian salmon in Spain | −0.8 |
| Norwegian salmon in Italy | −0.9 |
| Coffee in the Netherlands | −0.2 |
| Natural gas in Europe (short-run) | −0.2 |
| Natural gas in Europe (long-run) | −1.5 |
| US luxury cars in US | −1.9 |
| Foreign luxury cars in US | −2.8 |
| Basic cable TV in US | −4.1 |
| Satellite TV in US | −5.4 |
| Ocean shipping services (worldwide) | −4.4 |

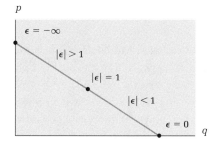
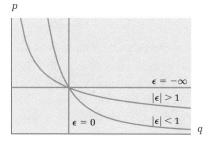

**FIGURE 2.3**
Demand elasticity

At this point, it should be clear that elasticity is not the same thing as slope, although slope is an input to it (recall that the slope is given by $dq/dp$). The difference between slope and elasticity is illustrated by the left and right panels in Figure 2.3. On the left panel, we have a curve with constant slope but varying elasticity; on the right panel, we have a series of curves with constant elasticity but varying slopes.

---

**TECHNICAL POINT: LOGARITHMS.** A useful variant of the elasticity formula uses logarithms. You might recall that:

$$d \left( \log q \right) = \frac{dq}{q}$$

where log stands for natural logarithm. Therefore,

$$\frac{\frac{dq}{q}}{\frac{dp}{p}} = \frac{d \log q}{d \log p}$$

If we do our usual approximation, replacing $d$'s with $\Delta$'s, we have:

$$\epsilon \approx \frac{\Delta \log q}{\Delta \log p}$$

The approximation is exact if the elasticity is constant along the demand curve; see Exercise 2.8.

---

■ **NUMERICAL EXAMPLE.** To see how the concepts of demand elasticity can be used in practice, consider the following example. Suppose you have access to historical sales data from the Yellow Note jazz label. When price was set at $10, $11, and $13, total units sold (thousands) were 6.31, 5.63, and 4.61, respectively. (As you can see, Yellow Note has not been a great commercial success.) Suppose that these historical data correspond to different points of the demand curve (that is, suppose that the demand curve has remained constant over these periods). This is a big — and possibly unrealistic — assumption, an assumption to which I will return later; but it will make our lives easier for the time being. Given this big if, how do we estimate the value of the demand elasticity at the price of $10?

We can approximate the value of the demand elasticity by the "percent change" formula applied to prices $10 and $11:

$$\epsilon \approx \frac{\Delta q}{\Delta p} \frac{p}{q} = \left( \frac{5.63 - 6.31}{11 - 10} \right) \left( \frac{10}{6.31} \right) = -1.08$$

This is an approximation, since we're using discrete changes. We could get a better approximation by using a finer price grid. In fact, the numbers in the present example were generated by a demand curve with constant elasticity $\epsilon = -1.2$. So, just as the true value, the estimate of $-1.08$ is greater than one in absolute value (that is, we correctly estimate that the demand for Yellow Note CDs is elastic); however, there is a considerable estimation error ($-1.08$ as opposed to $-1.2$).

How could I use the elasticity estimate to predict quantity demanded when price is \$13? Since $\epsilon \approx \frac{\Delta q/q}{\Delta p/p}$, we conclude that:

$$\frac{\Delta q}{q} \approx \epsilon \frac{\Delta p}{p}$$

Specifically, consider a variation in price from \$11 to \$13. This corresponds to $\Delta p/p = 2/11 = 18.18\%$. We therefore estimate that $\Delta q/q = -1.08 \times 18.18\% = -19.64\%$, which implies a value of $q$ given by $5.63 \times (1 - 19.64\%) = 4.53$. This overestimates the decrease in $q$: as we know, the true value is 4.61.

---

**LOGARITHMS (CONT).** Alternatively, we can do the above calculations using logarithms. First, we estimate the demand elasticity as:

$$\epsilon \approx \frac{\log 5.63 - \log 6.31}{\log 11 - \log 10} = \frac{-.1140}{.0953} = -1.20$$

In fact, given that the demand has constant elasticity, the logarithmic formula yields the *exact* value of the demand elasticity. Next, we can estimate the new value of $q$ when $p = 13$ by solving the equation:

$$\epsilon \approx \frac{\log 5.63 - \log q}{\log 11 - \log 13} = -1.20$$

The result is $q = 4.61$, the true value of $q$. Once again, we see that if the demand has constant elasticity, then the logarithms approach delivers more precise results.

---

The above numerical example shows how the value of the demand elasticity can be used to predict the change in quantity demanded following a change in price. Similarly, the value of $\epsilon$ can be used to predict the change in revenue (the product price $\times$ quantity). It can be shown that, if $|\epsilon| < 1$ (that is, if the demand is inelastic), then an increase in price leads to an increase in revenue; whereas, if $|\epsilon| > 1$ (that is, if the demand is elastic), then an decrease in price leads to an increase in revenue. This is a basic point, but one that some have missed: that to increase revenue in markets with elastic demand, you need to lower price, not raise it.

---

**ELASTICITY AND REVENUE.** Formally, the percent change in revenue induced by a (small) change in price is:

$$\frac{d(pq)}{pq} = \frac{q\,dp + p\,dq}{pq} = \frac{dp}{p} + \frac{dq}{q} = \frac{dp}{p} + \frac{dq}{dp}\frac{p}{q}\frac{dp}{p} = (1 + \epsilon)\frac{dp}{p}$$

That is, the percent change in revenue following a price change is $(1 + \text{elasticity}) \times (\%$ change in price). Since $\epsilon < 0$, the direct effect of the price change (the "1" term) and the indirect effect through changes in quantity demanded (the "$\epsilon$" term) have opposite signs. If demand is elastic ($|\epsilon| > 1$), then the demand effect is larger and an increase in price leads to lower revenue.

■ **CROSS-PRICE ELASTICITY.** We have seen that demand for a product depends not only on its own price, but also on the prices of other goods. For example, the demand for ski boots depends on the demand for skis: if skis get more expensive, we expect people to buy fewer skis — and fewer boots, too. As an alternative example, we expect the demand for commuter rail tickets to be influenced by the price of gasoline: if gasoline becomes more expensive, people drive their cars less and take the train more often.

Notice that, in the first example, the quantity demanded of good 1 (ski boots) decreases when the price of good 2 (skis) increases; whereas, in the second example, the quantity demanded of good 1 (rail tickets) increases when the price of good 2 (gasoline) increases. More generally, we summarize the sensitivity of demand to the price of another product with the **cross price elasticity**:

$$\epsilon_{12} \equiv \frac{\frac{dq_1}{q_1}}{\frac{dp_2}{p_2}}$$

That is, the cross price elasticity of product 1 with respect to product 2 is given by the ratio of the percent change in quantity demanded of product 1 to the percent change in the price for product 2.

The essential distinction here is between substitutes and complements. If the cross-price elasticity is positive, we say that the products are **substitutes**. Hence Coke and Pepsi are substitutes: if Coke becomes more expensive, we'd expect some people (but not all) to switch to Pepsi, thus increasing the quantity demanded of Pepsi. (I know that you would never do such thing, but some consumers just don't have any principles.) Conversely, if the cross-price elasticity is negative, we say the products are **complements**. For example, if gasoline price increases we expect people to drive less, which in turn decreases the quantity demanded of cars. In this sense, cars and gasoline are complement products.

Speaking of cars, Table 2.2 presents the values of direct and cross-price elasticities for selected car models. For example, the number 0.2 on the third column, second row means that a 1% increase in the price of the Accord leads to a $0.2 \times 1\%$ increase in Cavalier sales. Are the different car models complements or substitutes? What is the model closest to the Cavalier, in terms of demand? See Exercise 2.5 for more details.

**TABLE** 2.2 Automobile demand elasticities

| Model | 323 | Cavalier | Accord | Taurus | Century | BMW |
|---|---|---|---|---|---|---|
| Mazda 323 | −6.4 | 0.6 | 0.2 | 0.1 | 0.0 | 0.0 |
| Cavalier | 0.0 | −6.4 | 0.2 | 0.1 | 0.1 | 0.0 |
| Accord | 0.0 | 0.1 | −4.8 | 0.1 | 0.0 | 0.0 |
| Taurus | 0.0 | 0.1 | 0.2 | −4.2 | 0.0 | 0.0 |
| Century | 0.0 | 0.1 | 0.2 | 0.1 | −6.8 | 0.0 |
| BMW 735i | 0.0 | 0.0 | 0.0 | 0.0 | 0.0 | −3.5 |

■ **INCOME ELASTICITY.** Changes in income also affect demand. Higher income generally means greater demand for all products, but some products benefit more than others. We define the **income elasticity** of a product by:

$$\epsilon_y \equiv \frac{\frac{dq}{q}}{\frac{dy}{y}}$$

That is, the income elasticity of demand is given by the percent change in quantity demanded induced by a 1% change in income (represented by $y$).

Economists have names for products with different income elasticities. **Inferior goods** have negative income elasticities. Although inferior goods aren't all that common, it's fun to think of examples. Spam comes to mind, on the assumption that anyone with enough money would buy something else. **Normal goods** have positive income elasticities. Within normal goods, those with elasticities between zero and one are referred to as **necessities**, and those with elasticities greater than one as **luxuries**. Can you explain why?

■ **APPLICATION: DEMAND FOR GASOLINE.** Let us consider a specific example where the above concepts play an important role. Using historical data on gasoline price and consumption in the US from 2001–2006, the following relation was estimated:

$$\log q = -1.697 - 0.042 \log p + 0.530 \log y$$

where $q$ is gasoline consumption, $p$ is the price of gasoline, and $y$ is income.[2]

What is the price elasticity of gasoline demand? From the analysis above,

$$\epsilon = \frac{d \log q}{d \log p} = -0.042$$

Is gasoline demand elastic or inelastic? Well, since $|\epsilon| < 1$, we conclude that it is inelastic. No major surprises here: with the exception of New Yorkers, Americans need to drive to work, and there aren't many reasonable alternatives to get there (at least not in the short run).

What is the income elasticity of gasoline demand? The answer is:

$$\eta = \frac{d \log q}{d \log y} = 0.530$$

Is gasoline a normal good? Yes, since the income elasticity is greater than zero. In fact, since $\eta < 1$, gasoline is a necessity. Notice that the threshold from necessity to luxury is not purely arbitrary. In fact, if the income elasticity is greater than 1 then an increase in income implies that the *fraction* of income spent on that good increases. So, on average richer people spend more on gasoline ($\eta > 0$) but spend a lower proportion of their income on gasoline ($\eta < 1$).

This example helps explain an apparent "paradox," which is illustrated in the left panel of Figure 2.4. In the first decade of the millennium, the price of gasoline increased and so did consumption levels: compare, for example, the 2000 and 2010 data points. Doesn't this violate the regularity that demand curves are downward sloping; that is,

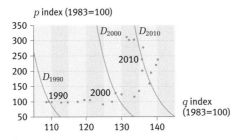 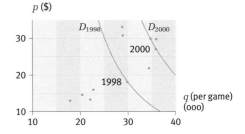

**FIGURE 2.4**
US gasoline consumption: yearly data (1990–2013) (left panel)
Shea Stadium ticket sales (1994–2004) (right panel)

that demand decreases when price increases? The answer is no, not when there are other factors varying at the same time. Specifically, income increased by so much in the early 2000s that, despite an increase in price, total consumption increased: the income effect dominated the price effect. The left panel in Figure 2.4 includes the estimated demand curves for the years 1990, 2000, and 2010. As can be seen, all are downward sloping, as theory predicts. What happens is that, since the demand curve itself shifted from year to year, the observed data points — the intersection of supply and demand — form what looks like a positively sloped line.

The right panel plots historical data of $p$ and $q$ for a different market: ticket sales for New York Mets games at Shea Stadium. The pattern is similar to that of gasoline demand: over the years, we observe both an increase in price and an increase in sales. In this case, the main variable shifting the demand curve is team quality, or the expectation of team performance in a given season. For example, in 1999 and 2000 the Mets made considerable investments in improving their team. This attracted many new fans, which corresponds to a northeast shift in the demand curve. Naturally, the business operations at the Mets were conscious that a better team allowed the organization to increase ticket prices without losing much demand; and so they did. The result was that, by 2000, price was higher but not so high as to undo the effect of the demand increase. All in all, the new equilibrium point — the new point where supply and demand intersect — lies to the NE of the initial point.

Given this combination of supply and demand shifts, it's not easy to estimate from market data the shape of the demand curve or the value of demand elasticity. In the next section I turn to this problem in greater detail.

## 2.3 ESTIMATING THE DEMAND CURVE

In an ideal world, firms would know the demands for their products. In practice, it's not so easy. One reason is that it's hard to get reliable market data: how much was bought by whom and at what price. Another reason is that it's inherently difficult to tease out

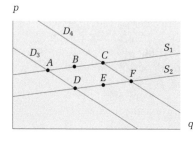
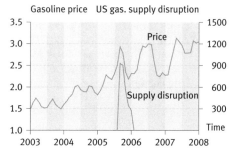

**FIGURE 2.5**
Identifying the demand curve with instrumental variables

the effect of price from the effect of other variables, especially when the latter might be changing at the same time as price (or, even worse, when they are not known to us).

I have colleagues who provide this service for a reasonable fee; but you should be aware of the main challenges in estimating the demand curve and the price elasticity of demand from actual data. A central problem is what econometricians refer to as the **identification problem.** Market data, such as that found in the two panels in Figure 2.4, result from a combination of demand-curve and supply-curve shifts. If only the demand curve shifted around, we would be able to identify the supply curve. If only the supply curve shifted, we would be able to identify the demand curve.

For example, consider the left panel in Figure 2.5. Suppose that the demand curve is fixed at $D_3$. As the supply curve shifts between $S_1$ and $S_2$, we observe equilibrium points $A$ and $D$. Based on these, we are able to correctly identify the shape of the demand curve. The problem is that, in practice, both curves shift around; and if we are not careful we may end up failing to identify either.

---

**IDENTIFYING THE DEMAND CURVE.** Consider the left panel in Figure 2.5. Suppose that, over time, the supply curve shifts between $S_1$ and $S_2$ and the demand curve between $D_3$ and $D_4$. Suppose there is an observable variable $x$ that is positively correlated with shifts in the supply curve: when $x = x_1$, $S = S_1$; when $x = x_2 > x_1$, $S = S_2$. The important question is whether the demand curve is also related to $x$. There are essentially three possibilities, which I consider next.

First, suppose that $x$ is also positively correlated with the demand curve: when $x = x_1$, the demand curve is given by $D_3$, and when $x = x_2$ the demand curve is given by $D_4$. In this case, the observable data consists of points $A$ and $F$; and if we were to use the observed points to estimate the demand curve, then we would grossly overestimate the value of elasticity (in absolute value).

Suppose instead that $x$ is negatively correlated with the demand curve: when $x = x_1$, the demand curve is given by $D_4$, and when $x = x_2$ the demand curve is given by $D_3$. In this case, the observable data consists of points $C$ and $D$. This is essentially what we find in the two panels in Figure 2.4: over time both $p$ and $q$ increase in tandem. In this case, if we were to use the observed points to estimate the demand curve, we would estimate a positive value of elasticity, which of course makes no sense.

Finally suppose that the shift in the demand curve are independent of the value of $x$: regardless of the value of $x$, the demand curve is equally likely to be at $D_3$ or $D_4$. In this case, if $x = x_1$ then the observable points are either $A$ or $C$ (average $B$); whereas, if $x = x_2$, then the observable points are either $D$ or $F$ (average $E$). Based on these average observations ($B$ and $E$), we are able to estimate the correct value of demand elasticity.

The critical step in the process of estimating demand elasticity is thus to find a variable $x$ that is correlated with shifts in the supply curve but *not* correlated with shifts in the demand curve.

Consider again the US gasoline market.[3] In 2005, hurricanes Katrina and Rita resulted in the temporary loss of several hundred thousand barrels of production in the Gulf of Mexico. The right panel in Figure 2.5 shows the difference between planned production and actual production in the US (supply disruption). As can be seen, gasoline price peaked when production disruptions peaked. Moreover, since the effect of hurricanes Katrina and Rita was relatively localized, it seems reasonable to assume that the overall US demand curve does not shift as a result of production disruptions.

Variables like this (production disruption) are ideal for the estimation of the demand curve. In econometrics jargon, we call them **instrumental variables**: they are correlated with the supply curve but uncorrelated with the demand curve. As a result, measuring the equilibrium points resulting from variation in instrumental variables such as production disruptions is akin to measuring various points along the demand curve, which in turn allows us to estimate its shape and the value of elasticity.[c]

---

■ **ALTERNATIVE PATHS TO ESTIMATING DEMAND.** Statistical analysis is not the only avenue for demand estimation. An alternative approach is to obtain data by means of surveys. One problem with this method is that we are never sure how accurate the responses are going to be: until your own money is at stake you don't have an incentive to think hard.

Still another approach is to do experiments in markets. Thus catalog companies sometimes send out catalogs to different customers in which some of the prices are different. These experiments run the risk of alienating customers (what if you find out you got the high price?), but you can see the value to the firm of knowing the demand for its products.

Finally, if you do not have historical data to estimate demand or the resources to experiment with price changes, you should at least have an idea of whether demand is more or less elastic depending on the characteristics of the good in question. In that spirit, here are some rules of thumb that might help in this process:

- Elasticities are higher (in absolute value) on luxuries than necessities. Compare, for example, food and Armani suits. Consider too the elasticities of the various products listed in Table 2.1.

- Elasticities are higher for specific products (e.g., the iPhone) than for a category as a whole (smartphones). Why is this so? Because when the price of a

c. Other candidate instrumental variables for the estimation of gasoline demand would be the war in Iraq and the 2002 labor strike in Venezuelan production facilities.

specific product rises, people are willing to buy fewer units. Some of this reduction leads to purchases of other products in the same category (e.g., Samsung
phones), some to a reduction in the category as a whole (smartphones). Only
the latter shows up in the elasticity of the category as a whole, so it's typically
less elastic.

- Elasticities are lower (in absolute value) in the short run than in the long run.
A good example is gasoline demand. Can you see why? Suppose, for example, that the government plans to levy a 100% tax on gasoline for the next
three years. In the next day or week consumers would probably still drive their
cars, but in the longer term their demand for gas could change for many reasons: they might buy more fuel-efficient cars, carpool, or take the bus or train
to work; perhaps some would work from home. As a result, the quantity of
gasoline demanded at the new price would gradually decrease. See Table 2.1
for another example: natural gas.

The price elasticity of demand tends to be higher (in absolute value) for luxuries;
for narrow product categories; and in the long run.

## 2.4  ARE CONSUMERS REALLY RATIONAL?

The economics edifice is built on a central premise: that agents (including firms and
consumers) are rational, optimizing agents. Specifically, the consumer behavior model
presented in Section 2.1 assumes that each consumer maximizes its utility function
subject to a budget constraint. It may seem over-restrictive to assume utility maximization: very few people think about functions when ordering coffee at Starbucks. The
economics defense is based on a simple (and beautiful) theorem: suppose your preferences are transitive; that is, if you prefer $a$ to $b$ and you prefer $b$ to $c$ then you prefer $a$ to
$c$. Then (and I'm simplifying things just a little bit) your behavior may be described as
resulting from the maximization of a utility function.
    The main challenge to the economics paradigm lies not on the deductive step
from rational ordering of alternatives ($a$ better than $b$ better than $c$) to utility maximization; but rather on the axiom that consumers (and agents, more generally) are able to
compare and order alternatives in a consistent way (e.g., satisfying transitivity). A central challenge to this assumption is given by **prospect theory**, the theory that preferences
depend on reference points.[4] For example, let $u_1$ be a given consumer's utility of having an apple and $u_0$ the utility of not having one. If price $p$ is lower than $u_1 - u_0$, then
I expect the consumer to buy an apple (if he hasn't done so yet); if price $p$ is greater
than $u_1 - u_0$, then I expect the opposite. So far, this is standard consumer theory. Now

suppose that utility depends on expectations as well. If a consumer was expecting not to have an apple, then the utility of having an apple is given by $u_1 + \mu_G (u_1 - u_0)$, where $\mu_G (u_1 - u_0)$ measures the extra benefit from "surprising oneself" by having an apple. By contrast, if the consumer was expecting to have an apple, then the utility from not having an apple is given by $u_0 + \mu_L (u_1 - u_0)$, where $\mu_L (u_1 - u_0)$ measures the extra benefit (possibly negative) from surprising oneself by not having an apple. Finally, if the consumer gets what she expected to get, then utility is simply given by $u_i$ (with $i = 1$ or $i = 0$ depending on whether the consumer has an apple or does not).

Experimental evidence suggests that consumers are more sensitive to losses than to gains. In terms of the current example, $\mu_L$ is negative (consumers dislike negative surprises) and moreover $\mu_L$ is greater than $\mu_G$ in absolute value (consumers dislike negative surprises more than they like positive ones). Then it can be shown that, for some prices $p$, a consumer whose reference point is to eat an apple will purchase one, whereas a consumer whose reference point is not to eat an apple will not purchase one. In other words, two consumers with the same utility function (the values $u_0, u_1$ and the coefficients $\mu_L, \mu_G$) make different choices simply because they hold different expectations.[5,d]

---

**Prospect theory example: formal analysis.** A consumer who expects to eat an apple compares $u_1 - p$, the utility from buying an apple, to $u_0 + \mu_L (u_1 - u_0)$, the utility from buying an apple. The former is greater than the latter if:

$u_1 - p > u_0 + \mu_L (u_1 - u_0)$

or simply

$p < (1 - \mu_L) (u_1 - u_0)$

A consumer who expects not to eat an apple compares $u_0$, the utility from not buying an apple, to $u_1 + \mu_G (u_1 - u_0) - p$, the utility from buying an apple. The former is greater than the latter if:

$u_0 > u_1 + \mu_G (u_1 - u_0) - p$

or simply

$p > (1 + \mu_G) (u_1 - u_0)$

If $\mu_L$ is negative and greater than $\mu_G$ in absolute value, then there exist values such that:

$(1 + \mu_G) (u_1 - u_0) < p < (1 - \mu_L) (u_1 - u_0)$

implying that the consumer buys an apple if it was expecting to have one and does not buy one if it was not expecting to have one.

---

A second area where the model of consumer rationality seems to fail is future-utility forecasting. For example, empirical evidence suggests that buying cold weather clothing is strongly influenced by the temperature of the day of purchase — even though, considering the durability of the item, a consumer's forecast of future utility from that item should not depend on current temperature.[6] Similarly, sometimes cellphone users purchase sub-optimal plans by incorrectly forecasting too-high consumption levels (e.g., they buy flat-rate plans when they would be better off with pay-per-use).[7]

Finally, many consumer transactions are considerably more complex than buying an apple. This is particularly true of financial instruments (mortgages, for example),

d. See Section 6.5 for another application of prospect theory.

which typically include many dimensions that even moderately literate consumers have a hard time evaluating.[e]

So where does this leave us — where does this leave economic theory? Ultimately, it's a question of perspective: the optimist sees the glass half full, the pessimist sees the glass half empty. Similarly, behavioral economists (the term used to refer to scholars who study decision biases by economic agents) stress the fact that, in many situations, the *homo rationalis* model fails to predict important patterns of consumer behavior; whereas mainstream economists (a designation that is likely to change in the future) stress the fact that, in many situations, the classical model does a pretty good job at describing consumer behavior.

## SUMMARY

• The demand curve gives the quantity demanded of a given good as a function of its price and of other factors; it can be derived from consumer preferences. • A change in price leads to a movement along the demand curve; a change in other factors leads to a shift in the demand curve itself. • Consumer surplus is the difference between willingness to pay and price. • The price elasticity of demand is the ratio between the percentage change in quantity and the percentage change in price, for a small change in price. • The price elasticity of demand tends to be higher (in absolute value) for luxuries; for narrow product categories; and in the long run.

## KEY CONCEPTS

• **preferences** • **indifference curve** • **budget set** • **utility maximization** • **demand function** • **inverse demand function** • **demand curve** • **willingness to pay** • **consumer surplus** • **price elasticity of demand** • **cross price elasticity** • **substitutes** • **complements** • **income elasticity** • **inferior goods** • **normal goods** • **necessities** • **luxuries** • **identification problem** • **instrumental variables** • **prospect theory**

## REVIEW AND PRACTICE EXERCISES

■ **2.1. FRUIT SALAD.** Adam and Barbara are big fruit salad fans (and both agree that the more the better). However, their tastes differ regarding the way the salad is made. For Adam, for each apple you throw in, there should be one and only one banana (if you give him more than one banana, he will throw it way). For Barbara, as long at it's fruit, it doesn't matter; in other words, all that counts is the number of pieces of fruit.

   (a)  Show what Adam's and Barbara's indifference curves look like.

   (b)  Are apples and bananas substitutes or complements?

e.  Section 14.4 continues this discussion.

■ **2.2. VILLAGE MICROBREW.** Village Microbrew raised its price from $10 to $12 a case (wholesale). As a result, sales dropped from 10,500 to 8,100 (in units). Based on your estimate of the demand elasticity, what percent change in sales would you predict if price were cut from $10 to $9? What demand level would this correspond to?

■ **2.3. DEMAND ELASTICITY.** Based on the values in Table 2.1, provide an estimate of the impact on sales revenues of a 10% increase in each product's price.

■ **2.4. SMARTPHONES.** The following pairs of price and quantity demanded for smartphones have been observed: (100, 600); (105, 590); (110, 575); (115, 550); and (120, 510).

(a) Calculate the approximate elasticity of demand when price is $105.

(b) Is the demand elasticity constant at all prices?

(c) How does the value of demand elasticity vary as price increases?

(d) If the monthly subscription fee for Internet access from a cell phone falls from $10 to $2, what would you expect to happen to the quantity of cell phones demanded at any given price? What effect would this Internet access price change have on the mobile phones' elasticity of demand?

■ **2.5. CARS.** Table 2.2 gives the "own" and cross-price elasticities for selected automobile models.[8] Specifically, each cell corresponds to the demand elasticity of the car model listed in the row with respect to changes in the price of the car model listed in column.

(a) Why are the "own" elasticities so high?

(b) Are the Accord and Taurus complements or substitutes?

(c) What are the Taurus's closest competitors?

(d) If GM lowers the price of its Chevy Cavalier, does it "cannibalize" its Buick Century sales?

(e) Why is the direct elasticity for the Mazda not lower than the elasticity for more expensive models (as the rule of thumb would suggest)?

(f) Suppose Honda sold 300k Accords in 2001. In 2002, the price of the Accord decreased by 2%, whereas the price of the Taurus decreased by 3%. What is the likely change in Accord sales?

■ **2.6. NETFLIX AND HULU.** Suppose the demand for Netflix is given by:

$$q_N = a - b_N p_N + b_B p_B$$

where $q_N$ is the number of Netflix subscriptions, $p_N$ the price of a Netflix plan, and $p_H$ the price of a Hulu plan.

CONSUMERS | 33

(a) What is the price elasticity of Netflix subscriptions?

(b) Suppose $a = 500$, $b_N = 10$, $b_H = 5$, and $p_H = p_N = 50$. What are $N$'s elasticity and cross-price elasticity? Are products $N$ and $H$ substitutes or complements?

(c) How much do consumers get in surplus at these prices?

■ **2.7. LAMBORGHINI.** The current US demand for the Lamborghini Gallardo SE is elastic; specifically, it is estimated that demand elasticity is given by $\epsilon = -3$. The current price is $p = \$120k$. Annual sales at this price amount to $q = 160$ (number of cars).

(a) What do you estimate would be the impact of an increase in price to $140k?

Suppose the cross price elasticity of the demand for Lamborghinis with respect to the price of the Maserati MC12 is $\epsilon_{LM} = .05$; and with respect to the price of gasoline, $\epsilon_{LG} = -.1$.

(b) What are the definitions of a substitute and of a complement? Are Maserati MC12 and gasoline substitutes or complements with respect to Lamborghinis? Can you think of other substitutes and complements to the Lamborghini Gallardo SE?

(c) Suppose that, in addition to the price increase considered in (a), there is also an increase in the price of the Maserati MC12 (from $110k to $115k); and an increase in the price of gasoline (from $2 to $2.8 per gallon). What do you estimate will be the new demand for the Lamborghini Gallardo SE?

## CHALLENGING EXERCISES

■ **2.8. CONSTANT ELASTICITY DEMAND.** Linear demand curves have constant slope, that is, constant derivative $dq/dp$. Consider now a demand curve with constant elasticity.

(a) Show that, if demand curve has the form $q = \alpha p^\beta$, then demand elasticity is constant.

(b) Consider two points from the demand curve, $(q_1, p_1)$ and $(q_2, p_2)$. Show that the expression $\Delta \log q / \Delta \log p$ gives the exact value of the demand elasticity.

## APPLIED EXERCISES

■ **2.9. DEMAND CURVE.** Find data on prices and quantities, as well as variables that shift the demand curve, from a particular market where you believe price is set exogenously. Estimate the demand curve and the value of demand elasticity. Discuss the assumptions you need to make in your estimation.

## NOTES

1. The various estimates of demand elasticities were obtained from the following sources: Trond Bjørndal, Kjell G. Salvanes, Daniel V. Gordon (1994), "Elasticity Estimates of Farmed Salmon Demand in Spain and Italy," *Empirical Economics* **19** (3), 419–428. Verboven, Frank, and Leon Bettendorf (2000), "Incomplete Transmission of Coffee Bean Prices: Evidence From the Netherlands," *European Review of Agricultural Economics* **27** (1), 1–16; Asche, Frank, Odd Bjarte Nilsen, and Ragnar Tveteras (2008), "Natural Gas Demand in the European Household Sector," *Energy Journal* **29** (3), 27–46; Berry, Steven, James Levinson, and Ariel Pakes (1995), "Automobile Prices in Market Equilibrium," *Econometrica* **63**, 841–890; Crawford, Gregory S., and Ali Yurukoglu (2012), "The Welfare Effects of Bundling in Multichannel Television Markets," *American Economic Review* **102** (2), 643–85. Kalouptsidi, Myrto (2014), "Time to Build and Fluctuations in Bulk Shipping," *American Economic Review* **104** (2), 564–608;

2. Hughes, Jonathan E., Christopher R. Knittel, and Daniel Sperling (2008), "Evidence of a Shift in the Short-Run Price Elasticity of Gasoline Demand," *The Energy Journal* **29** (1), 93–114.

3. Cf Endnote 2.

4. Kahneman, Daniel, and Amos Tversky (1979), "Prospect Theory: An Analysis of Decision under Risk," *Econometrica* **47**, 263–291.

5. Koszegi, Botond, and Matthew Rabin (2006), "A Model of Reference-Dependent Preferences," *Quarterly Journal of Economics* **121** (4), 33–65.

6. Conlin, Michael, Ted O'Donoghue, and Timothy J. Vogelsang (2007), "Projection Bias in Catalog Orders," *American Economic Review* **97** (4), 1217–1249.

7. Lambrecht, Anja, and Bernd Skiera (2006), "Paying Too Much and Being Happy about It: Existence, Causes, and Consequences of Tariff-Choice Biases," *Journal of Marketing Research* **43** (2), 212–223.

8. Source: Berry, Steven, James Levinson, and Ariel Pakes (1995), "Automobile Prices in Market Equilibrium," *Econometrica* **63**, 841–890.

# CHAPTER 3

# FIRMS

It takes two to tango. In markets, you must have at least one buyer and one seller. Frequently buyers are consumers; accordingly, in the previous chapter we studied consumer behavior in detail. Frequently, sellers are firms; accordingly, in this chapter we delve into the world of firm decision making.[a]

Firms are organizations; organizations are made up of people; and when there are people involved there are relationships, there are leaders and followers, there is trust and mistrust, there are explicit incentives and other sources of motivation; and there are complex processes of decision making, sometimes group decision making, sometimes hierarchical-based decision making.

Although parts of the economics discipline deal with these intricacies of organizational behavior, in this chapter (and in the book) I largely abstract from the internal workings of the firm and rather treat it as "blackbox," a process of transforming inputs into outputs. Specifically, the "box" that economists use corresponds to a mathematical object called the firm's production function.

In this context, I first look at the decision of selecting an optimal input mix as well as an optimal output level, assuming the firm is so small that it takes market input and output prices as given. Next, I consider the case when the firm is not an output-price taker and derive the firm's optimal rules for setting sales price.

The assumption of a firm as a "blackbox" that maximizes profits based on a production function is obviously a simplification. Is it a reasonable simplification? At the end of the chapter, I deal with a variety of questions regarding firm behavior: Do firms really maximize profits, as we assume throughout most of the book? What determines the boundaries of firms? Why do different firms perform differently? At this point you may think that these questions are obvious or uninteresting or both ("of course firms don't just maximize profits;" or "who cares what the firm's boundaries are;" or "isn't

a. Note that buyers are not always consumers: in business-to-business (B2B) transactions, for example, buyers are firms. Conversely, sellers are not always firms: on eBay, for example, many sellers are individuals, not firms. However, for the purpose of this chapter (and most of the book), I will treat sellers as firms and buyers as consumers.

it obvious that firms are different?"). Hopefully, by the end of the chapter you will agree that the time reading it was well spent; and that the economics' assumption of a production-function-based profit-maximizing firm is not so bad after all.

## 3.1  THE FIRM'S PRODUCTION, COST, AND SUPPLY FUNCTIONS

At the risk of oversimplifying, we can think of a firm as a process of transforming inputs into outputs. This is easier to see for a firm that makes actual things. For example, a bagel bakery uses water, flour, and other ingredients, together with machinery (an oven) and labor (someone has to put it all together), to produce tasty bagels. Firms that offer services also go through a similar process. For example, a consulting firm uses hours of labor — many, many hours, I'm told — together with some capital (mainly laptop computers) and materials (paper and paper clips), to produce solid advice to corporations that need it.

The firm's **production function** is the mapping that tells us, for a given set of inputs, how much output a firm is able to produce. Normally, this depends on the particular firm, as some firms are more efficient than others at transforming inputs into outputs. It also depends on the quality of inputs, for example skilled versus unskilled labor.

Formally, we denote the production function by $f(x_1, \ldots x_n)$, where $x_i$ the quantity of input $i$. For the purpose of this chapter, we consider two inputs: capital and labor. This is not to say that other inputs are not relevant: no matter how many ovens and oven operators you have, you cannot make bagels without flour. It's just that, for the purposes of illustrating the main principles, it suffices to consider two inputs. Moreover, in many examples (e.g., consulting services) these are indeed the main inputs into production (in other words, paper and paper clips are a small fraction of the consulting firm's operations).

What does the production function $f$ look like? One way to answer this question is to answer a related question: what combinations of inputs lead to a given level of output? The answer is given by the **isoquant** curves, which look a lot like the indifference curves introduced in the previous chapter.

Figure 3.1 shows two possible extremes regarding isoquant curves. On the left, we have the case of a production process that operates on fixed proportions. For example, Air France uses planes and pilots to produce transportation services. Each plane requires a pilot (for simplicity, I ignore co-pilots in the present analysis). Having more pilots than planes does not allow Air France to carry more passengers (assuming the planes are already used all the time). Likewise, having more planes than pilots doesn't help either (until Google or someone else comes up with a pilotless plane).

Fixed-proportion production processes lead to right-angle isoquants, as shown on the left panel of Figure 3.1: with one plane and one pilot the firm produces one unit

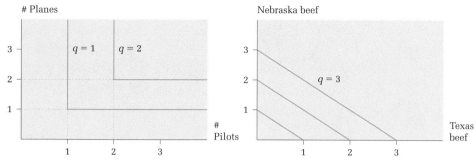

**FIGURE 3.1**
Production functions: two extreme cases

of output (if the plane carries 100 passengers, then let the output unit be hundreds of passengers). Given one plane, having more pilots does not help: total output is still one unit, and so all of these points belong to the same isoquant. With two planes and two pilots Air France can produce two units of output. More than two pilots given two planes or more than two planes given two pilots still leaves us at two units of output. More generally, the production function corresponding to fixed proportions is given by $f(x_1, x_2) = \min\{x_1, x_2\}$. We say that in this case inputs are **perfect complements**.

The right panel of Figure 3.1 shows the opposite extreme case: **perfect substitutes**. Suppose that McDonalds uses both Texas and Nebraska beef as input into its burgers. Moreover, for the purpose of this example, suppose that beef is the only ingredient into burgers (I am aware this is a strong assumption, but please bear with me). At the risk of offending the great states of Texas and Nebraska, it seems reasonable to assume that the quality of beef in these two states is similar. Therefore, the quantity and quality of McDonalds burgers depends on the total quantity of beef, not on the particular proportions of beef from Texas or Nebraska.

Perfect substitute inputs lead to straight isoquants, as in the right panel of Figure 3.1. One unit of output (burger) can be obtained with one unit of Texas beef and zero units of Nebraska beef; or one unit of Nebraska beef and zero units of Texas beef; or any combination therein.

Finally, the left panel in Figure 3.2 shows an intermediate case, that is, a case when inputs are neither perfect complements nor perfect substitutes. The particular isoquants in this figure are derived from a particular production function, which is known as the Cobb-Douglas production function and provides a good fit to the data in many settings. If capital ($K$) and labor ($L$) are the two main inputs in the production process, then the **Cobb-Douglas production function** is given by:

$$q = K^\alpha L^\beta$$

In the particular example depicted in Figure 3.2, I chose parameter values $\alpha = \frac{1}{2}$ and $\beta = \frac{1}{2}$ and plotted three different isoquants, corresponding to output levels 1, 2 and 3. Here's an interesting feature about these isoquants: for a given output level (e.g., $q = 4$), if I use less $L$ then I need to use more $K$ to compensate for the decrease in $L$;

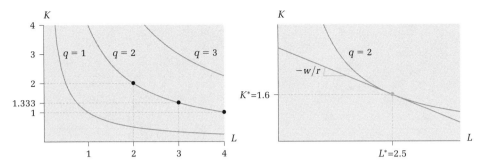

**FIGURE 3.2**
Isoquants and cost minimization

and the further I decrease $L$ the greater the increase in $K$ required to compensate for the decline in $L$. This latter property reflects the law of **diminishing marginal returns**, a feature that we saw in the context of consumer utility. It also works in terms of increases of $L$. Consider for example the isoquant corresponding to $q = 2$. One possible way of achieving this output level is to employ two units of $K$ and two units of $L$. By increasing $L$ to 3, I am able to drop $K$ from 2 to 1.333, a drop of .666. If I further increase $L$ from 3 to 4 (the same increment as before), I can now decrease $K$ from 1.333 to 1, a drop of .333. The fact that .333 is lower than .666 is just another case of diminishing marginal returns at work.

Based on the comparison of the two panels in Figure 3.1 and based on the preceding analysis, we conclude that:

> Reflecting decreasing marginal returns, isoquants are convex curves; the closer complements two inputs are, the more convex the corresponding isoquants are.

Understanding the degree of complementarity or substitutability between two different inputs is important for a variety of reasons. For example, in the past few decades desktop computers have become a common feature in our daily lives. What impact has this had on the firms' demand for labor? One way to rephrase this question is: if we increase the quantity of one particular input (IT, specifically desktop computers) what impact does this have on the demand for labor? As often is the case in economics, the answer is: it depends. In this case, it depends on the type of labor. For example, at university departments the number of secretaries has declined considerably. I typed this book and I type all of my papers directly on my computer. Had I been born 20 or 30 years earlier, I would probably have written a manuscript and asked someone in the "typing pool" to turn it into a typescript. In sum, we may say that secretarial services and desktop computers are largely substitute inputs. But there are other types of labor that are complements with respect to IT investments, including desktop computers. The most obvious one is IT specialists: more desktops in the organization means more desktop problems; more desktop problems require more people to solve those problems. In sum, we may say that IT specialists and desktop computers are largely complement inputs.

■ **PRODUCTIVITY.** The term **productivity** is used frequently to describe a firm's performance. Unfortunately, it means different things to different people and as a result may be a source of confusion. Some, for example, measure average labor productivity, which is given by $qp/L$, or revenue per worker ($q$ is number of units produced, $p$ is price per unit, and $L$ is number of workers). However, this may not be the best measure of firm performance. Consider two firms, both with the same production function. If the first firm has a higher level of capital than the second firm, then it will also have a higher level of labor productivity — though we might argue that, having the same production function, the two firms are equally productive.

In this sense, a better measure of performance would be that of **total factor productivity** (TFP). Suppose that: (a) market price is given (and is the same for all firms in the industry); (b) each firm has a Cobb-Douglas production function with inputs $K$ and $L$; (c) all firms have the same $\alpha$ and $\beta$ coefficients but differ with respect to a multiplying coefficient:

$$q_i = \xi_i K_i^\alpha L_i^\beta \tag{3.1}$$

The coefficient $\omega_i$ would then be a better measure of a firm's performance, namely its total factor productivity. In fact, given two firms using the same quantity of inputs, the firm with a higher $\omega_i$ is able to produce a higher output level.

---

**ESTIMATING TOTAL FACTOR PRODUCTIVITY.** Taking logarithms on both sides of the production function (3.1), we get:

$\ln q_i = \ln \omega_i + \alpha \ln K_i + \beta \ln L_i$

or simply

$\ln \omega_i = \ln q_i - \alpha \ln K_i - \beta \ln L_i \tag{3.2}$

It can be shown (cf Exercise 3.15) that a profit maximizing firm chooses input levels such that the ratio between input costs (e.g., $wL$ in labor) and total revenue (i.e., $pq$) is equal to the respective coefficient in a Cobb-Douglas function (e.g., $\beta$ for labor):

$\alpha = \frac{rK}{pq}$

$\beta = \frac{wL}{pq}$

The values of $r, w, K, L, p, q$ can all be obtained from observable data. Together with the estimates of $\alpha$ and $\beta$, (3.2) gives us an estimate of the each firm's total factor productivity.

---

■ **COST MINIMIZATION.** The parallel between producer theory and consumer theory is more general than the point I made earlier. In consumer theory, we have a consumer who transforms consumption into utility — a kind of production function. The consumer's problem we solved was to maximize utility given a certain income level and given prices for the various goods. In production theory, we ask a similar question: given a desired output level and given input prices, we determine the input mix that minimizes cost.

This problem is shown in the right panel of Figure 3.2. Suppose we want to achieve $q = 4$. Suppose moreover that the cost of capital is $r = 12.5$, whereas the cost of labor is $w = 8$. Then it can be shown (cf Exercise 3.16) that the optimal solution is $K = 1.6$ and $L = 2.5$, as shown in the figure. Graphically, the problem of cost minimization (right panel of Figure 3.2) is similar to the problem of utility maximization considered in Chapter 2. Consumers seek the highest utility level consistent with a certain budget set; firms seek the lowest cost consistent with a certain output level. In both cases, the solution is given by a point of tangency: in the case of consumers, the optimal solution corresponds to a point where the indifference curve is tangent to the budget line (which, as you will recall, has a slope equal to -1 times the ratio between the prices of the two goods in question); in the case of firms, the optimal solution corresponds to a point where the isoquant is tangent to a line with slope equal to -1 times the ratio of the two inputs' prices.

If the cost of capital is $r = 12.5$ and the cost of labor is $w = 8$; if the best input mix to produce two units of output is $K = 1.6$ and $L = 2.5$; then the lowest cost the firm needs to incur in order to achieve $q = 2$ is $12.5 \times 1.6 + 8 \times 2.5 = 40$. More generally, for a given set of input prices $r, w$ and for a given output level $q$, we can follow the same steps and obtain the minimum cost required to achieve $q$. In this particular example we would get $C(q) = 20\,q$ (cf Exercise 3.16), an expression we denote the cost function. The reason we get such a simple expression is that we are considering a simple production function and, more important, we are assuming that both $K$ and $L$ can be adjusted at will, an assumption that does not always hold true. In general, things can get a little messier, as we will see later.

Before doing so, I should mention that, just as consumers have demand functions for products, firms have demand curves for inputs; and just as consumer demand can be characterized by its direct and cross price elasticities, so the firm's demand for inputs can be more or less elastic with respect to its price and the price of other inputs. In particular, the cross-price elasticity of the demand for inputs depends on the shape of the production function. If the production function is close to the extreme of perfect complements (left panel in Figure 3.1), then an increase in the cost of capital, for example, leads to a lower demand for capital *and* a lower demand for labor (since the quantities of capital and labor move hand in hand); that is, an increase in the cost of capital leads to a lower demand for labor: a negative cross-price elasticity, which as we saw in Chapter 2 denotes complements.

By contrast, if the production function is close to the perfect substitutes case (right panel in Figure 3.1), then depending on the price ratio of inputs the firm either only uses capital or only uses labor.[b] An increase in the cost of capital, for example, either keeps the demand for labor at zero or, if the ratio $-w/r$ "crosses over" the slope of the isoquant, switches all of the capital demand into labor demand; that is, an increase in the price of capital leads to a higher demand for labor: a positive cross-price elasticity, which as we saw in Chapter 2 denotes substitutes.

To see how this works in practice, consider two different industries (building hydroelectric dams and building aircraft) and two different countries (US and India). One important difference between the US and India is that $w/r$ is considerably lower in India, mainly because labor costs are lower. In order to dig a dam, one can use many possible combinations of labor and machines (that is, we are closer to the perfect substitutes case in Figure 3.1). To the extent that these are close substitutes, in India the industry is very labor intensive (that is, the ratio $K/L$ is very low), whereas, in the US, the industry is very capital intensive (that is, the ratio $K/L$ is very high). By contrast, in order to build an aircraft, certain amounts of skilled labor *and* machinery are required (that is, we are closer to the perfect complements case in Figure 3.1). For this reason, the $K/L$ ratio is relatively similar in the US and India even though the $w/r$ ratio is much lower in India.

■ **Cost function.** As I mentioned earlier, the firm's **cost function**, typically denoted by $C(q)$, shows the least total cost of inputs the firm needs to pay in order to produce output $q$; that is, the cost of producing $q$ assuming the firm does so efficiently. The cost function $C(q)$ leads to a series of related cost concepts:

- **Fixed Cost** (FC). The cost that does not depend on the output level.
- **Variable Cost** (VC). That cost which would be zero if the output level were zero.
- **Total Cost** (TC). The sum of fixed cost and variable cost.
- **Average Cost** (AC) (also known as "unit cost"). Total cost divided by output level.
- **Marginal Cost** (MC). The cost of one additional unit. In other words, the total cost of producing $q + 1$ units minus the total cost of producing $q$ units of output. (Strictly speaking, this is the definition of incremental cost. The rigorous definition of marginal cost is the derivative of total cost with respect to the output level.)

To illustrate all of these cost concepts, let us consider a very simple example, that of a small, price-taking T-Shirt Factory. In order to produce T-shirts, a manager leases one machine at the rate of $20 per week. The machine must be operated by one worker. The hourly wage paid to that worker is as follows: $1 during weekdays (up to 40 hours), $2 on Saturdays (up to 8 hours), and $3 on Sundays (up to 8 hours). Finally, the machine — which is operated by the worker — produces one T-shirt per hour.

Assuming that current output ($q$) is 40 T-shirts per week, we have that:

- The fixed cost is given by the machine weekly lease. We thus have FC = $20.

- The variable cost is given by 40 T-shirts times one hour per T-shirt times $1 per hour, which equals $40.

- The average cost is (20+40)/40 = $1.50.

- The marginal cost is \$2. In fact, producing the 41st T-shirt in a given week would imply asking the worker to work on Saturday, which would be paid at the hourly rate \$2; and producing a T-shirt requires one hour of work.

These cost values were computed for a particular output level. However, both average cost and marginal cost depend on the output level. By computing the values of marginal cost and average cost for each output level, we get the marginal cost and average cost functions. Figure 3.3 depicts these functions for the particular case of the T-shirt factory. The more general case is given by the right panel in Figure 3.3.

What is the use of all of these cost concepts? Consider the following application. Suppose that Benetton, the sole buyer of T-shirts from our small factory, is offering a price of $p = \$1.80$ per T-shirt. Moreover, Benetton is willing to buy as many T-shirts as the factory wants to sell at that price (that is, the T-shirt factory is a price-taking firm). Given this offer, should the factory operate on Saturday?

At the current output of $q = 40$ T-shirts a week, average cost is given by \$1.50 (see above). This means that, at $p = \$1.80$, the factory is making money. It might seem that, for this reason, it is worth it to operate on Saturdays as well: "If you are making money at the current output level, produce more and you will make more money." As it turns out, this is wrong. What is relevant for the decision of whether or not to operate on Saturdays is the comparison between price and *marginal* cost, not the comparison between price and average cost. And since marginal cost of operating on Saturdays is \$2, it is not worth pursuing that strategy given that the selling price is only \$1.80.

In other words, although the factory is making money at output level $q = 40$ (because price is greater than average cost), profits would be lower if output were increased (because price is lower than marginal cost); the factory would lose money at the margin. (By "lose money at the margin" I mean lose money by producing an additional — a marginal — unit of output.)

Suppose now that Benetton (still the sole buyer) offers a price $p = \$1.30$ per T-shirt. No matter what the output level is, price falls below average cost. (Check this.) That is, no matter how much the factory produces, it will lose money. In fact,

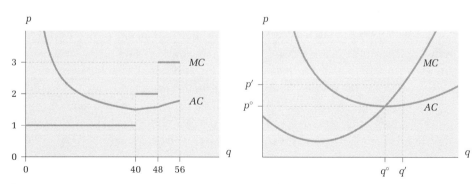

**FIGURE 3.3**
Marginal cost and average cost: T-shirt factory example (left) and general case (right)

$p < AC$ implies that $p \times q < AC \times q$, that is, revenues ($p \times q$) are less than total cost ($AC \times q = C$).

It follows that the optimal decision would be not to produce at all. (This comparison is based on the assumption that the firm has still not paid for the weekly machine lease.) To summarize,

> Marginal cost is the appropriate cost concept to decide how much to produce, whereas average cost is the appropriate cost concept to decide whether to produce at all.

The T-shirt factory example is a bit special in that there are only two factors of production and there isn't much flexibility in production. In general, the marginal cost and average cost functions would be continuous functions — or nearly continuous functions — as shown in the right panel of Figure 3.3. In this figure, $p^\circ$ denotes the minimum of the average cost function. For prices below this minimum, a price-taking firm would prefer not to produce at all. For values of $p$ greater than $p^\circ$, the optimal output level for a price-taking firm is given by the marginal cost function. For example, if $p = p'$, then optimal output is $q'$. More generally, a price-taking firm's **supply function** is given by the marginal cost function for values of price greater than the minimum of average cost.

## 3.2 PRICING

In the previous section we assumed that firms are price takers, like the small T-shirt factory that receives a take-it-or-leave-it offer from Benetton. However, most firms have *some* control over the price they set. Although they may have competitors, they can charge a higher or lower price, and generate less or more demand as a result. The question is then how high to set price. A high price generates more revenue per unit, but fewer units are sold. A low price generates less revenue per unit, but more units are sold. Which is best? As almost always in economics, the answer is: it depends! In the present context, it depends, as we will see, on the value of the price elasticity of demand as well as on the value of marginal cost.[c]

■ **OPTIMAL PRICING: THE INTUITION.** Before getting into more formal analysis, it may help to consider a specific numerical example, in fact, one that is — as they say in Hollywood — "inspired by true events." Rui, a young undergraduate economics major, got a summer job selling ice cream in Philadelphia. He operates his truck in a specific neighborhood of Philly, where he is the only vendor. After a few days of experimentation with different prices, he estimates that demand is given by the values in first two columns of Table 3.1. Rui's costs are as follows: each day he must pay $15 for the truck rental; in addition, he must pay the ice cream factory $3 per unit sold.

c. In the present section — in fact, until Chapter 8 — I will ignore the interaction between the firm's price and that of its competitors, either because they do not exist (monopoly) or because strategic interaction is not very important.

**TABLE 3.1** Ice cream pricing example

| price | demand | total revenue | total cost | incremental revenue | incremental cost | profit |
|---|---|---|---|---|---|---|
| 10.0 | 0.0 | 0.0 | 15.0 | | | −15.0 |
| 9.5 | 1.0 | 9.5 | 18.0 | 9.5 | 3.0 | −8.5 |
| 9.0 | 2.0 | 18.0 | 21.0 | 8.5 | 3.0 | −3.0 |
| 8.5 | 3.0 | 25.5 | 24.0 | 7.5 | 3.0 | 1.5 |
| 8.0 | 4.0 | 32.0 | 27.0 | 6.5 | 3.0 | 5.0 |
| 7.5 | 5.0 | 37.5 | 30.0 | 5.5 | 3.0 | 7.5 |
| 7.0 | 6.0 | 42.0 | 33.0 | 4.5 | 3.0 | 9.0 |
| 6.5 | 7.0 | 45.5 | 36.0 | 3.5 | 3.0 | 9.5 |
| 6.0 | 8.0 | 48.0 | 39.0 | 2.5 | 3.0 | 9.0 |
| 5.5 | 9.0 | 49.5 | 42.0 | 1.5 | 3.0 | 7.5 |
| 5.0 | 10.0 | 50.0 | 45.0 | 0.5 | 3.0 | 5.0 |
| 4.5 | 11.0 | 49.5 | 48.0 | −0.5 | 3.0 | 1.5 |

Based on these numbers, Rui assembled the values listed in Table 3.1. The third column shows total revenue for each price. This is simply price times quantity (first column times second column). The fourth column shows total cost: 15 plus three times the number of units sold (as given by the second column). The fifth and sixth columns will be discussed in detail below. Finally, the seventh column shows profit, the difference between the third and the forth columns.

Given all this information, the question at hand is: what price should Rui set?

Before continuing, notice that, since price and output are related by the demand function (as shown in the first two columns of Table 3.1), it is the same thing to choose the optimal price or to choose the optimal output level. That is, even though the seller is assumed to set price and consumers choose quantity as a function of price, we can think of the seller as choosing the optimal quantity it wants consumers to buy and then setting the corresponding price. In what follows, we treat the seller's decision as that of selecting an output level. Note also that, given the particular demand curve we consider, the sequence of declining prices in Table 3.1 corresponds to output increasing by units of one from row to row. This need not always be true, but it makes our life considerably easier.

So, to rephrase the earlier question: what level of unit sales should Rui optimally target? Economists like to think about these questions by reasoning in terms of incremental, or marginal, decisions. Specifically, let us first ask the question: is it better to sell one unit than to sell none (assuming the truck rental fee has already been paid)? Is it better to be in the first row (price equal to 10, zero sales), or the second one (price equal to 9.5, one unit of sales)?

In order to answer this question, we compute incremental revenue and incremental cost. The value of **incremental revenue** is shown in the fifth column of Table 3.1. For example, when setting price at 9.5, Rui is able to sell one unit. Compared to selling zero units (price equal to 10), this corresponds to an incremental revenue of 9.5, which is the difference between 9.5 (total revenue from selling one unit) and 0 (total revenue from selling no units). By the same token, the incremental revenue from selling three units instead of two is equal to $7.5 = 25.5 - 18$; and so forth. Similarly to incremental revenue, we can also compute the values of incremental cost, a concept introduced in the previous section. Specifically, the marginal cost of selling one unit is given by $3 = 18 - 15$. As can be seen in Table 3.1, this is also the marginal cost for all other units.

How do the concepts of incremental revenue and incremental cost help determine the optimal sales target? When considering the choice between selling zero units and selling one unit, Rui compares an incremental revenue of 9.5 to an incremental cost of 3. Since 9.5 is greater than 3, it is better to sell one unit than to sell none. Next we compare selling two units to selling one. The incremental revenue of the second unit is 7.5, whereas the incremental cost is only 3. Rui is therefore better off by selling two units than by selling only one. Continuing with this reasoning, we conclude that it is optimal to sell 7 units (by setting a price equal to 6.5). In fact, at this output level, a further increase to 8 would imply an incremental revenue of only 2.5, whereas the incremental cost would be 3.

The fact that a price of 6.5 and a sales target of 7 correspond to the optimal solution could also be gotten by simply looking that the rightmost column: the value of profit is maximal precisely in the column where price equals 6.5. However, the incremental revenue versus incremental cost reasoning helps derive an important rule in economics: the level of output should be chosen so that the value of incremental revenue is as close to incremental cost as possible. This may seem strange: if we want to maximize profit, then surely we want the difference between revenues and costs to be as high as possible. The solution to this apparent paradox is that that one thing is the difference between revenues and costs; and a different thing is the difference between incremental revenues and incremental costs. Below I return to this important issue.

■ **OPTIMAL PRICING: THE CALCULUS APPROACH.** We now develop the model of **optimal pricing** formally. Consider a firm facing a demand curve $D(p)$, where $p$ is the price set by the firm. It may help to think of the firm as being a monopolist, although the results that follow apply more generally as long as we know that $D(p)$ is the demand curve faced by the firm. We may also consider the demand curve in inverse form: in order to sell a quantity $q$, the seller must set a price $P(q)$, where $P(\cdot)$ is the inverse function of $D(\cdot)$. By producing $q$, the firm incurs a cost $C(q)$. Finally, it is assumed that the firm chooses a price to maximize profits.

Since for each price there is a unique quantity demanded and vice versa, it is equivalent to determine the optimal price or the optimal output level (from which the optimal price is obtained via the inverse demand function). I will follow this alternative path: I derive the optimal value of $q^*$ from which I then get $p^* = P(q^*)$.

If the inverse demand curve (price as a function of quantity) is $p = P(q)$, then revenue (expressed as a function of output, $q$) is:

$$R(q) = pq = P(q)\,q$$

Earlier I defined incremental revenue as the extra revenue obtained from selling an additional unit. If instead of one unit we consider an *infinitesimal* increase in output, then we obtain marginal revenue. Formally, **marginal revenue** is given by the derivative of revenue with respect to output level:

$$MR(q) = \frac{dR(q)}{dq} = \frac{d\left(P(q)q\right)}{dq} = P(q) + P'(q)\,q = p + P'(q)\,q$$

where $P'(q)$ denotes derivative of $p$ with respect to $q$ and I apply the derivative of product rule. Notice that:

$$MR(q) = p + P'(q)\,q < p$$

which follows from our standard assumption that demand declines as price increases (and hence $D'(p) < 0$, and hence $P'(q) < 0$). In words: the extra revenue a seller gets from increasing output level is less than the price at which the seller sells such additional output. (Why?)

The optimal output level can be found by maximizing profit, which we denote by the Greek letter $\pi$:

$$\pi(q) = R(q) - C(q)$$

We find the maximum of $\pi$ by setting the derivative equal to zero and then verifying that we have a maximum. The derivative equated to zero leads to:

$$\frac{d\pi(q)}{dq} = MR(q) - MC(q) = 0$$

or simply[d]

$$MR(q) = MC(q)$$

In words,

> The profit maximizing output level is such that marginal revenue equals marginal cost.

How do we go from the $MR(q) = MC(q)$ equation to the value of optimal price and output level? Suppose that demand is given by $q = a - bp$, whereas marginal cost is constant at $c$. First we derive the inverse demand curve, which is given by $p = \frac{a-q}{b}$. Total revenue is given by:

$$R = pq = \frac{a-q}{b}\,q$$

It follows that marginal revenue is:

$$MR = \frac{dR}{dq} = -\frac{1}{b}q + \frac{a-q}{b} = \frac{a-2q}{b}$$

d. A technical aside: To check that we have a maximum, we look at the second derivative, that is, $\partial\pi(q)/\partial q^2 = MR'(q) - MC'(q)$. If this is negative, then $MR = MC$ gives us a max. It's sufficient that $MC$ increase with $q$ (that is, $MC' > 0$) and $MR$ decrease with $q$ (that is, $MR' < 0$). For most of the problems I'll consider, I'll assume that $MR' < 0$ and $MC' \geq 0$ (thus allowing for the possibility that marginal cost is constant).

Next, we equate *MR* to $c$ (the value of marginal cost in the present instance) and solve with respect to $q$:

$$q = \frac{a - bc}{2}$$

Finally, by substituting this value for $q$ in the inverse demand function we obtain the optimal price level:

$$p = \frac{a - q}{b} = \frac{a - \frac{a-bc}{2}}{b} = \frac{a + bc}{2b}$$

Alternatively, we can simply write out the profit function:

$$\pi(q) = pq - cq = \frac{a - q}{b}\, q - cq = \frac{a}{b}\, q - \frac{1}{b}\, q^2 - cq$$

take the derivative with respect to $q$ and solve with respect to $q$. (Confirm that you get the same result.)

The left panel of Figure 3.4 depicts the optimal solution. We begin by plotting the inverse demand curve, which crosses the vertical axis at $a/b$ and the horizontal axis at $a$; as well as the marginal cost curve, which in the present example is simply constant at $c$. Next we derive the marginal revenue mapping. The vertical intercept of the marginal revenue curve is the same as the demand curve. (Can you explain why?) When the demand curve is linear, the intercept of the marginal revenue curve with the horizontal axis is given by $a/2$, that is, it is one half of the intercept of the demand curve. The optimal output level is given by the intersection of *MR* and *MC*, which takes place at $q^*$. Finally, optimal price $p^*$ can be obtained from $q^*$ and the inverse demand curve.

■ **ELASTICITY RULES.** The math is useful for some people because it is clear and concise. It is also useful for demonstrating an interesting relationship between seller margin and elasticity. Recall that marginal revenue is given by $MR = p + P'(q)\,q$. The optimality rule is that marginal revenue be equal to marginal cost. This implies:

$$p + P'(q)\,q = MC$$

Rearranging terms and dividing both sides by $p$ we get:

$$\frac{p - MC}{p} = -P'(q)\,\frac{q}{p}$$

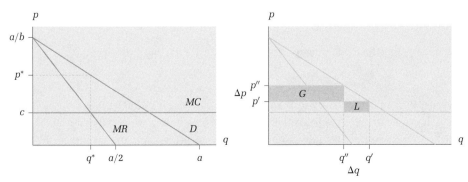

**FIGURE 3.4**
Optimal pricing

Notice that $P'(q) = \frac{dp}{dq}$, whereas $\epsilon$, the price elasticity of demand, is given by $\epsilon = \frac{dq}{dp}\frac{p}{q}$. Therefore, $P'(q)\frac{q}{p} = 1/\epsilon$. We thus conclude that:

$$\frac{p - MC}{p} = -\frac{1}{\epsilon} \qquad\qquad (3.3)$$

An equivalent expression is:

$$p = \frac{MC}{1 + \frac{1}{\epsilon}}$$

We refer to both equations as versions of the **elasticity rule** of optimal pricing. The elasticity rule is frequently referred to with reference to the **margin** (also known as the **Lerner index**[1]), defined as:

$$m = \frac{p - MC}{p} \qquad\qquad (3.4)$$

We know that firms should operate at a positive margin. But how large should this margin be? The answer is:

$$m = \frac{1}{-\epsilon}$$

In words, the elasticity rule states that:

> The lower the price elasticity of demand (in absolute value) the higher the price-cost margin should be set:

An alternative way to understand the elasticity rule is to consider a small increase in price. This is shown in the right panel of Figure 3.4, where I plot two different values of $p$: $p'$ and $p''$. How does profit change as we increase $p$ from $p'$ to $p''$? The good news is that the profit margin increases from $p' - c$ to $p'' - c$. This corresponds to a gain of $\Delta p\, q''$, the shaded area $G$. The bad news is that by increasing price sales drop from $q'$ to $q''$. This corresponds to a loss of $-\Delta q\,(p' - c)$, the shaded area $L$. How do these two areas compare? For very small variations in $p$ and $q$, small enough that $p$ is approximately equal to $p'$ and $p''$ and $q$ is approximately equal to $q'$ and $q''$, we can say that $L$ is less than $G$ if and only if $-\Delta q\,(p - c) < \Delta p\, q$. This is equivalent to:

$$\frac{p - c}{p} < -\frac{\Delta p}{\Delta q}\frac{q}{p}$$

If the change in price is very small (that is, infinitesimal), then this becomes:

$$m < \frac{1}{-\epsilon}$$

In words, if the margin is lower than the inverse of the elasticity (in absolute value), then an increase in price leads to an increase in profits. Likewise, if the margin is greater than the inverse of the elasticity, then a decrease in price leads to an increase in profits. (Check this.) We conclude that the only price such that profits cannot be further increased is given by the elasticity rule.

What if $-1 < \epsilon < 0$? Applying the elasticity rule $p = MC / \left(1 + \frac{1}{\epsilon}\right)$, we get a negative value for $p$, which does not make much sense. How does a firm maximize profit by setting a negative price? Let's think about the economics of the situation. If $\epsilon$ is less than 1 in absolute value, then an increase in price leads to an increase in revenue (as seen in Chapter 2: the decrease in quantity is very small compared to the increase in price). Since an increase in price implies a decrease in quantity (small as it may be), it also implies a decrease in cost (for cost is increasing in output). We thus conclude that, if $\epsilon$ is less than 1 in absolute value, then an increase in price leads to an increase in revenue and a decrease in cost; it thus leads to an increase in profit. It follows that, whenever $-1 < \epsilon < 0$, it is optimal for the seller to increase price.

In practice, we do observe goods that have a low price elasticity of demand (see Chapter 2 for examples). Does this imply a violation of the elasticity rule? Maybe yes, maybe not. Consider for example ConEdison, the electrical utility serving New York City. Consumer demand for electricity is inelastic, that is, $-1 < \epsilon < 0$; still, ConEdison does not increase price as the elasticity rule would suggest. The reason is not that ConEdison would not want to increase price, rather that regulation prevents it from doing so.

Consider now the case of milk sold in Manhattan. As we saw in Chapter 2, this is another example of a good with inelastic demand. Absent price regulation as in electricity, why isn't the price of milk higher? This time the reason is that, while the market price elasticity is less than 1 (in absolute value), the demand elasticity faced by each seller is considerably greater than 1 (in absolute value). In fact, to the extent that milk is a relatively homogeneous product, a small price increase by a small producer would reduce its demand to zero.

Finally, if the market demand for milk is inelastic, one might ask why don't milk sellers get together and jointly increase price (so that buyers have no alternative but to buy a similar quantity at a higher price). This time the reason is that such agreement would most likely be illegal, as we will see in Chapter 9.

---

**NUMERICAL EXAMPLE.** All roads lead to Rome, so goes the old adage.[e] In the present context, this means that there are different alternative paths to reach the optimal solution. Let us return to the ice cream pricing example and convince ourselves that this is indeed the case. If we try to fit a linear curve to the demand values in Table 3.1, we obtain a demand curve $q = 20 - 2p$. In terms of the notation on page 46, this corresponds to $a = 20$ and $b = 2$. Moreover, marginal cost is equal to $c$, which in the ice cream example becomes $c = 3$. What is optimal price? In the linear demand curve case, we saw that:

$$p^* = \frac{a + bc}{2b}$$

which in this case becomes $p = (20 + 2 \times 3)/(2 \times 2) = 6.5$, just as we derived earlier. Output, in turn, is given by $q = 20 - 2p = 7$.

What about the elasticity rule? First notice that, *at the optimal price level*, elasticity is given by:

$$\epsilon = \frac{dq}{dp} \frac{p}{q} = -b \frac{p}{q} = -2 \frac{6.5}{7} = -\frac{13}{7}$$

e. Actually, the original seems to be "Mille viae ducunt homines per saecula Romam" (A thousand roads lead men forever to Rome).

## BOX 3.1 MONSANTO'S ROUNDUP[2]

Monsanto's leading product, Roundup, is the trademarked name of glyphosate, a chemical herbicide developed and patented by the firm in the 1970s. Roundup is referred to as a nonselective herbicide, meaning it kills most plants. In the late 1990s, it became the best-selling agricultural chemical of all time and an enormously profitable product for Monsanto.

This success was the result of several factors. One was a conscious strategy to reduce price in the US, where patent protection gave it an effective monopoly until September 2000. (Prices were lower outside the US, where patents expired earlier: see the chart below, where $U$ stands for US and $O$ for overseas.) Between 1995 and 2000, Monsanto reduced the price by an average of 9% a year. When volume increased by an average of 22% a year, revenue and profits exploded. Glyphosate-based herbicides produced net sales for Monsanto of $2.4 billion in 2001 alone, nearly half the company's total.

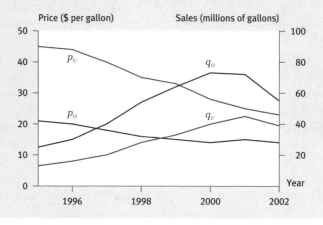

Also at the optimal price level, the margin is given by:

$$m = \frac{p - MC}{p} = \frac{6.5 - 3}{6.5} = \frac{3.5}{6.5} = \frac{7}{13}$$

Bingo! As expected, we confirm that $m = 1/(-\epsilon)$.

---

■ **MARGIN AND MARKUP.** Frequently, instead of price margins, price data are presented in terms of markups. The price **markup** is given by:

$$k \equiv \frac{p - MC}{MC}$$

How does the elasticity rule work in terms of markups? Notice that:

$$\frac{k}{1 + k} = \frac{\frac{p - MC}{MC}}{1 + \frac{p - MC}{MC}} = \frac{p - MC}{p} = m$$

Therefore, the elasticity rule may be written as:

$$\frac{k}{1+k} = \frac{1}{-\epsilon}$$

or alternatively,

$$k = \frac{1}{-\epsilon - 1}$$

(Check this.) As before, this formula makes it clear that, when $|\epsilon| < 1$, the elasticity rule does not apply: it is always optimal for the seller to increase price so long as $|\epsilon| < 1$.

---

**LOG-LINEAR DEMAND.** Consider a similar problem with a log-linear demand curve. This kind of demand curve is mathematically uglier, but is rather convenient because it has constant elasticity of demand. Moreover, in practice it is generally a much better approximation to the data than the linear demand curves we often use as examples. Let's say that the inverse demand is:

$$\log p = \log \alpha + \beta \log q$$

or

$$p = \alpha \, q^{\beta}$$

The price elasticity of demand is $\epsilon = \frac{1}{\beta}$. If marginal cost is a constant $c$, then profit is:

$$\pi(q) = p\,q - c\,q = \alpha\,q^{\beta+1} - c\,q$$

To find the optimal quantity we solve:

$$\frac{d\,\pi(q)}{d\,q} = (\beta + 1)\,\alpha\,q^{\beta} - c = 0$$

If you recall that $\alpha\,q^{\beta} = p$, this turns into:

$$p\left(1 + \frac{1}{\epsilon}\right) = c$$

which is equivalent to the elasticity rule.

---

■ **MULTIPRODUCT PRICING.** Most firms sell more than one product — some, like P&G or Unilever, sell much more than one product. If the demands for the various products are independent, then the above analysis applies to each of the products. If the demands are interrelated, however, then optimal pricing should take into account how the price of one product influences the demand for the other ones. For example, Philip Morris sells Marlboro and Cambridge cigarettes; Gillette sells razors and razor blades; Gristedes supermarkets sells a ton of products. What kind of pricing patterns would you expect to find in each of these examples?

A related phenomenon is that of dynamic pricing. The demand for movies, CDs, books, and the like is largely based on word-of-mouth dynamics. As Sony painfully learned, the demand for VCRs depends on the dynamics of standard setting (which we will get to in Chapter 16). Addiction can also be a important dynamic demand factor. You're probably thinking about drugs, but there are many other cases when habit formation plays an important role. What are the implications of such demand dynamics for optimal pricing?

A particularly interesting case of demand dynamics is durable goods, goods such that consumers have some flexibility regarding timing of purchase: whereas I need to buy lunch everyday, I can upgrade my car now or next year. Durable goods imply intertemporal product substitutes: if I buy a car now, my demand for cars next year drops (to close to zero). More on this in Chapter 6.

## 3.3 DO FIRMS MAXIMIZE PROFITS?[3]

One of the features of the "black-box" view of the firm is that firms maximize profits. How realistic is this assumption? In most modern corporations, management is separated from ownership; that is, the recipients of the firm's profits (owners) are not the agents whose decisions ultimately determine the firm's profit level (managers). Although we would expect managers to be motivated by the firm's success, profits are only one aspect of firm success. In general, the managers' objectives differ from the shareholders'. Does this imply that the assumption of profit maximization is wrong?

f. This argument suggests that monitoring by shareholders is more frequent when ownership is more concentrated. However, anecdotal evidence suggests that German banks, who own significant shares in other firms, do not monitor CEOs to any significant extent. Evidence from the US banking industry also suggests that shareholder concentration has little effect.[4]

g. We say that an agent is risk neutral if he or she is indifferent between receiving 100 for sure and receiving 0 or 200 with probability 50% each. More generally, a risk-neutral agent only cares about the expected value of each outcome. By contrast, a risk-averse agent would prefer a safe outcome to another outome with the same expected value but greater risk. Continuing with the same example, a risk-averse agent would prefer 100 for sure to the 0-or-200 gamble.

■ **INTERNAL DISCIPLINE.** Recognizing the difference in objectives, one thing shareholders can do is to appoint a manager with a contract that induces the latter to act in the former's interest. However, many corporations are owned by a large number of small shareholders. This considerably decreases the incentives for shareholders to act: the effort necessary in order to determine how to instruct managers is very high compared to the benefits a small shareholder would gain from better management.[f]

Boards of directors are supposed to solve, or at least attenuate, this problem. The board of directors has the discretion to appoint managers, fire them, set their salaries, correct them when and if necessary, and to do so in the interest of shareholders. But just as managers don't necessarily have the same objective as shareholders, so too boards of directors may have goals other than maximizing shareholder value. In fact, anecdotal evidence suggests that boards of directors are seldom independent and frequently defend the CEO's, not the shareholders', interests.

Even if shareholders can and are willing to control managers, there is still the problem that managers normally know better than shareholders what is best for the firm. In other words, there is a problem of asymmetric information. **Agency theory** is the area of economics that deals with this class of strategic interaction; that is, a principal who wants an agent to act in the principal's interest but possesses less information than the agent.

A critical result from agency theory is that, if the agent — the manager, in our case — is risk-neutral, then the optimal solution is for the manager to pay the shareholders an initial fee and then retain all of the profits: a management buyout.[g] In other words, the optimal solution is for ownership and management to be unified. Under this solution, the manager's decisions will be optimal from the owner's point of view — a trivial point.

The reason we observe separation between management and ownership is that managers are subject to financial constraints; and, more important, managers are risk-averse. The optimal contract between shareholders and managers is therefore one that balances the benefits from insuring the manager against risk, on the one hand, and the benefits from providing the manager with the right incentives, on the other hand. At one extreme, we have the solution outlined above (shareholders sell the firm to the manager), which entails maximum risk and maximum incentives. At the opposite extreme, we have a fixed wage or salary, which entails minimum risk and minimum incentives.

From a theoretical point of view, the optimal contract — the optimal balance between risk and incentives — is typically very complicated. Moreover, the solution turns out to depend greatly on the precise assumptions regarding the environment in which the firm operates. For these reasons, it is not surprising that actual contracts tend to be very simple: normally a combination of fixed wage and a profit-contingent compensation (e.g., stock options). Such contracts attenuate the agency problem of separation between ownership and management, but clearly do not completely solve it.

■ **LABOR MARKET DISCIPLINE.** Even if shareholders are unable to "punish" a manager for poor performance, the manager cannot avoid a negative reputation that follows poor performance. Since managers don't stay with the same firm forever, they are interested in creating a reputation for being good managers. This reputation effect may help provide managers with the proper incentives.

■ **PRODUCT MARKET DISCIPLINE.** Product market competition may also contribute to aligning shareholders' and manager's objectives. The idea is that, when product market competition is very intense, firms cannot survive unless they maximize profits. Under intense market competition, if the manager does not actively seek to maximize firm profits, the likelihood that the firm goes out of business — and the manager loses his or her job — is high. We should therefore expect the manager to put more effort into profit maximization in a situation where product market competition is tougher.[h]

A second reason why product market competition may increase the incentives for profit maximization is that competitors provide useful signals about the firm's productivity. In other words, they reduce the shareholders' informational disadvantage with respect to the manager. In a monopoly situation, a manager can always blame poor performance on a number of exogenous industry factors. Such strategy is less effective when there are competing firms and the latter perform well.

■ **CAPITAL MARKET DISCIPLINE.** One of the most compelling arguments in favor of the assumption of profit maximization is the role played by capital markets, namely the role played by mergers and acquisitions. The idea is quite simple: if a manager does not maximize profits, then the value of the firm is lower than its potential. In that case, a **raider** could acquire the firm, change management in order to maximize profits, and thus make a capital gain.[i] Notice that, in order for the disciplining effect of takeovers to

h. Exercise 3.19 formalizes this intuition.

i. This argument is not free from criticism. If a raider can change management in a profit increasing way, why can't current shareholders do the same? One possible answer is that the raider possesses information that shareholders do not: for example, the raider may be a firm from the same or a related industry. But if that is the case, then why would an individual shareholder sell his or her shares to the raider? Surely, if the raider is to change management and increase firm value, then the optimal strategy is not to sell the shares.

take place, it is not necessary for takeovers to actually take place — it is sufficient for the *threat* of takeover to be in place.

In summary,

> Although management and ownership are normally separated, there are reasons to believe that deviations from profit maximization cannot be too large. These reasons include management incentive contracts, labor market discipline, product market discipline, and capital market discipline.

The precise meaning of "not too large," that is, the extent to which profit maximization is a good approximation, remains an unresolved empirical question.

## 3.4  WHAT DETERMINES A FIRM'S BOUNDARIES?

Why should firms be of the size they are; why not smaller or bigger? What does economic analysis have to say about firm size? It may be useful to divide this into two questions: (a) what determines the horizontal extension of the firm and (b) what determines the degree of vertical integration. By horizontal extension I mean how much of a given product does a firm produce and how many different products it offers. By vertical integration, I mean how many stages of the production process take place within the firm. So, for example, by acquiring Skoda, SEAT, and Bentley, Volkswagen increased its horizontal stretch. Volkswagen would increase the degree of vertical integration if it were to acquire a tire manufacturer, for example (tires being one of the inputs into car manufacturing).

The horizontal size of the firm is largely determined by costs. If average cost is U shaped (cf Figure 3.3) and there is free entry into the industry, then firms will tend to produce at the level where average cost is minimized (cf Section 4.1). For example, there is an optimal size for a cement plant that minimizes cost. Plants of much smaller size or much larger size would probably incur a higher average cost and be unable to survive for very long. However, empirical evidence suggests average cost functions are U shaped with a flat bottom (that is, "saucer" shaped). This implies that there is a range of output levels which attain the minimum average cost. In other words, costs may not entirely allow us to pin down the size of the firm.

The problem becomes more complicated if we consider the distinction between plant and firm. Production costs are related to plant operation. Suppose there is a unique output level which minimizes plant average costs and that a given firm owns two plants. It is possible that the firm's average cost is similar to the average cost of a firm owning one plant only. If so, then multiplant firms create a new dimension of indeterminacy of firm size. This indeterminacy may be resolved if we take managerial costs into consideration: very large conglomerates may simply be too large to be managed efficiently. This brings us back to the idea of U-shaped cost curves, with the difference that the independent variable is now number of plants rather than output level.

■ **THE VERTICAL BOUNDARIES OF THE FIRM.**[5]  Perhaps a more interesting question regarding the boundaries of the firm is: why do we observe a great degree of vertical integration in some industries and very little in others? One of the most important decisions that a firm has to make is how to obtain its inputs: to make or to buy. In other words, to use the market (vertical separation) or to use the firm (vertical integration). The degree of vertical integration in a given industry results from the aggregation of these micro decisions at each stage of the production process. Understanding the nature of the make-or-buy decision contributes to understanding the nature of the firm as well as one the determinants of industry structure.

Consider the example of the US coal industry. About 80% of the coal is used for electricity generation. Since the transportation costs from mine to power generation plant are high, it pays to locate power plants near coal mines. Consider the decision of building a power plant near a coal mine. Since there are no other nearby sources of coal, we refer to such an investment as a **specific asset**: the power plant is worth a lot less if not coupled with this particular source of supply. For this reason, if the power plant owner is different from the coal mine owner, the relation between seller and buyer is subject to a **hold-up problem**: once the buyer pays for the relationship-specific asset, the seller can charge a higher price. One possible solution to this problem is vertical integration. In the US, mine-mouth power plants and the respective coal mine are typically owned by the same entity; and when they are not, the contractual relationship between seller and buyer is typically governed by long-term contracts.[6]

But vertical integration does not solve all of the incentive problems. If I buy from an external supplier, that supplier has strong incentives to perform: it knows that underperformance easily leads to supplier switching. If I buy the external supplier and make it part of my organization, that supplier (formerly external, currently internal) now has weaker incentives, for the threat of switching to another supplier is likely smaller.

Both the extremes of complete vertical integration and complete vertical separation imply incentive problems. Sometimes, the optimal solution may lie between the extremes. One possibility is that of **tapered integration**, whereby a given input is bought from an affiliated supplier *and* from an independent one. Examples of tapered integration include soft-drink bottling for the Coca-Cola and Pepsi-Cola companies; and crude oil supply to oil refineries. A second intermediate system is that of **franchising**, a system that has been used in a variety of industries, from fast-food (e.g., McDonald's) to designer clothing (e.g., Stefanel). Franchising combines the benefits of vertical integration (specific investments are paid by the mother company) with the benefits of vertical separation (franchisees retain most of the profit they generate, and thus have strong incentives to be efficient). Finally, the Japanese system of supplier contracting also corresponds to an intermediate solution: the firm and its suppliers establish a long-term, informal relationship that falls short of full-scale vertical integration but goes a long way towards providing suppliers with the right incentives to invest in assets specific to the relationship with their customers.

In other words, the definition of the boundaries of the firm is far from being a well-defined problem with a well-defined answer. Consider, for example, the Japanese *keiretsu*, that is, a family of firms, typically from related industries, with cross share-holdings. Should a keiretsu be considered a firm in and of itself? Probably not — but neither is it a simple collection of independent firms. Moreover, it is not uncommon to find two otherwise similar firms that differ significantly in the way they are organized. For example, the Italian clothes manufacturer Benetton depends largely on a franchise system for its retail sales, whereas Spanish rival Zara is wholy vertically integrated. Examples like these suggest that there may be other determinants of firm structure that lead some firms to choose differently from others.

While the problems of firm organization are extremely complex, both in theory and in practice, it seems safe to summarize that:

> The horizontal boundaries of the firm are largely determined by cost considerations (including managerial costs). The vertical boundaries result from the balance between investment incentives (specific assets) and performance incentives.

## 3.5 WHY ARE FIRMS DIFFERENT?

Casual observation of the real world reveals that firms are different from each other: different in size, different in scope, and so forth. In particular, we observe that firm performance (e.g., profit rate) varies enormously across firms. This is not entirely surprising if we consider that different firms may be of very different size or belong to different industries. Why should we expect the profit rate of Boeing to be the same as that of a coffee shop?

Empirical observation suggests, however, that firms in the same industry and of similar dimension also perform very differently. Only 20% of the variance in firm profit rates can be explained by variables that relate to firm size, the type of industry in which the firm operates, and so forth.[7] Moreover, differences in firm performance seem to be very persistent. If we consider a set of firms that are 20 or more years old, we will observe that the firms that are more profitable today were, on average, more profitable 20 years ago.[8]

What is the source of the 80% variability in firm performance that is left to explain? Why do some firms hold a **sustained competitive advantage**? It may be useful to consider the analogy with car racing; say, Formula One racing. It is quite clear that there are significant differences between different Formula One teams and that those differences seem to persist from race to race. One rather obvious explanation is that not all drivers have the same ability. In order for the Sauber team to match the performance of the Mercedes team, the former might need to recruit a driver like Nico Rosberg (who currently races for Mercedes). But such driver seems difficult to find. Likewise, in the world of business, there may be **impediments to imitation** that allow some firms to perform persistently better than others.[9] An obvious limit to imitation is given by legal restrictions. In the late 1960s and early 1970s, Xerox was the dominant player in the photocopier industry thanks to its patent on plain-paper photocopying. Once Xerox started licensing its technology, differences in performance with respect to competitors decreased considerably (see Chapter 15).

If Sauber cannot find another Nico Rosberg, it should at least be able to imitate the best features of the Mercedes car (which seems to be faster than the Sauber car, even controlling for driver skills). Most features of Formula One cars are not patented. However, there are so many aspects in which a Mercedes car differs from an Sauber car that it would be difficult to understand which one is responsible for the superior performance of the former. Something similar occurs with firms as organizations. For many years, Toyota's procurement system was considered clearly superior to its rivals'. However, the system involved so many different aspects that it was difficult to pin down what the crucial success factors were. More generally, the problem is even more serious: most of the features of any given organization are *tacit knowledge*, capabilities that are developed by experience and rarely written down; capabilities that are difficult to express formally as an algorithm or a set of rules. Even if one of Toyota's rivals were to recruit some key employees and managers from Toyota, the latter would have difficulty in expressing their knowledge in the new organization, let alone implementing it. In strategy jargon, we say this is a case of **causal ambiguity**.[10]

Finally, even at times when the Mercedes car/driver duo is slower than rivals, the Mercedes team has frequently turned out to be the winner. In these cases, success is largely due to **strategy**. Strategic or tactical decisions include whether to stop once or twice during a race, when to stop, what kind of tires to use, etc. — and how to react to the choices made by rival teams. In a business context, there are many dimensions in which strategy can have a lasting effect on firm performance: entry timing, capacity expansion, mergers and acquisitions, technological improvement, special contracts with customers and suppliers, not to mention pricing and advertising.

Of the three sources of competitive advantage listed above, strategy is the one we will focus on in the remaining chapters of the book. This is not to say that the other ones are not important. In fact, the argument can be made that firm **culture** — a broad term that would include tacit knowledge and other aspects which cannot be easily imitated — is an equally important source of competitive advantage. But the focus of industrial organization is on competition between firms, not so much the way a firm is internally organized.

A related source of heterogeneity across firms is the quality of its management. Empirical evidence suggests that (a) management quality is positively associated with firm performance ("management matters"); and (b) management quality varies considerably across firms. A recent study based on surveys of thousands of firms across the globe measured management quality by averaging a series of scores related to production logistics, inventories, performance evaluation, etc.[11]

Figure 3.5 plots the the distribution of values for the US and India. One first notice-able feature is the difference between the US and India. The average score for the US, $\mu_{US}$, is well above 3, whereas the average score for India, $\mu_I$, is well below 3. However, equally impressive is the variability of management quality within the US and within India. Some of the best-managed Indian firms are quite well managed: about 16% are better managed than the average US firm. By contrast, very few US firms have a score lower than 2, whereas about 20% of Indian firms fall below this threshold.

The preceding paragraph addresses point (b), that is, the idea that management quality varies considerably across firms. It does not address point (a), that is, the idea that management matters. To investigate the latter, one might regress firm performance (e.g., total factor productivity, as defined in Section 3.1), on the management quality score. Such a regression yields a large and statistical significant correlation. This is con-sistent with the proposition that management quality affects firm performance; how-ever, it does not imply that there is a causal relation. The best way to test causality is to run a **field experiment**. One such experiment randomly split Indian textile firms in two groups and offered one of the groups (treatment group) consulting services from Ander-son Consulting. As a result of these consulting services, the treatment group imple-mented important changes in its management practices, corresponding to an increase in the measurement quality score; moreover, these firms showed significant improvements in productivity (for example, a substantial drop in the number of defective products).

In conjunction with all of the factors mentioned above, one must also stress the importance of **history** in determining firm performance — and the persistence of differ-ences in firm performance. Consider the example of competition in the large commercial aircraft market during the 1970s. The three competitors were Boeing (B747), McDonnell Douglas (DC10), and Lockheed (L1011). One important aspect of competition in this

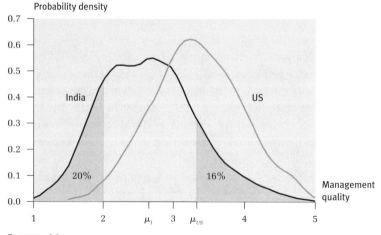

**FIGURE 3.5**
Management quality in India and in the US

industry is the existence of a steep **learning curve**: the more aircraft units a firm produces, the lower the cost of producing an aircraft unit. The name of the game is therefore to move down the learning curve as quickly as possible.

At the start, all three competitors maintained approximately equal market shares. But in the early 1970s, Lockheed's main engine supplier, Rolls-Royce, began to experience a series of technical and financial difficulties. This slowed down Lockheed's production rate and the speed at which it moved down the learning curve. When Lockheed tried to get back in the game, later in the 1970s, it was too late, for its competitors were already too competitive. McDonnell Douglas did not have much better luck. A series of crashes in 1980 severely hit consumer confidence in the DC10. In retrospect, this turned out to be a statistical coincidence, not the result of a fundamental problem with the DC10 design. But again, by the time McDonnell Douglas tried to get back in the game it was too late: Boeing had reached a superior degree of cost efficiency that allowed it to enjoy a sustainable competitive advantage over its rivals.[j]

This is an example where historical events (Rolls-Royce's problems in the early 1970s, the DC10 crashes in 1980) had an effect that lasted beyond the time when they occurred. In particular, these are events that, together with the learning curve phenomenon, have lead to a persistent asymmetry in firm performance between Boeing and its rivals. Other examples could be found, involving network externalities (see Box 16.3), consumer switching costs, and so forth. The point is that sometimes, instead of insisting on a general theory of firm heterogeneity, one simply has to accept the importance that history has in shaping an industry and the firms that it includes. I resume this discussion in Section 10.1. For now we conclude with a summary of the main points above:

> Firm performance varies a great deal. Firms are different because of impediments to imitation, causal ambiguity, firm strategy, management quality, or historical events.

## SUMMARY

• Reflecting decreasing marginal returns, isoquants are convex curves; the closer complements two inputs are, the more convex the corresponding isoquants are. • Marginal cost is the appropriate cost concept to decide how much to produce, whereas average cost is the appropriate cost concept to decide whether to produce at all. • The profit maximizing output level is such that marginal revenue equals marginal cost. • The lower the price elasticity of demand (in absolute value) the higher the price-cost margin should be set: • Although management and ownership are normally separated, there are reasons to believe that deviations from profit maximization cannot be too large. These reasons include management incentive contracts, labor market discipline, product market discipline, and capital market discipline. • The horizontal boundaries of the firm are largely

j.  Eventually, Lockheed exited from the civil aviation market. McDonnell Douglas, in turn, was later acquired by Boeing. In the meantime, Airbus appeared on the scene, challenging Boeing's dominance.

determined by cost considerations (including managerial costs). The vertical boundaries result from the balance between investment incentives (specific assets) and performance incentives. • Firm performance varies a great deal. Firms are different because of impediments to imitation, causal ambiguity, firm strategy, management quality, or historical events.

## KEY CONCEPTS

• production function  • isoquant  • perfect complements  • perfect substitutes  • Cobb-Douglas production function  • diminishing marginal returns  • productivity  • total factor productivity  • cost function  • fixed cost  • variable cost  • total cost  • average cost  • marginal cost  • supply function  • incremental revenue  • optimal pricing  • marginal revenue  • elasticity rule  • margin  • Lerner index  • markup  • agency theory  • raider  • specific asset  • hold-up problem  • tapered integration  • franchising  • sustained competitive advantage  • impediments to imitation  • causal ambiguity  • strategy  • culture  • field experiment  • history  • learning curve

## REVIEW AND PRACTICE EXERCISES

■ **3.1. DRAM FACTORY.** You own and operate a facility located in Taiwan that manufactures 64-megabit dynamic random-access memory chips (DRAMs) for personal computers (PCs). One year ago you acquired the land for this facility for $2 million, and used $3 million of your own money to finance the plant and equipment needed for DRAM manufacturing. Your facility has a maximum capacity of 10 million chips per year. Your cost of funds is 10% per year for either borrowing and investing. You could sell the land, plant, and equipment today for $8 million; you estimate that the land, plant, and equipment will gain 6% in value over the coming year. (Use a one-year planning horizon for this problem.)

In addition to the cost of land, plant, and equipment, you incur various operating expenses associated with DRAM production, such as energy, labor, raw materials, and packaging. Experience shows that these costs are $4 per chip, regardless of the number of chips produced during the year. In addition, producing DRAMs will cause you to incur fixed costs of $500k per year for items such as security, legal, and utilities.

(a) What is your cost function, $C(q)$, where $q$ is the number of chips produced during the year?

Assume now that you can sell as many chips as you make at the going market price per chip of $p$.

(b) What is the minimum price, $p$, at which you would find it profitable to produce DRAMs during the coming year?

■ **3.2. MP34U.** Music Ventures sells a very popular MP3 player, the MP34u. The firm currently sells one million units for a price of $100 each. Marginal cost is estimated to be constant at $40, whereas average cost (at the output level of one million units) is $90. The firm estimates that its demand elasticity (at the current price level) is approximately −2. Should the firm raise price, lower price, or leave price unchanged? Explain.

■ **3.3. KINDOFBLUE JEANS.** Two years ago, KindOfBlue jeans were priced at $72 and 121,000 units were sold. Last year, the price was lowered to $68 and sales increased to 132,000.

(a) Estimate the value of the demand elasticity.

(b) Based on your estimate of the demand elasticity, how many units would you expect to be sold if price were lowered by an additional $1?

(c) In order to increase *profits*, should price be lowered below $68? If your answer begins — as it should! — with "it depends," indicate as clearly as possible what additional information you would need and how you would base your answer on such additional information.

■ **3.4. EZJOINT.** After spending 10 years and $1.5 billion, you have finally gotten Food and Drug Administration (FDA) approval to sell your new patented wonder drug, which reduces the aches and pains associated with aging joints. You will market this drug under the brand name of EZjoint. Market research indicates that the demand elasticity for EZjoint is −1.25 (at all points on the demand curve). You estimate the marginal cost of manufacturing and selling one more dose of EZjoint is $1.

(a) What is the profit-maximizing price per dose of EZjoint?

(b) Would you expect the elasticity of demand you face for EZjoint to rise or fall when your patent expires?

Suppose that, after patent expiry, a generic version of EZjoint was introduced in the market (under the chemical name clorophospartane). Reacting to entry, EZjoint decided to *increase* price.

(c) Can this behavior be consistent with rational profit maximizing?

■ **3.5. LAS-O-VISION.** Las-O-Vision is the sole producer of holographic TVs, 3DTVs. The weekly demand for 3DTVs is $D(p) = 10200 − 100p$. The cost of producing $q$ 3DTVs per week is $q^2/2$ (note this implies that $MC = q$).

(a) What is Las-O-Vision's total revenue schedule?

(b) What is Las-O-Vision's marginal revenue schedule?

(c) What is the profit-maximizing number of 3DTVs for Las-O-Vision to produce each day? What price does Las-O-Vision charge per 3DTV? What is its daily profit?

■ **3.6. MONSANTO.** With reference to the discussion in Box 3.1:

(a) How do you know that cutting the price of Roundup was a good idea for Monsanto?

(b) How might you estimate the elasticity of demand and the profit-maximizing price for 1995? Do you think Monsanto set the right price?

(c) If cutting price was a good idea, why didn't Monsanto do it earlier?

■ **3.7. WINDOWS.** Microsoft is the dominant player in the market for desktop operating systems. Suppose each copy of Windows is sold for $50. Suppose moreover that the marginal cost of production and shipping is $5. What value of the demand elasticity is consistent with this price? Does it make sense? What elements of the OS market may be missing from the elasticity rule?

■ **3.8. PROFIT MAXIMIZATION.** Explain why the assumption of profit maximization is or is not reasonable?

■ **3.9. CAR PARTS.** Two parts in an automobile taillight are the plastic exterior cover and the light bulb. Which of these parts is a car company more likely to manufacture in-house? Why?

■ **3.10. JET ENGINES.** There are three main suppliers of commercial jet engines, Pratt & Whitney, General Electric, and Rolls-Royce. All three maintain extensive support staff at major (and many minor) airports throughout the world. Why doesn't one firm service each airport? Why do all three feel they need to provide service and support operations worldwide themselves? Why don't they subcontract this work? Why don't they leave it entirely to the airlines?

■ **3.11. SMART CAR.** The Smart car was created as a joint venture between Daimler-Benz AG and Swatch Group AG. Although Micro Compact Car AG (the name of the joint venture) was originally jointly owned, in November of 1998 Daimler-Benz AG took complete control by buying Swatch's share.[12] The deal put an end to a very stressed relationship between Daimler and Swatch. What does Section 3.4 suggest as to what the sources of strain might have been?

■ **3.12. FRANCHISE RETAILING.** Empirical evidence from franchise retailing suggests that, even when stores have similar characteristics, the mother company resorts to a mix between company-owned stores and franchised ones.[13] How can this be justified?

■ **3.13. BODY SHOP.** The UK Body Shop franchise network consists of three types of stores: franchised, company owned, and partnership stores. All stores that are distant from headquarters by more than 300 miles are franchised. More than half of the company-owned stores are within 100 miles of headquarters.[14] How can you explain these facts?

■ **3.14. INTEL.** Explain why Intel has maintained, if not increased, its competitive advantage with respect to rivals. Indicate the explanatory power of the different causes considered in the text (impediments to imitation, causal ambiguity, strategy, history).

## CHALLENGING EXERCISES

■ **3.15. INPUT SHARES.** Consider a firm with production function (Cobb-Douglas)

$$q = \xi K^\alpha L^\beta$$

Suppose that output price $p$ and input prices $r, w$ are given. Show that a profit maximizing firm chooses inputs levels such that the ratio between labor costs and total revenue $wL/pq$ is equal to $\beta$.

■ **3.16. COST MINIMIZING INPUT MIX.** Consider a firm with production function (Cobb-Douglas)

$$q = K^{\frac{1}{2}} L^{\frac{1}{2}}$$

Suppose that one unit of capital costs $r = 12.5$, whereas one unit of labor costs $w = 8$.

(a) Determine the optimal input mix that leads to an output of $q = 2$.

(b) Determine the firm's cost function, that is, the minimum cost required to produce output $q$.

■ **3.17. PRICING WITH CAPACITY CONSTRAINTS.** Consider again the case of a monopoly facing linear demand and constant marginal cost. Demand is:

$$q = a - bp,$$

and marginal cost is $MC = c$. Suppose moreover that the monopolist has a limited capacity of $K$. In other words, it must be $q \le K$. What is the optimal price?

■ **3.18. OPTIMAL BIDDING.** You are one of two companies bidding to try to win a large construction project. Call your bid $b$. You estimate that your costs of actually performing the work required will be $800k. You are risk neutral. You will win if and only if your bid is lower than that of the other bidder. You are not sure what bid your rival will submit, but you estimate that the rival's bid is uniformly distributed between $1 and $2 million.[k] What bid should you submit?

k. By "uniformly distributed between $a$ and $b$" we mean that all values between $a$ and $b$ are equally likely.

■ **3.19. COMPETITIVE PRESSURE.** Suppose that a firm's profits are given by $\pi = \alpha + \phi(e) + \epsilon$, where $\alpha$ denotes the intensity of product market competition, $e$ effort by the manager, and $\epsilon$ a random shock. The function $\phi(e)$ is increasing and concave, that is, $d\phi / de > 0$ and $d^2\phi / de^2 < 0$.

In order for the firm to survive, profits must be greater than $\underline{\pi}$. The manager's payoff is $\beta > 0$ if the firm survives and zero if it is liquidated, that is, if profits fall short of the minimum target. The idea is that if the firm is liquidated, then the manager loses his or her job and the rents associated with it.

Suppose that $\epsilon$ is normally distributed with mean $\mu$ and variance $\sigma^2$, and that $\mu > \underline{\pi}$. Show that increased product market competition (lower $\alpha$) induces greater effort by the manager, that is, $de / d\alpha < 0$.

## APPLIED EXERCISES

■ **3.20. PRODUCTIVITY.** Find firm level data on output and inputs (both quantity and prices). Use this information to estimate each firm's total factor productivity, following the method outlined in Section 3.1 (cf in particular Equation 3.2).

## NOTES

1. Lerner, A. P. (1934), "The Concept of Monopoly and the Measurement of Monopoly Power," *The Review of Economic Studies* **1** (3), 157–175.

2. Adapted from "A Weed Killer Is a Block to Build On," by David Barboza, *The New York Times*, August 2, 2001.

3. This section is partly based on Holmstrom, Bengt R, and Jean Tirole (1989), "The Theory of the Firm," in Schmalensee and Willig (Eds.), *Handbook of Industrial Organization*, Amsterdam: North-Holland

4. Hermalin, Benjamin E., and Michael S. Weisbach (1988), "The Determinants of Board Composition," *Rand Journal of Economics* **19**, 589–606; and Hermalin, Benjamin E., and Michael S. Weisbach (1998), "Endogenously Chosen Boards of Directors and Their Monitoring of the CEO," *American Economic Review* **88**, 96–118.

5. The theory presented in this section is based on Williamson, Oliver E. (1975), *Markets and Hierarchies*, New York: The Free Press; and on Grossman, Sanford J., and Oliver D. Hart (1986), "The Costs and Benefits of Ownership: A Theory of Vertical and Lateral Integration," *Journal of Political Economy* **94**, 691–719.

6. Joskow, Paul L. (1985), "Vertical Integration and Long-term Contracts: The Case of Coal-Burning Electric Generating Plants," *Journal of Law, Economics, and Organization* **1** (1), 33–80.

7. Schmalensee, Richard (1989), "Inter-Industry Studies of Structure and Performance," in Schmalensee and Willig (Eds.), *Handbook of Industrial Organization*, Amsterdam: North-Holland.

8. Mueller, Dennis (1986), *Profits in the Long Run*, Cambridge: Cambridge University Press.

9. Rumelt, Richard P. (1984), "Towards a Strategic Theory of the Firm," in R. Lamb (Ed), *Competitive Strategic Management*, Englewood Cliffs, NJ: Prentice Hall. Three other important references for this and the topics to follow are: Penrose, E. T. (1959), *The Theory of the Growth of the Firm*, Oxford: Blackwell; Wernerfelt, B. (1984), "A Resource-Based View of the Firm," *Strategic*

*Management Journal* **5**, 171–180; Dierickx, I., and K. Cool (1989), "Asset Stock Accumulation and Sustainability of Competitive Advantage," *Management Science* **35**, 1504-1511.

10. Rumelt, Richard P., op. cit.

11. Van Reenen, John, and Nick Bloom (2007), "Measuring and Explaining Management Practices Across Firms and Countries," *Quarterly Journal of Economics* **122**, 1351–1408.

12. *The Wall Street Journal Europe*, November 5, 1998.

13. See, for example, Affuso, Luisa (1998), "An Empirical Study on Contractual Heterogeneity Within the Firm: The "Vertical Integration-Franchise Contracts" Mix," University of Cambridge.

14. Source: Watts, Christophe F. (1995), "The Determinants of Organisational Choice: Franchising and Vertical Integration," M.Sc. dissertation, University of Southampton.

# CHAPTER 4

# COMPETITION, EQUILIBRIUM, AND EFFICIENCY

Markets are a frequent topic of discussion, if not argument. How do markets work? What exactly is the law of supply and demand? Is society better served with free markets? Are markets fair? Do market economies grow faster than centrally planned ones? It's impossible to answer all of these questions in a book chapter — or in an entire book, for that matter. That notwithstanding, the next pages should help you understand some of the main issues.

Understanding how markets work is important not just for arguing at cocktail parties: any piece of news that's fit to print on the front page of the *Financial Times* or the *New York Times* either pertains to a particular market or has important implications for what happens in a particular market. If this is not obvious to you now, read through the chapter and then check out today's newspaper.

I begin the chapter by reviewing the assumptions and the results of the so-called perfect competition model. Next I consider two extensions of this basic framework: competitive selection and monopolistic competition. Following that, I turn to one of the most important results in economics, a result that is so important we call it the Fundamental Theorem. An important exception to the theorem occurs in the presence of externalities, a phenomenon which I define and exemplify in the next section. Finally, I close the chapter with an introduction to economic regulation, which I will argue is both a consequence and a cause of imperfect competition.

## 4.1 PERFECT COMPETITION

The "perfectly competitive" industry, an industry with no barriers to competition, is a useful benchmark to consider. It is also a reasonable approximation to many important industries, including many sectors of agriculture, some parts of the labor market, and reasonably heavily traded financial securities. The main features of a competitive industry include:

- **Atomistic firms**. There are many competitors, all small relative to the market and unable to affect the market price through their actions.
- **Homogeneous product**. Competitors produce exactly the same product (and therefore compete head to head on price, the only relevant variable).
- **Perfect information**. Everyone (firms and consumers) knows about prices and product characteristics.
- **Free entry** and free access to technology. Other than the "normal" entry costs, there are no barriers to the establishment of a new firm. Imitation is possible: others can enter the business if they wish; and if they do, they incur the same costs as the incumbents do.[a]

Under these conditions, which we denote by "perfect competition," we'd expect intense competition, driving the entrants' profits to very low values. How reasonable is this? More so in some cases than in others. The characteristics of many commodity industries seem to match (at least approximately) the assumptions of the competitive model. And as the model predicts, profit rates tend to be relatively low and relatively similar across firms. However, there are also industries where differences in profit rates across companies can last for decades (cf Section 3.5 and 4.2). The key is to think of the perfect competition model as a benchmark that particular industries can be compared to.

The perfect competition benchmark is also helpful when studying possible violations of the underlying conditions. With one or few firms, we have a monopoly (which I discuss in Section 5.3) or an oligopoly (which I discuss in Chapters 8 and 9). With differentiated products, we moderate the impact of competition (a recurring theme) and open up the issue of product positioning (cf Section 4.3 and Chapter 14). With imperfect information, we create the possibility of branding, a brand often being a signal of quality (cf Chapter 14). With entry and access to technology, we raise the issues of scale economies (cf Chapter 10), entry preemption (cf Chapter 12), patent protection (cf Chapter 15) and network effects (cf Chapter 16). Stated differently: if a firm has a sustainable competitive advantage, that advantage must lie in the violation of one of the conditions of the perfect competition model (which I listed above). In fact, the subject of industrial organization is largely the study of what happens when one or more assumptions of the perfect competition model are violated.

■ **FIRM SUPPLY AND MARKET SUPPLY IN COMPETITIVE MARKETS.** Let's look more closely at a market or industry under conditions of perfect competition. First, each firm faces effectively a flat (infinitely elastic) demand curve: it can sell all it wants at the market price and can sell nothing at any higher price. Why? Because each firm is small relative to the whole market and has no impact on market price. People sometimes refer to the market as "atomistic," since each firm is assumed to be as small as an atom. In these circumstances a firm's total revenue is $R(q) = pq$; and since $p$ is given, the

a. There is a shorter version of this condition that is limited to free entry, that is, excludes the assumption of free access to technology. I will later discuss the model with this weaker assumption.

firm's marginal revenue is simply given by $p$. The usual profit-maximizing condition that marginal cost equals marginal revenue simplifies to:

$$MC(q) = p$$

Thus under these conditions, each firm's supply decision is governed by its marginal cost curve. It supplies the quantity at which marginal cost equals price, $MC(q) = p$.

For each value of $p$, the equation $MC(q_i) = p$ gives a value $q_i$, firm $i$'s supply. If we put all firms together, we sum their supply at each price, thus deriving the **industry supply curve**, which is given by $S(p) = q_1 + \ldots + q_n$.

■ **MARKET EQUILIBRIUM.** Whether considering long run or short run outcomes, in market settings the price of a product is the result of the interaction between buyers (demand) and sellers (supply). We refer to the point at which the supply and demand curves intersect as the **market equilibrium**.

Figure 4.1 illustrates this situation. The point $(q^*, p^*)$, where the supply curve crosses the demand curve, corresponds to the equilibrium output level and price, respectively. We say this outcome is an equilibrium in the sense that none of the market participants have an incentive to change their behavior: buyers are buying what they want at that price (the point is on the demand curve) and sellers are selling what they want (the point is on the supply curve).

If the price were higher than the equilibrium price, fewer people would want to buy than sell. The excess of sellers would tend to drive the price down. Conversely, if the price were lower than the equilibrium price, fewer people would be willing to sell than buy. The excess of buyers would cause the price to tend to rise to the equilibrium price. The tendency of price to move in the direction of equilibrium price — also known as market-clearing price — is frequently referred to as the **law of supply and demand**.

Price tends to move in the direction of equilibrium price (where supply equals demand).

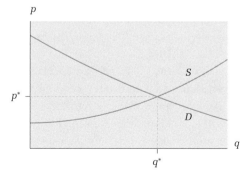

**FIGURE 4.1**
Market equilibrium

The law of supply and demand is not a law in the sense common to natural and exact sciences. However, the analogy can be useful. Consider, for example, the system formed by a pendulum hanging from a ceiling. Such system has an equilibrium: the vertical position. This is the point where the downward gravitational force is exactly compensated by the upward pull exerted by the string (by Newton's third law). Whenever the pendulum is not in the vertical position, a net force points in the direction of the rest point. By analogy, we can think of supply and demand as "forces" that push price up or down depending on whether the current price is below or above the equilibrium price. The equilibrium price, in turn, is the "rest point" of the system, the situation where the net force acting on price is zero.

In the real world, there are many exogenous factors (production technology, input costs, tastes, income, and so forth) shifting the supply and demand curves at all times. For this reason, the equilibrium point itself is constantly changing. In this sense, it is not very appropriate to talk about equilibrium as a "rest point." Nevertheless, finding the equilibrium is a helpful way of understanding in which direction we expect price to change in a given situation. I next turn to this issue.

■ **COMPARATIVE STATICS.** Often we are concerned about changes in market conditions. If the demand or supply curve shifts due to changes in various underlying factors, then a new equilibrium price is established. The term **comparative statics** is used by economists to describe the exercise of looking at what happens to equilibrium if an exogenous factor changes. We would represent this by shifting the supply or demand curves and noting the change in the equilibrium price and quantity. The most basic principle of comparative statics is that:

> (a) A rightward shift of the demand curve leads to an increase in quantity and an increase in price. (b) A rightward shift of the supply curve leads to an increase in quantity and a decrease in price.

(For the opposite shifts in demand or supply, just change the signs.) So, if I ask you what effect will event $y$ have on price and quantity in market $x$, the question to ask yourself is what $y$ implies in terms of shifts in the demand and supply curves of good $x$.

Consider for example the September 1999 earthquake in Taiwan. What impact would you expect it to have on the world market for DRAM (dynamic random access memory), both in terms of price and in terms of quantity? The relevant market for DRAM is the world, and Taiwan is one of the world's leading producers, accounting for about 10% of world output. An earthquake is likely to shut down a series of factories, which implies a northwest (or leftward) shift in the supply curve, as in the left panel of Figure 4.2 shows. The shift in supply leads to an increase in price and a decrease in quantity.

The right-hand panel in Figure 4.2 shows the world price of DRAM around the date of the Taiwan earthquake. Just before the earthquake, prices were around $7. Just

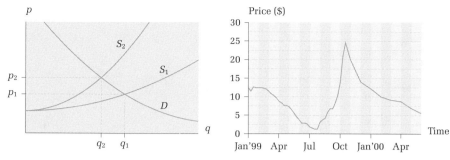

**FIGURE 4.2**

Impact of the 1999 Taiwan earthquake on the DRAM market. Source: *Financial Times* and author's calculations.

after the earthquake, in a matter of days, prices skyrocketed to values as high as $25. This seems a little too much considering that only a fraction of Taiwan's factories were affected, and Taiwan in turn represents less than 10% of world supply. One possible interpretation is that the earthquake also induced a sharp increase in speculative demand (brokers or computer manufacturers who stockpiled in anticipation of further price increases). This interpretation is consistent with the fact that prices declined considerably in the months after the initial spike.

By now we know how shifts in supply and demand lead to variations in quantity and price. An additional question is whether the shifts in supply and demand lead primarily to shifts in price or primarily to shifts in quantity. In other words, going beyond the sign of the changes in $p$ and $q$, we are now also interested in the size of such changes. If you work through an example using the supply and demand diagram, you'll see that the impact on price or quantity depends on the slopes of the supply and demand curves. Specifically, the effect of a shift in the supply curve depends on the slope of the demand curve. (This sounds a little strange, but it's true because the demand curve hasn't shifted, so the change in equilibrium is a movement along the demand curve.) If the demand curve is steep, price will change more than quantity in reaction to a shift in supply. By contrast, if the demand curve is flat then the impact of a shift in supply will be felt predominantly on quantity. For shifts in demand, the impact depends on the slope of the supply curve. The four panels in Figure 4.3 illustrate the four possible cases (demand or supply shifts with elastic or inelastic supply and demand, respectively). Can you think of examples that fit each of these cases? See Exercise 4.3.

Thus a key ingredient to any market analysis is an assessment of the slopes of the supply and demand curves: how sensitive the decisions of buyers and sellers are to changes in price. Consider the California electricity market. The capacity of local power plants can't be changed much without building new ones. Moreover, the high-voltage lines to bring in power from other states have limited capacity. Hence the supply curve is very steep (vertical?) and the impact of an increase in demand (the result of growth of the California economy) is reflected almost entirely in the price. In fact, during 2000 and 2001, a combination of increasing demand and limited supply sent wholesale prices up by a factor of 8 or 9.

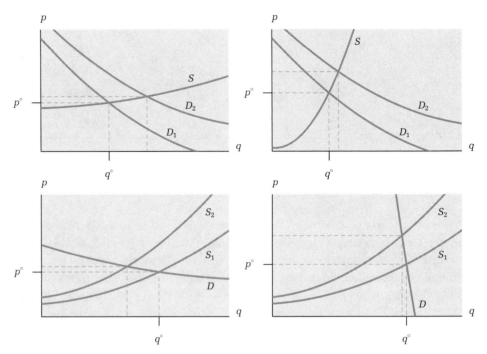

**FIGURE 4.3**
Price effect and output effect

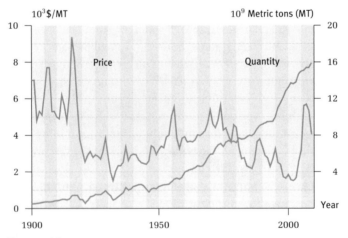

**FIGURE 4.4**
Copper: price and worldwide refinery production, 1900–2009.[1]

A second example is the copper market. As Figure 4.4 shows, over the last century quantity has increased substantially while price declined slightly. How is this possible? One explanation is that demand has increased as the world economy has grown, but supply has shifted, too, as new technologies make copper extraction more efficient. In other words, both the supply and demand curves have shifted to the right, with supply shifting slightly faster. Here's a practice exercise: as can be seen from Figure 4.4, the declining price trend was reversed during the beginning of the new millennium. What do you think were the main shifts in the supply and demand curves underlying the recent evolution of $p$ and $q$? Are these shifts likely to be temporary or permanent?

■ **SHORT-RUN AND LONG-RUN EQUILIBRIUM.** For the purpose of this chapter, I define the short-run as the period when the number of firms is fixed, whereas, in the long run, I also consider the possibility of entry and exit.

Consider an industry with a given number of firms (short-run) and a corresponding market supply curve. The intersection of supply and demand determines the equilibrium price. Depending on the number of firms in the market, the short-run equilibrium price may be above average cost (meaning firms are making above-normal profits), below (firms are losing money), or equal. Regardless of the firm profit level, firms are doing their best output choice given their prior choice to enter the market.

The upper panels of Figure 4.5 illustrate a possible short-run equilibrium. On the right panel, we have market demand and market supply, from which we determine equilibrium price and industry output in the short run ($p_{SR}$ and $Q_{SR}$). The left panel shows the problem faced by each firm (for the time being let's assume all firms are identical, that is, have the same cost function). Each firm takes price, $p_{SR}$, as given, and chooses output such that price equals marginal cost: $q_{SR}$ in the top left panel of Figure 4.5. In the particular case considered here, this corresponds to a point where price is greater than average cost, that is, a situation where firms make positive profits.

In the long run, we must also consider the possibility of firm entry and exit. Suppose that price is greater than average cost for all firms in the industry (as is the case in the top left panel of Figure 4.5). Then we would expect new firms to enter the industry.

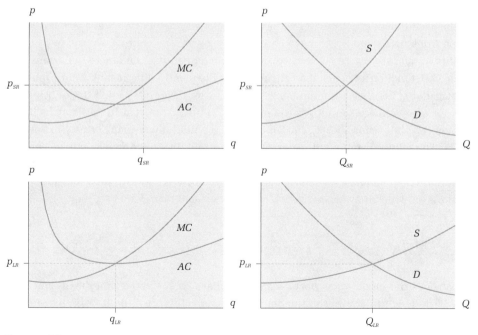

**FIGURE 4.5**
Short-run (upper panel) and long-run (lower panel) equilibrium under perfect competition

As a result, the market supply curve shifts to the right, driving down the price, as illustrated by comparing the top and bottom right panels in Figure 4.5.

Why does price decline when the supply curve shifts to the right? Were price to remain constant, some (or all) firms would be selling less than they would want to. They would then have an incentive to slightly lower then price and increase their demand. Given that, from a firm's perspective, demand is infinitely elastic, a slight decrease in price induces a large increase in demand. Following the **law of supply and demand**, this process continues until market supply and market demand are again balanced.[b]

This may take some time, but the ultimate effect is to drive firm profits down to zero (by which I mean zero economic profit, that is, normal profit levels). Conversely, if price is below average cost, then some firms leave the industry, the supply curve shifts to the left, and firms eventually attain a normal profit level.

The bottom panels in Figure 4.5 show the long-run equilibrium. Price is given by the intersection of market supply and market demand (right panel), and is also equal to the minimum of each firm's average cost (which is also equal to marginal cost at this particular output level).

> In the long-run equilibrium under perfect competition firms produce at the minimum average cost and make zero profits.

When I introduced the perfect competition model I included as one of the conditions that all firms have access to the same technology. An alternative version of the model excludes this assumption. If different firms have different cost structures, then in a long run competitive equilibrium (with many price-taking firms that are small relative to the overall market), the marginal firm will be one for which $p = MC = AC$. However, some firms lucky enough to have cost advantages will be earning a positive profit, a profit we refer to as a **rent**. Firms earn rents in competitive markets to the extent that their cost function is better than their rivals'. Frequently, this results from inputs or managerial skills that are impossible or hard to replicate (cf Section 3.5). For example, for many minerals mining is a commodity industry; but some mines may be lucky enough to find seams located near the surface, while others incur greater extraction costs. The marginal mine will be earning zero profit, but some mines may be earning positive profits. In this case, we would say these mines earn rents from their privileged location. (The challenge for managers is then to create or develop products, practices, or skills on which they can earn such rents. Easier said than done.)

## 4.2 COMPETITIVE SELECTION

What does the model of perfect competition have to say about entry, exit, and firm size? The long-run equilibrium under perfect competition is a limit point that industries converge to by means of successive entry and exit. If active firms make positive profits, then new firms are attracted to the industry. If, on the contrary, active firms make losses, then some of those firms exit. Finally, in the long-run equilibrium, price equals the minimum of the long-run average cost. Since technology (i.e., the cost function) is the same for all firms (because of the equal access assumption), each firm receives zero economic profits (i.e., earns a normal profit), and there is neither entry nor exit.

Concerning the size distribution of firms, the perfect competition model is either rather extreme or extremely scant: assuming plant-level average cost functions are U-shaped, all plants must be of the same size in the long run (i.e., there is only one output level that minimizes average cost). If the managerial costs of owning more than one plant are positive, then each firm owns one plant only, and all firms are of the same size. If, on the contrary, managerial costs are zero, then there exists a virtually uncountable number of possible industry configurations, all of which are consistent with the model.[c,2]

The empirical evidence from various industries with "many" small firms is widely at odds with the above view of industry dynamics and industry structure. First, in any given period and industry, entry and exit take place simultaneously. Second, many firms earn higher than normal profit rates, even in the long run. Third, the size distribution of firms displays a number of regularities and is not concentrated on a single size. In the remainder of this section, I present data on these and related stylized facts; as well as a possible extension of the perfect competition model to account for the puzzling disparity between facts and theory.

■ **PROFITS IN THE LONG RUN.** Empirical evidence suggests that *profit rates are persistent in the long run*, contrary to the implication of perfect competition. One author examined profit rates for a sample of 600 US firms from 1950 to 1972. He classified firms in groups of 100 according to average profits in the period 1950–1952 and computed average profit rates in the whole 23-year period for each of the groups. The hypothesis that profits converge to the competitive level in the long run would imply that inter-group differences be insignificant on average. However, the data rejects that any pair of averages is equal. In other words, average differences in profitability across the groups persist even after 23 years.[3]

■ **PRODUCTIVITY.** Within four-digit SIC industries in the US manufacturing sector, on average a plant in the 90th percentile has total factor productivity close to twice of that of a plant in the 10th percentile.[d] In other words, with the same inputs, a plant in the 90th percentile produces nearly twice as much as a plant in the 10th percentile.[4] In countries like China and India, that ratio is even greater: close to 5:1.[5] Moreover, productivity levels are highly correlated across time (the autoregressive coefficients are on the order of 0.6 to 0.8).[6] In sum, the data suggests that some firms and plants have superior skills in using inputs, allowing them to produce much higher output levels with the same quantity of inputs — and giving them a greater chance of survival.

c. In fact, there may be economies of scale in multiplant firms — e.g., large-scale purchasing discounts — that counteract increased managerial costs. But this would take back to a U-shaped cost curve and the prediction that all firms have the same number of plants.

d. See Section 3.1 for a definition of total factor productivity. Industries are classified in groups, sub-groups, sub-sub-groups, and so forth. For each subdivision, one digit is added to the classification. So, a five-digit classification is more detailed than a four-digit one.

■ **ENTRY AND EXIT RATES.** The perfect competition model predicts that, in any given period, there will either be entry into an industry (active firms are earning supra-normal profit rates); or exit from that industry (active firms are earning infra-normal profit rates). The empirical evidence suggests that, in any given period and industry, *entry and exit take place simultaneously*, with the gross entry and exit rates being much higher (typically one order of magnitude higher) than the *net* entry rate.[e]

Table 4.1 presents data from several countries. For example, in Norway and in the period 1980–85, the average gross entry rate for a four-digit industry was 8.2%, whereas the average exit rate was 8.7%. The difference, $8.2 - 8.7 = -.5\%$, an approximation of the average net entry rate, is one order of magnitude lower than either the gross entry or the gross exit rate.

■ **SIZE, GROWTH, AND SURVIVAL.** Empirical evidence suggests that entrants and exiters' average size is much smaller than industry average size. From a sample of eight countries, one obtains values between 6.7% (US) and 44.9% (UK) for entrants. That is, the average entrant's size in the US is 6.7% the average incumbent's size. For exiters, the rates vary between 6.9% (US) and 61.2% (UK).[8]

Several empirical studies indicate that expected growth rates are decreasing in size and in age. In other words, it is mainly small, young firms that grow fast. The same occurs with respect to survival rates: it is mainly young and small firms that exit.[f]

■ **FIRM SIZE DISTRIBUTION.** The model of perfect competition implies that all firms are of the same size (assuming U-shaped cost curves) or that almost any size distribution is consistent with the model (assuming constant returns to scale). The data however

e. By "one order of magnitude greater" we mean with one extra digit, i.e., about 10 times larger.

f. Note that the evidence regarding growth rates, presented in this paragraph, is consistent with the evidence regarding relative size, presented in the preceding paragraph.

**TABLE 4.1** Annual gross entry and exit rates (%).[7]

| Country | Gross entry | Gross exit | Time period | Data* |
|---|---|---|---|---|
| Belgium/Man | 5.8 | 6.3 | 80–84 | 130/3/E/E |
| Belgium/Serv | 13.0 | 12.2 | 80–84 | 79/3/E/E |
| Canada | 4.0 | 4.8 | 71–79 | 167/4/E/S |
| FRG | 3.8 | 4.6 | 83–85 | 183/4/F/S |
| Korea | 3.3 | 5.7 | 76–81 | 62/4,5/F/S |
| Norway | 8.2 | 8.7 | 80–85 | 80/4/F/S |
| Portugal | 12.3 | 9.5 | 83–86 | 234/5/E/E |
| U.K. | 6.5 | 5.1 | 74–79 | 114/4/F/S |
| US | 7.7 | 7.0 | 63–82 | 387/4/F/S |

* Number of industries/aggregation level (no. digit industries)/firm or establishment level/employment or sales data.

exhibit significant regularities in the firm-size distribution. The histograms in Figure 4.6, for example, display the distribution of manufacturing firm size for selected countries.[8] Although these countries are very different in total size, the distributions look remarkably alike. Similar results are obtained with sectoral distributions.

■ **A MODEL OF COMPETITIVE SELECTION.**[10]  In order to explain these stylized facts, we need to relax some of the assumptions of the perfect competition model. In this section I maintain the assumptions that (i) firms are price takers; (ii) the product is homogeneous; (iii) information about prices is perfect. However, in contrast with the perfect competition model, I now assume that: (iv) firms must pay a sunk cost in order to enter; (v) not all firms have access to the same technology.

Specifically, suppose that *different firms have different productivity levels*, which in turn corresponds to different cost functions: more efficient firms have a lower marginal cost schedule. These differences may result from a variety of factors. For example, some managers are more efficient in organizing resources than others (more on this later).

Suppose moreover that *each firm is uncertain about its own productivity level*. When a firm first enters an industry, it has only a vague idea of what its productivity is. As time goes by, and based on each period's experience, the firm gradually forms a more precise estimate of its true efficiency. In each period, the firm chooses optimal output based on its current expectation of efficiency; basically, the output level such that price is equal to expected marginal cost.

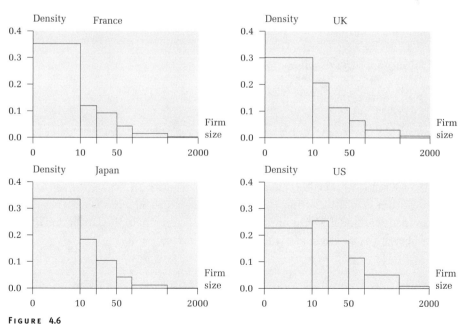

**FIGURE 4.6**
Firm size distribution, where size is measured by number of employees.[9]

g. Each bar on a histogram gives the frequency with which a given firm size occurs. For example, the first bar in the histogram for France indicates that most firms in France have less than 10 employees: the area of the first bar is greater than the total area of the remaining bars.

Given the above elements, we conclude that firms that get a series of bad signals (high production costs) gradually become "pessimistic" about their efficiency level, gradually decrease their output, and, eventually, may decide to exit the industry (as variable profit does not compensate for the fixed cost). By contrast, firms that receive a series of good signals (low production costs) remain active and gradually increase their output.

This model of **competitive selection** is consistent with several of the stylized facts described in the previous section. First, the model implies that *different firms earn different profit rates, even in the long run*; although, arguably, this is a bit of a tautology, for we *assumed* that different firms have different cost functions. Second, the model is consistent with the stylized fact of *simultaneous entry and exit in the same industry*. Firms that accumulate a series of very unfavorable productivity signals hold a very unfavorable estimate of their own efficiency. As a result, their expected value from remaining active is negative, which in turn leads them to exit. New entrants have no information regarding their efficiency. Their expected efficiency is therefore much better than the exiting firms': no news is better than bad news. This justifies that their expected value from being active is positive, in fact, greater than the entry cost. In summary, it is possible for a firm with no information about its efficiency to enter while a firm with unfavorable information about its efficiency exits.

Efficient firms are firms with a low marginal cost function. Since firms equate price to (expected) marginal cost, it follows that more efficient firms sell a higher output. Together with the previous results, this implies that exiters (the active firms with lowest expected efficiency) are also the firms with lower output. By selection, the firms that remain active have an efficiency higher than average. In particular, higher than the average entrant's. It follows that entrants' output is lower than the surviving firms' average output. In this way, the model is also consistent with the stylized fact that *firms that enter and firms that exit are smaller than average*.

> Variability of and uncertainty about firm efficiency reconciles the competitive model with empirical observation regarding (a) simultaneous entry and exit; (b) relative size of entrants/exiters vis-a-vis incumbents.

Finally, the competitive selection model is also consistent with the empirical observation that the firm size distribution is neither single-valued nor indeterminate, as the perfect competition model would imply. In fact, a given population distribution of efficiency levels implies a particular distribution of firm sizes.

---

**A MODEL OF COMPETITIVE SELECTION.** Consider a competitive market where each firm is characterized by a parameter $\theta$. Consistent with the previous discussion, we can think of $\theta$ as the firm's estimate of the value of its efficiency parameter. Specifically, the variable cost of a type-$\theta$ firm is given by $q_t^2/\theta$. That is, more efficient firms have a higher $\theta$. The profit for a type-$\theta$ firm is given by:

$$\Pi(q; \theta) = pq - \frac{q^2}{\theta}$$

At the beginning of each period, each firm decides whether to remain remain active or exit. Next, active firms decide how much to produce, which they do by solving:

$$\max_q \quad pq - \frac{q^2}{\theta}$$

By assumption, firms are price takers (the first assumption of the perfect competition model). Therefore, the first-order condition for profit maximization is given by:

$$p = 2\frac{q}{\theta}$$

or

$$q^* = \tfrac{1}{2}\,\theta\,p$$

In words: more efficient firms produce higher output levels. In fact, empirical evidence shows that, within a given industry, higher productivity firms produce a higher output.

Substituting $q^*$ for $q$ in the profit function, and simplifying, we get:

$$\Pi^*(\theta; p) = \tfrac{1}{4}\,\theta\,p^2$$

(Check this.) This implies that not only output but also profits are an increasing function of $\theta$. It follows that the firms that decide to exit are the firms with lower $\theta$. This is also consistent with empirical evidence: firms that exit are typically smaller than average. Since firm size is correlated with firm efficiency, this implies that firms that exit have lower $\theta$.

---

At this point, it may be worth to point out that the competitive selection model does not depend on firms being asymmetric with respect to costs. We could alternatively assume that some firms make products that are better than others. Consider, for example, the laser industry. Most new firms in this industry are spinouts from existing firms. Typically, a scientist/engineer from one firm leaves it to form his or her own firm. This industry is an interesting example because (a) it illustrates a source of variation across firms (scientific know how); and (b) it suggests that differences across firms need not be limited to cost differences.

However, it must be admitted that the above characterization of the firm size distribution is, to a great extent, tautological: the distribution of efficiency levels is *assumed* rather than derived; a more satisfactory model would also explain the distribution of efficiency levels.[h]

## 4.3   MONOPOLISTIC COMPETITION

One of the criticisms frequently addressed to the model of perfect competition is that it is based on the assumption of product homogeneity, that is, the assumption that all

h. One possibility is to assume that firms invest in R&D and that efficiency levels result from these R&D investments. A completely different approach to understanding the firm size distribution is to consider a model of dynamic stochastic growth where different growth rates results in a distribution of firm sizes. Suppose, for example, that there is a set of laser machine manufacturers and that, in each period, a new machine is demanded in the market. Suppose moreover that each of the existing firms receives each new order with equal probability. It can be shown that a process of this sort implies a distribution of firm size, in fact, one that approximates the empirically observed distribution fairly well. I return to this in Chapter 10.

firms produce the same product. If we think about industries such as shampoo or small restaurants we conclude that the assumption of product homogeneity is clearly wrong. Nevertheless, these industries share several features with the perfect competition model: there are typically many competitors, and entry and exit are relatively easy.

The **monopolistic competition** model attempts to characterize industries such as shampoo or small restaurants.[11] We say there is monopolistic competition when the following assumptions hold: (a) There is a large number of firms, so that the impact of each firm upon its rivals is negligible (as in the perfect competition model); (b) Due to product differentiation, the demand curve faced by each firm is not horizontal, that is, each firm is a price maker, not a price taker; (c) There is free entry and free access to all available technologies (as in the perfect competition model). In summary, *the monopolistic competition model maintains all of the assumptions of perfect competition except that of product homogeneity.*

One of the main learning points of the monopolistic competition model is that abandoning the assumption of product homogeneity implies abandoning some of the results of the perfect competition model, while maintaining others. This is illustrated in Figure 4.7. Let us first consider the short-run equilibrium, that is, the equilibrium when the number of firms is given. On the left panel of Figure 4.7, $d$ is the demand curve for a typical firm and $MR$ the corresponding marginal revenue curve;[i] $AC$ is the average cost curve and $MC$ the corresponding marginal cost curve. A profit maximizing firm will choose an output level such that marginal revenue equals marginal cost, that is, an output of $q_{SR}$.

At the short-run output level on the left panel in Figure 4.7, the price received by each firm, $p_{SR}$, is greater than average cost, $AC(q_{SR})$. This is a feature of the particular short-run equilibrium I selected, that is, there could be a different short-run equilibrium for which price were lower than average cost; it all depends on the number of firms in the market in the short run.

Whichever is the case, so long as price is different from average cost, the short-run equilibrium is not a long-run equilibrium. If $p > AC(q_{SR})$, as on the left panel of Figure 4.7, then outside firms are willing to enter the market. In fact, all firms have access to the same technology, and each firm is so small that its impact upon other

i. I use lowercase $d$ to indicate that this is the demand curve faced by each firm, not the market demand curve.

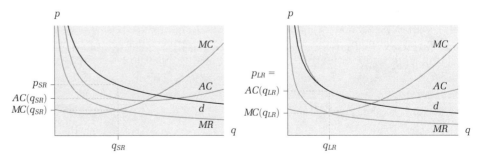

**FIGURE 4.7**
Equilibrium under monopolistic competition: short-run and long-run

firms is negligible. This implies that a potential entrant expects profits of approximately the same amount as the typical incumbent's, that is, $\pi = (p_{SR} - AC(q_{SR})) \, q_{SR}$. If, on the contrary, $p < AC(q_{SR})$, then incumbent firms earn negative profits and would do better by exiting the market.

The long-run equilibrium is then the situation in which (a) firms maximize profits, so that marginal revenue equals marginal cost; and (b) firms make zero profits (that is, price equals average cost), so that no active firm wishes to become inactive or vice-versa. The right panel in Figure 4.7 depicts such an equilibrium.

> Equilibrium profits under monopolistic competition are zero, but firms do not produce at the minimum of their average cost.

The monopolistic competition model suggests that *perfect competition is best thought of as an approximation*. It is true that very few industries, if any, satisfy the extreme assumptions of the perfect competition model, in particular the assumption of product homogeneity. However, if the product is approximately homogeneous, then outcomes are approximately like those of perfect competition. In fact, as the degree of product differentiation decreases, the residual demand faced by each firm becomes flatter and flatter, and the point at which price equals average cost (long-run equilibrium) becomes closer and closer to the point where price equals marginal cost, as in the perfect competition model.

## 4.4   EFFICIENCY

Perhaps it's not immediately obvious, but trade creates surplus. If trade is voluntary, this has to be true, or people wouldn't do it. Consider a specific example. Jane is a big iPhone 6 fan and would be willing to pay up to $1,200 for it. It costs Apple $200 to make one, and the sale price is $600. In this situation, Jane makes a "profit" of $1,200 − $600 = $600, which we refer to as consumer surplus. Apple, in turn, makes a variable profit of 600 − 200 = $400 from its sale to Jane, a value we refer to as producer surplus. All in all, the transaction creates a total value of $1,000, the difference between Jane's value for the iPhone 6 and Apple's production cost.

The crucial point is that the moment Apple produces this particular unit of the iPhone 6 it does not create as much value as when it sells it to Jane, whose valuation equals $1,200, far more than it cost Apple to produce it. Naturally, when creating and producing the iPhone 6 Apple has in mind that there are consumers like Jane who value the smartphone highly; but without trade such value is not realized.

The left panel of Figure 4.8 generalizes the concept. For buyers, the (inverse) demand curve represents their willingness to pay. The difference between the demand curve and market price (area $A$) is thus surplus to buyers; we call it **consumer surplus**. Similarly, the (inverse) supply curve measures the price at which sellers are willing to sell. The difference between price and the supply curve (area $B$) is thus surplus to sellers; we call it **producer surplus**.[j] Total surplus generated by trade, the sum of areas $A$ and $B$, measures the increase in economy-wide value that results from production and trade: going back to our example, it measures how much better the economy is with the existence of the iPhone 6.

■ **EFFICIENCY.** Just as justice is to law and health to medicine, efficiency is a central concept in economics, in particular microeconomics. We may distinguish different types of efficiency. The first version, **allocative efficiency**, requires that resources be allocated to their most efficient use. Suppose that the left panel of Figure 4.8 provides a good approximation of the iPhone 6 market. At price $p'$, only $q'$ units are sold. This implies that there are a number of disgruntled consumers who would be willing to buy an iPhone 6 but do not do so because the price is too high; specifically, those consumers whose willingness to pay is less than $p'$. Of these consumers, some would be willing to pay more than it costs to produce an iPhone. This is specifically the case of the consumers of units $q'$ to $q^*$, where $q^*$ is the output level such that marginal cost equals willingness to pay. In total, the degree of allocative inefficiency when output is $q'$ is given by the area $C$.

But there is more to efficiency. Take an average European firm and a firm in India operating in the same industry. Chances are that, valuing inputs at the same input prices, the Indian firm produces at a higher cost than the European firm; that is, chances are that the Indian firm has lower productivity (cf Chapter 3).[k] Low productivity results from using the wrong input mix or from making a suboptimal use of existing inputs. In graphical terms, low productivity implies a higher marginal cost curve. This is illustrated in the right panel of Figure 4.8, where two marginal cost curves are depicted. The area between the high marginal cost curve ($S_H$) and the low marginal cost curve ($S_L$), which we assume is the lowest cost possible, measures the extent of inefficiency in production associated to $S_H$. More generally, **productive efficiency** refers to how close the actual production cost is to the lowest cost achievable.

j. Producer's surplus is nothing but the value of variable profit. By subtracting fixed costs from producer's surplus, we get net profits.
There is an interesting analogy between producer's and consumer's surplus. The firm's marginal cost can be interpreted as its "willingness to sell" for each unit, that is, the minimum the firm would require to sell that unit. This is analogous to the consumer's willingness to pay. One important difference, however, is that the firm's "willingness to sell" is normally increasing when the number of units increases, whereas the consumer's willingness to pay is decreasing.

k. The actual production cost of the firm in India may very well be lower, due to the fact that production inputs, especially labor, as cheaper in India than in Europe.

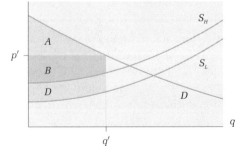

**FIGURE 4.8**
Trade, surplus, and efficiency

So far I have only been concerned with static efficiency effects. In some cases, however, dynamic efficiency is at least as important as static efficiency. Take the case of smartphones. More important then having the right number of iPhones produced and sold, and more important than the efficiency in the production of the iPhone, is the fact that the iPhone exists at all. More generally, the rate of introduction of new products, as well as the improvement in the production techniques of existing ones, is the basis of an industry's **dynamic efficiency**.

We can summarize the preceding discussion by stating that:

> *Allocative efficiency* requires that output be at the right level. *Productive efficiency* requires that such output be produced in the least expensive way given the available set of technologies. *Dynamic efficiency* refers to the improvement over time of products and production techniques.

One should also mention that, strictly speaking, productive efficiency and dynamic efficiency are also cases of allocative efficiency. For example, a firm that lacks efficiency in production is a firm that fails to allocate the right mix of production inputs, which in turn results in a higher cost than the minimum necessary for producing a given output level. However, we normally use the term allocative efficiency — or simply efficiency — to characterize the output level as it compares to the surplus-maximizing output level.

■ **THE FUNDAMENTAL THEOREM.** Why do economists (and sometimes even policy makers) wax lyrical about markets? One reason (and there are other perhaps more compelling ones) is that competitive markets are efficient, meaning that:

> In a competitive market the equilibrium levels of output and price correspond to the maximum total surplus.

To economists this is a sufficiently important and striking result that it has won the (somewhat grandiose) designation **the Fundamental Theorem**.

The Fundamental Theorem is about static efficiency, both allocative and productive efficiency. Productive efficiency is maximized because, due to competition, inefficient firms (that is, firms with marginal cost functions higher than $S_L$ in the right panel of Figure 4.8) are forced out of the market (that is, fail to make positive profits at the prevailing equilibrium price). As Warren Buffett aptly put it, "only when the tide goes out do you discover who's been swimming naked." In the present context, this might be rephrased as "only when the tide of perfect competition takes place do you discover which firms are not clothed with the garb of productive efficiency." (And no, I don't expect this sentence to help me towards a Pulitzer Prize.)

Allocative efficiency, in turn, is maximized because, from the equilibrium output level $q^*$, any change in $q$ implies a loss in surplus: if $q < q^*$, then there are consumers whose willingness to pay is higher than marginal cost who do not make a purchase (as shown on the left panel of Figure 4.8); if $q > q^*$, then there are consumers whose willingness is lower than marginal cost who do make a purchase. In other words, so long as the demand curve ("willingness to pay") lies above the marginal cost curve ("willingness to sell"), an increase in output increases total surplus; conversely, if the demand curve lies below the marginal cost curve, then a decrease in output increases total surplus. Maximum surplus (and allocative efficiency) is achieved at the point where marginal cost equals willingness to pay, which corresponds to the market equilibrium. This is shown in Figure 4.9.

The Fundamental Theorem may be rephrased with reference to the famous (or infamous) "invisible hand" of the competitive market. Though buyers and sellers may have disparate and conflicting preferences and abilities, the price mechanism ensures that those consumers who value goods most receive them, and those firms for whom it is cheapest to produce the goods produce them.[1]

This no doubt is a good thing; however, a few observations or caveats are worth highlighting. First, the Fundamental Theorem is a statement about efficiency rather than equity, that is, it concerns the size of total surplus, not its distribution. In particular, note that in calculating total surplus we value consumer and producer surplus equally. Presumably, we attach value to profits because they are eventually returned to the firm's shareholders. However, inasmuch as shareholders tend to be wealthier as a group than consumers, many would argue that firms' profits ought not to be weighted as much as consumer benefits. For example, institutional arrangements or regulations that raised consumer surplus by the equivalent of $20 million and decreased firms' profits by $25 million may be judged to improve welfare even at a cost of $5 million in terms of total surplus.

Another important caveat is that the Fundamental Theorem applies to competitive markets, which, as outlined earlier in the chapter, correspond to some fairly strong assumptions. When producers or consumers are large enough to affect market prices; products are differentiated; there is less than perfect information about price and quality; entry into the industry is restricted; or there are market externalities (a concept I will introduce in Section 5.1) then the Fundamental Theorem does not necessarily hold. More on this in the next sections and in the next chapter.

1. The idea of the price system (under perfect competition) as an effective allocative system — including the "invisible hand" metaphor — were developed at length by the great eighteenth century author Adam Smith. Note that the competitive system achieves productive efficiency by means of a sort of "natural selection" mechanism (only the efficient firms survive). In this sense, it's closer to the ideas of Darwin than it is to Smith's.

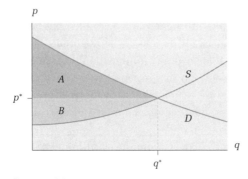

**FIGURE 4.9**
The Fundamental Theorem

Finally, I should stress that the Fundamental Theorem (as stated above) is about static efficiency, about the optimal allocation of resources in an economy with a given set of goods. The Fundamental Theorem is not a statement about dynamic efficiency. It is difficult to measure dynamic efficiency, even more difficult to compare it to static efficiency. For this reason, industrial economists have tended to pay more attention to static efficiency than to dynamic efficiency. The bias towards static efficiency is not innocuous. As we will see in Chapter 15, there is often a trade-off between static and dynamic efficiency, that, increasing static allocative efficiency may come at the cost of dynamic efficiency.

■ **COMPETITIVE SELECTION AND EFFICIENCY.** Let us return to the model of competitive selection introduced in Section 4.2. For all its differences with respect to perfect competition, competitive selection maintains one important property: efficiency. First, notice that each firm's output decision in each period is efficient: price equal to expected marginal cost is the most efficient output decision, that is, the one that maximizes total surplus. Moreover, it can be shown that the firm's entry and exit decisions are also optimal from a social point of view. The basic idea is the same as in the model of perfect competition: a very small firm has a negligible impact on other firms and on price. It follows that it internalizes all of the costs and benefits from entering or exiting the industry: what is good for the firm is good for society.

It might seem inefficient to have firms entering and exiting the industry simultaneously. But we must remember that firms are uncertain about their efficiency. The only way to determine a firm's efficiency is actually to enter the industry.

Similarly to perfect competition, market equilibrium under competitive selection is efficient.

Notice in particular that the rate of firm turnover (the number of firms entering and exiting the industry divided by the total number of firms) is efficient: a central planner would not want to increase or decrease it. At first, it might seem that simultaneous entry and exit is a waste of resources — to the extent that there are entry costs. However, those entry costs are the price to pay for the firm turnover process to select the more efficient firms.

■ **MONOPOLISTIC COMPETITION AND EFFICIENCY.** Comparing the long-run equilibria under perfect competition and monopolistic competition, we notice one important similarity and one important difference. Common to both models is the feature that, *due to free entry, profits are zero in the long run*. However, this zero-profit equilibrium implies that price equals the minimum average cost in the perfect competition model, whereas *under monopolistic competition price is greater than the minimum average cost*. To put it differently, price equals marginal cost under perfect competition, whereas *price is greater than marginal cost under monopolistic competition*.

Under free entry, the propositions "price is greater than the minimum of average cost" and "price is greater than marginal cost" are equivalent (cf Exercise 4.12). However, they imply two different (though related) sources of allocative inefficiency: (a) The fact that price is greater than the minimum of average cost implies that, by reallocating production across firms, it is possible to reduce total industry cost. Specifically, if the goal is to minimize cost per unit then each firm produces too small an output under monopolistic competition (cf Figure 4.7): for the same output level, total costs would be lower if there were fewer firms with each producing at a higher output level. (b) The fact that price is greater than marginal cost implies that, by increasing output, total surplus increases: at the margin, what consumers are willing to pay (price) is greater than what firms have to pay (marginal cost).

Under perfect competition, we have both zero profits (price equal to average cost) and efficiency (price equal to marginal cost). This coincidence has led many to equate zero profits with efficiency. The monopolistic competition model shows that such equivalence is, in general, unwarranted. Zero profits are the result of free entry.[m] Both the models of perfect competition and monopolistic competition are based on the assumption of free entry, and therefore result in zero profits. Productive efficiency is achieved when production costs are minimized. Such minimization takes place under perfect competition (because firms are price takers), but not under monopolistic competition (where firms are price makers).

Finally, notice that allocative inefficiency under monopolistic competition (price greater than marginal cost and the minimum of average cost) does not necessarily imply overall inefficiency; one must also consider the benefits from product variety. If each firm were to produce at the level $q$ such that average cost is minimized, and if price were to equal average cost (and marginal cost), then the number of active firms would be lower than under the long-run monopolistic competition equilibrium. But, assuming that consumers value variety (which is consistent with the assumption that individual demands are downward sloping), then such a move would imply a loss of consumer utility. This loss of product variety must be weighed against the gain in terms of production costs when determining how attractive the long-run equilibrium is. More on this in Chapter 10.

## SUMMARY

m. To be more precise, zero profits result from free entry *and* equal access to the best available technologies. The case when the first condition holds but not the second was addressed in Section 4.2.

• Price tends to move in the direction of equilibrium price (where supply equals demand). • (a) A rightward shift of the demand curve leads to an increase in quantity and an increase in price. (b) A rightward shift of the supply curve leads to an increase in quantity and a decrease in price. • In the long-run equilibrium under perfect competition firms produce at the minimum average cost and make zero profits. • Variability of and uncertainty about firm efficiency reconciles the competitive model with empirical observation regarding (a) simultaneous entry and exit; (b) relative size of entrants/exiters vis-a-vis incumbents. • Equilibrium profits under monopolistic competition are zero, but firms do not produce at the minimum of their average cost. • *Allocative efficiency* requires that output be at the right level. *Productive efficiency* requires that such output be produced in the least expensive way given the available set of technologies. *Dynamic efficiency* refers to the improvement over time of products and production techniques. • In a competitive market the equilibrium levels of output and price correspond to the maximum total surplus. • Similarly to perfect competition, market equilibrium under competitive selection is efficient.

## KEY CONCEPTS

• atomistic firms • homogeneous product • perfect information • free entry • industry supply curve • market equilibrium • law of supply and demand • comparative statics • law of supply and demand • rent • competitive selection • monopolistic competition • consumer surplus • producer surplus • allocative efficiency • productive efficiency • dynamic efficiency • the Fundamental Theorem

## REVIEW AND PRACTICE EXERCISES

■ **4.1. VITAMIN C.** Vitamin C is a generic vitamin that is produced by many companies: brand names are not very important, entry is easy. A good friend — a world-renowned orthopedic surgeon from New Jersey — tells you that he is about to publish in *The New England Journal of Medicine* (a highly respected and widely quoted medical journal) a study indicating that daily doses of 500 mg of vitamin C tends to improve the muscle tone and increase the physical stamina of adults, with no adverse side effects. Though a very good doctor, he is woefully ignorant about the basic workings of markets and wants to know what is likely to happen, and why — in the short run and in the long run — to the price of vitamin C, to the quantity sold, to the profits of the producers, and to the number of firms that produce it. Summarize what you would tell him.

■ **4.2. COMPARATIVE STATICS: ASPARTAME, OIL.** For each of the following, use a supply and demand diagram to deduce the impact of the event on the stated market. Would you expect the impact to be primarily on price or quantity? Feel free to mention issues that you don't think are captured by a traditional supply and demand analysis.

(a) Event: The FDA announces that aspartame may cause cancer. Market: Saccharin. (Note: aspartame and saccharin are low-calorie sweeteners.)

(b) Event: Oil price increases. Market: California electricity.

■ **4.3. COMPARATIVE STATICS: PRICE AND QUANTITY EFFECTS.** Consider following events and markets:

• OPEC reduces oil output [market: oil]

- Unusually rainy winter in New York City [market: umbrellas in NYC]

- Soccer Champions League final in Madrid [market: Madrid hotels]

- Unusually low catch of sole fish [market: sole fish]

Which of the four corresponds to the four cases considered in Figure 4.3?

■ **4.4. KIDNEY TRANSPLANTS.** Suppose that in a given state — let's call it state X — a few recent kidney transplant malpractice suits have led to punitive damage awards of unprecedented levels. What impact do you expect this to have in the market for kidney transplant services in state X? To the extent that you can, and making the necessary assumptions as you go along, indicate the expected effects on price and quantity; the relative magnitude of these effects; and any possible differences between short-run and long-run effects.

■ **4.5. BOOK PUBLISHING.** The technology of book publishing is characterized by a high fixed cost (typesetting the book) and a very low marginal cost (printing). Prices are set at much higher levels than marginal cost. However, book publishing yields a normal rate of return. Are these facts consistent with profit maximizing behavior by publishers? Which model do you think describes this industry best?

■ **4.6. LAUNDRY DETERGENT.** The market for laundry detergent is monopolistically competitive. Each firm owns one brand, and each brand has effectively differentiated itself so that it has some market power (i.e., faces a downward sloping demand curve). Still, no brand earns economic profits, because entry causes the demand for each brand to shift in until the seller can just break even. All firms have identical cost functions, which are U-shaped.

Suppose that the government does a study on detergents and finds out they are all alike. The public is notified of these findings and suddenly drops allegiance to any brand. What happens to price when this product that was brand-differentiated becomes a commodity? What happens to total sales? What happens to the number of firms in the market?

■ **4.7. T-SHIRT PRINTING.** The custom T-shirt printing business has many competitors, so that the perfect competition model may be considered a good approximation. Currently the market demand curve is given by $Q = 120 - 1.5\,p$, whereas the market supply is given by $Q = -20 + 2\,p$.

(a) Determine the market equilibrium.

Suppose there is a T-shirt craze that increases demand by 10% (that is, for each price, demand is now 10% greater than it was before the price increase).

(b) Determine the new demand curve.

(c) Determine the change in equilibrium quantity.

(d) If your answer to the previous question is different from 10%, explain the difference in values.

Now go back to the initial demand curve and suppose there is an increase in the cost of blank T-shirts, an essential input into the business of selling custom T-shirts. Specifically, for each unit by each supplier, the production cost goes up by 10%.

(e) Determine the new supply curve.

(f) Determine the change in equilibrium price.

(g) If your answer to the previous question is different from 10%, explain the difference in values.

■ **4.8. SALES TAX.** Consider an industry with market demand $Q = 550 - 20p$ and market supply $Q = 100 + 10p$. Determine the equilibrium price and quantity. Suppose the government imposes a tax of $6 per unit to be paid by consumers. What is the impact on equilibrium price and quantity? What if the sales tax is paid by the seller instead of the buyer?

■ **4.9. SALES TAX WITH STEEPER DEMAND.** Consider again Exercise 4.8. Suppose that demand is instead given by $Q = 280 - 2p$.

(a) Show that the equilibrium levels of $p$ and $q$ are the same as in the initial equilibrium of Exercise 4.8.

(b) Determine the impact of a $6 sales tax in terms of the price effectively paid by buyers and sellers.

(c) Compare the results in (b) to those in Exercise 4.8. Explain the economic intuition.

■ **4.10. CAR PRICES IN EUROPE.** Sales taxes on car purchases in Europe vary from 0% to more than 200%.[12] The UK is one of the countries with lowest taxes, whereas Denmark is one of the countries with highest taxes.

(a) In which countries do you expect consumer prices to be the highest?

(b) In which countries do you expect pre-tax consumer prices to be the highest?

By law, if a consumer buys a car in country $x$ and then registers the car in country $y$, the consumer receives a refund from the tax paid in country $x$ and then pays the corresponding tax in country $y$.

(c) What is the optimal car buying strategy for a European who does not mind to purchase abroad?

## CHALLENGING EXERCISES

■ **4.11. ELECTRICITY SUPPLY.** Consider an electricity market where there are three suppliers, each with constant marginal cost (a reasonable approximation in electricity generation). Firm 1 has a capacity of 200 and $MC = 5$. Firm 2 has a capacity of 100 and $MC = 8$. Firm 3 has a capacity of 100 and $MC = 10$. Suppose that suppliers act as price takers.

(a) Determine the industry supply curve.

(b) Suppose that market demand is given by $Q = 540 - 20p$. Determine the market equilibrium. Is this equilibrium a long-run equilibrium?

(c) Suppose that (i) demand falls to $D(p) = 400 - 20p$; (ii) Firm 3 reduces its $MC$ to 8; (iii) Firm 2 reduces its $MC$ to 7. What happens to equilibrium profits in each case?

■ **4.12. AVERAGE AND MARGINAL COST.** Show that, in a long-run equilibrium with free entry and equal access to the best available technologies, the comparison of price to the minimum of average cost or the comparison of price to marginal cost are equivalent tests of allocative efficiency. In other words, price is greater than the minimum of average costs if and only if price is greater than marginal cost.

Show, by example, that the same is not true in general (hint: consider a monopolist with constant average and marginal cost $c$).

## APPLIED EXERCISES

■ **4.13. MARKET SUPPLY.** Find firm level data on marginal cost and capacity (e.g., electricity power plants). Estimate the firm and market supply curves under the assumption that firms are price takers.

## NOTES

1. Source: US Geological Survey.

2. Lucas, Robert (1978), "On the Size Distribution of Business Firms," *Bell Journal of Economics* **9**, 508–523.

3. Mueller, Dennis (1986), *Profits in the Long Run*, Cambridge: Cambridge University Press.

4. Syverson, Chad (2004), "Product Substitutability and Productivity Dispersion," *Review of Economics and Statistics* **86** (2), 534–550.

5. Hsieh, Chang-Tai, and Peter J. Klenow (2009), "Misallocation and Manufacturing TFP in China and India," *Quarterly Journal of Economics* **124** (4), 1403–1448.

6. Foster, Lucia, John Haltiwanger, and Chad Syverson (2008), "Reallocation, Firm Turnover, and Efficiency: Selection on Productivity or Profitability?," *American Economic Review* **98** (1), 394–425

7. Source: Cable, John, and Joachim Schwalbach (1991), *International Comparisons of Entry and Exit*, in Geroski and Schwalbach (Ed.), *Entry and Market Contestability*, Oxford: Basil Blackwell.

8. Source: Cable and Schwalbach, op. cit.

9. Source: Van Ark, Bart, and Erik Monnikhof (1996), "Size Distribution of Output and Employment: A Data Set For Manufacturing Industries in Five OECD Countries, 1960s-1990," OECD Economics Department Working Paper No. 166.

10. Several models have been proposed to account for the main stylized facts (including those presented in the previous section). The model I present here is adapted from Jovanovic, Boyan (1982), "Selection and Evolution of Industry," *Econometrica* **50**, 649–670. Other important contributions include Lippman, Stephen, and Rumelt, R. (1982), "Uncertain Imitability: An Analysis of Interfirm Differences in Efficiency under Competition," *Bell Journal of Economics* **13**, 418–438; Hopenhayn, Hugo (1992), "Entry, Exit, and Firm Dynamics in Long Run Equilibrium," *Econometrica* **60**, 1127–1150; and Ericson, Richard and Ariel Pakes (1989), "Markov-Perfect Industry Dynamics: A Framework for Empirical Work," *Review of Economics Studies* **62**, 53–82.

11. Chamberlin, Edward H. (1933), *The Theory of Monopolistic Competition*, Cambridge, Mass: Harvard University Press; Robinson, Joan V. (1933), *The Economics of Imperfect Competition*, London: Macmillan; 2d ed., 1969.

12. Source: European Parliament, "Car Taxes: The Less I Pollute, the Less I Pay," 27-06-2006.

# CHAPTER 5

# MARKET FAILURE AND PUBLIC POLICY

The perfect competition model is based on so many assumptions that it is not difficult to find examples where it fails. In this chapter, I consider three important sources of "market failure:" externalities, imperfect information, and market power. Externalities exist when the actions of an economic agent (consumer, firm, etc.) have an impact on other agents that go beyond the effect on market price. This may seem a bit vague, but hopefully the examples in Section 5.1 will make things clear; for now, let me just say that pollution and climate change provide a prominent example of externalities. The idea of imperfect information should be more straightforward: sometimes firms don't know everything about consumers and consumers don't know everything about firms. Health care is an example that comes to mind, but as we will see in Section 5.2 there are many, many more examples. Finally, market power refers to firms that have the ability to set prices, sometimes very high prices: your local supermarket, your airline, and your cable provider are just three examples; I am sure you can think of more examples (and I will suggest a few in Section 5.3).

One half of the chapter is devoted to these sources of market failure, whereas the other half focuses on public policy instruments to correct situations of market power: market regulation (Section 5.4), competition policy (Section 5.5), and firm regulation (Section 5.6).

## 5.1 EXTERNALITIES AND MARKET FAILURE

Where can you find beer for 5 cents a bottle? My best answer: try a class reunion with 100 diners. Let me explain. When you and your 99 colleagues go out for a meal, chances are you will decide to split the total bill: it would be far too complicated to keep

100 individual tabs. When it comes to decide whether to order that second or third beer, if you are an economist, then the way you'll reason is as follows: one more beer, five more dollars on the total tab; that's five cents for me — not a bad deal! Lest you think this is a purely theoretical consideration, economists have actually estimated this effect: even for a party as small as four, splitting the bill may lead to an increase in the total tab by as much as 40%.[1]

In economics, this problem is referred to as the **free riding problem**. The point is that an agent's decisions (for example ordering an extra beer at a split-the-bill dinner) does not take into account the costs imposed on other agents (99% of that extra beer is effectively paid by them). As a result, the total quantity consumed at the dinner is likely to be higher than socially efficient: even if the marginal cost of a beer is, say, 30 cents, there will be a lot of beer consumed for which willingness to pay is lower than social cost.

■ **TYPES OF EXTERNALITIES.** More generally, we say there is an **externality** when an agent's actions have an effect on other agents that goes beyond the market transaction per se. This effect can be negative (e.g., when I smoke people around me suffer) or positive (e.g., when I plant flowers in my yard, everyone who passes by benefits). I next consider some of the most common types of externalities.

- The **tragedy of the commons** is the situation where a common resource is overused with respect to the socially optimal level. The name dates back to the grazing fields in England that were shared by several flock owners; but there are some more recent and economically important cases, such as fisheries and clean air. For example, when a fishing boat decides how much cod to catch in New Foundland, the owner compares his own benefits and his own costs, ignoring the effect that this will have on the overall stock of cod. In this case, the market equilibrium involves an output level that is too high from a social point of view, possibly even leading to species extinction or at least over-fishing.[a]

- Here's an externality that most of us complain about on a daily basis: **congestion**. If you are used to fly out of a busy airport like New York's LaGuardia or London's Heathrow, you know the drill: "Good morning folks, this is your captain speaking, we are now number 17 for takeoff." Which means an extra half hour taxiing on the tarmac. Excessive congestion results from an externality: when an airline decides to schedule a flight during rush hour, it does not take into account the extra delay it will impose on all flights departing right after.

- I've been giving examples of negative externalities, but there are also examples of positive externalities. An extreme case is given by **public goods**. If I build a park, I create a benefit for myself, but others can enjoy it at no extra

a. The tragedy of the commons may also be felt in a large multi-division organization where division managers and heads are rewarded only for the performance of their own divisions, thus failing to take into account the impact of their actions on the firm as a whole. See Exercise 5.6.

cost — a positive externality.[b] National defense, health, and education are also examples of investments and expenses that have some element of public good.[c]

As these examples show, externalities abound. This is bad news for the Fundamental Theorem, and it begs a number of questions: how poorly does the market solution work in the presence of externalities? Are there any means of restoring optimality — or something close to optimality — in the presence of externalities? I begin with the economists' favorite solution to the problem: externality-correcting taxes.

■ **SOCIAL COST AND PIGOU TAXES.** In markets with externalities, the Fundamental Theorem fails to hold: market price is no longer the right guide for consumers and producers; something else besides the "invisible hand" is required to establish social efficiency. What is this "something else"? Many economists will tell you that the solution is to apply a **Pigou tax**.

To motivate the idea, consider the problem of climate change. We may dispute the precise numbers, but we all agree that industrial production is an important factor in carbon dioxide emissions, which in turn contribute to climate change and related effects. What does this mean in economics terms? Figure 5.1 depicts the supply and demand curves in a given industry. Recall that, in a competitive industry, the supply curve reflects the sellers' marginal cost curves, whereas the demand curve — specifically, the inverse demand curve — reflects the buyers' willingness to pay for the product in question. The free market equilibrium implies price $p^\circ$ and output $q^\circ$. By the Fundamental Theorem, this is the output level such that a marginal buyer's willingness to pay is just equal to the marginal seller's marginal cost: there is no trade that would increase total gains from trade; total surplus is maximized.

Suppose however that each unit of output implies a social marginal cost of $c(q)$, that is, a value that changes as $q$ changes (in the figure, and in most real-world cases,

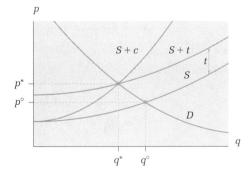

**FIGURE 5.1**
Market equilibrium and social optimum with externalities

b. In other words, public goods are non-rival (and non-excludable) goods: the consumption by one person does not impede the consumption of the same good by another person.

c. One important distinction is between public goods with exclusion and public goods with no exclusion. For example, I can restrict access to a park that I build, but it would be hard to stop residents in a given area from enjoying clean air, if clean air is provided.

the social marginal cost is increasing in $q$). Then the total marginal cost of producing a $q$th unit is given the sum of production marginal cost and social marginal cost, the curve $S + c$ in Figure 5.1. By the same reasoning as in the Fundamental Theorem, the socially optimal output level — the level that maximizes net benefits, including the extra social marginal cost — is given by the point where $S + c$ crosses the demand curve. This corresponds to output level $q^*$. Not surprisingly, $q^*$ is lower than $q^\circ$: whenever there is a negative externality, the equilibrium output level is greater than the socially optimal output level.

Is there any hope for the market? Enter economist Arthur C. Pigou, whose answer is yes, so long as we impose an output tax (if the externality is negative) or a output subsidy (if the externality is positive).[d] Consider Figure 5.1 again. Suppose that a tax $t$ is levied on suppliers for each output unit. This implies an upward shift in the supply curve, from $S$ to $S + t$. The market equilibrium is now given by $q^*$, the socially optimal output level.

A relative success story in applying Pigou's ideas is taxation of gasoline consumption in Europe, where a Pigou tax has shifted consumption levels closer to the social optimum. See Box 5.1 for details. A less successful story is the idea of a "Google tax," which is gaining traction in several European countries. See Box 5.2 for details. The idea is to tax Internet content aggregators (such as Google) that list snippets of content (e.g., news items) created by others. The "Google tax" is more about fairness than it is about efficiency. In fact, Pigou would recommend that both newspapers and Google be *subsidized*, since both content creation and links to content create a positive externality (see Box 5.2). However, such policy would face tremendous difficulties (e.g., deciding who will pay for the subsidy).

■ **ALTERNATIVE SOLUTIONS TO THE EXTERNALITY PROBLEM.** Notwithstanding economists' preferences, Pigou taxes are by no means the only way to deal with externalities. One important alternative is direct **regulation** of the externality-creating activity. For example, smoking creates an externality in the sense that it bothers — and harms — nearby non-smokers. In many countries around the world, this problem has been solved simply by banning smoking in public places.

In many settings, social norms play the role of government regulations. Even if you are splitting the restaurant bill, you will probably not order the Beluga caviar with Dom Perignon champagne on the side. Why not? Often going out to restaurants is a repeated game (cf Chapter 7): we tend to go out with the same groups of friends or colleagues, and so a norm of behavior (with a consequent threat of punishment) can arise. If you order caviar, it may be last time you do so with this group of friends, so think twice about it.

d. I am assuming that the amount of pollution is proportional to output. More generally, the tax should be on the amount of the polluting amount.

■ **THE COASE THEOREM.** One of the most creative ways of solving the inefficiency created by externalities may be to let the interested parties negotiate. The **Coase Theorem** — named after its originator, economist Ronald Coase — states that, if **property rights** are

## Box 5.1 Approaches to reducing gasoline consumption: US and EU

In 2013, 1 liter of gasoline cost €1.53 at an average European Union (EU) pump, of which 58% corresponded to taxes and duties. In the United States, average price at the pump was $3.49 per gallon. Considering that one gallon equals 3.785 liters and that the yearly average exchange rate was 0.783 euros per dollar, this comes to about €.72 per liter, about one half of the price in Europe. For US readers, the European price was about $7.40 per gallon, about twice the US price.

Not surprisingly, gasoline consumption (both per person and per car) is much lower in the EU than in the US. Arguably, the value of $q$ in Europe is much closer to $q^*$ in the EU than in the US (cf Figure 5.1). This is partly because the price elasticity of the demand for gasoline is different from zero, but also because the demand for cars is very different in the EU than in the US. Reacting to high gasoline prices and the demand for low-consumption cars, European cars are smaller and consume less gasoline than their American counterparts. In 2013, average fuel efficiency in the US was 32 miles per gallon, whereas the EU showed a whopping 45. For European readers, this corresponds to 5.2 liters per 100 kilometers (EU) against 7.6 liters per 100 kilometers (US).

Various US governments have made efforts to increase automobile fuel efficiency, for example enacting Corporate Average Fuel Efficiency (CAFE) standards, regulations that force automakers a minimum average fuel efficiency. However, the regulated firms have managed to keep the minimum standards at "reasonable" levels. Moreover, various loopholes make CAFE standards less effective than one might think: for example, gas-guzzling SUVs are treated as light trucks (and thus excluded from the average), which effectively provides an "escape" for consumers and manufacturers who want to avoid regulation.

In sum, fuel efficiency policy suggests that price may be a better instrument than quantity regulation. It also provides an example of how the market-based US may at times be less market-based then the more government-centered EU. Finally, having established how the US and the EU differ in the way they regulate gasoline consumption, one is naturally led to the question of why they differ: Section 5.4 provides a partial answer.

properly assigned and negotiations are costless, then all externalities will be "internalized," so that the market solution (cum negotiations) leads to an efficient solution.[2]

Consider, for example, the case of a steel plant dumping waste in the river. Society might decide that (a) downstream parties have a property right to clean water, or (b) that the plant has the right to dispose of its waste as it sees fit. Property rights can be established in either way. But once those rights have been clearly established (and so long as they are properly enforced), then individuals can bargain over how to exercise those rights. If downstream parties have the right to clean water, then the steel plant can pay them in order to get permission to pollute. Alternatively, if the plant has the property rights, then downstream parties can compensate the steel plant to restrict its pollution inducing activities.

**BOX 5.2 THE EUROPEAN "GOOGLE TAX"**

If you "Googled" "ebola" in Spain sometime in October 2014, you would probably find a link to the newspaper *El País*, as well as a snippet of the news item in question. If you clicked through the link you'd be directed to the site containing the complete story. In the process, several firms made money off your clicks and eyeballs: *El País* included ads on the page where the story was displayed; Google, too, included ads on the search page you started from; and online ads are paid for (a lot, since they tend to be targeted).

In October 2014, Günther Oettinger, the EU's incoming Digital Commissioner, floated the idea of an EU-wide "Google-tax." This tax would require Internet search engine providers to pay a fee for displaying copyrighted materials on their sites. "If Google takes intellectual property from the EU and makes use of it, the EU can protect this property and demand that Google pay for it," said Oettinger.

This would not be the first attempt by European regulators to extract rents from the Internet giant. In 2006, a Belgium court ordered Google to pay Copiepresse, a consortium of Belgium newspapers, for the right to include news snippets on its search pages, "under penalty of a daily fine of €2,000,000 per day of delay." Google complied — not by paying but rather by removing the links from its pages. This led to a sharp decrease in advertising revenues for the Copiepresse affiliated newspapers. After several years of "link wars," the Belgians eventually caved in: in 2011, Copiepresse allowed Google to re-include their sites in Google's searches.

The newspapers claim their content is being stolen; Google defends itself by asserting that each month it originates billions of views to newspapers' websites. It may be that both are right, that is, both parties stand to gain from snippet display and links to the content source; as author Cory Doctorow aptly put it, "the net is the natural home of positive externalities." At the same time, it can be argued that Google makes relatively more money than the linked sites: many users coming from Google are known as "one hit wonders," users who are more likely to hit the "back" button than to continue browsing the site they were directed to from Google.

In October 2014, Spain created a "Google tax" similar to the Belgian one. The "link wars" are far from over.

Suppose that the value that the plant gets from the opportunity of dumping waste in the river is greater than the cost it imposes on downstream residents. Then, in equilibrium, negotiations will lead to an agreement whereby waste dumping takes place. Notice that this equilibrium is achieved regardless of the initial property rights allocation. If the factory owns the rights, then residents have no incentive to buy the rights from the factory. If, in turn, the residents own the rights, then the factory will make them a proposal they cannot refuse. Conversely, if the value that the plant gets from the opportunity of dumping waste in the river is greater than the cost it imposes on downstream residents, then in equilibrium negotiations will lead to an agreement whereby waste dumping does take place. Once again, this outcome arises regardless of the initial property rights allocation.

The reasoning underlying the Coase Theorem serves as an additional illustration of the difference between efficiency and fairness. The Fundamental Theorem and the

Coase Theorem are about efficiency: resource allocation that maximizes gains from trade (total surplus). These theorems have little to say about fairness. From an efficiency point of view, it makes no difference who owns the rights to a clean river (factory or residents). This is not to say, however, that both property rights allocations are equally fair.

Here's another example of the difference between efficiency and fairness: many cities around the world have banned smoking from public places, including bars. But suppose that some fabulously wealthy person came to town and really, really wanted to light up in a small bar, to the point where he was willing to pay $1 million to each person in the bar. Would it be efficient to let him do so? Would it be fair?

This section can be summarized by stating that:

> Market externalities imply market failure. Pigou taxes and other mechanisms may reestablish equilibrium efficiency.

In the remainder of the book we will come across various instances of externalities. Particularly important are externalities in competition (cf Chapter 8) and externalities in the relation between firms along the value chain (cf Chapter 13).

## 5.2 IMPERFECT INFORMATION

Suppose you want to buy a 2010 Honda Accord. By consulting the Internet or some other source, you find out that the value of a very well kept car is about $20,000. In practice, you know that some owners were not that careful, so that the actual value could be anywhere between $20,000 and $0 (zero being a really bad lemon). For simplicity, let's assume that, from the perspective of an uninformed buyer (you), the value could be anywhere between $0 and $20,000. This means that, on average, you should be willing to pay $10,000 (or less, if you are risk averse, a possibility I presently ignore).

Suppose that sellers, unlike you, are informed about the real value of the car they consider selling. If you are unwilling to pay more than $10,000 for a car, then the sellers whose cars are in best condition (and thus are worth more) will be unwilling to sell. For example, suppose that all sellers whose cars are worth more than $12,000 decide to stay out. If that is the case, and if you find out about it, then you shouldn't be willing to pay more than $6,000. But wait: if this is all that you are willing to pay, then more sellers are unwilling to sell, again those whose cars are in better condition.

This unraveling process of **adverse selection** may go on and on, possibly to the extreme that the market collapses completely.[3] That's a rather unfortunate outcome. As we saw in Section 4.4, under perfect competition all beneficial trades take place. In the present context, there may be many socially profitable trades (where the value of a specific car is greater for buyer than for seller) that do not take place. The key departure from the Fundamental Theorem (Section 4.4) is that perfect competition assumes perfect information, whereas in the present case you (the buyer) are uninformed about the seller's product quality. Absent this situation of **asymmetric information**, each car's price would reflect its quality and a trade take place if and only if the buyer's valuation is greater than the seller's.

Unfortunately, this problem is not limited to buying used cars. A particularly important case of asymmetric information and adverse selection is provided by health insurance markets. The situation is illustrated by Figure 5.2. Suppose that consumers (that is, patients) can be ordered in terms of health risk (from very healthy to very sick). Healthier people are willing to pay less for a given health insurance policy. So, for a given price, only the consumers whose health risk is greater than a certain threshold choose to purchase health insurance.

So far there is nothing special about health insurance. For example, only consumers whose valuation for potato chips is higher than price choose to buy potato chips. One important characteristic of health insurance, however, is that the seller's *cost* depends on the buyer's *type*. Specifically, the cost of serving a specific consumer is greater the greater that consumer's health risk. As a result, the consumers who choose to buy insurance are precisely the consumers whose cost of providing insurance is highest.

This implies that the marginal cost of serving the $q$th consumer is decreasing, as shown in Figure 5.2. It also implies that the average cost of serving the first $q$ consumers (that is, the riskiest $q$ consumers) is declining and greater than the marginal cost, as shown in Figure 5.2.[e]

The competitive equilibrium corresponds to the point where, by means of entry and exit, price is driven to the point where price equals average cost (and firms make zero economic profits). This is given by $(q^e, p^e)$ in Figure 5.2. By contrast, the social optimum level of $q$ corresponds to the point where price equals marginal cost. This is given by $(q^o, p^o)$ in Figure 5.2. As can be seen, $q^e < q^o$, so the competitive equilibrium implies under-provision of health insurance. Specifically, the social inefficiency of the competitive equilibrium may be measured by the are of the shaded triangle $A$. This corresponds to all of the trades such that willingness to pay is greater than (marginal) cost, trades that would be efficient but do not take place.

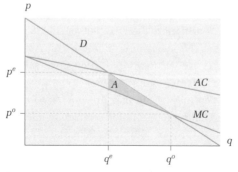

e. If marginal cost is lower than average cost, then average cost is decreasing, and vice-versa.

**FIGURE 5.2**

Equilibrium and social optimum in the health insurance market[4]

**ADVERSE SECTION: FORMAL ANALYSIS.** Suppose that consumer (patient) types are given by $\theta$, which is uniformly distributed between 0 and 1. A consumer of type $\theta$ is willing to pay $\theta$ for health insurance: $\theta = 0$ corresponds to a consumer who is so healthy that he or she is not willing to pay anything for health insurance; $\theta = 1$, by contrast, corresponds to a very sick person who, due to his or her poor health, is willing to pay 1 for health insurance. Finally, suppose that the cost of providing health insurance to a consumer of type $\theta$ is given by $c_0 + c_1 \theta$, where both $c_0$ and $c_0 + c_1$ are greater than 0 and less than 1.

If the price of insurance is $p$, then consumers with $\theta > p$ buy insurance. Since $\theta$ is uniformly distributed between 0 and 1, it follows that $1 - p$ consumers buy insurance, that is, the demand curve is given by $q = 1 - p$.

The healthiest of the set of consumers who buy insurance has $\theta = p$, so it costs $MC = c_0 + c_1 \theta = c_0 + c_1 p$ to serve this consumer. Since $q = 1 - p$, we have $p = 1 - q$, and so $MC = c_0 + c_1 (1 - q)$. It costs $c_0 + c_1$ to serve the least healthy consumer. It follows that, on average, it costs $AC = c_0 + c_1 \frac{1}{2} (1 - q + 1) = c_0 + c_1 (1 - \frac{1}{2} q)$ to serve the consumers who buy health insurance when price is $p$.

The socially efficient solution corresponds to offering health insurance until the demand curve crosses the marginal cost curve, that is, until $1 - q = c_0 + c_1 (1 - q)$. This is true when:

$$q = q^o = \frac{1 - c_0 - c_1}{1 - c_1}$$

The competitive market equilibrium, in turn, corresponds to the point where the demand curve crosses the average cost curve, that is, $1 - q = c_0 + c_1 (1 - \frac{1}{2} q)$, which corresponds to:

$$q = q^e = \frac{1 - c_0 - c_1}{1 - \frac{c_1}{2}}$$

Comparing the above expressions, we can see that $q^e < q^o$: in the competitive equilibrium, the value of $q$ is lower than the socially optimal value.

I should note that the opposite of adverse selection — **advantageous selection** — is also possible, though not as common. Estimates from the Israeli auto insurance market suggest that riskier drivers (that is, drivers who are more prone to accidents) are typically drivers with less risk aversion (that is, for a given level of risk they are less willing to buy insurance).[5] If the variation in risk aversion is sufficiently large — as is the case in Israel — then, for a given price, the drivers who are willing to pay for insurance are on average less risky than the total population. This implies that the average cost of insurance car drivers is *increasing* with $q$, the opposite of Figure 5.2. It also implies that marginal cost is greater than average cost and that equilibrium output is greater than the social optimum: $q^e > q^*$.

Finally, one should also mention another implication of market asymmetric information: **moral hazard**. Consider the market for an expensive smartphone. Some consumers are risk averse and purchase theft insurance. The problem with this is that, once you are insured, your incentives to be careful about not having your phone stolen are lower. Insurance companies know this, of course, and adjust their premiums accordingly. You can see how the adverse-selection market unraveling (as in, for example, the market for lemons) could also take place in the context of moral hazard.[f]

## 5.3 MONOPOLY

In the previous chapter we looked at the equilibrium of a market where there are many buyers and many sellers. Now we consider another extreme, namely the case when there is one seller only: a monopolist (we continue assuming that there are many buyers).

Monopolies may exist for various reasons. First, they may be granted by the government. For example, by government decree Electricité de France (EdF) held the monopoly in electricity generation in France until 1999, at which time it was forced by a European Directive to open up 20% of its business to competitors. A common form of government granted right which may lead to a monopoly outcome is a **patent**. For example, until November 2011 Pfizer held a patent on the cholesterol-reducing drug Atorvastatin, which it sold under the name Lipitor. Similarly to patents, a **copyright** confers on its owner exclusive rights over the expression of a creative work. For example, the use of Mickey Mouse's image is an exclusive held by Disney (for now).

A second source of monopoly is the nature of the cost or demand function. For example, due to strong indirect **network effects** (which we will discuss in detail in Chapter 16), the video cassette recorder (VCR), for which various alternative designs were created, ended up in a de facto monopoly in terms of design (with VHS beating Betamax and other alternatives).

Frequently, a monopoly or near monopoly position is the result of more than one factor. Consider for example the case of Intel. One reason for its success is that, over the years, it has led the industry in terms of product quality and efficient production (cf Chapter 15). It also helps that the set-up costs required to create a production facility (a fab) are so high that it would be difficult for an alternative company to rival Intel in size; that is, economies of scale play an important role (cf Chapters 3, 10). AMD is indeed a rival to Intel, but of much smaller size. In fact, some might argue that one of the reasons why AMD does not grow to become a closer competitor to Intel is to be found in Intel's aggressive pricing strategies (cf Chapter 12).

■ **MONOPOLY POWER AND INEFFICIENCY.** The competitive and monopoly equilibria are contrasted in Figure 5.3. Suppose there are two industries with the same demand and market marginal cost curve. The difference between the two industries is that, in the first one (left) there are many small sellers, so that the market is competitive; whereas in the second one (right) there is only one seller (the monopolist).

Under perfect competition, equilibrium price is determined by the intersection of the demand and supply curves. Since the (inverse) demand curve measures consumer willingness to pay and the (inverse) supply curve measures marginal cost, the equilibrium point is the point at which willingness to pay is just equal to marginal cost. All

f. Moral hazard problems appear at various points in this book, including Section 3.3 (I did not explicitly mention the term "moral hazard," but the agency problem is partly a moral-hazard problem); Section 9.1 (collusion is, to some extent, a moral hazard problem); and Section 13.1 (vertical integration raises issues of moral hazard).

trades in a competitive market (points to the left of $q_C$) are such that willingness to pay is greater than marginal cost; and there is no trade such that willingness to pay is higher than marginal cost that does not take place. This is the essence of the Fundamental Theorem: all efficient trades take place (see Section 4.4).

Not so under monopoly (see Section 3.2). As can be seen from the right panel in Figure 5.3, equilibrium output under monopoly, $q_M$, is lower than the efficient level, $q_C$. In other words, all trades corresponding to $q_M < q < q_C$ fail to take place under monopoly. These trades would be efficient, that is, the buyer willingness to pay is greater than marginal cost. High airfares, for example, mean that there are potential fliers who refrain from buying tickets even though the cost of carrying them as passengers would be low. From a social point of view, it would be efficient to fly many of these potential travelers: although the value they derive from flying is lower than price (hence they don't fly), that value is greater than the cost of flying (which is much lower than price). In sum, monopoly implies an efficiency loss. This loss is measured by the shaded area $C$, which adds up all of the lost surplus $p - MC$ from "missing" efficient trades. (This area is frequently referred to as a **Harberger triangle**, although as you can see it is only a triangle if both the demand and the marginal cost curves are linear.)

While economists tend to focus on the **allocative inefficiency** implied by monopoly pricing (that is, the area $C$, also known as **excess burden**), many policy makers and most politicians focus on another implication of market power: to the extent that monopoly price is greater than marginal cost, market power implies a transfer from consumers to firms. This can be seen by comparing the relative magnitude of the areas $A$ and $B$ in the two panels of Figure 5.3: the ratio $A/B$ is much greater under monopoly than under competition. To the extent that society places a greater weight on consumer welfare than on firm welfare, it sees market power as problematic.

But there is more, as we saw in Sections 1.2 and 4.4: insulated from competition, monopolists may tend to "coast" and make less effort to reduce costs (a phenomenon known as X-inefficiency)."[g] In fact, the evidence suggests that firms in more competitive markets are also more productive; and that most of this variation is accounted by X-inefficiency.[6] Then market power also implies a loss of **productive efficiency**, that is,

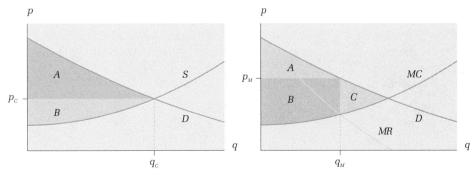

**FIGURE 5.3**
Competitive and monopoly market equilibria

g. As mentioned in Section 4.4, productive efficiency refers to how close the actual production cost is to the lowest cost achievable. X-inefficiency is one possible source (though not the only one) of productive inefficiency total output is not produced at the lowest cost possible. By contrast, under perfect competition (as we saw in Section 4.4) inefficient firms fail to survive in an equilibrium where price equals the minimum of average cost of the most efficient technology.

Finally, to the extent that monopoly rights create rents, they may induce wasteful resource competition for those rents. For example, many commodity exporting developing countries suffer from a significant resource shift into the commodity exporting industry and away from other industries where the marginal value of those resources would be higher. In other words, **rent seeking** must be added to the social cost of monopoly.

Not everything about monopoly is bad: in Chapter 15 we will see how the rate of innovation may be greater when the industry is dominate by large, quasi-monopoly firms (though this is debatable). In Chapter 16 we will see how a monopoly market structure may be beneficial in markets with strong network effects (it's better to have one operating system rather than a myriad operating systems each with a tiny market share).

■ **DOMINANT FIRMS.** Pure monopolies are fairly rare. Aside from utilities, one is hard pressed to find a good example of a firm that controls 100% of its market (for a reasonable market definition). It is not uncommon, however, to find industries where one of the firms commands a market share of 50% or more, whereas a set of smaller firms divide the remainder of the market among themselves. Examples include the mainframe computer industry in the '60s and '70s, IBM being the dominant firm; computer microprocessors, since the 1980s, Intel being the dominant firm; and desktop operating systems since the 1980s, with Microsoft (Windows) being the dominant firm. Normally, the dominant firm holds some competitive advantage with respect to rivals, either by reason of lower costs or higher quality (or better reputation for quality).

Consider a third example, that of long-distance telecommunications in the US in the second half of the 1980s. AT&T competed against two smaller rivals: MCI and Sprint. Until the early to mid-1990s, there were two important differences between AT&T and its competitors. First, most of the rivals had a smaller capacity than AT&T's. Second, rivals were not subject to the same type of regulation that the former monopolist was.[h] As a result, AT&T's competitors could change prices more quickly and more easily.

For this reason, AT&T was, in some sense, a price leader. Whichever price was set, competitors would typically follow by pricing at the same level or slightly lower. Table 5.1 illustrates this point: most price changes effected by MCI and Sprint in the period 1987–1994 followed price changes by AT&T; and the prices set by AT&T's rivals tended to be just below those of the former monopolist.[i]

Suppose that consumers choose the firm offering the lowest price and that the small carriers are capacity constrained, having a total capacity of $K$. This situation is depicted in Figure 5.4. Whichever price AT&T sets (above marginal cost), the small carriers will set a slightly smaller price and sell up to capacity. In practice, this implies that AT&T is faced with the **residual demand** $D_R$, obtained from market demand $D$ by moving it $K$ units to the left, where $K$ is the total capacity of the small competitors.

h. In 1996, AT&T ceased to be subject to price regulation. Moreover, the rivals' capacity and market share increased considerably.

i. MCI changed its rates in the same month as AT&T in 5 out of 12 price changes. Sprint set the same rates as AT&T from 1991 to 1994 (although it reacted to the latter's changes with some lag).

Given the residual demand $D_R$, AT&T's optimal price is derived in the usual way, by equating marginal revenue to marginal cost ($MC$). This results in an optimal price $p_D$ and output $q_D$. Notice that, so long as $K$ is small, $p_D$ is close to $p_M$, the monopoly price. This suggests that a dominant firm behaves in a way that is similar to a monopolist.

In reality, things are a bit more complicated. Long-distance telecommunications is not a homogeneous product, or at least is not perceived as such by consumers. In fact, AT&T's advantage resulted primarily from a large base of loyal consumers who perceived AT&T's service as superior. This caveat notwithstanding, the above model illustrates the idea that:

> The monopoly model provides a good approximation to the behavior of dominant firms.

■ **MONOPOLY AND MONOPOLY POWER.** Are there any monopolies? In the beginning of the chapter, I suggested the example of utilities (electricity, telephone, etc.). But most of these have been privatized, deregulated, and/or open to competition in most Western countries, so that it seems more and more difficult to find an example of a pure monopoly. Or is it?

**TABLE 5.1** Long-distance telephone rates: AT&T, MCI and Sprint[8]

| | AT&T | | MCI | | Sprint | |
|---|---|---|---|---|---|---|
| Date rate changed | New rate | Months after | New rate | Months after | New rate |
| January 87 | .298 | 2 | .289 | 2 | .289 |
| January 88 | .265 | 2 | .256 | 2 | .259 |
| January 89 | .254 | 0 | .244 | 0 | .250 |
| January 90 | .233 | 1 | .223 | 1 | .228 |
| January 91 | .228 | 1 | .222 | 5 | .228 |
| July 91 | .227 | 5 | .223 | 1 | .227 |
| January 92 | .228 | 0 | .224 | 2 | .228 |
| June 92 | .227 | 0 | .225 | 5 | .227 |
| February 93 | .228 | 1 | .225 | 2 | .228 |
| August 93 | .229 | | | | |
| September 93 | .235 | 0 | .234 | 1 | .235 |
| January 94 | .256 | 0 | .255 | 0 | .256 |

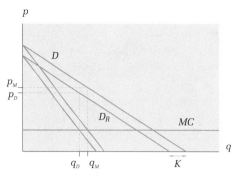

**FIGURE 5.4**
Dominant-firm optimal price

Consider the case of Apple. Apple is the sole manufacturer of the Apple MacIntosh line of personal computers.[j] That is, Apple is the monopoly supplier of the MacIntosh PC. But calling Apple a monopolist would be an artifact of a very contrived market definition. It would probably make more sense to talk about the market for personal computers, in which case a host of Windows-based computers should be included, leaving Apple with a modest 10% or so market share.

Simplistic as it might be, this example illustrates the point that defining monopoly based on a market share calculation is bound to run into problems of market definition. Different market definitions lead to potentially very different market shares. But why should we attach so much importance to market share when assessing a monopoly? Consider the two graphs in Figure 5.5. In both cases we have, by assumption, a monopoly, that is, a firm with a 100% market share. However, the degree of **monopoly power,** defined as the ability to sell at a price substantially above cost, is much lower in the right-hand side case, the case when demand is more elastic. The general point is that:

> The degree of monopoly power is inversely related to the demand elasticity faced by the seller.

This definition of monopoly power seems more sensible than the one based on market share. For instance, suppose that the firm on the left-hand side of Figure 5.5 commands a market share of 90%, whereas the one on the right-hand side is a pure monopoly (100% market share). Even though, in terms of market share, the firm on the right is more of a monopoly, in terms of monopoly power the firm on the left seems more of a monopoly.

The value of demand elasticity depends on many factors, some static, some dynamic. This makes it difficult to judge the extent of monopoly power in actual situations. Take for example Microsoft in the market for operating systems. In terms of market share, there is no question that Microsoft is a near monopolist (a dominant

j. For a while, Apple allowed other firms to manufacture the MacInstosh — or "Mac clones" — but this is currently not the case.

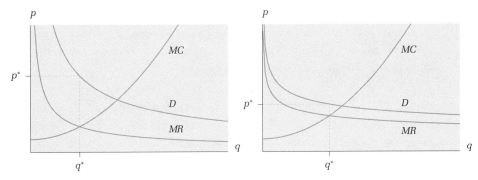

**FIGURE 5.5**
Demand elasticity and optimal margin

firm). But does it truly have monopoly power? Box 5.3 addresses this question in greater detail.

## 5.4 REGULATION

In the Section 5.1 I suggested the idea of a Pigou tax as a means to "fix" a market externality. A Pigou tax is an example of a government regulation. More generally, we may define **regulation** as a *government intervention in economic activity using commands, controls, and incentives.*[8]

There are many, many types of government regulations that affect firms and markets (some argue too many). Examples include pre-marketing approval of medical drugs, credit card disclosure requirements, media ownership limits, occupational licensing, minimum wages and maximum prices. Given all this variety, it may help to organize government regulations into categories. One possible classification runs as follows:

**(a)** Market regulation affects directly the workings of the price mechanism. A Pigou tax is an example of a market regulation. Another example is given by the European Union's policy of purchasing butter so as to stabilize the price of butter.

**(b)** Entry regulation refers to rules determining firm entry into a market (e.g., the requirement to obtain a license). For example, in order to work as a real-estate agent you need to be certified by the government (in the US, by the state). In Section 10.5 I will discuss this at length.

**(c)** Firm regulation is the case when a firm — typically a public utility — is subject to direct oversight by the government. For example, ConEdison needs permission from New York State in order to change its electricity rates. Section 5.6 deals with this type of regulation.

**(d)** Social regulation corresponds to rules that apply to firms, consumers, employers, etc. Examples include automobile safety standards, equal opportunity employment standards, and product labeling standards. This type of regulation, important as it is, lies beyond the scope of this book.

Why is there government regulation, in particular economic regulation? The question may seem obvious or stupid — or both. However, understanding the origins of regulation may help understand its nature. At its best, market regulation may be understood as an attempt by a well-intentioned government to reestablish optimality in the presence of market failure; market failure, in turn, may result from externalities, imperfect information, and market power (which I covered in Sections 5.1-5.3 of this chapter). Under this view, known as the **normative theory** of regulation, consumers (and voters), faced with the negative effects of market failure, "demand" (as it were) regulation from their political leaders.

A more skeptical — and possibly more realistic — perspective is that regulation is demanded not by consumers but rather by firms. Consider for example the US peanut program. Since 1949, the US government limits the number of farmers who can sell peanuts in the country; imports are also severely restricted. In addition, there is a support mechanism that guarantees a minimum price received by each farmer. Altogether, these regulations result in a domestic price 50% higher than the rest of the world. Clearly, this is not regulation at the service of the consumer. More likely, this is an instance of the so-called **capture theory** of regulation, according to which market regulation is a tool employed by firms to better serve their own interests.

How do firms get away with something like that? In part, the reason is that the benefits from regulations such as the peanut program are highly concentrated in a few agents (the farmers), whereas the costs are spread throughout a large number of agents (the consumers). Estimates for the 1980s indicate that the peanut program implied an annual cost of $1.23 per consumer and an annual benefit of $11,100 per farmer. The incentives for farmers to lobby for the program are as strong as the incentives for consumers to be outraged are weak.

Regulatory capture is facilitated by the so-called "revolving doors" problem, the common personnel turnover between regulatory agencies and regulated firms. For example, in 2011 Meredith Attwell Baker left the US Federal Communications Commission (where she was a commissioner) to join Comcast, one of the FCC's primary regulation targets; Linda Fisher was Deputy Administrator of the US Environmental Protection Agency from 2001–2004, in between jobs at Monsanto and DuPont, both companies with a huge stake in environmental regulations; and Henry Paulson, formerly Goldman Sachs' CEO, joined the US government as Treasury Secretary under the Bush administration. Many countries have rules that limit the extent of the "revolving door" phenomenon, but one must weigh the costs against the obvious benefits: the best informed regulators are precisely the former managers of the firms they are supposed to regulate.

Which is the right perspective: the normative or the capture theory of regulation? Clearly, many regulations such as the peanut program seem to protect firms more than the consumer; but many other regulations — environmental regulations come to mind — are strongly opposed by firms and supported by the public in general. All in all, it seems safe to say that regulation is like politics: a balancing act of interests and influences.

## 5.5 COMPETITION POLICY AND ANTITRUST

In Chapter 4 I established that, in perfectly competitive industries, the market equilibrium is efficient. Unfortunately, there is no such thing as a perfectly competitive market. The assumption that most obviously fails in many real-world markets is arguably the assumption that there is a very large number of firms, so that each of them is too small to influence market price.

In Section 5.3 I considered the opposite extreme in terms of market structure: monopoly (and its close relative, dominant firm). In this section, I provide an introduction to the public policy instruments that address market failure due to monopoly power. The section's title, "competition policy and antitrust," suggests that there are two types of such policy. In fact, competition policy and antitrust are essentially the same; **competition policy** is the term most commonly used in Europe, whereas **antitrust** the term most commonly used in the US.[k]

The oldest and most commonly accepted form of competition policy relates to so-called horizontal agreements, in particular **price fixing**. Consider for example the art auction market. Together, Christie's and Sotheby's control nearly 100% of the market. While the industry is not a monopoly, the tantalizing possibility is that the firms behave as a monopoly, namely by jointly determining the price (i.e., buyers' and seller's commissions) as if they were a monopolist. This is not simply a theoretical possibility: it happens quite frequently, as we will see in Chapter 9.

Many monopolies are created by means of mergers and acquisitions. One important role of **merger policy** is precisely to prevent excessive concentration of market shares. Over the past few decades, the US, the EU and other countries have developed sets of guidelines regarding what mergers should be allowed and what mergers should be blocked (or whether the merger should be allowed if some concessions are made by the merging parties). In Chapter 11 we will go over these in greater detail.

Finally, in many cases a monopoly or a dominant firm may be inevitable. While monopoly is not per se illegal, abuse of such a monopoly or dominant position is. Large firms such as IBM, Microsoft, Intel, or Google are constantly under the eye of antitrust authorities who want to make sure the giants play fair (that is, refrain from **abusive practices**) and the competition playing field is as level as possible. More on this in Chapter 12.

To sum up,

> The main areas of competition policy are price fixing, merger policy, and abuse of dominant position.

k. In other countries, such as China, Japan, and Russia, the term "anti-monopoly policy" is also used.

**BOX 5.3 MICROSOFT: MONOPOLY AND MONOPOLY POWER[9]**

The legal battle between Microsoft and the US Justice Department is an interesting instance of the concepts of monopoly and monopoly power. There is little doubt that Microsoft holds a position of near monopoly in the market for operating systems. The Windows operating system is used in about 80% of the world's personal computers. Hewlett-Packard's operations manager claims that "absolutely there is no choice" when it comes to selecting an operating system for its Pavillon computers. The world depends on Windows.

Yet, Microsoft claims it "cannot charge a monopoly price because it faces competition from rival operating systems, potential entrants, its own installed base and pirated software." In other words, Microsoft has a (near) monopoly market share but virtually no monopoly power, it claims. Richard Schmalensee, one of Microsoft's main witnesses in the 1998–2001 antitrust case, calculates that an unchallenged-monopoly profit maximizing price would fall in the $900 to $2,000 range. Since Microsoft is a profit maximizing concern and charges substantially less than that, the argument goes, it follows that Microsoft has no monopoly power.

However, it seems difficult to deny that Microsoft has used its monopoly power in operating systems to extend its dominant position to other areas of business. Alleged anticompetitive practices include exclusionary agreements with PC markers and online service and content providers. For example, in 1997 Microsoft forced an agreement on Intuit Inc. that prohibited the financial-software maker from promoting Netscape's browser. This sort of agreements, together with the policy of bundling Windows with Microsoft's Internet Explorer, eroded Netscape's market share in the browser market to an extent that would probably not have been reached if Microsoft didn't control the operating systems market.

The institutions of antitrust policy vary from country to country. In the US, the most relevant players are the Department of Justice and the Federal Trade Commission. In addition, sectoral regulators such as the Federal Communications Commission, the Department of Transportation or the Federal Reserve Board may have a say, for example, in matters related to mergers. Finally, courts (especially district courts and the Supreme Court) also play a central role.

In Europe, competition policy is largely centralized in the European Commission's Competition Directorate, known as DG Comp. In addition, each country has its own competition policy authority. The assignment of cases to national or European regulators is broadly determined by the size of the operation in question (e.g., the turnover of the firms involved) and whether the case is of an international nature.

## 5.6 FIRM REGULATION[10]

If fixed costs are very large — or, more generally, if scale economies are very significant — then competition may simply not be a viable alternative. An extreme situation is given by a **natural monopoly**, the case when the cost structure is such that costs are minimized with one supplier only. In these cases, direct **firm regulation** of the monopolist (or dominant firm) may be the optimal solution.

Let us start by considering the simplest case of monopoly regulation. There is a firm with a cost function given by $C = F + cq$, where $F$ is the fixed (capital) cost and $c$ marginal cost (for simplicity, I assume marginal cost to be constant). Absent regulation, the monopolist sets price at the monopoly level, $p_M$, as shown in the left panel of Figure 5.6. Since the social optimum would be to set price at marginal cost level, monopoly pricing implies that output is lower than socially optimal; and that total surplus is lower than the highest value possible by an amount equal to the area of the triangle $E$. As for the monopolist, it receives a *variable* profit $\pi = q_M (p_M - c)$, so that net profit is given by $\pi - F$.

A first natural solution for a regulator is to force the monopolist to set price equal to marginal cost: $p_R = c$, where $R$ stands for "regulated." In this case, output is given by $q_R$ and maximum allocative efficiency is achieved (i.e., the area $E$ is equal to zero). One problem with marginal cost pricing is that it may imply negative profits for the firm. This is certainly the case when marginal cost is constant: variable profit, $\pi$, is zero, and total profit is therefore $-F$.

Clearly, a firm that makes losses of $F$ cannot survive. To solve this problem, the regulator might give the firm a subsidy of $F$. However, this would likely create additional problems. First, in order to obtain the value $F$ the regulator may need to raise taxes elsewhere in the economy; and the efficiency cost implied by these taxes, $E'$, may be greater than the efficiency cost that marginal cost pricing is supposed to eliminate, $E$. Second, the possibility of transfers from the regulator to the regulated firm gives the former more discretion, and opens the door to the possibility of regulatory capture (see Section 5.4). By **regulatory capture** I mean the situation whereby firms invest resources into influencing the regulator's decisions, to the point that regulation reflects the objective of profit maximization rather than that of welfare maximization. In fact, even if the regulator is not actually influenced, the use of resources attempting to do so is socially wasteful.[1]

Given the problems of marginal cost pricing, an interesting alternative is that of **average cost pricing**. Under this regime, the firm is forced to set the lowest price

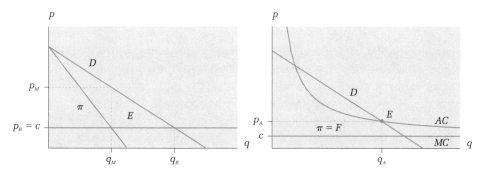

**FIGURE 5.6**
Unregulated and regulated monopoly

1. See also the discussion on rent seeking presented in Chapter 1, as well.

consistent with making non-negative profits; that is, price is equal to average cost. This situation is depicted in the right panel of Figure 5.6, where $p_A = AC(q_A)$ and $q_A = D(p_A)$. As can be seen, this solution is intermediate between those of marginal cost pricing and unregulated monopoly.

In the United States, the mechanism that in the past has been used most often to regulate utilities is that of **rate-of-return regulation**. This is a mechanism whereby prices are set so as to allow the firm a fair rate of return on the capital it invests. Roughly speaking, this corresponds to average cost pricing.[m]

One major problem with rate-of-return regulation is that it gives the firm very little incentive for cost reduction. In fact, lowering cost implies that the allowed price will be accordingly lowered, leaving the firm with the same rate of return. In practice, there is a gap between the time when the firm reduces its cost and the time when the new regulated prices take effect — what might be called a **regulatory lag** — and this may provide the firm some transitory gains; but the mechanism of rate-of-return is fundamentally flawed when it comes to incentives for cost reduction.

In the terminology of regulation theory, we say that rate-of-return regulation is a **low-power incentive mechanism**: price varies in the same measure as cost, a fact which minimizes the incentives for cost reduction. At the other extreme, we have the most **high-power incentive mechanism**: price is set beforehand and does not change at all even if cost changes. Roughly speaking, this is the essence of the **price cap regulation** mechanism. This mechanism provides maximal incentives for cost reduction: a $1 saving in costs implies a $1 increase in profits.[11]

Or does it? Imagine that the regulator sets a price, or a price path, for a period of five years. During that period, the firm invests heavily in cost reduction. By the end of the five-year period, the firm's cost is, say, one-half of what it was initially. It is difficult to imagine how the regulator can ignore the extent of this cost reduction at the time of setting the price cap for the new five-year period. In fact, the greater the cost reduction achieved by the regulated firm during the first five-year period, the lower the price cap set for the second five-year period.

Following this line of argument, a somewhat extreme appraisal of price-cap regulation is to view it as rate-of-return regulation with a long regulatory lag (five years in the previous example). The discussion is then focused on the length of the period that the regulator commits to a price cap (or a price path). Ten years would seem like a reasonable period, sufficient to make price cap regulation substantially different from rate-of-return regulation. But the experience of several countries — including the United Kingdom, where the mechanism was first implemented — suggests that revisions of the price cap normally occur at smaller intervals. This in turn casts some doubt over the effectiveness of price-cap regulation as an incentive scheme.

Another problem with price cap regulation is that it creates little incentives for the provision of product or service quality, an aspect I have ignored until now. Unable to increase price, the regulated firm may have an incentive to reduce quality, thereby effectively increasing price "per unit of quality."

m. If there is only one output, then this is exactly the same mechanism as average cost pricing.

Finally, implementing price cap regulation raises the problem of determining the price cap. A very high price cap implies the allocative inefficiency of a price greater than marginal cost (in addition to a transfer from consumers to the regulated monopolist). A very low price cap may not be sustainable, as the regulated firm suffers losses. More generally, a high-power incentive scheme — of which price-cap regulation is an extreme — implies a high degree of risk for the regulated firm. In this sense, rate-of-return regulation is a better mechanism: the risk for the regulated firm is minimal. In summary:

> A high-power regulation mechanism provides strong incentives for cost reduction but little incentives for quality provision. In addition, it implies a high degree of risk for the regulated firm and requires strong commitment on the part of the regulator.

■ **ESSENTIAL FACILITIES AND ACCESS PRICING.**[12]  Competition is the best way of recovering the allocative inefficiency lost under monopoly pricing. Regulation, in turn, is the best alternative when, due to natural monopoly conditions, competition is not feasible. The question is then when and to what extent we are in a natural monopoly situation.

In recent decades, the classification of many industries as natural monopolies has been questioned. Take for example electricity. It is generally agreed that the basic network for the transmission of electric power is a natural monopoly: the costs of keeping two parallel networks would be much too high. However, there is little evidence of natural monopoly at the stage of electricity generation. Natural gas and railways are also examples of industries where only one segment of the value chain is subject to natural monopoly (the gas transportation network and the railway track network, respectively). Still another example is given by telecommunications, where the natural monopoly would be the local network.[n]

Suppose that competition is allowed in the parts of those industries where natural monopoly is not an issue (electricity generation, long-distance telecommunications, and so on). The problem that typically arises is that these parts cannot exist independently from the part that is a natural monopoly: an electricity generator needs the distribution network to sell its power; a long-distance carrier needs to receive and send its calls through the local network; and so on. Specifically, what we have is a monopolist (e.g., the local telecommunications operator) selling services to firms in the competitive segment (e.g., long-distance telecommunications) who in turn sell to the final consumer. In these cases, we say that the monopolist is an upstream **bottleneck** and that the monopolist's assets or output are an **essential facility**. Seen from this perspective, the list of examples goes beyond that of public utilities (as considered above). An airport, for example, is an essential input for transportation services into a certain city. While there may be many competing airlines (downstream firms), there is frequently only one airport in

n. The latter example is open to debate, however. Some argue that not even the local network is a natural monopoly; and in the age of cell phones many argue whether that matters at all.

each city, the owner of which is the upstream firm. In summary, essential facilities are a fairly common situation.

The regulation of essential facilities shares the same problems as those of monopoly regulation (which I addressed in the first part of this section). Moreover, it is frequently the case that the owner of an upstream essential facility also competes downstream. For example, France Telecom owns the essential facility (local network) and competes in the market for long-distance telecommunications. This type of situation raises a number of additional issues.

One possible concern is that the upstream firm may use its monopoly power to extend it downstream, thus creating monopoly power at the downstream level as well. For one reason or another, the upstream firm may be unable to extract from the downstream competitors all of the monopoly rents in the value chain. By foreclosing its downstream competitors from the market, the upstream firm is then able to recapture its maximal monopoly profits.

From a social welfare point of view, foreclosure would seem to decrease consumer welfare (and total welfare): consumers pay a higher price and have less product variety to choose from. One way to avoid this is to force the upstream firm to divest its interests in the downstream market. For example, AT&T was broken up in 1984, resulting in a long-distance carrier (the new AT&T) and a series of regional telecom operators (the so called "Baby Bells"). Competition was opened in the downstream markets (long-distance), while monopoly was preserved in the upstream, local, markets.[o]

However, as we saw in Chapter 3, there may be important efficiency gains from vertical integration. For example, if the US government had barred the merger between GM and Fisher Body in the 1920s, it is likely that the industry would have become less efficient, on account of the difficulty to contract for investments in specific assets. As in many other instances of industrial organization, we have a trade-off between efficiency and market power.

A regulatory alternative to divestiture consists of allowing the upstream firm to compete downstream but to prevent it from discriminating against downstream competitors. In most European countries, this was the chosen solution in the case of telecommunications.[p] One of the central aspects of this alternative is the regulation of the **access price**, the price paid by downstream firms to access the essential facility.

The **Efficient Component Pricing Rule** (ECPR) has been proposed as a means to achieve this end.[14] It states that the wholesale price offered to an independent downstream firm cannot be higher than the difference between $p$, the final price set by the integrated firm, and the marginal cost of the integrated firm at the downstream stage.

To motivate these ideas, consider a European cable provider who owns the TV broadcasting rights for the national soccer league. In many European countries, this would be considered an essential facility: it would be difficult to attract a cable TV subscriber if the provider did not include the sports channel that features the league games. Potentially, this places the cable provider at an advantage with respect to competing cable providers who do not own the critical sports channel. Let $c_i$, $i = 1, 2$, be the marginal cost of cable provider $O_i$ (think of $O$ as meaning "operator"). Let $p_1$ be the

o. Subsequently, the 1996 Telecommunications Act also allowed for the possibility of local operators entering into long-distance telecommunications.

p. Box 5.4 looks at the cases of France and Germany.

**BOX 5.4 A TALE OF TWO MARKET DEREGULATIONS**[13]

France and Germany provide an interesting contrast of the path towards telecommunications deregulation. Both countries started from a similar initial situation, with a large, state-owned operator controlling virtually all of the country's telecommunications. Both countries allowed new competitors to enter the market at about the same time. Beyond this, the differences are more significant than the similarities.

One of the most important steps in the deregulation process is the "interconnection decision," that is, determining the amount of money a competitor has to pay in order to use the incumbent's local network. In France, a distinction was made between new competitors that built their own networks and those that didn't: the latter were required to pay a higher access fee. No such distinction was made in Germany. This gave bare-bones resellers an advantage in Germany, at least during the first year. In fact, these firms did not have to make significant investments and nevertheless were able to access the Telekom network at the same price as other new entrants.

The treatment of new competitors in Germany is more favorable in several respects. For example, German customers wishing to try a new long-distance carrier can do so by simply dialing the access code and then the desired number. They are billed in a single Deutsche Telekom statement, which then transfers the corresponding amount to the new competitor. No such "call-by-call" option is available in France.

The most significant difference between Germany and France is, however, the *level* of the access fees. Before the interconnection decision was made in Germany, Deutsche Telekom asked for a fee of 6.5 pfennig per minute. Competitors pushed for a one-pfennig rate. The German regulator followed an unexpected route: it took the average of the access fee in 10 countries and came up with the value of 2.7 pfennigs. That this value was unexpectedly low is proved by the fact that Deutsche Telekom's stock dropped by 7.7% in a single day and a further 6% a few days later. After one year of competition, 51 new rivals entered the market to steal about one-third of Deutsche Telekom's long-distance business. During the same period, France Telecom lost a mere 3% market share.

Deutsche Telekom's CEO claims his competitors are nothing but "arbitragers" who simply use the low access fees to piggyback on Telekom's network. In fact, few carriers invested in their own network during the first year after deregulation. In December 1998, the German regulator reacted to this problem by allowing Deutsche Telekom to charge higher access fees to resellers who don't build their own network, a distinction the French regulator made from the start.

The importance of the interconnection decision shows in the numbers. Whereas Deutsche Telekom's stock had its ups and downs, France Telecom's shares soared 103% during the first year of full competition. In contrast, long-distance charges in Germany have fallen by nearly 90% in one year, and local competition exists in more than one dozen cities. Rates in Germany have gone from among the highest in the world to among the lowest in the world. Rates in France have also dropped, but by much less than in Germany.

cable subscription price charged by the integrated cable provider (the one that owns the sports channel). The ECPR states that the maximum wholesale price that $O_1$ (the integrated firm) can charge $O_2$ (the independent cable operator) is given by $w = p_1 - c_1$. The idea is that, at this wholesale price, $O_2$'s price-cost margin is:

$$p_2 - (c_2 + w) = (p_2 - p_1) + (c_1 - c_2)$$

(Notice that $O_2$'s marginal cost now includes two components: the direct marginal cost $c_2$ and the wholesale price $w$.)

From the above equation, we conclude that, if $O_2$ were to set a competitive price with respect to the rival, say, $p_2 = p_1$, then it would receive a *positive margin if and only if* $c_2 < c_1$. This is the idea of the ECPR: it allows the independent downstream firms to survive if and only if they are competitive with respect to the vertically integrated firm. The point is that, *if the ECPR is applied, then production efficiency is maximized.*

However, it is far from clear that the ECPR will bring any clear benefit. Suppose that cable operators are equally efficient, that is, $c_1 = c_2$. It can be seen that $O_1$'s optimal price is $p_1 = p^M$, the monopoly price. Consistently with the ECPR, the access price would then be set at $w_2 = p^M - c_1$. At this wholesale price, the best the downstream firm can do is to sell at $p^M$ for a margin of zero. Whichever amount $M_2$ sells, the manufacturer receives full monopoly profits; and consumers pay monopoly prices. In other words, although the ECPR implies productive efficiency, it has no bite with respect to price levels. In fact, prices are set at the same level as an unrestricted monopoly.[q,15]

Despite these limitations, the ECPR is popular among regulators. One of the most clear examples of application of the ECPR rule is given by New Zealand telecommunications in the 1990s. The Telecom Corporation of New Zealand (TCNZ) was then the main telecommunications operator, holding a monopoly over the local network. Rival operator Clear Communications challenged TCNZ in court, arguing that the latter's access charges were predatory (cf Section 12.3), that is, were unfairly forcing Clear Communications out of the industry. Clear Communications argued that Telecom ought to charge an access price in line with the actual cost of providing access. Telecom in turn wished to apply the ECPR rule, which, as seen above, may imply an access fee substantially higher than the cost of providing access. Ultimately, the case was decided in London, where the Lords of the Judicial Committee of the Privy Council upheld Telecom's view.[16]

q. To avoid this problem, some authors have proposed a solution whereby the essential facility owner is subject to a price-index cap. The price index includes both the final price set by the integrated firm and the access price charged to downstream competitors. This implies that, if the integrated firm wants to increase the final price, it has to decrease the access price, and vice-versa.

## SUMMARY

• Market externalities imply market failure. Pigou taxes and other mechanisms may reestablish equilibrium efficiency. • The monopoly model provides a good approximation to the behavior of dominant firms. • The degree of monopoly power is inversely related to the demand elasticity faced by the seller. • The main areas of competition policy are price fixing, merger policy, and abuse of dominant position. • A high-power regulation mechanism provides strong incentives for cost reduction but little incentives for quality provision. In addition, it implies a high degree of risk for the regulated firm and requires strong commitment on the part of the regulator.

## KEY CONCEPTS

• free riding problem • externality • tragedy of the commons • congestion • public goods • Pigou tax • regulation • Coase Theorem • property rights • adverse selection • asymmetric information • advantageous selection • moral hazard • patent • copyright • network effects • Harberger triangle • allocative inefficiency • excess burden • productive efficiency • rent seeking • residual demand • monopoly power • regulation • normative theory • capture theory • competition policy • antitrust • price fixing • merger policy • abusive practices • natural monopoly • firm regulation • regulatory capture • average cost pricing • rate-of-return regulation • regulatory lag • low-power incentive mechanism • high-power incentive mechanism • price cap regulation • bottleneck • essential facility • access price • Efficient Component Pricing Rule

## REVIEW AND PRACTICE EXERCISES

■ **5.1. FRONT YARDS.** Front yards, if well tended, generate positive externalities for a house's neighbors. Do you think this is an important externality? Is the market solution inefficient?

■ **5.2. AT&T.** The long-run demand elasticity of AT&T in the period 1988–1991 was estimated to be around -10.[17] Assuming the estimate is correct, what does this imply in terms of AT&T's market power at the time?

■ **5.3. MONOPOLY POWER.** "The degree of monopoly power is limited by the elasticity of demand." Comment.

■ **5.4. WINDOWS.** Is the Windows operating system an essential facility? What about the Intel Pentium microprocessor? To what extent does the discussion in Section 5.6 on essential facilities (vertical integration, access pricing) apply to the above examples?

## CHALLENGING EXERCISES

■ **5.5. CARBON TAX.** Consider an industry with demand $q = 1 - p$ and supply $q = p$. Suppose that each unit of output implies one unit of $CO_2$ added to the atmosphere and a marginal social cost of $e$, where $e$ is the total level of emmissions.

(a) What is the level of $CO_2$ emission at the market equilibrium?

(b) What is the socially optimal level of $CO_2$ emissions?

(c) Determine the Pigou tax that achieves the social optimum.

■ **5.6. COMMON FACILITY.** Different divisions within a firm frequently compete for a common resource. Suppose that divisions 1 and 2 of a given firm share a common facility $F$. Let $y_i$ be the service level used by division $i$ ($i = 1, 2$). Division $i$'s gross benefit in terms of improved divisional earnings is given by $y_i - 0.25 y_i^2 - 0.1 (y_1 + y_2)$.

(a) What are the equilibrium levels of $y_i$ if the various divisions act separately?

(b) What are the optimal levels of $y_i$ from an overall firm point of view?

(c) Explain the difference between the results in (a) and (b).

(d) How can equilibrium and optimality be reconciled?

## APPLIED EXERCISES

■ **5.7. EXTERNALITY.** Choose a market or an industry (or another situation from economic life). Determine what externalities there might be in consumption or production. Propose ways in which these externalities can be corrected ("internalized"). Compare your proposed solution to reality and explain the differences.

## NOTES

1. See Gneezy, U., E. Haruvy, and H. Yafe (2004), "The Inefficiency of Splitting the Bill: A Lesson in Institution Design," *The Economic Journal* **114**, 265–280.

2. Coase, Ronald H (1960), "The Problem of Social Cost," *Journal of Law and Economics* **3**, 1–44.

3. See Akerlof, George A (1970), "The Market for 'Lemons': Quality Uncertainty and the Market Mechanism," *Quarterly Journal of Economics* **84** (3), 488–500.

4. Adapted from Einav, Liran, and Amy Finkelstein (2001), "Selection in Insurance Markets: Theory and Empirics in Pictures," *Journal of Economic Perspectives* **25** (1), 115–138.

5. See Cohen, Alma, and Liran Einav (2007), "Estimating Risk Preferences from Deductible Choice," *American Economic Review* **97** (3), 745–788.

6. Backus, Matt (2012), "Why is Productivity Correlated with Competition?," Cornell University.

7. Source: MacAvoy, Paul W. (1996), *The Failure of Antitrust and Regulation to Establish Competition in Long-Distance Telephone Services*, Cambridge, Mass.: MIT Press, Table 5.2.

8. See Baron, David (2010), *Business and Its Environment (Sixth Edition)*, Prentice Hall.

9. Adapted from "Big Friendly Giant," *The Economist*, January 30, 1999; and Mark Boslet, "Economist Calls Microsoft a Monopoly," *The Wall Street Journal Europe*, January 6, 1999.

10. This section is partly based in Armstrong, Mark, Simon Cowan, and John Vickers (1994), *Regulatory Reform: Economic Analysis and British Experience*, Cambridge, Mass.: MIT Press.

11. Cabral, Luís, and Michael H. Riordan (1989), "Incentives for Cost Reduction Under Price Cap Regulation," *Journal of Regulatory Economics* **1**, 93–102.

12. This section is partly based on Rey, Patrick, and Jean Tirole (1997), "A Primer in Vertical Foreclosure," University of Toulouse.

13. Adapted from several articles in *The Wall Street Journal Europe*, December 28, 1998; January 8–9, 1999.

14. Willig, Robert (1979), "The Theory of Network Access Pricing," in Trebing (Ed.), *Issues in Public Utility Regulation*, Michigan State University Public Utilities Papers. Baumol, William (1983), "Some Subtle Issues in Railroad Regulation," *Transport Economics* **10**, 341–355.

15. Laffont, Jean-Jacques, and Jean Tirole (1996), "Creating Competition through Interconnection: Theory and Practice," *Journal of Regulatory Economics* **10**, 227–256.

16. Armstrong, Mark, Chris Doyle, and John Vickers (1996), "The Access Pricing Problem: A Synthesis," *Journal of Industrial Economics* **44**, 131–150.

17. Ward, Michael R. (1995), "Measurements of Market Power in Long Distance Telecommunications," Federal Trade Commission, Bureau of Economics Staff Report.

CHAPTER **6**

# PRICE DISCRIMINATION

A word of advice for air travelers: never ask your fellow passenger what fare he or she paid. One of you is bound to become quite upset. In fact, unless both passengers booked their tickets together and at the same time, most likely they will have paid different fares for the very same flight. Strictly speaking, what each passenger purchased was not *exactly* the same good. For example, one ticket may charge an extra fee for changing the return date, whereas the other one has no such restrictions. However, the very high differences in price hardly seem justified by the small differences in the terms of sale.

The practice of *setting different prices for the same good*, whereby the relevant price in each case depends on the quantity purchased, on the buyer's characteristics, or on various sale clauses, is known as **price discrimination**. Other than airlines, examples of price discrimination include toothpaste, computer software, and electricity, to name just a few.

In this chapter, I explain why firms want to price discriminate — and why they may be unable to do so. Then I classify the various types of price discrimination policies and study different ways in which firms can implement them. I conclude by looking at some legal aspects related to price discrimination.

■ **WHY PRICE DISCRIMINATE?** Figure 6.1 should be familiar from Section 5.3. For a given (linear) demand curve, and constant marginal cost, the figure depicts the optimal price for a monopolist selling one product. The optimal output level $q^M$ is given by the intersection of marginal revenue with marginal cost, and the optimal price $p^M$ is given by the demand curve and the optimal output level $q^M$. At this price and output level, the seller makes a profit given by $(p^M - c)\, q^M$ (ignoring fixed costs).

Optimal pricing is a balancing act: by setting a higher price, the seller would receive a greater margin, $p - c$, per unit sold; but by setting a higher price, the seller

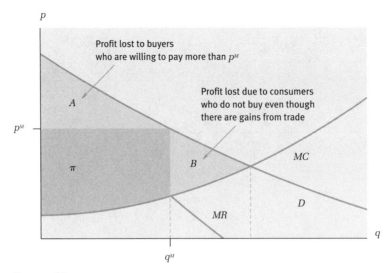

**FIGURE 6.1**
Lost revenue under simple pricing

would also sell fewer units. The values $p^M, q^M$ strike the right balance — the one that maximizes profit. Nevertheless, in this situation the seller is "leaving money on the table." First, there are consumers who pay $p^M$ but would be willing to pay more than that. Second, there are consumers who would be willing to pay more than cost $c$ but don't buy at all because their valuation is lower than price $p^M$.

The goal of price discrimination is to get a slice of this untapped revenue source: selling for a higher price to consumers whose willingness to pay is higher; and selling for a lower price to consumers whose willingness to pay is lower.

This is easier said than done, as we will see below. But suppose that the seller (a) knows each consumer's valuation and (b) is able to charge a different price from each consumer. A classical example if that of a small-town doctor who has good knowledge of the town's inhabitants, including information on their financial status. Based on this knowledge, the doctor evaluates the patient's willingness to pay before each visit and sets the fee accordingly. Another example is given by aircraft: although manufacturers post list prices for each aircraft, in practice each airline pays a different price for each aircraft. Both of these examples correspond to **customer markets**, that is, markets where sales terms are tailored to each individual customer.[a]

The situation when the seller has perfect information about each buyer's valuation and is able to set a different price to be paid by each buyer is known as **perfect price discrimination**. Although relatively infrequent, perfect price discrimination is a useful benchmark to understand the effects of price discrimination more generally. Under the assumptions of prefect price discrimination, the optimal policy is to sell at a price equal to the willingness to pay by each consumer whose valuation is greater than the seller's marginal cost. This results in a new equilibrium where the seller makes more money

a. See also Section 6.4 for other aspects of customer markets.

than under uniform price; specifically, seller profit is given by the area of the large triangle between the demand and marginal cost curves. In other words, the seller effectively increases profit by the shaded areas in Figure 6.1, that is, areas $A$ and $B$.

■ **ARBITRAGE AND PRICE DISCRIMINATION.** Suppose you are a car dealer and try to sell the Hyundai Sonata for $18,000 to regular customers and for $13,000 to students. You can figure what would happen: an entrepreneurial student would start a part-time business of buying cars at the student price and reselling them at the regular price. The point is that, when segmenting a market and setting different prices to different segments, one must beware of the possibility of **resale**.

More generally, in a perfectly competitive market, the **law of one price** must prevail; that is, there cannot be two different prices for the same product. If there were two different prices, then arbitrage would take place, just as in the above Hyundai Sonata example.[b] By contrast, in the real world it is very common to observe more than one price set for what is apparently the same product, while little or no arbitrage occurs. This is because most real-world markets are not perfectly competitive.

We conclude that, in order for more than one price to prevail in equilibrium, there must be some market friction. Examples of such market frictions include:

(a) Physical impossibility of resale. This is the reason why price discrimination is more frequent in services than in physical products: have you ever seen anyone reselling a haircut?

(b) Transactions costs. If RiteAid offers three tubes of toothpaste for the price of two, you could potentially buy a multiple of three and then sell them individually at the single tube price; but this would imply such a hassle that it's probably not worth the effort.

(c) Imperfect information. Consumers may simply not know about the different prices. More on this in Chapter 14.

(d) Legal restrictions. For example, in most countries it is illegal to resell electricity, so sellers can price discriminate without fear of resale. More on this in Section 6.5.

To summarize the above points:

> Price discrimination allows the seller to create additional consumer surplus and to capture existing consumer surplus. Its success requires that resale be expensive or impossible.

One additional dimension regarding price discrimination is **fairness**. Rightly or wrongly, frequently consumers perceive the practice of charging different prices to different consumers as unfair. Even if a firm can materially and legally implement a strategy

b. Arbitrage refers to the practice of buying and selling in order to profit from a price difference; an arbitrageur is an agent who engages in such practice.

of market segmentation and price discrimination, negative consumer perception may make it practically infeasible. Box 6.5 deals with an illustrative example of the pitfalls of price discrimination and fairness: DVD pricing at Amazon. I will return to this issue in Section 6.5.

■ **COST DIFFERENCES AND PRICE DISCRIMINATION.** In the definition of price discrimination we stated "different prices for the same product." But then, is a BMW in the US the same product as a BMW in Germany? Even if it is from a consumer's perspective, it certainly is not from a producer's perspective, for it costs more to sell a German car in the US than to sell it in Germany, on account of transportation costs and import tariffs. For this reason, the fact that the price of a BMW is higher in the US than in Germany would not constitute sufficient evidence of price discrimination.

An alternative test for price discrimination is that *the ratio of prices across markets is different from the ratio of marginal costs*. For example, if a hard cover book sells for $30 and the corresponding paperback sells for $10, then we have a case of price discrimination, for the $20 difference can hardly be accounted for by the cost of a hard cover.[1] Although a hard cover and a paperback version of the same book are not *exactly* the same product, they are sufficiently *similar* that the ratio test should be considered a sufficient indicator of price discrimination.

■ **TYPES OF PRICE DISCRIMINATION.** There are many different ways that sellers can price discriminate; some classification is therefore useful. The key question is how much firms know about consumers. For example, the New York Metropolitan Opera can set a special price for students and require them to show a student ID at the door. In this case, the seller can exactly determine whether the buyer belongs to a certain market segment (students in this case) and charge accordingly. We refer to this situation as **selection by indicators**. In addition to student discounts, examples of selection by indicators include country specific prices (e.g., Levi's in Bulgaria are cheaper than the same Levi's sold in England); membership discounts; and reduced train fares for the elderly.

In other instances, the seller has some information about the buyers' preferences but cannot observe the characteristics of each particular buyer. Even then it is possible to effectively discriminate between different buyers by offering a menu of selling options that include various clauses in addition to price. Consider, for example, discount airfares. These are reduced airfares that impose a series of constraints on the buyer (e.g., advance purchase and ticket change fees). Frequently, business trips are booked without much advance notice and require some flexibility regarding flight times. For this reason, discount fares allow the seller to indirectly discriminate between business travelers and leisure travelers. In this case we say that there is **self selection** on the part of the buyers.

> Sellers can price discriminate either based on observable buyer characteristics or by inducing buyers to self-select among different product offerings.

A note on semantics. Price discrimination has traditionally been classified into first-, second- and third-degree price discrimination.[2] Under the original definition, first-degree price discrimination corresponds to perfect price discrimination (introduced earlier in the chapter); second-degree price discrimination is the case when price depends on quantity purchased but not on the identity of the consumer; and third-degree price discrimination takes place when different prices are set in different market segments (though unit price does not depend on quantity). I prefer the terminology "selection by indicators" and "self selection" and will follow it for the remainder of the chapter.

## 6.1 SELECTION BY INDICATORS

As discussed above, selection by indicators corresponds to the situation when the seller divides buyers into groups, setting a different price for each group. This practice is also known as **market segmentation**. One common form of market segmentation is based on geographical location. For example, in 2012 a 51-week digital subscription to the *Economist* cost $126.99 in the US and $209.99 in China. £117, €125 and Y18,000, respectively). Another example, discussed in Box 6.1, is pricing of cars in Europe.

However, market segmentation need not be based on geographic location; for example, many products and services are sold at special prices for students or the elderly. Yet another example: subscriptions to the *American Economic Review* vary according to the subscriber's annual income.

The simplest model of market segmentation consists of a monopolist selling to two separate markets. The seller's profit function is then given by:

$$\Pi(p_1, p_2) = p_1 D_1(p_1) + p_2 D_2(p_2) - C\Big(D_1(p_1) + D_2(p_2)\Big)$$

where $p_i$ is price in market $i$, $D_i$ demand in market $i$, and $C(\cdot)$ production cost. Profit maximization implies that $MR_1 = MR_2 = MC$ (why?), where $MR_i$ is marginal revenue in market $i$ and $MC$ is marginal cost. This in turn implies the well-known **elasticity rule**:

$$p_1\left(1 + \frac{1}{\epsilon_1}\right) = p_2\left(1 + \frac{1}{\epsilon_2}\right) = MC$$

where $\epsilon_i \equiv \frac{\partial q_i}{\partial p_i} \frac{p_i}{q_i}$ is the price elasticity of demand. It follows that:

> Under discrimination by market segmentation, a seller should charge a lower price in those market segments with greater price elasticity.

A model like this explains, among other things, why the export price may be lower than the price set for the domestic market. For example, Chilean wines are cheaper in New York than in Santiago de Chile, even though the cost of selling in New York is higher than the cost of selling in Santiago (there are additional transportation costs, import

## BOX 6.1 PRICE DISCRIMINATION IN THE EUROPEAN CAR MARKET[3]

A series of studies by the European Bureau of Consumers Unions shows that pretax prices for identical car models may vary by over 90% across countries. The following table presents estimates for the margins of a few models in a few countries.

| Relative markups of selected cars in selected European countries (in %) | | | | | |
|---|---|---|---|---|---|
| Model | Belgium | France | Germany | Italy | U.K. |
| Fiat Uno | 7.6 | 8.7 | 9.8 | 21.7 | 8.7 |
| Nissan Micra | 8.1 | 23.1 | 8.9 | 36.1 | 12.5 |
| Ford Escort | 8.5 | 9.5 | 8.9 | 8.9 | 11.5 |
| Peugeot 405 | 9.9 | 13.4 | 10.2 | 9.9 | 11.6 |
| Mercedes 190 | 14.3 | 14.4 | 17.2 | 15.6 | 12.3 |

These differences can be interpreted in different ways: it may be that the level of collusion is greater in some countries than in others; or that import quotas differ across models and country; or simply that spatial price discrimination is at play.

Econometric evidence suggests that price discrimination is indeed quite important: demand elasticities are different in different countries, and manufacturers set different prices accordingly. Specifically, one pattern that is noticeable from the numbers above is that markups are higher in the country where each car is produced (e.g., Fiat in Italy). This may correspond to a national bias that is reflected in a lower demand elasticity (e.g., Italian buyers are so keen on Fiat cars that their demand is very inelastic).

Not everything is spatial price discrimination: the disparity of markups for Japanese cars (e.g., the Nissan Micra) likely results from the very restrictive import quotas imposed by France and Italy.

duties, and so on). This would be optimal when the demand elasticity in the export market is sufficiently greater than the elasticity in the domestic market to the point of compensating for the higher cost of selling to the export market. This phenomenon is not limited to wine or to Chile: in general, demand elasticities tend to be lower (in absolute value) in the domestic market, a feature of the demand function known as **home bias**.

---

**EXAMPLE.** At a small-town college campus, Joe's Pizza serves both faculty and students. At lunchtime only students come into Joe's, whereas in the evening only faculty come in. Students have a constant demand elasticity of $-4$, whereas faculty have a constant demand elasticity of $-2$. Finally, marginal cost is $6 per pizza. What are the optimal prices at lunch and dinner time?

It will be profitable to charge one price $p_L$ at lunch time and a different price $p_D$ at dinner time. To determine exactly what these prices should be recall the elasticity rule for a monopolist, which implies that you should charge:

$$p_L \left(1 - \frac{1}{4}\right) = 6$$

$$p_D \left(1 - \frac{1}{2}\right) = 6$$

Solving these equations we get $p_L = \$8$ and $p_D = \$12$.

Now suppose both faculty and students visit Joe's Pizza throughout the day. What challenges do you face to maintain the same revenue as before? The above scheme would not work in this alternative setting: faculty would pay the lower price at lunch and you would lose the students' custom at dinner. What alternatives are possible?

---

As mentioned in Section 3.2, the elasticity rule is a useful way to find optimal prices when demand elasticity is constant at all points of the demand curve. If demand elasticity is not constant, then we need to "manually" solve the problem of profit maximization in order to find optimal prices. This holds both for finding the optimal single price and the optimal price per market segment. The next example shows how this is done.

---

**EXAMPLE.** BioGar has developed Xamoff, an over-the-counter medicine that reduces exam-related anxiety. A patent currently protects Xamoff from competition. BioGar is now thinking of entering the European market but wonders whether it should charge the same price in the two markets. They estimate that the demand curves have the form:

$$q_i = a_i - b_i p_i$$

In the US (market $i = 1$), the parameters are $a_1 = 12$ and $b_1 = 2$. In the EU (market $i = 2$), the parameters are $a_2 = 4$ and $b_2 = 1$. The marginal (and average) cost per unit is $c = 1$. All of these units are millions.

One first question of interest is how much BioGar could gain by charging different prices in the two markets. To address this question, consider first the problem of setting one uniform price. Total demand at price $p_1 = p_2 = p$ is:

$$Q = q_1 + q_2 = (a_1 + a_2) - (b_1 + b_2)p = A - Bp$$

(The idea is to save ourselves some writing by defining $A = a_1 + a_2$ and $B = b_1 + b_2$.) To find profit as a function of output $Q$, we solve for price $p = (A - Q)/B$ and substitute:

$$\pi(Q) = pQ - cQ = \frac{A - Q}{B}Q - cQ = \frac{A}{B}Q - \frac{1}{B}Q^2 - cQ$$

To maximize, we differentiate with respect to $Q$ and equate to zero, which yields:

$$Q = \frac{A - cB}{2} = 6.5$$

Price is:

$$p = \frac{A - Q}{B} = 3.17$$

Finally, quantities are $q_1 = 5.67$ and $q_2 = 0.83$, and profit $\pi = 14.08$.

Next we find the best prices in the two markets separately. The presumption is that we can avoid "parallel" imports from Europe (which we guess is the

### BOX 6.2 TICKET DEMAND AT THE METS

In 2002, the baseball team New York Mets decided to switch from uniform to tiered pricing. Up until then, all tickets for a given seat cost the same regardless of the game being played. However, all baseball games are not equal: it's not the same to play the Yankees on Sunday or the Royals on Wednesday — with no offense to either team or weekday.

Under the new regime, games were classified by tier: gold, silver, bronze and value; soon after the platinum tier was added. This raises two important pricing questions: first, how to assign games to tiers; and second, how to set prices for each tier. The second question was rather difficult to answer: with no historical variation in prices it was impossible to estimate the demand elasticity (see Section 2.3).

The first question may be rephrased as: what makes baseball fans go to the ballpark? Clearly having a good team helps — but it's not the only factor. Based on ticket sales at the New York Mets' Shea Stadium during the 1994–2002 seasons, a statistical regression can be performed where the dependent variable is the number of tickets sold. The following table displays the estimated coefficients of such a regression for a specific section of the Mets' stadium: Upper Reserved.[*]

| | |
|---|---|
| Weekend | 1078.63 |
| Evening | −905.58 |
| Season opener | 8196.82 |
| July | 2410.27 |
| August | 1425.13 |
| September | 1555.44 |
| October | 3774.67 |
| Yankees | 9169.82 |
| Constant | 401.53 |

Each dependent variable is a "dummy," or indicator, variable, taking the value 0 or 1. For example, if the game is played on a weekend, then — everything else constant — 1,078.63 more tickets were sold on average. Considering that the Upper Reserve capacity is about 17,000 seats, these are economically significant coefficients: for example, playing against the New York Yankees leads to an increase in ticket sales equivalent to more than one half of capacity. It is thus no surprise that to watch the Mets play the Yankees you must pay platinum prices.

---

[*] All estimated coefficients are statistically significant at the 2% level; year dummies are also included but not reported; $N = 651$, $R^2 = 0.44$.

cheap location) back to the US. Following a similar logic as in the single-price case, we have:

$$\pi(q_1, q_2) = \frac{a_1 - q_1}{b_1} q_1 + \frac{a_2 - q_2}{b_2} q_2 - c(q_1 + q_2)$$

Next we differentiate with respect to $q_1$ and $q_2$ (one at a time) and set each derivative equal to zero. The result is:

$$q_i = \frac{a_i - c\,b_i}{2}$$

or $q_1 = 5$, $q_2 = 1.5$. The prices are now $p_1 = 3.5$ and $p_2 = 2.5$, and profit $\pi = 14.75$. We conclude that, by setting different prices in Europe and in the US, profits increase from 14.08 to 14.75, an increase of about 4.76%.[c]

For you own enlightenment: Verify that the elasticity rule applies to each market.

■ **THE LIMITS OF MARKET SEGMENTATION.** As the previous example suggests, setting different prices in the two different market segments gives the seller a greater profit than setting the same price in both market segments. Why not then continue segmenting the market into smaller and smaller slices? Specifically, suppose that the market is segmented geographically (one of the most common sources of market segmentation). We start with the US East and West regions. But we could then go on to a division by states, and then by county, and so forth. The problem with such fine segmentation is that either (a) the elasticity in each submarket is very similar to that of the neighboring submarkets, in which case you don't get much out of market segmentation; (b) elasticities vary a lot across neighboring submarkets, in which case you fall prey to the resale or arbitrage problem. For example suppose that Hyundai dealers in Fairfield, CT, set a price that is 5% lower than dealers in neighboring New Haven, CT, county. This would be a difference of about $1,000 — worth the cross-county trip.

■ **THE INTERNET, BIG DATA, AND PRICE DISCRIMINATION.** It's a bit of a cliché to say that the Internet has changed the way we do things, and price discrimination is no exception. In the pre-Internet era, sellers used primarily geographic and demographic indicators to segment markets. Nowadays, sellers who have access to cookies, for example, are able to gather considerably more information about each consumer; we are now much closer to the perfect discrimination extreme that I alluded to earlier, when the seller knows each consumer's valuation and accordingly charges a different price to each consumer.

For example, one study examined purchases of the DVD service Netflix in 2005 in the US.[4] (Before streaming became more common, DVD rentals were still the norm. Netflix allowed subscribers to borrow a certain number of DVDs from their collection; Blockbuster was Netflix's main competitor in this market.) By correlating consumer purchases with individual characteristics, we observe that demographics explain each consumer's choice to some extent. However, consumer characteristics such as use of the Internet (number of websites visited) or broadband access explain a much greater portion of each consumer's choice (about one order of magnitude more).

Another example is given by Orbitz.com, a travel website that is known to steer customers toward more expensive offerings (e.g., more expensive hotels) if they logged on from a Mac computer. Mac computers cost more than Windows-based computers; also, on average Mac users earn a higher income than Windows users. One thus expects

c. For completeness, we also need to confirm that BioGar is better off by selling in both markets. The maximum price at which consumers will make any purchase — also known as the choke price — is given by $a_i/b_i$. This value is higher in the US than in the EU. It is theoretically possible that the optimum is to set a price such that demand in the EU is zero. See Exercise 6.8 for details.

the willingness to pay of a consumer who uses a Mac to be greater, which in turn justifies this type of strategy.

But the Internet is a two-way street: if sellers know more about buyers, buyers also know more about sellers. Price comparison sites such as Google shopping allow buyers easy access to the prices set by various sellers for a given item. This makes it more difficult for sellers to customize prices. Similarly, in the pre-Internet era catalog sellers such as L.L. Bean were able to ship different catalogs with different prices to different consumers. Now that consumers can check prices online, catalog customization is more difficult to implement.

## 6.2 SELF SELECTION

There are many examples in which the seller knows that the population of potential consumers is divided into groups, but cannot identify which group each consumer belongs to. For example, airlines know that people fly for business or for leisure motives, and that the willingness to pay is higher among business travelers. However, it would be difficult to identify business travelers directly, especially if the fare they are charged is higher than the fare paid by leisure travelers. Imagine the sales agent asking, "Are you traveling for business purposes? The reason I ask is, if you say yes then I will charge you more." You can see it just wouldn't work.

More generally, price discrimination by self-selection is the situation when the seller does not directly identify the consumer as belonging to a particular group. The seller *indirectly* sorts consumers by group by offering different "deals" or "packages." These can be combinations of fixed and variable fees, different combinations of price and quality, different combinations of price and quantity, and so forth. Consumers in turn self-select according to the group they belong to.

■ **VERSIONING AND DAMAGED GOODS.** Discount airfares are an example of price discrimination by self-selection. Because these fares imply a number of restrictions — e.g., a Saturday night stay in the place of destination — business travelers are unlikely to purchase such fares. Airlines are thus able to sort out low-valuation leisure travelers (and most academics), who will change their schedule to take advantage of the discount fares.

A similar phenomenon takes place in consumer electronics. Consider for example the Kindle Fire. In 2012, the top four hits at an Amazon.com search corresponded to four versions with prices ranging from $115 (Kindle Fire Full Color 7″, Multi-Touch Display Wi-Fi) to $299 (Kindle Fire HD 8.9″, Dolby Audio, Dual-Band Wi-Fi, 16GB). If Amazon offered one version only — say priced at $150 and with a medium amount of features — then it would lose sales margin from some high-end consumers (willing to pay more than $150), as well as sales from some low-end consumers (unwilling to buy at $150). Thus price discrimination by versioning leads to a higher revenue for the seller.[d]

One extreme form of versioning occurs when firms reduce the quality of some of their existing products in order to price discriminate, that is, firms produce **damaged**

d. These prices were checked in October 2012. Needless to say, both the price values and the product characteristics were soon out of date — it's life in the technology lane. However, the basic features of the pricing scheme are likely to remain valid for a long time.

**goods**. For example, Pex and Apex airfares are normal economy fares with additional restrictions, such as the requirement of a Saturday night stay. These restrictions create no particular benefit to the airlines; they are simply a means of reducing the quality of the service provided. Another example is student versions of software packages: for some time, Mathematica's student version consisted of the standard software together with a special flag that prevented the use of a math coprocessor (even if the computer had one). Still another example is provided by Microsoft's Office Home and Business 2010 Suite, which comes in two versions: one can be transferred to a portable computer and is priced at $279.99; a second one corresponds to the same software but can only be used in one computer and is sold for $199.99.

Dupuit, a nineteenth century French engineer and economist, remarks on the practice of the three-class rail system:

> It is not because of the few thousand francs which would have to be spent to put a roof over the third-class carriages or to upholster the third-class seats that some company or other has open carriages with wooden benches … What the company is trying to do is prevent the passengers who can pay the second-class fare from traveling third-class; it hits the poor, not because it wants to hurt them, but to frighten the rich … And it is again for the same reason that the companies, having proved almost cruel to third-class passengers and mean to second-class ones, become lavish in dealing with first-class passengers. Having refused the poor what is necessary, they give the rich what is superfluous.[5]

Box 6.3 provides additional examples of damaged goods.

In order for versioning to work, the seller must take into account an important constraint: the seller must be careful not to set prices so different that the high-end consumers prefer to buy the low-end product. That would defeat the whole purpose of versioning as a means for price discrimination. To understand how this works, consider the following numerical example.

---

**EXAMPLE.** We had the "baby Mac," then the iMac; it's now time for the "baby iMac." As head of marketing of Apple Computer, you decided you can do better than the current situation. Last year, the company sold one million iMacs for $1,500 each. This is the most you can get from the market segment that currently buys the iMac. According to a marketing study, there is a second market segment of two million people willing to pay up to $500 for a stripped-down version of the iMac. Your market researchers also tell you that (a) the first segment would be willing to pay up to $800 for the stripped down version, (b) the second segment would be willing to pay no more than $600 even for the full-fledged version of the iMac. Finally, your production people tell you that it costs $300 to produce an iMac, be it the standard version or the stripped-down version.

What is your optimal pricing policy? A first possible strategy (benchmark) is to only sell the full version and charge $1,500. This would lead to selling one million units, for a total profit of $(1,500 - 300) \times 1\,\text{m} = \$1.2\,\text{bn}$. A second possible strategy would be to hit each segment by charging $500 for the stripped-down version and $1,500 for the full version. But would this work? No: high-end consumers get zero value from buying the full version (it's priced

**BOX 6.3 INTEL, IBM AND SONY DAMAGE THEIR PRODUCTS[6]**

The practice of selling lower quality, in fact, "damaged," goods as a means to price discriminate between high-valuation and low-valuation consumers is common among several high-tech firms.

- Intel's 486 generation of microprocessors came under two versions: the 486DX and the 486SX. While there were significant differences in performance, "the 486SX is an exact duplicate of the 486DX, with one important difference — its internal math coprocessor is disabled ... [The 486SX] sold in 1991 for $333 as opposed to $588 for the 486DX."

- "In May 1990, IBM announced the introduction of the LaserPrinter E, a lower cost alternative to its popular LaserPrinter. The LaserPrinter E was virtually identical to the original LaserPrinter, except that the E model printed text at five pages per minute (ppm), as opposed to 10 ppm for the LaserPrinter ... The LaserPrinter uses the same 'engine' and virtually identical parts, with one exception: ... [it includes] firmware [which] in effect inserts wait states to slow print speed."

- Sony recently introduced a new digital recording-playback format intended to replace the analog audiocassette, but offering greater convenience and durability: [the MiniDisc]. Minidiscs are similar in appearance to 3.5-inch computer diskettes, and come in two varieties: prerecorded and recordable. The latter, in turn, "come in two varieties: 60-minute discs and 74-minute discs. The list prices for these discs are currently $13.99 and $16.99. Despite the difference in price and recording length, the two formats are physically identical ... A code in the table of contents identifies a 60-minute disc and prevents recording beyond this length, even though there's room on the media."

at exactly their value), but $800 - 500 = \$300$ from the stripped-down version. Thus they would buy the stripped-down version. An alternative strategy is to charge $1,200 for the full version (think of it as slightly less than $1,200) and $500 for the stripped-down version. This will lead high-end users to pay $1,200 and low-end users to pay $500. Total profit is now $(500 - 300) \times 2\,\text{m} + (1,200 - 300) \times 1\,\text{m} = \$1.3\,\text{bn}$, an improvement over the current solution.

What if production cost were $400?

The above pattern is a general pattern in self-selection mechanisms (which, incidentally, crop up in other parts of economics). How do we get to the value $1,200 for the full version? Basically, we must make sure a high-end consumer has no incentive to go for the deal that is intended for the low-end consumer. We call this the **incentive constraint**. By choosing the stripped-down version a high-end consumer gets a surplus of $300 = 800 - 500$. By choosing the full version, they get a surplus of $1,500 - p$. The incentive constraint is that $1,500 - p \geq 800 - 500$, or simply $p \leq 1,200$. Since profit is greater the greater $p$ is (all else constant), we choose $p = 1200$. How do we get to the value $500 for the stripped-down version? Basically, since this version is intended for the low-end consumer, price cannot be greater than the low-end consumer willingness to pay. We call this the **participation constraint**.

In general, prices are such that the "low type" gets a net surplus of zero (whatever it takes for the type to "participate," that is, to purchase). The "high type," in turn, makes a strictly positive surplus, the minimum that is consistent with the incentive constraint. The surplus obtained by the high type is sometimes referred to as **information rent**. In fact, if the seller could identify each seller's type, it could set prices to extract the entire consumer surplus (as in perfect price discrimination). Since the seller does not know the consumer's type, the seller must leave some of the rents with the consumer, an information rent.

■ **BUNDLING.** Movie distributors frequently force theaters to acquire "bad" movies if they want to show "good" movies from the same distributor. Photocopier manufacturers offer bundles that include the copier itself as well as maintenance; they also offer the option of buying the copier and servicing it separately. These are examples of **tie-in sales**, or **bundling**, an alternative strategy for sorting consumers and price discriminate between them. A distinction can be made between **pure bundling**, whereby buyers must purchase the bundle or nothing (as in the case of movie distributors) and **mixed bundling**, whereby buyers are offered the choice between purchasing the bundle or one of the separate parts (as in the case of photocopier and after-sales service).

As a motivating example for the analysis that follows, consider the pricing of the Microsoft Office Home and Business 2012. This is a software "suite" that comprises a series of different applications: Word, Excel, Powerpoint, OneNote, and Outlook. In 2012, Excel, Outlook, and Powerpoint cost $139.99 if purchased separately; OneNote cost $79.99; and Word is distributed for free. The price for the full suite, in turn, was $199.99. How can this be a profitable strategy for Microsoft? To address this question, let us consider a simple numerical example.

---

**EXAMPLE.** ACME Software owns two different applications: a word processor and a spreadsheet. Some users are mainly interested in a word processor ("writers"), some work exclusively with spreadsheets ("number crunchers"), and a third group uses both word processors and spreadsheets ("generalists").

The table below summarizes the willingness to pay for each application by each type of software user. It also indicates the number of users of each type. Based on this table we can determine the software company's optimal price policy.

| User Type | Number of users | Willingness to pay for | |
| --- | --- | --- | --- |
| | | Word processor | Spreadsheet |
| Writer | 40 | 50 | 0 |
| Number cruncher | 40 | 0 | 50 |
| Generalist | 20 | 30 | 30 |

Since the costs of producing software are all fixed (that is, do not depend on the number of copies sold), the software company is effectively interested in maximizing revenues.

One possible strategy for revenue maximization is to sell each application separately. If that were the case, then the optimal price would be $50. At this price, the company sells 40 copies of each application and earn revenues of $2,000 per application, or a total of $4,000. The alternative price under the strategy of individual-application selling is $p = 30$. In this case, sales would be $60 per application and revenue $1,800 per application, which is less than 2,000.

Consider now the following alternative strategy: in addition to selling each application separately (at a price of $50), for a price of $60 the software company also sells a package (a "suite") comprising both applications. From the perspective of the "writer" and the "number cruncher" types this makes no difference. They will still prefer to buy their preferred application for $50. True, for a mere extra $10 they would be able to acquire a second application; but the extra utility of doing so would be zero. The main difference with respect to the initial case is that the suite will be purchased by "eclectic" types who, at $50 per application, would not be willing to buy; but, at $60 for the package, are. As a result, the seller now receives a total revenue of $4,000 from individual-application sales plus $1,200 (20 times 60) from suite sales, a 30% increase in revenue over the no-bundling case.

---

■ **INTERTEMPORAL PRICE DISCRIMINATION.** Non-durable goods, like groceries or bus rides, are defined by a demand flow: in each period, consumers need to purchase a certain amount. By contrast, the decision to buy a **durable good** is one where timing is of the essence. I can buy a computer today or wait for a few months (and in the meantime hold on to the one that I currently own). A similar reasoning applies to buying a car and other related products.

Pricing durable products involves one additional dimension of price discrimination: time. By setting different prices now and in the future, a monopolist may be able to engage in price skimming: to sell both to high-valuation buyers at a high price and to low-valuation buyers at a low price — the dream of any monopolist (as we saw when discussing Figure 6.1). The idea is that valuation and impatience are normally correlated. Suppose that I launch a new smartphone today and price it at $600; and then lower the price to $400 six months from now. Hopefully, this pricing pattern will lead high high-valuation buyers to buy now and lower valuation consumers to wait for six months.

Unfortunately, the hope that high-valuation buyers will make a purchase now may be just that — hope. In fact, a rational buyer should put itself in the seller's shoes and figure that it will be in the latter's interest to lower prices in the future. Since even high-valuation buyers prefer to pay low prices, the outcome of the high-price-today-and-low-price-tomorrow strategy may turn out to be that most buyers prefer to wait for the future low price. The seller's price discrimination strategy will then have backfired in several ways: first, sales are much slower; and second, average price is much lower than it would have been if the seller had simply set the monopoly price in both periods.

In other words, the possibility of setting different prices in each period, at first sight an advantage to the seller, may turn out to be its "curse," for total profits are then lower. [e]

> When selling a durable good, sellers may prefer to commit not to price discriminate over time. In fact, due to "strategic" purchase delays, profits may be lower under price discrimination.

In the limit, the waiting game may unravel to the point that the seller is forced to lower prices from the get-go, a possibility that is known as the **Coase conjecture**.[7]

There are a number of ways in which the seller can avoid the durable-goods "curse." One is to commit not to lower price in the future. Chrysler, for example, for a while offered a "lowest-price guarantee:" if, in the future, it lowered the price of a given car model, it would refund all previous buyers for the difference. The incentive not to lower price in the future is then so strong that buyers have little reason to expect prices will come down in the future; and thus have little incentive to delay purchases.[f]

Alternatively, the seller may decide not to sell the durable good, only to lease it. This is what Xerox did with its photocopiers in the late 1960s to early 1970s, a time when it commanded substantial market power in the industry. A no-sale, lease-only policy effectively turns a durable good into a non-durable one: buyers need to pay the lease every period they want to use a photocopier; there is no use in delaying the time for getting a photocopier in the hope of saving on purchase price.

Still another way of avoiding strategic purchase delays is to introduce some sort of product differentiation that further separates high-valuation from low-valuation buyers. For example, book publishers normally start with a hard-cover edition, which is sold at a high price in the first period; and then, perhaps two years later, a paperback edition is released at a much lower price.

Finally, the seller may simply acquire a reputation for not lowering prices "arbitrarily." In the 1990s, Apple Computer enjoyed the reputation of a high-end, high-price seller. Waiting for a cheap Mac was simply not a viable buyer strategy. The introduction of the iPod and iPhone product lines in the 2000s brought in new revenue opportunities for Apple — and new pricing challenges as well. Box 6.4 looks at one particular case: the pricing of the first generation iPhone.

## 6.3 NON-LINEAR PRICING

Frequently, consumers must decide not only whether to buy a given product but also how much to buy of it. Examples range from utilities (electricity, water, telephone services, etc.) to the size of a cup of soda or the number of scoops in an ice cream cone. If Häagen Dazs, for example, sells one scoop for $2 and two scoops for $3, then the price per scoop is, respectively, $2 and $1.50. In cases like this we say the seller practices **non-linear pricing**. The idea of linear pricing is that Figure 6.1, which I initially presented as

e. From the *Wall Street Journal*: commenting on the sad state of the personal computer industry, someone remarked that "the industry has set a trap for itself. 'Everybody folds their arms and says, "I'll just wait for the next price cut,"' says one consultant."

f. Notice the irony of the lowest-price "guarantee:" although at first it may seem to protect the consumer, the end-result is that the latter pays a higher price than it would absent any guarantee.

a motivation for setting different prices to different consumers, also applies to individual consumers, to the extent that they make the choice of how much to consume of a product. If this is the case, then linear pricing may "leave money on the table;" and non-linear pricing is a strategy for capturing some of that back.

Moreover, to the extent that different consumers purchase different quantities of the same product, non-linear pricing also creates the possibility of charging different consumers different unit prices. This effectively corresponds to price discrimination by self-selection, just like versioning or bundling — but it is sufficiently important to justify a separate subsection.

Before we get to the general, more realistic case, it helps to consider the simpler case when all consumers have the same demand curve.

g. Strictly speaking, the amount paid, $f + p\,q$, is a linear function of the quantity bought. The key point is that price per unit, $p + f/q$, is not constant.

■ **HOMOGENEOUS CONSUMERS.** Consider the pricing problem of a golf club owner. Suppose all golfers have the same demand curve, say $D$ in Figure 6.2. The simplest case of non-linear pricing, the one I will focus on for most of this section, is a **two-part tariff**: a fixed part $f$, which each consumer must pay regardless of quantity purchased, and a variable part $p$, proportional to the quantity purchased.[g] Continuing with the golf club example, think of $f$ as the annual membership fee and $p$ the greens fee you must play each time you play 18 holes. Would the club owner gain from setting a two-part tariff? If so, what would the optimal values of $f$ and $p$ be?

If marginal cost is constant at $c$ (the additional maintenance cost each time a golfer plays the course) and if the club owner were to set a uniform price, that is, independent of quantity, then the optimal value would be $p^M$. This is the monopoly price derived in Section 3.2, the point where marginal revenue equals marginal cost. Under this solution, profits are given by $A$ (that is, the area of rectangle $A$).

Now suppose that the club owner sets a two-part tariff. Whatever the value of $p$ (the fee for playing golf), the seller should set $f$ (the annual membership) at the maximum value such that golfers are still willing to join the club; anything else would leave money on the table. This maximum is given by consumer surplus, $CS(p)$, the area under the demand curve and above price. For example, for $p = p^M$, consumer surplus is given by area of the triangle $B$, that is, $CS(p^M) = B$. Note that if, instead of $p^M$, price is equal to marginal cost $c$, then we have $CS(c) = A + B + C$.

Let $\pi(p)$ be the golf course's variable profit as a function of the price it sets, that is, $\pi(p) = (p - c)D(p)$. Total profit is given by variable profit, $\pi(p)$, plus the fixe fee, $f$:

$$\Pi(p) = \pi(p) + f$$

It is optimal for the club to set a fixed fee (membership fee) equal to the consumer surplus corresponding to price $p$, that is, $f = CS(p)$. Therefore, we have:

$$\Pi(p) = \pi(p) + CS(p)$$

But this is exactly the total surplus $W(p)$, that is, $\Pi(p) = W(p)$. This implies one important result:

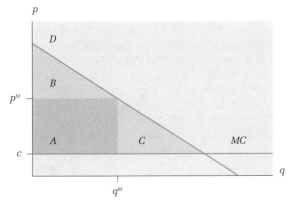

**FIGURE 6.2**
Two-part tariff

> If the seller can set a two-part tariff and all consumers have identical demands, then the (variable) price that maximizes total profits is the same that maximizes total surplus, that is, a price equal to marginal cost.

The optimal fixed part is then the consumer surplus corresponding to $p = c$, that is, $f = CS(p) = CS(c) = A + B + C$. Notice that the introduction of a two-part tariff (a) increases profits from $A$ to $A + B + C$ (the seller makes no money at the margin but receives a large fixed fee); (b) increases total surplus from $A + B$ to $A + B + C$ (a larger quantity is sold, as efficiency would dictate); increases gross consumer surplus from $B$ to $A + B + C$ (the marginal price drops from monopoly price, $p^M$, to marginal cost, $c$); but decreases net consumer surplus (net of the fixed fee) from $B$ to zero (all of the gross consumer surplus is captured by the monopolist via the fixed fee). In other words, total efficiency increases but consumer welfare decreases as a result of non-linear pricing. In Section 6.5, when examining the public policy issues created by price discrimination, I will show that the trade-off between social efficiency and consumer welfare is one of the main issues to be considered.

---

**EXAMPLE.** Monthly individual demand for hours at the NPNG (no pain no gain) gym is $q = 15 - 2.5\,p$, where $p$ is price per hour. (All individuals have the same demand curve.) Marginal cost is zero.

 Suppose first that the seller is restricted to charging a price per hour of gym use; what is then the optimal price? The inverse demand is given by $p = 6 - q/2.5$. Marginal revenue is therefore given by $MR = 6 - q/1.25$. Since marginal cost is zero, optimal price is given by $MR = 0$, which leads to $q = 7.5$, which in turn corresponds to $p = 3$. Profit per customer is then given by $3 \times 7.5 = 22.5$ (note that this is variable profit and does not take into account any fixed cost that might be incurred).

 Suppose now that the gym can charge a monthly fee. Following the logic of two-part tariffs, it should charge an hourly fee equal to the marginal cost, $p = 0$, in which case demand will be 15; and a fixed fee equal to the consumer surplus at this price, that is,

$$f = \frac{1}{2}(15 \times 6) = 45$$

Now profit per customer is $45, a clear improvement over linear pricing.

---

Although the above result was derived for a particular set of assumptions (all consumers are identical), one can make the general point that:

> A monopolist's optimal two-part tariff consists of a positive fixed fee and a variable fee that is lower than monopoly price. Total surplus is therefore greater than under uniform pricing.

■ **MULTIPLE CONSUMER TYPES AND MULTIPLE TWO-PART TARIFFS.** Given that there are different types of consumers, it is natural to assume that the seller sets different two-part tariffs. If the seller could identify directly each consumer's type, then the solution would
be quite simple: the seller would set $p = c$ and $f = CS_i(c)$, where $CS_i(p)$ is the consumer surplus for a type $i$ consumer. The problem is that in most real-world cases the
seller cannot directly observe the consumer type; and, even if that were possible, price
discrimination of this type (imposing different two-part tariffs on different consumers)
would most likely be considered illegal.

But suppose the seller offers consumers the *choice* of different two-part tariffs.
Continuing with the example of a telecom operator, this would correspond to offering different optional *calling plans*, a common practice around the world. Could this
improve the seller's profit? Consider the set of two-part tariffs suggested earlier: one
calling plan with $p = c$ and $f = CS_1(c)$, intended to be chosen by type 1 consumers;
and another calling plan with $p = c$ and $f = CS_2(c)$, intended to be chosen by type 2
consumers. This menu of calling plans would not work. Both consumers would strictly
prefer to adopt the first calling plan: the marginal price is the same and the fixed fee is
smaller for the first plan.

If the seller wants consumers to be sorted across different calling plans, then it
must make sure that type 2 consumers have no incentive to adopt the first calling plan.
Moreover, the seller must make sure that each consumer type prefers to pay the fixed fee
and consume its optimal quantity than not consuming at all. In the economics jargon,
which I introduced in page 132, the seller must take into account (a) incentive constraint
(type $i$ prefers plan $i$ to plan $j$); and (b) the participation constraint (each consumer
prefers some plan vis-a-vis no plan at all). In fact, this analysis generalizes the principles
presented in the previous section. For example, when versioning, the seller must make
sure that the high-valuation buyer does not prefer the stripped-down version (incentive
constraint); and that the low-valuation buyer prefers buying to not buying (participation
constraint).

Let us return to the problem of setting a menu of calling plans. It can be shown that
the optimal menu of calling plans consists of $f_1 = CS_1(p_1)$, $p_1 > c$; and $f_2 > f_1, p_2 = c$. In
words, the high-consumption types pay a relatively high fixed fee but a low marginal
fee, $p_2 = c$. The low-consumption types, in turn, pay a lower fixed fee, $f_1 = CS_1(p_1)$, but
a higher marginal fee, $p_1 > c$. The optimal value of $f_2$ is the highest value of $f_2$ such that
the incentive constraint is satisfied:

$$CS_2(p_2) - f_2 = CS_2(p_1) - f_1$$

The left-hand side gives the net value that a type 2 obtains from choosing plan 2,
whereas the right-hand side gives the value that a type 2 obtains from choosing plan 1.

Finally, the value of $p_1$ is obtained so as to maximize seller's profit, knowing that
revenues are obtained from charging fixed fees as well as marginal fees. Exercise 6.15
considers a specific (and challenging) numerical example.

It is important to understand that consumers of type $i$ choose the calling plan
$(f_i, p_i)$ because they want to. That is, given the menu of calling plans $(f_1, p_1)$, $(f_2, p_2)$,

type 1 consumers prefer plan 1 and type 2 consumers prefer plan 2. For this reason, the seller does not need to identify the group each consumer belongs to: consumers are sorted out by self-selection.

In comparison with the one-type case, this solution differs in two ways. First, low types pay a price that is greater than marginal cost ($p_1 > c$), which implies that the solution is less efficient than it would be if the seller could identify buyer types directly. Second, high-consumption buyers pay a fixed fee that is less than their willingness to pay, that is, $f_2 = CS_2(p_1) < CS_2(p_2)$, where $CS_2(p_2)$ is the willingness to pay. As a result, the seller's profit is lower than it would be were it able to differentiate consumers directly. The loss of profits is the price the seller must pay in order to sort buyers by means of self-selection. The loss can be divided into two parts. First, by setting $p_1 > c$, a deadweight loss is created — the triangle formed by the demand curve and the marginal cost curve, between $q_1(p_1)$ and $q_1(c)$. Second, by setting $f_2 < CS_2(c)$, the seller leaves some of the surplus with the high-use consumers. However, unlike the $p_1 > c$ case, this is simply a transfer, not a social efficiency loss.

Finally, notice that, if the seller can identify consumer types directly, then the latter receive a net payoff of zero. Under price discrimination by self-selection, however, high-use consumers have a strictly positive payoff. Economists sometimes refer to this payoff as the information rent earned by these consumers (the party that is better informed).

## 6.4 AUCTIONS AND NEGOTIATIONS

In recent years, with eBay and other online sellers, many people have become familiar with auctions. The practice is hardly new, however: for example, after a military victory Roman soldiers would often auction off the spoils of war.

Why would anyone care to auction an object (a bottle of wine, a used car, or a corporation, to give a few common examples) rather than sell it for a fixed price? Suppose I know there are two interested buyers and that their valuations are either $100 or $150, each with equal probability. For simplicity, suppose that their valuations are either *both* $100 or *both* $150. Finally, suppose that they know their valuations, whereas I, the seller, do not; all I know is that each value is equally likely.

If I choose to set a fixed price, then there are two candidates: $100 or $150. If I set $p = 100$, then I get 100 for sure. If I set $p = 150$, then I get 150 with probability 50% and nothing with probability 50%. This results in an expected value of $75, which is lower than $100. I thus conclude that, if I am to set a fixed price, I might as well choose $p = 100$.

Now suppose that I run an auction, specifically an ascending price auction. I start by calling out the number 100. If the buyers' valuation is 100, one or both of them will make a sign of acceptance. As I ask for higher bids, they will be silent and the auction ends with a winning bid of $100. If however the buyers' valuation is $150, then they will continue outbidding each other until the price reaches $150. The bottom line: with probability 50%, I will make $100, and with probability 50% I will make $150, which results in an expected value of $125, clearly better than the best fixed-price policy.

This example is based on a variety of simplifying assumptions, but you can see how and why auctions may be a good idea. In a sense, an auction is the ultimate strategy for price discrimination by self-selection: I know the distribution of buyers' valuations but not the precise value of each buyer's valuation; I thus want to create a mechanism whereby buyers' actions lead them to pay a price that is related to their valuation.

■ **TYPES OF AUCTIONS.** Auctions come in many different shapes and sizes. Perhaps the one you are most familiar with is the **ascending price auction** (also known as the English auction).[h] Christie's and Sotheby's, for example, use this auction to sell art. You start at a low price, ask for higher bids and continue on until no bidder wants to outbid the highest extant bid.

Alternatively, you might start with a high price and then gradually decrease it until a bidder makes a sign, at which point such bidder is declared the winner and pays the price at the moment the sign was made. This alternative mechanism is known as — you might have guessed it — the **descending price auction**. It is used in the Netherlands for selling flowers, for example. Perhaps for this reason it is also known as the Dutch auction. However, we find descending price auctions in other countries and for other products.

But there is more. For example, for a long time countries like France and Spain have awarded water supply monopoly franchises by means of an auction. Typically, these auctions require bidders to submit a sealed bid. The highest bid is then selected and the bidder pays the amount specified in the bid. This is known as the **first-price auction**. You might think, "obviously the bidder pays the amount specified in the bid," but it's actually not obvious. For example, in the 1990s radio spectrum rights were sold in New Zealand using a **second-price auction**: bidders submitted sealed bids, the highest bid won, but the price paid by the winning bidder was the second highest bid.[i]

Given all this variety of auction formats, a natural question to ask is which one is best, namely in terms of raising seller revenue. As often is the case in economics, the answer is: it depends. If the buyers' valuations are independent, it turns out that several auction designs yield *on average* the same revenue level: ascending, descending, first price, and second price auction.[j] This suggests that the choice of auction may be dictated by considerations other than revenue. For example, one advantage of the descending price auction is that auctions take place faster and at a constant pace. Perhaps for this reason they are frequently used in the sale of goods such as flowers and fish.[k]

■ **BIDDING STRATEGY.** I've been discussing a seller's strategy, namely the seller's choice of auction mechanism. What about the buyer's strategy? A bidding strategy amounts to a tradeoff similar to that of a monopoly seller. In Section 3.2, I showed that, by increasing price, a seller collects a higher margin but sells to fewer customers. The elasticity

h. The term "auction" is derived from the Latin verb augeo ("I increase" or "I augment").

i. The logic behind requiring the highest bidder to pay the second highest bid is that it encourages bidders to bid their true valuation. Can you see why?

j. By independent valuations I mean statistically independent; that is, if I know the distribution of valuations, then knowing one bidder's valuation tells me nothing about another bidder's valuation.

k. However, in Tokyo's famous fish market ascending auctions, not descending auctions, are used.

rule (or the $MR = MC$ rule) indicates the optimal balance between these two considerations. Similarly, a higher bid increases my chances of winning the auction but lowers the margin I will get, namely the difference between my valuation and the bid I pay. The optimal bid strikes the right balance between these two goals, just like monopoly pricing. See Exercise 6.17 for details.[1]

Earlier I mentioned the case when valuations are independent. In most real-world cases, however, there is some positive correlation of valuations across bidders. For example, suppose that the Italian government auctions the rights to use the radio spectrum for wireless telecommunications purposes; and suppose that there are two bidders, an Italian telecommunications operator and a international one. It seems reasonable to assume the Italian bidder has better knowledge about the value of owning the spectrum license than the international one. Moreover, the uncertainty regarding valuation is likely correlated across bidders: for example, if the market turns out to be smaller than expected, then it is smaller for both bidders. In this context, the less informed bidder must beware of what auction theorists refer to as the **winner's curse**: if I (the uninformed bidder) win the auction, it's because my rival (the informed bidder) submitted a lower bid. If my rival submitted a low bid, it's because the value of the object is probably low; in sum, if I win the auction, it's probably because the value is lower than expected.

Seasoned bidders learn to take this effect into account. This results in relatively lower bids by uninformed bidders and, as a result, lower probability of winning the auction. For example, when the US auctions the rights for oil drilling in a given area, most of the time the winning bidder is a firm that already owns the rights to adjacent areas. This may be justified by cost considerations, but careful economic analysis suggests that information asymmetries also play an important role: if a firm has been drilling an adjacent area, it's bound to have better information about the quantity of oil in the ground.[8]

■ **MULTI-OBJECT AUCTIONS.** Throughout the world, government treasuries issue debt by selling millions of bonds worth more than $4 trillion.[9] There are two ways in which this sale can take place. One is an auction where each bidder declares how much it is willing to pay for a given number of securities. The highest bids are then collected up to the point where the total amount demanded equals the amount offered for sale. Finally, the winning bidders get the amounts they demanded and pay the bids they offered. This is known as a **discriminatory auction** (each bidder pays a different price). Alternatively, the same set of bidders get the same number of securities but the price they pay equals the lowest winning bid. This is known as the **uniform price auction**.

It's tempting to conclude that the discriminatory auction serves the seller's interests better: after all, in the uniform price auction all but one bidder pay less than they bid for. However, we must take into account that bidders are bound to adjust their bids as the seller changes the rules from discriminatory to uniform. In fact, research applied to treasury auctions in Turkey and in the Czech Republic suggests that the uniform price auction performs better, if only slightly.[10]

The problem of selling multiple objects gets more complicated when, unlike government bonds, the objects are different from each other but related in value. Take for

1. This exercise assumes a certain belief by a bidder about the other bidder's bidding strategy. The issue of beliefs in a strategic context is addressed in Chapter 7. Specifically, its application in the context of bidding games is illustrated by Exercise 7.11.

example radio spectrum licenses. Radio broadcasting and wireless telephony require dedicated portions of the radio spectrum. Starting in the 1990s, various countries initiated the practice of allocating these spectrum licenses based on auctions. For example, in 1994 the US Federal Communications Commission offered to sell 99 licenses corresponding to 48 regions of the US territory. The complexity of this type of auctions stems from the fact that the value of a license to use the radio spectrum in New York City, for example, may depend on also holding a license in New Jersey. How should this be taken into account in designing the appropriate auction? Different countries opted for different designs, and the resulting average bids differed considerably, from as low as $2.6 per inhabitant (Switzerland, November 2000) to as high $107.2 per inhabitant (UK, April 2000).[11]

One mechanism that has proved reasonably good is the **simultaneously ascending auction**.[12] In each round, bidders are allowed to submit bids for each object on the block. Each new bid must be higher than the previous highest bid plus a minimum increment. The overall auction ends when, after a period of time, no new bids are submitted for any existing object.

■ **NEGOTIATIONS.** So far we've considered two possible extremes in the process of price formation: posted prices, where the seller sets the price; and auctions, where buyers, through their bidding behavior, effectively set prices. What about the case when both seller and buyer set prices? Suppose the seller sets a price at which it is willing to sell. The buyer chooses not to purchase but instead makes a counter-offer. At that point, the seller may accept the counter-offer or, if it rejects the counter-offer, make the buyer a new offer; and so on. This is an example where price is determined by a bilateral negotiation process between seller and buyer.

Although auctions have been around for a long time, it's fair to say that, until recently, they were not a very common transaction method. By contrast, haggling over prices is as old as trade is. If you visit a bazaar in Istanbul or a street market in Beijing, you might still find buyers and sellers routinely arguing over prices. In today's economy, however, negotiations between buyer and seller are especially common in customer markets (cf page 122), including in particular business-to-business (B2B) transactions. For example, if Singapore Airlines wants to buy an Airbus 380, the buyer doesn't simply go to the Airbus website and check the list price. Rather, a long negotiations process takes place until the terms of sale are finally agreed upon.

Sometimes, posted prices, auctions, and negotiations co-exist in a given market. For example, eBay, which originally started as an online auction site, currently allows the seller to post a price ("buy it now") or for seller and buyer to negotiate over price by submitting sequential offers and counter-offers.

One combination that is particularly frequent is auctions followed by negotiations and fixed prices: Suppose a homeowner wants to redo her kitchen. She might ask three contractors for bids and choose the lowest bid. However, between the time the contractor is chosen and the moment the project is done, multiple job changes will be requested. In some cases, this is reflected in a new total price that is computed based on fixed prices.

For example, if the buyer wants to add a standard extra part to all kitchen cabinets, then the contractor charges the extra cost based on that part's list price. If however the buyer asks for more complicated changes, then the parties need to renegotiate the overall terms.

So, which is better: posted prices, auctions, or negotiations? Let's consider a specific example: in 1993, the senior executives of Paramount decided to sell the company to Viacom through a process of direct and exclusive negotiation. It was known that there was at least another interested bidder, QVC. Nevertheless, Paramount's board decided to lock QVC out of the negotiations and claimed that Paramount's shareholders benefitted by such strategy. Most economists would disagree: it can be shown that, if a seller has multiple potential buyers lined up, then auctions are generally a better way of selling an item. So, if Paramount's board wanted to maximize shareholder value, it should probably have run an auction with Viacom and QVC as bidders rather than lock into negotiations with one of the potential buyers.[13]

By contrast, if there is only one buyer, then a posted price or a negotiations process may be better. Also, there may be additional reasons that tilt the scales in favor of one method or another. For example, most car buyers have an aversion to haggling. For this reason, some dealers prefer to commit to a posted price policy rather than negotiating price on a case-by-case basis — if you can make that a credible commitment.[m]

## 6.5 IS PRICE DISCRIMINATION LEGAL? SHOULD IT BE?

I mentioned earlier that the extreme case of perfect price discrimination provides a useful framework for the welfare analysis of price discrimination. Figure 6.2, which illustrates the effects of a two-part tariff, also depicts the difference between simple pricing and perfect price discrimination. A monopolist that cannot price discriminate sets price $p^M$, thus selling output $q^M$. Under this solution, profits are given by $A$ and consumer's surplus by $B$; total surplus is thus $A + B$. Consider now the case when the seller can discriminate between different buyers. The price charged to each buyer is given by the latter's willingness to pay. The monopolist will thus sell to all buyers whose willingness to pay exceeds marginal cost, that is, to all buyers from 0 to $q^D$. The monopolist's profit is now given by $A + B + C$, whereas consumer's surplus is zero; total surplus is therefore $A + B + C$.

There are several relevant points in the comparison between the solutions with and without price discrimination:

m. I return to the issue of aversion to haggling in Section 6.5. Issues of commitment are formally treated in Section 7.2.

**(a)** *Total welfare is greater under price discrimination* ($A + B + C$ as opposed to $A + B$).

**(b)** *Consumer welfare is lower under price discrimination* (zero as opposed to $B$).

**(c)** *Different consumers pay different prices under price discrimination.*

**(d)** *More consumers are served under price discrimination (specifically, all consumers between $q^M$ and $q^D$ are served under price discrimination but not under uniform price).*

Although this is a very simple, extreme example, it serves to illustrate the main trade-offs implied by price discrimination. First, the trade-off between efficiency (point (a), which favors price discrimination) and consumer welfare (point (b), which favors uniform pricing). Second, the trade-off between "fairness" (point (c), which favors uniform pricing) and the objective of making the good accessible to as many consumers as possible (point (d), which favors price discrimination).[n] If distribution concerns are not very important, then a case can be made in favor of price discrimination, for it increases total efficiency. However, if distribution between firms and consumers, as well as across consumers, is an important issue, then a case can be made for disallowing price discrimination.

This analysis is a bit simplistic, and several qualifications are in order. First, *it may happen that total efficiency decreases as a result of price discrimination.* For example, if perfect price discrimination is costly, it may be that the gains for the seller do not compensate the losses imposed on consumers. Likewise, it can be shown that spatial price discrimination decreases efficiency when demand curves are linear, for example.

Second, *there are cases when price discrimination implies a strict Pareto improvement:*[o] both the seller *and* consumers are made better off (more specifically, some are equally well off and some are strictly better off as a result of price discrimination). The examples of damaged goods and bundling, presented in Section 6.2, prove this point.

Third, the effects of price discrimination go beyond producer and consumer surplus. In particular, the evidence suggests that, on average, *consumers dislike paying different prices* (thus the piece of advice I started the chapter with). Some car dealers promise "no haggling" terms of sale, partly because consumers dislike the process of haggling, partly because they dislike the idea of paying a different price than other customers. In this sense, the main thrust of **prospect theory** of consumer behavior applies here: consumers like paying a lower price than others, but much more than that they dislike paying a higher price than others.[p] Or, to put it differently, consumers perceive price discrimination as a **fairness** issue. The case of Amazon's DVD pricing, summarized in Box 6.5, illustrates one instance of this.

■ **LEGAL MATTERS.** The analysis is further complicated by the fact that, both in the US and in Europe, public policy towards price discrimination has been driven by considerations that differ from the principles of economic efficiency outlined above. In the US, the main concern has been to prevent price discrimination from injuring competition. In particular, the **Robinson-Patman Act** states that:

> It shall be unlawful for any person engaged in commerce . . . to discriminate in price between different purchasers of commodities of like grade and quality . . . where the effect of such

n. There is no good simple term to designate this. In telecommunications, the expression "universal service" is used.

o. A Pareto improvement is a change that harms no one and helps at least one person.

p. See Section 2.4 for more on prospect theory.

---

### Box 6.5 Amazon.com's pricing experiment[14]

In the summer of 2000, an Amazon.com customer ordered the DVD of Julie Taymor's *Titus*, paying $24.49. The next week he went back to Amazon.com only to find that price had jumped to $26.24. He decided to make an experiment: he cleared all identifiers (e.g., cookies) from his computer and tried again: the price fell to $22.74.

Before long, a heated discussion got started at the web site DVDTalk.com. An Amazon spokesperson admitted their price varying strategy, but added that "it was done to determine consumer responses to different discount levels. This was a pure and simple price test." However, most consumers were not convinced by the explanation and were sure this was a case of "unfair" price discrimination.

One analyst put it best when he stated that "Amazon knows who has the ability and perhaps the incentive to pay more based on demographics, on purchasing history, on income and urgency. The variable that they're deficient on is which customers won't mind paying more. They don't know the level of outrage."

Eventually, Amazon.com admitted its practice. One spokesperson stated that "dynamic pricing [i.e., price discrimination] is stupid, because people will find out. Fortunately, it only took us two instances to see this."

---

discrimination may be substantially to lessen competition or tend to create a monopoly in any line of commerce.

However, for decades no case has been tried in the US on the basis of the Robinson-Patman act.

In the European Union, a classical case of price discrimination is that of *United Brands*, which sold bananas in different European countries. Although the transportation costs to each country differ by very little, the wholesale prices charged in each country differed a great deal. At one point, the price in Denmark was more than two times the price in Ireland. United Brands argued that it only adapted its prices to what each market could bear — the essence of market segmentation. The European Commission decided that such practice was in breach of **Article 102** of the Treaty of Rome, which forbids the **abuse of dominant position**.[q] More generally, it stated that:

> the Commission has the firm intention of systematically applying Article 86 [later renumbered Article 102] against undertakings in a dominant position which directly or indirectly impose discriminatory or unfair prices, ...[on account of] the injury which these practices can cause to the user and the consumer.

Ultimately, one suspects that the real goal behind the prohibition of spatial price discrimination is that of achieving a single market, where no "major differences between prices for identical goods or services ... persist over a lengthy period." A later decision by the European Court of Justice seems to confirm this view. Silhouette, an Austrian maker of eyeglass frames, refused to sell its glasses to Hartlauer, a discount store chain. Hartlauer bought 21,000 Silhouette eyeglass frames in Bulgaria at a low price and announced its sale in Austria. The European Court judged that Silhouette's trademark

q. This ruling was important, among other things, because "abuse of dominant position" is a rather vague concept for which no clear definition has been given.

rights extend to the point of limiting the import of its products from other countries (also known as buying in the gray market). This was an important decision for various reasons. UK supermarket chains, for example, have sold Levi's, Adidas, and Nike products imported from countries where prices are lower.[15] This is one instance of the point made at the beginning of the chapter: if resale is easy, then price discrimination is difficult. By allowing manufacturers to limit the imports of their products into the European Union, the *Silhouette* decision essentially facilitates price discrimination between EU and non-EU countries.

In summary, it would appear that the European Union is very concerned with price discrimination within Europe but not so much between Europe and the rest of the world. In fact, EU law dictates that a manufacturer has no right to restrict the subsequent sale of trademarked goods within the EU after their initial sale.

By contrast to the European Union, the US Supreme Court has taken the view that, once a company sells a product, it has no rights to restrict its subsequent resale unless the product is altered in a way that may mislead consumers. In other words, parallel imports are allowed. Price discrimination between the US and the rest of the world is therefore relatively more difficult.

■ **Net neutrality.** A hot question regarding public policy towards the Internet is the issue of net neutrality. At the risk of oversimplifying things, the Internet can be divided into its backbone — a network of fiber optic connections that covers each country — and a series of Internet Service Providers (ISP), some connecting content providers such as Google or iTunes to the Internet (backbone ISP), some connecting individual consumers such as you and me to the Internet (residential ISP). In the US, the backbone is owned by telecommunications companies such as AT&T. The precise definition of net neutrality depends somewhat on who's defining it. However, most would agree that it refers to the principle that ISPs and governments should treat all Internet data equally, that is, not discriminating or charging differentially by user, content, site, platform, application, etc.

As I showed earlier, allowing price discrimination may be a good thing or a bad thing: setting different prices for different uses may lead to a more efficient allocation of limited resources (e.g., a Skype conversation vis-a-vis downloading a movie). However, discrimination may make some consumers worse off — and it may be a means for anti-competitive behavior. As often is the case in economics, it's all about trade-offs.

Not surprisingly, ISPs oppose net neutrality. One argument they use for price discrimination is that, unless they are allowed to charge more from users who can pay more (e.g., Google), then they will lack the incentives to continue investing in Internet infrastructure, an issue I will return to in Section 15.4.

By contrast, some of the biggest champions of net neutrality are content providers such as Netflix, a US-based movie streaming service. They are afraid — probably rightly so — that discrimination may place them at a competitive disadvantage. For example, Comcast, one of the largest ISPs, owns a third of Hulu, one of Netflix's main competitors in content provision. Although Comcast is only a silent partner in Hulu, it would come as no surprise if they offered Hulu better terms than Netflix for access to Comcast's consumers. But there's more: allowing ISPs to freely charge content providers is likely to lead to higher average charges, which in turn will be passed on to the final consumer to some extent. These and other related issues form the core of Chapter 13.

■ **Privacy.** Another hot question regarding public policy towards the Internet is the issue of privacy. There are many aspects to it; price discrimination is one of them. Consider the case of Orbitz to which I made reference in Section 6.1. Its market research shows that people who use Mac computers spend about 30% more on hotels than others. Given that, the Orbitz engine shows Mac users more expensive hotels than Windows users. Orbitz's defense of its policy: given that you own a Mac, you are more likely to be interested in relatively more expensive hotels; therefore, we provide a better service by identifying the consumer's operating system. Still, some Mac users might be upset with this and prefer to remain anonymous (as far as their operating system is concerned).

A potentially more serious threat to privacy is the use of **cookies**, small files placed by a website in a user's web browser that record information about the user's visit. Understandably, many consumers fear that some organization may come to possess information on their entire browsing history, click by click. Accordingly, the European Union and other countries now place severe restrictions on the use of cookies (e.g., users must be notified and allowed to opt out). However, cookies allow for sellers to know each user's preferences better, which in turn may lead to important efficiency gains. For example, the accuracy of search engines such as Amazon's depends largely on observing browsing histories. In sum, as frequently happens in economics the issue of cookies is a collection of trade-offs.

## Summary

• Price discrimination allows the seller to create additional consumer surplus and to capture existing consumer surplus. Its success requires that resale be expensive or impossible. • Sellers can price discriminate either based on observable buyer characteristics or by inducing buyers to self-select among different product offerings. • Under discrimination by market segmentation, a seller should charge a lower price in those market segments with greater price elasticity. • When selling a durable good, sellers may prefer to commit not to price discriminate over time. In fact, due to "strategic" purchase delays, profits may be lower under price discrimination. • If the seller can set a two-part tariff and all consumers have identical demands, then the (variable) price that maximizes total profits is the same that maximizes total surplus, that is, a price equal to marginal cost. • A monopolist's optimal two-part tariff consists of a positive fixed fee and a variable fee that is lower than monopoly price. Total surplus is therefore greater than under uniform pricing.

## KEY CONCEPTS

• price discrimination • customer markets • perfect price discrimination • resale
• law of one price • fairness • selection by indicators • self selection • market
segmentation • home bias • damaged goods • incentive constraint • participation
constraint • information rent • tie-in sales • bundling • pure bundling • mixed
bundling • durable good • Coase conjecture • non-linear pricing • two-part tariff
• ascending price auction • descending price auction • first-price auction
• second-price auction • winner's curse • discriminatory auction • uniform price
auction • simultaneously ascending auction • prospect theory • fairness
• Robinson-Patman Act • Article 102 • abuse of dominant position • net neutrality
• cookies

## REVIEW AND PRACTICE EXERCISES

■ **6.1. PERFECT PRICE DISCRIMINATION.** Consider a monopolist with demand $D = 120 - 2p$
and marginal cost $MC = 40$. Determine profit, consumer surplus, and social welfare in
the following two cases: (a) single-price monopolist; (b) perfect price discrimination.

■ **6.2.** *The Economist.* First-time subscribers to *The Economist* pay a lower rate than
repeat subscribers. Is this price discrimination? Of what type?

■ **6.3. CEMENT.** Cement in Belgium is sold at a uniform delivered price throughout the
country, that is, the same price is set for each customer, including transportation costs,
regardless of where the customer is located. The same is practice is also found in the
sale of plasterboard in the United Kingdom.[16] Are these cases of price discrimination?

■ **6.4. FULTON FISH MARKET.** A study of the New York fish market (when it was the Fulton
fish market) suggests that the average price paid for whiting by Asian buyers is significantly lower than the price paid by White buyers.[17] What type of price discrimination
does this correspond to, if any? What additional information would you need in order
to answer the question?

■ **6.5. COUPONS.** Supermarkets frequently issue coupons that entitle consumers to a
discount in selected products. Is this a promotional strategy, or simply a form of price
discrimination? Empirical evidence suggests that paper towels are significantly more
expensive in markets offering coupons than in markets without coupons.[18] Is this consistent with your interpretation?

■ **6.6. GETGOING.COM.** In 2013, the travel booking site GetGoing was offering a "Pick Two, Get One" deal: customers would select two flights — to different cities — and make a purchase before finding out where they would be heading. GetGoing would then select one of the destinations. Explain how this can be a profitable strategy for GetGoing.

■ **6.7. COCA-COLA.** In 1999, Coca-Cola announced that it was developing a "smart" vending machine. Such machines are able to change prices according to the outside temperature.[19] Suppose, for the purposes of this problem, that the temperature can be either "High" or "Low." On days of "High" temperature, demand is given by $Q = 280 - 2p$, where $Q$ is number of cans of Coke sold during the day and $p$ is the price per can measured in cents. On days of "Low" temperature, demand is only $Q = 160 - 2p$. There is an equal number days with "High" and "Low" temperature. The marginal cost of a can of Coke is 20 cents.

(a) Suppose that Coca-Cola indeed installs a "smart" vending machine, and thus is able to charge different prices for Coke on "Hot" and "Cold" days. What price should Coca-Cola charge on a "Hot" day? What price should Coca-Cola charge on a "Cold" day?

(b) Alternatively, suppose that Coca-Cola continues to use its normal vending machines, which must be programmed with a fixed price, independent of the weather. Assuming that Coca-Cola is risk neutral, what is the optimal price for a can of Coke?

(c) What are Coca-Cola's profits under constant and weather-variable prices? How much would Coca-Cola be willing to pay to enable its vending machine to vary prices with the weather, i.e., to have a "smart" vending machine?

■ **6.8. SAL'S SATELLITE.** Sal's satellite company broadcasts TV to subscribers in LA and NY. The demand functions are given by:

$$Q_{NY} = 50 - \frac{1}{3}P_{NY}$$
$$Q_{LA} = 80 - \frac{2}{3}P_{LA}$$

where $Q$ is in thousands of subscriptions per year and $P$ is the subscription price per year. The cost of providing $Q$ units of service is given by:

$$TC = 1,000 + 30Q$$

where $Q = Q_{NY} + Q_{LA}$.

(a) What are the profit-maximizing prices and quantities for the NY and LA markets?

(b) As a consequence of a new satellite that the Pentagon developed, subscribers in LA are now able to get the NY broadcast and vice versa, so Sal can charge only a single price. What price should he charge?

(c) In which situation is Sal better off? In terms of consumers' surplus, which situation do people in LA prefer? What about people in NY? Why?

■ **6.9. STADIUM PRICING.** Stanford Stadium has a capacity of 50k and is used for exactly seven football games a year. Three of these are OK games, with a demand for tickets given by $D = 150k - 3p$ per game, where $p$ is ticket price. (For simplicity, assume there is only one type of ticket.) Three of the season games are not so important, the demand being $D = 90k - 3p$ per game. Finally, one of the games is really big, the demand being $D = 240k - 3p$. The costs of operating the stadium are essentially independent of the number of tickets sold.

(a) Determine the optimal ticket price for each game, assuming the objective of profit maximization.

Given that the stadium is frequently full, the idea of expanding the stadium has arisen.[r] A preliminary study suggests that the cost of capacity expansion would be $100 per seat per year.

(b) Would you recommend that Stanford go ahead with the project of capacity expansion?

■ **6.10. SPOKENWORD.** Your software company has just completed the first version of SpokenWord, a voice-activated word processor. As marketing manager, you have to decide on the pricing of the new software. You commissioned a study to determine the potential demand for SpokenWord. From this study, you know that there are essentially two market segments of equal size, professionals and students (one million each). Professionals would be willing to pay up to $400 and students up to $100 for the full version of the software. A substantially scaled-down version of the software would be worth $50 to consumers and worthless to professionals. It is equally costly to sell any version. In fact, other than the initial development costs, production costs are zero. Although you know there are two market segments, you cannot directly identify a consumer as belonging to a specific market segment.

(a) What are the optimal prices for each version of the software?

Suppose that, instead of the scaled-down version, the firm sells an intermediate version that is valued at $200 by professionals and $75 by students.

(b) What are the optimal prices for each version of the software? Is the firm better off by selling the intermediate version instead of the scaled-down version?

r. Ignore the fact that Stanford Stadium used to hold 90,000 seats and was thought to be too big.

■ **6.11. SoS.** SoS (Sounds of Silence, Inc.) prepares to launch a revolutionary system of Bluetooth-enabled noise-cancellation headphones. It is estimated that about 800,000 consumers would be willing to pay $450 for the headphones; an additional 1,500,000 consumers would be willing to pay $250 for the headphones. Though SoS knows this marketing information, it cannot identify a consumer as belonging to one group or the other.

SoS is considering the launch of a stripped-down version of the headphones (the stripped-down version uses wires instead of bluetooth). The 800,000 high-valuation consumers would only be willing to pay $325 for the stripped-down version. The remaining 1,500,000 consumers don't particularly care about bluetooth vs. wire connections; they are willing to pay the same $250 for either version.

Both the bluetooth version and the stripped-down version cost the same to produce: $100 per unit.

(a) Determine the optimal pricing policy assuming that SoS only sells bluetooth-enabled headphones.

(b) Determine the optimal pricing policy assuming that SoS offers the two versions.

(c) Suppose that SoS finds out that the estimate regarding the number of low-valuation users is overly optimistic. In fact, there are only 300,000 consumers who would be willing to pay $250. How would you change your answer to (a) and (b)?

■ **6.12. RAWDEAL.** RawDeal is the new sushi bar in the neighborhood. Their estimated marginal cost is 10 cents per sushi unit. RawDeal estimates that each consumer has a demand for sushi given by $q = 20 - 10p$, where $q$ is number of sushi units and $p$ is price in dollars per unit.

(a) Determine the optimal price per sushi unit.

(b) RawDeal is considering switching to an all-you-can-eat-sushi policy. Determine the optimal price per customer. How does profit compare to pricing per unit?

(c) Discuss other advantages and disadvantages of each pricing option.

(d) Ignoring implementation costs, what is the optimal two-part tariff for sushi (i.e., a fee at the door plus a price per sushi piece).

## CHALLENGING EXERCISES

■ **6.13. PRICING WITH LIMITED CAPACITY.** Consider the model of a monopolist with two markets presented earlier in the chapter. Suppose that the seller has a limited capacity and low marginal cost up to capacity. An example of this would be an airline with two types of passengers or a football stadium with two types of attendees.

Derive the conditions for optimal pricing. How do they relate to the case when there are no capacity constraints?

■ **6.14. BLACKINK.** *Printing Solutions*, the maker of the printer *BlackInk*, faces an important product design dilemma: deciding the speed of its popular laser printer. There are two market segments: Professionals are willing to pay up to $800 $(a - .5)$ for the printer, where $a$ is printer speed. Students, in turn, are willing to pay up to $100\,a$. Maximum printer speed corresponds to $a = 1$, whereas $a = 0$ corresponds to a worthless printer. There are one million professionals and one million students. It is equally costly to produce a printer with any level of $a$. In fact, other than the initial development costs, production costs are zero.

How many versions of the *BlackInk* should *Printing Solutions* sell? Which versions? What are the optimal prices of each version?

■ **6.15. MULTIPLE TWO-PART TARIFFS.** Consider the model of non-linear pricing introduced in Section 6.2. Suppose there are two types of consumers, in equal number: type 1 have demand $D_1(p) = 1 - p$, and type 2 have demand $D_2(p) = 2\,(1 - p)$. Marginal cost is zero.

(a) Show that if the seller is precluded from using non-linear pricing, then the optimal price is $p = \frac{1}{2}$ and profit (per consumer) $\frac{3}{8}$.

(b) Show that if the seller must set a single two-part tariff, then the optimal values are $f = \frac{9}{32}$ and $p = \frac{1}{4}$, for a profit of $\frac{9}{16}$.

(c) Show that if the seller can set multiple two-part tariffs, then the optimal values are $f_1 = \frac{1}{8}$, $p_1 = \frac{1}{2}$, $f_2 = \frac{7}{8}$, $p_2 = 0$, for a profit of $\frac{5}{8}$.

(d) Show that, like profits, total surplus increases from (a) to (b) and from (b) to (c).

■ **6.16. SALES.** Many retail stores set lower-than-usual prices during a fraction of the time (sale). One interpretation of this practice is that it allows for price discrimination between patient and impatient buyers.

Suppose that each buyer wants to purchase one unit per period. Each period is divided into two subperiods, the first and the second part of the period. Suppose there are two types of buyers, $i = 1, 2$. Each type of buyer is subdivided according to the part of the period they would ideally like to make their purchase. One half the buyers would prefer to purchase during the first part of the period, one half during the second part. A buyer of type $i$ is willing to pay $\overline{v}_i$ for a purchase during his or her preferred part of the period; and $\underline{v}_i$ for a purchase at another time.

Buyers of type 1, which constitute a fraction $\alpha$ of the population, are high-valuation, impatient buyers; that is, $\overline{v}_h$ is very high and $\underline{v}_h$ very low. High valuation implies that $\overline{v}_h$ is very high; impatience implies that $\underline{v}_h$ is very low: buyers of type 1 are not willing to buy at any time other than their preferred time. Buyers of type 2, by contrast, are very patient: $\bar{v}_l \approx \underline{v}_l$. Assume that $\alpha$ is relatively low; specifically, $\alpha < \bar{v}_l / \bar{v}_h$. To summarize: $\bar{v}_h > \bar{v}_l \approx \underline{v}_l > \alpha \bar{v}_h > \underline{v}_h \approx 0$.

(a) Show that, under a constant-price strategy, the seller optimally sets $p = \bar{v}_l$.

(b) Determine firm profits when it sets prices $p = \bar{v}_h$ and $p = \underline{v}_l$ in the first and second parts of the period, respectively. Show that profits are greater under the "sales" strategy.

■ **6.17. OPTIMAL BIDDING STRATEGY.** Consider a first-price auction with two bidders. Suppose Bidder 1 believes that Bidder 2's bid is some number between 0 and $\frac{1}{2}$, with all numbers equally likely. Show that Bidder 1's optimal bid is given by $b_1 = v_1/2$.

## APPLIED EXERCISES

■ **6.18. SELLING MECHANISMS FIELD EXPERIMENT.** Set up a seller identity in a online trading site (eBay, Taobao, Alibaba, etc.). Obtain a series of objects of uniform quality (e.g., sports trading cards, USB memory drives, etc.). Sell different units of the object using different selling mechanisms: fixed price, auction, negotiation. Compare the price obtained with each method and discuss the extent to which the differences can be explained by economic theory.

## NOTES

1. Stigler, George (1987), *Theory of Price*, New York: McMillan.

2. Pigou, A C (1932), *The Economics of Welfare*, 4th Edition, London: McMillan & Co.; Varian, Hal (1989), "Price Discrimination," in Schmalensee and Willig, *Handbook of Industrial Organization*, Amsterdam: North-Holland, p. 600; Tirole, Jean (1989), *The Theory of Industrial Organization*, Cambridge, Mass: MIT Press, p. 137–143.

3. Verboven, Frank (1996), "International Price Discrimination in the European Car Market," *Rand Journal of Economics* **27**, 240–268.

4. Benjamin Reed Shiller (2014), "First-Degree Price Discrimination Using Big Data," Brandeis University.

5. Ekelund, R. B. (1970), "Price Discrimination and Product Differentiation in Economic Theory: An Early Analysis," *Quarterly Journal of Economics* **84**, 268–278.

6. Deneckere, Raymond J., and R. Preston McAfee (1996), "Damaged Goods," *Journal of Economics and Management Strategy* **5**, 149–174.

7. Coase, Ronald (1972), "Durability and Monopoly," *Journal of Law and Economics* **15** (1), 143–49.

8. Hendricks, Kenneth, and Robert Porter (1988), "An Empirical Study of an Auction with Asymmetric Information," *American Economic Review* **78** (5), 865–883.

9. Bartolini, Leonardo and Carlo Cottarelli (1997), "Treasury Bill Auctions: Issues and Uses," in Mario I. Blejer and Teresa Ter-Minassian, (Eds.), *Macroeconomic Dimensions of Public Finance: Essays in Honour of Vito Tanzi*, London: Routledge, 1997, 267–336.

10. Hortaçsu, Ali and David McAdams (2010), "Mechanism Choice and Strategic Bidding in Divisible Good Auctions: An Empirical Analysis of the Turkish Treasury Auction Market," *Journal of Political Economy* **118** (5), 833–65; Kastl, Jacob (2011), "Discrete Bids and Empirical Inference in Divisible Good Auctions," *Review of Economic Studies* **78** (3), 974–1014.

11. Cramton, Peter (2002), "Spectrum Auctions," in Martin Cave, Sumit Majumdar, and Ingo Vogelsang, eds., *Handbook of Telecommunications Economics*, Amsterdam: Elsevier Science B.V., Chapter 14, 605–639.

12. Milgrom, Paul (2000), "Putting Auction Theory to Work: The Simultaneous Ascending Auction," *Journal of Political Economy* **108** (2), 245–272.

13. Bulow, Jeremy, and Paul Klemperer (1996), "Auctions Versus Negotiations," *American Economic Review* **86** (1), 180-194

14. David Streitfeld, "On the Web, Price Tags Blur," *Washington Post*, September 27, 2000.

15. *The Wall Street Journal Europe*, July 17–18, 1998.

16. Phlips, Louis (1983), *The Economics of Price Discrimination*, Cambridge: Cambridge University Press, pp. 23–30.

17. Graddy, Kathryn (1995), "Testing for Imperfect Competition at the Fulton Fish Market," *Rand Journal of Economics* **26**, 75–92.

18. Levedahl, J.W. (1986), "Profit-Maximizing Pricing of Cents-Off Coupons: Promotion or Price Discrimination?," *Quarterly Journal of Business and Economics* **25**, 56–70

19. *Financial Times*, October 28, 1999.

PART **TWO**

OLIGOPOLY

# CHAPTER 7

# GAMES AND STRATEGIES

Suppose it's early in 2010. Two major Hollywood studios, Warner Bros. and Fox, are considering when to release their promising blockbusters targeted at younger audiences: Warner Bros.' *Harry Potter* and Fox's *The Chronicles of Narnia*.[a] There are two possibilities: November or December. Everything else equal, December is a better month; but having the two movies released at the same time is likely to be bad for both studios.

The dilemma faced by Warner Bros. and Fox illustrates the problem of *interdependent decision making*: Warner Bros.' payoff depends not only on its own decision but also on the decision of another player, Fox. Economists study this type of situations as if Warner Bros. and Fox were playing a *game*.[b]

A game is a stylized model that depicts situations of strategic behavior, where the payoff of one agent depends on its own actions *as well as* on the actions of other agents.[c] The application of games to economic analysis is not confined to movie release dates. For example, in a market with a small number of sellers the profits of a given firm depend on the price set by that firm *as well as on the prices set by the rival firms*. In fact, price competition with a small number of firms is a typical example of the world of games and strategic behavior.

This type of situation introduces a number of important considerations. The optimal choice for a player — its optimal strategy — depends on what it expects other players will choose. Since other players act in a similar way, when conjecturing what another player will do, I may need to form a belief about what the other player's belief regarding my behavior is; and so forth. Moreover, if the strategic interaction evolves over a number of periods, I should also take into account that my actions today will have an impact on the other players' beliefs and actions in the future. In summary, payoff interdependence introduces a host of possibilities for strategic behavior — the object of game theory.

a. Specifically, *Harry Potter and the Deathly Hallows: Part I*; and *The Chronicles of Narnia: The Voyage of the Dawn Treader*.

b. In the US, the game resulted in Warner Bros. and Fox choosing November 19 and December 10 as release dates, respectively.

c. Economic analysis is based on the use of models. Models are stylized representations of reality, highlighting the particular aspects of interest to the analyst. Being stylized is not a defect of models, rather it should be seen as a requisite: a completely realistic model would be as useful as an exceedingly detailed description of reality, so complete that its main features would be buried in the abundance of detail. For the same reason, a stylized map can be more helpful than a satellite photo, though in some sense it is less realistic. It is helpful to keep this point in mind when judging the very stylized nature of some of the games and models presented in this text.

■ **ELEMENTS OF GAME THEORY.** The basic element of game theory and applied game theory is a game. A **game** consists of a set of players; a set of rules and actions (who can do what when); and a set of payoff functions (the utility each player gets as a result of each possible combination of strategies). Figure 7.1 depicts a simple game which exemplifies these ideas. There are two players, Player 1 and Player 2. Player 1 has two possible choices, *T* and *B*, which we represent as Player 1 choosing a row in the matrix represented in Figure 7.1. Player 2 also has two possible choices, *L* and *R*, which we represent by the choice of a column in the matrix in Figure 7.1. Finally, Players 1 and 2 make their choice simultaneously.

For each combination of strategies by each player, the respective matrix cell shows the payoffs received by each player. In the lower left corner, the payoff received by Player 1; in the top right corner, the payoff received by Player 2. A crucial aspect of a game is that each player's payoff is a function of the strategic choice by *both* players. In Figure 7.1, this is represented by a matrix, where each cell corresponds to a combination of strategic choices by each player. This form of representing games is know as **normal form**. Later we will consider alternative forms of representing a game.[d]

■ **SIMULTANEOUS VS. SEQUENTIAL DECISIONS.** One final point regarding the game in Figure 7.1 is the "rule" that both players choose their strategies simultaneously. This rule will be maintained throughout a number of examples in this chapter — in fact, throughout much of the book. I should thus clarify its precise meaning. In real life, very seldom do agents make decisions at *precisely* the same time. A firm will make a strategic investment decision this week; its rival will do it in two or three weeks' time. So how realistic is the assumption that players choose strategies at the same time? Suppose that there is an observation lag, that is, suppose that it takes time for Player 2 to observe what Player 1 chooses; and likewise, suppose that it takes time for Player 1 to observe what Player 2 chooses. In this context, it is perfectly possible that players make decisions at different times but that, when decisions are made, neither player knows what the other player's choice is. In other words, *it is as if players were simultaneously choosing strategies.*[e] Naturally, the assumption that observation lags are very long does not always hold true. Later in the chapter, we will find examples where an explicit assumption of sequential decision making is more appropriate.

d. Normally, in games represented by a matrix (normal form) we assume that players move simultaneously. However, that need not be the case. More on this in Chapter 12.

e. In other words, we may distinguish two concepts of time: calendar time and game-theory time. Players' choices may be sequential in calendar time and simultaneous in game-theory time.

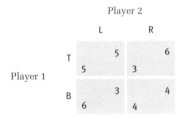

**FIGURE 7.1**
The "prisoner's dilemma" game

## 7.1 NASH EQUILIBRIUM

A game is a model, a stylized description of a real-world situation. The purpose of formulating such a model is to understand (and predict) behavior patterns, in this case strategic behavior patterns. In other words, we would like to "solve" the game, that is, determine the strategies we expect each player to follow. This can be important for descriptive analysis (understanding why a certain player chooses a certain strategy) as well as for prescriptive analysis (advising a player what strategy to choose). In this section, I consider various possible avenues for "solving" a game.

■ **DOMINANT AND DOMINATED STRATEGIES.** Consider again the game in Figure 7.1. What strategies would we expect players to choose? Take Player 1's payoffs, for example. If Player 1 expects Player 2 to choose $L$, then Player 1 is better off by choosing $B$ instead of $T$. In fact, $B$ would yield a payoff of 6, which is more than the payoff from $T$, 5. Likewise, if Player 1 expects Player 2 to choose $R$, then Player 1 is better off by choosing $B$ instead of $T$. In this case, Player 1's payoffs are given by 4 and 3, respectively. In summary, Player 1's optimal choice is $B$, *regardless of what Player 2 chooses.*

Whenever a player has a strategy that is better than any other strategy regardless of the other players' strategy choices, we say that the first player has a **dominant strategy**.

> A dominant strategy yields a player the highest payoff regardless of the other players' choices.

If a player has a dominant strategy and if the player is rational — that is, payoff maximizing — then we should expect the player to choose the dominant strategy. Notice that all we need to assume is that the player is rational. In particular, we do not need to assume that the other players are rational. In fact, we do not even need to assume the first player knows the other players' payoffs. The concept of dominant strategy is very robust.

The structure of the game presented in Figure 7.1 is very common in economics, in particular in industrial organization. For example, strategies $T$ and $L$ might correspond to setting a high price, whereas $B$ and $R$ correspond to setting a low price. What is interesting about this game is that (a) both players are better off by choosing $(T, L)$, which gives each player a payoff of 5, then choosing $(B, R)$, which gives each player a payoff of 4; however, (b) Player 1's dominant strategy is to play $B$ and Player 2's dominant strategy is to play $R$; (c) for this reason, players choose $(B, R)$ and receive (4,4), which is less than the commonly beneficial outcome (5,5).

In other words, the game in Figure 7.1, which is commonly known as the **prisoner's dilemma**, depicts the *conflict between individual incentives and joint incentives.* Jointly, players would prefer to move from $(B, R)$ to $(T, L)$, boosting payoffs from (4,4) to (5,5). However, individual incentives are for Player 1 to choose $B$ and for

Player 2 to choose $R$. In Chapters 8 and 9, I will show that many oligopoly situations have the nature of a "prisoner's dilemma." I will also show ways by which firms can escape the predicament of lowering payoffs from the "good" outcome (5,5) to the "bad" outcome (4,4).

Consider the game in Figure 7.2. There are no dominant strategies in this game. In fact, more generally, very few games have dominant strategies. We thus need to find other ways of "solving" the game. Consider Player 1's decision. While Player 1 has no *dominant* strategy, Player 1 has a **dominated strategy**, namely $M$. In fact, if Player 2 chooses $L$, then Player 1 is better off by choosing $T$ than $M$. The same is true for the cases when Player 2 chooses $C$ or $R$. That is, $M$ is dominated by $T$ from Player 1's point of view. More generally,

> A dominated strategy yields a player a payoff which is lower than that of a different strategy, regardless of what the other players do.

The idea is that, if a given player has a dominated strategy and that player is rational, then we should expect that player not to choose such a strategy.

Notice that the definition of a dominated strategy calls for there being another strategy that dominates the strategy in question. A strategy is not necessarily dominated even if, for each opponent strategy, we can find an alternative choice yielding a higher payoff. Consider Figure 7.2 again and suppose that Player 1's payoff from the $(T, R)$ strategy combination is $-3$ instead of 1. Then, for each possible choice by Player 2, we can find a choice by Player 1 that is better than M: if Player 2 chooses L, then T and B are better than M; if Player 2 chooses C, then T is better than M; and if Player 2 chooses R, then B is better than M. However, $M$ is *not* a dominated strategy in this alternative game: there is no other strategy for Player 1 that guarantees a higher payoff than $M$ *regardless* of Player 2's choice.[f]

The concept of dominated strategies has much less "bite" than that of dominant strategies. If Player 1 has a dominant strategy, we know that a rational Player 1 will

f. In fact, if Player 1 believes Player 2 chooses C with probability 2/3 or R with probability 1/3, then the expected payoff from choosing T or B is negative, whereas the expected payoff from choosing M is zero.

**FIGURE 7.2**
Dominated strategies

GAMES AND STRATEGIES | 163

choose that strategy; whereas if Player 1 has a dominated strategy all we know is that it will not choose that strategy; in principle, there could still be a large number of other strategies Player 1 might choose. Something more can be said, however, if we successively eliminate "dominated" strategies. (The justification for quotation marks around "dominated" will soon become clear.)

Suppose that Player 2 knows Player 1's payoffs and, moreover, knows that Player 1 is rational. By the reasoning presented earlier, Player 2 should expect Player 1 not to choose M. *Given that Player 1 does not choose M,* Player 2 finds strategy C to be "dominated" by R. Notice that, strictly speaking, C is not a dominated strategy: if Player 1 chooses M then C is better than R. However, C is dominated by R *given* that M is not played by Player 1.

We can now take this process one step further. If Player 1 is rational, believes that Player 2 is rational, and believes that Player 2 believes that Player 1 is rational, then Player 1 should find T to be a "dominated" strategy (in addition to M). In fact, if Player 2 does not choose C, then strategy T is "dominated" by strategy B: if Player 2 chooses L, Player 1 is better off with B; if Player 2 chooses R, again, Player 1 is better off with B. Finally, if we take this process one step further, we conclude that L is a "dominated" strategy for Player 2. This leaves us with the pair of strategies (B, R).

As in the first example, we have reached a single pair of strategies, a "solution" to the game. However, the assumptions necessary for iterated elimination of "dominated" strategies to work are more stringent than in the case of dominant strategies. Whereas in the first example all we needed to assume was that players are rational, payoff maximizing agents, we now assume that each player believes that the other player is rational.

To understand the importance of these assumptions regarding rationality, consider the simple game in Figure 7.3. Player 2 has a dominated strategy, L. In fact, it has a dominant strategy, too (R).[g] If Player 1 believes that Player 2 is rational, then Player 1 should expect Player 2 to avoid L and instead play R. Given this belief, Player 1's optimal strategy is to play B, for a payoff of 2. Suppose, however, that Player 1 entertains the possibility, unlikely as it might be, that Player 2 is not rational. Then B may no longer be its optimal choice, since there is a chance of Player 2 choosing L, resulting in a payoff of −100 for Player 1. A more general point is that, in analyzing games,

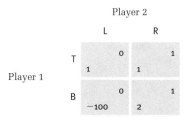

**FIGURE 7.3**
Dubious application of dominated strategies

g. In a 2x2 game, if a player has a dominant strategy, she also has a dominant strategy.

It is not only important whether players are rational: it is also important whether players believe the other players are rational.

■ **ABSOLUTE AND RELATIVE PAYOFF.** The game in Figure 7.3 also raises the issue of what rationality really means. In game theory, we take it to imply that players seek to maximize their payoff. However, many students of game theory, faced with the game in Figure 7.3, expect Player 2 to choose *L*: while it implies a lower payoff for Player 2 (0 instead of 1) it also gives Player 1 a very negative payoff. In other words, the outcome $(B, L)$ looks favorable to Player 2 in the sense that Player 2 "wins" by a very favorable margin. Given that Player 1 chooses B, Player 2 would get a greater payoff by choosing R, but it would "lose" to Player 1, in the sense that it would then receive a lower payoff than Player 1.

Although this is a frequent interpretation of games like that in Figure 7.3, it differs from the game theory approach. Instead, we assume that each rational player's goal is to maximize his or her payoff. It is quite possible that one component of a player's payoff is the success (or lack thereof) of rival players. If that is the case, then we should include that feature explicitly as part of the player's payoff. For example, suppose that the values in Figure 7.3 correspond to monetary payoffs; and that each player's payoff is equal to the cash payoff plus a relative performance component computed as follows: earning one extra dollar more than the rival is equivalent to earning 10 cents in cash. Then the relevant game payoffs, given that Player 1 chooses *B*, would be $(-110, +10)$ (if Player 2 chooses *L*) and $(2.1, 0.9)$ (if Player 2 chooses *R*).[h]

■ **NASH EQUILIBRIUM.** Consider now the game in Figure 7.4. There are no dominant or dominated strategies in this game. Is there anything we can say about what to expect players will choose? In this game, more than in the previous games, it is apparent that each player's optimal strategy depends on what the other player chooses. We must therefore propose a conjecture by Player 1 about Player 2's strategy and a conjecture

h. It would follow in this case that *R* is no longer a dominant strategy for Player 2 and as a result that Player 1 is better off by choosing *T*.

**FIGURE 7.4**
A game with no dominant or dominated strategies

by Player 2 about Player 1's strategy. A natural candidate for a "solution" to the game is then a situation whereby (a) players choose an optimal strategy given their conjectures of what the other players do and (b) such conjectures are consistent with the other players' strategy choice.

Suppose that Player 1 conjectures that Player 2 chooses $R$; and that Player 2 conjectures that Player 1 chooses $B$. Given these conjectures, Player 1's optimal strategy is $B$, whereas Player 2's optimal strategy is $R$. In fact, if Player 1 conjectures that Player 2 chooses $R$, then $B$ is Player 1's optimal choice; any other choice would yield a lower payoff. The same if true for Player 2. Notice that, based on these strategies, the players' conjectures are consistent: Player 1 expects Player 2 to choose what in fact Player 2 finds to be an optimal strategy, and vice-versa. This situation is referred to as a **Nash equilibrium**.[1]

Although the concept of Nash equilibrium can be defined with respect to conjectures, it is simpler — and more common — to define it with respect to strategies.

> A pair of strategies constitutes a Nash equilibrium if no player can unilaterally change its strategy in a way that improves its payoff.

It can be checked that, in the game in Figure 7.4, $(B, R)$ is a Nash equilibrium and no other combination of strategies is a Nash equilibrium. For example, $(M, C)$ is not a Nash equilibrium because, given that Player 2 chooses $C$, Player 1 would rather choose $B$.

■ **BEST RESPONSES.** A useful way to find a game's Nash equilibrium is to derive each player's best response. Player 1's **best response** is a mapping that indicates Player 1's best strategy for each possible strategy by Player 2. The left panels in Figure 7.5 shows

| Player 2's strategy | Player 1's best response |
|---|---|
| L | T |
| C | B |
| R | B |

| Player 1's strategy | Player 2's best response |
|---|---|
| T | R |
| M | {L,C} |
| B | R |

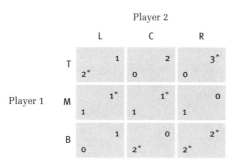

**FIGURE 7.5**
Best responses

Player 1's (top) and Player 2's (bottom) best-response mapping. For example, if Player 2 chooses $L$, then Player 1 gets 2 from playing $T$, 1 from playing $M$, and 0 from playing $B$. It follows that Player 1's best response to Player 2 choosing $L$ is given by $T$; and so forth. Regarding Player 2's best response, notice that, if Player 1 chooses $M$, then $L$ and $C$ all are equally good choices for Player 2 (and better than $R$). For this reason, Player 2's best response corresponds to the set $\{L, C\}$.

How are best responses related to Nash equilibrium? Let $BR_1(s_2)$ and $BR_2(s_1)$ be Player 1's and Player 2's best response mappings, respectively. A Nash equilibrium is then a pair of strategies $s_1^*$ and $s_2^*$ such that $s_1^*$ is the best response to $s_2^*$ and vice-versa. Continuing with the game described in Figure 7.4, a helpful way of representing these best response mappings is to go back to the game matrix and mark with an asterisk (or some other symbol) the payoff values corresponding to a best response. This is done in the matrix on the right-hand side of Figure 7.5. A Nash equilibrium then corresponds to a cell where both payoffs are marked with an asterisk. As can be seen from Figure 7.5, in our example this corresponds to the pair of strategies $(B, R)$ — which confirms our previous finding.

---

**CONTINUOUS VARIABLES.** In this introductory chapter, I only consider games where players chose among a finite number of possible actions and strategies. However, consider a gas station's pricing strategy. There are many different values of price it can choose from. If we assume only a few possible values — for example, \$2, \$3, and \$4 per gallon — we may artificially limit the player's choices. If instead we assume each and every possible price to the cent of the dollar, then we end up with enormous matrices.

In situations like this, the best solution is to model the player's strategy as picking a number from a continuous set. This may be too unrealistic in that it allows for values that are not observed in reality (for example, selling gasoline at $\$\sqrt{2}$ per gallon). However, it delivers a better balance between realism and tractability.

Suppose that player $i$ chooses a strategy $x_i$ (for example, a price level) from some set $S$ (possibly a continuous set). Player $i$'s payoff is a function of its choice as well as its rival's: $\pi_i(x_i, x_j)$. In this context, a pair of strategies $(x_i^*, x_j^*)$ constitutes a Nash equilibrium if and only if, for each player $i$, there exists no strategy $x_i'$ such that $\pi_i(x_i', x_j^*) > \pi_i(x_i^*, x_j^*)$.

An equivalent definition may be given in terms of best response mappings. Let $BR_i(x_j)$ be player $i$'s best response to player $j$'s choice. Then a Nash equilibrium is a pair of strategies $(x_i^*, x_j^*)$ such that, for each player $i$, $x_i^* \in BR_i(x_j^*)$.

In Chapter 8 I will use this methodology to determine the equilibrium of some oligopoly games.

---

i. For the sake of rigor, two qualifications are in order: first, existence of Nash equilibrium applies to all games except some very special cases. Second, equilibria sometimes require players to randomly choose one of the actions (mixed strategies), whereas I have only considered the case when one action is chosen with certainty (pure strategies).

■ **MULTIPLE EQUILIBRIA AND FOCAL POINTS.** Contrary to the choice of dominant strategies, application of the Nash equilibrium concept always produces an equilibrium.[i] In fact, there may exist more than one Nash equilibrium. One example of this is given by the game in Figure 7.6, where both $(T, L)$ and $(B, R)$ are Nash equilibria. A possible

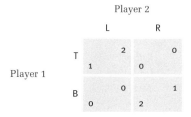

**FIGURE 7.6**
Multiple Nash equilibria

illustration for this game is the process of standardization. Strategies $T$ and $L$, or $B$ and $R$, correspond to combinations of strategies that lead to compatibility. Both players are better off under compatibility. However, Player 1 prefers compatibility around the standard ($B$-$R$), whereas Player 2 prefers compatibility over the other standard. More generally, this example is representative of a class of games in which (a) players want to coordinate, (b) there is more than one point of coordination, (c) players disagree over which of the two coordination points is better.[j]

Equilibrium multiplicity can be problematic for an analyst: if the game's equilibrium is a natural prediction of what will happen when players interact, then multiplicity makes such prediction difficult. This is particularly the case for games that have not only two but many different equilibria. Consider the following example: two people are asked to choose independently and without communication where and when in New York City they would try to meet one another. If they choose the same meeting location, then they both receive $100; otherwise they both receive nothing.[2] Despite the plethora of possible meeting and time locations, which correspond to a plethora of Nash equilibria, a majority of subjects typically choose Grand Central Station at noon: the most salient traffic hub in New York City and the most salient time of the day.

Although there is an uncountable number of Nash equilibria in the "meet me in New York" game, some are more "reasonable" than others. Here, "reasonable" is not meant in the game theoretic sense: all equilibria satisfy the conditions for a Nash equilibrium. Rather, it is meant in the sense that, based on information that goes beyond the game itself, there may be **focal points** on which players coordinate even if they do not communicate.[k] Game theory and the concept of Nash equilibrium are useful tools to understand interdependent decision making; but they are not the only source of useful information to predict equilibrium behavior.

## 7.2 SEQUENTIAL GAMES[l]

In the previous section, I justified the choice of simultaneous-choice games as a realistic way of modeling situations where observation lags are so long that it is as if players were choosing strategies simultaneously. When the time between strategy choices is

j. Standardization problems are further discussed in Sections 16.3 and 16.4.

k. One game theorist defined a focal point as "each person's expectation of what the other expects him to expect to be expected to do" (cf Endnote 2).

l. This and the next section cover relatively more advanced material which may be skipped in a first reading of the book.

sufficiently long, however, the assumption of sequential decision making is more real-istic. Consider the example of an industry that is currently monopolized. A second firm must decide whether or not to enter the industry. Given the decision of whether or not to enter, the incumbent firm must decide whether to price aggressively or not. The incumbent's decision is taken *as a function* of the entrant's decision. That is, first the incumbent observes whether or not the entrant enters, and then decides whether or not to price aggressively. In such a situation, it makes more sense to consider a model with sequential rather than simultaneous choices. Specifically, the model should have the entrant — Player 1 — move first and the incumbent — Player 2 — move second.

The best way to model games with sequential choices is to use a game tree. A **game tree** is like a decision tree only that there is more than one decision maker involved. An example is given by Figure 7.7, where strategies and payoffs illustrate the case of entrant and incumbent described above. In Figure 7.7, a square denotes a **decision node**. The game starts with decision node 1. At this node, Player 1 (entrant) makes a choice between $e$ and $\bar{e}$, which can be interpreted as "enter" and "not enter," respectively. If the latter is chosen, then the game ends with payoffs $\pi_1 = 0$ (entrant's payoff) and $\pi_2 = 50$ (incumbent's payoff). If Player 1 chooses $e$, however, then we move on to deci-sion node 2. This node corresponds to Player 2 (incumbent) making a choice between $r$ and $\bar{r}$, which can be interpreted as "retaliate entry" or "not retaliate entry," respectively. Games which, like Figure 7.7, are represented by trees are also referred to as games in **extensive form.**[m]

This game has two Nash equilibria: $(e, \bar{r})$ and $(\bar{e}, r)$. Let us first check that $(e, \bar{r})$ is indeed a Nash equilibrium, that is, no player has an incentive to change its strategy given what the other player does. First, if Player 1 chooses $e$, then Player 2's best choice is to choose $\bar{r}$ (it gets 20, it would get $-10$ otherwise). Likewise, given that Player 2 chooses $\bar{r}$, Player 1's optimal choice is $e$ (it gets 10, it would get 0 otherwise).

Let us now check that $(\bar{e}, r)$ is an equilibrium. Given that Player 2 chooses $r$, Player 1 is better off by choosing $\bar{e}$: this yields Player 1 a payoff of 0, whereas $e$ would yield $-10$. As for Player 2, given that Player 1 chooses $\bar{e}$, its payoff is 50, regardless of which strategy it chooses. It follows that $r$ is an optimal choice (though not the only one).

Although the two solutions are indeed two Nash equilibria, the second equilib-rium does not make much sense. Player 1 is not entering because of the "threat" that

m. From this and the previous sections, one might erroneously conclude that games with simultaneous choices must be represented in normal form and games with sequential moves in extensive form. In fact, both simultaneous and sequential choice games can be represented in both the normal and extensive forms. However, for simple games like those considered in this chapter, the choice of game representation considered in the text is more appropriate.

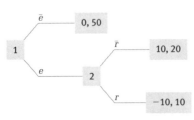

**FIGURE 7.7**
Extensive-form representation: the sequential-entry game

Player 2 will choose to retaliate. But, is this threat credible? If Player 1 were to enter, would Player 2 decide to retaliate? Clearly, the answer is "no": by retaliating, Player 2 gets $-10$, compared to 20 from no retaliation. We conclude that $(\bar{e}, r)$, while being a Nash equilibrium, is not a reasonable prediction of what one might expect to be played out.

One way of getting rid of this sort of "unreasonable" equilibria is to solve the game backward; that is, to apply the principle of **backward induction**. First, we consider node 2, and conclude that the optimal decision is $\bar{r}$. *Then*, we solve for the decision in node 1 *given the decision previously found for node 2*. Given that Player 2 will choose $\bar{r}$, it is now clear that the optimal decision at node 1 is $e$. We thus select the first Nash equilibrium as the only one that is intuitively "reasonable."

Solving a game backward is not always this easy. Suppose that, if Player 1 chooses $e$ at decision node 1 we are led not to a Player 2 decision node but rather to an entire new game, say, a simultaneous-move game as in Figures 7.1 to 7.6. Since this game is a part of the larger game, we call it a **subgame** of the larger game. In this setting, solving the game backward would amount to first solving for the Nash equilibrium (or equilibria) of the subgame; and then, given the solution for the subgame, solving for the entire game. Equilibria which are derived in this way are called **subgame-perfect equilibria**.[3] For simple game trees like the one in Figure 7.7, subgame-perfect equilibria are obtained by solving the game backwards, that is, backwards induction and subgame perfection coincide.

■ **THE VALUE OF CREDIBLE COMMITMENT.** In the game of Figure 7.7, the equilibrium $(\bar{e}, r)$ was dismissed on the basis that it requires Player 2 to make the "incredible" commitment of playing $r$ in case Player 1 chooses $e$. Such threat is not credible because, *given* that Player 1 has chosen $e$, Player 2's best choice is $\bar{r}$. But suppose that Player 2 writes an enforceable and not renegotiable contract whereby, if Player 1 chooses $e$, then Player 2 must choose $r$. The contract is such that, were Player 2 not to choose $r$ and choose $\bar{r}$ instead, Player 2 would incur a penalty of 40, lowering its total payoff to $-20$.[n]

The situation is illustrated in Figure 7.8. The first decision now belongs to Player 2, who must choose between writing the bond described above (strategy $b$) and not doing anything (strategy $\bar{b}$). If Player 2 chooses $\bar{b}$, then the game in Figure 7.7 is played. If instead Player 2 chooses $b$, then a different game is played, one that takes into account the implications of issuing the bond.

Let us now compare the two subgames starting at Player 1's decision nodes. The one on top is the same as in Figure 7.7. As we then saw, restricting to the subgame perfect equilibrium, Player 2's payoff is 20. The subgame on the bottom is identical to the one on top except for Player 2's payoff following $(e, \bar{r})$. The value is now $-20$ instead of 20. At first, it might seem that this makes Player 2 worse off: payoffs are the same in all cases except one; and in that one case payoff is actually lower than initially. However, as I will show next, Player 2 is better off playing the bottom subgame than the top one.

Let us solve the bottom subgame backward, as before. When it comes to Player 2 to choose between $r$ and $\bar{r}$, the optimal choice is $r$. In fact, this gives Player 2 a payoff of

n. This is a very strong assumption, as most contracts are renegotiable. However, for the purposes of the present argument, what is important is that Player 2 has the option of imposing on itself a cost if it does not choose $r$. This cost may result from breach of contract or from a different source.

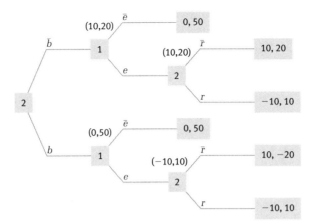

**FIGURE 7.8**
The value of commitment

10, whereas the alternative would yield $-20$ (Player 2 would have to pay for breaking the bond). Given that Player 2 chooses $r$, Player 1 finds it optimal to choose $\bar{e}$: it is better to receive a payoff of zero than to receive $-10$, the outcome of $e$ followed by $r$. In sum, the subgame on the bottom gives Player 2 an equilibrium payoff of 50, the result of the combination $\bar{e}$ and $r$.

We can finally move backward one more stage and look at Player 2's choice between $b$ and $\bar{b}$. From what we saw above, Player 2's optimal choice is to choose $b$ and eventually receive a payoff of 50. The alternative, $\bar{b}$, eventually leads to a payoff of 20 only.

This example illustrates two important points. First it shows that:

A credible commitment may have significant strategic value.

By signing a bond that imposes a large penalty when playing $\bar{r}$, Player 2 credibly commits to playing $r$ when the time comes to choose between $r$ and $\bar{r}$. In so doing, Player 2 induces Player 1 to choose $\bar{e}$, which in turn works in Player 2's benefit. Specifically, introducing this **credible commitment** raises Player 2's payoff from 20 to 50. Therefore, the value of commitment in this example is 30.

The second point illustrated by the example is a methodological one. If we believe that Player 2 is credibly committed to choosing $r$, then we should model this by changing Player 2's payoffs or by changing the order of moves. This can be done as in Figure 7.8, where we model all the moves that lead to Player 2 effectively precommitting to playing $r$. Alternatively, this can also be done as in Figure 7.9, where we model Player 2 as choosing $r$ or $\bar{r}$ "before" Player 1 chooses its strategy. The actual choice of $r$ or $\bar{r}$ may occur in time after Player 1 chooses $e$ or $\bar{e}$. However, if Player 2 pre-commits

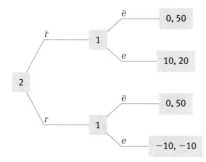

**FIGURE 7.9**
Modeling Player 2's capacity to precommit

**FIGURE 7.10**
A game with long-run and short-run strategy choices: timing of moves

to playing $r$, we can model that by assuming Player 2 moves first. In fact, by solving the game in Figure 7.9 backward, we get the same solution as in Figure 7.8, namely the second Nash equilibrium of the game initially considered.

■ **SHORT-RUN AND LONG-RUN.** To conclude this section, I should mention another instance where the sequence of moves plays an important role. This is when the game under consideration depicts a long-term situation where players choose both long-run and short-run variables. For example, capacity decisions are normally a firm's long-term choice, for production capacity (buildings, machines) typically lasts for a number of years. Pricing, on the other hand, is typically a short-run variable, for firms can change it relatively frequently at a relatively low cost.

When modeling this sort of strategic interaction, we should assume that players choose the long-run variable first and the short-run variable second. Short-run variables are those that players choose *given* the value of the long-run variables. And this is precisely what we get by placing the short-run choice in the second stage.

This timing of moves is depicted in Figure 7.10. This figure illustrates yet a third way of representing games: a time-line of moves. This is not as complete and rigorous as the normal-form and extensive-form representations we saw before; but it proves useful in analyzing a variety of games.

In a real-world situation, as time moves on, firms alternate between choosing capacity levels and choosing prices, the latter more frequently than the former. If we want to model this in a simple, two-stage game, then the right way of doing it is to place the capacity decision in the first stage and the pricing decision in the second stage. The same principle applies more generally when there are long-run and short-run strategic variables. In the following chapters, we will encounter examples of this in relation to capacity/pricing decisions (Chapter 8), entry/output decisions (Chapter 10), and product positioning/pricing decisions (Chapter 14).

## 7.3 REPEATED GAMES

Many real-world situations of strategic behavior are repeated over an extended period of time. Sometimes, this can be modeled by an appropriate static model. For example, in the previous section we saw how a two-stage game can be used to model competition in long-term and short-term variables. Consider, however, the strategic phenomenon of **retaliation**, that is, the situation whereby a player changes its action in response to a rival's action. Clearly, this cannot be achieved in a static, simultaneous-move game, for in such a game there is no time for a player to react to another player's actions.

A useful way to model the situation whereby players react to each other's moves is to consider a repeated game. Consider a simultaneous-choice game like the one in Figure 7.1. Since in this game each player chooses one action only once, we refer to it as a **one-shot game**. A **repeated game** is defined by a one-shot game — also referred to as **stage game** — which is repeated a number of times. If repetition takes place a finite number of times, then we have a finitely repeated game, otherwise we have an infinitely repeated game.

In one-shot games, strategies are easy to define. In fact, strategies are identified with actions. In repeated games, however, it is useful to distinguish between actions and strategies. Consider again the game depicted in Figure 7.1, a version of the "prisoner's dilemma." As we saw earlier, it is a dominant strategy for Player 1 to choose $B$ and it is a dominant strategy for Player 2 to choose $R$; the unique Nash equilibrium thus implies a payoff of 4 for each player.

Now suppose that this one-shot game is repeated indefinitely. Specifically, suppose that, after each period actions are chosen and payoffs distributed, the game ends with probability $1 - \delta$. For simplicity, suppose that players assign the same weight to payoffs earned in any period. Now the set of *strategies* is different from the set of actions available to players in each period. In each period, Player 1 must choose an action from the set $\{T, B\}$, whereas Player 2 must choose an action from the set $\{L, R\}$; these sets are the players' action sets. Strategies, however, can be rather complex combinations of "if-then" statements where the choice at time $t$ is made dependent on what happened in previous periods; in other words, strategies can be history dependent. Given the conditional nature of strategies, the number of strategies available to a player is considerably greater than the number of actions it can choose from.

Specifically, consider the following strategies for Players 1 and 2: if in the past Player 1 chose $T$ and Player 2 chose $L$, then continue doing so in the current period. If at any time in the past either of the players made a different choice, then let Player 1 choose $B$ and Player 2 choose $R$ in the current period.

Can such a pair of strategies form a Nash equilibrium? Let us first compute the equilibrium payoff that Player 1 gets playing the equilibrium strategies. Recall that $(T, L)$ induces a payoff of 5 for Player 1. Total expected payoff is therefore given by:

$$V = 5 + \delta\, 5 + \delta^2\, 5 + \dots = \frac{5}{1 - \delta}$$

Notice that I successively multiply payoffs by $\delta$ for this is the probability that the game will continue on (that is, after each period is played, the game ends with probability $1 - \delta$). Now consider the possibility of deviating from the equilibrium strategies. If at a given period a given player chooses $B$ instead of $T$, then expected payoff is given by:

$$V' = 6 + \delta\, 4 + \delta^2\, 4 + \dots = 6 + \frac{4\,\delta}{1 - \delta}$$

In order for the proposed set of strategies to be a Nash equilibrium, it must be that $V \geq V'$, that is,

$$\frac{5}{1 - \delta} \geq 6 + \frac{4\,\delta}{1 - \delta}$$

which is equivalent to $\delta \geq \frac{1}{2}$. Given the symmetry of the payoff function, the computations for Player 2 are identical to those of Player 1. We thus conclude that, if the probability that the game continues on into the next period, $\delta$, is sufficiently high, then there exists a Nash equilibrium whereby players pick $T$ and $L$ in every period (while the game is still going on).

Intuitively, the difference between the one-shot game and the indefinitely repeated game is that, in the latter, we can create a system of intertemporal rewards and punishments that induces the right incentives for players to choose $T$. In one-shot play, the temptation for Player 1 to play $B$ is too high: it is a dominant strategy, it yields a higher payoff regardless of what the other player does. In repeated play, however, the short-term gain achieved by choosing $B$ must be balanced against the different continuation payoff each choice induces. The equilibrium strategies are such that, if Player 1 chooses $B$ in the current period, then it gets 4 in every subsequent period. We thus have a gain of 1 in the short run ($6 - 5$) against a loss of 1 in every future period ($5 - 4$). Whether future periods matter or not depends on the value of $\delta$. If $\delta$ is very high, then the loss of 1 in every future period counts very heavily, and Player 1 prefers to stick to $T$ and forego the short-term gain from choosing $B$.

We conclude that:

> Because players can react to other players' past actions, repeated games allow for equilibrium outcomes that would not be an equilibrium in the corresponding one-shot game.

As I will show in Chapter 9, this idea of "agreements" between players that are enforced by mutual retaliation plays an important role in explaining the workings of cartels and collusive behavior. More generally, many agreements in a variety of social situations are based not on formal contracts but rather on the trust that stems from repeated relationships. For example, in the diamond districts in Antwerp, New York City, and Tel-Aviv many high-value transactions are based on unwritten contracts, sometimes referred to as **relational contracts**.

Even more generally, the phenomenon of cooperation in society is frequently explained as the equilibrium of a prisoner's dilemma: individually and in the short run, each society member has an incentive to take advantage of the others. In practice, however, he or she refrains from doing so because the costs from being shunned by other members in the future outweigh the short-term gains.

To conclude, a note on concepts and terminology. There are two different interpretations for the role played by the parameter $\delta$ introduced earlier. One is that the game will end in finite time but the precise date when it will end is unknown to players; all they know is that, after each period, the game ends with probability $1 - \delta$. This is the interpretation I considered in this section and corresponds to the term *indefinitely*-repeated game. An alternative interpretation is that the game lasts for an infinite number of periods and that players discount future payoffs according to the discount factor $\delta$: a dollar next period is worth $\delta$ dollars in the current period. This is the interpretation corresponding to the term "*infinitely*-repeated game."[o] Formally, if players are risk-neutral, then the two interpretations lead to the same equilibrium computation. I prefer the indefinitely-repeated game interpretation and terminology. However, it is rarely used.

## 7.4   INFORMATION

Consider the pricing dilemma faced by a health insurance company: a low price leads to small margins, but a high price runs the risk of attracting only high-risk patients. What should the insurance company do? Specifically, consider the following sequential game between an insurance company and a patient. First the insurance company decides whether to charge a high premium or a low premium; then, the patient decides whether or not to accept the company's offer.

So far, this looks like a sequential game like the ones considered in Section 7.2. But now we add a twist: the patient may either be a low-risk patient or a high-risk patient; moreover, the patient knows what type he is but the insurance company does not. Specifically, the insurance company believes that with probability 10% the patient is a high-risk patient. For a high-risk patient, health insurance is worth $20,000 a year, whereas for a low-risk patient, the value is $3,000. For the insurance company, the cost of providing insurance is $30,000 for a high-risk patient and $1,000 for a low-risk patient.

Notice that, based on the prior probabilities that the patient is high or low risk, the insurer estimates that the average valuation is given by $10\% \times 20 + 90\% \times 3 = 4.7$, whereas the average cost of insuring a patient is given by $10\% \times 30 + 90\% \times 1 = 3.9$. Based on these average, the insurance company is considering two possible prices:

$4,500 (a price that is below average valuation but above average cost) or $30 (a price that covers cost regardless of patient type).[p]

How do we model this situation as a game? First, notice that, to the extent that actions are sequential, it will be easiest to model the interaction between insurer and patient based on a game tree (as I did in Section 7.2). One important difference with respect to the basic sequential games considered earlier is that we now have uncertainty to consider: specifically, the patient may be high risk (probability 10%) or low risk (probability 90%). Moreover, insurer and patient are differently informed regarding risk: specifically, I consider the extreme case where the patient knows exactly his type but the insurer only has prior probabilistic beliefs.

In order to model games where there is **uncertainty** and **asymmetric information**, we introduce a new "player" into the game; we call this player **Nature**. Nature is not a player like other players: it has no strategic motives, and its actions are limited to choosing different branches of a game tree according to predetermined probabilities. This may seem a bit strange, but the example we are considering may help clarify things.

Figure 7.11 shows the game tree for the insurer-patient game. First, the insurer must decide whether to set a price of $4.50 or $30. Regardless of what the insurer chooses, the next move is by Nature, which "decides" whether the patient is high-risk or low-risk according to the probabilities considered earlier. Finally, given the insurer's choice *as well as* Nature's choice, the patient either accepts or rejects the insurer's offer.

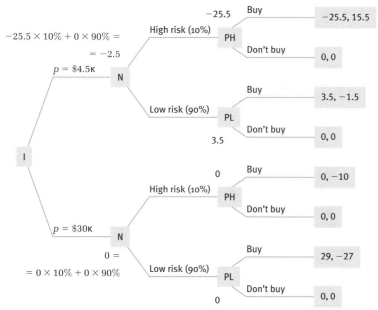

**FIGURE 7.11**
Sequential game with asymmetric information

p.  Below I consider other possibilities.

For ease of reading the tree, I use two different names for the patient, depending on his type: *PH* or *PL* for high-risk or low-risk patient, respectively.

As in Section 7.2, I proceed by solving the game backwards. If $p = 4.5$, then the patient accepts the offer if he is high-risk but rejects the offer if he is low risk. If $p = 30$, in turn, then neither a high-risk patient nor a low-risk patient accept the offer.

Moving back one step, we compute the expected value for player $I$ given Nature's move: if $p = 4.5$, then $I$'s expected payoff is given by $-25.5 \times 10\% + 0 \times 90\% = -2.5$; if $p = 30$, then expected payoff is simply 0. Finally, given these expected payoffs we can solve for $I$'s optimal strategy, which is $p = 30$.

In sum, equilibrium strategies are as follows: the insurer chooses $p = 30$; the patient accepts the offer $p = 4.5$ if he is high risk and rejects the offer if $p = 4.5$ and he is low-risk or if $p = 30$ (regardless of risk type).

There are a lot of interesting economics regarding this game, but for now I will focus on the game theory elements.[q] First, we model uncertainty by creating the player Nature. Second, we model asymmetric information by placing the informed player's nodes *after* Nature's move and the uninformed player's nodes *before* Nature's move. This is an important modeling choice. Consider an alternative possibility: neither the insurer nor the patient himself know the level of risk; all they know is the prior probabilities, namely that the probability of being high risk is 10%. Figure 7.12 depicts the tree corresponding to this alternative game. Now the order of moves is different: first, $I$ choses the price; next, $P$ decides whether or not to accept the offer; and finally, $N$ determines whether $P$ is high or low risk.

Solving the game backwards, we see that the equilibrium corresponds to: $I$ offers a price $p = 4.5$; $P$ accepts a $p = 4.5$ offer but rejects a $p = 30$ offer (and Nature chooses patient type as before). This is a very different outcome than in the game considered in Figure 7.11. As we saw in Section 7.2, the order of moves matters, namely when commitment matters; we now have one additional reason why the order of moves is important: if Nature is involved, then changing the order of moves changes the nature of information, that is, who knows what when.

■ **STANDARD GAMES WITH ASYMMETRIC INFORMATION.** The game between insurer and patient corresponds to a typical situation of asymmetric information, namely the case when an uninformed player (e.g., an insurer) must make a move (e.g., offer insurance policy terms) before the informed player (e.g., the patient) gets to make its move (e.g., accept or reject the offer). The equilibrium of such games typically involves what economists refer to as **adverse selection**. Let us go back to the game in Figure 7.11. By setting a low price, $p = 4.5$ the insurer offers a deal that is acceptable for an average patient. However, no patient is average: in practice, low-risk patients turn down the offer, and all the insurer gets is high-risk patients, in which cases revenues fail to cover cost.

There are many real-world examples that feature adverse selection. For example, a buyer who makes an offer for a used car should take into account that the offer will only be accepted by sellers who own cars of poor quality (which they know better than the

q. In Section 5.2, I discuss the issue of equilibrium in the insurance market, though not using the formal game-theory apparatus.

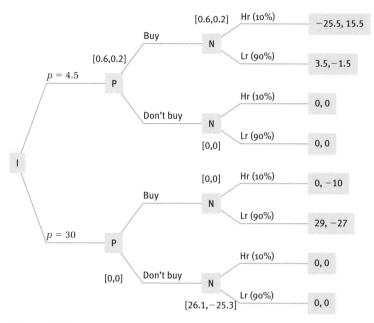

**FIGURE 7.12**
Sequential game with uncertainty but no asymmetric information

buyer). On a lighter note, in Groucho Marx's autobiography we learn that, in response to an acceptance letter from a club, "I sent the club a wire stating, 'PLEASE ACCEPT MY RESIGNATION. I DON'T WANT TO BELONG TO ANY CLUB THAT WILL ACCEPT PEOPLE LIKE ME AS A MEMBER'." Can you see why Groucho was playing an adverse selection game? How does club membership relate to health insurance?

As I mentioned earlier, adverse selection results from models where the uninformed party makes the first move. Consider now the opposite case, that is, the case when the informed party makes the first move. As a motivating example, think of a firm that enters the market for luxury luggage. The firm would like to reduce price to gain market share, but worries that this might be interpreted by customers as a sign of low quality. The key word here is "signal." In fact, asymmetric information games where the informed party moves first are frequently referred to as **signaling games**. In Section 12.3 I discuss a particularly important signaling game: the reputation building game, where a player's actions in the first period indirectly provide information about his type, which in turn has an effect on how the game is played in the second period. In Chapter 14 I consider a different application of the same principles and develop a model of advertising as a signal of quality.

Finally, the **principal-agent** problem provides an additional example of a game with asymmetric information. Consider an employer who wants to encourage his sales team to work hard but cannot observe whether or not they are doing all they can. What steps can he take to ensure that they work hard? A similar problem occurs in the relation between a board of directors and a firm's manager (cf Section 3.3). Still another example is given by the relation between a regulator and a regulated firm (cf Section 5.6). What these examples have in common is a principal (employer, shareholder, regulator) who would like to induce a specific behavior from an agent (employee, manager, regulated utility) but cannot directly observe the agent's actions or the agent's type. In the former case, known as **moral hazard** (or hidden action) the agent has better information only with respect to the action that he takes but that the principal does not observe. The key in games of moral hazard is that even though the principal might not observe the agent's actions, she might be able to observe outcomes that are related to actions (for example, output, an observable, is a function of effort, an unobservable). Then the principal might want to set up a reward system based on observables.

## SUMMARY

• A dominant strategy yields a player the highest payoff regardless of the other players' choices. • A dominated strategy yields a player a payoff which is lower than that of a different strategy, regardless of what the other players do. • It is not only important whether players are rational: it is also important whether players believe the other players are rational. • A pair of strategies constitutes a Nash equilibrium if no player can unilaterally change its strategy in a way that improves its payoff. • A credible commitment may have significant strategic value. • Because players can react to other players' past actions, repeated games allow for equilibrium outcomes that would not be an equilibrium in the corresponding one-shot game.

## KEY CONCEPTS

• game • normal form • dominant strategy • prisoner's dilemma • dominated strategy • Nash equilibrium • best response • focal points • game tree • decision node • extensive form • backward induction • subgame • subgame-perfect equilibria • credible commitment • retaliation • one-shot game • repeated game • stage game • relational contracts • uncertainty • asymmetric information • Nature • adverse selection • signaling games • principal-agent • moral hazard

## REVIEW AND PRACTICE EXERCISES

■ **7.1. DOMINANT AND DOMINATED STRATEGIES.** What are the assumptions regarding player rationality implicit in solving a game by elimination of dominated strategies? Contrast this with the case of dominant strategies.

■ **7.2. THE MOVIE RELEASE GAME.** Consider the example at the beginning of the chapter. Suppose that there are only two blockbusters jockeying for position: Warner Bros.'s *Harry Potter* and Fox's *Narnia*. Suppose that blockbusters released in November share a total of $500 million in ticket revenues, whereas blockbusters released in December share a total of $800 million.

(a) Formulate the game played by Warner Bros. and Fox.

(b) Determine the game's Nash equilibrium(a).

■ **7.3. ERICSSON VS. NOKIA.** Suppose that Ericsson and Nokia are the two primary competitors in the market for 4G handsets. Each firm must decide between two possible price levels: $100 and $90. Production cost is $40 per handset. Firm demand is as follows: if both firms price at $100, then Nokia sells 500 and Ericsson 800; if both firms price at $90, then sales are 800 and 900, respectively; if Nokia prices at $100 and Ericsson at $90, then Nokia's sales drop to 400, whereas Ericsson's increase to 1,100; finally, if Nokia prices at $90 and Ericsson at $100 then Nokia sells 900 and Ericsson 700.

(a) Suppose firms choose prices simultaneously. Describe the game and solve it.

(b) Suppose that Ericsson has a limited capacity of 800k units per quarter. Moreover, all of the demand unfulfilled by Ericsson is transferred to Nokia. How would the analysis change?

(c) Suppose you work for Nokia. Your Chief Intelligence Officer (CIO) is unsure whether Ericsson is capacity constrained or not. How much would you value this piece of info?

■ **7.4. E.T.** In the movie *E.T.,* a trail of Reese's Pieces, one of Hershey's chocolate brands, is used to lure the little alien out of the woods. As a result of the publicity created by this scene, sales of Reese's Pieces trebled, allowing Hershey to catch up with rival Mars. Universal Studio's original plan was to use a trail of Mars' M&Ms, but Mars turned down the offer. The makers of *E.T.* then turned to Hershey, who accepted the deal.

Suppose that the publicity generated by having M&Ms included in the movie would increase Mars' profits by $800,000 and decrease Hershey's by $100,000. Suppose moreover that Hershey's increase in market share costs Mars a loss of $500,000. Finally, let $b$ be the benefit for Hershey's from having its brand be the chosen one.

Describe the above events as a game in extensive form. Determine the equilibrium as a function of $b$. If the equilibrium differs from the actual events, how do you think they can be reconciled?

■ **7.5. E.T. (CONTINUATION).** Return to Exercise 7.4. Suppose now that Mars does not know the value of $b$, believing that either $b = \$1,200,000$ or $b = \$700,000$, each with probability

50%. Unlike Mars, Hershey knows the value of $b$. Draw the tree for this new game and determine its equilibrium.

■ **7.6. HERNAN CORTÉZ.** In a message to the king of Spain upon arriving in Mexico, Spanish navigator and explorer Hernan Cortéz reports that, "under the pretext that [our] ships were not navigable, I had them sunk; thus all hope of leaving was lost and I could act more securely." Discuss the strategic value of this action knowing the Spanish colonists were faced with potential resistance from the Mexican natives.

■ **7.7. HDTV STANDARDS.** Consider the following game depicting the process of standard setting in high-definition television (HDTV).[4] The US and Japan must simultaneously decide whether to invest a high or a low value into HDTV research. If both countries choose a low effort than payoffs are (4,3) for US and Japan, respectively; if the US chooses a low level and Japan a high level, then payoffs are (2,4); if, by contrast, the US chooses a high level and Japan a low one, then payoffs are (3,2). Finally, if both countries choose a high level, then payoff are (1,1).

(a) Are there any dominant strategies in this game? What is the Nash equilibrium of the game? What are the rationality assumptions implicit in this equilibrium?

(b) Suppose now the US has the option of committing to a strategy ahead of Japan's decision. How would you model this new situation? What are the Nash equilibria of this new game?

(c) Comparing the answers to (a) and (b), what can you say about the value of commitment for the US?

(d) "When pre-commitment has a strategic value, the player that makes that commitment ends up 'regretting' its actions, in the sense that, given the rivals' choices, it could achieve a higher payoff by choosing a different action." In light of your answer to (b), how would you comment this statement?

■ **7.8. FINITELY REPEATED GAME.** Consider a one-shot game with two equilibria and suppose this game is repeated twice. Explain in words why there may be equilibria in the two-period game which are different from the equilibria of the one-shot game.

■ **7.9. AMERICAN EXPRESS'S SPINOFF OF SHEARSON.** In 1993, American Express sold Shearson to Primerica (now part of Citigroup). At the time, the *Wall Street Journal* wrote that,

> Among the sticking points in acquiring Shearson's brokerage operations would be the firm's litigation costs. More than most brokerage firms, Shearson has been socked with big legal claims by investors who say they were mistreated, though the firm has made strides in cleaning up its backlog of investor cases. In 1992's fourth quarter alone, Shearson took reserves of $90 million before taxes for "additional legal provisions."[5]

When the deal was completed, Primerica bought most of Shearson's assets but left the legal liabilities with American Express. Why do you think the deal was structured this way? Was it fair to American Express?

■ **7.10. SALE OF BUSINESS.** Suppose that a firm owns a business unit that it wants to sell. Potential buyers know that the seller values the unit at either $100 million, $110 million, $120 million, ... $190 million, each value equally likely. The seller knows the precise value, but the buyer only knows the distribution. The buyer expects to gain from synergies with its existing businesses, so that its value is equal to seller's value plus $10 million (In other words, there are gains from trade.) Finally, the buyer must make a take-it-or-leave-it offer at some price $p$. How much should the buyer offer?

## CHALLENGING EXERCISES

■ **7.11. FIRST-PRICE AUCTION.** Consider the following auction game. There are two bidders who simultaneously submit bids $b_i$ for a given object. Bidder $i$ values the object at $v_i$; it knows its own value but not the other bidder's value. It is common knowledge that valuations $v_i$ are uniformly drawn from the unit interval, that is, $v_i \sim U[0,1]$.

    (a) Suppose that Bidder 1 expects Bidder 2's bid to be uniformly distributed between 0 and $\frac{1}{2}$. What is Bidder 1's optimal bid function (that is, bid as a function of valuation $v_1$)?

    (b) If Bidder 2 expects Bidder 1 to follow the strategy derived in part (a), what is Bidder 2's belief about Bidder 1's bid levels?

    (c) Determine the bidding game Nash equilibrium (assuming there is only one).

■ **7.12. AD GAMES.** Two firms must simultaneously choose their advertising budget; their options are $H$ or $L$. Payoffs are as follows: if both choose $H$, then each gets 5; if both choose $L$, then each gets 4; if firm 1 chooses $H$ and firm 2 chooses $L$, then firm 1 gets 8 and firm 2 gets 1; conversely, if firm 2 chooses $H$ and firm 1 chooses $L$, then firm 2 gets 8 and firm 1 gets 1.

    (a) Determine the Nash equilibria of the one-shot game.

    (b) Suppose the game is indefinitely repeated and that the relevant discount factor is $\delta = .8$. Determine the optimal symmetric equilibrium.

    (c) (challenge question) Now suppose that, for the first 10 periods, firm payoffs are twice the values represented in the above table. What is the optimal symmetric equilibrium?

■ **7.13. Finitely repeated game.** Suppose that the game depicted in Figure 7.1 is repeated $T$ times, where $T$ is known. Show that the only subgame perfect equilibrium is for players to choose $(B, R)$ in every period.

■ **7.14. Centipede.** Consider the game in Figure 7.13.[6] Show, by backward induction, that rational players choose $d$ at every node of the game, yielding a payoff of 2 for Player 1 and 0 for Player 2. Is this equilibrium reasonable? What are the rationality assumptions implicit in it?

■ **7.15. Advertising levels.** Consider an industry where price competition is not very important: all of the action is on advertising budgets. Specifically, total value $S$ (in dollars) gets splits between two competitors according to their advertising shares. If $a_1$ is firm 1's advertising investment (in dollars), then its profit is given by:

$$\frac{a_1}{a_1 + a_2} S - a_1$$

(The same applies for firm 2). Both $a_1$ and $a_2$ must be non-negative. If both firms invest zero in advertising, then they split the market.

(a) Determine the symmetric Nash equilibrium of the game whereby firms choose $a_i$ independently and simultaneously.

(b) Determine the jointly optimal level of advertising, that is, the level $a^*$ that maximizes joint profits.

(c) Given that firm 2 sets $a_2 = a^*$, determine firm 1's optimal advertising level.

(d) Suppose that firms compete indefinitely in each period $t = 1, 2, \ldots$, and that the discount factor is given by $\delta \in [0, 1]$. Determine the lowest value of $\delta$ such that, by playing grim strategies, firms can sustain an agreement to set $a^*$ in each period.

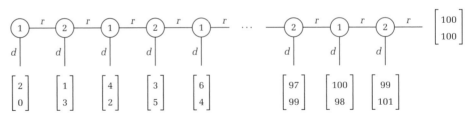

**Figure 7.13**
The centipede game. In the payoff vectors, the top number is Player 1's payoff, the bottom one Player 2's.

## APPLIED EXERCISES

■ **7.16. LABORATORY EXPERIMENT.** Run a laboratory experiment to test a specific prediction from game theory. First, convene a group of willing subjects (you may need to clear the experiment with the human subject review board at your institution). Second, write detailed instructions to explain to subjects what they are supposed to do. To the extent that it is possible, attach a financial reward to the subjects' performance in the experiment. Third, run the experiment and carefully keep track of all of the subjects' decisions. Finally, compare the observed results with the theoretical predictions, and discuss any differences there might exist between the two. (If a dedicated laboratory does not exist in your institution, use the classroom and your colleagues as a subject pool.)

## NOTES

1. Nash, John (1951), "Non-Cooperative Games," *Annals of Mathematics* **54**, 286–295.

2. A version of this experiment was first reported in Schelling, Thomas (1960), *The Strategy of Conflict*, Cambridge, MA: Harvard University Press.

3. Selten, Reinhard (1965), "Spieltheoretische Behandlung eines Oligopolmodells mit Nachfrageträgheit," *Zeitschrift für die gesamte Staatswissenschaft* **121**, 301–324, 667–689.

4. This exercise is adapted from Dixit, Avinash K., and Barry J. Nalebuff (1991), *Thinking Strategically*, New York: W W Norton.

5. *The Wall Street Journal*, March 9, 1993.

6. This game was first proposed by Rosenthal, Robert (1981), "Games of Perfect Information, Predatory Pricing and the Chain-Store Paradox," *Journal of Economic Theory* **25**, 92–100.

# OLIGOPOLY

So far, we have looked at the extreme market structures of monopoly and perfect competition. These are useful points of reference. However, empirical observation suggests that most real-world markets fall somewhere between the extremes. Normally, we find industries with a few (more than one) firms, but less that the "very large number" usually assumed by the model of perfect competition. The situation where there are a few competitors is designated by **oligopoly** (**duopoly** if the number is two).

One thing the extremes of monopoly and perfect competition have in common is that each firm need not worry about rivals' reactions. In the case of monopoly, this is trivial as there are no rivals. In the case of perfect competition, the idea is that each firm is so small that its actions have no significant impact on rivals. Not so in the case of oligopoly. Consider the following excerpt from a news article:

> In a strategic shift in the US and Canada, Coca-Cola Co. is gearing up to raise the prices it charges its customers for soft drinks by about 5%. The price changes could help boost Coke's profit.
>
> Important to the success of Coke and its bottlers is how Pepsi-Cola responds. The No. 2 soft-drink company could well sacrifice some margins to pick up market share on Coke, some analysts said.[1]

As this example suggests, in contrast with the extremes of monopoly and perfect competition, an important characteristic of oligopolies is the strategic interdependence among competitors: an action by Firm 1, say Coke, is likely to influence Firm 2's profits, say Pepsi, and vice versa. For this reason, Coke's decision process should take into account what it expects Pepsi to do, specifically, how Coke expects its decision to impact on Pepsi's profits and, consequently, how it expects Pepsi to react. Part II of this book is dedicated to the formal analysis of oligopoly competition. We begin in this chapter with some simple models that characterize the process of interdependent strategic decision-making under oligopoly: the Bertrand model and the Cournot model.

## 8.1 THE BERTRAND MODEL

Pricing is probably the most basic strategy that firms must decide on. The demand received by each firm depends on the price it sets. Moreover, when the number of firms is small, demand also depends on the prices set by rival firms. It is precisely this interdependence between rivals' decisions that differentiates duopoly competition (and more generally oligopoly competition) from the extremes of monopoly and perfect competition. When Lenovo, for example, decides what prices to set for its PCs, the company has to make some conjecture regarding the prices set by rival Dell (as well as other rivals); and based on this conjecture determine the optimal price, taking into account how demand for the Lenovo PC depends on both the Lenovo price and the Dell price.[a]

In order to analyze the interdependence of pricing decisions, we begin with the simplest model of duopoly competition: the Bertrand model.[2] The model consists of two firms in a market for a homogeneous product and the assumption that firms simultaneously set prices. We also assume that both firms have the same constant marginal cost, $MC = c$.[b]

Since the duopolists' products are perfect substitutes (the product is homogeneous), and since firms have no capacity constraints, it follows that whichever firm sets the lowest price gets all of the demand. Specifically, if $p_i$, the price set by firm $i$, is lower than $p_j$, the price set by firm $j$, then firm $i$'s demand is given by $D(p_i)$ (the market demand), whereas firm $j$'s demand is zero. If both firms set the same price, $p_i = p_j = p$, then each firm receives one half of market demand, $\frac{1}{2} D(p)$.

■ **THE DISCRETE BERTRAND GAME.** Let us first consider the case when sellers are restricted to a limited set of price levels. Specifically, suppose that market demand is given by $q = 10 - p$, marginal cost constant at 2, and sellers can only set integer values of price: 3, 4, and 5. Figure 8.1 describes the game in normal form (similarly to the games introduced in Chapter 7): Firm 1 chooses a row (5, 4, or 3), whereas Firm 2 chooses a column (5, 4, or 3). For each possible combination, profits are determined according to the rules described in the preceding paragraph. For example, if both firms set $p = 5$, then total demand is $q = 10 - 5 = 5$; and each firm's profit is given by $\pi = \frac{1}{2} 5 (5 - 2) = 7.5$. If Firm 1 sets $p_1 = 4$ whereas Firm 2 sets $p_2 = 5$, then Firm 1 captures all of the market demand, which is now given by $q = 10 - 4 = 6$. It follows that $\pi_1 = 6 (4 - 2) = 12$, whereas $\pi_2 = 0$. The remaining cells of the game matrix are obtained in a similar manner. (Check this.)

What is the game's equilibrium? First notice that there is no dominant strategy. I can however derive each firm's best response and from this derive the game's Nash equilibrium. Firm 1's best response mapping is as follows: if Firm 2 sets $p_2 = 5$, then Firm 1's optimal price is $p_1 = 4$; if Firm 2 sets $p_2 = 4$, then Firm 1's optimal price is $p_1 = 3$; and finally, if Firm 2 sets $p_2 = 3$ then Firm 1's optimal price is $p_1 = 3$. In words, Firm 1's best response is to undercut Firm 2 — unless Firm 2 is already setting the

a. Moreover, in a dynamic setting, Lenovo must also take into account that current price choices will likely influence the rival's future price choices. This we will focus on in Chapter 9.

b. The Bertrand model is more general than the simplified version presented here, but the main ideas are the same.

Firm 2

|  | 5 | 4 | 3 |
|---|---|---|---|
| **5** | 7.5 / 7.5 | 12 / 0 | 7 / 0 |
| **4** | 0 / 12 | 6 / 6 | 7 / 0 |
| **3** | 0 / 7 | 0 / 7 | 3.5 / 3.5 |

Firm 1

**FIGURE 8.1**
Bertrand game with limited number of price choices

lowest price. As a result, the Nash equilibrium corresponds to both firms setting the lowest price: $\widehat{p}_1 = \widehat{p}_2 = 3$.

Notice that, while the game is not, strictly speaking, a prisoner's dilemma, it does share some of the features of the prisoner's dilemma game (cf Section 7.1). Specifically, (a) both firms are better off by setting a high price; (b) however, given that both firms set a high price, both firms have an incentive to undercut the rival.

The above game is based on a number of simplifying assumptions. In particular, I am restricting firms to set prices at integer values (3, 4, or 5). What if Firm 1 could undercut $p_2 = 5$ by setting $p_1 = 4.99$? In the next paragraphs, I consider the more general case when firms can set any value of $p_i$, in fact any real value. As I will show, the main qualitative results and intuition remain valid. In fact, in some sense the result will be even more extreme.

■ **THE CONTINUOUS CASE.** Suppose that firms can set any value of $p$ from 0 to $+\infty$, including non-integer values. Now we are unable to describe the game as a matrix of strategies (there are infinitely many strategies). However, we can derive, as before, each firm's best response mapping, from which we can then derive the Nash equilibrium. Recall that firm $i$'s best response $p_i^*(p_j)$ is a mapping that gives, for each price by firm $j$, firm $i$'s optimal price. The only novelty with respect to the discrete case is that the values of $p_j$ and $p_i$ now vary continuously.

Suppose that Firm 1 expects Firm 2 to price above the monopoly price. Then Firm 1's optimal strategy is to price at the monopoly level. In fact, by doing so Firm 1 gets all of the demand and receives monopoly profits (the maximum possible profits). If Firm 1 expects Firm 2 to price below monopoly price but above marginal cost, then Firm 1's optimal strategy is to set a price just below Firm 2's:[c] pricing above would lead to zero demand and zero profits; and pricing below gives firm $i$ all of the market demand, but lower profits the lower the price is. Finally, if Firm 1 expects Firm 2 to price below marginal cost, then Firm 1's optimal choice is to price higher than Firm 2, say, at marginal cost level.

c. What does "just below" mean? If $p_1$ could be any real number, than "just below" would not be well defined: there exists no real number "just below" another real number. In practice, prices have to be set on a finite grid (in cents of the dollar, for example), in which case "just below" would mean one cent less. This points to an important assumption of the Bertrand model: Firm 1 will steal all of Firm 2's demand even if its price is only one cent lower than the rival's.

Figure 8.2 depicts Firm 1's best response, $p_1^*(p_2)$, in a graph with each firm's strategy on each axis. Consistent with the above derivation, for values of $p_2$ less than $MC$, Firm 1 chooses $p_1 = MC = c$. For values of $p_2$ greater than $MC$ but lower than $p^M$, Firm 1 chooses $p_1$ just below $p_2$. Finally, for values of $p_2$ greater than monopoly price, $p^M$, Firm 1 chooses $p_1 = p^M$.

Since Firm 2 has the same marginal cost as Firm 1, its best response is identical to Firm 1's, that is, symmetric with respect to the 45° line. In Figure 8.2, Firm 2's best response is given by $p_2^*(p_1)$.

As we saw in Section 7.1, a Nash equilibrium is a pair of strategies — a pair of prices, in the present case — such that no firm can increase profits by unilaterally changing price. In terms of Figure 8.2, this is given by the *intersection of the best responses*, that is, point N. In fact this is the point at which $p_1 = p_1^*(p_2)$ (because the point is on Firm 1's best response) and $p_2 = p_2^*(p_1)$ (because the point is on Firm 2's best response). As can be seen from Figure 8.2, point N corresponds to both firms setting a price equal to marginal cost, $\widehat{p}_1 = \widehat{p}_2 = MC = c$.

Another way of deriving the same conclusion is to think about a possible equilibrium price $p'$ greater than marginal cost. If both firms were to set that price, each would earn $\frac{1}{2}D(p')(p' - MC)$. However, setting a slightly smaller price, one of the firms would be able to almost double its profits to $D(p' - \epsilon)(p' - \epsilon - MC)$, where $\epsilon$ is a small number. This argument holds for any possible candidate equilibrium price $p'$ greater than marginal cost. We thus conclude that the only possible equilibrium price is $p = c$. In summary,

Under price competition with homogeneous product and constant, symmetric marginal cost (Bertrand competition), firms price at the level of marginal cost.

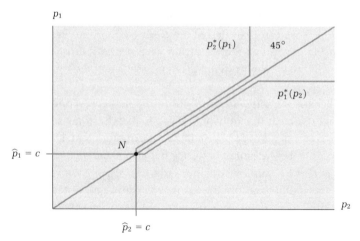

**FIGURE 8.2**
Bertrand model: best responses and equilibrium

---

### BOX 8.1 DIGITAL YELLOW PAGES: FROM MONOPOLY TO DUOPOLY TO OLIGOPOLY[3]

In 1987, Nynex began offering in digital form the entire telephone directory for the area the company then served (New York and New England). With a list price of $10,000, the CD product was primarily targeted at retailers, government departments, and financial service operators.

Soon after, Jim Bryant, the Nynex executive in charge of developing the new Nynex product, decided to leave the company and found Pro CD, a company devoted to publishing white and yellow page directories in electronic form.

Fearing competition, Nynex declined to offer the required data for Pro CD to compile his listing. Undeterred by this obstacle, Bryant sent physical copies of the directories to Asia, where he outsourced the task of typing them from scratch (and retyping, to check for errors). All in all, Pro CD created a mega-directory with more than 70 million entries.

Facing competition in the market for electronic directories, Nynex was forced to lower its price. By the early 1990s, sale prices were in the hundreds of dollars, down from the original $10,000 price tag. Meanwhile, additional entrants joined Pro CD in challenging Nynex's initial monopoly. By 2000, a complete directory could be bought for a mere $20.[d]

---

Notice that this result is valid even with only two competitors (as we have considered above). This is a fairly drastic result: as the number of competitors changes from one to two, the equilibrium price changes from the monopoly price to the perfect competition price. Two competitors are sufficient to guarantee perfect competition.

From a consumer welfare point of view, Bertrand competition is a tremendous boon. From the seller's point of view, however, it is a rather unattractive situation: the **Bertrand trap**, as some call it. Consider for example the case of encyclopedias.[4] *Encyclopedia Britannica* has been, for more than two centuries, a standard reference work. Until the 1990s, the 32-volume hardback set sold for $1,600. Then Microsoft entered the market with *Encarta*, which it sold on CDs for less than $100. *Britannica* responded by issuing its own CD version as well. By 2000, both *Britannica* and *Encarta* were selling for $89.99. While this is still far from the Bertrand equilibrium (price equal to the cost of the CDs) it is certainly closer to Bertrand than the initial, monopoly-like price of $1,600. Box 8.1 describes another example of how even one competitor can drive prices down tremendously.

Another example of pricing down to marginal cost is given by the airline industry at various moments during its tumultuous history. For example, in the spring of 1992 American Airlines announced a new "value pricing" plan. It replaced complex discounts with a simple, four-tier price system; and it cut fares considerably. AA was hoping that its competitors would follow its move, thus achieving a much needed period of stability. However, TWA and USAir announced even bigger fare cuts. American matched these, and in some cases surpassed them. The rest of the industry had no choice but to

d. Eventually, Pro CD became the first company to compile all of the published telephone directories in the United States and Canada. In 1996, it merged with Acxiom, a company that integrates data, services, and technology to create and deliver customer and information management solutions.

go along. The industry found itself plunged into a full-fledged price war, the collective cost of which (in a matter of months) was about four billion dollars.[5]

■ **AVOIDING THE BERTRAND TRAP.** There are many real-world markets where the number of firms is small — two or a few more — and firms compete on price, and still firm profits are positive — sometimes very large. (Can you think of some?) This seems to contradict the Bertrand model's prediction. How can we explain this apparent contradiction between theory and empirical observation? Put differently: if you consult with a firm competing in a price-setting duopoly, how do you help your client avoid the Bertrand trap? In what follows, I consider four different solutions, two of which I will develop in later chapters, two of which I will cover in the remainder of this section.

1. **PRODUCT DIFFERENTIATION.** The Bertrand model assumes that both firms sell the same product. If instead firms sell differentiated products, then duopoly price competition does not necessarily drive prices down to marginal cost as predicted by the Bertrand model. In fact, undercutting the rival does not guarantee that a firm will get total market demand. Take, for example, the cola market. In the US and in many other countries, Pepsi and Coke are the two main competitors. Brand allegiance tends to be very high and cross-price elasticity tends to be relatively close to zero. By lowering its price, Coke may increase its sales a bit, but it will certainly not capture all of the market demand (as assumed under Bertrand competition). The issues of product differentiation and brand allegiance are examined in Chapter 14.

2. **DYNAMIC COMPETITION.** The Bertrand model assumes that firms compete in one period only; that is, price is chosen once and for all. One of the likely consequences of undercutting a rival's price is that the latter will retaliate by lowering its price too, possibly initiating a price war. For example, if the BP gas station lowers its price today, it may attract additional customers who were previously filling up at the Exxon gas station across the street; but before long the Exxon gas station is bound to respond. In that case, undercutting does not guarantee a firm total market demand, except perhaps in the very short run. The possibility of retaliation is not considered in the Bertrand model because of its static nature. In the next chapter, I will consider dynamic games and show that, even when firms set prices and the product is homogeneous, there exist equilibria where price is strictly greater than marginal cost.

3. **ASYMMETRIC COSTS.** One important assumption in the simple version of the Bertrand model I considered above is that both firms have the same marginal cost. As I will show below, if one of the firms has a lower marginal cost (a "cost leader") then it is no longer true that both firms earn zero profits.

4. **CAPACITY CONSTRAINTS.** By undercutting the rival, a Bertrand duopolist receives all of the market demand. But what good is this if the firm does not have sufficient capacity to satisfy all of this demand? In other words, one important assumption of the Bertrand model is that firms have no capacity constraints. Below I show that, if there are capacity constraints, then the nature of competition may change considerably.[e]

■ **PRICE COMPETITION WITH DIFFERENT COSTS.** Consider the Portuguese wholesale gasoline market. There are essentially two sellers (that is, two supply sources): Galp, which owns all of the country's refineries; and imports. Typically, the import price is greater than Galp's cost. As a result, Galp supplies all retailers at the import price and effectively maintains a 100% market share in wholesale gasoline sales (that is, imports represent a very small share of total sales). In sum, although the product is relatively homogeneous and competition is based on price, Galp sells at a positive margin, the reason being that Galp has a lower marginal cost than its competitors.

The simple version of the Bertrand model I considered before assumed that both firms had the same marginal cost. Suppose now that one of the firms, say Firm 1, has a lower marginal cost than its rival. The situation is depicted in Figure 8.3. The best response curves are derived as before: firm $i$ undercuts the rival all the way down to the rival's marginal cost — that is, all the way down to firm $i$'s marginal cost. In this case, since Firm 1 has a lower marginal cost, its best response mapping extends to lower values than Firm 2's. As a result, the point where the two best responses cross — the Nash equilibrium of the game — is given by $p_2 = MC_2$ and $p_1 = MC_2 - \epsilon$; that is, Firm 1 just undercuts Firm 2 (who prices at marginal cost) and gets all of the market demand.

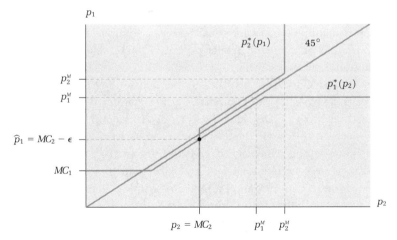

**FIGURE 8.3**
Bertrand equilibrium with different marginal costs

e. More generally, if marginal cost is increasing, then the price-equals-marginal-cost Bertrand equilibrium no longer holds. The case of capacity constraints can be thought of as the limit case of increasing marginal cost.

In other words, one way out of the Bertrand trap is to be a cost leader. For years, Dell managed to make considerable profits in a highly commoditized industry (desktop computers). Part of Dell's secret was to create a very efficient supplier system which effectively gave it a lower marginal cost. Unfortunately, others can play that game too: frequently, competitive advantages based on cost leadership are short lived.

To conclude this section, I should mention that the Bertrand model extends easily to the case when there are more than two firms (as is the case in the desktop computer and other industries). Basically, pick the two firms with the lowest marginal cost and apply the analysis above. For example, if Firm 1 has marginal cost $c_1 = 53$, whereas firms 2 and 3 have marginal cost $c_2 = c_3 = 55$, then Firm 1 sets $p_1 = 55$ and captures the entire market. If instead Firm 2 has $c_2 = 53$, then Firms 1 and 2 set $p_1 = p_2 = 53$ and share the market. And so on.

■ **PRICE COMPETITION WITH CAPACITY CONSTRAINTS.** Suppose now that each firm is constrained by its capacity, $k_i$. That is, firm $i$ cannot sell more than $k_i$: if its demand turns out to be greater than $k_i$, then its sales are $k_i$ only. Otherwise, we maintain the same assumptions as before: firms simultaneously set prices, marginal cost is constant (zero, for simplicity), and the product is homogeneous.

Under Bertrand competition, if Firm 2 were to set a price greater than Firm 1's, its demand would be zero. The same is not necessarily true if Firm 1 is capacity constrained. Suppose that $p_2 > p_1$ and that $D(p_1) > k_1$, that is, Firm 1 is capacity constrained. Firm 1's sales will be given by $k_1$: it will sell as much as it can. Firm 2's demand, in turn, will be given by $D(p_2) - k_1$ (or zero, if this expression is negative). $D(p_2)$ would be Firm 2's demand if it had no competition. Having a rival price below, some of that demand will be stolen, specifically, $k_1$. However, if $k_1$ is small enough, a positive residual demand will remain.[f]

f. For aficionados only: the above expression for firm $i$'s residual demand, $D(p_i) - k_j$, is only valid under the assumption that the customers served by firm $j$ are the ones with the greatest willingness to pay.[6]

g. $D(p)$, the direct demand curve (or simply demand curve), corresponds to taking price as the independent variable, that is, quantity as a function of price; $P(Q)$, the inverse demand curve, corresponds to taking quantity as the independent variable, that is, price as a function of quantity. See Section 2.1.

The situation of price competition with capacity constraints is illustrated in Figure 8.4. $D(p)$ is the demand curve. Two vertical lines represent each firm's capacity. In this example, Firm 2 is the one with greater capacity: $k_2 > k_1$. The third vertical line, $k_1 + k_2$, represents total industry capacity.

Let $P(Q)$ be the inverse demand curve, that is, the inverse of $D(p)$.[g] Moreover, let $P(k_1 + k_2)$ be the price level such that, if both firms were to set $p = P(k_1 + k_2)$, total demand would be exactly equal to total capacity. This price level is simply derived from the intersection of the demand curve with the total capacity curve. I will now argue that the equilibrium of the price-setting game consists of both firms setting $p_i = P(k_1 + k_2)$. In other words, firms set prices such that total demand equals industry capacity.

Let us consider Firm 2's optimization problem assuming that Firm 1 sets $p_1 = P(k_1 + k_2)$. Can Firm 2 do better than setting $p_2 = p_1 = P(k_1 + k_2)$? One alternative strategy is to set $p_2 < P(k_1 + k_2)$. By undercutting its rival, Firm 2 receives all of the market demand. However, since Firm 2 is already capacity constrained when it sets $p_2 = P(k_1 + k_2)$, setting a lower price does not help: on the contrary, Firm 2 receives lower profits by setting a lower price (same output sold at a lower price).

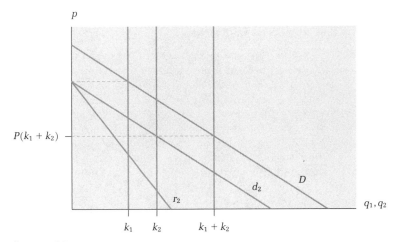

**FIGURE 8.4**
Capacity constraints

What about setting a price higher than $P(k_1 + k_2)$? The idea is that, since Firm 1 is capacity constrained when $p_1 = P(k_1 + k_2)$, Firm 2 will receive positive demand even if it prices above Firm 1. Figure 8.4 depicts Firm 2's residual demand, $d_2$, under the assumption that $p_2 > p_1$ and $p_1 = P(k_1 + k_2)$: Firm 2 gets $D(p_2)$ minus Firm 1's output, $k_1$, so $d_2$ is parallel to $D$, the difference being $k_1$. The figure also depicts Firm 2's marginal revenue curve, $r_2$. As can be seen, marginal revenue is greater than marginal cost (zero) for every value of output less than Firm 2's capacity. This implies that setting a higher price than $P(k_1 + k_2)$, which is the same as selling a lower output than $q_2 = k_2$, would imply a lower profit: the revenue loss (the positive marginal revenue) is greater than the cost saving (the value of marginal cost, which is zero).

A similar argument would hold for Firm 1 as well: given that $p_2 = P(k_1 + k_2)$, Firm 1's optimal strategy is to set $p_1 = P(k_1 + k_2)$. We thus conclude that $p_1 = p_2 = P(k_1 + k_2)$ is indeed an equilibrium. Notice that, if capacity levels were very high, then the above argument would not hold; that is, it might be optimal for a firm to undercut its rival's price. However, if capacities are relatively small, then the result obtains that *equilibrium prices are such that total demand equals total capacity*.[7] In summary:

> If total industry capacity is low in relation to market demand, then equilibrium prices are greater than marginal cost.

Conversely, if industry capacity is very high, then an equilibrium with positive margins may turn into the Bertrand trap we saw earlier. Box 8.2 summarizes the case of World-Com and the long-distance telecommunications industry: a glut of fiber optic capacity

**BOX 8.2 WORLDCOM AND THE US TELECOMS PRICE WARS[8]**

After merging with MCI in 1998, WorldCom became one of the leading players in the global telecom industry. Central to WorldCom's strategy was tapping into the Internet's rapid growth by expanding fiber optic capacity. The company's mantra — shared by many industry analysts — was that Internet traffic was doubling every 100 days.

Unfortunately, WorldCom was not the only game in town: "In 1998 anyone who announced plans to lay fiber could get $1 billion from Wall Street, no questions asked." And many did. Moreover, the estimates of the growth in Internet traffic turned out to be wildly exaggerated: what happened in the early 1990s was no longer true by the late 1990s.

As a result, the telecom industry imploded. Excess capacity fueled vicious price wars. Many startups filed for bankruptcy, dumping their capacity on the market at bargain-basement prices. Meanwhile, the long-reliable long-distance voice market lost share to wireless. WorldCom wasn't immune to these events, and its stock price fell by 70% during 2000.

One analyst summarized the events as follow: "WorldCom's main transgression was to pour gasoline on the Internet fire. The technological revolution was pretty powerful as it was, but WorldCom made it much worse than it would have been."

pushed prices down to marginal cost, leading many firms to bankruptcy and sowing the seeds of WorldCom's eventual demise.

## 8.2 THE COURNOT MODEL

In the previous section, we concluded that, if firms' sales are limited by the capacity they built beforehand, then in equilibrium firms set prices such that total demand just clears total capacity. The same applies for the choice of output level, to the extent that firms must first produce a certain amount and then set prices to sell the output previously produced. This analysis can be taken one step back: what output levels should firms choose in the first place? Suppose that output decisions are made simultaneously before prices are chosen. Based on the above analysis, firms know that, for each pair of output choices $(q_1, q_2)$, equilibrium prices will be $p_1 = p_2 = P(q_1 + q_2)$. This implies that firm $i$'s profit is given by $\pi_i = q_i(P(q_1 + q_2) - c)$, assuming, as before, constant marginal cost.

The game where firms simultaneously choose output levels is known as the Cournot model.[9] Specifically, suppose there are two firms in a market for a homogeneous product. Firms choose simultaneously the quantity they want to produce. The market price is then set at the level such that demand equals the total quantity produced by both firms.

As in Section 8.1, our goal is to derive the equilibrium of game played between the two firms. Also as in Section 8.1, I do so in two steps. First, I derive each firm's optimal choice given its conjecture of what the rival does, that is, the firm's best response. Second, I put the best response mappings together and find a mutually consistent combination of actions and conjectures.

Suppose that Firm 1 believes Firm 2 is producing quantity $q_2$. What is Firm 1's optimal quantity? The answer is provided by Figure 8.5. If Firm 1 decides not to produce anything, then price is given by $P(0 + q_2) = P(q_2)$. If Firm 1 instead produces $q_1'$, then price is given by $P(q_1' + q_2) = 0$. More generally, for each quantity that Firm 1 might decide to set, price is given by the curve $d_1(q_2)$, which is referred to as Firm 1's **residual demand**: it gives all possible combinations of Firm 1's quantity and price *for a given a value of $q_2$*.

Having derived Firm 1's residual demand, the task of finding Firm 1's optimum is now similar to finding the optimum under monopoly, which I have already done in Section 3.2. Basically, we must determine the point where marginal revenue equals marginal cost. Marginal cost is constant by assumption and equal to $c$. Marginal revenue is a line with twice the slope of $d_1(q_2)$ and with the same vertical intercept.[h] The point at which the two lines intersect corresponds to quantity $q_1^*(q_2)$, Firm 1's best response to Firm 2's strategy.

Notice that Firm 1's optimum, $q_1^*(q_2)$, depends on its belief of what Firm 2 chooses. In order to find an equilibrium, I am interested in deriving Firm 1's optimum for other possible values of $q_2$. Figure 8.5 considers two other possible values of $q_2$. If $q_2 = 0$, then Firm 1's residual demand is effectively the market demand: $d_1(0) \equiv D$. The optimal solution, not surprisingly, is for Firm 1 to chose the monopoly quantity: $q_1^*(0) = q^M$, where $q^M$ is the monopoly quantity. If Firm 2 were to chose the quantity corresponding to perfect competition, that is $q_2 = q^c$, where $q^c$ is such that $P(q^c) = c$, then Firm 1's optimum would be to produce zero: $q_1^*(q^c) = 0$. In fact, this is the point at which marginal cost intercepts the marginal revenue corresponding to $d_1(q^c)$.

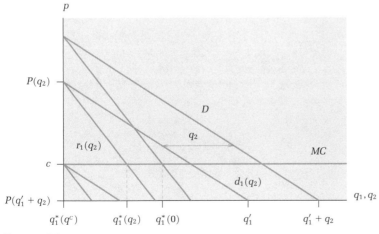

h. This results from our assumption that demand is linear. In general, the marginal revenue curve has the same intercept as the demand curve and a higher slope (in absolute value), not necessarily twice the slope of the demand curve.

**FIGURE 8.5**
Firm 1's optimum

It can be shown that, given a linear demand and constant marginal cost, the function $q_1^*(q_2)$ — Firm 1's best response mapping — is also linear. Since we have two points, we can draw the entire function $q_1^*(q_2)$. This is done in Figure 8.6. Notice that the axes are now different from the previous figures. On the horizontal axis, I continue measuring quantities, specifically, Firm 2's quantity, $q_2$. On the vertical axis, I now measure Firm 1's quantity, $q_1$, not price.

---

**ALGEBRAIC DERIVATION.** Throughout this chapter, in parallel with the graphical derivation of equilibria, I also present the corresponding algebraic derivation. Except for some results in the next section, algebra is not necessary for the derivation of the main results; but it may help, especially if you are familiar with basic algebra and calculus. Let me start with the algebraic derivation of Firm 1's best response. Suppose that (inverse) demand is given by $P(Q) = a - bQ$, whereas cost is given by $C(q) = cq$, where $q$ is the firm's output and $Q = q_1 + q_2$ is total output.

Firm 1's profit is:

$$\pi_1 = Pq_1 - C(q_1) = \left(a - b(q_1 + q_2)\right)q_1 - cq_1$$

The first-order condition for the maximization of $\pi_1$ with respect to $q_1$, $\partial\pi_1/\partial q_1 = 0$, is:

$$-bq_1 + a - b(q_1 + q_2) - c = 0$$

or simply:

$$q_1 = \frac{a-c}{2b} - \frac{q_2}{2}$$

Since this gives the optimum $q_1$ for each value of $q_2$, I have just derived the Firm 1's best response, $q_1^*(q_2)$:

$$q_1^*(q_2) = \frac{a-c}{2b} - \frac{q_2}{2} \tag{8.1}$$

---

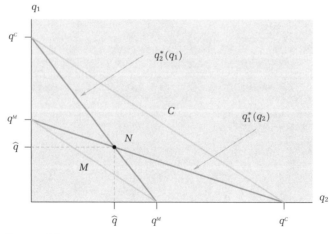

**FIGURE 8.6**
Cournot model: best responses and equilibrium

We are now ready for the last step in our analysis, that of finding the equilibrium. An equilibrium is a point at which firms choose optimal quantities given what they conjecture the other firm does; and those conjectures are correct. Specifically, an equilibrium will correspond to a pair of values $(q_1, q_2)$ such that $q_1$ is Firm 1's optimal response given $q_2$ and, conversely, $q_2$ is Firm 2's optimal response given $q_1$.

I have not derived Firm 2's best response. However, given our assumption that both firms have the same cost function, we conclude that Firm 2's best response, $q_2^*(q_1)$, is the symmetric of Firm 1's. I can thus proceed to plot the two best responses in the same graph, as in Figure 8.6.

As in the case of the Bertrand model (see Section 8.1), the equilibrium point in the Cournot model is then given by the intersection of the best response mappings, point $N$. In fact, this is the point at which $q_1 = q_1^*(q_2)$ (because the point is on Firm 1's best response) and $q_2 = q_2^*(q_1)$ (because the point is on Firm 2's best response).[i]

**ALGEBRAIC DERIVATION (CONT.).** I now proceed with our algebraic derivation. In equilibrium, it must be that Firm 1 chooses an output that is optimal given what it expects Firm 2's output to be. If Firm 1 expects Firm 2 to produce $q_2^e$, then it must be $\widehat{q}_1 = q_1^*(q_2^e)$. Moreover, in equilibrium Firm 1's conjecture regarding Firm 2's choice should be correct: $q_2^e = \widehat{q}_2$. Together, these conditions imply that $\widehat{q}_1 = q_1^*(\widehat{q}_2)$. The same conditions apply for Firm 2, that is, in equilibrium it must also be the case that $\widehat{q}_2 = q_2^*(\widehat{q}_1)$. An equilibrium is thus defined by the system of equations:

$$\widehat{q}_1 = q_1^*(\widehat{q}_2)$$
$$\widehat{q}_2 = q_2^*(\widehat{q}_1)$$

Equation (8.1) gives Firm 1's best response. I can thus write the first equation of the above system as:

$$\widehat{q}_1 = \frac{a-c}{2b} - \frac{\widehat{q}_2}{2}$$

Since the two firms are identical (same cost function), the equilibrium will also be symmetric, that is, $\widehat{q}_1 = \widehat{q}_2 = \widehat{q}$.[j] We thus have:

$$\widehat{q} = \frac{a-c}{2b} - \frac{\widehat{q}}{2}$$

Solving for $\widehat{q}$, this yields:

$$\widehat{q} = \frac{a-c}{3b}$$

■ **MONOPOLY, DUOPOLY, AND PERFECT COMPETITION.** Duopoly is an intermediate market structure, between monopoly (maximum concentration of market shares) and perfect competition (minimum concentration of market shares). One would expect equilibrium price and output under duopoly also to lie between the extremes of monopoly and perfect competition.

This fact can be checked based on Figure 8.6. Recall that each firm's best response intercepts the axes at the values $q^M$ and $q^C$. Therefore, a line with slope $-1$ intersecting the axes at the farther extremes of the best response mappings unites all points such

i. The equilibrium concept I am using here is that of Nash equilibrium, or Nash-Cournot equilibrium, thus the notation $N$. In general, more than one equilibrium can exist. However, when the demand curve is linear and marginal cost is constant, there exists one equilibrium only.

j. For aficionados: in general, the fact that a game is symmetric does not imply that its equilibrium is symmetric as well. However, when best responses are linear as in the present case, symmetry of the model implies symmetry (and uniqueness) of the equilibrium.

that $\widehat{q}_1 + \widehat{q}_2 = q^C$ (line $C$ in Figure 8.6). Likewise, a line with slope $-1$ intersecting the axes at the closer extremes of the best response mappings unites all points such that $\widehat{q}_1 + \widehat{q}_2 = q^M$ (line $M$ in Figure 8.6). We can see that the Cournot equilibrium point, $N$, lies between these two lines. This implies that total output under Cournot is greater than under monopoly and lower than under perfect competition.

To summarize,

> Under output competition (Cournot), equilibrium output is greater than monopoly output and lower than perfect competition output. Likewise, the duopoly price is lower than the monopoly price and greater than the price under perfect competition.

See Exercise 8.18 for the analytical version of this idea.

To conclude this section, I should mention that the Cournot equilibrium extends to the case of firms with different marginal costs as well as to the case when there are more than two competitors, both of which are quite relevant in the real world. Below I consider the $n$ firm case when all firms have the same cost. In Section 8.4 I derive the equilibrium of a Cournot duopoly with different marginal costs. Finally, Exercise 8.15 takes you through the more general case of an $n$ firm Cournot oligopoly with asymmetric firms.

---

**THE $n$ FIRM CASE.** Suppose, as before, that (inverse) demand is given by $P(Q) = a - bQ$, whereas cost is given by $C(q) = cq$, where $q$ is a given firm's output and $Q = q_1 + q_2 + \ldots + q_n$ is total output in an $n$ firm Cournot oligopoly.

Firm 1's profit is:

$$\pi_1 = P q_1 - C(q_1) = (a - bQ) q_1 - c q_1$$

The first-order condition for the maximization of $\pi_1$ with respect to $q_1$, $\partial \pi_1 / \partial q_1 = 0$, is:

$$-b q_1 + a - b Q - c = 0$$

In a symmetric equilibrium, $q_1 = q_2 = \ldots = q$, whereas $Q = nq$. Therefore, the above equation becomes:

$$-bq + a - bnq - c = 0$$

or simply:

$$q = \frac{a - c}{(n + 1) b}$$

Substituting back into the inverse demand curve we get:

$$p = \frac{a + nc}{n + 1}$$

which shows that, as $n \to \infty$, $p \to c$, that is, as the number of competitors grows large, the equilibrium price under Cournot competition converges to the competitive price level (which is also the equilibrium under Bertrand competition).

---

■ **A "DYNAMIC" INTERPRETATION OF THE COURNOT EQUILIBRIUM.** It is easy to understand why the Cournot equilibrium is a stable solution: no firm would have an incentive to choose a different output. In other words, each firm is choosing an optimal strategy given the strategy chosen by its rival. But: is the Cournot equilibrium a realistic prediction of what will happen in reality?

The equilibrium concept we have used is that of Nash equilibrium, first introduced in Section 7.1. There I presented a variety of possible justifications for the concept of Nash equilibrium. Here I present an argument, first proposed by Cournot himself, which is similar to the idea of elimination of dominated strategies.

Although the Cournot model is a static game, consider the following dynamic interpretation. At time $t = 1$, Firm 1 chooses some output level. Then, at time $t = 2$, Firm 2 chooses the optimal output level given Firm 1's output choice. At time $t = 3$, it's again Firm 1's turn to choose an optimal output given Firm 2's current output; and so on: Firm 1 chooses output at odd time periods, and Firm 2 at even time periods.

Figure 8.7 gives an idea of what this dynamic process might look like. We start from a point in the horizontal axis ($q_2^\circ$, Firm 2's output at time zero). At time $t = 1$, we move vertically towards Firm 1's best response (Firm 1 is optimizing). At time $t = 2$, we move horizontally to Firm 2's best response (Firm 2 is optimizing). At time $t = 3$, we move again vertically toward Firm 1's best response. And so on. As can be seen from the figure, the dynamic process converges to the Cournot equilibrium. In fact, *no matter what the initial situation, we always converge to the Nash equilibrium.* This is reassuring, insofar as it provides an additional motivation for the idea of Cournot equilibrium.

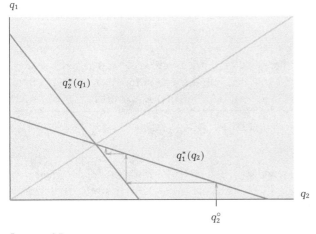

**FIGURE 8.7**
Convergence to Cournot equilibrium

## 8.3 BERTRAND VS. COURNOT

The two models of duopoly competition presented in the previous sections, though similar in assumptions, are in stark contrast when it comes to predicted behavior. The Cournot model predicts that price under duopoly is lower than monopoly price but greater than under perfect competition. The Bertrand model, by contrast, predicts that duopoly competition is sufficient to drive prices down to marginal cost level, that is, two firms are sufficient to bring price down to the price level under perfect competition.

This contrast suggests two questions: which model is more realistic? Why should we consider more than one model instead of just choosing the "best" one? The answer to both questions is that industries differ; and some industries are more realistically described by the Cournot model, whereas other industries are more realistically described by the Bertrand model.

Specifically, suppose that firms must make capacity (or output) decisions in addition to pricing decisions. In this context, the crucial aspect that selects Cournot or Bertrand as the right model is the relative timing of each decision (output and pricing). As I showed in Section 7.2, games with two strategic decisions are best modeled as two-stage games, with the long-run decisions taken in the first stage and the short-run decisions taken in the second one. The idea is that short-run decisions (second stage) are taken *given* the values of long-run decisions (first stage).

Suppose that capacity or output is a long-run decision with respect to prices. In other words, suppose that it is easier to adjust price than it is to adjust capacity or output. Then, the "right" model is one where firms first set capacity and output; and then prices. From the analysis of the previous sections, we know this corresponds to the Cournot model.

By contrast, suppose that output is a short-run decision with respect to prices, that is, it is easier to adjust output levels than it is to adjust prices. Then, the "right" model is one where firms first set prices and then output levels. Although we have not presented the Bertrand model as such, this is essentially what it corresponds to. In the Bertrand model, firms simultaneously set prices and receive demand based on those prices. Implicitly, this assumes that firms produce an output exactly equal to the quantity demanded, that is, output is perfectly adjusted to the quantity demanded at the prices (initially) set by firms.

To summarize:

> If capacity and output can be adjusted easily, then the Bertrand model describes duopoly competition better. If output and capacity are difficult to adjust, then the Cournot model describes duopoly competition better.

Most real-world industries seem closer to the case when capacity is difficult to adjust. In other words, capacity or output decisions are normally the long-run variable, prices being set in the short run. Examples include wheat, cement, steel, cars, computers. Consider, for instance, the market for video-game consoles. On August 1999, Sony cut the price of its system from \$129 to \$99. *One hour* after Sony's price-change press release, Nintendo published its own release announcing a price cut to match Sony's.[10] Another example is given by car services in New York City: in the summer of 2014, Gett began offering its customers rides anywhere in Manhattan for \$10. Uber, a rival service, swiftly lowered their own fares by 20%. Lyft, a third company, began offering three free rides to new customers.[11] In both of these examples prices appear to adjust more easily than quantities. The Cournot model would then seem a better approximation to industry behavior.

There are, however, situations where capacities — or at least output levels — adjust more rapidly than prices. Examples include software, insurance, and banking. A software company, for example, can easily produce additional copies of its software almost on demand; sometimes, in fact, it will simply ship a copy electronically. In this sense, the Bertrand model would provide a better approximation than the Cournot model.[k]

■ **ESTIMATING OLIGOPOLY EQUILIBRIA.** Is there any way we can estimate the nature of competition by looking at market data? The short answer is: yes, but it can be quite tricky. In what follows, I present a somewhat longer answer.

Consider the Bertrand model with equal and constant marginal costs. As I showed in Section 8.1, in equilibrium price is equal to marginal cost. This implies that, if cost changes by \$1, then price also changes by \$1. In other words, the Bertrand model implies a **pass through** rate of 1. Suppose instead that we have a Cournot duopoly with equal and constant marginal costs and with inverse demand given by $P(Q) = a - bQ$. As I showed in Section 8.2, in equilibrium each firm's output is given by $\widehat{q} = \frac{a-c}{3b}$. This in turn implies an equilibrium price of $\widehat{p} = \frac{a+2c}{3}$. (Check this.) Thus a \$1 increase in cost implies an increase in equilibrium price of \$$\frac{2}{3}$; in other words, the pass through rate is now $\frac{2}{3}$.

If we have data on prices and quantities for different values of cost — either due to geographical variation or due to variation over time — then we can in principle test between these two models (assuming linear demand). In fact, we might as well add collusion to the pile: if the two firms were to select prices and quantities as a monopoly, then their optimal price would be $p = \frac{a+c}{2}$, as I showed in Section 3.2. This time we would predict a pass-through rate of 50%.

The problem with this approach is that it depends on what assumption we make regarding the demand curve. Suppose that, instead of linear demand, we have constant-elasticity demand. As I showed in Section 3.2, a monopolist (or a duopoly acting as a monopoly) would set price at $p = c/(1 + 1/\epsilon)$, where $\epsilon$ is the price elasticity of demand. Suppose for example that $\epsilon = -2$. Then we have $\partial p/\partial c = 2$. (Check this.) In other words, the pass-through rate for a monopolist is now 2. More generally, while the pass-through rate under Bertrand (or under perfect competition) is always 1, under Cournot or monopoly the pass through rate depends on the shape of the demand curve.

k. There are, however, other aspects to be taken into account in an industry like software: product differentiation (cf Chapter 14) and network effects (cf Chapter 16).

If we have information about costs, then our task becomes a lot simpler. If the Bertrand equilibrium better describes market interaction — and if marginal costs are similar across firms — then we should observe price close to marginal cost; whereas, under Cournot competition or monopoly behavior, we should observe price greater than marginal cost. There is still an important statistical inference problem: a positive price-cost margin results from a certain degree of monopoly pricing and from a certain demand elasticity; what is the relative contribution of each for the observed data?

## 8.4   THE MODELS AT WORK: COMPARATIVE STATICS

What is the use of solving models and deriving equilibria? Models are simplified descriptions of reality, a way of understanding a particular situation. Once we understand how a given market works, we can use the model to run a **counterfactual**, that is, to predict how the market changes as a function of changes in various exogenous conditions, e.g., the price of an input or of a substitute product. This exercise is known in economics as **comparative statics**: the meaning of the expression is that we compare two equilibria, with two sets of exogenous conditions, and predict how a shift in one variable will influence the other variables. The word "statics" implies that we are not predicting the dynamic path that takes us from one equilibrium to the other, but rather answering the question, "once all of the adjustments have taken place and we are back in equilibrium, what will things look like."

In this section, I look at some examples of how the Cournot and Bertrand models can be used to perform comparative statics. Some of the practice and challenge exercises at the end of the chapter take the idea of comparative statics a few steps further.

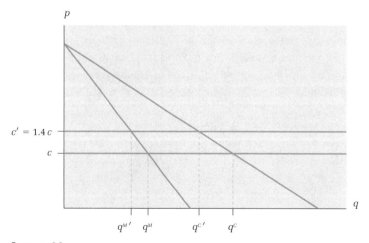

**FIGURE 8.8**
Optimal solution after increase in marginal cost

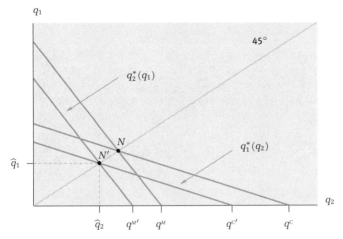

**FIGURE 8.9**
Cournot equilibrium after increase in marginal cost ($N'$)

■ **INPUT COSTS AND OUTPUT PRICE.** Suppose the market for transatlantic flights between London and New York is served by two firms, American Airlines (AA) and British Airways (BA). Both firms have the same marginal cost, which can be divided into labor costs (50%) and fuel (50%), and is initially at $300. Suppose fuel costs go up by 80%. What will happen to transatlantic airfares between London and New York?

Suppose AA and BA compete *à la* Cournot. This assumption might be justified, in line with the discussion in the previous section, by the fact that firms must decide beforehand how much capacity (aircraft) to allocate to the market.

Looking back at the graphical derivation of the Cournot equilibrium (page 195), we see that each firm's best response depends on its marginal cost.[1] We should thus compute a new best response based on the higher value of marginal cost. In Figure 8.8, we compute the new $q_1^*(0)$ (that is, $q^{M'}$), and the new value $q^{c'}$ such that $q_1^*(q^{c'}) = 0$, the two extreme points of the best response. Based on these extreme points, we can draw the new best response. This is done in Figure 8.9. Notice how, under Cournot competition, an increase in marginal cost implies a downward shift of the best response. This is an important fact which will reappear in different applications.

By symmetry, we know that both firms will experience the same shift in their best response. We thus have everything that is needed in order to determine the new equilibrium, which is depicted in Figure 8.9. The new equilibrium point is denoted by $N'$. For comparison, the previous equilibrium, $N$, is also shown. As expected, each firm's output as well as total output are lower in the new equilibrium; it follows that price is higher.

**ALGEBRAIC DERIVATION.** Let us now solve the problem algebraically. As we saw in Section 8.2, the equilibrium output in a (symmetric) Cournot equilibrium is

1. Firm 1's best response depends on the rival's output but not on the rival's marginal cost. *In equilibrium*, the rival's output will depend on its marginal cost, so that, *indirectly*, Firm 1's output will depend on Firm 2's marginal cost. However, when we talk about the best response, what is important is whether Firm 1's output depends *directly* on Firm 2's marginal cost, which is not the case.

given by:

$$\widehat{q} = \frac{a - c}{3\,b}$$

Total output is therefore:

$$\widehat{Q} = 2\,\frac{a - c}{3\,b}$$

Substituting in the demand function, we obtain equilibrium price:

$$\widehat{p} = a - b\widehat{Q}$$
$$= a - b\,2\,\frac{a - c}{3\,b}$$
$$= \frac{a + 2\,c}{3} \qquad\qquad (8.2)$$

We thus have:

$$\frac{d\widehat{p}}{dc} = \frac{2}{3}$$

In economics jargon, we say that the **pass through rate** is $\frac{2}{3} \approx 66\%$. To put a dollar value on the price change, note that an 80% increase in fuel costs implies a $80\% \times 50\% = 40\%$ increase in marginal cost, or a $40\% \times 300 = \$120$ increase. This increase in marginal cost is experienced by both firms. It follows that price increases by $\frac{2}{3} \times 120 = \$80$.

---

■ **EXCHANGE RATE FLUCTUATIONS AND MARKET SHARES.** Consider a duopoly with two different firms from two different countries. For example, two producers of microchips, one in Japan (Firm 1) and one in the US (Firm 2). The market for microchips is in US dollars (that is, all sales are made in US dollars). However, the costs of the Japanese firm are paid in Japanese yen. (The American firm's costs are in US dollars.)

Suppose that firms compete *à la* Cournot. In fact, this is one case where the reduced-form interpretation of the Cournot model seems appropriate: firms set production capacities and then set prices (given capacities), the result of the two-stage game being identical to Cournot competition.

In an initial equilibrium, both firms have the same cost and the market is divided equally between the two. Moreover, equilibrium price is $p = \$24$. One question which comparative statics might help to answer is: what is the impact on market shares of a 50% devaluation of the yen?

Since the market is in US dollars, a shift in the exchange rate will change the Japanese firm's marginal cost *in dollars*, while keeping the US firm's marginal cost constant. Specifically, suppose that both firms start with marginal cost $c$. Then the Japanese firms marginal cost will change to $c/e$ as a result of the devaluation, where $e$ is the exchange rate in yen/$.

For example, suppose marginal cost was initially \$12 for the US firm and ¥1200 for the Japanese firm; and that the initial exchange rate was 100 Y/$. This implies that the Japanese firm's marginal cost in US dollars was $1200/100 = \$12$. A 50% devaluation of the yen means that \$1 is now worth Y150. The Japanese firm's marginal cost in US dollars is now $1200/150 = \$8$. We thus have to compute the new equilibrium where one of the firm's marginal cost is lower.

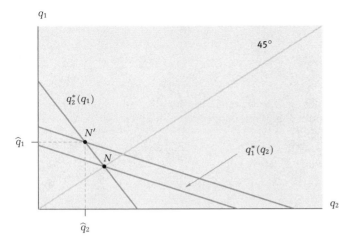

**FIGURE 8.10**
Cournot equilibrium after exchange rate devaluation

In the previous application, we saw that an increase in marginal cost implies a downward shift in the best response. By analogy, we now deduce that the Japanese firm's best response will shift upwards as a result of the reduction in its marginal cost (in US dollars). Since only the Japanese firm's best response has changed, we are now ready to determine the equilibrium shifts resulting from a yen devaluation. This is done in Figure 8.10, where the Japanese firm's output is measured on the vertical axis and the American firm's on the horizontal one. As can be seen, the new equilibrium point $N'$ is above the $45°$ line, that is, the Japanese firm's output is now greater than the American firm's. This is not surprising, as the Japanese firm has decreased its cost (in US dollars), whereas the US firm's cost remained unchanged.

---

**ALGEBRAIC COMPUTATION.** The graphical analysis has the limitation that it is difficult to determine the precise value of market shares. The best strategy is then to solve the model algebraically, which I do now. The first thing I must do is to determine the Cournot equilibrium for the asymmetric case. From Section 8.2, we know that a firm's best response is given by:

$$q_1^*(q_2) = \frac{a - c}{2b} - \frac{q_2}{2}$$

where $c$ is marginal cost. Let Firms 1 and 2 marginal cost now be given by $c_1$ and $c_2$, respectively. The two best response mappings are then given by:

$$q_1^*(q_2) = \frac{a - c_1}{2b} - \frac{q_2}{2}$$

$$q_2^*(q_1) = \frac{a - c_2}{2b} - \frac{q_1}{2}$$

Substituting the first equation for $q_1$ in the second and imposing the equilibrium condition $q_2 = q_2^*(q_1)$, we get:

$$q_2 = \frac{a - c_2}{2b} - \frac{\frac{a-c_1}{2b} - \frac{q_2}{2}}{2}$$

Solving for $q_2$, we get:

$$\widehat{q}_2 = \frac{a - 2c_2 + c_1}{3b}$$

Likewise,

$$\widehat{q}_1 = \frac{a - 2c_1 + c_2}{3b} \tag{8.3}$$

(The latter expression is obtained by symmetry; all we have to do is to interchange the subscripts 1 and 2.) Total quantity is given by:

$$\widehat{Q} = \widehat{q}_1 + \widehat{q}_2 = \frac{2a - c_1 - c_2}{3b} \tag{8.4}$$

Finally, Firm 1's market share. $s_1$, is given by:

$$s_1 = \frac{q_1}{q_1 + q_2} = \frac{a - 2c_1 + c_2}{2a - c_1 - c_2} \tag{8.5}$$

It can be shown that $s_1 > s_2$ if and only if $c_1 < c_2$. (Can you do it?) It follows that, by decreasing its cost below its rival, the Japanese firm's market share is greater than the American's.

---

**CALIBRATION.** I would like to go beyond the expression on the right-hand side of (8.5) and put an actual number to the value of $s_1$. So far, all I know is that, initially, $c_1 = c_2$, whereas, after the devaluation, $c_2$ remains constant at \$12, whereas $c_1$ drops to $12/1.5 = \$8$. As can be seen from (8.5), I need to obtain the value of $a$ in order to derive the numerical value of $s_1$. The process of obtaining specific values for the model parameters based on observable information about the equilibrium is know as **model calibration**.

Earlier, I determined that, in a symmetric Cournot duopoly,

$$p = \frac{a + 2c}{3}$$

where $c$ is the value of marginal cost and $a$ the intercept of the inverse demand curve. Solving with respect to $a$ and plugging in the values observed in the initial equilibrium, I get:

$$a = 3p - 2c = 3 \times 24 - 2 \times 12 = 48$$

Given this value of $a$ and given $c_1 = 8$ and $c_2 = 12$, I can now use (8.5) to compute the Japanese firm's market share:

$$s_1 = \frac{48 - 2 \times 8 + 12}{2 \times 48 - 8 - 12} \approx 58\%$$

In summary, a 50% devaluation of the yen increases the Japanese firm's market share to 58% from an initial 50%.

---

■ **NEW TECHNOLOGY AND PROFITS.** Consider the industry for some chemical product, a commodity that is supplied by two firms. Firm 1 uses an old technology and pays a marginal cost of \$15. Firm 2 uses a modern technology and pays a marginal cost of \$12. In the current equilibrium, price is at \$20 per ton and output 13 million tons. How much would Firm 1 be willing to pay for the modern technology?

Quite simply, the amount that Firm 1 should be willing to pay for the technology is the difference between its profits with lower marginal cost and its current profits.

We thus have to determine Firm 1's equilibrium profits in two possible equilibria and compute the difference. In a way, this problem is the reverse of the one examined before. In the case of exchange-rate devaluation, we started from a symmetric duopoly and moved to an asymmetric one. Now, we start from an asymmetric duopoly (Firm 2 has lower marginal cost) and want to examine the shift to a symmetric duopoly, whereby Firm 1 produces at the same marginal cost as its rival.

---

**ALGEBRAIC DERIVATION.** From (8.4), we know that total output is given by:

$$\widehat{Q} = \widehat{q}_1 + \widehat{q}_2 = \frac{2a - c_1 - c_2}{3b}$$

Substituting in the demand function, we get:

$$\widehat{p} = a - b\widehat{Q} = \frac{a + c_1 + c_2}{3} \tag{8.6}$$

(Notice that, in the particular case when $c_1 = c_2 = c$, we get (8.2), the equilibrium price in the symmetric duopoly case.)

Given the expressions for Firm 1's output (8.3) and for equilibrium price (8.6), I can now compute Firm 1's equilibrium profits:

$$
\begin{aligned}
\pi_1 &= p\,q_1 - c_1\,q_1 \\
&= \frac{a + c_1 + c_2}{3}\,q_1 - c_1\,q_1 \\
&= \left( \frac{a + c_1 + c_2}{3} - c_1 \right) q_1 \\
&= \left( \frac{a + c_1 + c_2}{3} - c_1 \right) \frac{a + c_2 - 2c_1}{3b} \\
&= \frac{a + c_2 - 2c_1}{3} \cdot \frac{a + c_2 - 2c_1}{3b} \\
&= \frac{1}{b}\left( \frac{a + c_2 - 2c_1}{3} \right)^2
\end{aligned}
$$

Finally, the value that Firm 1 would be willing to pay for the improved technology would be the difference in the value of the above expression with $c_1 = 15$ and $c_1 = 12$. In order to determine the precise value, we need, once again, to calibrate the model.

By analogy with the previous application, we can invert the price equation (8.6) to obtain:

$$a = 3p - c_1 - c_2$$

Since $p = 20$, $c_1 = 15$, $c_2 = 12$, this implies that $a = 3 \times 20 - 15 - 12 = 33$. Moreover, (8.4) can be inverted to obtain:

$$b = \frac{2a - c_1 - c_2}{3Q}$$

Since $Q = 13$, it follows that $b = (2 \times 33 - 15 - 12)/(3 \times 13) = 1$. Therefore, in the initial equilibrium, Firm 1's profits are given by:

$$\widehat{\pi}_1 = \left( \frac{33 + 12 - 2 \times 15}{3} \right)^2 = \left( \frac{15}{3} \right)^2 = 25$$

whereas, with the new technology, profits would be given by:

$$\widehat{\widehat{\pi}}_1 = \left( \frac{33 + 12 - 2 \times 12}{3} \right)^2 = \left( \frac{21}{3} \right)^2 = 49$$

I conclude that Firm 1 should be willing to pay $49 - 25 = 24$ for the new technology. Given the units I worked with (price in \$ per ton and quantity in million tons) this would be \$24 million.

---

Let us go back to where we started this section. Why is it useful to perform comparative statics? Take for example the last application considered above. The question we posed was: how much would Firm 1 (the inefficient firm) be willing to pay for an innovation that reduces marginal cost to 12 (the efficient firm's cost level)? Our analysis produced an answer to this question: Firm 1 would gain 24 from adopting the more efficient technology.

Is it worth going through all the algebraic trouble to get this answer? A simpler estimate for the gain might be the following: take Firm 1's initial output as given and compute the gain from reducing marginal cost. Since initial output is 5 (check), this calculation would yield the number $5 \times (15 - 12) = 15$. This number greatly underestimates the true gain of 24. Why? The main reason is that, upon reducing marginal cost, Firm 1 becomes much more competitive: not only does it increase its margin, it also increases its output.

Let us then consider an alternative simple calculation. Since Firm 1 will have a marginal cost identical to Firm 2's, we can estimate the gain by the difference between Firm 2's and Firm 1's initial profits. Firm 2's output (in the initial equilibrium) is 8 (check), whereas price is given by 20; its profit is thus $8 \times (20 - 12) = 64$. Firm 1, in turn, is starting from a profit of $5 \times (20 - 15) = 25$. We would thus estimate a gain of $64 - 25 = 39$. This time we are grossly overestimating the true value. Why? The main reason is that, when Firm 1 lowers marginal cost, duopoly competition heats up and price drops. As a result, Firm 2's profit (which is now equal to Firm 1's) also drops. In other words, the number $\pi_2 - \pi_1$ overestimates the gain from technology adoption because it omits the effect of increased competition.

The advantage of the equilibrium analysis — that is, comparative statics — is that it takes into account all of the effects that follow from an exogenous change, such as a reduction in one of the firm's marginal cost. Taking the initial equilibrium values as constant may lead to gross misestimation of the impact of an exogenous change, especially if the change is significant in magnitude (as in the present example).

■ **EXCHANGE RATES AND SALES MARGIN.** A French pharmaceutical firm is the sole domestic producer of a given generic antidepressant. Its marginal cost is €2 per dose. Demand in France is given by $Q = 400 - 50\,p$ ($Q$ in millions of doses, $p$ in €). There is a second producer in India whose marginal cost is INR 150 (including transportation cost to France). The French regulatory system implies that firms must commit to prices for one year at a time. Production capacity can be easily adjusted, since the firms produce several other medical drugs. Suppose that the Indian rupee is devalued by 20% from its initial value of INR 50/€. What impact does this have on the French firm's profitability?

Given the nature of price and output decisions, the Bertrand model seems appropriate for modeling competition between the French and the Indian firm (Firms 1 and 2, respectively). Initially, the Indian firm's marginal cost in € is given by 150/50 = €3. Since this is greater than the French firm's marginal cost, we conclude that the French firm sets a price $p_1$ = €3 (or perhaps a tad lower), which in turn implies a total profit of:

$$\pi_1 = (400 - 50 \times 3) \times (3 - 2) = 250 \quad (\text{million } €)$$

When the rupee devalues by 20%, the new exchange rate becomes $50 \times (1 + 20\%) = 60$. It follows that the Indian firm's marginal cost expressed in € becomes 150/60= € 2.5. This is still greater than € 2, so the French firm still corners the market. Its new profit level is given by:

$$\pi_1 = (400 - 50 \times 2.5) \times (2.5 - 2) = 137.5$$

which corresponds to a 45% drop in profits.

■ **LABOR COSTS AND PROFITS.** I conclude with an example which, to use Hollywood's lingo, is "inspired" by true events in the US auto industry ("inspired" normally means a number of things were made up).[12] First, the facts: in the early 1990s, Ford initiated a capital investment program which led to the substitution of robots for labor. In 1993, United Auto Workers (UAW, the main labor union) initiated wage negotiations with Ford. It was expected that, whichever agreement was reached between UAW and Ford, a similar deal would later be struck with GM and Chrysler, Ford's US rivals.[m] In this context, negotiations between Ford and UAW imply several effects on Ford's profitability: they directly determine Ford's cost, which in turn determines its competitiveness; but indirectly they also determine Ford's rivals' costs, which in turn has an effect on Ford's profits.

Does Ford benefit from negotiating a lower wage? In terms of the direct effect, the answer is yes: a lower wage implies a lower marginal cost, which in turn translates into higher output, market share, and profit. However, a lower wage implies that rivals GM and Chrysler also benefit from a lower wage. This in turn increases the rivals' competitiveness and decreases Ford's output, market share and profit. Which effect dominates?

Suppose that GM and Chrysler's marginal cost is given by $c_i = z + w$, where $w$ is the wage rate and $z$ denotes non-labor marginal costs (and $i = G, C$, which stand for GM and Chrysler, respectively). Ford's marginal cost, in turn, is given by $c_F = z + (1 - \alpha) w$, where $\alpha$, a value between 0 and 1, reflects labor savings resulting form investment in robotics. In all three cases I use the same value $w$, which corresponds to the assumption that Ford's negotiation with UAW set the industry standard.

The earlier question can then be rephrased as follows: how does Ford's equilibrium profit depend on the value of $w$? In what follows I will show that, if $\alpha$ is high enough, then Ford's profit is *increasing* in $w$, that is, the higher wage it agrees with UAW, the higher its equilibrium profit. The idea is that, having made such a large investment

m. The UAW negotiations pattern is still observed in the present. In September 2015, about 36,000 UAW members negotiated an agreement with Fiat Chrysler. The agreement was expected to be followed by a similar deal with General Motors and Ford.

in robotics (high $\alpha$), Ford's profit is less sensitive to increases in $w$ than are the rivals'. This in turn implies that the indirect effect of **raising rivals' costs** dominates the direct effect of lowering Ford's margin.[n]

---

**FORMAL ANALYSIS.** The advantage of equilibrium analysis is that it takes into account all of the direct and indirect effects of an exogenous change (e.g., a change in $w$). Suppose that the Cournot model adequately describes industry competition. Suppose also that (inverse) demand is given by $p = a - bQ$, where $Q$ is total output. Then it can be shown (Exercise 8.15) that Ford's equilibrium profit is given by:

$$\widehat{\pi}_F = \frac{1}{b} \left( \frac{a + c_G + c_C - 3c_F}{4} \right)^2$$

Substituting the marginal cost functions given above, we get:

$$\widehat{\pi}_F = \frac{1}{b} \left( \frac{a - z - w(1 - 3\alpha)}{4} \right)^2$$

It follows that $\widehat{\pi}_F$ is increasing in $w$ if and only if $w(1 - 3\alpha)$ is decreasing in $w$, which in turn is true if and only if $\alpha > \frac{1}{3}$. In words, if Ford's investment in robotics decreases its dependency on labor by one-third or more, then Ford's equilibrium profit increases when wages increase.

---

Back to the facts: in 1993, Ford agreed to what was then generally considered a fairly liberal wage and benefits package with the UAW. This seems consistent with the fact that $\alpha$ was significantly greater than zero, to the point that Ford's profitability did not change, or even increased, as a result of an increase in $w$.

## SUMMARY

• Under price competition with homogeneous product and constant, symmetric marginal cost (Bertrand competition), firms price at the level of marginal cost. • If total industry capacity is low in relation to market demand, then equilibrium prices are greater than marginal cost. • Under output competition (Cournot), equilibrium output is greater than monopoly output and lower than perfect competition output. Likewise, the duopoly price is lower than the monopoly price and greater than the price under perfect competition. • If capacity and output can be adjusted easily, then the Bertrand model describes duopoly competition better. If output and capacity are difficult to adjust, then the Cournot model describes duopoly competition better.

## KEY CONCEPTS

n. In Section 12.2 I will return to the issue of raising rivals' costs.

• oligopoly • duopoly • Bertrand trap • residual demand • pass through
• counterfactual • comparative statics • pass through rate • model calibration
• raising rivals' costs

# REVIEW AND PRACTICE EXERCISES

■ **8.1. BERTRAND IN THE REAL WORLD.** The Bertrand model of price competition suggests that, under a given set of conditions, firms make zero economic profits even if there are only two firms. However, there are many instances of industries with a small number of competitors where firms appear to earn more than zero economic profits.

Give an example of an industry dominated by a couple of firms where profits are significant. Explain why the predictions of the Bertrand model are not borne out.

■ **8.2. BERTRAND AND ZERO PROFITS.** According to Bertrand's theory, price competition drives firms' profits down to zero even if there are only two competitors in the market. Why don't we observe this in practice very often?

■ **8.3. E-COMMERCE.** E-commerce represents an increasing fraction of economic transactions in many different industries. Does e-commerce create a Bertrand trap? What is special about e-commerce (and, more generally, the new economy) that makes the Bertrand trap a dangerous trap? How can e-commerce firms avoid the trap?

■ **8.4. PRICE DISCRIMINATION.** A monopolist is generally better off by price-discriminating. What about a duopolist? Consider the special case when Market A is Firm 1's "strong" market, whereas Market B is firm 2's "strong" market.

■ **8.5. COURNOT MODEL ASSUMPTIONS.** Three criticisms are frequently raised against the use of the Cournot oligopoly model: (i) firms normally choose prices, not quantities; (ii) firms don't normally take their decisions simultaneously; (iii) firms are frequently ignorant of their rivals' costs; in fact, they do not use the notion of Nash equilibrium when making their strategic decisions. How would you respond to these criticisms? (Hint: in addition to this chapter, you may want to refer to Chapter 7.)

■ **8.6. COURNOT VS. BERTRAND.** Which model (Cournot, Bertrand) would you think provides a better approximation to each of the following industries: oil refining, Internet access, insurance. Why?

■ **8.7. BYEBYECOLD.** You are currently the sole seller of ByeByeCold, a revolutionary drug that almost instantly eliminates cold symptoms. Although the production cost is only $.10 per dose, you sell ByeByeCold for $1.39 per dose, for a total profit of $900 million a year. You are currently considering licensing ByeByeCold to a second producer. Neither you nor your competitor have any significant capacity constraints. One of your managers suggested, since the firm would be sharing the market with a competitor, it would be appropriate to charge a flat fee that covers half the current profits plus a generous margin; the value of $700 million was suggested. An alternative proposal would be to set a royalty fee of $.50 per dose. What is your opinion?

■ **8.8. FRENCH GENERICS MANUFACTURER.** Consider the "exchange rates and sales margin" problem in Section 8.4. Suppose that a retailing campaign costing € 80m is expected to increase demand by 40%. Suppose also that the current rupee/euro exchange rate is 50 INR/€. Should the French firm go ahead with the campaign? One macroeconomics expert tells you that "it is likely that the rupee will appreciate in the near future." How would this influence your decision?

■ **8.9. KARMANIA AUTOMOBILES.** There are two auto producers in Karmania, F1 and F2. The cars they produce are essentially identical. The market inverse demand curve is given by $p = a - bQ$, where $p$ is price (in thousands of dollars); $Q$ market output (in thousands of units); and $a$ and $b$ are parameters. It is estimated that $a = 25$ and $b = .1$. Both F1 and F2 have a marginal cost of $10,000 per car.

Competition in the Karmania auto market works as follows. At the beginning of each year, both firms simultaneously and independently decide how many cars to produce. Then the market price adjusts so that supply equals demand.

(a) Determine F1's best response mapping.

(b) Determine the equilibrium of the game played between F1 and F2.

(c) Suppose that an increase in incomes shifts demand to $p = 28 - 0.1\, Q$. What do you expect will happen to price and the number of cars sold?

■ **8.10. ETHANOL.** In the ethanol industry, each firm chooses what output to produce and price is determined by aggregate output. Market demand is given by $Q = 1500 - 2\,p$, where $Q$ is in million tons and $p$ in $/ton. There are two producers and their marginal costs are constant and given by $c_1 = 340$, $c_2 = 420$ (both in $/ton).

(a) Determine equilibrium price, output, and market shares.

Firm 2 is currently considering two possible strategies: (a) a public opinion campaign that would cost $1.15 billion and shift the demand curve to $Q = 1520 - 2\,p$; (b) a capital investment of $4.9 billion that would reduce marginal cost $c_2$ to 400 $/ton.

(b) Are investments (a) and (b) worthwhile in isolation? Are they worthwhile if taken together? Justify your answer.

■ **8.11. NATURAL GAS.** Suppose there are only two natural gas producers in Kabralkstan. In each period, firms determine how much natural gas to sell; market price is then determined by total demand and total supply. Marginal cost is given by 77 for Firm 1 and 74 for Firm 2. Currently, Firms 1 and 2 are producing 170 and 200, respectively, whereas market price is 94.

By making an important discovery in the process of hydraulic fracturing (or "fracking"), Firm 2 managed to cut its marginal cost from 74 to 68.

(a) What impact do you expect Firm 2's cost reduction to have on its market share?

Some studies suggest that Firm 2's new production process may not be environmentally sound.

(b) How much would Firm 1 be willing to pay in support of a campaign to (successfully) prevent Firm 2 from using its new fracking process?

## CHALLENGING EXERCISES

■ **8.12. WOLFRAMIUM.** Suppose there are two producers of wolframium in the world. Wolframium is a homogenous product. Producers set prices simultaneously and capacity constraints are not binding at the current levels of world demand. Both producers have a marginal cost of $900 per metric tonne. One producer is located in the US, the other one in Mexico. Demand for wolframium is exclusively found in the US. It is estimated that, at $p = \$1,000$, world demand for woframium is 130,000 metric tons per year, and that demand elasticity is $\epsilon = -.5$.

(a) Suppose the government imposes an import tax of 20% on wolframium imports. What are equilibrium price and profits?

(b) Suppose a third producer enters the wolframium industry. It is located in China and has a marginal cost of $600 per metric ton. What impact does this have on the equilibrium prices and profits?

■ **8.13. SHIPBUILDING.** The world shipbuilding industry is dominated by three countries/regions: Japan, Europe, and China. Demand for ships is given by $p = a - bQ$, where $b$ has been estimated by industry participants to equal 0.42. Before 2006, the world quarterly production of ships was 19 bulk carriers per quarter. The average price of a bulk carrier was US $17.8 million. Country market shares were as follows: China 24%, Europe 8%, Japan 68%.

(a) Assuming that the industry is well described by a Cournot game played between countries, estimate each country's production marginal cost before 2006.

In 2006, China introduced a government plan to guide the development of its shipbuilding industry. After 2006, the number of Chinese shipyards increased dramatically. The same happened with China's ship production rate: its market share jumped to 50%, while Europe's dropped to 5% and Japan's to 45%. World Trade Organization (WTO) agreements prohibit government industrial subsidies. Thus, complaints by WTO members led to an investigation to find out if the Chinese government subsidized shipbuilding and if so by how much.

(b) Suppose that a production subsidy of $z$ implies a decrease in China's marginal cost from $c$ to $c - z$. Use the pre- and post-2006 data to estimate $z$.

(c) Compute consumer surplus and profits by country. Who was hurt and who gained from China's production subsidies?[13]

■ **8.14. STRATEGIC TRADE POLICY.** Suppose a given country's domestic market is supplied by two firms competing a la Cournot: Firm 1, a domestic firm, and Firm 2, a foreign firm. Demand is given by $p = a - Q$, where $Q$ is total output, and marginal costs by $c_1$ and $c_2$, where we assume $c_i < a$ $(i = 1, 2)$. Suppose that the domestic government levies an import tariff $t$ to be paid by firm 2 for every unit sold in the domestic market.

(a) Determine the equilibrium values of $q_i$ for a given value of $t$.

(b) Show that a small import tariff increases domestic welfare, where the latter is defined as the sum of consumer surplus, the domestic firm's profit, and import revenues.

(c) Show that, the more efficient the foreign firm, the greater the increase in domestic welfare from an import tariff. Discuss.

(d) Show that, if $c_1$ is not very different from $c_2$, then a small import tariff decreases world welfare, where the latter is defined as the sum of consumer surplus, and the profits of the domestic and foreign firms.

(e) In light of the above results, what can be an important role of the World Trade Organization (WTO)?

■ **8.15. COURNOT WITH $n$ ASYMMETRIC FIRMS.** Consider an industry with $n$ output setting firms, each with constant marginal cost $c_i$ and fixed cost $F_i$. Market demand is given by $p = a - bQ$, where $Q = \sum_{i=1}^{n} q_i$.

(a) Show that firm $i$'s best-response mapping is given by $q_i^*(Q_{-i}) = \frac{a-c_i}{2b} - \frac{1}{2} Q_{-i}$, where $Q_{-i} \equiv \sum_{j \neq i} q_j$.

(b) Show that, in equilibrium, total output is given by $\widehat{Q} = \left( na - \sum_{i=1}^{n} c_i \right) / (b(n+1))$. (Hint: add up all $n$ first-order conditions for profit maximization.)

(c) Show that equilibrium price is given by $\widehat{p} = \left( a + \sum_{i=1}^{n} c_i \right) / (n+1)$

(d) Show that, in equilibrium, firm $i$'s output level is given by $\widehat{q}_i = \left( a - nc_i + \sum_{j \neq i} c_j \right) / (b(n+1))$

(e) Show that, in equilibrium, firm $i$'s profit is given by $\widehat{\pi}_i = \left( a - nc_i + \sum_{j \neq i} c_j \right)^2 / (n+1)^2 / b - F_i$

(f) Show that, in equilibrium, consumer surplus is given by
$$CS = \frac{1}{2b}\left(na - \sum_{i=1}^{n} c_i\right)^2 / (n+1)^2$$

■ **8.16. ELASTICITY RULE (REPRISE).** Show that the elasticity rule derived in Chapter 3, that is $(p - MC)/MC = -1/\epsilon$, holds under Cournot competition with linear demand and costs, where $MC$ is firm $i$'s marginal cost and $\epsilon$ its demand elasticity (not the market elasticity).

■ **8.17. EFFICIENCY LOSS UNDER COURNOT.** Consider a market where two firms simultaneous set quantities of a homogeneous product with demand given by $Q = 37.5 - P/4$. Each firm has constant marginal cost equal to 30.

(a) Determine equilibrium output and price.

(b) Compute the efficiency loss as a percentage of the efficiency loss under monopoly.

■ **8.18. EQUILIBRIUM PRICE UNDER COURNOT.** Show analytically that equilibrium price under Cournot is greater than price under perfect competition but lower than monopoly price.

■ **8.19. COURNOT WITH INCREASING MARGINAL COST.** Consider a duopoly for a homogenous product with demand $Q = 10 - P/2$. Each firm's cost function is given by $C = 10 + q(q + 1)$.

(a) Determine the values of the Cournot equilibrium.

(b) Recompute the equilibrium values assuming that one of the firms — say, firm 2 — has a cost function given by $C = 10 + q(q + 1)$.

■ **8.20. CEMENT.** Two firms compete (a la Cournot) in the cement market. Demand for cement is given by $Q = 450 - 2P$. Firm 1's marginal cost is constant at 50, Firm 2's at 40. A technological innovation allows firms to reduce marginal cost by 6.

(a) How much would each firm be willing to pay for the innovation if it were the only competitor to acquire it?

Suppose the innovation costs 600. Consider a "metagame" where firms first simultaneously decide whether to acquire the innovation and then compete a la Cournot with whatever marginal cost results form the first stage.

(b) What is the equilibrium of the $2 \times 2$ game played by firms at the technology choice stage?

## APPLIED EXERCISES

■ **8.21. MODEL CALIBRATION.** Choose an industry for which you can find firm level data on prices and market shares, and for which the Cournot model seems a good approximation.

(a) Making the necessary assumptions, estimate each firm's marginal cost and margin.

(b) Use the estimated model to run the counterfactual whereby one of the firm's cost declines by 5%.

## NOTES

1. *The Wall Street Journal*, November 16, 1999.

2. The Bertrand model was first introduced by J. Bertrand, "Théorie Mathématique de la Richesse Sociale," *Journal de Savants* (1883), 499–508.

3. Sources: Shapiro, Carl, and Hal Varian (1999), *Information Rules*, Harvard Business School Press. *Computer Business Review*, 16 November 1987. See http://www.cbronline.com/news/nynex_puts_phone_book_on_cd (visited October 2012). Walter R. Baranger, *Taking In the Sites; Number, Please? 3 Routes to Phone Listings*, The New York Times, August 07, 1995.

4. This example is adapted from Shapiro, Carl, and Hal Varian (1998), *Information Rules: A Strategic Guide to the Network Economy*, Cambridge, Mass.: Harvard Business School Press.

5. James Surowiecki, "Priced to Go," *The New Yorker*, November 9, 2009.

6. See Davidson, Carl, and Raymond Deneckere (1986), "Long-run Competition in Capacity, Short-run Competition in Price, and the Cournot Model," *Rand Journal of Economics* **17**, 404-415; and Herk, Leonard F. (1993), "Consumer Choice and Cournot Behavior in Capacity-constrained Duopoly Competition," *Rand Journal of Economics* **24**, 399–417.

7. If capacity costs are sufficiently high, then firms' capacity levels will surely be sufficiently low that the above result holds. However, it can be shown that, even if capacity costs were low, the same would be true. See Kreps, David M. and José A. Sheinkman (1983), "Capacity Precommitment and Bertrand Competition Yield Cournot Outcomes," *Bell Journal of Economics* **14**, 326–337.

8. Sources: Andy Kessler, "Bernie Bites the Dust," *The Wall Street Journal*, May 1, 2002. Ken Belson, "WorldCom's Audacious Failure and Its Toll on an Industry," *The New York Times*, January 18, 2005.

9. Cournot, Agustin, *Recherches sur les Principes Mathématiques de la Théorie des Richesses* (1838). English translation edited by N. Bacon, New York: Macmillan, 1897.

10. Source: *The Wall Street Journal*, August 17, 1999.

11. *The Wall Street Journal*, October 10, 2014.

12. Weisman, Dennis L (2007), "An Instructional Exercise in Cost-Raising Strategies, and Perfect Complements Production," *Journal of Economic Education* **38** (2), 215–221.

12. Myrto Kalouptsidi graciously provided data and background information for this exercise. See also Kalouptsidi, Myrto (2014), "Detection and Impact of Industrial Subsidies: The Case of World Shipbuilding," NBER Working Paper 20119.

13. Myrto Kalouptsidi graciously provided data and background information for this exercise. See also Kalouptsidi, Myrto (2014), "Detection and Impact of Industrial Subsidies: The Case of World Shipbuilding," NBER Working Paper 20119.

CHAPTER **9**

# COLLUSION AND PRICE WARS

One of Adam Smith's most frequently cited passages of *The Wealth of Nations* states that:

> People of the same trade seldom meet together, even for merriment and diversion, but the conversation ends in a conspiracy against the public, or in some contrivance to raise prices.[1]

There is a reason why this is the case: in any of the oligopoly structures we have considered so far, total profits, in equilibrium, are lower than monopoly profits. This drop in profits results from the **externality** inherent to the process of imperfect competition: when, for example, a firm chooses quantity under Cournot competition, it maximizes its own profit, not taking into account the fact that part of the increase in profits from a higher output level is obtained at the expense of the rival firm's profits. It is therefore natural that firms attempt to establish agreements between themselves with a view at increasing their **market power**. In fact, it is in general possible to find alternative solutions such that all firms are better off (normally at the expense of consumers). This type of behavior is generically denoted by **collusion** and is the focus of this chapter.

**Cartel** agreements are a particular institutional form of collusion. The increase in oil prices in October 1973, decreed by the OPEC (the oil cartel), is a classic example of cartel behavior. However, collusive behavior does not need to be based on public and institutional agreements. Frequently, collusion results from **secret agreements** — secret not least because they are illegal (in Europe, by article 101 of the Treaty of the European Union; in the US, by the Sherman Act).

A classic example of collusion by secret agreements is the US electrical goods industry in the 1950s — especially with respect to goods, such as turbine generators, that were sold through "competitive" bidding. As a result of a criminal investigation, a number of details of the agreement became known: there was an elaborate process to determine which firm should be the winner of each tender and at what price, the prices that the designated bidding losers should set, and so on.[2]

Finally, collusion may simply result from **tacit agreements** which are attained for some historical reason or simply because they are natural focal points. For example, in the UK and in December 1996, a particular Sony TV set model was being sold for £499.99 by most sellers around Oxford Street (one of them, Harrods, was selling for £500). This price is significantly higher than marginal cost (as evidenced by the price set by some discount sellers). The price of £499.99 may have been reached by agreement between retailers (possibly with Sony acting as a coordinator between retailers) or simply because £499.99 is a "natural" discount on a natural "round" number—a focal point.[a]

For the most part of this chapter, I will consider agreements with the objective of restricting supply (or increasing price). However, collusion may also refer to other decisions: restricting advertising expenditures, setting the level of service quality (cf European airlines until the 1990s), or limiting each firm's territory. A good example of the latter is the chemical industry cartel in the 1920s. According to the agreement — which was declared illegal around 1930 — ICI would concentrate on the UK and the Commonwealth countries, German firms in Europe, and DuPont in America.

## 9.1 STABILITY OF COLLUSIVE AGREEMENTS

Consider a homogeneous-product duopoly where firms simultaneously set prices, marginal cost is constant, and there are no capacity constraints. If firms were to set prices once and for all, then this industry would correspond to the Bertrand model. From the previous chapter, we know that the equilibrium in such industry would consist of both firms setting price equal to marginal cost.

A more realistic model should consider the possibility of firms changing their prices over time. Specifically, suppose that time is divided into a series of periods $t = 1, 2, ...$, and that, in each period, firms simultaneously set prices. In other words, suppose that firms play a Bertrand game in each of an infinite series of periods. In the jargon of game theory, we say that firms play a **repeated game**, a concept I introduced in Section 7.3.

What is the equilibrium of such dynamic game? Clearly, one possible equilibrium consists of firms playing according to the Nash-Bertrand equilibrium in each period, ignoring at each stage what the previous history of the industry was. In fact, if Firm 1 knows that Firm 2 will set price equal to marginal cost in every period, regardless of what Firm 1 does, then the optimal response is to set price equal to marginal cost as well.

There can be other equilibria, however. Suppose that firms play the following **grim strategies**.[3] In the first period, both firms set price at the monopoly level, $p^M$, and share monopoly profits equally ($\frac{1}{2} \pi^M$). In each subsequent period, firms observe the price history before setting their own prices. If historical prices have all been at the monopoly level, that is, if both firms have "respected" the collusive agreement, then each firm sets

a. See Section 7.1 for a discussion of focal points in game theory. I will return to this issue in Section 9.5.

$p^M$ in the current period. Otherwise, they set price at the level of marginal cost. To put it differently: Firm 1 will set $p = p^M$ so long as Firm 2 sets $p = p^M$ as well. The moment Firm 1 observes its rival setting a different price, it "punishes" the deviation by reverting (forever) to price at the marginal cost level.[b]

In order to determine whether such strategies form an equilibrium we must check whether the firms' **no-deviation constraints** are satisfied. If both firms stick to their equilibrium strategy, then Firm 1's expected discounted payoff is given by:

$$\frac{1}{2} \pi^M + \delta \frac{1}{2} \pi^M + \delta^2 \frac{1}{2} \pi^M + ... \qquad (9.1)$$

where $\delta$ is the **discount factor**, that is, the value of $1 one period into the future compared to $1 now. Simplifying (9.1), we get:

$$V = \frac{1}{2} \pi^M \frac{1}{1 - \delta} \qquad (9.2)$$

where $V$ denotes discounted (net present value) equilibrium payoff or value.

If Firm 1 deviates by setting $p_1 \neq p^M$ in some period $t$, then its future payoff is zero since, by assumption, both firms revert thereafter to pricing at marginal cost. Since future payoffs are not a function of *what* the deviation was, but only *whether* there was a deviation at all, it follows that the best deviation for Firm 1 is the one that maximizes short-run profits. The price that maximizes Firm 1's short-run profits is $p^M - \epsilon$, where $\epsilon$ is a very low number: by slightly undercutting Firm 2's price, Firm 1 gets all of the demand and a total profit of approximately $\pi^M$.[c] It thus follows that the payoff from the optimal deviation is:

$$V' = \pi^M \qquad (9.3)$$

(Short-run monopoly profits plus zero future profits.) The condition that the proposed strategies form an equilibrium is then that $V \geq V'$. Pulling (9.2) and (9.3) together, we get:

$$\frac{1}{2} \pi^M \frac{1}{1 - \delta} \geq \pi^M$$

or simply:

$$\delta \geq \frac{1}{2} \qquad (9.4)$$

In words: if the discount factor is sufficiently high, then there exists a Nash equilibrium of the repeated game whereby firms set monopoly price in every period under the "threat" that, if any firm ever deviates from this price level, then both firms revert to pricing at marginal cost level forever.

■ **THE DISCOUNT FACTOR.** As mentioned earlier, the discount factor measures how much $1 one period into the future is worth compared to $1 now. Normally, $0 < \delta < 1$. There are several reasons why $\delta < 1$. One is the opportunity cost of time: given one period of time, an investor might use $1 to gain $(1 + r)$ next period, where $r$ is the interest rate per period. In this sense, we would compute $\delta$ as:

$$\delta = \frac{1}{1 + r}$$

b. Note that, since Firm 2 knows that its deviation implies that Firm 1 reverts to pricing at marginal cost, Firm 2 will also set price at marginal cost level following a deviation by itself. Thus the designated strategy calls for firms to revert to pricing at marginal cost whenever *some* firm sets price different from monopoly price in the past.

c. The exact value of Firm 1's payoff would be smaller than $\pi^M$, as it needs to undercut its rival. But since $\epsilon$ can be arbitrarily small, I assume that the profit from deviation is equal to $\pi^M$.

In the above equation, the relevant rate is the rate corresponding to the period between successive decisions. Specifically, suppose that $r$ is the annual rate and that the frequency with which firms change their prices is given by $f$ (times per year). Then, we would have:

$$\delta = \frac{1}{1 + r/f}$$

Another important factor to take into account in the computation of $\delta$ is the probability that the payoff in the next period will be received at all. For example, if two pharmaceutical firms were to collude, they would have to consider the (likely) possibility that, before the next period, a third firm would discover a superior drug that would essentially eliminate the market for the first two firms. In other industries (cement, for example), this possibility would be rather remote. Specifically, let $h$ be the probability (or hazard rate) that the industry will cease to "exist" one period later. Then, we compute the discount factor as:

$$\delta = \frac{1 - h}{1 + r/f}$$

The opposite effect of an industry disappearing is for that industry to grow. Suppose that demand is growing at a rate $g$. This implies that, everything else constant, profits are greater in period $t + 1$ than in period $t$ by a factor $1 + g$. One way to represent this formally is to assume a "constant" profit function but a discount factor such that a \$ one period in the future is worth *more* than a \$ in the current period, by a factor $1 + g$, on account of industry growth. The discount factor would then be:

$$\delta = \frac{(1 + g)(1 - h)}{1 + r/f} \tag{9.5}$$

Notice that $\delta$ is increasing in $f$, $g$; and decreasing in $h$, $r$.

Given this derivation of the value of $\delta$, Condition (9.4) can be interpreted as follows:

> Collusion in normally easier to maintain when firms interact frequently and when the probability of industry continuation and growth is high.

So, for example, regarding the value of $f$: collusion between two service stations that set gas prices on a daily basis is likely to be easier than collusion between two summer holiday resorts where rates are set on an annual basis. And regarding the value of $h$: collusion between two pharmaceutical firms in a given therapeutical market where products become obsolete at a fast rate is likely to be more difficult than collusion in the cement industry, where most likely the market will remain unchanged in the next period.

■ **WHY DON'T FIRMS COLLUDE MORE OFTEN?** In Section 8.1 I showed that, under the assumptions of Bertrand competition, two firms are enough for equilibrium prices to be driven down to marginal cost level — the Bertrand trap. Earlier in this section I also showed that, under repeated interaction and for a low enough interest rate (and no

## Box 9.1 The diamond cartel

De Beers Consolidated Mines Ltd. was established in the 1870s. Since then, the firm, owned by the Oppenheimer family, has maintained a remarkable control over the world diamond industry. DeBeers owns all of the diamond mines in South Africa and has interests in other countries as well. However, in terms of mining, its share of the world market is relatively small, especially since the discovery of massive mines in Russia. The key to De Beers's market control is the Central Selling Organization (CSO), its London-based marketing arm.

The CSO serves as an intermediary between the mines and the diamond cutters and polishers. More than 80% of the world's diamonds are processed by the CSO, although only a fraction of these originate from DeBeers mines. CSO staff classify the diamonds by category (there are literally thousands of types of diamonds). This is a highly skill-intensive task in which De Beers has unmatched expertise. The CSO also regulates the market to achieve price stability, building up its stocks during periods of low demand and releasing those same stocks during periods of high demand.

The very high margins earned by De Beers are a constant temptation for mining companies, who figure that the same margins might be earned by selling directly to diamond cutters. What stops them from doing so? First, many of the diamond producers see the current cartel structure as a benefit to the whole industry. In addition to stabilizing prices, De Beers plays the crucial role of advertising diamonds. Both price stabilization and advertising are "public goods" at the industry level: every producer benefits, although only De Beers pays for it.

A second reason for compliance with De Beers's dominance is the fear of retaliation following cartel defection. In 1981, President Mobutu announced that Zaire, the world's largest supplier of industrial diamonds, would no longer sell diamonds through the CSO. At the same time, contacts were set up with two Antwerp and one British broker. Two months later, about one million carats of industrial diamonds flooded the market, and the price fell from $3 to less than $1.80 per carat. Although the source of this supply surplus remains unknown, many believe the move was De Beers's way of showing who's in control.

For De Beers, this was a costly operation; but it was a case of "it's not the money, it's the principle." And the point was made: in 1983, Zaire requested the renewal of its old contract with De Beers. In fact, the contract it ended up with was less favorable than the original one.

capacity constraints), it may be possible to sustain monopoly prices even if firms set prices simultaneously.

In other words, if without repetition we were led to a puzzle (zero margins even with only two firms), we now have the opposite puzzle, as it were: the model predicts that firms can almost always collude to set monopoly prices. Why don't firms collude more often in practice, since, as the above analysis suggests, such strategy would be an equilibrium and increase the firms' profits? In fact, suppose that the annual interest rate is 10% and suppose that firms set prices on a monthly basis. Then it can be shown that, even if there are *dozens* of symmetric price setting firms, there exists an equilibrium such that all firms set monopoly prices in every period! Why doesn't this happen more often?

One possible explanation is that antitrust policy is a binding constraint on the firms' actions. For one, explicit cartel agreements are illegal. But even tacit collusion agreements may run into problems with antitrust authorities, as I will show in Section 9.5.

A second explanation is suggested by the analysis above. The discount factor that should be used for the purpose of determining the equilibrium conditions includes, in addition to the value of time, the probability of continuation. Consider an industry with a very high turnover rate, that is, a high rate of entry and exit. In this context, the probability that a given firm exits the market in each period is high, and accordingly its discount factor is small. This in turn implies that only for unreasonably low values of the interest rate is it an equilibrium for firms to set monopoly prices. In other words, if a firm expects to exit the industry with a high probability, then its incentives to deviate from a collusive agreement are also very high, for there is little to lose, in terms of expected future profits, from "cheating" on a collusive agreement today.

A third explanation why collusive agreements of the sort presented above are not more common is that they are really not an equilibrium. To be sure, they form a Nash equilibrium. The point, however, is that such equilibrium is unreasonable and unrealistic. Suppose that cheating from the monopoly pricing agreement is punished with a infinite price war, as assumed above. Suppose that one of the firms actually cheats and a reversion to a price war takes place. One can imagine the deviating firm would have an incentive to approach its rival and try to convince it that there are mutual gains from abandoning the price war and reverting to collusive pricing. But if firms were to agree on this — and it seems reasonable they would — then the threat of engaging in a price war in the first place would no longer be credible. And cheating from monopoly pricing might after all be profitable, breaking the monopoly pricing equilibrium.

A fourth reason why collusion may in practice be more difficult than the model above would predict is that not all prices are observed with precision. In a world of imperfect observability, the possibility of secret price cuts must be taken into account. And, as I will show in the next section, this possibility makes collusive agreements more difficult to sustain.

To summarize, few real-world collusive agreements work exactly like the model presented above. However, the main intuition, namely that each firm's decision involves a trade-off between short-run gains and medium- to long-term losses, is the essence of the problem of cartel stability. Box 9.1 presents the example of the diamond industry. Although this is, in many respects, a very peculiar industry, it does illustrate the main points developed in this section.

## 9.2   PRICE WARS

By comparison to the models in the previous chapter (Cournot and Bertrand), adding dynamics brings in a fair amount of realism to the analysis of duopoly competition. For example, zero margins are not the only outcome when there are two price-setting competitors. Even so, the model presented in the previous section is too stylized to explain various industry pricing patterns. In particular, one common observation is that industry prices oscillate between high levels (close to the collusive price level described in the previous section) and low levels (close to the competitive price level described in the previous chapter). For example, the market for rail shipping, discussed in Box 9.2, seems (at least historically) to exhibit this pattern, as can be seen from the figure inserted in the box. However, the model presented in the previous section predicts that, along the equilibrium path, prices are always at the monopoly level. In this section, I consider extensions of that model in an attempt to explain the observed patterns.

■ **SECRET PRICE CUTS.**[5] Ready-mixed concrete and ocean shipping are examples of **customer markets**. These are industries where each customer is sufficiently large that prices are negotiated on a case-by-case basis.[d] For this reason, collusive agreements are difficult to monitor: although firms may agree on what prices to set, the temptation to secretly cut prices for a particular customer is significant. In fact, what deters firms from cheating on a collusive agreement is the threat of reversion to a "bad" equilibrium. But if deviations from the prescribed equilibrium cannot be directly observed, then the deterrence effect is greatly decreased.

Suppose that demand fluctuates and that these fluctuations cannot be perfectly observed. All that each firm can observe is the price it sets and the demand it receives. If a firm receives unexpectedly low demand, it is faced with a guessing problem: its low demand may result from low overall demand, or it may result from some rival having undercut prices with respect to the agreed-upon level. Should the firm punish its rival when it receives low demand? Could it not be punishing an "innocent" competititor?

Suppose firm $i$ decides not to punish firm $j$, on the assumption that its low demand resulted from a market downturn, not firm $j$'s cheating. Can this be an equilibrium? Clearly not: if that were firm $i$'s strategy, then firm $j$ would be better off by secretly cutting prices and blaming firm $i$'s low demand on market conditions. Suppose instead that each time firm $i$ receives low demand it reverts to an infinite price war, on the assumption that low demand resulted from firm $j$'s cheating. Such harsh punishment would most likely suffice to keep firm $j$ from offering secret price cuts. But that is little consolation, for, sooner or later, a market downturn would imply low demand for firm $i$ regardless of firm $j$'s behavior. The industry would revert into an indefinite price war even if no cheating on the agreement had occurred.

Finally, consider an intermediate solution: each time firm $i$ or firm $j$ receives low demand, they move into a price war for $T$ periods, upon which they revert back to pricing at the collusive level. Let $T$ be sufficiently large such that no firm has an incentive to undercut the rival. In fact, if the future is sufficiently important for each firm (that is, if the discount factor $\delta$ is sufficiently closer to 1), then such $T$ exists. We thus have an equilibrium with collusion phases alternating with price war phases, just as empirical observation suggests. Notice that, *although price wars occur in equilibrium, no firm cheats in equilibrium.* That is, price wars are a necessary "evil" for collusion to take

d. See Chapter 6 for more on customer markets.

**Box 9.2 COLLUSION AND PRICE WARS: THE JOINT EXECUTIVE COMMITTEE, 1880–1886**[4]

"The Joint Executive Committee (JEC) was a cartel which controlled eastbound freight shipments from Chicago to the Atlantic seaboard in the 1880s. It was formed in April 1879 by an agreement of the railroads involved in the market. The firms involved publicly acknowledged this agreement, as it preceded the passage of the Sherman Act (1890) and the formation of the Interstate Commerce Commission (1887)" which formally prohibited this kind of agreements (cf Section 9.5). "A separate agreement was reached for westbound shipments on the same railroad lines, primarily because of the essential physical differences of the products being transported."

The internal enforcement mechanism adopted by the JEC was a variant of the trigger price strategy discussed in the first part of Section 9.2. "There were several instances in which the cartel thought that cheating had occurred, cut prices for a time, and then returned to the collusive price." The figure below shows the evolution of price in the period 1880–1886.

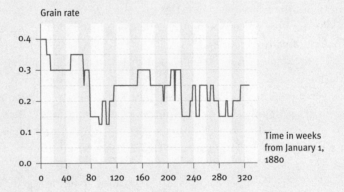

"The assumption that a homogeneous good was sold seems to have been approximately satisfied ... Lake steamers and sail ships were the principal source of competition for the railroads, but at no point did they enter into an agreement with the JEC. The predictable fluctuations in demand that resulted from the annual opening and closing of the Great Lakes to shipping did not disrupt industry conduct. Rather, rates adjusted systematically with the lake navigation season."

Therefore, the conduct of the JEC from 1880 to 1886 is largely consistent with the first model of collusive equilibrium described in the first part of Section 9.2, "as price wars were caused by unpredictable disturbances, rather than by entry or predictable fluctuations in demand."

place: if firms never engaged in price wars, the incentives for cheating would be too great for the collusive agreement to be stable.

If price cuts are difficult to observe, then occasional price wars may be necessary to discipline collusive agreements.

Exercise 9.19 (a rather challenging one) formalizes this idea.

■ **DEMAND FLUCTUATIONS.** The previous model is based on the somewhat extreme assumption that demand fluctuations (or the demand received by rival firms) are not observable. Suppose instead that demand fluctuates over time but that, in each period, the state of demand is observed by all firms. If firms collude with each other, how will prices fluctuate with demand? A collusive equilibrium, as we saw before, must be such that firms have no incentive to undercut their rivals' price. In other words, the difference between future collusive profits and future profits in case of a price war must be sufficiently large so as to deter a firm from pursuing the short-term gains of cheating on the collusive agreement.

Suppose that demand shocks are independent across periods. This implies that, in terms of future demand levels, the future looks the same in every period, regardless of the current state of demand. Consequently, expected future profits from collusion (or punishment) are the same regardless of the current state of demand. *Current profits*, however, do depend on the current state of demand. In particular, the gains from cheating on the cartel agreement are greater when demand is higher.[e] This implies that the constraint that no firm wants to cheat on the collusive agreement is more serious when demand is high. In order to achieve an equilibrium, it may be necessary to reduce price during periods of high demand. In fact, if price is lower, the gains from cheating are also lower.[f] In a number of settings, this may result in an equilibrium where *prices are lower in periods when demand is higher*. Exercise 9.20 (a rather challenging one) formalizes this idea.

The above model implies that prices move counter-cyclically, that is, price wars take place during booms. The first model presented in this section predicts that firms enter into a price war following a period of low demand. The stark contrast between the predictions of the two models shows how important different assumptions can be. In the first model, I assumed that demand shocks are not observable, whereas in the second one I assumed that, before choosing prices in each period, firms observe that period's demand shock.

Empirical evidence suggests that both sets of assumptions are realistic approximations to different industries; and that different industries evidence patters of pro- or counter-cyclical price movements. Based on yearly data from 1947–1981, it can be shown that the price of cement varies counter-cyclically: a 1% increase in GDP is associated with a decrease in the relative price of cement between .5 and 1%.[6] This evidence is consistent with the second model. By contrast, the market for eastbound freight shipments from Chicago to the Atlantic seaboard, during the period 1880–1886, provides a good example of the first model and of its empirical prediction.[7]

■ **FIRM HETEROGENEITY.** The two models presented above, for all of their differences, have one thing in common: price wars are a coordinated action by all firms in the industry as part of a collusive equilibrium. In other words, price wars are necessary in order to maintain long-term collusion in the industry. However, many price wars observed in

e. Recall that, under duopoly competition with a homogeneous product and constant marginal cost, a firm that undercuts its rival doubles its profit. If demand is higher, then this gain is also higher.

f. The argument is similar to the previous footnote.

practice fail to fit into this behavior category. Consider, for example, the airline industry. Industry analysts suggest that the main cause for price wars are the financial troubles of individual carriers: "Fares are dictated not by the strongest, but by the financially troubled," claims an airline executive.[8]

A simple model that would explain behavior of this type must be based on some form of asymmetry between firms. Suppose, for example, that each firm's discount factor starts by being $\bar{\delta}$. However, with some probability, a firm's discount factor may switch to a lower value, say, $\underline{\delta}$. A lower value of $\delta$ means that the future is less important for the firm. As I showed in Section 9.1, one of the elements that goes into a firm's discount factor is the probability that the future will not exist (the hazard rate $h$ in Equation 9.5). A firm that is in a difficult situation (financially or otherwise) has a lower discount factor than a firm which is doing well. The former attributes a higher probability to exiting the industry.

If the difference between $\bar{\delta}$ and $\underline{\delta}$ is sufficiently high, it may be that collusion is possible among "patient" firms ($\delta = \bar{\delta}$) but not among "impatient" firms ($\delta = \underline{\delta}$). Notice that, in equilibrium, no firm can have an incentive to deviate if a high price is to be maintained: all firms must therefore have $\delta = \bar{\delta}$. As soon as a firm sees its $\delta$ turn from $\bar{\delta}$ to $\underline{\delta}$, that firm will deviate and initiate a price war: although the short-run gains from deviation remain the same, the long-run (expected) gains from sticking to the collusion agreement are now much lower.

Price wars need not necessarily be initiated by the weaker firms, however. Consider the case of the British newspaper industry. In July 1993, Rupert Murdoch reduced the price of the *Times* from 45 pence to 30 pence. Ten months later, the price was further dropped to 20 pence, less than one-half the starting level. This aggressive strategy launched the entire broadsheet newspaper market into a price war that lasted for more than 18 months. Although most newspapers increased circulation (especially the *Times*), the price war had a marked negative impact on average industry profitability.

The most likely reason why Murdoch cut the *Times*' price in 1993 is that circulation was deteriorating rapidly, falling below 360,000. By May 1995, circulation was well above 650,000. At that point, Murdoch sent the signal for putting an end to the price war: at a press conference, he stated that prices "will probably have to be corrected" in response to a 30–40% increase in newsprint costs which have "changed the economics of the industry."[9] Was it the increase in costs, or was it the fact the *Times* had recaptured a more comfortable market share after two years of reduced prices?

Even if this price war reflected the *Times*'s weak market share in 1993, Murdoch might not have taken the initiative if his financial position were not as strong as it was. In fact, an alternative explanation for his strategy is that, by cutting prices, he was simply attempting to drive rivals out of the market.[8]

A more recent example is given by cloud services. In March 2014, Google reduced its prices by 30 to 85%, throwing the entire cloud computing market into a price war. Although these actions may reflect the weakness of Google's cloud-computing compared to traditional in-house servers and data centers, it is clear that Google would not have taken the initiative had their financial position not been as strong as it is.[10]

g. In Section 12.3 I look at this strategy in greater detail.

In sum, the airline, newspaper and cloud computing examples show that price wars can be unilaterally initiated by one firm. However, whereas in the airline case it's the weaker firm that gets the price war started, in the latter ones it's the stronger player that cuts prices first.

## 9.3 FACTORS THAT FACILITATE COLLUSION

In Section 9.1, I derived some of the conditions that make an industry more prone to collusive agreements. In particular, I mentioned frequency of interaction and market growth. Moreover, some of the cases considered — the diamond industry, for example — suggest that the severity and credibility of punishments also play an important role. Section 9.2 introduced another important factor, namely the probability of detection of a deviation from collusive agreements. In this section, I continue the discussion of factors that may facilitate the formation and maintenance of collusive agreements.

■ **MARKET STRUCTURE AND COLLUSION.** In the previous sections, I maintained (for simplicity) the assumption of a symmetric duopoly. This assumption is unlikely to be satisfied by most real-world examples. Normally, there are more than two firms with asymmetrically distributed market shares. How does the number of firms and the distribution of market shares influence the likelihood of collusive behavior?

One idea is that collusion is more likely in concentrated industries than in fragmented ones. First, it is easier to *establish* a collusive agreement when there are few competitors than when there are many competitors. In fact, both bargaining theory and anecdotal evidence suggest that agreements are more difficult to reach the greater the number of interested parties. Moreover, it is easier to *maintain* a collusive agreement with fewer competitors. Consider the case of repeated price competition, presented in Section 9.1 for the case of two firms. If there were $n > 2$ competitors, profit per firm would be smaller. However, the profit that a price cutter would gain would still be the same. Consequently, the temptation to cut prices is relatively greater when there are more competitors, and collusion is more difficult to sustain. This point is further developed in Exercise 9.17.

A second aspect relating to market structure is symmetry between firms. It is normally easier to maintain collusion among similar firms than among asymmetric ones.[h] To understand why, consider a price-setting duopoly where one firm has a cost advantage over the other one. For example, Firm 1's constant marginal cost is $c$, whereas Firm 2's is given by $\overline{c}$, which is greater than $c$ but lower than the low cost firm's monopoly price. The efficient collusive agreement is for Firm 1 to set its monopoly price and for Firm 2 to set a higher price and sell zero. In fact, this is the price and market share allocation that maximizes joint profits. However, such an agreement is clearly not stable, for Firm 2 would have an incentive to undercut Firm 1 and make some positive profit in the short run. Note that this is true regardless of the value of the discount factor,

h. The diamond industry is an important exception to this rule. Given the peculiar nature of the product (diamonds), the leadership of one of the firms (DeBeers) has played an essential role in maintaining high prices, basically by maintaining — through advertising and stock management — the perception that diamonds are scarce (though they are not).

for in the efficient solution Firm 2 makes zero profits. It follows that *no punishment can detain Firm 2 from deviating,* as it has nothing to lose.

An alternative solution might be for both firms to price at the same (high) level. This would alleviate the problem of Firm 2 wanting to deviate, but it might create a new problem: Firm 1 may now want to deviate. First, Firm 1's gains from deviation are very large, for it sells at a large margin. Second, the punishment Firm 2 might be able to impose on Firm 1 is likely to be smaller: even if Firm 2 sets price at marginal cost, Firm 1 can still make positive profits.[i]

The bromide industry during the turn of the twentieth century provides an interesting illustration of this point. Between 1885 and 1914, a period when the industry was dominated by a cartel, six price wars occurred. Two of these wars took place right after publicly announced violations of the cartel agreement. Clearly, these were not equilibrium price wars in the sense explained in the previous section. Rather, they resulted from disagreement among cartel members regarding the distribution of profits. If all firms were symmetric, then profit distribution would be a simple issue: the natural solution is then for profits to be equally distributed. If firms are asymmetric, however, then the cartel is subject to an additional strain, namely agreement on profit distribution.[11]

> Collusion is normally easier to maintain among few and similar firms.

■ **MULTIMARKET CONTACT.**[12]  Theoretical analysis and empirical evidence suggest that firms which compete with each other in several markets have a greater propensity to collude, and/or collude to a greater extent. For example, it has been estimated that multimarket contact has a significant positive impact on airfares (see Box 9.3).

Why would multimarket contact increase the chances of collusion? Perhaps the best way to begin addressing this question is to see why multimarket contact might *not* improve the chances of collusion. Consider a price-setting homogeneous-product duopoly where marginal cost is constant and the same for both firms. If firms set prices at the monopoly level, $p^M$, then each receives $\frac{1}{2}\,\pi^M$, where $\pi^M$ is monopoly profits. If one of the firms were to set a slightly lower price, then it would receive all of the monopoly profits, that is, twice as much. The worse price war to punish such deviation would consist of setting price at marginal cost forever, that is, zero profits. Collusion is therefore possible if and only if:

i.  Strictly speaking, Firm 2 can impose an equally severe punishment on Firm 1: by setting $p_2 = c$, Firm 2 forces Firm 1 to zero profits. The problem is that in the process Firm 2 makes losses, which in many real-world settings may be difficult to sustain.

$$\frac{1}{1-\delta}\,\frac{1}{2}\,\pi^M \geq \pi^M$$

The left-hand side is the discounted stream of half monopoly profits in each period, whereas the right-hand side is monopoly profits in one period only. Solving this equation we get $\delta \geq \frac{1}{2}$.

Consider now the case when the firms compete in two identical markets, each of which is described as in the previous paragraph. What is now the lowest value of the discount factor such that collusion is stable? The future cost of a deviation is now

## Box 9.3 Multimarket contact between US airlines[13]

In air travel, a market might be defined as the flight connection between two different cities. In this sense, airlines compete in several markets, and competing airlines overlap in the markets that they cover. Consider, for example, the top 1,000 routes in the US. Define average contact in each market as the average number of other markets in which the competing airlines face each other.

For example, consider a particular route which, in 1988, was serviced by American, Delta, and Northwest. During that year American and Delta appear jointly in 527 of the top 1,000 routes, while American and Northwest were present in 357 routes and Delta and Northwest in 323 routes. Average route contact would then be (527+357+323)/3=402.3.

Statistical evidence shows that this variable has a significant positive impact on airfares, controlling for a host of other factors. This in turn suggests that airlines use competition in other routes as a means to collude in a given route. Price cutting in a particular route might lead to a profit increase in the short run. However, not only would this lead to a price war in that route, it would also lead to more severe price competition in other routes as well.

greater: a price war in both markets. But the benefits from deviation are also greater: increased profits in both markets. In fact, the new stability condition is:

$$\frac{1}{1-\delta} \frac{1}{2} \pi^M + \frac{1}{1-\delta} \frac{1}{2} \pi^M \geq \pi^M + \pi^M$$

which again implies $\delta \geq \frac{1}{2}$. In words, if the different markets are simply a replication of each other, then multimarket contact seems to have little effect: the potential punishment from a deviation increases, but so does the benefit, in fact in exactly same proportion.

Now suppose that each firm has a cost advantage in one of the markets. For example, in Market 1 Firm 1's cost is $\underline{c}$, whereas Firm 2's is $\overline{c} > \underline{c}$; and in Market 2 Firm 2's cost is $\underline{c}$, whereas Firm 1's is $\overline{c}$. One possible interpretation is that each firm is located in a different country and $\overline{c} = \underline{c} + t$, where $t$ is the transportation cost from one country to the other.

As seen in the previous subsection, the efficient collusive agreement in Market 1 is for Firm 1 to set its monopoly price and for Firm 2 to set a higher price and sell zero. The reverse is true in Market 2. Taken in isolation, such agreements are clearly not stable. However, if we consider the two markets together, then the situation is quite different. Firm 1 might be able to convince Firm 2 not to undercut its monopoly price in Market 1 with the threat that it would undercut Firm 2 in the latter's market if that were to happen. In fact, suppose that the punishment from deviation would be for firms to engage in a price war whereby price equals the high marginal cost, $\overline{c}$.[j] One can easily show that if the discount factor is sufficiently high, then firms will be able to collude and set prices at the monopoly level (see Exercise 9.18). Multimarket contact matters.

j. It can be shown that this constitutes an equilibrium of the static price game.

**Box 9.4 Multimarket contact in the dog food industry**[14]

With dozens of millions of dogs to feed, the pet food industry represents an important dollar value. In the US alone, dog food sales exceed $3 billion a year. There are essentially five segments in the dog food market: dry, moist, snack, canned, and soft-dry.

In 1986, Quaker Oats, a dominant player in the moist segment, acquired the financially stressed Anderson Clayton. This was not an entirely peaceful acquisition. In fact, Quaker's move preempted a bid by Ralston Purina, a competitor of Quaker's and a dominant player in the dry dog food segment (49.7% market share).

Quaker sold all of Anderson Clayton's divisions except Gaines, owner of a number of brands in different segments. This acquisition strengthened Quaker's position in the moist segment, increasing its total market share from 27.9 to 80.7%. It also increased Quaker's presence in the dry segment, bringing total market share to 19.8%.

Responding to Quaker's move, Ralston Purina acquired Benco Pet Food's Inc., Quaker's main rival in the moist market. One industry analyst commented that this move "was to put Quaker on notice a little bit; to say 'Hey, we can come at you in your strong area if you come after us in our strong area'." Quaker responded by launching a semi-moist product named *Moist 'n Beefy*, a clear attack at Ralston's (ex Benco's) *Moist & Meaty* brand. Ralston Purina, in turn, introduced a dry dog food called *Grrravy*, a clear attack on Quaker's *Gravy Train* brand.

Collusion is normally easier to maintain when firms compete in more than one market.

One example that illustrates this kind of reasoning is that of the chemical industry in the 1920s (discussed in the introduction). According to the collusive agreement — which was declared illegal around 1930 — ICI would concentrate on the UK and the Commonwealth countries, German firms in Europe, and DuPont in America. A more recent example, discussed in Box 9.4, is that of the dog food industry, where two segments — dry and moist dog food — are dominated by two different firms.[k]

■ **Institutional factors.** In addition to structural factors such as the number of firms and the number of markets in which firms interact, there are a number of institutional factors which may particularly facilitate collusion (these are also known as **facilitating practices**). By institutional factors I mean rules or regulations imposed either by the firms of by the government. An important instance of such regulations is given by **most-favored-customer** clauses. These clauses bind firms not to offer a discount to a particular customer without offering the same discount to every other customer within a period of time. At face value, this appears to be a clause that protects the customer — in particular, it protects the customer against paying a higher price than other customers. However, an important effect of the clause is that it lowers the incentive for a firm to price aggressively: although a price cut may allow the firm to capture market share from

k. Actually, Box 9.4 illustrates the consequences of the breakdown of a multimarket agreemnt.

## Box 9.5 The market for large turbine generators[15]

Turbine generators are complicated pieces of machinery used to convert steam into electrical power. Typical buyers are electrical utilities; the main sellers are General Electric and Westinghouse. Large turbine generators are produced to order. Sellers are chosen either by direct negotiation (typical of investor-owned utilities) or as the result of sealed bids (typical of government-owned utilities).

As mentioned on page 217, a secret collusive agreement between the main competitors in the electrical goods industry (including turbine generators) was discovered and dismantled in the 1950s. As a result of the cartel breakdown, prices for large turbine generators declined by 50% between 1958 and 1963.

In May 1963, GE announced a new pricing policy for turbine generators. The policy was based on a *price book* which contained objective rules for determining the price of each turbine generator. GE announced that, from then on, it would sell at the published prices *without exception*. Moreover, it instituted a *most-favored customer clause*: in the event GE were to sell for a price lower than the book price, every customer in the previous six months would be entitled to the same discount. The credibility of GE's new policy was strengthened by their decision to hire an accounting firm to monitor compliance with the pricing rules.

Within less than a year, Westinghouse followed GE's policy of publishing a price book and offering a price protection clause. Except for a brief episode of price cutting in 1964, the prices charged by both companies remained stable and identical until 1975. At this time, the US Department of Justice decided that the policies followed by GE and Westinghouse tended to stabilize prices and were thus in violation of antitrust laws (the Sherman Act, in particular). As a result, it proposed to GE and Westinghouse a consent decree whereby the latter would abstain from such practices as "offering a price protection policy" or "revealing to any person ... a price book or price list relating to large turbine-generators."

its rival, a price cut also implies the cost of reimbursing previous customers who were charged a higher price. Finally, since firms have a lower incentive to cut prices, collusive pricing arrangements are more stable than if no clause is imposed. In other words, a business practice which at first could be thought of as a protection against high prices ends up implying precisely that: high prices. The market for large turbine generators in the 1960s and 1970s provides an interesting example of this idea: see Box 9.5 for details. See Exercise 9.16 for a similar clause, namely price-matching guarantees.

In the US and until 1986, railroads had the freedom to establish rates and enter into confidential agreements with grain shippers. Legislation passed in 1986 required that certain terms of the contract be disclosed. The empirical evidence suggests that the effect of this legislation was to increase prices.[17] At first, legislation that increases market **transparency** appears to protect buyers. However, the effect of transparency may be to facilitate price coordination. The idea is that, if prices are made public, then monitoring a collusive agreement is much easier than if prices are private information. This is consistent with the analysis in the previous section, namely the situation of collusion with secret price cuts.

**Box 9.6 Collusion in the Danish ready-mixed concrete market**[16]

The structure of the ready-mixed concrete industry in Denmark can roughly be described as a collection of fairly tight regional oligopolies with a few firms active in most regional markets and most firms active in only one or two regional markets. Until 1993, list prices were frequently subject to individual, confidential discounts of considerable amount. This situation led industry observers and competition policy authorities to suggest that pricing behavior in the industry was far from the perfectly competitive ideal.

In response, the Danish Competition Council decided, in October 1993, to gather and regularly publish actual transaction prices set by individual firms in three regional markets for two particular grades of ready-mixed concrete. Presumably, the purpose of such publications was to improve information on the buyer side (i.e., among building contractors), whereby seller competition would be stimulated and average transactions prices fall.

The result of the change in regulation was, however, different from what was intended. In the Aarhus market, for example, prices evolved as shown in the figure below. First, price dispersion between firms decreased dramatically (compare January 1994 to November 1995). Second, the average price level increased significantly.

The data suggests that making all prices public information helped firms coordinate on a collusive equilibrium. The requirement to publish prices ceased soon after the period reported below.

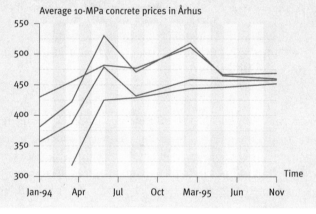

Average 10-MPa concrete prices in Århus

A similar example, described in Box 9.6, is given by ready-mixed concrete in Denmark. In 1994, the Danish government ordered that all transaction prices for ready-mixed concrete be made public. This resulted in smaller price variability, but also higher average prices.

## 9.4 EMPIRICAL ANALYSIS OF CARTELS AND COLLUSION

There are various sources of information regarding the workings of cartels and, more generally, collusive agreements. First, for a time cartels were legal, and their modus operandi was reasonably well known to outsiders. This is the case, for example, of the rail shipping cartel (cf Section 9.2) and the bromide cartel (cf Section 9.3). Second, many illegal cartels are discovered and prosecuted by competition policy authorities; and court proceedings typically reveal a wealth of information regarding cartel operations. Finally, just as we can test between different models of oligopoly competition (see Section 8.3), we can also use historical market data to estimate the degree of collusion. I next review a few illustrative examples which, together, should provide a better understanding of collusion in practice.

□ **THE SUGAR CARTEL.**[18] In the 1910s and 1920s, the US cane sugar industry was suffering from falling margins and excess capacity. In December 1927, a trade association was formed to facilitate collusion among the leading 14 firms (which together comprised nearly all refining capacity). The agreement was maintained until 1936, at which point the US Supreme Court ruled its practices illegal.

The sugar cartel consisted of a "Code of Ethics" — complemented by a series of "Code Interpretations" — which covered various aspects of sugar distribution and marketing. The focus was on creating as much transparency as possible, so as to detect deviations clearly. For example, prices and other sales terms had to be publicly announced. By contrast, collusion on price was implicit rather than explicit.

The cartel was fairly successful: margins increased from about 5% to about 10%. There were some deviations from the tacitly agreed upon price levels; however, harsh punishments only took place in response to massive cheating. This leniency with respect to small deviations may have resulted from the high degree of communication among cartel members.

□ **THE LYSINE AND CITRIC ACID CARTELS.**[19] Lysine is a product added to pigs and poultry livestock feed. From 1990–1995, the five leading firms established a cartel agreement. Lysine is a customer market (see Chapter 6, that is, prices are typically agreed upon by means of bilateral negotiations. Perhaps for this reason the cartel terms were based on sales quotas: each month, sales reports were sent to the Japanese firm Ajinomoto, which acted as the cartel's central coordinator. Firms that exceed their quota were forced (by the threat of a cartel breakdown) to "buy-back" from firms with sales below their quotas. Perhaps not surprisingly, some firms lied in their reports so as to avoid "punishment" ("there is no honor among thieves," as they say).

Citric acid is primarily used in the food and beverage industry (other uses include household cleaning products, pharmaceuticals, cosmetics, and some industrial products). From 1991–1995, the five leading producers — which together accounted for about two-thirds of the global market — operated a cartel similar to the lysine's: market allocations were agreed upon and monthly sales reported to the cartel coordinator, which in this case was the Swiss firm Hoffmann LaRoche.

The lysine and citric acid cartels suggest that, if information about individual firms is good enough, then a system of individual punishments may work better than an industry-wide price war as suggested by the models presented in Section 9.2.

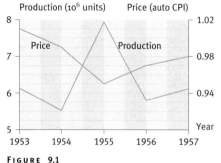
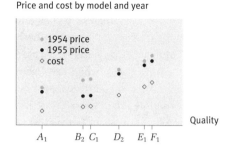

**FIGURE 9.1**

The 1955 price war in the US auto industry

☐ **COLLUSION IN THE US AUTO INDUSTRY.**[20]  The left panel of Figure 9.1 shows the evolution of price and output in the US auto industry during the mid 1950s. Clearly, 1955 was a special year: prices were lower and output level considerably greater than in the adjacent years. A tantalizing possibility is that the sharp shift in $p$ and $q$ resulted from the temporary breakdown in the industry's ability to collude (tacitly?) on high prices. How can we decide, based on the available data, if 1955 corresponded to a "price war" of the type considered in Section 9.2?

The right panel in Figure 9.1 describes a possible strategy for **statistical identification** of a change in the degree of collusion. Suppose that different car models can be characterized by quality level, which is measured along the horizontal axis.[l] Suppose that two producers, 1 and 2, offer a series of models: $A$, $C$, $E$, and $F$ by Firm 1; and $B$ and $D$ by Firm 2. On the vertical axis I measure both prices in 1954 and 1955 as well as per unit cost, which I assume is the same in both years.

The identification strategy is to note that, if two competing car models are sufficiently apart, then a change in the degree of collusion should have no effect on price-cost margins. Similarly, for two car models that are close to each other in product space but belong to the same supplier, a change in the degree of collusion should have no effect. A breakdown in collusion should be detected in the pricing of competing models that are close to each other in product space: for example, models $B_2$ and $C_1$ in the right panel of Figure 9.1. The empirical evidence from 85 different car models is consistent with this interpretation: in 1955, the degree of collusion was significantly lower than in 1954 or 1956.

l.  This is obviously a simplifying assumption. In Section 14.1 I will treat this issue in greater detail.

m.  The terms "antitrust" and "competition policy" are used in approximately the same meaning. The term "antitrust" usually refers to the US tradition, whereas the term "competition policy" usually refers to the European tradition.

## 9.5   PUBLIC POLICY

As I mentioned at the beginning of the chapter, firms have a natural incentive to come together and agree on setting high prices. A significant fraction of public policy related to industry competition (antitrust policy, competition policy) is directed precisely towards fighting the tendency for sellers to "conspire" against the consumer.[m]

As discussed in Section 5.3, there are various reasons why price fixing should be (and is) illegal. From an allocative efficiency point of view, the optimal solution is for firms to set prices at marginal cost level. Any deviation from this solution implies a welfare loss, one that grows with the difference between price and marginal cost at an increasing rate.[n]

Moreover, even if the allocative efficiency losses were not very significant, an increase in price implies a transfer from buyers to sellers — which frequently means a transfer from consumers to firms. In fact, it's fair to say that this has been the primary motivation behind public policy against price fixing: while economists have a tendency to stress allocative efficiency considerations — with little regard to distributional issues — policymakers in turn typically place a greater weight on consumer welfare than on total welfare. In the case of price fixing, the difference in motivation does not matter a great deal, for both lead to the same conclusion. The same is not true, however, in other areas of public policy (for example, mergers, as I will show in Section 11.3).

Price fixing is illegal in most countries of the world. In Europe, for example, the prohibition stems from Art. 101 of the **Treaty of the European Union**, which states that:

> The following shall be prohibited ...: (a) directly or indirectly fix purchase or selling prices ... (b) limit or control production ... (c) share markets or sources of supply ...

In the US, price fixing is illegal by virtue of the **Sherman Act**, which was passed in 1890:

> Section 1. Every contract, combination in the form of trust or otherwise, in restraint of trade or commerce ... is declared to be illegal.
>
> Section 2. Every person who shall monopolize, or attempt to monopolize, or combine or conspire with any other person or persons, to monopolize any part of the trade or commerce ... shall be deemed guilty of a felony ...

In most other countries, similar forms of legislation are in place. Every company, even if it does not operate in more than one country, is potentially subject to the oversight of a number of price-fixing watchdogs: in the US, the Federal Trade Commission (FTC) and the Department of Justice (DoJ); in Europe, the European Commission's Directorate-General for Competition (or simply DG Comp) and various country-level competition policy agencies, such as the UK's Office of Fair Trade (OFT) and Germany's Federal Cartel Office (Bundeskartellamt). The list extends to many other countries, including Japan's Fair Trade Commission, China's Ministry of Commerce, and Brazil's Conselho Administrativo de Defesa Econômica.

■ **EXPLICIT AND TACIT COLLUSION.** As described in Box 9.5, in 1963 GE and Westinghouse initiated a period of more than a decade of high and stable prices. There is no evidence that, during this period, GE maintained any direct contact with Westinghouse. Moreover, GE and Westinghouse later denied that their intent had been to stabilize prices. Rather, they justified their identical prices as the result of conscious parallelism or the exercise of price leadership by GE, none of which violates US antitrust laws.[o]

Economists and lawyers at the DOJ did not buy into this story, but it was not easy — certainly not obvious — how to construct an anticompetitive argument to condemn the duopolists. It took more than a decade before the DOJ revisited the case.

n. If demand is linear and marginal cost constant, then the efficiency loss is a quadratic function of the difference between price and marginal cost.

o. Conscious parallelism is the situation when, absent an actual agreement between firms, prices move in parallel, typically with one firm acting as a price leader and its rivals then following suit.

Threatening to sue GE and Westinghouse, the DOJ was able to effectively force the companies to stop their pricing practices.

This GE-Westinghouse case marks a watershed in antitrust thinking. The new antitrust doctrine argues that an agreement between firms does not require a smoke-filled-room type of conspiracy: the agreement can also be established through a "public communication of pricing system." Publishing a price book and announcing price changes ahead of time may be construed as an invitation for the rival to do the same; and as a result may have the same effect as meeting the rival face to face.

In this regard, an interesting test was provided by the 1994 airline tariff publishing (ATP) case.[21] Major airlines are linked by computer ticket reservation systems. The US DOJ argued that such common systems allow airlines to effectively "communicate" and "coordinate" pricing plans by means of fare change announcement. For example, a given airline might announce that its fares would increase in a week's time. The other airlines could then follow by announcing a fare increase effective the same date; or by not doing so, in which case the first airline could reverse its initial announcement. The result, similar to the GE-Westinghouse system, was a pattern of uniform fares and parallel fare changes across airlines.

■ **JURISDICTION.** One important point to keep in mind regarding price fixing legislation — and competition policy more generally — is that their application is not limited to the firms headquartered in each particular jurisdiction. For example, in the 1980s the European Economic Community (EEC, the European Union's predecessor) sued a series of companies in the wood pulp industry for alleged price fixing. Among the defendants were several US companies that argued that they could not be prosecuted by a non-US entity. The EEC in turn argued that it could regulate conduct taking place outside its territory as long as it had repercussions inside its territory. In a 1988 milestone decision, the courts sided with the EEC, effectively adopting an **effects doctrine**.[22]

The same is true in the US, where prosecutors do not "discriminate in the enforcement of the antitrust laws on the basis of the nationality of the parties."[23] In fact, as of October 2012, of the 21 Sherman Act violation cases prosecuted by the US DOJ that led to fines of more than $100 million, only two involved a US firm (Archer Daniels Midland Co. in 1996 and UCAR International Inc. in 1998). The remaining 19 involved companies from Taiwan, Switzerland, Japan, Korea, France, the Netherlands, UK, Germany, Luxembourg, Chile, and Brazil.[24]

Regarding jurisdiction, an important point to mention is the possibility of extradition. The US Department of Justice found Romano Pisciotti, an Italian national and former executive of Parker ITR, guilty of bid rigging in the sale of marine hoses in the US and elsewhere. When traveling from Nigeria to Italy in June 2013, Mr. Pisciotti made a stopover in Germany. There he was arrested and, in April 2014, extradited to the US, where he was sentenced by a federal district court to serve 24 months in prison and to pay a $50,000 fine. In the past, many foreign executives were formally accused of antitrust violations. However, by declining to appear in the US to face cartel charges, they were free from any punishment. The Pisciotti case marks the first successful extradition ever that is based on an antitrust charge (in this case bid rigging, which is a crime both in the US and in Germany).

■ **Leniency programs.** Leniency programs promise special treatment to price-fixing violators who approach anti-cartel authorities — if they are the first to do so. Although the original leniency program was instituted in the US, today many jurisdictions around the world have implemented their own programs, including the EC, the UK, South Korea, and Japan.

Consider the example of Virgin Atlantic (VA) and British Airways (BA).[25] In August 2004, BA decided to increase its passenger "fuel surcharge," an extra tariff placed on tickets to compensate for high oil prices. BA wanted to sound out VA on the price increase. In fact, the two firms exchanged information at least six times between August 2004 and January 2006. Meanwhile, fuel surcharges increased in tandem from £5 to £60 ($10 to $110).

In 2007, a number of investigations were in place regarding fuel surcharges to cargo clients. Fearing that the investigation would turn to passenger fuel surcharges, Virgin lawyers decided it would be better to move early. After an anonymous phone call established that VA would gain immunity under the UK leniency program, Virgin provided the UK's Office of Fair Trade (OFT) with large amounts of information, including phone records and interviews with staff members. BA was beaten to the clock and eventually was sentenced to fines in the hundreds of millions of dollars; VA in turn received a thank you note.

Leniency programs are not immune to criticism. For example, many question the fairness of letting one guilty party walk out unpunished while another one suffers severe penalties — maybe even jail sentences — for the very same offense. Notwithstanding this and other limitations, leniency programs have proved very powerful tools to discover and prosecute secret cartels. Can you see why? (Hint: think about the prisoner's dilemma.) See Exercise 9.10 for more on this.

■ **NON-PRICE HORIZONTAL AGREEMENTS.** Not all agreements between firms amount to conspiracies against consumers. In fact, many may work to the consumers' greater benefit. For example, in 1982 the Semiconductor Research Corporation (SRC) was founded by companies such as Intel, AMD, IBM, and Texas Instruments to "to provide competitive advantage to its members," namely through applied research programs. While these projects benefit its members, some of the benefits are likely to be passed on to consumers. For this reason, entities such as the SRC are either immune or nearly immune to antitrust prosecution. For example, the US National Cooperative Research and Production Act of 1984 reduces potential antitrust liabilities of research joint ventures (RJV) and standards development organizations (SDO). The problem is that such agreements also create a much improved set of circumstances for firms to collude to fix prices.[p]

p. The particular case of R&D agreements is addressed in greater detail in Section 15.4.

■ **INDUSTRY ASSOCIATIONS AND INFORMATION EXCHANGE.** Industry associations allow firms to exchange information regarding costs, demand, or even prices. Information exchange per se does not violate any of the laws against price fixing. But, as Box 9.6 suggests, information exchange may facilitate price fixing, or at least implicit collusion. Consider the case of ocean shipping. Shipping lines contend that information exchange is necessary to stabilize rates and service. In fact, they have been granted a number of exemptions from US antitrust law based on this defense. However, buyers argue that information exchange allows sellers to charge more than they would otherwise.

▪ **COMPETITION POLICY IN DEVELOPING COUNTRIES.** By looking at antitrust legislation around the world, we find a consensus that collusion is and should be illegal. In practice, however, the intensity with which the legislation is enforced varies considerably: for example, as a general rule antitrust enforcement has been stricter in the US than in most other countries.

In this respect, a note regarding developing countries is in order. As an economy undergoes a process of deregulation and growth, competition policy issues become relatively more important. However, frequently the "culture" of competition policy lags behind economic growth. Consider the case of Brazil, where the Conselho Administrativo de Defesa Econômica (CADE) has fought cartel behavior for years. A list of cases compiled by CADE shows businesses forming cartel agreements with complete unawareness of competition legislation.

> The cases range from retailers that register price fixing agreements in the notary to guarantee that no party will violate the illegal deal, to resellers that publish price increase charts in the newspaper, alleging "transparency," and even some who resort to CADE itself to complain that members of a cartel violated private deals and caused "losses" to other industry companies.[26]

Clearly, a solid competition policy must begin with a solid process of education in competition policy. It is therefore reassuring that newly formed regulators such as the Competition Authority of Kenya include as part of their mandate to "promote public knowledge, awareness and understanding of the obligations, rights, and remedies under the [Competition] Act."

▪ **SELECTED RECENT CASES.** Most antitrust and competition policy is based on precedent, that is, decisions made in previous related cases. I next list a series of recent cases which, together, provide an overview of some of the direction of public policy toward collusion.

☐ **CHOCOLATE.** In a 2008 class-action suit in Canada, lawyers representing chocolate consumers successfully argued that several major manufacturers conspired to increase prices. From court proceedings, it was revealed that discussions were held at trade shows and association events. The total settlements from the case amounted to C$23.2 million (Canadian dollars), from C$3.2 million paid by Mars to C$9 million paid by Nestlé. Mars and Nestlé still face criminal charges from a separate case initiated by Canada's Competition Bureau. As in the US and the UK, price-fixing is a crime in

Canada. Unlike Mars and Nestlé, Hershey was left off the hook courtesy of the Canadian leniency program.

A class-action suit was also initiated in the US. Although the evidence from the Canadian case was quite solid, the US case was struck down. The deciding judge opined that "nothing scandalous or improper has been discovered within our borders, and no evidence permits a reasonable inference of a price-fixing agreement."

Meanwhile, in a separate case the German Cartel Commission found a similar set of firms guilty of price fixing, meting out fines for a total of over €60 million. This time Mars was able to dodge any financial penalty as one of the initial whistleblowers.

The chocolate price-fixing cases provide a good example of the limits of transporting evidence across jurisdictions. Similarly, it shows that leniency programs are jurisdiction specific. Finally, we have here an illustration of the difference and complementarity between government initiated cases (e.g., German Cartel Commission) and private suits. In same countries, like Canada, it's perfectly possible that both proceed in parallel.

☐ **APPLE AND E-BOOK PUBLISHING.** Amazon has established itself as a leading discount book seller; e-books are no exception: typically, Amazon sells them for $9.99 (and a loss from a wholesale price between $10 and $15). Publishers have not been happy with the system, which, in their own words, erodes margins and is destroying the business.

Apple's entry in e-books, which essentially coincided with the launch of the iPad, was thus received as a sign of hope. Apple promised to "liberate" publishers from the Amazon's "shackles" by introducing an alternative system: the agency model. The idea is that publishers set prices and the retailer (e.g., Apple) charges a fee (30% in Apple's case). Moreover, Apple imposed on publishers a Most Favored Nation (MFN) clause: if they were to sell to a different retailer (meaning Amazon) at a lower price, then Apple's sale price would be equally reduced.

In April 2012, the US DOJ sued Apple and the major publishers, arguing that the agency model, together with the MFN clause, facilitated collusion in e-book pricing. In fact, it all but eliminated the publishers' incentives to lower prices below the Apple-recommended $14.99; it's as if Apple served as a "coordination device" for price fixing.

In December 2013, Hachette, HarperCollins, Simon & Schuster, Macmillan, and Penguin agreed to settle while denying any wrongdoing. Apple, by contrast, refused to settle and the case was taken to court, which found that Apple violated antitrust law in helping raise the retail price of e-books. As of the writing of this book, the case is still on appeal.

The Apple decision does *not* imply that the agency model or MFC clauses are illegal *per se*. However, it solidifies the doctrine that collusion is not limited to smoke-filled room price fixing: facilitating practices too can be deemed anticompetitive (compare to the GE and Westinghouse case discussed in Box 9.5).

☐ **LIBOR SETTING.** The London InterBank Offered Rate (LIBOR or Libor) is a benchmark rate that some of the world's leading banks charge each other for short-term loans. Many financial institutions, mortgage lenders, and credit card agencies set their own rates relative to the Libor; it is estimated that more than $350 trillion in financial instruments are tied to it.

For each of the major currencies, a set of 11 to 18 banks submit (daily) a series of rates at which they would be prepared to lend money to one another (from overnight to one-year rates). The four highest and four lowest rates are dropped, an average is taken of the remaining rates, and the Libor rate is set.

Beginning with a short 2008 article that later turned into a longer study, the *Wall Street Journal* reported on a major case of interest rate manipulation: it was discovered that banks were falsely inflating or deflating their rates so as to profit from trades. As a expert noted, "this dwarfs by orders of magnitude any financial scam in the history of markets."

In December 2013, the EU fined a group of global financial institutions a combined €1.7 billion ($2.3 billion) to settle charges, the largest combined fine in EC history. Meanwhile, the US DOJ and the Canadian Competition Bureau opened criminal investigations into price fixing.

□ **Labor contracts in Silicon Valley.** Beginning in 2013, the US DoJ filed a series of civil antitrust suits against Adobe, Apple, eBay, Google, Intel, Intuit, Lucasfilm, and Pixar. The claim: that these firms established a series of "no cold call" agreements: for example, senior executives of eBay and Intuit agreed not to recruit employees from each other.

The relevant district court found that the agreements, if proven, would amount to a naked horizontal market allocation agreement, thus manifestly anticompetitive and per se unlawful. Eventually, a series of settlements was reached.

These cases are interesting in showing that illegal horizontal practices are not restricted to sellers' actions. Buyer collusion — a form of **monopsony power** — also constitutes a violation of the Sherman Act. Nor are illegal horizontal practices limited to setting prices: any horizontal agreement that limits the degree of competition — such as an agreement not to poach the rival's customers or employees — is per se illegal.

□ **Synthetic rubber.** In November 2006, the European Commission (EC) fined ENI and Versalis €272.25 million for participating in the synthetic rubber cartel. The fine includes a 50% increase due to recidivism: both firms had already participated in polypropylene (1986) and PVC II (1994) cartels. In January 2008, Bayer and Zeon were also fined for cartelization. Bayer's and Zeon's fines were reduced by 30 and 20%, respectively, under the EC leniency program. However, Bayer's fine was increased by 50% because it had been fined for cartel activity in a previous commission decision.

This case is not particularly important as a doctrine-making precedent. However, it illustrates the system of positive and negative incentives — sticks and carrots — implicit in the European system: extra fines for recidivism, leniency for cooperation. At the time of the Bayer decision, then Competition Commissioner Neelie Kroes stated:

> This is the fourth cartel decision in the synthetic rubber industry in just over three years. I hope that this is the last.

If you ask me, I would call this wishful thinking: commodity cartels are plenty and probably will never end (recall Adam Smith's sentence that opens the chapter). Commissioner Kroes' statement is particularly wishful thinking if we recall that, in the European Union, price fixing is only a civil offense. Perhaps things would be different if, following the US tradition, it were also deemed a criminal offense.

■ **OVERALL ASSESSMENT OF PUBLIC POLICY TOWARD PRICE FIXING.** Has public policy against price fixing worked? The data clearly shows that the laws have bite: many firms are fined for violating price-fixing laws; and where price fixing is a criminal offense (e.g., in the US), many jail sentences are meted out.[q] But has cartel busting brought lower prices to consumers?

It is not easy to answer this question. Consider the example of Christie's and Sotheby's. Their main business is to auction fine art and other valuables. Their customers are the buyers and the sellers brought together by the auction houses. The "prices" that the two auction houses charge are (essentially) seller commission fees and buyer commission fees (also known as buyer penalties). In the mid 1990s, Christie's and Sotheby's engaged in a secret agreement to fix seller commission fees at higher and non-negotiable levels. Eventually, the cartel was discovered and broken up: civil and criminal suits were brought against the houses; and the defendants were found guilty and sentenced in 2000. It is safe to say that no secret cartel exists between Christie's and Sotheby's these days. However, the commission fees they charge are as high as ever, arguably higher than the high levels attained when there was a cartel!

However, fine art auctions is not the only cartel in the world; and in many other cases cartel busting did result in lower prices. Moreover, one must not forget the deterrent effect of public policy against price fixing. While it is very difficult to measure this effect, it is reasonable to assume that many firms are dissuaded from fixing prices by the threat of being prosecuted. Long live antitrust and competition policy!

## SUMMARY

• Collusion in normally easier to maintain when firms interact frequently and when the probability of industry continuation and growth is high. • If price cuts are difficult to observe, then occasional price wars may be necessary to discipline collusive agreements. • Collusion is normally easier to maintain among few and similar

q. In the US, more than 50% of the criminal defendants accused of price fixing end up serving jail sentences.[27]

firms. • Collusion is normally easier to maintain when firms compete in more than one market.

## KEY CONCEPTS

• externality • market power • collusion • cartel • secret agreements • tacit agreements • repeated game • grim strategies • no-deviation constraints • discount factor • customer markets • facilitating practices • most-favored-customer • transparency • statistical identification • Treaty of the European Union • Sherman Act • effects doctrine • leniency programs • monopsony power

## REVIEW AND PRACTICE EXERCISES

■ **9.1. TACIT COLLUSION.** Industries A and B can be characterized by a series of parameters: $n$, the number of firms, is 8 in both industries; $r$, the annual interest rate, is 10% in both countries; $f$, the frequency with which firms interact (number of times per year), is 1 in industry A and 12 in industry B; $g$, the industry growth rate, is 10% in industry A and $-30\%$ in industry B; finally, $h$, the likelihood that the industry will continue in existence into the next period, is 80% in industry A and 100% in industry B.

In which of the two industries do you think tacit collusion is more likely to take place? Briefly justify your answer.

■ **9.2. $n$ FIRM OLIGOPOLY.** Consider a price-setting oligopoly with $n$ firms, all with constant marginal cost $c$. Suppose market demand is given by $D(p)$ and the discount factor is .8. Determine the maximum number of firms such that there exists an equilibrium with monopoly pricing.

■ **9.3. REPEATED INTERACTION.** Explain why collusive pricing is difficult in one-period competition and easier when firms interact over a number of periods.

■ **9.4. AIRBUS AND BOEING.** Boeing and Airbus seem to cycle between periods of severe price competition and pledges that they will not sink into another war. Based on the analysis of Section 9.1, why do you think it is so difficult for aircraft manufacturers to collude and avoid price wars?

■ **9.5. PRICE WARS.** "Price wars imply losses for all of the firms involved. The empirical observation of price wars is therefore a proof that firms do not behave rationally." True or false?

■ **9.6. AIRLINE FARE WARS I.** Empirical evidence from the US airline industry suggests that fare wars are more likely when carriers have excess capacity, caused by GDP growth falling short of its predicted trend. Fare wars are also more likely during the spring and summer quarters, when more discretionary travel takes place.[28] Explain how these two observations are consistent with the theories presented in Section 9.2.

■ **9.7. AIRLINE FARE WARS II.** A 1998 news article reported that:

> Delta Air Lines and American Airlines tried to raise leisure air fares 4% in most domestic markets, but the move failed Monday when lone-holdout Northwest Airlines refused to match the higher prices.
>
> The aborted price boost illustrates the impact Northwest's woes already are having on the industry. Months of labor unrest ... are prompting passengers to book away from the fourth largest carrier.[29]

What does this say about the nature of price dynamics in the airline industry?

■ **9.8. PAPER PRODUCTS.** In the third quarter of 1999, most North American paper and forest-products companies experienced an improvement in their results. The industry, analysts said, was in a cyclical upswing: not only was demand increasing at a moderate pace; more important, the industry practiced restraint in keeping low production levels, thus providing support for higher prices.[30]

How do you interpret these events in light of the models presented in Section 9.2?

■ **9.9. EXPORT CARTELS.** In 1918, the US Congress passed a low allowing American firms to form export cartels. Empirical evidence suggests that cartels were more likely to be formed in industries where American exporters had a large market share, in capital-intensive industries, in industries selling standardized goods, and in industries that enjoyed strong export growth.[31] Discuss.

■ **9.10. CARTEL LENIENCY.** Many antitrust authorities throughout the world have implemented leniency programs targeted at busting secret cartels. These programs offer immunity from prosecution to firms who blow the whistle on their co-cartel conspirators. These programs have proven extremely successful: in the US, from 1993 to 2000 the total amount of fines for anti-competitive behavior increased by twentyfold.

Show how the leniency programs first implemented by the US Department of Justice and later replicated in many countries changes the rules of the game played between firms in a secret cartel.

■ **9.11. CORPORATE LENIENCY.** A study of the European corporate leniency program shows that the likelihood of a firm becoming the chief witness increases with its character as repeat offender, the size of the expected basic fine, the number of countries active in one group, as well as the size of the firm's share in the cartelized market.[32] Are these results consistent with the discussion of these programs in the text?

■ **9.12. IVY LEAGUE.** The endowments of the Ivy League universities have increased significantly in recent decades. This wealth notwithstanding, for years the universities managed to refrain from using financial incentives as a means to compete for students: the manual of the Council of Ivy League Presidents stated that the schools should "neutralize the effect of financial aid so that a student may choose among Ivy Group institutions for non-financial reasons." In 1991, the Justice Department argued that this amounted to price collusion and forced the agreement to end. However, no significant price competition took place until 1998, when Princeton University started offering full scholarships for students with incomes below $40,000. Stanford, MIT, Dartmouth, and Cornell followed suit. Allegedly, Harvard sent a letter to accepted 1998 applicants stating that "we expect that some of our students will have particularly attractive offers from the institutions with new aid programs, and those students should not assume that we will not respond."[r]

How do you interpret these events in light of the theories discussed in this chapter?

■ **9.13. SPANISH HOTELS.** Based on data from the Spanish hotel industry, it was estimated that the rate set by hotel $i$ in market $k$ is positively influenced by a variable that measures the intensity of multimarket competition between hotel $i$ and its competitors in market $k$: the more markets $m \neq k$ in which firm $i$ and its competitors meet, the greater the measure of multimarket contact. It was also observed that the measure of multimarket contact is highly correlated with hotel chain size, that is, the larger hotel $i$'s chain, the greater the measure of multimarket contact for firm $i$.[33]

Provide two interpretations for the positive coefficient of multimarket contact on hotel rates, one based on collusion, one based on a different effect.

■ **9.14. RAILROADS.** In 1986, the US Congress enacted a regulation (PL99-509) requiring railroads to disclose contractual terms with grain shippers. Following the passing of the legislation, rates increased on corridors with no direct competition from barge traffic, while rates decreased on corridors with substantial direct competition.[34] How do you interpret these events?

■ **9.15. MULTIMARKET CONTACT.** Consider the model of multimarket contact presented in Section 9.3: Firm 1 has cost $\underline{c}$ in Market 1, while Firm 2 has a cost $\overline{c}$. The situation is reversed in Market 2. Demand is the same in both markets: consumers are willing to buy $q$ units for a price of up to $p^M$ (that is, for $p \leq p^M$, quantity demanded does not depend on price). It is assumed that $\underline{c} < \overline{c} < p^M$. In each period, firms set prices in both markets simultaneously.

Determine the minimum value of the discount factor such that the optimal collusive solution is stable.

■ **9.16. PRICE-MATCHING GUARANTEES.** In some industries firms offer price-matching guarantees (also known as meet-the-competition clauses): if some rival offers a price lower than firm $i$, then firm $i$ is forced to offer the same price to all of its customers. Consider a price-setting, homogenous-product oligopoly and suppose that all firms have constant marginal cost $c$ and offer the same price-matching guarantee. Specifically, firms simultaneously set prices (as in the Bertrand model); and if some firm sets a lower price than other firms, then all firms must match that price. Show that any price between cost and monopoly price can be obtained as the play of a Nash equilibrium.

## CHALLENGING EXERCISES

■ **9.17. NUMBER OF COMPETITORS.** Consider an $n$ firm homogeneous-good oligopoly with constant marginal cost, the same for all firms. Let $\bar{\delta}$ be the minimum value of the discount factor such that it is possible to sustain monopoly prices in a collusive agreement. Show that $\bar{\delta}$ is decreasing in $n$. Interpret the result.

■ **9.18. TWO MARKETS.** Consider the model of multimarket contact presented in Section 9.3. Determine the minimum value of the discount factor such that the optimal collusive solution is stable.

■ **9.19. SECRET PRICE CUTS.** This exercise formalizes the model of secret price cups presented in Section 9.2.[35] Suppose that all consumers are willing to pay $u$ for the (homogeneous) product sold by two duopolists. In each period, demand can be high (probability $1 - \alpha$) or low (probability $\alpha$). When demand is high, $h = 1$ units can be sold at price $u$ (or any lower price). When demand is low, only $l = 0 < h$ units can be sold. The probability that demand is high or low in each period is independent of what it was in the previous period. Moreover, *firms are unable to observe the state of market demand*; all they can observe is whether *their own* demand is high or low. Finally, for simplicity, assume that production costs are zero.

Consider the following equilibrium strategies. Firms start by setting $p = u$. If they receive a positive demand (namely, $\frac{1}{2}$), then they continue to set $p = u$, that is, they remain in the "cooperative phase". If however one of the firms (or both) receives zero demand, then both firms enter into a "price war:" they set $p = 0$ during $T$ periods and, after this period, revert to $p = u$ again (the cooperative phase).[s] Let $V$ be the net present value of a firm in equilibrium (starting in a period where collusion takes place).

(a) Show that:

$$V = (1 - \alpha)\left(\frac{u}{2} + \delta V\right) + \alpha\, \delta^{T+1} V$$

(b) Show that the best a firm can do by deviating is to get:

$$V' = (1 - \alpha)\, u + \delta^{T+1} V$$

(c) Show that the condition that the prescribed strategy constitutes an equilibrium is given by:

$$1 \le 2(1 - \alpha)\,\delta + (2\alpha - 1)\,\delta^{T+1}$$

(d) What is then the optimal equilibrium?

s. Notice that, if a firm receives zero demand, then it is common knowledge that a price war is going to start, that is, it is common knowledge that one of the firms receives zero demand. In fact, either demand is low, in which case both firms receive zero demand, or one of the firms deviates from $p = u$, in which case the deviating firm knows that the rival receives zero demand.

■ **9.20. DEMAND FLUCTUATIONS.** This exercise formalizes the model of demand fluctuations considered in Section 9.2.[36] The new model is similar to the model in Exercise 9.19, with the difference that we now assume that in each period, before setting prices, firms observe the state of demand.[t] We also make the simplifying assumption that $\alpha = \frac{1}{2}$, that is, the high- and the low-demand states are equally likely.

(a) Show that, if the discount factor is sufficiently large, specifically, if $\delta > \frac{2h}{3h+l}$, then there exists an equilibrium where firms set monopoly price in every period (similarly to Section 9.1).

(b) Suppose now that the discount factor $\delta$ is lower than, but close to, the threshold derived in the previous answer. Show that, while there exists no equilibrium where firms set monopoly price in every period, there exists an equilibrium where firms set monopoly price during periods of low demand and a lower price during period of high demand.

## APPLIED EXERCISES

■ **9.21. MULTIMARKET CONTACT.** Choose a pair of firms from a given industry. Determine the extent to which there is multimarket contact between these firms and how it may help them soften competition.

## NOTES

1. See Book I, Chapter 10, para. 82 in Adam Smith (1776), "An Inquiry into the Nature and Causes of the Wealth of Nations," London: W. Strahan.

2. See Box 9.5 and Fuller, John (1962), *The Gentlemen Conspirators: The Story of the Price-Fixers in the Electrical Industry*, New York: Grove Press, 1962.

3. This kind of equilibria, as they apply to oligopoly competition, were first proposed by Friedman, James (1971), "A Noncooperative Equilibrium for Supergames," *Review of Economic Studies* **28**, 1–12.

4. Adapted and quoted from Porter, Robert H. (1983), "A Study of Cartel Stability: The Joint Executive Committee, 1880–1886," *Bell Journal of Economics* **14**, 301–314.

5. This subsection follows the analysis proposed by Green, Ed and Robert Porter (1984), "Noncooperative Collusion Under Imperfect Price Information," *Econometrica* **52**, 87–100. These authors in turn follow the seminal work by Stigler, George (1964), "A Theory of Oligopoly," *Journal of Political Economy* **72**, 44–61.

6. Rotemberg, Julio, and Garth Saloner (1986), "A Supergame-Theoretic Model of Price Wars During Booms," *American Economic Review* **76**, 390–407.

7. See Box 9.2 and Porter, op. cit. See also Ellison, Glenn (1994), "Theories of Cartel Stability and the Joint Executive Committee," *Rand Journal of Economics* **25**, 37–57.

8. *Aviation Week and Space Technology*, January 11, 1993. For econometric evidence on this claim, see Busse, Meghan R. (1997), "Firm Financial Conditions and Airline Price Wars," Yale School of Management.

t. Firms can also observe past decisions by rival firms.

9. *Financial Times,* 1 February 1995.

10. *The Economist*, August 30, 2014.

11. Levenstein, Margaret C. (1997), "Price Wars and the Stability of Collusion: A Study of the Pre-World War I Bromine Industry," *Journal of Industrial Economics* **45**, 117–137.

12. The following analysis draws partly on Bernheim, B. Douglas and Michael D. Whinston (1990), "Multimarket Contact and Collusive Behavior," *Rand Journal of Economics* **21**, 1–26.

13. Adapted from Evans, W. N., and I. N. Kessides (1994), "Living by the 'Golden Rule': Multimarket Contact in the US Airline Industry," *Quarterly Journal of Economics* **109**, 341–366.

14. Adapted from Toby Stuart, "Cat Fight in the Pet Food Industry," Harvard Business School Case No. 9-391-189.

15. Adapted from Porter, Michael (1980), "General Electric Vs. Westinghouse in Large Turbine Generators," Harvard Business School Case No. 9-380-129.

16. Text and data adapted from Albæk, Svend, Peter Møllgaard, and Per B Overgaard (1997), "Government-Assisted Oligopoly Coordination? A *Concrete* Case," *Journal of Industrial Economics* **45**, 429–443.

17. See Fuller, Stephen W, Fred J Ruppel, and David A Bessler (1990), "Effect of Contract Disclosure on Price: Railroad Grain Contracting in the Plains," *Western Journal of Agricultural Economics* **15** (2), 265–271.

18. Adapted from Genesove, David, and Wallace P. Mullin (2001), "Rules, Communication, and Collusion: Narrative Evidence from the Sugar Institute Case," *American Economic Review* **91** (3), 379–398.

19. Adapted from Harrington, Joseph E., and Andrzej Skrzypacz (2011), "Private Monitoring and Communication in Cartels: Explaining Recent Collusive Practices," *American Economic Review* **101** (6), 2425–2449.

20. Adapted from Bresnahan, Timothy F. (1987), "Competition and Collusion in the American Automobile Industry: The 1955 Price War," *Journal of Industrial Economics* **35** (4), 457-82.

21. See Borenstein, Severin, "Rapid Price Communication and Coordination: The Airline Tariff Publication Case (1994)," in J. Kwoka and L. White (Eds.), *The Antitrust Revolution*, 3rd Ed., 1999.

22. Ahlstrom Osakeyhtio and Others vs. Commission of the European Communities (Judgment September 27).

23. US Department of Justice and Federal Trade Commission, Antitrust Enforcement Guidelines for International Operations, April 1995; at http://www.justice.gov/atr/public/guidelines/internat.htm, visited October 2012.

24. http://www.justice.gov/atr/public/criminal/sherman10.html, visited October 2012.

25. Adapted from Cabral, Luís (2009), "Leniency Programs: Virgin Atlantic and British Airways," case study.

26. Basile, Juliano, and Lucas Marchesini (2014), "Small Antitrust Cases Show How Widespread Violations in Brazil Are," *Valor Internacional*, September 15.

27. See http://www.justice.gov/atr/public/criminal/264101.html.

28. Morrison, Steven A., and Clifford Winston (1996), "Causes and Consequences of Airline Fare Wars," *Brookings Papers on Economic Activity* (Microeconomics), 205–276.

29. *The Wall Street Journal Europe*, August 12, 1998.

30. *The Wall Street Journal*, October 11, 1999.

31. Dick, Andrew (1997), "If Cartels Were Legal, Would Firms Fix Prices?," Antitrust Division, US Department of Justice.

32. Hoang, Cung Truong, Kai Hüeschelrath, Ulrich Laitenberger, and Florian Smuda (2014), "Determinants of Self-Reporting Under the European Corporate Leniency Program," University of St. Gallen and ZEW Centre for European Economic Research.

33. Fernández, Nerea, and Pedro Marín (1998), "Market Power and Multimarket Contact: Some Evidence from the Spanish Hotel Industry," *Journal of Industrial Economics* **46**, 301–315.

34. See Schmitz, John, and Stephen W. Fuller (1995), "Effect of Contract Disclosure on Railroad Grain Rates: An Analysis of Corn Belt Corridors," *The Logistics and Transportation Review* **31**, 97–124.

35. This model is adapted from Tirole, Jean (1989), *The Theory of Industrial Organization*, Cambridge, Mass: MIT Press, who in turn presents a simplification of the model proposed by Green and Porter, op. cit.

36. This model is adapted from Rotemberg, Julio, and Garth Saloner (1986), "A Supergame-Theoretic Model of Price Wars During Booms," *American Economic Review* **76**, 390–407.

ENTRY AND MARKET STRUCTURE

CHAPTER **10**

# MARKET STRUCTURE

How many firms would you expect to find in a given industry? How large would you expect those firms to be? These are hard questions to answer, and as we saw in Section 4.2 the perfect competition model has little to offer as an answer: if there are constant returns to scale (that is, average cost is constant), then *any* number and size distribution of firms is possible (so long as each firm is sufficiently small for the assumption of price-taking behavior to hold).[1] Not much prediction power here.

But let us look at the empirical evidence. The left panel in Figure 10.1 depicts data on market concentration (measured by C4, the total market share of the top four firms) in a number of sectors in France and in Germany. That is, for each sector, a point is marked such that the horizontal coordinate is the value of C4 in France and the vertical coordinate is the value of C4 in Germany. For example, if in a given sector the four largest French firms hold 40% of the market, whereas the four largest German firms hold 60% of the market, then a point (.4,.6) appears in the diagram. The right panel in Figure 10.1 represents a similar diagram, this time for France and Belgium.

If the reality of the firm size distribution were as unpredictable as the model of perfect competition suggests, then we would expect the diagrams to be just a chaotic cloud of points. However, the first diagram shows a remarkable regularity, with most points close to the 45° line. In words, for each industry, the value of C4 in France is very similar to the value of C4 in Germany. This suggests that there are industry-specific factors which determine each firm's size.

In contrast with the left panel in Figure 10.1, the right panel shows that most points are above the diagonal. In words, for each sector, the value of C4 tends to be greater in Belgium than in France. One important difference between the two panels is that, whereas the left panel refers to two economies of similar size (both in population and in GDP), the right panel compares two countries of very different size (France being some five times bigger than Belgium). Together, these diagrams suggest that market size, in addition to industry-specific factors, is an important determinant of market structure.

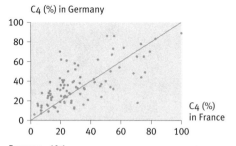

**FIGURE 10.1**
Industry concentration in France, Germany and Belgium[2]

In this chapter, I focus precisely on how technology and market size, as well as competition and market power, influence firm size and industry concentration. Before that, however, I deal with issues of measurement.

■ **MEASURING MARKET CONCENTRATION AND MARKET POWER.** In Chapter 8, I considered mostly symmetric oligopoly models. In this context, the number of firms, $n$, is a good indicator of industry structure: the lower $n$, the more concentrated the industry is. Specifically, $1/n$ might be a good measure of concentration, a measure that varies from 0 (minimum concentration) and 1 (maximum concentration, monopoly).

In practice, different firms have different market shares, and a simple firm count misses out important information regarding market structure and industry concentration. For example, five firms of the same size is not the same thing as one with 96% and the remaining four with 1% each. In this context, an alternative to counting the number of firms is to measure the coefficient $C_m$, the sum of the market shares of the largest $m$ firms. In particular,

$$C_4 \equiv \sum_{i=1}^{4} s_i$$

where firms are ordered by market shares (Firm 1 is the largest firm, and so on). The value of $C_4$ varies between zero (minimum concentration) and one (maximum concentration); or between zero and 100, if we measure market share by percentage points (that is, from 0 to 100).

Still another alternative measure of market concentration is the Herfindahl-Hirschman index (sometimes referred to as the **Herfindahl index**, sometimes $HHI$, sometimes $H$), which is given by:

$$H \equiv \sum_{i=1}^{n} s_i^2$$

The value of $H$ varies between zero (minimum concentration) and one (maximum concentration, i.e., monopoly). If market shares are measured in percent points, then the value of $H$ varies between zero and 10,000.

The Herfindahl index provides a better measure of market concentration, as I will show later. However, it is more difficult to compute: it requires knowledge of the market share of all firms in the industry, whereas $C_4$, for example, only requires knowledge of the market shares of the four largest firms.[a]

We are also interested in measuring market power. Up to now, I did so by computing the price cost margin: either $p - MC$ or $(p - MC)/p$ or $(p - MC)/MC$. This is fine if all firms have the same costs. If costs vary from firm to firm, then so do margins (even if market price is the same for all firms, which is the case when the product is homogeneous). What is then market power in the industry as a whole? The natural generalization of the margin is the **Lerner index**, defined as the weighted average of each firm's margin, with weights given by the firm's market share:

$$L \equiv \sum_{i=1}^{n} s_i \frac{p - MC_i}{p} \tag{10.1}$$

where $s_i$ is firm $i$'s market share.[3,b] Obviously, if all firms have the same marginal cost, then the Lerner index is simply the (common) margin set by all firms, as considered before.

## 10.1 ENTRY COSTS AND MARKET STRUCTURE

My first goal is to determine the relation between technology, market size, and industry concentration. I begin by considering a simple model in which all firms are of the same size. For this reason, determining concentration is equivalent to determining the number of firms. C4, for example, is given by $4/n$; that is, if all firms are of the same size, then the market share of the four largest firms is equal to the ratio of four to the number of firms. Changes in C4 can therefore be measured by changes in $n$.

Suppose that a generic firm, firm $i$, has a cost function given by $C = F + c q_i$ and that the demand curve is given by $Q = (a - P) S$. In this equation, $S$ stands for market size. I am therefore allowing two different markets (e.g., the market for a given product in two different countries) to be identical once differences in size are taken into account.

It can be shown (cf Exercise 10.9) that, for a Cournot equilibrium, each firm's profit is given by:

$$\Pi(n) = S \left(\frac{a - c}{n + 1}\right)^2 - F \tag{10.2}$$

A **free-entry equilibrium** is characterized by a set of active firms such that (i) no active firm wishes to leave the market and (ii) no inactive firm wished to enter the market. Specifically, the equilibrium number of firms, $\hat{n}$, has to be such that $\Pi(\hat{n}) \geq 0$ (no active firm wishes to exit) and $\Pi(\hat{n} + 1) \leq 0$ (no inactive firm wishes to enter).[c] Equating the right-hand side of (10.2) to zero, and solving for $n$, we get:

$$n = (a - c)\sqrt{\frac{S}{F}} - 1 \tag{10.3}$$

a. However, even if we lack information on the market shares for some of the firms, we can still find a lower and an upper bound for the value of $H$. See Exercise 10.14.

b. I first introduced the Lerner index in Section 3.2. Then I considered the case of one seller only; in this case the Lerner index corresponds to the seller's margin. Equation (10.1) considers the general $n$-firm case, of which (3.4) is the particular case when $n = 1$.

c. Notice that, if $\Pi(n') = 0$, then both $\hat{n} = n' - 1$ and $\hat{n} = n'$ form an equilibrium. Since $\Pi(n') = 0$ is only true "by coincidence" (that is, non-generically) I will henceforth assume that there exists a unique solution to the system $\Pi(\hat{n} + 1) \leq 0 \leq \Pi(\hat{n})$.

Hence, the equilibrium value of $n$ is given by:

$$\widehat{n} = \left[ (a - c)\sqrt{\frac{S}{F}} - 1 \right] \tag{10.4}$$

where $[x]$ (expression $x$ in square brackets) denotes the highest integer lower than $x$ (the characteristic function). That is, if (10.3) gives $n = 32.4$, for example, then $\widehat{n} = [32.4] = 32$.

■ **MARKET SIZE AND CONCENTRATION.** Equation (10.4) states that the number of firms is an increasing function of market size (here measured directly by $S$ and indirectly by $a$) and an inverse function of both fixed and variable costs ($F$ and $c$). None of this is very surprising. Note, however, that the relation between $S$ and $\widehat{n}$ is not proportional. In fact, *for high values of $\widehat{n}$, the relation between $S$ and $\widehat{n}$ is approximately quadratic*: in order to double the number of firms, market size must increase four-fold; conversely, if market size doubles, the number of firms increases by only 40% (specifically, by $\sqrt{2} - 1$).

What explains this non-proportional relationship? If market price were constant (with respect to the number of firms), then the relation between size and number of firms would be proportional: double market size and you double the number of firms. However, as the number of firms increases, the market becomes more competitive, that is, the margin $p - c$ decreases. As a result, variable profit per unit of market size also decreases, which in turn limits the number of firms the market can sustain.

> Due to increased price competition, the equilibrium number of active firms varies less than proportionally with respect to market size.

■ **MINIMUM EFFICIENT SCALE AND CONCENTRATION.** As mentioned earlier, one of the determinants of market structure is the firm's cost structure. In particular, the fact that most firms have a U-shaped average cost curve is an important determinant of market structure. A firm in the left-hand side of the U, that is, a firm with decreasing average cost, is said to operate under **increasing returns to scale**. (The model considered in this section, where costs are given by $F + cq$, is an extreme case in which average cost is always decreasing.)

In order to measure the relation between increasing returns to scale and market structure, we first need to measure the degree of increasing returns to scale. There are several ways of doing this. One is to use the concept of **minimum efficient scale**, the minimum scale at which a firm's average cost is, say, within 10% of the minimum.[d] In the model considered in this section, total cost is $C = F + cq$. Average cost is therefore $AC = F/q + c$. The minimum of average cost is $c$. Let the minimum efficient scale (MES) be the minimum scale such that average cost is equal to $c'$. Equating $AC = c'$ and solving for $q$, we get:

$$\text{MES} = \frac{F}{(c' - c)}$$

d. Strictly speaking, MES is defined as the lowest output level such that average cost is minimized; the definition I consider here is slightly more general. For the special case when $C = F + cq$ (constant marginal cost), MES = $\infty$ according to the strict definition.

It is natural to interpret changes in MES as changes in the value of $F$: an increase in $F$ by a factor $\lambda$ implies an increase in MES by the same factor $\lambda$. In this sense, Equation 10.4 shows how market structure changes when MES changes (that is, when $F$ changes). If MES increases by a factor of 2, then the number of firms decreases by a factor of approximately $\sqrt{2}$. The intuition for this is exactly the inverse of an increase in market size by a factor of 2. In fact, if both market size and the MES increase by the same amount, then the equilibrium number of firms remains constant. For this reason, when comparing the structure of different industries, it is common to consider as an explanatory variable market size divided by MES, or MES divided by market size.

■ **SCALE ECONOMIES AND CONCENTRATION.** An alternative way of measuring increasing returns to scale is the coefficient of scale economies, defined as the ratio of average cost over marginal cost: $\rho \equiv AC/MC$. If this ratio is greater than one, that is, if average cost is greater than marginal cost, then we say that there are **economies of scale**; if the ratio is less than one, then we say there are **diseconomies of scale**. It can be shown that average cost is greater than marginal cost if and only if average cost is decreasing. Therefore, economies of scale or increasing returns to scale are the same thing.[e]

How does market structure depend on the degree of scale economies? As with minimum efficient scale, we would expect an industry to be more concentrated if the degree of scale economies is greater (or the MES higher). For the cost function considered above, $C = F + cq$, we have:

$$\rho \equiv \frac{AC}{MC} = \frac{\frac{F}{q} + c}{c} = 1 + \frac{F}{cq} \qquad (10.5)$$

If we think of two industries that differ in the value of $F$, then the industry with the greatest degree of scale economies is more concentrated. In fact, from (10.5), the industry with greater $F$ has greater degree of scale economies; and, from (10.4), the industry with greater $F$ has a smaller number of firms in the free-entry equilibrium.

> Concentration is generally greater the greater the minimum efficient scale (or the greater the degree of scale economies).

Both the minimum efficient scale and economies of scale are instances of **barriers to entry**. A generalization of the above point is therefore that concentration is greater the higher the barriers to entry are. (I should add, however, that the precise definition of a barrier to entry is a highly controversial issue. Not all authors would agree that economies of scale constitute a barrier to entry.)

■ **HISTORY MATTERS.** The model presented at the beginning of this section makes a number of implicit assumptions regarding the entry process. It assumes that (a) all firms have access to the same unique available technology (corresponding to the cost function $C = F + cq$); (b) firms have perfect information regarding the market (in particular, they all know the demand function); and (c) the entry process itself is well coordinated;

e. See Exercise 10.11. See also the definition of economies of scale in Chapter 3.

in particular, we assume that firms make their entry decisions sequentially, knowing what previous decisions earlier entrants have made.

Based on the above assumptions, we can predict exactly the equilibrium number of firms for a given a set of parameter values that characterize the industry (that is, the values of $a, c, F$, and other possible parameters in a more complex model). Moreover, the equilibrium predicted is symmetric; that is, all firms are of the same size.

Alas, the evidence of most real-world industries fails to match these predictions. One can find examples of industries that seem to share the same set of parameters but exhibit very different market structures. Consider for example the prepared soups industry in the US and in the UK. Although the two markets differ in size, they are very similar in terms of their state of development, the composition of demand across categories (canned versus dried), and so on. Campbell was the first entrant in the United States, having established operations in 1869. In the UK, Heinz established an initial lead in the 1930s. Although Campbell made an attempt at entering the UK market and Heinz the US market, the current picture is still that Campbell dominates the US market (63% share), while Heinz has a very small share (it mostly sells through retailers' own labels); and Heinz dominates the UK market (41% share), while Campbell has a fairly small share (9%).[4]

One should also add that most industries include firms of different sizes. For example, the US car market includes three domestic firms of different sizes and a variety of importers of different size too. And the European mineral water industry is dominated by three firms of different sizes.[f]

To close the gap between the predictions of the theoretical model and empirical observation, we must go beyond the assumptions listed above. First we must consider that often not all firms have access to the same technology. For some period of time, Dupont maintained a cost advantage over its rival producers of titanium dioxide. This was due to the fact that Dupont held exclusive patent rights over a lower-cost production process. Even after those patents expired, Dupont maintained much of that advantage due to the fact that it had moved down the **learning curve**; in other words, it transformed a **first-mover advantage** into a **sustainable competitive advantage**.

Even when all firms have access to the same technology, if there are several available technologies, then there may be several possible free-entry equilibria. For example, in the steel industry there are (roughly speaking) two different production processes, one with a high MES (regular mills) and one with a low MES (mini-mills). In terms of the notation of the model introduced earlier, regular mills have a high $F$ and a low $c$, whereas mini-mills have a low $F$ and a high $c$. Unless one of the technologies clearly dominates the other one (lower $F$ *and* lower $c$), one can find (under Cournot competition) different combinations of $n_1$ regular mills and $n_2$ mini-mills that would constitute a free-entry equilibrium.[g] Currently, operating profit per ton is approximately the same for mini-mills and major mills, although the latter are about four times bigger than the former. This suggests that none of the technologies dominates the other one, so that the above assumption is satisfied.

Imperfect information about market conditions may also influence market structure in ways not considered in the model above. For example, several oil companies

f. Some refer to this market strcuture as a **triopoly**.

g. This possibility is illustrated in Exercise 10.13.

built large refineries in the early 1970s. After the 1973 oil shock and subsequent demand cuts, there was excess capacity in the oil refining industry; that is, the value of $n$ was greater than the value given by (10.4); or, in other words, capacity was greater that it would be if firms had known in advance about the oil shock.

In addition to forecasting mistakes, market structure may also be influenced by coordination mistakes. Consider the case of commercial aircraft. In the late 1960s, Lockheed and McDonnell Douglas were considering whether to enter the market for large commercial aircraft. Since Boeing had just entered with the B747, there was only room for one more firm ($\hat{n} = 2$, according to Equation 10.4), and both Lockheed and McDonnell Douglas knew it. The question was therefore which of the two should enter. After a long "waiting game" played between the two, both ended up entering the market, only to make huge losses from which they never recovered. In other words, the actual value of $n$ was greater than the "equilibrium" value predicted by (10.4); an entry "mistake" led to too many firms in the market.[h]

Within the same industry, the opposite example is given by the "waiting game" played between Boeing and Airbus in the super jumbo market segment. In 1988, engineers at Airbus began to study the feasibility of a ultra-high-capacity airliner (UHCA). The project was announced at the 1990 Farnborough Air Show, promising 15% lower operating costs than the 747-400. Although there was demand for one such super jumbo, all parties agreed there was no room for two; so Boeing and Airbus began studying the possibility of a joint design. However, in 1994 Airbus decided it was going solo instead, whereas Boeing changed its mind to focus on a super-stretched version of the B747. Then both firms delayed their entry decision, until in late 2000 Airbus formally decided to launch an €8.8 billion program to build the then-called A3XX.[i] All in all, the outcome of this waiting game was that Airbus' A380 was developed a decade later than it might have been developed was it not for the coordination "mistake" that led to too little entry (too slow entry) with respect to the equilibrium level predicted by Equation (10.4).

Finally, history may determine market structure through the effect of **agglomeration economies**. Why is Silicon Valley in Silicon Valley? In other words, why are there so many high tech firms in and around Palo Alto, California, compared to other parts of the US and the world? One possible explanation is that the concentration of technology ventures results from industry agglomeration: first, there was Hewlett-Packard and a handful of other firms; these attracted new technology firms that wanted to be close to other technology firms; these in turn attracted new ones, and so forth, creating a "snowball" effect that led to the current concentration of talent.[j] I will return to this issue in Chapter 16.

In summary,

> The particular historical details of the evolution of an industry may in some cases determine the long-run market structure in ways that go beyond simple technology determinants.

h. For more on this example, see Section 3.5.

i. The first A380 was unveiled in Toulouse in January 2005. The final cost estimate was €11 billion.

j. I should add that this is a highly controversial point: after all, both Hewlett Packard and many subsequent Silicon Valley firms were founded by faculty or alumni of Stanford University, which casts doubt over the assertion that concentration is an endogenous, "snowball" type of phenomenon.

### Box 10.1 Evolution of the US beer industry[5]

The structure of the US beer industry has undergone significant changes since the 1950s. Initially, the most populated segment of the size distribution was 101–500 thousand barrels. Half a century later, we observe a bimodal distribution: there is a greater number of very large breweries (from 2 to 22 in the 4,000+ range); and there is also a greater number of microbreweries (from 68 to 83 in the 10–100 range).

Several factors have contributed to this evolution. First, the rise of national television effectively created a national market (the fraction of US households with a TV set jumped from 9% in 1950 to 87% in 1960 to 95% in 1970).

Second, the construction of the interstate highway system (which began during the Eisenhower administration) decreased transportation costs significantly, thus allowing for the growth of "shipping brewers."

Third, technology evolved in the direction of increasing economies of scale. For example, in 1966 the minimum efficiency scale in bottling was 0.82 million barrels per year; by 1987, that number had increased to 2.18 million.

Fourth, as incomes increases, so does consumers' demand for variety. From 1959 to 1989, US per capita income nearly doubled. Until the 1970s, traditional domestic beers were relatively undifferentiated lagers. Since then, a variety of microbrewers have emerged (these are also known as craft brewers). The number of imports has also increased (as has the number of brands offered by the macroproducers, e.g. Miller).

#### Surviving Breweries by Capacity: 1959–2006

| Capacity (10³ barrels) | 1959 | 1967 | 1975 | 1983 | 1989 | 1998 | 2001 | 2006 |
|---|---|---|---|---|---|---|---|---|
| 10 – 100 | 68 | 36 | 10 | 15 | 8 | 77 | 81 | 83 |
| 101 – 500 | 91 | 44 | 19 | 12 | 7 | 19 | 19 | 19 |
| 501 – 1000 | 30 | 35 | 13 | 2 | 3 | 1 | 1 | 4 |
| 1001 – 2000 | 18 | 18 | 13 | 13 | 5 | 4 | 2 | 2 |
| 2001 – 4000 | 8 | 10 | 12 | 9 | 6 | 7 | 5 | 3 |
| 4001+ | 2 | 4 | 15 | 23 | 20 | 20 | 20 | 22 |

Chapter 16 includes additional examples where history has an important role in the determination of market structure.

To conclude this section, I should mention that, to the extent that exogenous factors change over time, so does industry structure. Box 10.1 illustrates this idea by describing the evolution of the US beer industry, where a variety of changes — particularly changes in technology — had led to considerable shifts in industry structure.

■ **EVOLUTION OF NEW INDUSTRIES.** The evolution of new industries deserves particular mention because of a number of observed regularities. While there are differences from case to case, one frequently observes a period of fast growth in the number of firms followed by a period of consolidation. Sometimes, the latter takes the form of a sudden "shakeout" whereby the number of competitors declines drastically even as total industry output increases. For example, in the early 1910s the US auto industry comprised more than 200 firms; before the end of the decade, that number had dropped to less than 130; by the mid-1920s, it was less than 50; and by 1942 there were fewer than 10 American manufacturers.

A more recent example is provided by a global high-tech industry: hard disk drives (HDD).[6] Figure 10.2 illustrates dramatic changes in its market structure over a period of four decades. The first decade witnessed a high entry rate, on the back of the growing demand from the newly born personal computer (PC) industry, which accounted for most of the HDD demand. During the second decade, the number of active firms remained more or less constant at around 30. New firms kept on entering the market, but just as many incumbent firms chose to exit, leading to a high turnover but a low net entry rate. This peak phase coincided with the technological shift from the 5.25-inch to the 3.5-inch HDD.

The HDD industry matured during the 1990s and experienced a shakeout, whereby the number of active firms dropped precipitously. The demand for HDD continued to increase as Microsoft released Windows 95 and the Internet grew exponentially. However, many HDD makers were unable to keep up with the rising cost of product innovations and had no choice but to exit. New entry ceased by the mid-1990s. As of 2000, 10 major firms across the globe survived the shakeout, but only three remained in the market in 2014. This final phase of industry consolidation differed from the shakeout that preceded it in one important aspect: before 2000, approximately one in every five exits was the result of a merger; by contrast, all exits since 2000 proceeded through mergers rather than bankruptcy or liquidation. Thus the history of the

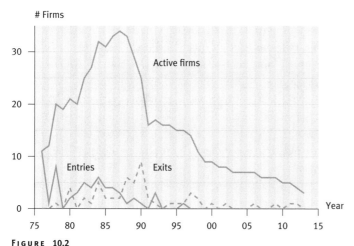

**FIGURE 10.2**
Evolution of the US hard drive industry

HDD industry highlights the roles of market size, innovation costs, as well as mergers in shaping the evolution of market structure in the long run.[k]

## 10.2 ENDOGENOUS VS. EXOGENOUS ENTRY COSTS

The structure of the beer industry in Portugal is not very different from the US: in Portugal, aside from some very small firms, there are two large firms that control the market (Centralcer, Unicer). In the US, the industry is dominated by three firms (Anheuser Bush, Miller, Coors), one relatively large, one medium size, and one relatively small.

Considering that the US economy is 30 to 50 times bigger than the Portuguese economy, and based on the model presented in the previous section, one would expect a much greater difference in the equilibrium number of firms. Specifically, one would expect the number of firms in the US to be $\sqrt{30}$ to $\sqrt{50}$ times bigger than in Portugal (five to seven times bigger, respectively).

Why is the number of firms in the US three, and not 10 (that is, $2 \times 5$) or 14 (that is, $2 \times 7$), as the model in the previous section would suggest? One important aspect of the beer industry which the model did not consider is *advertising*. Advertising expenditures are a very large fraction of sales, both in the US and in the Portugal. In fact, the value of advertising *as a percentage of sales* is not very different between the two countries. But since the volume of sales is much higher in the US than in Portugal, so is the volume of advertising. In order to enter the US beer industry and compete with the likes of Budweiser and Miller Lite, a new entrant would need to pay a much greater entry cost than an entrant into the Portuguese beer industry. In other words, when advertising is an important part of a firm's strategy, *entry costs are endogenous*, specifically, endogenous with respect to market size.

The comparative statics of industries with **endogenous entry costs** are somewhat different from the model in the previous section. The idea of the model in the previous section is that, because of price competition, as market size increases by a factor of two there will be room for less than twice as many firms. (In the specific case of Cournot competition, the number of firms can only increase by the square root of two as market size doubles.) If entry costs are increasing in market size, then we have an *additional* reason whereby the number of firms does not increase as much as market size. A bigger market induces firms to make bigger investments. Since these investments are costly, the net "pie" in terms of industry profits grows by less than market size. As a result, even if competition were not to increase (as in the previous section), the number of firms would increase by less than market size.

Let us consider an example which, though somewhat simplistic and extreme, serves to illustrate this point. A given country decides to deregulate its telecommunications sector. The main source of revenues in this industry is (by assumption) wireless telephony, for which a new technology has recently been developed. The government plans to allocate one exclusive license for the right to develop this new technology, the revenues of which are estimated at $S$. One of the conditions for obtaining the license is

k. The next chapter is devoted specifically to mergers.

that the candidate be already established as a telecommunications company; in order to do so, companies must pay an entry cost $F$.

We will consider two different forms of allocating the license. First, assume that the winner of the license is decided by means of a lottery. (In the US and in several countries this method was used until the 1990s.) If there are $n$ potential grantees, then each gets the license in a lottery with probability $1/n$. Knowing this beforehand, each potential entrant expects a revenue of $S/n$ (that is, $S$ with probability $1/n$). By analogy with the previous section, the equilibrium number of entrants is given by the zero-profit condition, $\pi = S/n - F = 0$. We thus get:

$$\widehat{n} = \left[ \frac{S}{F} \right]$$

In words, the number of firms is proportional to market size, $S$. This is consistent with the result in the previous section: if there is no price competition, as I am now assuming, then twice as large a market implies twice as large a number of firms.

Consider now a different method of allocating the license: an auction. Since the late 1980s, different variations of this method have been implemented in different countries, beginning with New Zealand and including Australia, the US, and several European and South American countries. Suppose that, upon paying the fixed cost $F$, each firm must bid for the right to exploit the license. Bids are submitted simultaneously, and the highest bid gets the license (and pays the proposed bid).

If there is more than one entrant, then the bidding game played between firms is similar to Bertrand competition, only that now it's the highest bid, not the lowest price, that wins. Under Bertrand competition, the equilibrium is given by all firms setting prices at the level of marginal cost. By analogy, the equilibrium of the bidding game is for all firms to submit a bid equal to the value of the license, $S$. (If all firms were to bid less then $S$, then it would pay for a firm to bid just a little higher.) If there is only one entrant, then it will bid zero (or whatever the minimum bid is), and receive the license with probability one.

Just as under Bertrand competition the equilibrium profit is zero, each firm's expected payoff in the bidding game is also zero (gross of entry cost): if a firm loses the bidding, then its payoff is clearly zero; if a firm wins the license, then its payoff is $S$, the value of the license, minus $S$, the bid that it has to pay; zero payoff again. Naturally, if there is only one contender for the license, then expected payoff is $S$ minus the value of the minimum bid admissible.

Predicting the above outcome beforehand, no firm would be willing to enter if it expected that there would be another entrant, *no matter what market size is*. In other words, the equilibrium of the entry game is for one firm only to enter, regardless of the value of $S$. If only one firm enters, then it will not have to bid all the way up to $S$ in order to win the license, and a positive net profit will result from entry.

The reason for the result that $\widehat{n} = 1$, for any value of $S$, is the following: while the value of winning the license increases as $S$ increases, so do the bids submitted by firms increase in the same amount. It follows that the value of being in the market (when $n > 1$) does not change as $S$ increases: it is always zero.

This is in stark contrast with the case considered before (lottery allocation), where the number of firms was proportional to market size. The difference between the two cases lies on the assumption regarding the way the license is allocated. If a lottery is used, then the only entry cost is $F$, an exogenous cost. Since there is no price competition, we get the law of proportional change (of number of firms with respect to market size). If the license is auctioned, however, then total "entry" costs are given by $F + B$, where $B$ is the bid for the license, an endogenous entry cost. The fact that $B$ increases proportionately with $S$ implies that the number of firms remains constant.

While this is an extreme example, the general point holds that:

> If entry costs are endogenous, then the number of firms is less sensitive to changes in market size.

Exercise 10.17 illustrates this point.

Finally, I should mention that there can be various sources of endogenous entry costs. In this section I considered two: advertising and bidding for a government license. However, any situation where firms engage in an "escalation war" for grabbing a share of the market (or the entire market) is likely to involve some degree of entry cost endogeneity. Another important instance of endogenous entry costs is given by R&D expenditures. For example, if firms race to be the first to patent a new medical drug which will give them a monopoly over a certain therapeutical market, then it is likely that much of the increase in the value of the market will be competed away in the patent race, so that the number of entrants does not change that much. Additional examples of this sort are found in Chapters 15 and 16.

■ **EMPIRICAL EVIDENCE.** The hypothesis implied by the above analysis is that, when endogenous entry costs are important, the relation between market size and industry concentration is flatter than when entry costs are exogenous. By the same token, the relation between concentration (e.g., C4) and market size is flatter when entry costs are endogenous. (Under symmetry, C4=4/$n$; if $n$ varies less with market size, so does C4.)

The ideal method for testing this hypothesis is to obtain data for a given industry in different, separated markets (e.g., different countries). However, this creates the difficulty of obtaining data for sufficiently many different separated markets. An alternative strategy is to collect data for a few markets and a few industries with similar degree of entry cost endogeneity. The problem with this alternative approach is that is implies putting apples and oranges in the same bag. However, if we believe that the main difference between industries is in the degree of scale economies (or the size of MES), then we can adjust the data and consider size divided by MES (for example) as an explanatory variable. As I showed earlier, the equilibrium number of firms is a function of the ratio between $S$ and $F$, which suggests that using adjusted market size when comparing different industries may be a reasonable strategy.

TABLE 10.1 Advertising/retail sales ratios for a selection of industries and countries (France, Germany, Italy, Japan, UK, US)[4]

| Low-adv industries | A/RS (%) | High-adv industries | A/RS (%) |
|---|---|---|---|
| Salt | 0.26–0.45 | Frozen food | 1.2–7.1 |
| Sugar | 0.06–0.24 | Soup | 2.7–6.0 |
| Flour | 0.17–0.96 | Margarine | 2.3–10.2 |
| Bread | 0.02–0.42 | Soft drinks | 1.2–5.4 |
| Processed meat | 0.30–0.70 | RTE cereals | 8.34–12.9 |
| Canned vegetables | 0.29–0.71 | Mineral water | 1.5–5.0 |
| | | Sugar confectionery | 1.4–6.0 |
| | | Chocolate confectionery | 2.9–6.5 |
| | | R&G coffee | 1.9–16.7 |
| | | Instant coffee | 2.2–11.1 |
| | | Biscuits | 1.9–8.0 |
| | | Pet foods | 4.0–8.4 |
| | | Baby foods | 0.9–4.2 |
| | | Beer | 1.0–5.43 |

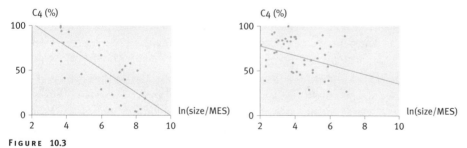

FIGURE 10.3
Industry size and industry concentration: homogeneous-good industries (left) and differentiated-good industries (right)[7]

Table 10.1 presents data for a series of 20 industries and five countries. Based on the values of the advertising/sales ratio, we can classify the different industries into "homogeneous-product" and "advertising-intensive" industries. We can then plot the values of size/MES and concentration, as in Figure 10.3, splitting the sample into homogenous-product and advertising-intensive industries (left and right panel, respectively). The hypothesis put forward above implies that the relation between concentration and size is flatter in the latter case, that is, when entry costs are endogenous. Roughly speaking, the data seem to agree with this prediction.

Notice however what we have presented fairly specific models of entry and competition (Cournot, license auction, etc.). The precise relation between market size and market structure will depend on the precise nature of entry and market competition. It this therefore not surprising that we cannot find a very precise relation in the left panel of Figure 10.3. What can be shown, however, is that the lower bound of a scatter diagram with concentration and size/MES in the axes is flatter when entry costs are endogenous. In this sense, the empirical evidence is quite striking: the lower bound of the plot in the right panel of Figure 10.3 is close to a horizontal line, whereas the lower bound of the plot in the left panel of Figure 10.3 is a downward-sloping line.[4]

## 10.3 INTENSITY OF COMPETITION, MARKET STRUCTURE, AND MARKET POWER

In the previous section and in the previous chapters I have considered quite a range of models of competition (e.g., collusion, Cournot, Bertrand); quite a range of market structures (from one or a few large firms to many tiny ones); and quite a range of market outcomes (e.g., from zero to high margins). A natural question to ask is: are these related in any interesting way? The short answer: yes, but in ways that are sufficiently complicated to render cross-industry comparisons difficult if not impossible. The longer answer follows.

■ **INTENSITY OF COMPETITION DETERMINES INDUSTRY STRUCTURE.** So far I considered variations in market size as well as variations in the nature of technology (as reflected in the cost function) as determinants of market structure. For analytical purposes, I assumed that oligopoly competition takes place as in the Cournot model. Clearly, all industries are not Cournot-like: in some industries, behavior is closer to the Bertrand model, where equilibrium price is equal to (the second-lowest) marginal cost, whereas in other industries behavior is closer to the monopoly model, where the equilibrium price maximizes industry revenues. I now show that, in addition to technology and market size, the nature of competition plays a crucial role in shaping market structure.

Consider the Swedish pharmaceutical industry. Each month, sellers bid for the right to be the sole supplier (during a one-month period) of each generic drug. Depending on how strict the government rules are, the market share obtained by the winning bid can be somewhere from 50 to 70%. In other words, market competition is close to Bertrand competition: the lowest price takes most of the market demand. Clearly, the immediate impact of forcing the adoption of the lowest cost drug is to lower average price. However, an additional effect of increasing the intensity of competition is to reduce the number of competitors, as indeed the empirical evidence suggests.

A very different example is given by the Kenyan banking industry. In this case, price competition is quite soft: average spreads (the difference between lending rates deposit rates) are very high (even correcting for inflation) and the experience of recent years suggests that interest rates do not vary with the number of competitors. Since margins are so high, entry into banking is very attractive: currently, there are more than 40 banks in Kenya.

These two examples suggest that the intensity of competition has an effect on market structure: if competition is close to Bertrand (generic drugs in Sweden), then the tendency is for the number of competitors to decrease; if competition is close to monopoly (banks in Kenya), then the tendency is for the number of competitors to increase.

---

**PRICE REGULATION AND MARKET STRUCTURE.** As a formal illustration of this point, consider a certain industry X and compare its market structure across different countries. Suppose that technology and market size are the same in all countries. Suppose also that, in each country, market price is exogenously set by a regulator at a level $p$ which varies from country to country: in some countries, $p$ is set very close to marginal cost, and we say that competition is very intense; in other countries, $p$ is set very close to monopoly price, and we say that competition is weak. How does equilibrium market structure depend on the level of competition as measured by regulated price $p$?

For simplicity, suppose that each firm's cost function is given, as before, by $C = F + c\,q$. If there are $n$ firms in the industry, then each firm's profit is given by $\frac{1}{n}(p - c)\,D(p) - F$. Ignoring for a second the fact that the number of firms must be an integer, we expect firms to continue streaming in until:

$$\frac{1}{n}(p - c)\,D(p) - F = E$$

where $E$ is the entry cost. Since the value of $n$ must be an integer, the equilibrium number of entrants is given by:

$$\widehat{n} = \left[\frac{1}{E + F}(p - c)\,D(p)\right]$$  (10.6)

where, as before, $[x]$ denotes the highest integer lower than $x$ (the characteristic function). So long as $p$ is lower than monopoly price, total variable profits $(p - c)\,D(p)$ are increasing in $p$, and so is the value of $\widehat{n}$. We thus conclude that, the more competitive the industry is — in the sense that it is subject to a "strong" regulator who sets a low price $p$ — the lower the equilibrium number of firms.

---

In sum, empirical evidence and formal analysis suggest that:

The more intense market competition is, the lower the number of equilibrium firms.

Exercise 10.5 illustrates some of these issues.

■ **MARKET CONCENTRATION DETERMINES MARKET POWER.** In the previous subsection, I considered variations in the degree of competition (from Bertrand to collusion) and determined their effect on market structure. Now, I fix the nature of competition; specifically

I assume — as in Section 10.1 — that firms compete à la Cournot; and I examine how variations in market structure affect market performance.

Consider a general Cournot model with $n$ firms, each with a cost function $C_i(q_i)$. It can be shown (Exercise 10.10) that:

$$L = \frac{H}{-\epsilon} \tag{10.7}$$

where $\epsilon$ is the industry price elasticity of demand and $L$ and $H$ are as defined above.

This is not just a beautiful formula (if you are into that sort of thing); it is an important result, since it generalizes the idea that the greater concentration is (as measured by $H$), the greater the degree of market power (as measured by $L$). It allows us to answer questions like the following:

> Consider two markets with identical demands. In one market, there are two firms with identical market shares. In the other market, there is one firm with a 70% market share and two small firms with 15% each. Assuming that both markets are in a Cournot equilibrium, where is market power the greatest?

The answer is, from (10.7), whichever market has the greatest concentration, as measured by the Herfindahl index. In this particular example, we have, in the first market, $H = 50^2 + 50^2 = 5,000$, whereas in the second market $H = 70^2 + 15^2 + 15^2 = 5,350$. In words, market power is greater in the second market (even though $n$ is greater); the difference, however, is very small.[1]

■ **CONCENTRATION AND MARKET POWER: EMPIRICAL ESTIMATION.** As I mentioned in Chapter 1, for decades mainstream industrial organization was grounded on the so-called **Structure-Conduct-Performance paradigm** (SCP). The SCP paradigm provides a system for the analysis of a given industry. The industry is characterized by its structure (e.g., how concentrated it is), conduct (that is, the behavior of its firms), and performance (market power, allocative efficiency, and so on). Moreover, the SCP paradigm propounds that there is a causal relationship between structure, conduct, and performance: structure influences conduct; and both structure and conduct influence performance.

1. Several reasons why structure influences conduct were proposed in the previous chapters. For example, I argued that collusion is easier among a small number of firms; likewise, it is easier to reach a price-fixing agreement when firms are similar to each other; and so on.

2. The relation between conduct and performance should be clear: the more competitively firms behave, the lower the degree of market power and the greater allocative efficiency. Compare, for example, the Bertrand solution to collusive price setting.

3. The argument that structure influences performance is eloquently exemplified by Equation (10.7) on page 266: fixing behavior (Cournot), the more concentrated an industry is, the greater the degree of market power.

1. Equation (10.7) also generalizes the discussion on demand elasticity and market power, the fact that $L$ is decreasing in the absolute value of $\epsilon$. See Section 5.3.

For a long time, industrial economists were concerned with the empirical implications of the above paradigm. Specifically, if performance is a function of structure and conduct; and conduct, in turn, is a function of structure; then we can simplify the above into a relation between performance (say, market power) and structure (say, concentration).

The direct relation between concentration and market power is positive, as derived in the previous section (Equation 10.7). The relation between concentration and non-competitive behavior is positive, as argued in the previous chapter. Finally, by definition, the relation between non-competitive behavior and market power is also positive. Putting all of these together, there should be a positive relationship between concentration and market power.

We thus have a testable implication, which we may call the **structure-performance hypothesis**, namely a positive relation between concentration and market power. To test this hypothesis, we need data on concentration and on market power. The former is normally easy to obtain (e.g., market shares based on sales data). Measuring the Lerner index, the index of market power we have been considering, is more difficult; in fact, it is normally impossible. However, if marginal cost is constant and equal to $c_i$, then firm $i$'s profit rate, $r_i$, is equal to firm $i$'s margin, $m_i$:

$$r_i \equiv \frac{R_i - VC_i}{R_i} = \frac{p\,q_i - c_i\,q_i}{p\,q_i} = \frac{p - c_i}{p} = m_i$$

where $VC_i = c_i\,q_i$ denotes firm $i$'s variable cost. Consequently, as an approximation the Lerner index (the average of every firm's $m_i$) can be measured by the average variable profit rate.[m]

Accordingly, in the past many economists gathered data on concentration and profit rates for a number of industries and estimated the statistical relation between those variables.[8] That is, suppose we have data on the average profit rate in industry $i$ as well as on concentration in that industry. Then we would expect industries with higher concentration to exhibit higher average profit rates, that is, a positive coefficient in the regression of profit rate on concentration.

Alas, the result of this statistical effort is not very encouraging.[9] Most studies find a very weak link between structure and performance. However, before dismissing the theoretical analysis that has brought us to the structure-performance hypothesis, we must say that there are important data measurement problems which may at least partially explain the poor results. For example, accounting profit rates may be a poor proxy for margins, especially where firms operate in various industries (which requires allocating variable cost to each separate industry).

In terms of methodology, the test of the structure-performance hypothesis suffers from an additional important limitation. Basically, it ignores the possibility of reverse causal links in the relation between structure, conduct, and performance. As Equation (10.6) shows, the greater the intensity of competition (lower $p$), the lower the number of equilibrium entrants (that is, the higher industry concentration). This implies the opposite prediction of Equation (10.7), which suggests that, the greater industry concentration ($H$), the greater market power ($L$).

m. If fixed costs are zero, then this is equal to the average profit rate.

The critical difference between the two approaches is that Equation (10.7) takes market structure as given (that is, as an exogenous variable) and the degree of competition as an endogenous variable (that is, the dependent variable). In Equation (10.6), by contrast, the degree of competition is the exogenous variable, whereas market structure (the number of firms) is assumed to be endogenous (the dependent variable). In other words, in Equation (10.7) concentration causes market power; in Equation (10.6), market power causes concentration.

In practice, it is likely that both the direct and the reverse effects in the SCP paradigm are important. This may explain why the statistical relation between concentration and profitability is not very significant: it may simply be the sum of two effects with opposite signs.[n]

■ **THE COLLUSION AND EFFICIENCY HYPOTHESES.** Suppose that the feedback effect of performance on structure is not very important. Suppose moreover that statistical estimation yields a positive effect of structure on performance (as some studies did indeed find). We still have a problem of interpretation to solve, as I will show next.

The **collusion hypothesis** is that concentration implies market power through increased collusion between firms. If this is the case, then policy makers should be concerned with anything that increases industry concentration — a merger, for example. In fact, as we will see in Section 11.3, concentration indices play an important role in the policy analysis of mergers. Roughly speaking, a merger that increases concentration significantly is usually not allowed because it would increase market power to the detriment of consumers.

An alternative interpretation for the positive relation between structure and performance is the **efficiency hypothesis**, normally associated with the Chicago school.[10] Consider a symmetric oligopoly (all firms have the same marginal cost), and suppose that one of the firms improves its productive efficiency, thus reducing its marginal cost. A lower marginal cost by one of the firms implies a redistribution of market shares, whereby both concentration and market power increase, just like in the collusion hypothesis. However, while under the collusion hypothesis the increase in market power is mainly associated with a decrease in allocative efficiency, under the efficiency hypothesis the increase in market power is mainly associated with an increase in productive efficiency (the transfer of market share from relatively inefficient firms to a more efficient one). It is quite possible that society is better off in the new situation, even though both concentration and market power are greater. The policy implications of this alternative hypothesis are nearly the opposite of the collusion hypothesis.

Empirical studies based on firm-level data show that firm profit rates are positively associated with market shares: larger firms are more profitable — or, alternatively, more efficient firms grow to bigger sizes. This does not prove, but is consistent with, the efficient hypothesis of the relation between concentration and performance.

n. There are statistical ways to distinguish between the two effects, and attempts at doing so have been made. Even then, the empirical results are not very encouraging; that is, they do not provide any clear support for either effect.

## 10.4 ENTRY AND WELFARE

The model of perfect competition shows that, if there is free entry and if a number of other conditions are satisfied, then the equilibrium is socially efficient. If all of the other conditions are satisfied, then absence of free entry (e.g., barriers to entry) implies inefficiency. However, if the other conditions of the perfect competition model fail (e.g., price-taking behavior fails), then it is no longer necessarily the case that free entry is desirable from the perspective of economic efficiency.[11]

This point is illustrated in Figure 10.4, which depicts an industry with aggregate marginal cost $MC$ and demand $D(p)$. Suppose first that there are $n$ active firms, producing a total output $Q_n$ which is sold at price $p_n$. Suppose now that an extra firm enters the industry. The output produced by the entrant is $q_{n+1}$, whereas total output is now given by $Q_{n+1}$ and price by $p_{n+1}$. The change in gross surplus (not including entry costs) is given by areas $B$ plus $C$. The gross profit earned by the new entrant is given by areas $A$ plus $B$ (assuming the entrant has the highest marginal cost of all firms).

The way the figure is drawn, the increase in gross surplus (area $B$ plus $C$) is smaller than the gross profit earned by the latest entrant (area $A + B$). This implies an important potential divergence between the private and the social incentives for entry by the $n + 1$st firm. Suppose that the entry cost, $E$, is such that $B + C < E < A + B$. Then entry is profitable from a private perspective (positive net profits) but not from a social perspective (the increase in gross surplus does not compensate for the entry cost). In this circumstance, *free entry results in excessive entry*.

What is the reason for this divergence between private and social entry incentives? The key is that part of the profits earned by the entrant are "stolen" from the incumbent firms. Area $A$ measures (approximately) this **business stealing effect**, a transfer between firms which does not correspond to a benefit to society (although obviously it benefits the entrant).

Retail banking is one example where the above argument might be applied. In some European countries, due to regulation or lack of competition, margins can at times be very high (cf also the example of Kenya, referred to in the previous section). Moreover, given the relative homogeneity of retail banking services and the low elasticity of demand, it is likely that the business-stealing effect is significant. For this reason, one would expect the equilibrium number of banks and bank branches to be excessive from a social point of view. In Portugal, in the late 1980s and for a period of time, banks were required to pay a fee in order to open a new branch. While there were different political motives underlying this measure, one possible defense in terms of economic efficiency is precisely the business stealing entry externality.

Another example is given by broadcast radio.[12] In the US and in other countries, a large fraction of radio stations are thematic, that is, devoted to a particular type of music (or to talk shows). Empirical evidence suggests that the main effect of opening a new station is to divert listeners from other stations.[o] As a result, the market equilibrium features too many rock stations, to the detriment of other genres such as classical music.

o. These are free-to-air broadcasters: from the listeners' point of view, the only price is the cost of listening to commercials. While there is some competition on this dimension, it can be shown that the business stealing effect dominates.

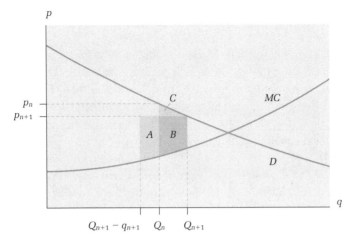

**FIGURE 10.4**
Entry and welfare

Still another example is given by real estate services in the US. Typically, brokers charge a 6% commission regardless of the price of the house sold. In other words, there is very little price competition, which implies that any profit opportunity is taken up in the form of additional entry. Empirical evidence shows that, when housing prices in a given city increase, more real-estate brokers enter the local market, which in turn leads to a drop in the number of houses sold per agent. However, the average real wage of brokers remains constant, that is, the increase in commissions exactly compensates for the decrease in the number of clients.[13] This is consistent with the idea that there is excessive entry in these markets: all that new entry is doing is competing away existing rents; that is, the business stealing effect dominates.

■ **PRODUCT DIFFERENTIATION, FREE ENTRY, AND EFFICIENCY.** The result of excessive entry is subject to an important qualification: if there is product differentiation, then entry implies, in addition to a decrease in price, an increase in product variety. The entrant is normally unable to capture all of the additional willingness to pay generated by the new product. That is to say, there is a positive externality from entrant to consumers. For example, if a new car firm enters the industry with an innovative car design, many consumers will be willing to pay more for the new car than it will be priced. In other words, some of the benefits from the new car design are not captured by its designer.

An extreme example of the positive entry externality is given by medical drugs targeted at relatively rare diseases, or diseases that are concentrated on populations with relatively low incomes. For regulatory or other reasons, it may be difficult for the seller to set high prices required to recoup research investments. This in turn may lead the firm to decide not to enter in the first place. The drug in question is then referred to as an "orphan drug." For example, around 2005 scientists from Canada and the US developed a vaccine against the Ebola virus. However, the project sat on the shelf, primarily because, until 2014, there were few Ebola cases and most were confined to poor countries.[14]

The analysis of the general problem (taking product differentiation explicitly into account) is rather complex. The conclusion, however, is rather simple and intuitive:

> If product differentiation is very important, or if competition is very fierce, then free entry implies insufficient entry from a social point of view. Conversely, if product differentiation is unimportant and competition is soft, then the business-stealing effect dominates, whereby the free-entry equilibrium entails excessive entry.

Exercise 10.18 formalizes this point.

■ **FIRM HETEROGENEITY, FREE ENTRY, AND EFFICIENCY.** Another qualification on the excessive entry result is that it does not focus on efficiency differences across firms. Empirical evidence shows that there is significant firm turnover in most industries, with lower productivity firms being replaced by higher productivity ones. In this context, a *dynamic* analysis of free entry should take into account the benefits from entry in terms of increased average productivity.[15]

For example, average productivity in the US telecom equipment industry increased drastically when the industry underwent a period of deregulation in the 1980s. Careful accounting and econometric estimation shows that most of the productivity gain was simply due to the reallocation of output from less efficient to more efficient firms (in particular, exiters and entrants). Box 10.2 explores this example in greater detail.

Another impressive example of the relation between entry and productivity growth is given by the US steel industry.[17] Between 1972 and 2002, total factor productivity in the steel sector increased by 28%, whereas the mean increase in the rest of the economy was only 7% (see Section 3.1 for a definition of total factor productivity). Total output in 2002 was at about the 1972 level; however, during this period employment decreased by 80%. For the past few decades, productivity growth in the steel sector was only second to IT.

The main determinant of the steel productivity miracle was entry by new firms with a new technology: the mini-mills (cf page 256). Not only did these new plants replace old, less productive firms; they also increased their own productivity over time. Together, these effects accounted for about one-half of the productivity increase in the three decades since 1972. In some sense, this is an underestimate of the total effect of entry. In fact, an important component of the overall improvement was the productivity increase by the incumbent firms using the old technology. To the extent that this improvement was in reaction to the new competition imposed by the mini-mills, we might say that the overall effect of entry accounts for more than one-half of the drastic productivity improvement.

**Box 10.2 DEREGULATION AND PRODUCTIVITY IN THE TELECOMMUNICATIONS EQUIPMENT INDUSTRY[16]**

"Beginning in the early 1970s, the [US] telecommunications industry entered into a period of rapid change. There were significant technological developments in telecommunications equipment and a gradual liberalization of the regulatory environment governing the provision of telecommunications services ...

The conditions restricting entry were [significantly] eroded in 1975 when the FCC [Federal Communications Commission] established a registration and certification program to allow for the connection of private subscriber equipment to the network ... [A second important event was] the 1982 Consent Decree ... implemented in January 1984, [which] called for the divestiture of AT&T's regional operating companies." The decree implied that the divested regional companies were no longer "forced" to purchase equipment form AT&T's subsidiary, Western Electric, thus creating an extra factor favoring entry.

From 1963 to 1987 the number of firms increased from 104 to 481. In addition to a rapid increase in the total number of firms, there was a considerable turnover, with both high entry rates and high exit rates. For example, almost 90% of the firms active in 1987 entered after 1972.

This turnover contributed to a reallocation of capacity and output between more efficient are less efficient firms. In order to measure how efficiently capacity is distributed among firms, we can compute the correlation between capital and productivity. A high correlation means that firms with higher levels of capital are more productive. For a given set of firms, this implies higher industry efficiency. A low (or negative) correlation results in firms with higher levels of capital and less efficiency, which leads to a lower industry efficiency.

The graph below shows that, except for the period 1981–1984, the correlation between productivity and capital, measured at the plant level, increased. This is consistent with the interpretation that entry and exit allowed for a more efficient allocation of capital among firms. To confirm this interpretation, it can be shown that the probability of a firm exiting is negatively correlated with its productivity. Since deregulation increased the probability of exit, it follows that deregulation increased the exit rate of low-productivity firms.

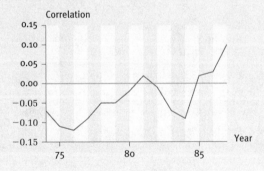

The telecommunications equipment and steel examples suggest the general point that:

> Firm entry and exit, as well as the reallocation of capital among incumbents, is an important component of industry productivity growth.

## 10.5 ENTRY REGULATION

In Section 5.4, I suggested two perspectives on the nature and origins of regulation: an optimistic view is that, faced with a particular market failure, a well-intentioned government agency directly intervenes in the market mechanism so as to restore the social optimum. A rather more skeptical view — one that, at times, is more realistic — is that incumbent firms lobby governments to enact measures that effectively protect their own interests.

The economic regulation of entry provides an excellent illustration of the dichotomy between the normative theory of regulation and the regulatory capture perspective. For example, charging a fee for opening a bank branch, especially in highly dense areas where the business stealing effect is significant, may help moderate excessive entry. Also, in a world of imperfect information requiring minimum qualifications for medical doctors to practice may alleviate the social costs of free entry by quacks. Such regulations seem motivated by the public interest and indeed appear to have an overall positive impact.

But consider instead the US peanut program, which I alluded to in Section 5.4. The argument can be made that the entry barriers created by the program imply far more costs to consumers than benefits to producers. Special interests, rather than the public interest, are the main force behind protectionist entry regulations such as this one.

The same applies to many regulations of qualifications: while requiring medical doctors to pass an exam seems to make a lot of sense, it seems hard to justify that more than 700 professions must go through the same process. In the 1950s, about 5% of all professions were subject to licenses; today, nearly one-third of the US workforce is licensed.[18] Consider the following extreme example: the state of Louisiana requires florists to obtain a government-issued license before they may create and sell floral arrangements. This means that aspiring florists must take a test, a test which is judged by current florists (that is, by the aspiring entrants' potential competitors). It also means spending $2,000 on a two-week, 80-hour course, and an additional $150 on a refresher course before the exam — not to mention many hours studying. Maybe George Bernard Shaw had a point when he wrote that "all professions are conspiracies against the laity."

One recent example that seems to fall on the regulatory capture camp is the car service Uber. The company began in San Francisco in March 2009 and by October 2014 had launched its operations in 215 cities in 45 different countries around the globe. In June 2014 it was valued at $18.2 billion. Wherever Uber has attempted to enter, it has faced strong resistance from established interests. In May 2011, the San Francisco Transportation Authority declared Uber an unlicensed taxi service and delivered a cease-and-desist letter. Later, Uber and the California Public Utilities Commission were able to craft a new category called "transportation network companies" to work around the licensing requirement. In Australia and Belgium, Uber drivers are required to be licensed taxi drivers, which effectively defeats the purpose of creating Uber in the first place. In Germany, a Frankfurt court went even further: not only did it declare Uber illegal, it also established a €250,000 fine and a six-month jail sentence for violators. However, a few weeks later the injunction was revoked.

Despite all of these setbacks, Uber has managed to enter a significant number of markets, and has done so successfully. In New York City, where taxis are difficult to find during rush hour, Uber has been well received by consumers, though perhaps not by taxi owners (see Box 10.3).

## Summary

• Due to increased price competition, the equilibrium number of active firms varies less than proportionally with respect to market size. • Concentration is generally greater the greater the minimum efficient scale (or the greater the degree of scale economies). • The particular historical details of the evolution of an industry may in some cases determine the long-run market structure in ways that go beyond simple technology determinants. • If entry costs are endogenous, then the number of firms is less sensitive to changes in market size. • The more intense market competition is, the lower the number of equilibrium firms. • If product differentiation is very important, or if competition is very fierce, then free entry implies insufficient entry from a social point of view. Conversely, if product differentiation is unimportant and competition is soft, then the business-stealing effect dominates, whereby the free-entry equilibrium entails excessive entry. • Firm entry and exit, as well as the reallocation of capital among incumbents, is an important component of industry productivity growth.

## Key concepts

• Herfindahl index • Lerner index • free-entry equilibrium • increasing returns to scale • minimum efficient scale • economies of scale • diseconomies of scale • barriers to entry • triopoly • learning curve • first-mover advantage • sustainable competitive advantage • agglomeration economies • endogenous entry costs

## Box 10.3 Better than gold: NYC taxi medallions

Ever asked yourself — perhaps on a rainy afternoon in Manhattan — why there aren't more taxi cabs in New York City? Part of the answer is that, in order to drive a cab in the Big Apple you need a license, a medallion. Currently, there are 13,237 medallions in the city. Since the 1950s, as the city grew in size, so did the demand for cab rides in Manhattan. However, as the figure below shows, the number of cabs has remained relatively constant. Since new medallions are rarely issued, the only way to enter the industry is to acquire an existing medallion. As the figure below shows, the going price increased very rapidly in the past few decades. In 2011, for the first time a medallion was sold for more than $1 million.[20]

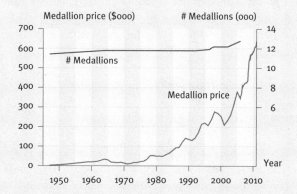

Asked about the high prices, Taxi and Limousine Commission Chairman David S. Yassky asserts that, "It's a lot of money, and it is an investment that someone would not make without being confident in the industry and the future of the city." Did he mean confidence in the industry or confidence in the commission's ability to lobby for a freeze on the number of medallions?

In January 2011, Mayor Bloomberg announced the issue of 18,000 "green cab" medallions, taxis that can pick up passengers in the outer boroughs of New York City (outside of Manhattan). An additional 2,000 yellow cab medallions were issued. Medallion prices, which at one point surpassed $1 million, dropped to about $800,000, both as a result in the increase in supply and the entry by car services such as Uber.

• Structure-Conduct-Performance paradigm • structure-performance hypothesis
• collusion hypothesis • efficiency hypothesis • business stealing effect

## Review and practice exercises

■ 10.1. Market size and market structure. Explain in words why the number of firms in a free-entry equilibrium may be less than proportional to market size.

■ **10.2. SINGLE MARKET.** Suppose that two countries, initially in autarchy, decide to create a single market. For simplicity, assume that, in both economies, there is only one product. Demand for this product is given by $D_i = S_i (a - p_i)$, $(i = 1, 2)$, where $S_i$ is a measure of country $i$'s size. Upon the creation of a single market, total demand is given by the horizontal sum of the two initial demands.

Assuming there is free entry and that firms compete a la Cournot, determine the equilibrium number of firms in autarchy and after the completion of the single market. Interpret the results.

■ **10.3. CALIFORNIA AND MONTANA.** The number of imported automobiles in California is four times higher than in Montana, in per capita terms. The population of Californian is mainly urban, whereas the population of Montana is mainly rural. How do demographic differences and the model presented in Section 10.1 explain the differences in consumption patterns?[21]

■ **10.4. MARKET SIZE AND MARKET STRUCTURE.** In some industries, the number of firms increases as market size increases. In other industries, the number of firms seems remarkably stable despite changes in market size. Discuss.

■ **10.5. RETAIL IN SWITZERLAND.** Retail in Switzerland is mostly dominated by highly profitable cartels. The Swiss authorities anticipate the gradual collapse of these cartels as the country becomes better integrated with the rest of Europe. OECD, by contrast, hold a more sceptical view, claiming that the collapse of cartels does not necessarily lead to more competitive markets; rather, they add, cartel breakdowns are frequently associated with an increase in concentration. Which prediction seems more reasonable? Are the two views inconsistent?

■ **10.6. MARKET DEFINITION AND MARKET STRUCTURE.** Consider the following goods: cement, mineral water, automobiles, retail banking. In each case, determine the relevant market boundaries and present an estimate of the degree of concentration.

■ **10.7. COST REDUCTION AND THE HERFINDAHL AND LERNER INDEXES.** Consider an industry where demand has constant price elasticity and firms compete in output levels. In an initial equilibrium, both firms have the same marginal cost, $c$. Then Firm 1, by investing heavily in R&D, manages to reduce its marginal cost to $c' < c$; a new equilibrium takes place.

(a) What impact does the innovation have on the values of $H$ and $L$?

(b) What impact does the innovation have on consumer welfare?

(c) What do the previous answers have to say about $L$ as a performance measure?

■ **10.8. BARRIERS TO ENTRY AND WELFARE.** "Barriers to entry may be welfare improving." What particular industry characteristics might make this statement valid?

# CHALLENGING EXERCISES

■ **10.9. NUMBER OF COMPETITORS AND EQUILIBRIUM PROFITS.** Derive equation (10.2).

■ **10.10. MARKET STRUCTURE AND MARKET POWER UNDER COURNOT COMPETITION.** Derive equation (10.7).

■ **10.11. SCALE ECONOMIES.** Show that the coefficient of scale economies, $AC/MC$, is greater than one if and only if average cost is decreasing.

■ **10.12. TECHNOLOGY AND MARKET STRUCTURE.** Consider an industry with market demand $Q = a - p$ and an infinite number of potential entrants with access to the same technology. Initially, technology is given by $C = F + cq$. A new technology allows for a lower marginal cost, $c' < c$, at the expense of a higher fixed cost, $F' > F$.

(a) What can you say about the effect of the new technology on equilibrium price?

(b) Suppose that $a = 10, F = 2, F' = 3, c = 2, c' = 1$. Determine equilibrium price under each of the two technologies.

■ **10.13. ALTERNATIVE PRODUCTION TECHNOLOGIES.** Consider an industry with a homogeneous product where firms set output (or capacity) levels and price is determined by total output (or capacity). Suppose there is a large number of potential entrants and that each firm can choose one of two possible technologies, with cost functions $C_i = F_i + c_i q_i$ $(i = 1, 2)$.

(a) Derive the conditions for a free-entry equilibrium.

(b) Show, by means of a numerical example, that there can be more than one equilibrium, with different numbers of large and small firms.

■ **10.14. HERFINDAHL INDEX BOUNDS.** Suppose you only know the value of the market shares for the largest $m$ firms in a given industry. While you do not possess sufficient information to compute the Herfindahl index, you can find a lower and an upper bound for its values. How?

■ **10.15. PRODUCT DIFFERENTIATION AND MARKET STRUCTURE.** Consider the monopolistic competition model, presented in Section 4.3. What is, according to this model, the relation between the degree of product differentiation and market structure?

■ **10.16. DOCTORS AND PLUMBERS.** Consider the structure of geographically isolated markets in the US (small towns) in the following businesses: doctors, dentists, plumbers. It can be shown that the minimum town size that justifies the entry of a second doctor is approximately 3.96 times the required size for the first doctor to enter. For plumbers, the number is 2.12. How can these numbers be interpreted?[22][21]

■ **10.17. ADVERTISING COSTS.** Consider the following model of entry into an advertising-intensive industry. To simplify the analysis, and to concentrate on the effects of advertising, suppose that there is no price competition. Specifically, the value of the market, in total sales, is given by $S$. (One can think of a demand curve $D(p)$ and an exogenously given price, whereby $S = pD(p)$.) $S$ is therefore a measure of market size.

Each firm must decide whether or not to enter the industry. Entry cost is given by $F$. If a firm decides to enter, then it must also choose how much to invest in advertising; let $a_i$ be the amount chosen by firm $i$. Finally, firm $i$'s market share, $s_i$, is assumed to be equal to its share of the industry total advertising effort:

$$s_i = \frac{a_i}{\sum_{j=1}^{n} a_j} = \frac{a_i}{A}$$

where $n$ is the number of firms in the industry and $A \equiv \sum_{i=1}^{n}$ is total industry advertising.

(a) Show that each firm $i$'s optimal level of advertising solves $S(A - a_i)/A^2 - 1 = 0$.

(b) Show that, in a symmetric equilibrium, $a = S(n-1)/n^2$, where $a$ is each firm's level of advertising.

(c) Show that equilibrium profit is given by $\pi = S/n^2 - F$.

(d) Show that the equilibrium number of entrants is given by the highest integer lower than $\sqrt{S/F}$.

(e) Interpret this result in light of the previous discussion on the effects of endogenous entry costs.

■ **10.18. ENTRY AND WELFARE.** Consider a homogeneous product industry with inverse demand function $P(Q)$ where every firm has the same cost function: $C(q)$. Suppose that firms decide sequentially whether or not to enter the industry and that the number of firms can be approximated by a continuous variable $n$. Show that, if (a) an increase in $n$ leads to a decrease in $q_n$ (the equilibrium output per firm when there are $n$ firms); and (b) equilibrium price is greater than marginal cost; then the equilibrium number of firms is too high from a social welfare point of view. Hint: derive the condition such that a firm is indifferent between entering and not entering; then show that, at that value of $n$, the derivative of social welfare with respect to $n$ is negative.

## APPLIED EXERCISES

■ **10.19. INDUSTRY EVOLUTION.** Choose an industry for which you can find historical data. Describe the industry's evolution in terms of number of firms and the firm size distribution. Explain what factores determined such evolution and how they relate to the discussion in the present chapter.

■ **10.20. AIRBNB.** Write a short essay on the birth and evolution of AirBnB. Focus on the legal difficulties the new service has experienced and compare the normative and capture theories of entry regulation as ways to explain the facts.

## NOTES

1. Robert E. Lucas, "Adjustment Costs and the Theory of Supply," *Journal of Political Economy* **75** (1967), 321–334.

2. Lyons, Bruce, Catherine Matraves, and Peter Moffatt (2001), "Industrial Concentration and Market Integration in the European Union," *Economica* **68** (269), 1–26.

3. Lerner, A. P. (1934), "The Concept of Monopoly and the Measurement of Monopoly Power," *The Review of Economic Studies* **1** (3), 157–175.

4. Sutton, John (1992), *Sunk Costs and Market Structure*, Cambridge, MA: MIT Press.

5. Adapted from Tremblay, Victor J., and Carol H. Tremblay (2005), *The U.S. Brewing Industry: Data and Economic Analysis*, Cambridge, MA: MIT Press; and Elzinga, Kenneth G. (2009), "The Beer Industry," in J. Brock (Ed.), *The Structure of the American Industry*, Upper Saddle River, NJ: Pearson Prentice Hall.

6. Igami, Mitsuru, and Kosuke Uetake (2014), "Shakeout with Merger: Consolidation of the Hard Disk Drive Industry (1976–2014)," Yale University.

7. Source: Table 10.1.

8. Bain, Joe (1951), "Relation of Profit Rate to Industry Concentration: American Manufacturing, 1936–1940," *Quarterly Journal of Economics* **65**, 293–324.

9. Schmalensee, Richard (1989), "Inter-Industry Studies of Structure and Performance," in Schmalensee and Willig, *Handbook of Industrial Organization*, Amsterdam: North-Holland.

10. Harold Demsetz, "Industry Structure, Market Rivalry, and Public Policy", *Journal of Law and Economics* **16** (1973), 1–9.

11. Mankiw, N. Gregory, and Michael D. Whinston (1986), "Free Entry and Social Inefficiency," *Rand Journal of Economics* **17**, 48–58; Spence, Michael (1976), "Product Selection, Fixed Costs, and Monopolistic Competition," *Review of Economic Studies* **43** (2), 217–35.

12. Berry, Steven T, and Joel Waldfogel (1999), "Entry and Social Inefficiency in Radio Broadcasting," *Rand Journal of Economics* **30**, 397–420.

13. Hsieh, Chang-Tai, and Enrico Moretti (2003), "Can Free Entry Be Inefficient? Fixed Commissions and Social Waste in the Real Estate Industry," *Journal of Political Economy* **111** (5), 1076–1122; Barwick, Panle Jia, and Parag Pathak (2014), "The Costs of Free Entry: An Empirical Study of Real Estate Agents in Greater Boston," forthcoming in *Rand Journal of Economics*.

14. Denise Gradyoct, "Ebola Vaccine, Ready for Test, Sat on the Shelf," *The New York Times*, October 23, 2014.

15. Vickers, John (1995), "Entry and Competitive Selection," Oxford University, December.

16. Olley, G. Steven, and Ariel Pakes (1996), "The Dynamics of Productivity in the Telecommunications Equipment Industry," *Econometrica* **64**, 1263–1297.

17. Collard-Wexler, Allan, and Jan De Loecker (2014), "Reallocation and Technology: Evidence from the US Steel Industry," forthcoming in *American Economic Review*.

18. Edlin, Aaron, and Rebecca Haw (2014), "Cartels by Another Name: Should Licensed Occupations Face Antitrust Scrutiny?," *University of Pennsylvania Law Review* **162** (5), 1093–1164.

19. Sources: New York City Taxi and Limousine Commision; Schaller Consulting.

20. Sources: New York City Taxi and Limousine Commision; Schaller Consulting.

21. Adapted from an exercise written by T. Bresnahan. See also Bresnahan, Timothy F., and Peter C. Reiss (1991), "Entry and Competition in Concentrated Markets," *Journal of Political Economy* **99**, 977–1009.

# HORIZONTAL MERGERS

Cemex, the Mexican cement company, was founded in 1906. Its first plant (Hidalgo, in Northern Mexico) had then a capacity of 33,000 tons. By 2013, Cemex was ranked the seventh largest cement company in the world, with operations in more than 50 countries and a total capacity of 76 million tons. How did Cemex get from point A to point B? Partly, it did so by building new capacity (organic growth). Mostly, it did so by acquiring existing companies: in 1987, Cemex purchased Cementos Anáhuac, a rival Mexican company; in 1992, it began its international expansion with the acquisition of Valenciana and Sanson, Spain's two largest cement companies. In a matter of a few years, Cemex was present in four continents.

In the previous chapter, I showed how entry and exit shape market structure. As the Cemex story suggests, the number of competitors — and more generally industry structure — is also the result of mergers and acquisitions. In fact, a merger can be thought of as an exit event: where there were two firms now there is only one.

Why do mergers and acquisitions take place? A brief look at a few examples will show that the causes are manifold.

- In the 1980s Sony purchased the film studio Columbia with the objective of creating "synergies" between two complementary producers. Columbia's collection of quality movies was seen as a guarantee of a minimum supply of "software" to complement the "hardware" offered by Sony (e.g., video players).

- Philip Morris and Kraft possessed a large number of food products sold through supermarket chains. Creating a new firm of greater size allowed Philip Morris and Kraft to increase their bargaining power with respect to retailers. This is important, for example, when it comes to obtaining shelf space for the launch of a new product.

- When Nestlé acquired Rowntree, its main goal was to enter the British market for chocolates. Rowntree owned a vast number of well-known brands (Smarties, After Eight, Kit Kat, etc.). Buying Rowntree allowed Nestlé to save the high costs of launching new brands.

- Another example also involving Nestlé is the joint venture with General Mills for the production and distribution of breakfast cereals in Europe. The main goal of this joint venture was to exploit the synergies between two complementary firms: Nestlé's distribution skills (especially in Europe) and General Mills production skills.

- In 2008, InBev agreed to buy Anheuser-Busch for a total value of $52 billion, leading to the newly-named Anheuser-Busch InBev, the world's largest brewer, bringing together brands such as Budweiser, Michelob, Stella Artois, Bass, and Brahma. InBev had been created in 2004 from the merger of the Belgian company Interbrew and Brazilian company AmBev.

In addition to these examples, where some strategic or efficiency seems to play a role, there are a number of cases where mergers and acquisitions are motivated for financial or tax reasons. For example, acquiring firms from different industries is equivalent to holding a diversified investment portfolio, thus reducing the parent company's overall risk.

In this chapter, I focus on **horizontal mergers**, that is, mergers or acquisitions between two firms within the same industry. From the examples given earlier, both the Phillip Morris-Kraft and Nestlé-Rowntree examples would quality as examples of horizontal mergers; not so the Sony-Columbia example (or the examples where mergers result from financial or tax reasons). Figure 11.1, which lists the largest mergers and acquisitions as of 2014, provides some additional examples, from which at least four would correspond to horizontal mergers (can you see which ones?). In Chapter 13, I consider the possibility of **vertical mergers**, that is, mergers between firms at different stages of the value chain (e.g., a gasoline refinery and a gas station). This still leaves out a considerable number of mergers and acquisitions (for example, conglomerate mergers). While these are great interest for corporate finance and other disciplines, they are relatively less important from the industrial organization point of view.[a]

## 11.1 ECONOMIC EFFECTS OF HORIZONTAL MERGERS

a. For simplicity, in this chapter I will often simply use the word "merger" even though I mean "horizontal merger."

Total output typically decreases (and price increases) as the result of a horizontal merger. In particular, there is a tendency for the combined output of the merged firms to decrease (thus leading to a price increase). Why? Before the merger, if firm $i$ were to decrease output by one unit, it would (a) lose $p - MC$, its selling margin; and (b) gain $q_i \Delta p$, where $q_i$ is its output and $\Delta p$ the increase in price that results from the output decrease. Since

| Rank | Year | Acquiror | Target | $ b | €b |
|---|---|---|---|---|---|
| 1 | 1999 | Vodafone AirTouch PLC | Mannesmann AG | 202.8 | 204.8 |
| 2 | 2000 | America Online Inc. | Time Warner | 164.7 | 160.7 |
| 3 | 2007 | Shareholders | Philip Morris Intl. Inc. | 107.6 | 68.1 |
| 4 | 2007 | RFS Holdings BV | ABN-AMRO Holding NV | 98.2 | 71.3 |
| 5 | 1999 | Pfizer Inc. | Warner-Lambert Co. | 89.2 | 84.9 |
| 6 | 1998 | Exxon Corp | Mobil Corp. | 78.9 | 68.4 |
| 7 | 2000 | Glaxo Wellcome PLC | SmithKline Beecham PLC | 76.0 | 74.9 |
| 8 | 2004 | Royal Dutch Petroleum Co. | Shell Transport & Trading Co. | 74.6 | 58.5 |
| 9 | 2000 | AT&T Inc. | BellSouth Corp. | 72.7 | 60.2 |
| 10 | 1998 | Travelers Group Inc. | Citicorp | 72.6 | 67.2 |

**FIGURE 11.1**
Largest M&A transactions as of 2014[1]

we start (before the merger) from an equilibrium situation, it must be that no firm would have an incentive to decrease (or increase) output. In other words, the positive and the negative effects of an output reduction exactly cancel out.

Consider now the situation after the merger between firms $A$ and $B$. Starting from the same output levels as before the merger, the newly formed firm $A\&B$ stands to gain from a reduction in output. In fact, while the loss in terms of lower output is still $p - MC$, the gain from an increased price is now $(q_A + q_B)\Delta p$. In other words, when firm $A$ lowers output, it now takes into account not only the effect of a higher price on its profits but also the effect on firm $B$'s profits. Therefore, unless the merger implies a significant reduction in the marginal cost of the combined firm $A\&B$, total output of the merging firms goes down.

The above analysis assumes that the mode of competition remains the same after the merger (e.g., Cournot before and Cournot after, though with a more concentrated industry). However, one of the implications of the merger may be precisely to change the industry's competition mode: a more concentrated industry (the result of the merger) may allow for a greater degree of collusion among competitors. We thus have a second reason why mergers may result in higher prices.

Mergers also have an impact on costs, normally referred to as **cost efficiencies**. These cost savings may be divided into two parts: fixed costs and variable costs. Savings in fixed costs typically result from eliminating duplicated functions in the new merged firm. For example, each firm only needs one back office. Although the merged firm is likely to require a bigger back office than either of the previous companies, it is also likely that the total size of the new back office be smaller than the sum of the two previous ones. As an example, the 2000 merger between Daimler and Chrysler was expected to create cost savings of $3 billion a year, mostly from fixed costs savings.[b]

b. As it turned out, the cost savings did not materialize, and the merger was eventually undone.

### BOX 11.1 THE HYUNDAI-KIA MERGER[2]

The Korean automobile industry was not imune to the 1997 Asian crisis: except for Hyundai, every automaker — Kia, Daewoo, Sangyong, Samsung — fell into serious financial distress. Kia declared bankruptcy in 1997 and was acquired by Hyundai (beating Samsung and Ford at the auction block).

The Hyundai-Kia (HK) merger promised a series of cost efficiencies, and soon the results began to show. Mong-Gu Chung, the eldest son of the then-owner of Hyundai, was appointed chairman and restructured business operations. The number of R&D centers was reduced from eight to two (the Namyang R&D Center for passenger car models, and the Junju R&D Center for commercial vehicles). A new business unit, Hyundai Mobis, was created in 2000 for the purpose of standardizing parts and modules across Hyundai and Kia plants. In this way, HK was able to consolidate production and take better advantage of scale economies. For example, the number of platforms (combination of underbody and suspensions with axles) declined considerably, as shown in the left panel below.

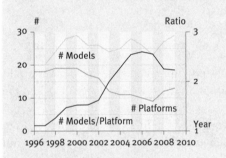
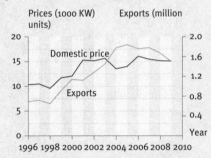

When reviewing the merger, the Korean Fair Trade Commission acknowledged the trade-off between the merger's negative effect (greater market power in the domestic market) and positive effect (greater cost efficiencies and competitiveness in export markets). The data on price and export share (right panel) seem consistent with this view.

Estimates of the merger's impact on welfare suggest that the price and cost effects approximately compensated for each other, so that total welfare remained relatively unchanged. However, the impact was not uniform: consumers were harmed by the merger, whereas the automakers' shareholders benefited.

Variable cost savings can result from different factors. For example, suppose that firm $A$ has good production expertise and poor distribution skills, whereas firm $B$'s advantage are the exact opposite: poor production expertise and good distribution skills. By merging, the firms combine the best of each firm's competitive advantages (some refer to effects of this sort as **merger synergies**). As an example, the joint venture between Nestlé and General Mills, which I alluded to earlier, combined complementary skills that lead to a lower marginal cost of producing and distributing breakfast cereals.

In sum, we have two main effects from a merger:

Mergers normally imply an increase in prices and a reduction in costs.

Box 11.1 describes an illustrative example, the merger between South Korean automakers Hyundai and Kia. As I will show in Section 11.3, these price and cost effects correspond to the main trade-off faced by policy makers when it comes to merger analysis.

---

**THE PROFIT EFFECT OF MERGERS: ANALYTICAL APPROACH.** Suppose we start from a situation with three firms, all with marginal cost $c_i = c$; and that Firms 2 and 3 merge, forming a new Firm 2 with cost function is $C = F' + c' q$, where $c' < c$. (Think of Firm 2 acquiring Firm 3 and keeping the former's name.)

There are three interested parties in the merger: first, the merging firms themselves; second the rival firms, in this case Firm 1; and finally, consumers. I first consider the effect of a merger on the merging firms' profits. In Chapter 8 (Exercise 8.15), I showed that Firm $i$'s profit under Cournot competition is given by:

$$\widehat{\pi}_i = \left( \frac{a - n c_i + \sum_{j \neq i} c_j}{n + 1} \right)^2 - F_i \tag{11.1}$$

Applying this formula, each firm's pre-merger profit is given by:

$$\pi_1 = \pi_2 = \pi_3 = \left( \frac{a - c}{4} \right)^2 - F$$

After the merger, the new Firm 2 (which resulted from the merger of 2 and 3) has a profit of:

$$\pi_2' = \left( \frac{a + c - 2 c'}{3} \right)^2 - F'$$

(Notice that, after the merger, $n = 2$, so that $n + 1 = 3$.) It follows that the combined profit of the merging firms changes by:

$$\pi_2' - (\pi_2 + \pi_3) = (2 F - F') + \left( \frac{a + c - 2 c'}{3} \right)^2 - 2 \left( \frac{a - c}{4} \right)^2 \tag{11.2}$$

There are four different effects to consider. First, fixed costs savings: to the extent that $F' < 2 F$, the merger implies fixed cost efficiencies.

The second effect can be seen in the numerator of the variable profit function. If $c' < c$, then $a + c - 2c' > a - c$. (Check this.) The more efficient a firm is, the greater its profits are.

The third effect can be seen in the fact the denominator of the variable profit function decreases from 4 to 3 (more generally from $n + 1$ to $n$, where $n$ is the initial number of firms). A merger implies a decrease in the number of competitors. Fewer competitors imply less competition, which in turn translates into higher profits.

So far, I showed three effects that are favorable to the merging firms. There is, however, one important negative effect: by merging, two profits are turned into one. In fact, the last term in (11.2) is multiplied by 2 (pre-merger variable profits), whereas the second-to-last term is not (post-merger variable profits). This fourth effect is clearly negative. In fact, if $F = 0$ and $c = c'$, such that there are no cost efficiencies, then the merging firms' change in profits is given by:

$$\pi_2' - (\pi_2 + \pi_3) = \left( \frac{a - c}{3} \right)^2 - 2 \left( \frac{a - c}{4} \right)^2 = (a - c)^2 \left( \frac{1}{9} - \frac{2}{16} \right)$$

which is negative. So, unless there are fixed cost redundancies that can be eliminated by the merger ($F > 0$) or variable cost synergies ($c' < c$), the merging parties actually reduce their combined profit as a result of the merger. Notice that this is true even though the market becomes less competitive, which is to the firm's benefit.

---

Not every firm decreases its output as a result of a merger. In fact, for the *non-merging firms* the opposite is true. Before the merger, if firm $C$ were to decrease output by one unit, it would (a) lose $p - MC$, its selling margin; and (b) gain $q_C \Delta p$. After the merger, (b) remains the same but (a) is now greater. If firm $C$ was indifferent between decreasing and increasing output before the merger, it now strictly prefers to increase, which in turn results in an increase in profit (higher margin and higher market share).

In fact, there is a sense in which non-merging firms are the main beneficiaries from the merger: without having to incur any costs, they see the number of their competitors decrease by one. The non-merging firms are, as it were, free riding on the output reduction (and price increase) initiated by the merging firms. As a well-known author put it, "the promoter of a merger is likely to receive much encouragement from each firm — almost every encouragement, in fact, except participation."[3]

This is not true in general, however. For example, if the merged firm becomes very efficient, specifically, if its marginal cost is substantially lower than before the merger, then it may happen that non-merging firms see their profits decrease. In terms of the analysis above, recall that I (implicitly) made the assumption that marginal cost remains unchanged as a result of the merger. Otherwise, effect (b) of an output reduction would increase and the merging firm $A\&B$ would no longer find it profitable to reduce output. The situation is then inverted: non-merging firms reduce their market share and profits as result of the merger.

> The value of non-merging firms may decrease or increase as the result of a merger, depending on the cost efficiencies generated by the merger.

The next four examples show that both situations are possible in practice:

- "British Petroleum PLC said it would buy Amoco Corp. in the largest industrial merger ever ... The accord has helped push up stock prices of most major oil companies. Mobil Corp., [for example,] was up $2.625 late Thursday at $69.375."[4]

- In March 2011, Western Digital announced that it would buy Hitachi, a merger between the first and third largest suppliers of computer disk drives. Stock prices for Seagate — the number three supplier — grew by 9% to $13.56.[5]

- Responding to the announcement of a proposed merger between British Airways and American Airlines, Virgin Atlantic — a smaller competitor in the London-US routes — painted its aircraft with the clear message "BA/AA No Way."[c]

- In the European defense industry, the merger between rivals GKN plc and Alvis plc put the pressure on Vickers, a third competitor. "Together, GKN and Alvis

c. In the case of Virgin Atlantic, an additional concern with the BA/AA merger is that Virgin Atlantic relative size would be even smaller. As I will show in Section 12.3, predatory practices are not unknown in this industry. A greater asymmetry in size between competitors may increase the likelihood of such an event.

will be in a far better position to call the shots as Europe undergoes defense and aerospace consolidation ... Some analysts have warned that could shut the door on Vickers."[6]

The first two example seems to fit the "free riding" story, whereby non-merging competitors benefit from the merger.[d] The third and fourth examples, however, suggest that the non-merging firms would be harmed by the merger.

---

**MERGER EFFECT ON NON-MERGING FIRMS: ANALYTICAL APPROACH.** Firm 1's profit, after the merger, is given by:

$$\pi_1' = \left( \frac{a + c' - 2c}{3} \right)^2 - F$$

The difference with respect to pre-merger profit is given by:

$$\pi_1' - \pi_1 = \left( \frac{a + c' - 2c}{3} \right)^2 - \left( \frac{a - c}{4} \right)^2 \tag{11.3}$$

We now have two effects. First, to the extent that $c' < c$, the numerator of the variable profit function is lower after the merger: $a + c' - 2c < a - c$. In other words, the non-merging firm loses from the merging firms' efficiency improvement. However, the denominator of the variable profit function is greater when the number of firms is decreased: the merger implies one firm less, and fewer competitors implies higher profits for everyone, including the non-merging firms.

If $c = c^k$, that is, if the merger implies no variable cost synergies, then $\pi_1' - \pi_1$ is positive. However, if for example $c$ is close to $a/2$ and $c'$ is close to zero (huge cost synergies), then $\pi_1'$ is close to zero, whereas $\pi_1$ was positive. So, outsiders have potentially a lot to lose from a merger that creates a more efficient firm.

---

Finally, consider the effect of a merger on consumer surplus. As I showed in previous chapters, equilibrium price under Cournot competition is (strictly) decreasing in the number of firms. Going from $n$ to $n - 1$ competitors implies an increase in price. More generally, an increase in concentration implies an increase in price. In other words, market price increases as a result of the merger. Consequently, if product differentiation is not very important — so that market price is the consumers's only concern — and if variable cost efficiencies are not too strong, then mergers imply a decrease in consumer welfare. However, if cost efficiencies are very strong, it is possible that consumers benefit from the merger.

---

**MERGER EFFECT ON CONSUMER SURPLUS: ANALYTICAL APPROACH.** In Exercise 8.15, I showed that consumer surplus under Cournot competition is given by:

$$CS = \frac{1}{2} \left( \frac{na - \sum_{i=1}^{n} c_i}{n+1} \right)^2 = \frac{1}{2} \left( \frac{n}{n+1} \right)^2 \left( a - \frac{1}{n} \sum_{i=1}^{n} c_i \right)^2$$

d. An alternative interpretation of the stock market movement is that other, similar "target" companies are now in play.

Therefore, the merger implies a change in consumer surplus by:

$$CS' - CS = \frac{1}{2}\left(\frac{2}{3}\right)^2 \left(a - \frac{1}{2}(c + c')\right)^2 - \frac{1}{2}\left(\frac{3}{4}\right)^2 (a - c)^2$$

As in the case of the non-merging firms, we have two effects to consider. First, part of the merger's synergies are passed on to consumers: since $c' < c$, we have $a - \frac{1}{2}(c + c') > a - c$. Second, a smaller number of firms implies an increase in market power: $CS'$ includes the factor $\frac{2}{3}$, which is lower than $\frac{3}{4}$. If $c'$ is much lower than $c$, then the positive effect dominates and consumers gain from the merger. If $c' \approx c$, then the market power effect dominates and consumers are harmed by the merger.

---

■ **EMPIRICAL EVIDENCE.** As someone once said, "it's difficult to make predictions, especially about the future."[e] One way to evaluate the effects of horizontal mergers is to look back at consummated mergers and observe what happened to prices. Alas, it's difficult to disentangle the effect of the merger from changes that coincided with the merger's occurrence but were not the result of the merger. In other words, to the extent that correlation and causality can be easily confused, it's difficult to "predict" even the past.

It's difficult but it's not impossible. Box 11.2 briefly discusses the methodology and the results of one particular case, the Miller-Coors merger. In this particular case, it's estimated that the merger had a negligible effect on price. However, a survey of 15 other studies of mergers that took place in the airline industry from 1986 to 2009 reports price effects that range from negative 19% to positive 26%.[8] It's not so much a case of economists disagreeing over what they measure as it is a case of different mergers having differential impacts. This leads naturally to the question of when should mergers be allowed to proceed, a question I discuss in Section 11.3. Before that, I extend the analysis in this section by considering dynamic aspects of merger strategy.

## 11.2 HORIZONTAL MERGER DYNAMICS

In the previous section, I considered the case when one single horizontal merger takes place. In reality, however, we observe patterns of merger activity over time. For example, globally mergers are highly procyclical, slightly leading the business cycle. At the industry level, we observe that many mergers take place in reaction to, or in anticipation of, other mergers. In this section, I discuss various dynamic issues of horizontal mergers.

e. I ignore the exact source of this quote; some scholars trace it back to Denmark in the late 1930s.

## Box 11.2 The Miller-Coors joint venture[7]

In October 2007 Miller and Coors — the second and third largest firms in the US beer industry — announced they planned to combine their operations. Although the merger substantially increased concentration in an already concentrated industry, it also came with the promise of significant cost savings. Prior to the merger, Coors was brewed in only two locations, whereas Miller was brewed in six locations. By moving the production of Coors beer into Miller plants, the joint venture could lower average shipping costs. Taking these efficiencies into account, the US Department of Justice approved the joint venture in June 2008. Was that the right decision?

The impact of the merger — both in terms of change in concentration and in terms of change in shipping distances — varied considerably from market to market. This variation allows for the statistical estimation of the impact of the merger. Controlling for a variety of other factors, it can be estimated that: (a) in markets where the Herfindahl index increased more, prices tended to increase more; (b) in markets where the average shipping distance decreased more, prices tended to decrease more.

These estimated effects are consistent with the analysis in Section 11.1. Their average impact on price changes is plotted in the figure below, where the two vertical lines represent the dates at which the merger was announced and then approved.

By 2011, three years after the merger took place, increases in concentration resulting from the merger (change in $H$) had caused a 2% increase in price ($p$). However, decreases in distribution costs resulting from the merger (change in shipping distance $d$) had caused a 2% decrease in price. While these are estimates are subject to statistical error, the overall picture is consistent with the view that, as far as consumer prices are concerned, the impact of the joint venture was minor (that is, the net effect on prices was very close to zero).

■ **PREEMPTIVE MERGERS.** In some industries, larger conglomerates compete for targets to acquire. In this context, the primary goal of an acquisition may be to preempt a rival from doing so.[f] For example, some analysts claim that:

> Google bought Waze not just because the company offers a potentially good product that Google can link to its own dominant map service, but possibly because its purchase keeps Waze out of the hands of its rival Facebook, which was also a rumored bidder.[9]

When preemption motives are very strong, it's even possible that a firm engages in a merger that decreases value — if the alternative is to suffer even more were the target acquired by a rival.[10]

■ **MERGER WAVES.** Frequently, mergers occur in waves: periods of intense merger activity in a given industry alternate with periods of relative stability. There are several explanations for this phenomenon, some based on exogenous causes, some based on endogenous causes. Consider, for example, the radio broadcasting industry. Among other things, the US 1996 Telecommunications Act raised ownership caps in local markets and abolished cross-market ownership restrictions of radio stations. As a result, between 1996 and 2006 the US radio broadcasting industry experienced an unprecedented merger wave, as can be seen in Figure 11.2. At wave's peak, more than 20% of stations changed ownership per year and about 14% changed programming formats.[11]

Alternatively, an industry merger wave may be caused by endogenous factors. For instance, the US supermarket business underwent a process of rapid consolidation during the 1990s. Some argue that this merger wave was primarily driven by the need to cut costs and remain competitive with Wal-Mart, which flooded the industry with its low-cost distribution model. As several firms merged together, the pressure to cut costs

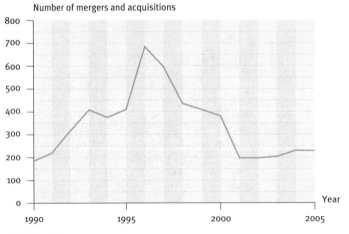

f. In the next chapter, I will look at preemption motives in greater detail.

**FIGURE 11.2**

Mergers and acquisitions of US radio stations[12]

become even greater, which in turn lead to further mergers in the unending quest to achieve cost efficiencies. In September 1999 alone,

> Kroger has made a $13 billion offer for Fred Meyer; ... Safeway has announced plans to buy Dominick's Supermarkets for $1.8 billion; and Canada's Empire has said it would buy a rival chain, Oshawa, for $900 million. [In the previous month], Albertson's snapped up American Stores for $12 billion. Meanwhile Kmart, a discount retailer, said this week that it needs to find a supermarket chain to be its partner."[13]

More recently, Madison Avenue's 2013 mega-merger between Publicis Groupe SA and Omnicom Group Inc. was expected to spark a new consolidation wave in the advertising industry.[14]

To understand endogenous merger wave effects, let us return to the big-firm-buys-small-target situation I considered earlier in the context of preemptive mergers. Suppose that the number of targets is limited and that there is some value in waiting and obtaining better information about target values. In this context, when one of my rivals acquires a target, the number of available targets becomes smaller, which in turn increases the relative value of acquiring a target (as opposed to waiting). As a result, my rival's acquisition may prompt me to jump into an acquisition myself — and a merger wave is in the making.[15,g]

> Merger waves may result from exogenous events (e.g., industry deregulation) or from endogenous events (e.g., a merger between two large firms).

■ **MERGERS AND ENTRY.** I have just argued that a merger between firms $x$ and $y$ may induce firms $v$ and $w$ to merge. However, more likely than that, a merger between firms $x$ and $y$ may induce entry by firm $z$. Consider again the US radio broadcasting industry. As I mentioned earlier, many mergers have taken place in the past decades. For each of the 88 markets in which the US is divided, Figure 11.3 contrasts entry rates in periods following a merger as compared to periods prior to the merger.[h] The contrast is remarkable: in most markets (72%), mergers are followed by higher entry rates.[i] For example, suppose that two adult-music stations merge and that in the next year a competing non-music station becomes an adult-music station. Then we record the event as an entry into the adult-music market.[j]

If you think about it, this is not entirely surprising: I mentioned earlier that a merger may be thought of an firm exit: when firms $x$ and $y$ merge, it's as if one of the firms had exited the market. (This is particularly clear when the acquirer is the bigger firm and keeps its name.) But if an exit takes place and if barriers to entry are not very high, then it is quite possible that the free-entry equilibrium requires entry by a new firm.

g. See Exercise 11.6 for an illustration of an alternative approach to strategic merger waves.

h. The number of radio licenses varies very little (only occasionally does the Federal Communications Commission issues new licenses). Entry does not refer to the issuance of new radio licenses, rather to the music format chosen by an existing licensed radio station.

i. For better visualization, a few markets with very high or very low values are omitted.
Naturally, other factors influence the net entry rate into radio broadcasting; but it can be shown that, even considering additional factors, the pattern persists, that is, entry rates are higher after a merger takes place.

j. Alternatively, a "dark" station — that is, a licensed station that has previously gone off-air — may restart broadcasting. This too would be recorded as an entry event.

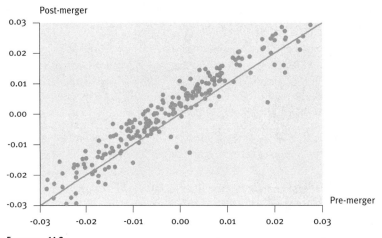

**FIGURE 11.3**
Entry in US radio station markets (monthly net entry rates)[11]

> If barriers to entry are not very high, then mergers tend to be followed by new firm entry.

The idea may be rephrased as follows: together, mergers and entry jointly create "self-correcting" dynamics. If one pulls down the number of firms, the other corrects the move by pushing up the number of firms. This pattern plays an important role in public policy toward mergers, which is the focus on the next section.

## 11.3 HORIZONTAL MERGER POLICY

There are essentially three interested parties in a horizontal merger: the merging firms, the non-merging firms, and consumers. Broadly speaking, Section 11.1 suggests that consumers in general lose from the merger; non-merging firms may gain or may lose; and merging firms, finally, are expected to gain from the merger, at least in expected terms (or else they wouldn't merge).

The task for public policy is to evaluate the relative importance of each gain and loss; and then to assess the overall merger effect, taking into account the relative weight given to firm profits and to consumer welfare. This task is especially hard when it comes to estimate cost savings. In fact, most of the information necessary for such evaluation lies with the merging firms; and the merging firms have a strategic incentive to distort such information, in the hope of convincing policy makers that the overall effect of the merger is positive.

One of the few general policy rules is that the greater the price increase, the less desirable a merger is. The idea is simple: a higher price implies a consumer loss that is less than compensated by a gain for firms (the difference being the allocative inefficiency caused by the gap between price and marginal cost). Moreover, policy makers normally give more weight to consumer welfare than to firm profits. So, even if there were no allocative efficiency loss, a higher price would imply a transfer from consumers to firms, a negative effect (from a policy maker's perspective).

How can a policy maker estimate the likely increase in price following a merger? In Section 10.3 I showed that, for a given mode of competition, equilibrium price is increasing in market concentration. So a merger between two large firms is likely to imply a greater increase in price than a merger between two small firms. Moreover, collusion is more likely in concentrated industries; so a switch to collusive behavior is more likely to take place as a result of a merger.

It is important to distinguish these two channels of price increase. The first one, known as the **unilateral effect** of the merger, is essentially a function of the increase in concentration. The idea is that the merger implies a reduction in the number of purchasing choices available to consumers. This is particularly relevant if products are differentiated (a possibility I consider in Chapter 14), but also in the homogenous-goods case.

The second channel of price increases motivated by a merger, the **collusion effect**, also depends on the *distribution* of market shares. An example will help clarify this distinction: in February 1992, the food products manufacturer Nestlé made a bid for Perrier S.A., Europe's leading producer of mineral water. Market shares prior to the merger were as follows: Perrier, 35.9%; BSN, 23%; Nestlé, 17.1%; others, 24%. The Nestlé/Perrier merger would thus create a leading producer with 53% of the market and a second firm with only 23%. Nestlé anticipated that the European Commission would not be very keen on such an increase in concentration, in particular on having a single firm with such a large market share. It therefore proposed the Commission that, together with the merger, it would transfer Volvic, one of the Nestlé/Perrier water sources, to rival BSN. Taking this asset transfer into account, the foreseeable post-merger market shares would be: Nestlé/Perrier, 38%; BSN (with Volvic), 38%; others, 24%.

The commission approved the merger with the conditional asset transfer. The idea is that anticompetitive concerns are less significant in a 38–38 dominant duopoly than in a 53–23 one. However, such presumption is far from obvious: the argument can be made that collusion between Nestlé/Perrier is made much easier if they hold similar market shares than in they are very different in size.[16] Although the unilateral effect of the merger (increased concentration and price) is likely to be greater without the asset transfer, the collusion effect (increased collusion) is likely to be greater with the asset transfer.

How does one go about estimating the price effect of a merger? One possibility is to estimate the impact of the merger on concentration and then apply a formula like Equation 10.7, which relates concentration to price. The practical problem of this approach is that, in order to compute the concentration index, one first needs to compute market shares; and, in order to compute market shares, one first needs to define the market; and the latter is far from trivial.

For example, in 1996 Staples and Office Depot — the two largest US chains of office supplies superstores — proposed to merge together. The merger was eventually disallowed by the US district court, ruling in favor of the Federal Trade Commission, which argued that the merger would increase market power in the industry, to the detriment of consumers. In fact, if the relevant market definition is "office superstores," then Staples and Office Depot would combine for a market share of more than 70%. However, if the relevant industry definition is "stores that sell office supplies," then the combined market shares of the two firms would be much lower.

Disagreement between firms and merger authorities concerning market definition is very common. It shows how difficult and inexact the science of market definition is. For this and for other reasons, antitrust authorities such as the US Federal Trade Commission (FTC) have come to favor the more direct approach of estimating the impact of a merger on consumer prices. For example, in examining the Staples/Office Depot proposed merger, the FTC concluded that prices in cities with little or no competition between superstore chains are up to 15% higher than in cities where there is competition. This provides a benchmark estimate of how much prices would increase as a result of the merger in cities where only Staples and Office Depot operate (of which, as it turns out, there is a fair number).

A second general rule for merger policy is that the smaller the relative size of the merging firms, the more likely the overall impact of the merger is positive. There are two reasons for this rule. First, the smaller the merging firms are, the lower the price increase caused by the merger. For example, going from 20 to 19 firms implies a lower increase in price than going from three to two firms.

The second reason is that a merger between small firms indicates that efficiency gains are likely to be significant. I showed before that, under Cournot competition, nonmerging firms "free ride" on the merging firm's output reduction. The fact that two small firms want to merge likely signals that cost efficiencies are sufficiently significant to counteract this free-riding effect.[17]

> The smaller the size of the merging firms, the more likely the total effect of a merger is positive.

In the US, the Department of Justice (DOJ) and the FTC follow horizontal merger guidelines that indicate thresholds of industry concentration, as well as changes in industry concentration, that determine the agencies' expected position with respect to a merger.

Most government authorities responsible for merger analysis have a set of rules or guidelines which include the ideas above and other related ones: the US Merger Guidelines (most recently updated in 2010) or the European Union's Regulation 89/90, for example. Ultimately, what matters is the relative weight given to each of the interested parties, for there will always be gainers and losers.

■ **DYNAMICS ASPECTS OF MERGER POLICY.** In the previous section, I considered the possibility of strategic merger waves, whereby the merger of two industry participants puts pressure on their competitors to follow a similar path. Such dynamic considerations should also be part of a policy maker's decision process: approving a merger today may have an impact on future mergers as well.

I showed in the previous section that mergers, which in a sense amount to firm exit, may be followed by a compensating entry flow. In other words, if industry entry is relatively easy, then post-merger entry partly corrects for the market power effect of a merger. For this reason, policy makers are normally more lenient towards mergers in industries where entry is easy: in such industries the price effect cannot be very significant; otherwise, entry would take place and counteract the merger's negative effect.

An additional dynamic effect in merger policy is regulator reputation. Consider again the Korean automobile manufacturing industry. In approving the Hyundai-Kia merger (see Box 11.1), the Korean Fair Trade Commission (KFTC) implicitly placed a significant weight on the cost efficiencies created by the merger, as well as its subsequent effect on exports. Different merger authorities have different priorities; contrary to the US, for example, the Korean authority follows a policy that combines competition policy concerns with industrial policy concerns (e.g., the creation of a "national champion"). If this was not clear to industry participants, it probably became clear after the 1998 Hyundai-Kia decision.

After the Hyundai-Kia merger took place, there were a series of additional changes: Renault acquired Samsung in 2000; GM acquired Daewoo in 2002; and Sangyong merged with Shanghai Motors in 2005. It is quite possible that this additional wave of mergers and acquisitions was at least partly due to the perception that the KFTC would be lenient in its merger review.

■ **MERGER POLICY IN PRACTICE.** In most countries in the world, merging firms are required to notify their plans with the appropriate government regulator or agency. This is especially true if the merging parties' sales revenue falls above a certain threshold. In the US, both the DOJ and the FTC must be notified. In Europe, the merging firms must notify the national competition authority if the merger only has an impact within the country; otherwise, the European Commissions DG Comp must be notified. In other countries, there is typically a government department or agency in charge of competition policy (sometimes one specialized on mergers). For example, in China the Anti-Monopoly Bureau, part of the Ministry of Commerce (MOFCOM), is in charge of merger control (but not of, say, price fixing or abusive practices, which fall under the purview of other government ministries).

Typically, the agency has a period of time to declare whether it has any antitrust concerns with the operation. In most cases, the agency says nothing and the merger goes through. For example, in the US and from 2002–2012, more than 15,000 mergers were notified but less than 750 were taken to the next phase, and of these only 65 were turned into a challenge case.[18] The next phase typically consists of a request for more information to be provided to the regulator, which in turn leads to a closer scrutiny of the proposed merger.

If there is a "case" — that is, a merger which is deemed to have potentially serious anti-competitive implications — then the agency may try to negotiate possible remedies with the interested parties. These remedies may be **behavioral remedies** (for example, prices cannot be increased more than $x\%$ during the next $n$ years); or **structural remedies** (for example, sell assets $y$ and $z$ to a competitor). Sometimes the remedies are initially proposed by the merging parties (anticipating possible objections by the agency). In other occasions, the merging parties respond to the agency's proposal with a remedy package counteroffer.

As a result of the case, various outcomes are possible. If the agency and the interested parties agree on a set of remedies, then the merger goes through. If they do not, then the merger is blocked. The precise meaning of a blocked merger depends on the particular jurisdiction. In the US, the DOJ and the FTC lack the power to unilaterally prevent the merger from taking place. Normally, their threat of asking a court to do so is sufficient. Sometimes it is not, and the case it tried in court. In Europe, both national agencies and the European Commission have the power to block a merger. The merging parties can then appeal the decision to national or European courts if they wish. In other countries, the system of authority tends to be closer to the European system than the American system.

■ **SELECTED CASES.** In the US — and increasingly in the European Union and other countries — competition policy is largely determined by precedent. For this reason, it is worthwhile considering some historically important decisions regarding proposed mergers.

☐ **STAPLES AND OFFICE DEPOT.** I mentioned this case earlier, but there are a few additional points worth mentioning. In 1996, Staples and Office Depot announced their plans to merge. The FTC asked for the companies to divest a series of stores as a remedy. Staples disagreed with the proposed remedy, and the case was taken to court in 1997. The court sided with the FTC, and the merger was blocked.

This case illustrates the fact that in the US — unlike the European Union and other countries — the regulator does not have the authority to block the merger unilaterally: if the merging parties disagree from the regulator's decision, then the case proceeds to court. This case also illustrates the FTC's willingness to fight till the end (it was a difficult court battle), as well as the court's willingness to accept economic analysis arguments regarding merger effects (for example, the statistical analysis referred to earlier).

☐ **BSKYB/ITV.** In 2006, British Sky Broadcasting Group (BSkyB), a UK pay-TV broadcaster, announced the acquisition of 17.9% of ITV, a UK free-to-air TV broadcaster. The UK Competition Commission (CC) concluded that such acquisition would lessen competition considerably, and ordered BSkyB to reduce its shareholding to below 7.5%.

Specifically, the CC found that, on the basis of past voting patterns (and considering that BSkyB would be the largest shareholder), the acquisition gave BSkyB the ability to block special resolutions proposed by ITV's management. As such, a relevant merger situation was created.

This decision is important, among other reasons, because it suggests that even partial shareholdings may be considered to have anticompetitive effects similar to a full merger.

□ **SIRIUS AND XM RADIO.** In 2001, Sirius and XM began broadcasting satellite radio, offering competing commercial free services for $10/month. The subscriptions included multiple thematic channels (music, talk, sports, etc.) and were mostly used by car drivers. By the end of 2006, the two companies had 17 million subscribers but no profits to show. In February 2007, Sirius and XM proposed to merge into a single satellite radio supplier.

The merger was approved by the US Department of Justice (DoJ) in March 2008, and by the FCC in July 2008. Besides the long decision period (it was the longest merger investigation in US history), there are a few points worth mentioning. First, sometimes, in addition to the relevant antitrust agency (the DOJ in this case), a merger may also need to be approved by the relevant sectoral agency (in this case, the Federal Communications Commission). Second, mergers into monopoly are rarely approved. However, a case can be made that consumers have alternatives to satellite radio (that is, the relevant market definition may not be satellite radio). Moreover, this merger implied combining two different technologies into one, which may imply important synergies both in terms of lower cost and in terms of a better service. Last but not least, the alternative to approving the merger might very well be for the two firms to go bankrupt, which might be a worse outcome even from the consumers' perspective. This is sometimes referred to as the **failing firm merger defense**.

□ **RYANAIR AND AER LINGUS.** In 2007, Ryanair attempted to acquire Irish rival Aer Lingus. The European Commission (EC) blocked the acquisition on the grounds that it would imply a high risk of price increases: it would have led to overlaps on more than 30 routes from/to Ireland, thus implying reduced choice for consumers. This decision was one of the commission's first prohibition decisions to be supported by extensive survey and quantitative data analysis to underpin the basic economic argument.

Ryanair filed an application for annulment of the decision with the General Court of the European Union. However, in 2010 the court ruled in the commission's favor. Undeterred by this and other defeats, in 2013 Ryanair reformulated its proposal, including a "remedies package" that, it claimed, clearly addressed all of the commission's objections. However, the EC again blocked the bid.

□ **CONTAINER SHIPPING: THE P3 NETWORK.** In 2014, the world's three biggest container shipping companies (AP Moller-Maersk, Mediterranean Shipping Company, and CMA

CGM) proposed to form an alliance (the so-called P3 Network). By pooling their 250 ships, they hoped to reduce costs and increase demand in various transatlantic routes.

In June of that year, China blocked the agreement. In a statement posted on its website, China's commerce ministry estimated that the alliance would control 47% of container traffic on Asia-Europe routes, "greatly increasing market concentration."

China's rejection is one of the most high-profile cases in its six-year-old merger review system history. It is also an interesting example of how merger policy (and more generally competition policy) is becoming a global issue in a global world.

## SUMMARY

• Mergers normally imply an increase in prices and a reduction in costs. • The value of non-merging firms may decrease or increase as the result of a merger, depending on the cost efficiencies generated by the merger. • Merger waves may result from exogenous events (e.g., industry deregulation) or from endogenous events (e.g., a merger between two large firms). • If barriers to entry are not very high, then mergers tend to be followed by new firm entry. • The smaller the size of the merging firms, the more likely the total effect of a merger is positive.

## KEY CONCEPTS

• horizontal mergers • vertical mergers • cost efficiencies • merger synergies • unilateral effect • collusion effect • behavioral remedies • structural remedies • failing firm merger defense

## REVIEW AND PRACTICE EXERCISES

■ **11.1. MERGERS AND OUTPUT LEVEL.** "The combined output of two merging firms decreases as a result of the merger." True or false?

■ **11.2. MERGERS IN THE PAPER INDUSTRY.** One of the efficiencies created by mergers in the paper industry results from reorganization of production. A machine is more efficient the narrower the range of products it produces, among other reasons because the length of each production run can be made longer.

The paper industry underwent a wave of mergers in the 1980s. Of the firms that merged, about two-thirds increased their market share as a result of the merger. Assuming that (i) firms compete by setting production capacity and (ii) paper products are relatively homogeneous across firms, explain how the previous paragraph explains the pattern of changes in market shares. Which firms would you expect to increase their market share?[19]

■ **11.3. BAE AND GE.** "The renewed prospect of a link-up between British Aerospace PLC and the Marconi defense arm of General Electric Co. PLC of the UK has led to revived talks between the top defense companies in Germany and France."[20] Discuss.

■ **11.4. THE HP-COMPAQ MERGER.** In 2001, HP acquired Compaq. The merger had an impact on two different markets: desktop PCs and servers. Pre-merger market shares in the desktop PC market were as follows: Dell, 13; Compaq, 12; HP, 8; IBM, 6; Gateway, 4. Pre-merger market shares in the servers market were as follows: IBM, 26; Compaq, 16; HP, 14; Dell, 7.[21]

(a) Determine the value of *HHI* in each market before the merger.

(b) Assuming market shares of each firm remain constant, determine the value of *HHI* after the merger.

(c) Considering the values determined above and the DoJ merger guidelines, was the Department of Justice right in allowing the merger to take place?

■ **11.5. MERGER AND THE HERFINDAHL INDEX.** Consider an industry with demand $Q = a - p$ where three identical firms that compete a la Cournot. Each firm's cost function is given by $C = F + cq$. Suppose two of the firms merge and that the merged firm's cost function is given by $C = F' + c'q$, where $F < F' < 2F$.

(a) Determine each firm's market share before and after the merger

(b) Suppose that $a = 10$ and $c = 3$. Determine the Herfindahl index after the merger takes place when (i) $c' = 2$ and (ii) $c' = 1$. Compare this to the post-merger Herfindahl index calculated based on pre-merger market shares. Why do these values differ?

■ **11.6. MERGER WAVE.** Consider an industry where firms compete by setting output levels (Cournot). Market demand is given by $D = 150 - P$, marginal cost is constant and equal to 50, and fixed cost is 150 (the same for all firms).

(a) Show that profits per firm are given by 961, 475, and 250 as the number of firms is equal to 2, 3, or 4.

Suppose that a merger leads to a new firm with the same fixed cost and the same marginal cost.

(b) Suppose that initially there are four firms. Show that a merger between Firms 1 and 2 is unprofitable.

(c) Suppose that Firms 3 and 4 decide to merge, forming Firm 3&4. Show that now a merger between Firms 1 and 2 is profitable.

## Challenging exercises

■ **11.7. Entry by acquisition.** A large fraction of industry entry corresponds to acquisition of incumbent firms. For example, from a sample of 3,788 entry events, about 70% were acquisitions.[22] Econometric analysis suggests that entry by acquisition is more common in more concentrated industries.[23] Can you explain this observation?

Suggestion: consider a Cournot oligopoly with $n$ symmetric firms. Determine the maximum that an entrant would be willing to pay for one of the incumbent firms. Determine also the minimum that an incumbent would require from a buyer, *knowing that the alternative to selling the firm is for the entrant to create a new firm.* Show that the difference between the two values above is greater when the industry is more concentrated.[24]

What other factors would you expect to influence the "build or buy" decision when entering an industry?

## Applied exercises

■ **11.8. Merger event study.** Find time-series stock market data for all firms in an industry where a (horizontal) merger has taken place. Determine whether and how stock price reacts to merger announcements as well as the actual merger. Are these movements consistent with the theory presented in this chapter? How can you use changes following merger announcement as well as changes following merger consummation to tease out various effects from the merger? What limitations do you think an event study of this type has, in general and in the specific merger application under consideration? Extra credit: find data on prices and costs pre- and post-merger; use it to refine your analysis of merger impact.

## Notes

1. Source: Institute of Mergers, Acquisitions, and Alliances

2. Ohashi, Hiroshi, and Yuta Toyama (2014), "Effects of Domestic Merger on Exports: The Case Study of the 1998 Korean Automobiles," University of Tokyo and Northwestern University.

3. George Stigler, "Monopoly and Oligopoly by Merger," *American Economic Review Proceedings*, May 1950, 40, 479–489.

4. *The Wall Street Journal Europe*, August 14–15, 1998.

5. *Wall Street Journal*, March 8, 2014.

6. *The Wall Street Journal Europe*, September 16, 1998.

7. Adapted from Ashenfelter, Orley, Daniel Hosken, and Matthew Weinberg (2014), "Efficiencies Brewed: Pricing and Consolidation in the US Beer Industry," Princeton University, Federal Trade Commission and Drexel University.

8. Ashenfelter, Orley, Daniel Hosken, and Matthew Weinberg (2014), "Did Robert Bork Understate the Competitive Impact of Mergers? Evidence From Consummated Mergers," NBER Working Paper 19939, forthcoming in *Journal of Law and Economics*.

9. Steven Davidoff Solomon, "New Buying Strategy as Facebook and Google Transform Into Web Conglomerates," *New York Times*.

10. Molnar, Jozsef (2007), "Pre-Emptive Horizontal Mergers: Theory and Evidence," Research Discussion Papers 17/2007, Bank of Finland.

11. Jeziorski, Przemysław (2014), "Estimation of Cost Efficiencies from Mergers: Application to US Radio," forthcoming in *Rand Journal of Economics*.

12. Przemysław Jeziorski.

13. *The Economist*, October 31st, 1998.

14. *The Wall Street Journal*, July 30, 2013.

15. Toxvaerd, Flavio (2008), "Strategic Merger Waves: A Theory of Musical Chairs," *Journal of Economic Theory* **140** (1), 1–26.

16. Compte, Olivier, Frederic Jenny, and Patrick Rey (2002), "Capacity Constraints, Mergers and Collusion," *European Economic Review* **46**, 1–29.

17. This point was formalized by Farrell, Joseph, and Carl Shapiro (1990), "Horizontal Mergers: An Equilibrium Analysis," *American Economic Review* **80**, 107–126.

18. Kwoka, John E. (2013), "Does Merger Control Work? A Retrospective on US Enforcement Actions and Merger Outcomes," *Antitrust Law Journal* **78**, 629–34.

19. Pesendorfer, Martin (2003), "Horizontal Mergers in the Paper Industry," *Rand Journal of Economics* **34** (3), 495–515.

20. *The Wall Street Journal Europe*, January 15–16, 1999.

21. Source: Bank of America report, October 2001. Data for 2001Q2.

22. Porter, Michael (1987), "From Competitive Advantage to Corporate Strategy," *Harvard Business Review*, May-June, 43–59.

23. Caves, Richard E., and Sanjeev Mehra (1986), "Entry of Foreign Multinationals into US Manufacturing Industries," in Porter (Ed.), *Competition in Global Industries*, Cambridge, MA: Harvard Business School Press.

24. This exercise is adapted from Gilbert, Richard, and David Newbery (1992), "Alternative Entry Paths: The Build or Buy Decision," *Journal of Economics and Management Strategy* **1**, 127–150.

# CHAPTER 12

# MARKET FORECLOSURE

easyJet is one of the European success stories of the past decades. Following (to a great extent) the example of Southwest Airlines, easyJet started operating low-cost, no-frills air services between different European cities, initially using London-Lutton as its main hub. Soon after entering the London-Amsterdam segment, KLM, which held 40% of the market, responded by matching easyJet's low fares. For KLM, likely this amounted to pricing below cost, and implied serious losses for easyJet on that particular route. Although easyJet survived this incumbent response, it seems plausible that KLM's tactics were directed at inducing easyJet to exit the market. This is by no means the only threat that small starting airlines must be wary of. In early 1998, British Airways (BA) launched its own discount fare airline, named Go. Although BA's move may be interpreted as taking advantage of a business opportunity (growth in demand for low-fare flights), an alternative interpretation is that Go's main goal was to "eliminate" as much as possible the competition BA suffered from small, low-fare airlines.[1] Ironically, Go was spun off in a management buyout in 2001, and the following year it was acquired by easyJet (which merged it into its own operations).

In Chapter 10, I assumed that entry and exit decisions are made in a non-strategic way: firms simply compare expected benefits from entering the market to the cost of entering into that market. That is, they perform a simple viability study. The examples in the previous paragraphs suggest that entry and exit decisions are also the result of strategic decisions: in industries with a small number of players, entrants must take into account directed retaliation by incumbent firms. Likewise, incumbent firms should play more than the passive role of waiting for potential entrants to decide whether or not to enter the market.

In this chapter, I examine situations where entry and exit result from strategic behavior by both incumbent and entrant firms. I first consider what preemptive strategies an incumbent firm can deploy in order to deter entry by potential rivals. Among the possible entry deterrence strategies, I consider capacity expansion, product proliferation, and long-term contracts. Second, I analyze possible incumbent strategies to induce the exit of firms that have already entered, with a particular focus on bundling and predatory pricing. Finally, I look at public policy related to strategic entry and exit behavior.

## 12.1 ENTRY DETERRENCE

In the early 1970s, DuPont drastically increased its production capacity of titanium dioxide. As Box 12.1 explains in detail, this was an attempt to deter capacity expansion as well as entry by rival firms, even if at the cost of lower profits in the short run. Can this be an optimal strategy?

Specifically, consider the following game played between DuPont and a potential competitor. First the incumbent firm decides what capacity to build, knowing that the incumbent will later produce at capacity level. Next, *having observed the incumbent's choice*, the rival firm (entrant) decides whether to enter and, if so, what capacity level to choose. Figure 12.1 gives payoff levels as a function of each firm's strategy. I consider three possible capacity levels for the incumbent: 40, 44, 48. Regarding the entrant, I consider three capacity levels too (24, 26, 28), as well as the option of not entering, which I denote as choosing capacity 0. One important note regarding the values in Figure 12.1 is that the entrant's payoff is gross of entry cost (that is, the entrant's net payoff is given by the value in Figure 12.1 minus the entry cost).

The game under consideration is one of sequential choices, that is, the entrant chooses its capacity upon observing the incumbent choices. As I mentioned in Chapter 7, such games are normally represented by a game tree. However, with three choices for one player and four for the other, this leads to a tree with 12 branches. For this reason, in this and in other games with more choice nodes, we can solve the game

|  | Entrant | | | |
|---|---|---|---|---|
|  | 0 | 24 | 26 | 28 |
| 40 | 0 / 1920 | 768 / 960 | 780 / 880 | 784 / 800 |
| Incumbent 44 | 0 / 1936 | 672 / 880 | 676 / 792 | 672 / 704 |
| 48 | 0 / 1920 | 576 / 768 | 572 / 672 | 560 / 576 |

**FIGURE 12.1**
Incumbent-entrant capacity game: payoffs

## BOX 12.1 DUPONT AND THE TITANIUM DIOXIDE INDUSTRY[2]

Titanium dioxide ($TiO_2$) is a white chemical pigment employed in the manufacture of paint, paper, and other products to make them whiter or opaque. The primary raw material for the production of $TiO_2$ is either ilmenite ore or rutile ore.

By 1970, there were seven firms in the industry: a large firm, DuPont, and six smaller ones. During the 1960s, DuPont used mainly ilmenite, whereas its rivals used mainly rutile. In 1970, a sharp increase in the price of rutile ore created a significant cost advantage for DuPont with respect to its rivals: at 1968 ore prices, Dupont had a cost advantage of 22%; at 1972 prices, this advantage averaged 44%. Moreover, stricter environmental regulation meant that several of DuPont competitors would have to incur large costs in order to continue production.

DuPont found itself with a competitive advantage in several dimensions. First, its production process used a cheaper input than most of its rivals. Second, its production process complied better with environmental standards. Third, because of the cost advantage, the firm was in better financial shape, thus better positioned to expand capacity.

A task force was formed at DuPont to study how to turn these advantages to the firm's greater benefit. The result was the strategy of expanding capacity at a pace sufficient to satisfy all of the growth in demand in the ensuing years. The idea was that *by expanding rapidly, DuPont would discourage expansion (or entry) by rival firms*. It was the task force's conviction that deterrence of competitive expansion was necessary if DuPont was to establish a dominant position: according to the plan, DuPont's market share would increase from 30% in 1972 to 56% in 1980 and perhaps 65% in 1985.

### Titanium dioxide US capacity: 1972–1982

|  | 1972 | 1973 | 1974 | 1975 | 1976 | 1977 | 1982 |
|---|---|---|---|---|---|---|---|
| Dupont | 265 | 354 | 367 | 421 | 425 | 425 | 520 |
| Rival firms | 504 | 545 | 549 | 560 | 562 | 489 | 409 |

World demand, which had expanded at a whopping 7.7% per year from 1962 to 1972, barely changed from 1972 to 1982. Partly for this reason, partly as a result of Dupont's strategy, various rival firms abandoned expansion plans or simply scrapped existing capacity. By 1985, five of the firms competing with DuPont in the domestic market had exited: three by acquisition, one by complete cessation of operations, and one by shutting down its US plants. DuPont never reached the 65% target, but its domestic market share surpassed 50%, as the table above shows.

Dupont's motto may be "miracles of science." Its rise to dominance in the $TiO_2$ industry, however, was more of a "miracle of strategy."

directly by examining the payoff matrix and taking into account the fact that players move sequentially. In sum, the fact that we analyze the game as a payoff matrix does not imply that the game is one of simultaneous moves.

Taking into account that we are dealing with a sequential move game, we first look at the second mover's optimal choice for each possible choice by the first mover; and then determine the first mover's optimal choice. Suppose that entry cost is low, say, $500. Then no matter what the incumbent does, the entrant is better off by entering, since its gross profits are always greater than $500. Specifically, the entrant's optimal output if the incumbent sets capacity 40, 44, or 48 is given by 28, 26, and 24, respectively. Anticipating this reaction by the entrant, the incumbent's optimal capacity choice is given by 40. We refer to this case as **entry accommodation**.

Suppose now that entry cost is equal to $600. Now, if the incumbent chooses capacity 48, then the entrant is better off by not entering. In fact, no matter what capacity the entrant chooses, its gross profit is always lower than its entry cost. It follows that the incumbent's optimal capacity choice is 48. We refer to this case as **entry deterrence**.

Finally, suppose that the entry cost is high, say, $700. Now, if the entrant chooses capacity 44 or 48, then the entrant prefers not to enter: no matter what capacity it chooses, its gross profit does not compensate for the entry cost. It follows that the incumbent's optimal capacity is 44. We refer to this case as **blockaded entry**.

I next take you through a similar analysis but in a more formal and general way. If math is not your forte, you should skip to the next main point (shaded text on page 308).

---

**THE STACKELBERG MODEL.** Consider a homogeneous product industry with inverse demand $p = a - bQ$, where $Q$ is total output. There are two firms, 1 and 2, which constant marginal cost $c_1$ and $c_2$, respectively. Just as in the Cournot model, price is determined by total industry output. Unlike the Cournot model, suppose now that Firm 1 first sets $q_1$ and then Firm 2, *having observed Firm 1's choice*, sets $q_2$. This model, known as the Stackelberg model, is appropriate for situations when there is a natural asymmetry between firms, so that one acts as a natural market "leader."[3]

As usual, we solve sequential games backwards (cf Section 7.2). Taking Firm 1's output choice as given, Firm 2 maximizes:

$$\pi_2 = \left(a - b(q_1 + q_2)\right)q_2 - c_2 q_2$$

The first-order condition is given by:

$$a - c_2 - bq_1 - 2bq_2 = 0$$

which implies the best-response mapping:

$$q_2^*(q_1) = \frac{a - c_2}{2b} - \tfrac{1}{2}q_1$$

Plugging this into Firm 2's profit function and simplifying we get:

$$\pi_2^*(q_1) = \frac{1}{4b}\left(a - c_2 - bq_1\right)^2 \tag{12.1}$$

(Check this.) Anticipating Firm 2's choice, Firm 1's profit is given by:

$$\pi_1 = \left(a - b\left(q_1 + q_2^*(q_1)\right)\right)q_1 - c_1 q_1$$
$$= \tfrac{1}{2}\left(a + c_2 - 2c_1 - bq_1\right)q_1$$

(Check this.) Maximizing with respect to $q_1$ yields:

$$q_1^S = \frac{a + c_2 - 2c_1}{2b}$$

$$\pi_1^S = \frac{1}{8b} \left( a + c_2 - 2c_1 \right)^2$$

Finally, plugging this back into Firm 2's output and profit we get:

$$q_2^S = \frac{a - 3c_2 - 2c_1}{4b}$$

$$\pi_2^S = \frac{1}{16b} \left( a - 3c_2 + 2c_1 \right)^2$$

In the above expressions, the superscript $S$ stands for Stackelberg. Notice that, unlike the Cournot equilibrium, where two firms with the same cost earn the same equilibrium profit, in the Stackelberg equilibrium Firm 1 sets a higher output level and earns a higher profit than Firm 1: leadership has its benefits.

---

The Stackelberg model characterizes an incumbent's optimal strategy if entry is a given. In the terminology presented earlier, it corresponds to the strategy of entry accommodation. I next consider the entry deterrence strategy.

---

**ENTRY DETERRENCE IN CAPACITY SETTING GAMES.** Suppose for simplicity that capacity and output levels are the same. Suppose also that, in order to enter, Firm 2 must pay an entry cost $E$. From Equation (12.1), Firm 2 prefers not to enter if:

$$E \le \frac{1}{4b} \left( a - c_2 - bq_1 \right)^2$$

In order to deter entry, Firm 1 must set $q_1$ so that the above equality holds (or higher). This yields Firm 1's entry deterring capacity level:

$$q_1^D = \frac{1}{b} \left( a - c_2 - 2\sqrt{bE} \right) \tag{12.2}$$

(Higher levels would also work, but since Firm 1's profit is decreasing in $q_1$ at these levels, Firm 1 would prefer this capacity level.) Substituting $q_1^D$ for $q_1$ and 0 for $q_2$ in Firm 1's profit function, and simplifying, we get:

$$\pi_1^D = 2 \left( a - c_2 \right) \sqrt{\frac{E}{b}} - 4E$$

(Check this.) If $E$ is very low, then $\pi_1^D$ too is very low, and Firm 1 is better off accommodating entry, that is, setting $q_1 = q_1^S$ so as to get $\pi_1^S$. By contrast, if $E$ is sufficiently large, then $q_1^D < q_1^M = (a - c_1)/(2b)$, in which case Firm 1 is better off by setting monopoly output and ignoring potential competition (if the entrant would not enter at $q_1 = q_1^D$, then it won't enter at $q_1 = q_1^M > q_1^D >$ either).

---

Figure 12.2 provides still another approach to the problem of entry deterrence by capacity expansion. On the horizontal axis I map Firm 1's capacity level. On the vertical axis, I measure Firm 1 as well as Firm 2's profit. Specifically, $\pi_1^M$ is Firm 1's profit if it has no competition, that is, if it is a monopolist; $\pi_1^S$, in turn, is Firm 1's profit if Firm 2 enters and chooses a capacity level that maximizes Firm 2's profit given Firm 1's capacity level. As for Firm 2, I draw three profit curves, each corresponding to a different level of Firm 2's entry cost: $\pi_2^S$, $\pi_2^D$, and $\pi_2^B$, each corresponding to a higher level of entry cost.

Let us now consider Firm 1's capacity choice problem. In order for Firm 1 to deter entry, its choice of $q_1$ must be greater than the intercept of $\pi_2$ on the horizontal axis. By choosing such value of $q_1$, Firm 2 would be looking at a negative profit from entry, and

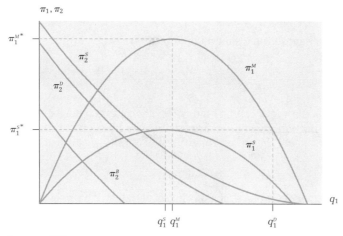

**FIGURE 12.2**
Entry deterrence by capacity expansion

thus chooses not to enter. The question is: does Firm 1 want to increase capacity so as to deter entry? If Firm 1 deters entry, then its profit will be given by the $\pi_1^M$ curve; whereas, if entry takes place, then Firm 1's profit is given by the $\pi_1^S$ curve. Therefore, if deterring entry requires Firm 1 to set $q_1$ greater than $q_1^D$, then Firm 1 prefers to choose $q_1 = q_1^S$ and accommodate entry. If deterring entry requires Firm 1 to set $q_1$ lower than $q_1^M$, then Firm 1 optimally sets $q_1 = q_1^M$, that is, it ignores the threat of entry and behaves as a monopolist. Finally, if entry deterrence requires Firm 1 to set a value of $q_1$ greater than $q_1^M$ but lower than $q_1^D$, then Firm 1 optimally sets the minimum $q_1$ required to deter entry.

The three $\pi_2(q_1)$ curves plotted in Figure 12.2 correspond to the three possible cases considered earlier: if entry cost is very low, so that $\pi_2(q_1) = \pi_2^A$, then we have accommodated entry; if entry cost is intermediate, so that $\pi_2(q_1) = \pi_2^D$, then we have entry deterrence; and finally, if entry cost is very high, so that $\pi_2(q_1) = \pi_2^B$, then we have blockaded entry.

The initial numerical example, the formal mathematical analysis, and Figure 12.2 all suggest an important point regarding firm strategy:

> An incumbent's optimal capacity choice depends on the level of entry costs. If entry costs are very high, then the incumbent should set monopoly capacity and ignore the threat of entry. If entry costs are very low, then the incumbent should choose capacity taking into account the entrant's best response. Finally, if entry costs are intermediate, then the incumbent should choose capacity large enough to induce the entrant not to enter.

Notice that the incumbent's optimal capacity is non-monotonic with respect to the entrant's entry cost: going back to the initial numerical example, notice that, as cost increases from $500 to $600 and then to $700, the incumbent's optimal capacity first

## Box 12.2 Games hospitals play[4]

In 1988, Medicare (the US health system for the elderly and chronically ill) announced it would likely increase the reimbursement offered to private hospitals for performing electrophysiological studies (a procedure to identify cardiac arrhythmias). A higher reimbursement rate makes the electrophysiological studies industry a more attractive entry target. Since the announcement was made about one year ahead of time, it also provided incumbent suppliers with a window of opportunity to prepare for possible entry.

The chart below plots the incumbent suppliers' output increase as a function of the number of competitors, that is, the number of other hospitals in the area who could begin offering the procedure if they so decided.

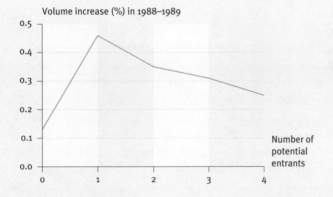

In words, the incumbent's reaction to Medicare's announcement was highest when there was one potential entrant and lowest when there was none or when there were many of them — a pattern that is consistent with theory's prediction.

increases from 40 to 48, then decreases from 48 to 44. The reason for this non-monotonicity is that there is a fundamental discontinuity in the entrant's strategy: as the incumbent increases its capacity, the entrant gradually decreases its capacity; however, beyond a certain level, the entrant's optimal capacity altogether drops to zero. As detailed in Box 12.2, the US healthcare industry provides an interesting illustration: the relation between incumbent's deterrence effort and the intensity of potential competition is inverse-U shaped. If there is no potential entry there is no deterrence (blockaded entry); and if there is a lot of potential entry again there is no deterrence (accommodated entry).

■ **Commitment, ex-ante optimality, and ex-post optimality.**[5]   In the above analysis, I was a little vague about the nature of each firm's strategy: I stated that firms choose capacity levels and then set output levels at capacity level. How reasonable is this assumption? If capacity costs are very high and marginal cost — given capacity — very low, then it seems reasonable that firms set capacity levels that are low compared to total market demand, so that the optimal choice is to use all available capacity.

But there is more: implicitly, I also assumed that the incumbent chooses a certain capacity level and sticks to it no matter what. In particular, the incumbent firm does not change its capacity even if the entrant decides to stay out. This turns out to be a very important assumption. To see why, consider the case of entry deterrence, which in the above example takes place when the entry cost is $600. By setting a capacity of 48, the incumbent induces the entrant not to enter. The incumbent's payoff is then given by $1,920. However, *given that the entrant stays out*, the incumbent is better off by choosing a capacity of 44 instead of 48, yielding an increase in profit from $1,920 to $1,936. But if the entrant anticipates that the incumbent will switch back to 44 (its ex-post optimal capacity level), then the entrant should enter, for given that capacity level the entrant is better off by entering and setting a capacity of 26. By the same token, if the entrant's entry decision is reversible, then the incumbent would then find it optimal to again increase capacity to 48, thus inducing the entrant's exit; and so on.

You get the idea: if players' choices are easily reversible, then the entire premise of sequentiality of moves with one move per player falls apart. It is therefore crucial that each player's choice be irreversible — or at least be believed to be irreversible. Irreversibility as the foundation of commitment is a general principle of game theory. In the present context (capacity decisions), irreversibility roughly corresponds to the "sunkness" of capacity decisions: once I built a plant, I cannot "unbuild" it and recoup the initial investment. In other words:

> Capacity preemption is a credible strategy only if capacity costs are high and sunk.

■ **ALTERNATIVE PREEMPTION STRATEGIES.** The Italian telecommunications industry, like those of many European countries, underwent a process of gradual deregulation, namely entry deregulation. Telecom Italia, at one point a protected monopoly, gradually had to account for competition from new entrants such as France Telecom. This situation seems similar to the one we considered before: an incumbent firm (the formerly protected monopolist) and a potential entrant (telecom operators from different countries).

As one looks more closely at this and related cases, however, one becomes aware of two important qualifications on the theoretical model of deterrence by capacity expansion. First, it is not only a matter of deterring vs. accommodating entry. Telecom Italia was probably aware that it was unable to avoid entry at *any time* in the future. However, different strategic investments made early on likely influenced the *time* at which entry did occur; and different entry times have different implications for Telecom Italia's profitability.

The second important difference of many real-world situations with respect to the simple model presented above is that incumbents have various available strategies other than just capacity expansion. Continuing with the telecommunications industry,

## Box 12.3 PGNiG AND THE POLISH ENERGY MARKET[6]

European markets are still fragmented, largely along national borders. One of the European Union's (EU) current goals is precisely to create a common EU energy market. Similarly to other former Soviet bloc members, Poland is lagging in energy market deregulation — and is thus subject to continuing pressure by the EU to get its act together.

PGNiG — Poland's leading gas utility — seems to be doing the best to turn the economic transition to its advantage. First, it created a German subsidiary to handle energy sales and trading. (This will facilitate the company's international trading and provide it with greater access to the larger European market.) Second, it reserved most of the pipeline capacity along the Czech and German borders through which Poland imports much of its gas. Finally, it reserved additional capacity from a new terminal that is being built along the Baltic coast.

These actions, combined with the company's continued control of the nation's gas storage facilities — an asset that is necessary for reliable gas supply — will likely serve to deter many would-be competitors for quite some time.

this time in the US, we observe that AT&T was able to slow down entry by virtue of its strong brand. Although its services were of comparable quality to its rivals (MCI and Sprint, mainly), and rates were, if anything, higher for AT&T, the former monopolist kept a very respectable market share, well in excess of 50%, for a long time. Still another telecommunications example of entry deterrence — discussed in greater detail in Box 12.3 — is that of PGNiG, Poland's leading gas utility.

I next look at a specific instance of an entry-deterrence strategy different from but similar to capacity expansion: product proliferation.

■ **PRODUCT PROLIFERATION.**[7] The ready-to-eat breakfast cereal industry may be characterized by relatively low economies of scale and relatively low levels of technology. In other words, entry into this industry is easy, from a technological point of view. Between the 1950s and the 1970s there was virtually no new firm entry, even though all of the incumbent firms (Kellogg, General Mills, General Foods, and Quaker Oats) made significant profits. Finally, while the number of firms did not change, the number of brands sold by the incumbent firms increased from 25 to about 80 (and keeps increasing).

Why are profits so high and no entry is observed, even though entry seems relatively easy? Why did the number of brands increase so rapidly, while the number of firms remained constant?

One possible explanation is that the incumbent firms "filled-in" the product space so as to eliminate any opportunity for profitable entry. Since there isn't much price competition (as the evidence suggests), high profit margins are an invitation to entry unless entrants cannot find any "market hole" where to position their product. In other words, the incumbents' **product proliferation** strategy effectively deters entry without the need to lower prices.

The strategy increasing variety is not limited to density in the product space; it also applies to density in geographical space. In this sense, an example is given by Staples, the US leader in the office supplies superstore industry. Referring to Staples' investment strategy, the company's CEO stated that:

> Staples was trying to build a critical mass of stores in the Northeast to shut out competitors ... By building these networks [of stores] in the big markets like New York and Boston, we have kept competitors out for a very, very long period of time.[8]

Together, the above examples suggest that:

> By increasing the density of product offerings, an incumbent may deter entry even when profit margins are high.

Exercise 12.2 illustrates this point.

Still another example of deterrence by product proliferation is given by Unilever in the impulse ice-cream industry. As of 2013, Unilever held a 66% share of the UK market. With a portfolio of literally dozens of ice cream products, Unilever makes it difficult for rivals to find a profitable entry or expansion strategy. Moreover, ice cream bars are stored in freezers supplied by Unilever under the contractual obligation that only Unilever brands be sold (see Section 12.4). This leads me to the next topic, the use of exclusive contracts as a deterrence strategy.

## 12.2 EXCLUSIVE CONTRACTS, BUNDLING, AND FORECLOSURE

In the previous section, I showed how increasing capacity or the density of product offerings may be an effective way of deterring rival entry. In this section, I consider a different class of rival foreclosure strategies: contracts.

■ **NAKED EXCLUSION.** In 1985, Monsanto acquired the patent rights for aspartame, an artificial sweetener used in diet colas and other soft drinks. The patent for aspartame, which Monsanto was selling under the Nutrasweet brand name, was due to expire in 1992, thus opening the way for new entrants. In addition to other entry deterrence strategies, which I detail in Box 12.4, Monsanto anticipated patent expiry by signing long-term contracts with Coca-Cola and Pepsi-Cola. Why would the soft drink manufacturers be interested in such contracts? Isn't it better to let new entrants come in and benefit from competition between suppliers?

One possibility is that, by signing up a sufficient number of buyers, the incumbent effectively makes entry unprofitable, a strategy that might be called **naked exclusion**.[9] Suppose that, due to scale economies, entry is only profitable if the entrant expects to attract a fraction of the market given by $\alpha$, a value between 0 and 1. Then the incumbent

## Box 12.4 THE ASPARTAME MARKET[10]

Aspartame is a low-calorie, high-intensity sweetener. It was discovered (by accident) in 1965, by a research scientist at G. D. Searle & Co. who was working on an anti-ulcer drug. Use of aspartame in soft drinks was approved by the US Food and Drug Administration (FDA) in 1983. Searle managed to extend the original patent to 1987 in Europe and 1992 in the US.

In 1985 Monsanto acquired Searle — and the aspartame patent with it. The soft-drink version of aspartame is sold by Monsanto under the brand name Nutrasweet. The potential market for such a product is enormous, especially considering the sales volume of Diet Coke and Diet Pepsi. It is thus not surprising that, in 1986, Holland Sweetener Company (HSC), a joint venture between a Dutch and a Japanese company, began building an aspartame plant, in anticipation of Nutrasweet's patent expiry.

When HSC started selling its own version of aspartame (generic aspartame, as opposed to the branded Nutrasweet version), Monsanto dropped the price of Nutrasweet from $70 to $22–$30 per pound. This meant negative profits for HSC, but also an enormous drop in Nutrasweet's European revenues. Monsanto's reaction might seem a bit excessive, especially considering that HSC's capacity was only 5% of the world market. However, Europe is only a small fraction of the world market: the US market alone is 10 times the European one. One interpretation of Nutrasweet's strategy is thus that, by fighting entry into a small market, it may "convince" potential entrants not to attempt entering other larger markets where the same incumbent is present. Moreover, production of aspartame is subject to a steep learning curve (Monsanto managed to cut costs by 70% over a period of 10 years). Nutrasweet's attack on HSC thus had the effect of slowing down HSC's move down the learning curve.

Partly as a consequence of Nutrasweet's strategy, HSC delayed its expansion plans and was not much of a competitor when the US market finally opened. Monsanto, however, did not take chances: just prior to the US patent expiry, both Coke and Pepsi signed long-term contracts with Monsanto.

might effectively foreclose the market by pursuing a **divide and conquer** strategy: a fraction $(1 - \alpha)$ of buyers are offered a contract with a price a little lower than the monopoly price in return for agreeing to exclusivity (that is, not buying from the entrant). The remaining $\alpha$ buyers, in turn, are asked to pay monopoly price. Both sets of buyers have no better option than to accept the terms imposed by the incumbent. In particular, if each buyer is small relatively to market size, then the alternative to accepting an exclusivity agreement is to pay a higher price. In fact, along the equilibrium path, entry never materializes, and so the exclusive contract offers a lower price in exchange for a promise that has no cost.

This extreme outcome — all buyers pay close to monopoly price, almost as if there was no threat of entry — depends on a series of assumptions, including the assumption that buyers are small. Clearly, this is not the case in the aspartame example: Coca-Cola and Pepsi-Cola are definitely not small buyers. However, you can see how a clever "divide and conquer" strategy may carry the incumbent a long way.

■ **BUNDLING.** In 1994, as the World Wide Web was taking its first steps, Jim Clark and Marc Andreessen founded the Mosaic Communications Corporation, the creator of web browser Netscape. Although Netscape was distributed for free to some end users, it was licensed to businesses. Together with the development of a variety of complementary plug-ins and applications, Netscape was able to generate a healthy revenue stream and a very successful IPO in August 1995. By then, Microsoft was releasing version 1.0 of Internet Explorer as a part of the Windows 95 distribution; that is, the browser was bundled with the operating system.

The browser wars were on. The Internet Explorer's market share rose very rapidly. According to Microsoft, this resulted from the superior quality of IE and its added features. According to Netscape, it was all the result of Microsoft's unfair bundling strategy. In 1998, the Justice Department, together with various US states, sued Microsoft for abuse of its dominant position. Years later, a similar case was initiated by the EU competition policy watchdog.

How can **bundling** or **tying** work as a foreclosure strategy? I will answer the question with a simple numerical example.[11] Suppose that Windows is the only operating system available and that all users value it at $50. Each computer user requires at most one Internet browser. There are three groups of users, each in equal number (for simplicity, one million each): IE fans are willing to pay $25 for IE and $10 for Netscape; Netscape fans are willing to pay up to $10 for IE and $25 for Netscape; and die-hard Netscape fans are willing to pay up to $10 for IE and $38 for Netscape. Finally, all pieces of software have zero marginal cost.

Consider first the situation when there is no bundling between Windows and IE. Clearly, it is optimal for Microsoft to price Windows at $50. Regarding Internet browsers, the equilibrium of the game where firms simultaneously set prices is for browsers to be sold for $25. At this price, Netscape fans buy Netscape and IE fans buy IE (and so Netscape captures two thirds of the browser market). Microsoft makes a gross profit of $175 million, $150 from the operating system (three million buyers, each paying $50); and $25 million from the browser (one million buyers, each paying $25). Netscape, in turn, makes a gross profit of $50 million (two million buyers, each paying $25 browser).

Before continuing, let us confirm that the $25 price point is indeed a Nash equilibrium. The best alternative for Microsoft would be to price its browser at a little less than $10. This would attract Netscape fans but not die-hard Netscape fans. (Die-hard Netscape fans pay $25 for something that is worth $38; this is better — for them — than IE at any positive price.) Microsoft would then earn about $20 million from selling its browser (two million buyers, each paying $10). This is worse than pricing the browser at $25. As to Netscape, setting a lower price, say $10, would imply a profit of $30 million (three million buyers, each paying $10 price). Setting a higher price, say $38, would imply a gross profit of $38 million (one million buyers, each paying $38 price). Either way, Netscape would make less than the gross profit of $50 million from selling its browser at $25.

Now suppose that Microsoft successfully commits to only selling the bundle Windows and IE. Moreover, suppose that it sets a price of $60 for the bundle. Notice that even Netscape fans are willing to pay that much ($50 for Windows, $10 for IE). This places Netscape in a difficult situation: in order to attract Netscape fans (as well as die-hard fans), Netscape must price at $15, the difference between $25 and $10. The idea is that Windows buyers already have the IE browser; therefore, Netscape fans will only purchase Netscape if the *additional* value of Netscape exceeds the price to pay. Alternatively, Netscape can price its browser at $28, the difference between die-hard Netscape fans valuation for Netscape ($38) and their valuation for IE ($10). It follows that Netscape is better off pricing at $15 for a gross profit of $30.

As for Microsoft, $60 is the best price to set. At this price, it sells three million bundles, for a total profit of $180 million. Microsoft could increase the bundle price to $75. However, at this higher price it would only sell to IE fans, thus getting a profit of $75 million.

Here lies the key to the issue of bundling and leveraging market power: if the goods are sold separately, Microsoft prefers to set a higher price for the IE and settle for attracting its browser fans only (one million). If however the goods are sold in a bundle, the opportunity cost for Microsoft to increase the price of its browser is that it loses browser sales *and* sales of the operating system. In other words, bundling the operating system with the browser commits Microsoft to become more aggressive in the browser market.

This is a problem for Netscape. As Microsoft switches to bundling, Microsoft's profit increases from $175 to $180 and Netscape's drops from $50 to $30. Netscape is a "victim" of Microsoft's commitment to aggressive pricing. Suppose that Netscape must pay an overhead cost greater than $30 million but lower than $50 million. Then, under separate pricing Netscape is able to cover the cost, but not when Microsoft bundles Windows with IE. In this sense, Microsoft's strategy may be seen as a way to foreclose competition in the browser market. Or, to put it differently, Microsoft **leverages** its power in the operating systems market to increase its dominance in the browser market.

I should add that the above story, while shared by many commentators of the Microsoft case, is far from universally accepted. In particular, notice that, even if Netscape does not abandon the field, Microsoft's optimal strategy is still to sell the Windows-IE bundle for $60. In other words, it's not obvious that Microsoft's bundling strategy is motivated by its desire to foreclose competition in the browser market. In fact, as I showed in Section 6.2 bundling and tying can be a means for price discrimination. More on this in Section 12.4.

> By bundling or tying the sales of two products, a dominant firm may leverage its power in one market to increase dominance in the other market.

■ **RAISING RIVALS' COSTS.** A more recent example of bundling-like foreclosure is given by Intel's **all-unit discounts**. In addition to an operating system, computers need a processor. Computers equipped with the Windows operating system use either Intel or AMD microprocessors. Intel is a much larger company, both in terms of number of units sold and in terms of product variety. For a period of time, Intel offered computer manufacturers a special deal: buyers receive a 15% discount if they buy exclusively from Intel. Michael Capellas, then CEO of Compaq, described the situation as "I had a gun to my head," one that effectively forced him to stop buying AMD chips. In the (relatively few) product categories where AMD offered a better price-quality deal, the all-unit discount proposed by Intel effectively made the relative price of AMD's product prohibitively high.

The all-unit discount strategy effectively increased the cost that computer manufactures such as Compaq must pay to purchase from AMD. In this sense, the Intel example provides an instance of the more general strategy of **raising rivals' costs**.[12] There are many incumbent strategies that achieve this effect. For example, an alternative interpretation of exclusive contracts is that they allow an incumbent to extract **entrant's surplus** through penalties for breach of contract.[13] Suppose there is a potential entrant of uncertain cost efficiency. Absent exclusive contracts, if the entrant's cost is low then entry takes place and the entrant earns a profit: an "entry surplus." The incumbent and the buyer can then "collude" and set an entry "price." This "price" is the fee that the buyer must pay the incumbent to be free from the exclusive contract. Given this breach penalty, the entrant is forced to set a lower price, low enough to attract a buyer who is contractually tied to the incumbent. This is good for the buyer, who ends up paying a lower price; and for the incumbent, who loses a customer but cashes in on the contract breach penalty. Finally, when the entrant is more efficient than the incumbent but not much more efficient, the contract effectively deters entry that would have taken place if no exclusivity clause were in place.[a] Exercise 12.4 formalizes this intuition.

Another instance of raising rivals' costs is the use of most favored nation (MFN) clauses in the health care industry. US health insurers agree with providers (e.g., hospitals) the price to be paid for certain procedures. Frequently, these contracts include the clause that other insurers cannot be offered a better price — or, if they are offered a better price, the difference must be paid to the first insurer. In fact, sometimes the contract clauses require providers to charge other insurers *higher* prices for the same procedure. In this way, MFN clauses effectively increase the cost paid by rival insurance companies, which in turn benefits the insurer imposing the clause.

> Contract exclusivity, selective discounts, and most-favored-nation clauses may be a way of raising rivals' costs and, as such, foreclosing competition.

a. This intermediate level of entrant efficiency — which leads to no entry — is analogous to the allocative inefficiency of monopoly pricing, when there is a potential buyer with valuation greater than cost but lower than monopoly price, that is, where an efficient sale fails to take place.

Raising rivals' costs is generally good for firms: even if it does not keep my rivals out of the market, it decreases their market share and increases my profitability. For example, in Section 8.4 I showed that an increase in firm $j$'s cost increases firm $i$'s profits, both under Bertrand competition and under Cournot competition. Even if my costs increase as well, so long as my rivals' costs increase more I might be better off. The case of labor negotiations in the US auto industry, described in Section 8.4, illustrates this possibility.

Is it possible that Ford was better off when it negotiated higher salaries with the unions? Yes, to the extent that Ford's deal also applies to GM and Chrysler; and to the extent that Ford uses less labor and more capital than its rivals.

This is one of the essential points in oligopoly theory (and game theory, more generally): a firm is not only concerned with, "What does this mean for my costs?" but also "What does this mean for my rivals' costs?" Not surprisingly, many instances of successful firm strategy are based on the effects they have on rivals costs. In addition to the examples listed above, one that is worth mentioning is the effect of environmental regulations. To the extent that these regulations include even partial "grandfathering" clauses (that is, clauses which exempt incumbent firms), you can see how incumbents might tolerate — in fact, encourage — stringent rules: to the extent that these rules increase potential rivals' costs, environmental regulation may be a cheap way of deterring entry.

## 12.3 PREDATORY PRICING

At the beginning of the chapter, I mentioned that the first difficulty encountered by easyJet upon entering the London-Amsterdam route was a price match by KLM, who at the time was carrying almost one-half of the passengers in that route. Arguably, KLM was engaging in **predatory pricing**: pricing below cost with the intent of driving easyJet out of the market. Eventually, a court case and a clever publicity campaign by easyJet's chairman, Stelio Haji-ioannou, put an end to KLM's aggressive strategy.

It is possible that, had KLM persisted with its low pricing for a longer period, easy-Jet would have found itself forced to exit the London-Amsterdam route. As it is, KLM's strategy may be explained by predatory pricing or simply by an incumbent's reaction to the arrival of a competitor. In fact, in a homogeneous-product market where firms do not collude, going from one to two competitors implies a price drop from monopoly price to marginal cost (cf Section 8.1). How can one be sure that KLM's price drop is not simply a shift from one equilibrium to another equilibrium (with exit not being at all intended)?

■ **THE CHICAGO SCHOOL AND THE LONG-PURSE THEORIES OF PREDATORY PRICING.** A more radical criticism of the predatory interpretation of KLM's strategy is that rational players should never exit when preyed upon; and, consequently, rational predators should never engage in predation. This view, associated with the Chicago school of thought, runs along the following lines. Suppose that there are two periods. In the first period, the incumbent must decide whether or not to set low prices. If it does, both incumbent and newly arrived prey make losses $L$ in the first period. (The first period can be thought as, say, the first year of the entrant's operation.) If the incumbent does not act aggressively, then both incumbent and entrant receive duopoly profits $\pi_D$. At the end of the first period, the entrant must decide whether or not to stay in the market. In the second period, if the entrant exits, then the incumbent receives monopoly profits $\pi_M$. Otherwise, the same situation as in the first period is repeated.

If the entrant decides to stay into the second period, then the incumbent's optimal strategy is clearly not to behave aggressively: the entrant's decision not to exit has already been made, and so, from the incumbent's perspective, it's a choice between positive profits $\pi_D$ and negative profits $-L$. Let us now consider the first period. Suppose the incumbent acts aggressively. The entrant will then be making losses $L$. Should it exit the industry? The answer is clearly "no". The incumbent's threat to keep prices is not credible: if the entrant remains in the market, the incumbent will eventually find it optimal not to behave aggressively. So the entrant should not exit. Even if it does not have enough cash to sustain a loss of $L$, the entrant should borrow from a bank: assuming that $\pi_D > L$, a bank should also see through the incumbent's incentives and conclude that staying in is a profitable strategy for the entrant; first-period losses are temporary. Finally, a rational incumbent that knows how a rational entrant behaves should avoid aggressive behavior in the first place: it does not induce any exit and costs a loss $L$ in the first period, instead of a gain $\pi_D$.

The Chicago argument is therefore that no predatory behavior should be observed in practice. If an incumbent responds to entry by lowering its price, this is simply the competitive effect of a decrease in concentration; something to be welcome, not feared.

The problem with this argument is that it relies too much on rationality and perfect information. Suppose that the entrant does not have enough cash to sustain losses in the first period. The only chance of survival in case the incumbent acts aggressively is for the entrant to borrow from a bank. According to the Chicago theory, a bank would always be willing to lend money, having seen through the equilibrium in the second period. Suppose now, perhaps more realistically, that the bank is not always willing to lend money. Specifically, the competing firms expect the bank to refuse a loan with probability $\rho$.

From the entrant's point of view, staying in the market while the incumbent is pricing low is a rational decision insofar as the initial loss, $L$, is less than what the entrant expects to gain in the future: $\pi_D$ times the probability that the bank will give a loan, $1 - \rho$. That is, the entrant should be willing to stay in the market so long as $(1 - \rho)\, \pi_D > L$.

From the incumbent's perspective, aggressive behavior in the first period may also be an optimal strategy. By accommodating entry the incumbent receives $\pi_D + \pi_D$, duopoly profits in each period. By behaving aggressively, the incumbent loses $L$ in the first period; in the second period, with probability $\rho$, it will get $\pi_M$, for the entrant will have exited, not having obtained additional funds from the bank; and with probability $1 - \rho$ the entrant will remain active, in which case the incumbent will settle for $\pi_D$ only. Simple calculations show that behaving aggressively in the first period is optimal for the incumbent if $\rho \pi_M > L + (1 + \rho)\, \pi_D$.

According to this alternative view, if the above conditions are satisfied, then: (i) predation is observed in practice; (ii) it is rational for the incumbent to be a predator and for the prey to resist aggressive behavior; (iii) $\rho$ percent of the times predation is successful in driving competition out of the market.

In this theory of predatory pricing the important difference between firms is not so much that one is the incumbent and the other a recent entrant. What is important is that one firm is financially constrained, needing to apply for a bank loan, whereas the other one is not. For this reason, the theory is known as the **long-purse** or **deep-pocket** theory of predatory pricing.[14]

■ **OTHER EXPLANATIONS OF PREDATORY PRICING.** There are at least three other explanations for why an incumbent might want to respond to entry by pricing aggressively. We now turn to these.

**LOW-COST SIGNALLING.**[15] For KLM, for example, pricing low might be a way of sending easyJet the "message" that KLM's costs are low and that, consequently, there is no room for an additional firm to make money in the same market.

One example of this "signalling" theory of predation is given by the American Tobacco Company. Between 1891 and 1906, American Tobacco acquired 43 small competitors (mostly regional firms), thus establishing a quasi-monopoloy. In most cases, before attempting to buy a rival, American Tobacco would engage in (allegedly) predatory pricing, effectively imposing losses on the target firm. It is estimated that the impact of these predatory actions was to lower the cost of buying rivals by up to 60%.[16] One interpretation of this number is that, by observing American Tobacco's low prices, a small regional firm would become convinced that American Tobacco's cost is low and thus the prospects of competing against it not very promising: thus the effect of settling for a lower price.

Another stylized fact derived from the analysis of the American Tobacco example is that the price paid for target firms acquired later was lower than the price paid for target firms acquired earlier by about 25% (everything else constant). This suggests that one of the effects of predation (and acquisition) is to create a "reputation" which in turn influences the outcome of future clashes between the large firm and small firms. To this alternative theory we turn next.

**REPUTATION FOR TOUGHNESS.**[17] By pricing aggressively, the incumbent may acquire a reputation for being "tough," so that in the future (or in other markets) no more entry will take place. The case of the aspartame industry, examined in detail in Box 12.4, is a good example: Monsanto retaliated against Holland Sweetener's entry into the European market by lowering prices substantially. One interpretation of this strategy is that Monsanto wanted to make sure that no competitors entered the US market, its most important territory, where the aspartame patent was due to expire later than in Europe.

Another example of the same explanation is given by British Airways (BA). In the 1970s, BA successfully (if at some cost) fought Laker Airways' entry into the transatlantic market.[b] In the 1980s, it took similar measures in response to entry by Virgin Atlantic, although with less successful results. In the 1990s, the "victims" were the likes of easyJet and, again, Virgin. One possible result of this series of aggressive actions is that BA has now gained the reputation for being a tough competitor, thus discouraging future entry into its markets.[c]

b. Laker Airways went out of business, but not before suing BA and several other airlines for conspiring to drive it out of the market. The case was eventually settled out of court.

c. As Virgin's President Richard Branson once stated, "the safest way to become a millionaire is to start as a billionaire and invest in the airline industry." Perhaps this sentiment is a reflection of several years competing against British Airways. A similar example in the context of the airline industry is given by the case of American Airlines' alleged predatory pricing against competitors in the Dallas/Forth Worth hub: see Chapter 1.

**GROWING MARKETS.**[18] A third explanation for predatory pricing applies to growing markets where long-term success requires a significant market share from early on. For example, in the market for operating systems it is important to start with a good installed base of adopters, so that third-party application software developers have an incentive to write software running on the operating system, so that new users in turn will be attracted and a sort of snowball effect takes place. The snowball effect also works in the opposite way: lacking a good starting installed base, an operating system may be doomed to failure.[d] In this context, predatory pricing early on may be successful in that it prevents rivals from achieving the critical market share necessary to survive in the market.

An example of this type of predatory pricing is cable TV competition in Sacramento, California.[19] In 1983, Sacramento Cable Television (SCT) was awarded a first franchise. In 1987, a second franchise was given to Cable America. The latter started off by laying down a cable system across 700 homes, a small fraction of the market, but planning to expand to the entire Sacramento area. Cable America's initial offering was 36 channels for a monthly fee of $10, which compared favorably to SCT's $13.50 for 40 channels. However, SCT quickly responded by selectively cutting its rates in the area where Cable America had entered: the new offer consisted of three months of free service and then continued service at $5.75 a month. After seven months, Cable America threw in the towel, unable to create a critical mass of subscribers that would justify further investment in programming and laying down additional cables.

To summarize,

> Predatory pricing may be a successful strategy when (i) the prey is financially constrained, (ii) low prices signal low costs or the predator's "toughness", and (iii) capturing a minimum market share early on is crucial for long-term survival. In all these cases, low pricing by the predator induces the prey to exit the market.

## 12.4 PUBLIC POLICY TOWARDS FORECLOSURE

d. The dynamics of markets of this sort, that is, markets where installed based is an important determinant of long-term firm success, are examined in greater detail in Chapter 16. Other examples where initial market share is an important target are learning curves and consumer switching costs. The latter are considered in Chapter 14.

Unlike price fixing (Section 9.5) or even mergers (Section 11.3), public policy towards dominant firms — and abuse of dominance by such firms — is a notably difficult endeavor. Section 2 of the US Sherman Act and Article 102 of the Treaty of the European Union prohibit anticompetitive practices by dominant firms. But: what exactly is an anticompetitive practice? When it comes to price fixing, matters are fairly clear. For other firm strategies, one can easily find both a pro-competitive and an anticompetitive explanation for a firm's strategy. Consider for example the practice of bundling. In Section 12.2 I argued that Microsoft's bundling of the Internet Explorer with the Windows operating system was likely motivated by, and had the effect of, forcing Netscape out of the market (or at least into a minor market share). However, in Chapter 6,

I argued that bundling may be a price discrimination strategy — and indeed a welfare increasing strategy as such. Which of the two explanations is valid?

Nor is the problem limited to bundling: quantity discounts, exclusive contracts, capacity expansion, low prices. In all cases, we can find a coherent story to justify such practices as welfare-increasing strategies by dominant firms. In this wide ranging gray area, policy makers must strike the right balance between false positives (deeming anticompetitive a practice that is not anticompetitive) and false negatives (failing to deem anticompetitive a practice that is anticompetitive). Not an easy task.

The policy uncertainty regarding dominant firms is reflected in — and in turn caused by — the enormous variation in legal precedent, both over time and especially across jurisdictions. I next present a few examples of recent cases in the US, EU, and elsewhere which illustrate this point.

□ **MICROSOFT.** In the early 1990s Microsoft forced computer manufacturers to accept a per-processor license contract which effectively foreclosed competing DOS suppliers. In 1991, the US Federal Trade Commission (FTC) initiated an investigation into Microsoft's practices, but that effort lost steam until the US Department of Justice took over. The Justice Department's effort was closely coordinated with a parallel investigation by the European Commission — a world's first — and led to Microsoft signing a 1995 consent decree. In it, Microsoft agreed to refrain from engaging in per-processor licencing or similar practices in the future.

Two years later, the US Department of Justice charged Microsoft with violating the 1995 consent decree by bundling Internet Explorer (IE) with Windows (as described in Section 12.2). In 2000, Judge Jackson, who initially handled the case, sided with the Department of Justice, arguing that Microsoft was guilty of a series of anticompetitive practices and recommending that it be split in two units (operating system and applications). In 2001, the Circuit Court of Appeals affirmed the monopolization claim but reversed other lower court's findings as well as the breakup remedy. Eventually, Microsoft settled with all of the plaintiffs.

Differently from the US, the European Commission's (EC) main case against Microsoft centered on issues of interoperability: the ability of third-party software developers to create applications that can "talk" properly with Windows. From 2003 to 2012, Microsoft repeatedly resisted the EC demands; was fined more than €1 million; appealed and lost the appeal of a series of decisions.

□ **INTEL.** Like Microsoft, Intel too has been the target of a number of lawsuits and investigations regarding abuse of dominant position. One interesting aspect of the Intel cases is the sheer number of plaintiffs and jurisdictions involved. As I mentioned in Section 12.2, the practice in question was to offer rebates to customers (PC manufacturers) who agreed not to purchase from Intel's rival. AMD, the rival in question, filed lawsuits or complaints in the US, Korea, Japan, and the EU. There were also various government initiated cases, including one by the New York attorney general, as well a series of class action suits filed by various private parties in various US jurisdictions.

The result of all of these cases varies: a 2005 suit in the US ended in a 2009 settlement whereby Intel compensated AMD for $1.25 billion, a 2007 investigation by the EC ended in the largest fine it ever imposed on a corporation: €1.44 billion, and a 2009 FTC investigation ended with a settlement whereby Intel agreed to stop offering all-unit discounts.

☐ **TETRA PAK.** In July 2013, China's State Administration for Industry and Commerce (SAIC) announced that it was launching an investigation against Tetra Pak for alleged abuse of market dominance through tying and discrimination. Tetra Pak was founded in Sweden and is currently headquartered in Switzerland. It is the world's largest manufacturer of aseptic packaging materials (used, for example, in milk cartons). The practice in question is to sell aseptic packaging materials bundled with consumables (a market where Tetra Pak is subject to stiffer competition).

This case is not especially important because of the issue at stake. In fact, Tetra Pak was previously accused and fined by the European Commission on the same grounds. Also, the alleged illegal practice falls squarely into the bundling category discussed in Section 12.2, for which there are other examples. What is special about this case is that it is the SAIC's first publicly announced investigation into abuse of dominance since China's Anti-Monopoly Law came into force in 2008. The expression "global antitrust policy" no longer means simply the US and the EU.

■ **PREDATORY PRICING.** Within the broad spectrum of competition policy directed at dominant firms, predatory pricing plays a particularly important role given the abundance of cases and legal doctrine. First, the theoretical debate as to whether predatory pricing *exists* in practice is still not completely settled. As I showed in Section 12.3, a price reduction by an incumbent in response to entry can be interpreted as a competitive response to new competition, rather than an attempt to drive that competition out of the market. However, recent theoretical and empirical developments are creating a consensus that there is such a thing as predatory pricing.

**IDENTIFYING PREDATORY BEHAVIOR.** Even if we agree that predatory pricing exists, we will still have to distinguish it from simple, straightforward, competitive behavior: more competition means lower prices and possibly exit, even if no firm is attempting to drive rivals out of the market. For example, some 5,000 roadside gas stations closed down in Britain during the 1990s, while average gas prices declined significantly. An investigation by the Office of Fair Trade concluded that the price decrease resulted from increased competition between the large incumbent firms and that no predatory intent was present; see Box 12.5.

In the US, a crucial step in distinguishing competition from predation is the so called **Areeda-Turner test**: prices should be regarded as predatory only if they fall below marginal cost. But this does not solve the problem: for example, a firm might very well price below short-run marginal costs with the sole purpose of moving down its learning curve (and with no anticompetitive intent).

## BOX 12.5 GAS STATIONS IN BRITAIN: COMPETITION OR PREDATION?

Between 1990 and 1998, some 5,000 roadside gas stations closed down in the UK. The Office of Fair Trade (OFT) initiated a detailed analysis of the industry and found no need to intervene to protect the losers from the gas price war.

"Excluding tax and duty, the price of ordinary unleaded gas has fallen from 15.3p per liter in February 1990 to 10.0p per liter in February 1998 ... The key dynamic in the market is the fierce rivalry between the oil majors, such as Shell and Esso, and the large supermarket chains, ... whose market share has grown from 5% to around 23% since 1990 ...

Supermarkets can offer keen prices because of their high volumes and low cost base ... Oil companies have responded by cutting their prices to match those of the supermarkets ... Predictably, not all of the smaller independent retailers have been able to withstand the competition. As a consequence there are around 5,000 fewer gas stations in the UK. today than in 1990 ...

Does this situation constitute predatory behavior on the part of the market leaders? The weight of evidence from the marketplace suggests not ... If successful predation had occurred, we would have seen much higher margins being earned now. In fact, between January 1991 and February 1998, gross margins in the market fell from around 6p to 4p per liter for both unleaded and leaded gas."[21]

Alternatively, one may look for post-exit price increases. If there is predatory intent, the prey must have a reasonable expectation of recouping short run losses in the long run, that is, after exit has taken place. In this respect, the case of Spirit Airlines vs. Northwest Airlines, described in greater detail in Box 12.6, is illustrative. When Spirit entered one of Northwest's markets, the latter responded by slashing its fares. Soon after Spirit exited, prices went back up, in fact, to higher levels that before Spirit's entry.[e]

**WELFARE EFFECTS.** Even if we are able to identify pricing with the clear intent of driving rivals out of the market, we still have to address the following question: why should predatory pricing be illegal? Even from a consumers' perspective, there is a trade-off to be taken into account: predatory pricing implies that, with some probability, the prey will exit the market, leaving the predator with monopoly or near-monopoly power. But against possible higher future prices we must weigh in lower short-run prices. These lower prices are not very relevant when the predator's price cuts are selective, as in the Sacramento cable TV case (only 700 customers benefited from the predator's price cuts). But consider instead the example at the beginning of the chapter: when easyJet entered the London-Amsterdam route, KLM retaliated by cutting fares. easyJet survived this attack. In the end, both easyJet and KLM lost with the price war episode. Who gained in the process? Clearly, consumers.

Going back to the Spirit Airlines case (cf Box 12.6): in 2000, Spirit sued Northwest, alleging that its practices were predatory and violated Section 2 of the Sherman Antitrust Act. Mark Kahan, Spirit's executive vice president, stated that Northwest's "strategy only made sense if their goal was to push us out of the market." To which Jon

e. Ironically, not too long before, Northwest (and Continental) sued American Airlines for alleged predatory pricing. Northwest and Continental claimed to have lost a total of $1 billion when forced to match the new lower fares set by American in the spring of 1992. Antitrust charges against American Airlines were cleared in the summer of 1993.

**Box 12.6 SPIRIT AIRLINES VS. NORTHWEST AIRLINES[22]**

In December 1995, Spirit Airlines started once-daily flights from Detroit to Philadelphia, with fares as low as $49 one way. Initially, Northwest did not respond to Spirit's entry. But when Spirit introduced a second daily nonstop flight in June 1996, Northwest dropped its fare to $49 — thus matching Spirit's — and added another daily flight.

Northwest's pricing and capacity strategy shifted demand away from Spirit, whose load factors dropped from as high as 88% to as low as 31%. In August 1996, Spirit canceled one of its daily flights. In September, it exited the Detroit-Philadelphia market altogether.

Northwest responded to Spirit's exit by raising its fares and reducing capacity.

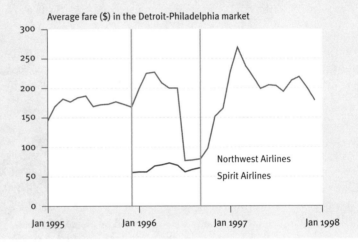

Average fare ($) in the Detroit-Philadelphia market

Austin, Northwest's spokesman, replied: "Spirit Air is complaining because we matched their prices. That is the central tenet of a free market." In some sense, both have a point.

Skepticism about the (alleged) negative effects of predatory pricing is especially relevant in industries with important network effects. The Macintosh operating system is worth little to a user when few other users adopt the same operating system, essentially because little software is developed for a system with few adopters. In this context, preventing predatory behavior may be a mixed blessing: a competitor is saved for the industry, but less standardization is achieved, with the obvious negative consequences in terms of network benefits. I will resume this discussion in Chapter 16.

**LEGAL TRADITION.** In practice, the US Supreme Court has clarified two conditions for illegal predatory pricing:[23] pricing below cost; and the intent of driving a rival out of the market, together with a reasonable expectation of recouping short run losses by means of higher future prices. At the same time, the court has repeatedly shown its skepticism about cases of predatory pricing: "Predatory pricing schemes are rarely tried, and even more rarely successful," wrote one judge.[24]

The analysis in Section 12.3 suggests that the Supreme Court's view is flawed when it implicitly assumes that predation is an unlikely event. Not only do we observe predation in practice, but we can also find convincing and rational explanations for its occurrence. However, distinguishing predation from competitive behavior is difficult. Moreover, the welfare analysis of predation reveals that its effects are ambiguous, even if we restrict our attention to consumer welfare. For this reason, the US courts may be right in not giving much weight to cases of alleged predation — although for different reasons than the stated skepticism about its existence.

The European legal tradition with regards to predation is less rich than the North American one. Predation would normally be considered an infringement of Article 102 of the Treaty of the European Union (EU), which forbids the abuse of a dominant position. Unlike the US, the European Commission (EC) typically does not require proof of intent and of a reasonable probability of recoupment as part of the proof of predatory pricing. Moreover, whereas in the US pricing below cost is a necessary but not sufficient condition, the EU doctrine essentially considers pricing below cost a sufficient but not necessary condition.

In one important case, AKZO Chemie BV, a Dutch chemical firm, was fined by the EC for alleged predatory action directed against Engineering and Chemical Supplies Ltd. (ECS), a small British firm. It should be noted that, a few years earlier, AKZO had threatened ECS it would cut prices in ECS's market unless ECS exited from the markets where it had recently entered, markets that were dominated by AKZO. The evidence of such threats was fairly solid: AKZO actually convened a meeting with ECS for the effect. The EC seems to have put a lot of weight on this past occurrence, as well as on the fact that AKZO is a much larger firm than ECS. By contrast, there was hardly any investigation of whether AKZO priced below cost or imposed any significant damage on ECS. Many critical analysts claim it did not.

## SUMMARY

• An incumbent's optimal capacity choice depends on the level of entry costs. If entry costs are very high, then the incumbent should set monopoly capacity and ignore the threat of entry. If entry costs are very low, then the incumbent should choose capacity taking into account the entrant's best response. Finally, if entry costs are intermediate, then the incumbent should choose capacity large enough to induce the entrant not to enter. • Capacity preemption is a credible strategy only if capacity costs are high and sunk. • By increasing the density of product offerings, an incumbent may deter entry even when profit margins are high. • By bundling or tying the sales of two products, a dominant firm may leverage its power in one market to increase dominance in the other market. • Contract exclusivity, selective discounts, and most-favored-nation clauses may be a way of raising rivals' costs and, as such, foreclosing competition. • Predatory pricing may be a successful strategy when (i) the prey is financially constrained, (ii) low prices signal low costs or the predator's "toughness", and (iii) capturing a minimum market share early on is crucial for long-term survival. In all these cases, low pricing by the predator induces the prey to exit the market.

## KEY CONCEPTS

- entry accommodation  • entry deterrence  • blockaded entry  • product proliferation  • naked exclusion  • divide and conquer  • bundling  • tying  • market power leverage  • all-unit discounts  • raising rivals' costs  • entrant's surplus  • predatory pricing  • long-purse  • deep-pocket  • Areeda-Turner test

## REVIEW AND PRACTICE EXERCISES

■ **12.1. STORE CLUSTERING.** "Tourists traipsing along a half-mile stretch of 23rd Street in New York pass five Starbucks outlets. In Tokyo, 7-Eleven boasts 15 stores within a similar distance of Shinjuku station."[25] Does it make any sense for stores to be clustered in this way?

■ **12.2. LC AND CS BURGERS.** LC Burgers is currently the sole fast-food chain in Linear city, a city that is one mile long and consists of one street, with one thousand consumers distributed uniformly along the street. The price for the BigLC, the only product sold by the LC Burger chain, is set nationally at $4, so that the local Linear city manager's decision is limited to choosing the number and location of its stores.

Each store costs $600,000 to open and lasts indefinitely. Each consumer buys one burger per week at the current price of $4. However, no consumer will walk for more than a quarter of a mile to buy a burger. Operating costs are $1 per burger. The interest rates is 0.1% per week. The market conditions are unchanging, so present discounted profits can be regarded as level perpetuities.

(a) Suppose that LC Burgers faces no competition and no threat of entry. How many stores should LC Burgers open, and at what locations?

CS Burgers is contemplating entering Linear city. CS Burgers' costs and price are the same as those of LC Burgers. Moreover, consumers regard the products at both chains as equally good, so, if both brands are in town, each consumers buys from the closest store.

(b) At what locations should CS Burgers open stores, given that LC Burgers has opened the locations found to be optimal in part (a)?

(c) Recognizing the threat of entry by CS Burgers, at what locations should LC Burgers open stores?

■ **12.3. GERMAN TELECOMMUNICATIONS.** In less than one year after the deregulation of the German telecommunications market at the start of 1998, domestic long-distance rates fell by more than 70%. Deutsche Telekom, the former monopolist, accompanied some of these rate drops by increases in monthly fees and local calls. MobilCom, one of the main competitors, feared it might be unable to match the price reductions. Following the announcement of a price reduction by Deutche Telekom at the end of 1998, shares of MobilCom fell by 7%. Two other competitors, O.tel.o and Mannesmann Arcor, said they would match the price cuts. VIAG Interkom, however, accused Telekom of "competition-distorting behavior," claiming the company is exploiting its (still remaining) monopoly power in the local market to subsidize its long-distance business.[26]

Is this a case of predatory pricing? Present arguments in favor and against such assertion.

# CHALLENGING EXERCISES

■ **12.4. EXCLUSIVE CONTRACTS AS A BARRIER TO ENTRY.** Suppose that there is one buyer who is willing to pay up to one unit of a given good for the price of 1. There is an incumbent seller with production cost $\frac{1}{2}$ (a value that is publicly known). Suppose there is a potential competitor to the seller. Unlike the incumbent seller, the potential entrant's cost is unknown to buyer and incumbent. Both expect it to be a value uniformly distributed in the $[0, 1]$ interval. The potential entrant, by contrast, is able to observe its cost and make an entry decision conditional on the observed value. If entry takes place, then the sellers play a price-setting game (with homogeneous product), whereby the low-cost firm sets a price just below the high-cost firm's cost.

(a) Show that the incumbent and the consumer's ex-ante expected payoffs are both given by $\frac{1}{4}$.

Now suppose that incumbent and consumer agree to an exclusive contract *before* the potential entrant makes its entry decision. The contract stipulates that the consumer buys the product from the incumbent (and only from the incumbent) at a price of $\frac{3}{4}$. Moreover, if the consumer were to buy from the entrant then it would pay the incumbent a penalty of $\frac{1}{2}$ for breach of contract.

(b) Show that both consumer and incumbent are better off with this exclusive contract.

# APPLIED EXERCISES

■ **12.5. BUNDLING.** Find examples of firm bundling strategies. Determine whether bundling is pro-competitive, anticompetitive, or relatively neutral with respect to competition.

## NOTES

1. See Sull, Don (1999), "easyJet: The $500 million gamble," *European Management Journal* **17**, 20–38.

2. Adapted from Ghemawat, Pankaj (1984), "Capacity Expansion in the Titanium Dioxide Industry," *Journal of Industrial Economics* **33**, 145–163; and Hall, Elizabeth A (1990), "An Analysis of Preemptive Behavior in the Titanium Dioxide Industry," *International Journal of Industrial Organization* **8**, 469–484.

3. See von Stackelberg, H (1934), *Marktform und Gleichgewicht*, Vienna: Springer.

4. Adapted from Dafny, Leemore (2005), "Games Hospitals Play: Entry Deterrence in Hospital Procedure Markets," *Journal of Economics and Management Strategy* **14** (3), 513–542.

5. For a rigorous analysis of the ideas in this subsection see Dixit, A. (1980), "The Role of Investment in Entry Deterrence," *Economic Journal* **90**, 95–106.

6. See *The Wall Street Journal*, March 15, 2013.

7. See Schmalensee, Richard (1978), "Entry Deterrence in the Ready-to-eat Breakfast Cereal Industry," *Bell Journal of Economics* **9**, 305–327.

8. Stemberg, Thomas G. (1996), *Staples for Success: From Business Plan to Billion-Dollar Business in Just a Decade*, Santa Monica, CA: Knowledge Exchange.

9. See Rasmusen, Eric B., J. Mark Ramseyer, and John S. Wiley, jr (1991), "Naked Exclusion," *The American Economic Review* **81** (5), 1137–1145; and Segal, Ilya R., and Michael D. Whinston (2000), "Naked Exclusion: Comment," *The American Economic Review* **90** (1), 296–309.

10. Adapted from Nalebuff, Barry J., and Adam M. Brandenburger (1996), *Co-opetition*, London: HarperCollinsBusiness.

11. The following analysis is broadly based on Whinston, Michael D. (1990), "Tying, Foreclosure, and Exclusion," *American Economic Review* **80**, 837-859.

12. See Salop, Steven C., and David T. Scheffman (1983), "Raising Rivals' Costs," *American Economic Review* **73** (2), 267–271.

13. See Aghion, Philippe, and Patrick Bolton (1987), "Contracts as a Barrier to Entry," *American Economic Review* **77**, 38–401.

14. For a rigorous analysis of the theory of predation based on financial contracting see Bolton, Patrick, and David S. Scharfstein (1990), "A Theory of Predation Based on Agency Problems in Financial Contracting," *American Economic Review* **80**, 93–106.

15. See Saloner, Garth (1987), "Predation, Mergers, and Incomplete Information," *Rand Journal of Economics* **18**, 165–186.

16. See Burns, Malcolm R. (1986), "Predatory Pricing and Acquisition Cost of Competitors," *Journal of Political Economy* **94**, 266–296.

17. See Kreps, David M., and Robert Wilson (1982), "Reputation and Imperfect Information," *Journal of Economic Theory* **27**, 253–279 and Milgrom, Paul R., and John Roberts (1982), "Predation, Reputation, and Entry Deterrence," *Journal of Economic Theory* **27**, 280–312.

18. See Cabral, Luís, and Michael H. Riordan (1994), "The Learning Curve, Market Dominance, and Predatory Pricing," *Econometrica* **62**, 1115–1140; and Cabral, Luís, and Michael H. Riordan (1997), "The Learning Curve, Predation, Antitrust, and Welfare," *Journal of Industrial Economics* **45**, 155–169.

19. See Hazlett, T. W. (1995), "Predation in Local Cable TV Markets," *Antitrust Bulletin* , 609–644.

20. Office of Fair Trading, *Fair Trading*, Issue 20 (1998).

21. Office of Fair Trading, *Fair Trading*, Issue 20 (1998).

22. Adapted from Elzinga, Kenneth, and David Mills (2009), "Predatory Pricing in the Airline Industry: *Spirit Airlines* v. *Northwest*," in J Kwoka and L White (Eds.), *The Antitrust Revolution*, Oxford: OUP, 2009.

23. *Brook Group Ltd. v. Brown & William Tobacco Corp.*, 113 S. Ct. 2578 (1993).

24. *Matsushita Electric Industrial Co. v. Zenith Radio Corp.*, 106 S. Ct. 1348 (1986).

25. *The Economist*, May 3, 2014.

26. *International Herald Tribune*, December 29, 1998.

**NON-PRICE STRATEGIES**

# VERTICAL RELATIONS

Although we normally think of firms as selling products and services to consumers, the fact is that most firms sell to other firms, not to final consumers. Cement producers sell cement to concrete producers, who then sell concrete to construction firms; TV set manufacturers sell TV sets to retailers, who then sell them to consumers; and so on.

There are several reasons why the relation between a manufacturer and a retailer is substantially different from the direct relation between a firm and the final consumer. First, the firm that sells directly to the consumer normally controls most of the variables that determine consumer demand: price, quality, advertising, sales service, and so on. The same is not true, however, for a manufacturer who sells through a retailer: there are many determinants of final demand which fall beyond the manufacturer's control. For example, the level of sales service and local advertising is normally controlled by the retailer. In particular, the *retail price*, an essential determinant of final demand, is set by the retailer, not the manufacturer. In summary *the demand faced by a manufacturer depends on the price it sets (the wholesale price) and on a host of other factors, most of which it does not directly control.*

A second reason why selling to a retailer is substantially different from selling to the final consumer is that *retailers compete with each other* (whereas consumers do not). In particular, each retailer cares about the wholesale price it has to pay the manufacturer *as well as the wholesale price paid by other retailers*. This is so because the wholesale price determines marginal cost (the retailer's marginal cost), and each firm's equilibrium profit is a function of all firms' marginal cost.

A third reason why selling to intermediate firms is different from selling to consumers is that the number of intermediate firms is small, whereas the number of final consumers is large; a firm that sells to the final consumer has more market power than a firm that sells to other firms. In fact, there are cases when most of the market power is on the buyer's side: large supermarket chains, for example, have a great degree of market power with respect to suppliers.

These reasons justify the separate treatment of **vertical relations** between firms. By "vertical relations" I mean relations between two firms in sequence along the value chain, as in the examples above. Normally, I will refer to the case of a manufacturer selling to one or several retailers. However, the analysis in this chapter applies more generally to cases when an **upstream firm** (e.g., cement producer, flour producer) sells to a **downstream firm** (e.g., concrete producer, bakery).

The chapter consists of three sections. First, I consider the possibility of vertical integration between upstream and downstream firms. Next, I discuss vertical restraints as a means to achieve similar results without the need to resort to full integration. Finally, I examine public policy towards vertical integration and vertical restraints.

## 13.1 VERTICAL INTEGRATION

Consider a structure consisting of an upstream firm ($M$) and a downstream firm ($R$). Firm $R$ is best thought of as a retailer, while firm $M$ could be the manufacturer of the product, a wholesaler, or the supplier of an important input to firm $R$. For example, $M$ could be an oil refiner and $R$ a gas station.

Suppose there is a demand for the final product (supplied by $R$), given by $D(p)$. Regarding the production technology, let us assume the simplest possible structure: in order to produce one unit of output, $R$ needs one unit of input. In fact, under the manufacturer/retailer interpretation this is the right assumption: in order to sell one TV set, a retailer must obtain exactly one TV set from the manufacturer. Suppose that $R$ has no costs in addition to the wholesale price, $w$, that it pays its supplier.[a] Finally, firm $M$ has a constant marginal cost $c$.

The situation is illustrated in Figure 13.1. Wanting to make a positive profit, the wholesaler sets $w$ above marginal cost $c$, that is $w > c$. The retailer, in turn, sets optimal output such that its marginal cost, $w$, equals its marginal revenue. This results in retail price $p^R$. In this equilibrium, firm $M$ earns a variable profit equal to area $A$, whereas firm $R$ earns a variable profit equal to area $B$. Together, the "vertical chain" (firms $M$ and $R$ combined) earn a profit $A+B$.

Now suppose that firms $M$ and $R$ are integrated as firm $M\&R$ with the single goal of maximizing joint profit. This new monopolist inherits firm $R$'s demand curve, $D(p)$, and firm $M$'s marginal cost, $c$. Its optimal choice is given the intersection of marginal revenue and marginal cost. This corresponds to output level $q^{M\&R}$ and retail price $p^{M\&R}$.[b]

In the vertical integration equilibrium, firm $M\&R$ makes a profit equal to areas $A + C$ in Figure 13.1. Since $C$ is greater than $B$, we conclude that firms $M$ and $R$ increase their joint profit by vertically integrating. The idea is that, under vertical integration, the wholesale price is simply a transfer price; therefore, it has no impact on retail price formation. For this reason, firm $M\&R$ is able to set the level of $p$ that maximizes total

a. Later, I will consider more complex contractual relationships between manufacturer and retailer; for the time being, I consider the simplest case of linear pricing (cf Section 6.3).

b. Retail price happens to be equal to firm $M$'s optimal wholesale price under vertical separation. This is true when the demand curve is linear, but is not true more generally.

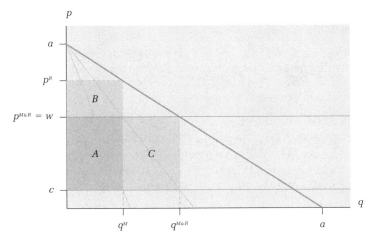

**FIGURE 13.1**

Double marginalization. If $M$ and $R$ are two different firms, then $M$ sets a wholesale price $w$ and $R$ sets a retail price $p^R$. If $M$ and $R$ are part of the same firm, then retail price is given by $p^{M\&R}$ (which, if the demand curve is linear, is equal to $w$).

value along the value chain. By contrast, under vertical separation, firm $M$ sets wholesale price $w$ above marginal cost $c$; and firm $R$ determines retail price $p$ based on a cost ($w$) that is higher than the "real" marginal cost ($c$).

We conclude that:

> If a manufacturer sets a wholesale price to a vertically separated retailer, then their joint profits are lower, and retail price is higher, than under vertical integration.

This problem, known as the **double marginalization problem**, provides a first justification for vertical integration.[1] Under vertical separation, there are two monopoly pricing decisions in effect. If the only contractual instrument that $M$ and $R$ can use is the wholesale price, then two monopoly margins will be added to marginal cost, resulting in a price that is greater than monopoly price. As a consequence, the combined profits of $M$ and $R$ are lower than if they were integrated. Exercise 13.7 illustrates this problem and more.

---

**DOUBLE MARGINALIZATION: FORMAL ANALYSIS.** The retailer's problem is identical to a monopolist with marginal cost $w$. Suppose final demand is given by $D = a - p$. From Section 3.2, we know that optimal price is given by:

$$p = \frac{a + w}{2}$$

which results in:

$$q = \frac{a - w}{2}$$

For the manufacturer, this implies a profit of:

$$\pi_M = (w - c)\, q = (w - c)\,\frac{a - w}{2}$$

## BOX 13.1 REGIONAL SPORTS NETWORKS[3]

Nearly 90% of the 116.4 million television households in the US subscribe to multichannel television. Distributors such as Comcast or TimeWarner negotiate affiliate fees with content providers such as Disney or ESPN. These are typically linear contracts; that is, they correspond to a per-subscriber fee.

Among the $30 billion per year in fees, about $4.1 billion correspond to regional sports networks (RSNs). RSNs are particularly interesting from an empirical research point of view because there is variation in ownership and carriage patterns. For example, in 2007, Comcast Sports Northwest (wholly owned by Comcast) was carried by Comcast but not by DirectTV or Dish; and independently-owned YES (Yankees Entertainment and Sports) was carried by TimeWarner and DirectTV but not by Dish.

This variation allows us to answer the question: does it matter if distributor and content provider are vertically integrated? The evidence suggests that, when there is vertical integration, (a) the price paid by consumers is lower; (b) the likelihood that the RSN is carried by the distributor is higher; and (c) the likelihood that the RSN is carried by rival distributors is lower.

---

The manufacturer's problem is identical to a monopolist with marginal cost $c$ and demand $q = \frac{1}{2}(a - w)$. From Section 3.2, we know that optimal price is given by:

$$w = \frac{a + c}{2}$$

Figure 13.1 considers the case when $c = 1$ and $a = 9$. This results in $w = 5$, $p^R = 7$, $q^M = 2$, and $q^{M\&R} = 4$. In terms of profit levels, $A = 8$, $B = 4$, and $C = 8$. (Check this.) It follows that vertical integration increases total profits by $C - B = 4$ (a 33% increase).[c]

---

The movie industry provides an example of the effects of double marginalization: in the 1940s and 1950s, US movie ticket prices were lower at theaters owned by studios.[2] Eventually, a US Supreme Court decision forced the studios to sell their theater assets. Clearly, the court judged that double marginalization was not the only relevant effect. I will return to this in Section 13.3.

Box 13.1 provides additional evidence, this time regarding the US cable TV industry. When distributor (firm $R$) and supplier (firm $M$) are owned by the same entity (vertical integration), the price paid by consumers is lower. This is consistent with the idea that vertical integration alleviates the double marginalization problem. The evidence also suggests that the likelihood that a given regional sports network is carried by a distributor (that is, the firm $M$'s product is sold by firm $R$) is greater under vertical integration. This too corroborates the double-marginalization-effect story, as shown in Exercise 13.6.

c. In fact, consumer welfare is also lower under vertical separation, since price is greater than monopoly price.

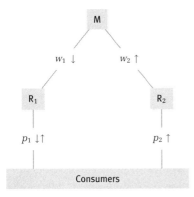

**FIGURE 13.2**
Vertical integration with downstream competition:
arrows indicate expected sign of change in variables following integration between M and $R_1$.

■ **DOWNSTREAM COMPETITION.**[4]  Things get a little more complicated if there is more than one downstream firm. Figure 13.2 depicts the case when an upstream firm (manufacturer) $M$ sells to two downstream firms (retailers) $R_1$ and $R_2$. Let $w_i$ be the wholesale price paid by retailer $R_i$ and let $p_i$ be its retail price. Suppose that firm $M$ merges with retailer $R_i$; what impact do we expect this to have on prices?

The first effect we would expect is a decrease in $w_1$. This corresponds to the double-marginalization effect considered earlier: once $M$ and $R_1$ have a single profit maximization goal, one of the intermediation margins, $w_1$, ceases to exist. There may still be a transfer price $w_1$ used for accounting purposes; but as a decision problem, firm $M\&R_1$ no longer considers two price margins.

The second effect we would expect is an increase in $w_2$. Firm $R_2$, which was a customer of firm $M$, is now also a *rival* of firm $M\&R_1$. An increase in $w_2$ has an effect on firm $M$'s revenues, an effect that previously firm $M$ was not taking into account. Now that firm $M$ is united to firm $R_1$, an increase in $w_2$ also has an effect on downstream competition: it puts pressure on $R_2$ to increase $p_2$, which in turn helps $R_1$, which in turn helps $M\&R_1$. In other words, an increase in $w_2$ is a way of **raising rivals' costs**, a strategy we discussed in Section 12.2.

Finally, when it comes to $p_1$ we find conflicting effects. Vertical integration eliminates double marginalization, which in turn provides a downward pressure on $p_1$ (as we saw earlier in this section). However, vertical integration also has a **competition softening** effect that tends to push price up. When $R_1$ considers an increase in price, it balances an increase in margin with a decrease in market share: the basic pricing trade-off we considered in Section 3.2. Now that $R_1$ is part of $M\&R_1$, it should consider an additional effect: by increasing price and losing market share, $R_1$ is giving $R_2$ some market share. This in turn implies that $R_2$ must order more input; and to the extent that $w_2 > c$, this extra input order increases the profits of the combined $M\&R_1$.

Overall, we expect the profits of $M\&R_1$ to increase and the profits of $R_2$ to decrease. Regarding consumers, we have conflicting effects: getting rid of double marginalization is good, but softening downstream competition is bad; in principle, the net effect can go either way.[d]

■ **INVESTMENT INCENTIVES.**[5]  So far we discussed pricing incentives along the value chain. In some cases investment incentives are also important. Suppose that firm $M$ comes up with a new electronic gadget worth $v$ to consumers, but consumers will only learn about it if firm $R$ makes an investment (for example, training its sales force to sell the new gadget). Alternatively, suppose that firm $R$ comes up with a new car model worth $v$ to consumers, but production is only possible if firm $M$ makes an investment (for example, designing and building a mould required to produce a car part). Suppose moreover that these investments are **specific assets**, a concept introduced in Section 3.4: the sales force training is only useful for selling firm $M$'s gadget; and the mould is only useful for making firm $R$'s car part.

Let us continue with the example of the car manufacturer $R$ outsourcing a part to manufacturer $M$. Frequently there are many contingencies which are difficult to predict and write a contract on (for example, how much it will it cost to produce the part or how many cars will be demanded). Accordingly, at some point in the future the exact terms of the transaction between $M$ and $R$ will need to be determined; whereas $M$'s investment decision must be made from the get-go. Then we have a problem.

Specifically, suppose that the investment costs $c = 5$, whereas the total value created by the investment is $v = 8$ (a value which is appropriated by firm $R$ upon sale). Clearly, this is a worthwhile investment. However, once the investment is made it is effectively a sunk cost, which in turn induces a **hold-up** problem (cf Section 3.4): suppose that $R$ makes a take-it-or-leave-it offer to $M$, either $p^H = 6$ or $p^L = 3$. The situation is represented by the game in Figure 13.3. The only subgame-perfect equilibrium of this game (cf Section 7.2) is for $R$ to offer $p^L$ and for $M$ to choose $\bar{a}$. This is an inefficient equilibrium: total payoff is zero, whereas the choice of $a$ would lead to a total payoff of 3.

In this context, vertical integration may help solve the hold-up problem created by investments in specific assets: suppose that $R$ acquires $M$. Now decisions such as the investment level, the number of parts, etc., are made by $R$, whereas $M$'s manager simply executes orders. Taking the $M\&R$ group together, $R$'s manager correctly determines that the investment $a$ is worthwhile (it costs 5 and generates benefits of 8); and accordingly, the efficient level of investment is chosen.

If vertical integration solves some problems, it may also create new ones. Continuing with the same example: upon acquisition by the downstream firm, $M$'s manager is at the orders of $R$'s manager. As we saw in Section 3.3, this creates an **agency** problem: Firm $R$'s manager wants Firm $M$ (now a division of $M\&R$) to act in $R$'s interest; but Firm $R$ may not know exactly what to order, since Firm $M$'s manager is better informed than Firm $R$'s manager.

d. All of the above analysis assumes that firms compete in prices. The case when firms are quantity setters in analyzed in Exercise 13.9.

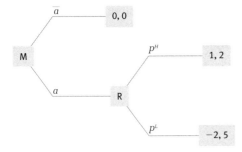

**FIGURE 13.3**
Specific assets and hold-up:
the upstream firm, M, decides whether to make an investment in a specific asset;
next, the downstream firm, R, decides what price to pay for the asset.

In sum,

> When investments in specific assets are at stake, vertical integration alleviates the hold-up problem but increases the agency problem.

The above analysis of the hold-up problem is based on a very stylized example. However, the basic ideas are far more general. For example, we could assume that, instead of a take-it-or-leave-it offer by $R$, firms $M$ and $R$ negotiate over transfer payments and split the cake (that is, the value at stake). If $M$ chooses $a$, then a value $v = 8$ is at stake. If $M$ and $R$ split the cake, then $R$ gets 4. This is still not sufficient to compensate for its initial investment of 5, so the unique subgame-perfect equilibrium is, again, for $M$ not to invest.[e]

■ **VERTICAL INTEGRATION: THE EVIDENCE AND MORE THEORY.** In many industries, the last decades of the twentieth century witnessed a significant increase in the practice of **outsourcing**, purchasing inputs from an outside supplier (even though those inputs are available internally). In fact, currently in the US almost one-half of upstream establishments make no internal shipments to their downstream integrated establishments.[6] This evidence runs counter to the idea of vertical integration as a means to increase efficiency in vertical transactions (namely by reducing double marginalization).

Much of the outsourcing shift was directed at foreign suppliers (that is, outsourcing took the form of offshoring). In this sense, one explanation for the trend is simply that firms were seeking cheaper suppliers. However, recently much of that outsourcing has shifted back to the US, and the lack on internal flows is still very noticeable.

If vertical ownership is not associated to vertical flows, why then do firms vertically integrate? One explanation is that integration allows for the internal transfer of intangible inputs such as management ability, marketing know-how, intellectual property, and R&D capital. This would then suggest that the effects of vertical integration

e. Exercise 13.10 considers still another, namely the case of a continuum of choices.

have less to do with strategic interaction in setting prices and output levels than with organizational efficiency issues.

However, before discarding strategic behavior as a driver of vertical integration, we should note that, even if vertical integration is not associated with internal flows, it does imply the *option* of internal flows. In other words, the advantage of being vertically integrated with a potential supplier is that it forces outsource suppliers to be more efficient and bid more aggressively — or else the buyer switches to the internal source.[7]

## 13.2 VERTICAL RESTRAINTS

In the previous section, we saw how vertical integration may increase the efficiency of pricing along a value chain. But: is vertical integration *required* for efficient pricing? In many cases it is not; in this section, I show how a variety of **vertical restraints** may also do the job.

■ **NONLINEAR PRICING.** Suppose that, in addition to determining a wholesale price, the upstream firm, $M$, can also set a fixed fee $f$ to be paid by the downstream firm, $R$, in case it wants to do any business with $M$. As in Section 6.3, we call the pair $(f, w)$ a **two-part tariff**. Often, the fixed fee is also called **franchise fee** (although, in fact, franchise contracts involve more than just setting a fixed fee). More generally, as in Section 6.3, contracts of this type are an example of a **nonlinear pricing**.[f]

Suppose that the manufacturer sets $w = c$ and $f = \pi^M$, where $\pi^M \equiv (p^M - c) D(p^M)$ is monopoly profit for a vertically integrated firm. In terms of Figure 13.1, this corresponds to setting a fixed fee equal to the area $A + C$. There are three points to notice about this nonlinear contract: first, from the point of view of the firms, this contract is efficient, that is, it maximizes their joint profits. This is so because the marginal cost taken into consideration by the retailer (the wholesale price $w$) is equal to the true marginal cost ($c$); accordingly, the retailer sets price at the optimal level, that is, at the level that a vertically integrated monopolist would set ($p^M$). Second, by pricing this way, the retailer receives total gross profits $\pi = \pi^M$ (gross of the franchise fee); therefore, it is willing to pay up to $f = \pi^M$ as a fixed fee. Finally, the manufacturer receives zero in terms of variable profit (because it sells at marginal cost) but is able to recover all monopoly profits through the fixed fee.

We thus conclude that,

> If nonlinear contracts are possible, then the optimal solution under vertical separation is identical to that under vertical integration.

In fact, a more general point is that, *allowing for fixed fees, the upstream firm's profit maximization problem is essentially equivalent to maximizing joint profits of the*

f. Strictly speaking, the amount paid, $f + wq$, is a linear function of the quantity bought. The key point of a nonlinear contract is that price per unit ($w + f/q$ in the case of a two-part tariff) is not constant.

*upstream and the downstream firms,* and then finding the maximum fixed fee that the downstream firm is willing to pay.

In practice, we observe many industries where linear pricing is the rule. This seems inconsistent with the above view that nonlinear pricing increases total profits along the value chain. This suggests that the above result (nonlinear pricing leads to efficiency) needs to be qualified in several ways. First, I assumed that there is no competition at each stage. If there are several downstream firms competing against each other, then the result that franchise fees are sufficient to capture monopoly profits may fail to hold. A second qualification is that we have considered the case of complete information. If the upstream firm does not know the downstream firm's costs, then it may be optimal to set a variable fee that is greater than average marginal cost.

Sometimes the number of manufacturers is very large with respect to the number of retailers. This seems especially true of grocery stores: in the Los Angeles area alone, for example, there are 15 varieties of green peas, 19 different kinds of mustard, and 12 brands of frozen pizza.[8] Most of the market power is therefore at the retailer level, not at the manufacturer level. Limited shelf space means that the opportunity cost of carrying one particular product is very high. The analysis of the previous section would predict that manufacturers set a high wholesale price and a fixed fee equal to variable profits minus fixed cost. But because the resulting margin is low and fixed costs are very high (the opportunity cost of shelf space is very high), the fixed fee paid by the retailer may actually be negative. In other words, it may be the manufacturer that has to pay the retailer for shelf space. In fact, **slotting allowances**, fees paid by manufacturers to obtain retailer patronage, are a common practice in these markets.[g]

■ **RESALE PRICE MAINTENANCE.**[9]  Consider the market for consumer electronics: personal computers, smartphones, and so on. These are complex products for which sales effort is important: consumers gain a good deal from the service provided at the point of sale. Now suppose that one retailer makes a large investment in sales effort, so that it attracts a large number of consumers to its store; and suppose also that a second retailer makes no investment in sales effort but sells at a lower price than the first retailer. One possible outcome is that many price-conscious consumers will visit the first retailer to learn about the available products; and then visit the second retailer to purchase the preferred product at a low price.

This situation entails an important **externality** (cf Section 5.1): the investment in sales effort by the first retailer benefits both retailers. In fact, if most consumers are price conscious, then the investment benefits mostly the second retailer, who free rides on the first one. As a consequence, the incentives for investment in retailer service quality are very low. Finally, the manufacturer suffers from this, for final demand depends to a great extent on sales effort.

**Resale price maintenance (RPM)**, the practice whereby the manufacturer imposes a minimum price on retailers, provides a way out of this dilemma. If the minimum price is effectively enforced, then every retailer sticks to it, that is, every retailer prices at the

g. Slotting allowances are also known as *street money* or *placement allowances.*

uniform minimum level; and then the free-riding problem disappears: not even price-conscious consumers gain from purchasing from a different retailer than the first one they visit. Therefore, the benefits from increased sales accrue to the retailer who makes the corresponding investment.

■ **EXCLUSIVE TERRITORIES AND EXCLUSIVE DEALING.** Advertising provides a similar instance of an inter-retailer externality. Suppose that a car dealer pays for local TV advertising. Advertising expenditures increase demand, which in turn benefits all the car dealers selling the same car model, not just the dealer who paid for the advertising costs. That is, if there is a second dealer selling the same car in the same area, then part of the increase in sales goes to that second dealer. In this case, RPM would probably not do the job of correcting the externality, but other vertical restraints might. A specific alternative is to award **exclusive territories**. This is a vertical restraint whereby each retailer is assigned a given territory that other retailers have no access to. For example, car manufacturers have an exclusive dealer in each European country. The German Fiat dealer, for instance, is not allowed to sell cars in France. Exclusive territories do the job because, if the dealer's advertising campaign is confined to its exclusive territory, then there is no longer an inter-retailer externality.

Externalities may also occur between manufacturers. Continuing with the car dealerships example: it is often the case that manufacturers invest resources in training salespeople working in dealerships. Some of this training is specific to the manufacturer's cars, but some is more general (e.g., the art of car selling). If dealers were to work with more than one manufacturer, then there would be an inter-manufacturer externality: part of the training investment made by one manufacturer benefits the rival manufacturer. One way of solving this externality is to impose on retailers the vertical restraint of **exclusive dealing**, whereby the retailer cannot work but with one manufacturer.

> Vertical restraints such as resale price maintenance, exclusive territories, and exclusive dealing allow upstream and downstream firms to internalize the effects of demand-increasing investments.

## 13.3 PUBLIC POLICY

In the previous sections, I suggested a variety of reasons why vertically-related firms may want to merge or establish contracts that regulate transactions between upstream and downstream players. Are vertical mergers and vertical restraints good for consumers? Should policy makers care about it?

Unlike horizontal mergers, where the presumption is that the transaction leads to higher equilibrium prices, when it comes to vertical integration the effect is ambiguous. As we saw in Section 13.1, the double marginalization effect suggests that prices may decrease as a result of a vertical merger; but the competition softening effect suggests that they may increase; moreover, a vertical merger may lead to foreclosure, which in turn may lead to higher prices in the long run. Whichever effect dominates is likely to depend on each industry's particulars. Consistent with this view, the US and EU non-horizontal policies are generally more permissive than the corresponding horizontal merger policies.

Similar to vertical integration, the effect of vertical restraints on consumer welfare is ambiguous. Consider the case of Unilever, the dominant player in Europe's impulse ice cream market. In the late 1980s Mars, one of the world's largest confectioners, decided that if you can sell chocolate you can also sell chocolate ice cream. This was no small threat to Unilever, which at the time stepped up enforcement of its freezer exclusivity policy: basically, Unilever provided retail outlets with a freezer for free or at a very low cost; and the retailer in turn had to agree to store and display only Unilever products in such freezer. Over the next two decades or so, Mars sued Unilever in multiple European countries; and both the European Commission as well as various national competition authorities initiated their own investigations. These various cases recognize the costs and benefits of exclusive dealing contracts: they may harm competition but may also provide better incentives for the dominant firm to invest. The actual outcome of the various cases and investigations varied enormously: sometimes Unilever won, sometimes Mars won, and in some cases the parties settled out of court. This variation in outcomes reflects the ambiguity of public policy with respect to vertical restraints such as exclusive dealing.

Another example is given by cable TV. As indicated in Box 13.1, when a cable distributor owns a content provider, such distributor is more likely to carry the content in question, whereas rival distributors are less likely to carry the content. If the first effect is consistent with vertical integration alleviating the double-marginalization problem, the second effect indicates that foreclosure may also result from vertical integration. In some US markets, the adverse foreclosure effect is prevented by imposing program access rules.

In addition to foreclosure, one concern with vertical restraints is the possibility of collusion. Consider for example an industry with several upstream and downstream firms who compete à la Bertrand. Equilibrium wholesale price and retail price are set at marginal cost level, $w = c$ and $p = w = c$. Suppose now that manufacturers impose (or the industry agrees on) a minimum retail price equal to monopoly price $p^M$. Clearly, this implies a shift from competitive pricing to monopoly pricing.

To summarize,

> Vertical restraints may facilitate collusion or lead to competitor foreclosure.

To conclude: the number of effects involved in vertical relations is large (double marginalization, investment externalities, foreclosure, collusion, etc.). Moreover, the number of possible settings is also very large (one or many upstream or downstream firms; linear or nonlinear contracts; vertical integration or vertical separation; etc.). Given all this variety, it's likely that public policy with regard to vertical relations will continue to incorporate an important case-by-case component.

## SUMMARY

• If a manufacturer sets a wholesale price to a vertically separated retailer, then their joint profits are lower, and retail price is higher, than under vertical integration. • When investments in specific assets are at stake, vertical integration alleviates the hold-up problem but increases the agency problem. • If nonlinear contracts are possible, then the optimal solution under vertical separation is identical to that under vertical integration. • Vertical restraints such as resale price maintenance, exclusive territories, and exclusive dealing allow upstream and downstream firms to internalize the effects of demand-increasing investments. • Vertical restraints may facilitate collusion or lead to competitor foreclosure.

## KEY CONCEPTS

• **vertical relations** • **upstream firm** • **downstream firm** • **double marginalization problem** • **raising rivals' costs** • **competition softening** • **specific asset** • **hold-up** • **agency theory** • **outsourcing** • **vertical restraints** • **two-part tariff** • **franchise fee** • **nonlinear pricing** • **slotting allowances** • **externality** • **resale price maintenance** • **exclusive territories** • **exclusive dealing**

## REVIEW AND PRACTICE EXERCISES

■ **13.1. MCDONALD'S.** Empirical evidence suggests that McDonald's restaurants that are wholly owned by the parent company charge lower prices than do independent franchise ones. How can this difference be explained?

■ **13.2. RESALE PRICE MAINTENANCE.** The following industries are known to practice or have practiced resale price maintenance: fashion clothing, consumer electronics, fine fragrances. In each case, indicate the probable motivation for RPM and the likely welfare consequences.

■ **13.3. VERMONT CASTINGS.** Vermont Castings is a manufacturer of wood-burning stoves, a somewhat complex product. One of Vermont Castings's dealers once complained about the terms of the relations between the manufacturer and dealers, stating that "the worst disappointment is spending a great deal of time with a customer only to lose him to Applewood [a competing retailer] because of price." Specifically, the dealer lamented "the loss of three sales of V.C. stoves ... to people whom we educated and spent long hours with."[10]

How do you think this problem can be resolved? How would you defend your solution in an antitrust/competition policy court?

■ **13.4. EXCLUSIVE TERRITORIES IN THE EUROPEAN UNION.** Should the European Union outlaw the practice of exclusive territories in car dealerships? Why or why not?

■ **13.5. EXCLUSIVE DEALING IN BEER SALES.** Beer producers are wont to impose an exclusive dealing clause on retailers. Discuss the efficiency and market power effects of this practice.

## CHALLENGING EXERCISES

■ **13.6. CABLE TV.** Evidence from the US cable TV industry suggests that the likelihood that a given network is carried by a distributor is greater when the network is owned by the distributor (see Box 13.1). Consider the analysis of double marginalization in Figure 13.1. Suppose that there the distributor must pay a cost $F$ in order to carry a given network (this could correspond to the opportunity cost of adding a channel to the distributor's lineup, for example the profit lost from not being able to carry a different channel). Show that there exist values $F$ such that the distributor will carry the network if and only if it owns the network.

■ **13.7. WINTEL.** Consider the following highly simplified picture of the personal computer industry. A large number of price-taking firms assemble computer systems; call them "computer OEMs" (Original Equipment Manufacturers). Each of these firms must buy three inputs for each computer system that it sells: (1) a variety of components that are themselves supplied competitively and collectively cost the computer OEM $500 per computer; (2) the Windows operating system, available only from Microsoft, at a price $p_M$, to be discussed below; and (3) a Pentium microprocessor, available only from Intel, at a price $p_I$, also to be discussed below. Since each computer system requires precisely one operating system and one microprocessor, the marginal cost of a computer to an OEM is $500 + p_M + p_I$. Assume that competition among OEMs drives the price of a computer system down to marginal cost, so we have $p = 500 + p_M + p_I$, where $p$ is the price of a computer system. The demand for computer systems is given by $Q = 100,000,000 - 50,000\,p$. Microsoft is the sole supplier of the Windows operating system for personal computers. The marginal cost to Microsoft of providing Windows for one more computer is zero. Intel is the sole supplier of the Pentium microprocessors for personal computers. The marginal cost to Intel of a Pentium microprocessor for one more computer system is $300.

(a) Suppose that Microsoft and Intel simultaneously and independently set the prices for Windows and Pentium chips, $p_M$ and $p_I$. What are the Nash equilibrium prices, $\widehat{p}_M$ and $\widehat{p}_I$?

Now suppose that Microsoft and Intel sit down to negotiate an agreement to sell Windows and Pentium chips as a package to computer OEMs for a package price of $p_{MI}$.

(b) What package price would maximize Microsoft's and Intel's combined profits? By how much would an agreement between Microsoft and Intel boost their combined profits?

(c) Would final consumers benefit from such an agreement between Microsoft and Intel, or would they be harmed? What about computer OEMs? Relate your answer to your calculations in parts (a) and (b), and explain the economic principles underlying your answer.

■ **13.8. TWO-PART TARIFFS.** Suppose that a manufacturer sells to $n$ retailers by means of a two-part tariff $(f, w)$: a fix fee $f$ and a wholesale price $w$. Explain the intuition of the result that the greater the degree of retailer competition, the greater the optimal wholesale price.

■ **13.9. DOWNSTREAM COURNOT COMPETITION.** Consider an industry with one upstream firm and $n$ downstream firms that compete à la Cournot. Show that the optimal wholesale price is strictly between marginal cost and monopoly price.

■ **13.10. ASSET SPECIFICITY AND VERTICAL INTEGRATION.** The value created by the collaboration between firms $M$ and $R$ is given by $v = \sqrt{e_M} + \sqrt{e_R}$, where $e_M$ and $e_R$ are investments (in \$) by firms $M$ and $R$. After investment levels have been chosen, $M$ and $R$ negotiate the division of $v$, each firm keeping 50%.

(a) Determine the equilibrium values of $e_i$ $(i = M, R)$.

(b) Suppose that Firm $M$ and $R$ merge. Determine Firm $M\&R$'s optimal choices of $e_i$.

(c) Compare total payoff under vertical separation and under vertical integration.

(d) Comment on your answer to the previous question in light of the discussion in Section 13.1, Box 13.1, and Section 5.1.

## NOTES

1. Spengler, Joseph (1950), "Vertical Integration and Antitrust Policy," *Journal of Political Economy* **58**, 347–352.

2. Gil, Ricard (2015), "Does Vertical Integration Decrease Prices? Evidence from the Paramount Antitrust Case of 1948," *American Economic Journal: Economic Policy* **7** (2), 1–1.

3. Adapted from Crawford, Gregory S., Robin S. Lee, Michael D. Whinston, and Ali Yurukoglu (2015), "The Welfare Effects of Vertical Integration in Multichannel Television Markets," Working Paper.

4. The analysis in this section is partly adapted from Chen, Yongmin (2001), "On Vertical Mergers and their Competitive Effects," *Rand Journal of Economic* **32** (4), 667–685.

5. Some of the ideas in this section go back to Williamson, Oliver (1975), *Markets and Hierarchies: Analysis and Antitrust Implications*, New York: Free Press.

6. Atalay, Enghin, Ali Hortaçsu, and Chad Syverson (2014), "Vertical Integration and Input Flows," *American Economic Review* **104** (4), 1120–1148.

7. Loertscher, Simon, and Michael H. Riordan (2014), "Outsourcing, Vertical Integration, and Cost Reduction," Working Paper.

8. Shaffer, Greg (1991), "Slotting Allowances and Resale Price Maintenance: A Comparison of Facilitating Practices," *Rand Journal of Economics* **22**, 120–135.

9. This subsection is partly based on Mathewson, Frank, and Ralph Winter (1984), "An Economic Theory of Vertical Restraints," *Rand Journal of Economics* **15**, 27–38.

10. Mathewson, Frank, and Ralph Winter (1998), "The Law and Economics of Resale Price Maintenance," *Review of Industrial Organization* **13**, 57–84.

# CHAPTER 14

# PRODUCT DIFFERENTIATION

The US credit card industry is composed of over 4,000 firms (typically, banks that issue credit cards). The good that is offered is, at least apparently, close to homogeneous. The number of consumers is large (75 million). The 10 largest firms (credit card issuers) hold a combined 20% market share. There are no significant barriers to entry, and a fair number of firms operate at the national level, so that the geographic definition of the US as the relevant market seems reasonable. There is no sign of an explicit price-fixing agreement between the different credit-card issuers.

Given this set of circumstances, many would feel inclined to identify the credit card industry as an example of near-perfect competition. However, the evidence is greatly at odds with such expectation. First, interest rates are very insensitive with respect to changes in marginal cost (the money market rate), which is not consistent with perfect competition.[a] Second, from 1983 to 1988 rates of return in the credit card business were three to five times higher than the normal rate of return in other lines of banking business.

One first possible explanation for this discrepancy is that credit card users are subject to switching costs. Many consumers obtain their first credit card through the bank they have an account with. Changing to a different card may imply a series of costs, e.g., opening an account with a different bank. Moreover, before applying for a new credit card, the consumer needs to obtain information regarding the card's terms and conditions. This too is a cost of getting a new credit card (if nothing else, the time lost in finding out what the terms and conditions are). Similarly to switching costs, consumers may simply be unaware of the existence of better deals, perhaps because of the cost of finding out about alternative offers. High search and switching costs may allow the seller to set a higher price without losing many customers, thus justifying the evidence from credit cards.

a. Under perfect competition a one-dollar change in marginal cost implies a one-dollar change in price.

A second explanation is that the good "credit card" is in fact not a homogeneous product, rather a **differentiated product**. This may result from differences in quality (some credit cards offer better services) or from differences in the status that is associated with a certain credit card. For example, the services and the status associated with an American Express card are not the same as with a Visa card. Moreover, not all Visa cards are identical, or seen by consumers as identical.[1] As with switching costs, product differentiation allows sellers to increase price without the substantial loss in sales that would take place in a homogeneous-product scenario.

In this chapter, I consider cases when the assumptions of homogeneous product and perfect information fail to hold. Section 14.1 deals with characterizing and estimating the demand for differentiated products, whereas Section 14.2 focuses on oligopoly competition in markets for differentiated products. Frequently, products are differentiated not so much by virtue of their physical characteristics but rather by the consumers' perception of each product. This motivates Section 14.3, devoted to advertising and branding. As mentioned earlier in this introduction, consumer search and switching costs may turn a homogeneous-product industry into one that effectively operates like a differentiated-product industry. This motivates Section 14.4, where consumer information and behavior is the main source of departure from the homogenous-product, perfect-information paradigm. Finally, Section 14.5 deals with public policy issues related to advertising and product differentiation.

## 14.1 DEMAND FOR DIFFERENTIATED PRODUCTS

In the previous chapters — in particular in Chapter 8 — we assumed that oligopoly competition takes place in a homogenous-product industry. This is a reasonable assumption for industries such as copper, but probably not for industries such as cars: a Toyota is not the same thing as a Volkswagen, and even within the Toyota family we find significant differences across models.

Consider the housing market. In a sense, this is the opposite extreme of a commodity market: each house has unique characteristics; even if two different houses were built in the same way, their different locations would make them different products. Despite this variation, each house may be described by a host of objective (and mostly measurable) characteristics: location, total area, number of floors, style, etc. Suppose that all consumers agree on how much each characteristic is worth; and that one seller dominates the market. Both of these are strong assumptions that I will relax later. For now, I note that under these conditions we can estimate the value of each characteristic simply by running a statistical regression of price as a function of characteristics. In fact, sale price reflects the buyers' willingness to pay, and the latter is simply a function of the quantity of each characteristic.

Table 14.1 shows the result of such a regression for houses sold in Madison, Wisconsin.[3] The bottom row with dots indicates that the list of explanatory variables

TABLE 14.1 Determinants of (logarithm of) house prices in Madison, Wisconsin[2]

| Variable | Units | [min,max] | Coefficient | p value |
|---|---|---|---|---|
| Total area | squared feet | [336,9145] | .0003446 | 0.000 |
| Total area squared | (squared feed)$^2$ | [112896,8.36E+07] | −2.19e-08 | 0.000 |
| Central air | Yes=1, No=0 | [0,1] | .0365447 | 0.000 |
| Amp rating | Ampere | [30,500] | .0002067 | 0.000 |
| ... | ... | ... | ... | ... |

Notes: $N = 15849$; $R^2 = 0.9246$; Adj $R^2 = 0.9223$

exceeds the ones listed in the table (in fact, dozens of explanatory variables are considered). The dependent variable is the logarithm of price (measured in US $); therefore, changes in the dependent variable can be interpreted as approximate percent changes in price level. For example, if the variable "central air" switches from 0 to 1 (that is, if the house has central air conditioning), then logarithm of price changes by .0365, that is, price increases by approximately 3.65%. Similarly, if total area increases from 1,000 to 2,000 square feet, then log price increases by $.0003446 \times (2000 - 1000) - 2.19E\text{-}08 \times (2000^2 - 1000^2) \approx .3446$, that is, price increases by 34.46%. Finally, notice that $R^2 = .92$. This means that more than 90% of the variation in house prices can be explained by observable and measurable characteristics.

In cases like Diet Coke and Diet Pepsi, we may estimate demand by directly estimating two demand curves and explicitly taking into account that each demand depends on the prices of both products. This works well when there is a small number of differentiated products. For houses in Madison, Wisconsin, such approach is not feasible: we would have thousands of demand curves and many, many thousands of elasticities to estimate (e.g., how the demand for house #9,234 depends on the price of house #13,293). In this context, the **characteristics approach** to product demand allows for an approach that is both realistic and feasible: instead of estimating the demand for each individual house, we estimate the demand for each characteristic. The implicit prices of each characteristic (such as size and air conditioning), measured by regressions such as the above, are referred to as **hedonic prices**. Having estimated the demand for each characteristic, we can then better estimate the demand for a particular house, that is, a house with a particular set of characteristics.

Easier said than done: in practice, many complications are likely to arise. Take the case of cars, for example. First, unlike the assumption I made earlier, cars are not sold by a single monopolist (I will consider the issue of competition in the next section). More important, all consumers do not value car characteristics equally. A more realistic model of consumer demand allows for the possibility that the utility coefficient of a given characteristic — for example, car size — varies from consumer to consumer: a larger household is likely to place a higher weight on the car-size characteristic than a smaller household.

**Characteristics approach: formal analysis.** Suppose the utility of a consumer of type $i$ for car $j$ is given by:

$$u_{ij} = b_{i1} v_{j1} + \ldots + b_{in} v_{jn} - p_j + \epsilon_{ij} \tag{14.1}$$

where $b_{ik}$ is consumer $i$'s valuation for characteristic $k$ ($k = 1, \ldots, n$) and $v_{jk}$ is how much car $j$ has of characteristic $k$. Finally, $\epsilon_{ij}$ measures consumer- and model-specific preferences that are not captured by product characteristics.

Suppose each consumer purchases at most one car and that the option of not buying any car yields utility $u_{i\ell}$. Given the above utility function, the likelihood that a consumer of type $i$ buys car $j$ is given by:

$$\mathbb{P}(u_{ij} > u_{i\ell}) \quad \forall \, \ell \neq j$$

where $\mathbb{P}$ denotes probability

---

Estimating the distribution of these utility coefficients can be a difficult endeavor. If we have data on individual purchases, the task is relatively easier: we estimate how each buyer's demographic characteristics influence the buyer's choice of car, and thus estimate the relation between buyer characteristics (e.g., household size) and valuation of product characteristics (e.g., car size). Finally, the distribution of buyer characteristics leads to a distribution of buyer demands for product characteristics.

The task is more complicated when only aggregate market shares are available, but even then we can use product characteristics and average demographics to estimate the desired relation. For example, if average household size is greater in Utah than in Nevada; and if — everything else constant — larger cars are more highly demanded in Utah than in Nevada; then we can infer that, on average, larger households prefer larger cars.

Table 14.2 shows the results of this approach to estimating the demand for automobiles in the US.[4] The second and third columns show the lowest and the highest value of each characteristic found among the 997 models considered. For example, the least powerful car in the sample is the 1985 Plymouth Gran Fury (really!), with 0.170 HP/Weight; whereas the most powerful is the 1989 Porsche 911 Turbo, with 0.948 HP/Weight.

The fourth and fifth columns show the mean and standard deviation of the utility coefficients. Perhaps surprisingly, on average consumers don't put much weight on horse power or fuel efficiency. However, a consumer whose valuation of horse power is one standard deviation above the mean — that is, a consumer with $b_{ih} = 4.628$, where

**Table 14.2** Product characteristics and consumer valuations

| Characteristic | Min $v_{jk}$ | Max $v_{jk}$ | Average $b_{ik}$ | St. Dev. $b_{ik}$ |
|---|---|---|---|---|
| HP/Weight | .170 | .948 | $\approx 0$ | 4.628 |
| Air Cond. | 0 | 1 | 1.521 | 0.619 |
| Miles Per $ | 8.46 | 64.37 | $\approx 0$ | 1.050 |
| Size | .756 | 1.888 | 3.460 | 2.056 |

$h$ refers to horse power — is willing to pay $(.948 - .170) \times 4.628 = \$3,600$ more for a Porsche ($v_h = .948$) than for a Plymouth ($v_h = .170$) *solely on account of horse power*.

If the average value of $b_h$ is close to zero and the standard deviation positive, then for some consumers a higher value of HP/Weight is utility-decreasing — perhaps an overly-concerned parent buying a car for a teenage child. More generally, some product characteristics are widely considered a good thing, whereas for other product characteristics individual perceptions differ radically across consumers — as the saying goes, "there is no accounting for taste."[b] I return to this issue in the next section.

The results also allow us to compare the relative importance of each characteristic. For example, having air-conditioning as a standard feature is worth as much as an additional 1.521/3.460=.44 units of size. (This is approximately the difference in size between a medium-sized car and a small car.)

---

**CHARACTERISTICS APPROACH AND DEMAND CURVE: FORMAL ANALYSIS.** Having estimated the various characteristic utility coefficients, we can now evaluate consumer demand. Specifically, consider the demand of a consumer whose valuations are given by the averages in Table 14.2: 0 for HP/Weight and Miles per $; 1.521 for AC; and 3.46 for size. Suppose such consumers were to compare the Nissan Sentra to the Ford Escort. Neither one has AC; as to size, the Sentra's value is 1.092 and the Escort's 1.116. In this simple case, utility provided by the Sentra is given by $1.092 \times 3.46 = 3.778$, whereas utility provided by the Escort is given by $1.116 \times 3.46 = 3.861$. (I omit the constant term of the utility function; for comparison purposes this makes no difference.)

Suppose, for example, that the value of $\epsilon_{ij}$ in (14.1) has the distribution function $\exp(\exp(\epsilon_{ij}/\sigma))$.[c] Suppose also for simplicity that the Sentra and the Escort are the consumer's only options. Then it can be shown that the Sentra's market share *among consumers with average valuation coefficients* is given by:

$$s_s = \frac{\exp(3.378/\sigma)}{\exp(3.378/\sigma) + \exp(3.861/\sigma)} \qquad \text{(14.2)}$$

If we add up these market shares for all types of consumers (and weigh them by the number of each consumer type), we finally obtain the Sentra's overall market share.

In the process of estimating the distribution of $b_k$ (the consumers' valuation for characteristic $k$) we can also estimate the variance of the random term $\epsilon_{it}$ (measured by $\sigma$).[d] Recall that $\epsilon_{it}$ measures consumer utility that is not explained by measurable product characteristics. As $\sigma \to \infty$, we see from (14.2) that $s_s \to \frac{1}{2}$. This is the case when measurable product characteristics have little to say about market shares (think fine fragrances, for example). At the opposite extreme, as $\sigma \to 0$, even a slight difference in product characteristics swings demand from one product to the other.

---

Finally, the results can be used to produce a matrix of price elasticities for all 997 models. A selection of these is presented in Table 14.3. Not surprisingly, the results indicate that the cross elasticity between the Nissan Sentra and the Ford Escort is greater than the cross elasticity between the Nissan Sentra and the Toyota Lexus. More generally, the

b. For Latin aficionados, *de gustibus non est disputandum*.

c. This is known as the Weibull or type I extreme value distribution.

d. For statistics aficionados: the variance of $\epsilon_{ij}$ is actually given by $\frac{6}{\pi} \sigma^2$, so a higher $\sigma$ means a higher variance.

**TABLE 14.3** Price elasticities of demand for selected auto models

|  | Nissan Sentra | Ford Escort | Toyota Lexus | BMW 735i |
|---|---|---|---|---|
| **Nissan Sentra** | −6.5282 | 0.4544 | 0.0008 | 0.0000 |
| **Ford Escort** | 0.0778 | −6.0309 | 0.0008 | 0.0000 |
| **Toyota Lexus** | 0.0002 | 0.0010 | −3.0847 | 0.0322 |
| **BMW 735i** | 0.0001 | 0.0005 | 0.0926 | −3.5151 |

Notes: (i) quantity change in row, price change in column; (ii) sample includes 77 subcompact and compact

models (including Sentra, Escort); and 24 luxury models (including Lexus, 735i)

characteristics approach provides a quantitative idea of the relevant submarkets within a given market.

## 14.2 COMPETITION WITH DIFFERENTIATED PRODUCTS

In the previous section, I showed how to model and measure consumer demand in a world with differentiated products. The next step is to understand how firms compete in markets with product differentiation. I consider the case when price is the main strategic variable, as in the Bertrand model (cf Section 8.1); differently from the Bertrand model, I assume that the product is not homogeneous, so that it's not enough to price lower than the rival in order to capture all market demand.

This section is essentially divided into two parts, one dealing with vertical differentiation, one with horizontal differentiation. Vertical product differentiation corresponds to the case when consumers unanimously prefer more of a given characteristic (even if the intensity of such preference varies). As an illustration, take the car characteristics example from the previous section (in particular the results presented in Table 14.2). On average, buyers are willing to pay an extra $1,521 for a car with AC. Different buyers differ in how much they would pay for AC (the standard deviation is $619) but most think of AC as a good thing.

By contrast, horizontal differentiation refers to the case when different buyers' preferences for a given characteristic have different signs; that is, some think it's a good thing, some think it's a bad thing. Consider, for example, the horse-power-per-unit-of-weight characteristic. On average buyers do not seem to care about it, but each individual buyer cares a lot: the standard deviation of the coefficient is greater than $4,000 per unit of HP/W, which implies that some buyers like powerful cars whereas some other buyers dislike powerful cars.

The distinction between vertical and horizontal differentiation is far from clear-cut. Let us go back to the AC characteristic: with an average valuation of $1,521 and a standard deviation of valuations of $619, it's unlikely that a buyer have a negative valuation for AC. It is however possible — and maybe even plausible — that a tiny small

Net utility

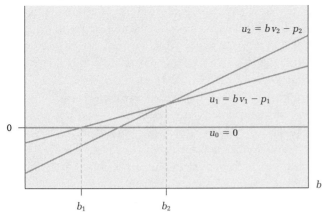

$u_2 = b\,v_2 - p_2$

$u_1 = b\,v_1 - p_1$

$u_0 = 0$

$b$

$b_1$  $b_2$

**FIGURE 14.1**
Demand with vertically-differentiated products

fraction of buyers strictly prefer cars without AC.[e] If you think hard enough you will probably come up with reasons why. Strictly speaking, that would make AC a horizontal differentiation characteristic. However, common sense dictates that we should think of AC as a vertical differentiation characteristic.

■ **VERTICAL PRODUCT DIFFERENTIATION.** The simplest version of the framework considered in the previous section consists of a duopoly where firms offer products that are differentiated according to one characteristic only — for example, car quality, to continue with the example from the previous section.[f] Moreover, *all* consumers agree that more of this characteristic (higher quality) is better — though not all may agree on how much a quality increase is worth in dollar terms.

The timing (the "rules of the game") are similar to the Bertrand model (cf Section 8.1): firms simultaneously set prices $p_i$; consumers choose which firm they want to buy from; and finally firms produce and supply the amount demanded, where each unit costs $c$ to produce.[g] We refer to this model as the model of **vertical product differentiation**, where "vertical" refers to the fact that all agree that a higher value of $v$ implies a better product.

Let $v_j$ $(j = 1, 2)$ be the amount of the relevant characteristic that firm $j$'s car has. For simplicity, I will refer to $v_j$ as $j$'s quality. Without loss of generality, suppose that $v_2 > v_1$ (that is, Firm 2's car is better). Let $b$ be the value (in $) that a given consumer attributes to car quality. Consistent with the previous section, suppose that $b$ varies from consumer to consumer (that is, there is a distribution of values of $b$, possibly correlated with consumer characteristics such as household income). Finally, let $p_i$ be the price set by firm $i$.

Consumers purchase at most one car from one of the firms. There are three possible options: not buying a car, which yields a net utility of $u_0 = 0$; buying a car from Firm 1,

e. If the preference coefficient were normally distributed, than the probability of that happening would be approximately half of a percent. For statistics aficionados: that's the probability of a standardized normal distribution being greater than 1521/619.

f. Alternatively, we can think of the case when there are several characteristics (acceleration, fuel efficiency, etc.), so long as they are correlated across car makes.

g. As we saw in Section 8.3, choosing price as the main strategic variable amounts to assuming that quantities can adjust easily to demand levels; that is, capacity constraints are not very important.

which yields a net utility $u_1 = b\,v_1 - p_1$; or buying a car from Firm 2, which yields a net utility $u_2 = b\,v_2 - p_2$. Notice that $u_0$ is not a function of $b$; by contrast, $u_1$ and $u_2$ are increasing in $b$: consumers who value the relevant characteristic more are willing to pay more for the product in question. However, the rate at which net utility changes with $b$ differs across products: although higher $b$ consumers value cars more, this increase is particularly significant for the higher-quality car (Firm 2's car).

As a result, consumers may be divided into three categories, as shown in Figure 14.1: (i) those with $b < b_1$ prefer not to buy any car, since $u_1 < u_0$ and $u_2 < u_0$; (ii) those with $b > b_1$ and $b < b_2$ prefer to buy from Firm 1, since $u_1 > 0$ and $u_1 > u_2$; (iii) finally, those with $b > b_2$ prefer to buy from Firm 2, since $u_2 > u_0$ and $u_2 > u_1$.

Determining the Nash equilibrium of the model graphically is not as easy as in the Bertrand case (cf Section 8.1). However, Figure 14.1 shows that, unlike the Bertrand case, a small change in price does not imply a big change in demand. Moreover, it is not sufficient for one firm to price lower than its rival for the firm to capture all market demand.

**VERTICAL PRODUCT DIFFERENTIATION: FORMAL ANALYSIS.** Suppose that $b$ is uniformly distributed in the $[\underline{b}, \overline{b}]$ interval. Suppose that $\overline{b}$ is sufficiently high with respect to prices so that all consumers prefer to make a purchase (in terms of Figure 14.1, this means $b_1 < 0$); and that the total number of consumers is given by 1 (one million, for example). In terms of Figure 14.1, Firm 1's demand is given by $b_2$, whereas Firm 2's demand is given by $1 - b_2$. The value of $b_2$ results from solving solving $u_1 = u_2$. This yields:

$$q_1 = b_2 = (p_2 - p_1)/(v_2 - v_1)$$
$$q_2 = 1 - q_1$$

Solving the system of first-order conditions for maximizing $\pi_i = (p_i - c)\,q_i$ we get:

$$\widehat{p}_1 = \tfrac{1}{3}(\overline{b} - 2\,\underline{b})(v_2 - v_1)$$
$$\widehat{p}_2 = \tfrac{1}{3}(2\,\overline{b} - \underline{b})(v_2 - v_1)$$

Substituting in the profit function and simplifying, we get:

$$\widehat{\pi}_1 = \tfrac{1}{9}(\overline{b} - 2\,\underline{b})^2(v_2 - v_1)$$
$$\widehat{\pi}_2 = \tfrac{1}{9}(2\,\overline{b} - \underline{b})^2(v_2 - v_1)$$

There are several things to notice about this model's equilibrium. First, the higher-quality firm sets sets a higher price. This makes sense: we're in the world of value for the money. Second, as mentioned earlier, higher-valuation consumers purchase the higher-quality product: all consumers agree that Firm 2 offers a better product than Firm 1; however, higher valuation consumers are more sensitive to quality changes than lower valuation consumers. In other words, in terms of value for the money, low-valuation and high-valuation consumers reach different conclusions.

■ **PRODUCT POSITIONING.** So far, I assumed that product qualities are given. Suppose however that firms get to choose their product's quality level. Specifically, suppose that

$v_2$ is given and consider Firm 1's choice of quality $v_1$. The model's analytical solution suggests that Firm 1's profit *decreases* as its quality level increases. At first, this seems counterintuitive: all consumers prefer higher-quality to lower-quality products (that is, all consumers agree that more of $v$ is a good thing). However, even if Firm 1 does not need to pay any extra for higher quality, its profits decline as quality increases.

In order to solve this puzzle, it helps to divide the effect of an increase in $v_1$ into two effects: the direct effect and the strategic effect. The **direct effect** of an increase in $v_1$ corresponds to the change in $\pi_1$ that takes place if prices remain constant at their initial equilibrium level. The **strategic effect** corresponds to the effect of the equilibrium price adjustments following an increase in $v_1$.

---

**DIRECT EFFECT AND STRATEGIC EFFECT (CHALLENGING).** Mathematically, the distinction between direct and strategic effect corresponds to the distinction between partial and total derivative:

$$\frac{d\pi_1}{dv_1} = \frac{\partial \pi_1}{\partial v_1} + \frac{\partial \pi_1}{\partial \widehat{p}_1}\frac{d\widehat{p}_1}{dv_1} + \frac{\partial \pi_1}{\partial \widehat{p}_2}\frac{d\widehat{p}_2}{dv_1}$$

$$= \frac{\partial \pi_1}{\partial v_1} + \frac{\partial \pi_1}{\partial \widehat{p}_2}\frac{d\widehat{p}_2}{dv_1}$$

Note that the second term on the right-hand side of the first equation is zero: since $\widehat{p}_1$ is Firm 1's optimal price, it must be that $\partial \pi_1 / \partial \widehat{p}_1 = 0$ (otherwise $\widehat{p}_1$ would not be optimal because the first-order condition would not be satisfied). We are thus left with two terms. The first term, $\partial \pi_1 / \partial v_1$, corresponds to the direct effect and is positive: keeping prices constant, a higher quality $v_1$ leads to a higher profit $\pi_1$. The second term, $(\partial \pi_1 / \partial \widehat{p}_2)(d\widehat{p}_2 / dv_1)$, corresponds to the strategic effect: a higher $v_1$ makes Firm 2 more aggressive, that is, $d\widehat{p}_2 / dv_1 < 0$; and such price cut has a negative impact on Firm 1's profit, that is, $\partial \pi_1 / \partial \widehat{p}_2 < 0$.

---

The intuition that higher quality is better for consumers and thus should also be good for the seller corresponds to a positive direct effect: if prices were to remain constant, Firm 1's profits would increase if its quality were to increase. However, for the lower-quality firm to increase its quality level means to make $v_1$ closer to $v_2$; and the closer $v_1$ and $v_2$ are, the more competitive pricing will be. In the limit when $v_1 = v_2$ we are back to Bertrand competition: firms set prices equal to marginal cost and earn zero profits.

■ **HORIZONTAL DIFFERENTIATION.** Consider a one-mile-long beach with two ice cream vendors, one at each end. Both venders offer the same product, but they offer it at different locations. For this reason, consumers value their ice cream options differently. Since the physical product is the same, consumer choice amounts to comparing price and location.

The situation exemplified by the ice cream example is actually more general. First, it generalizes to any situation wherein sellers and buyers are physically located at different places and a transportation cost must be paid by buyers in order to purchase from a specific seller (gas stations, restaurants, steel mills, etc.). Second, *by analogy*, it also

Price, transportation cost, valuation

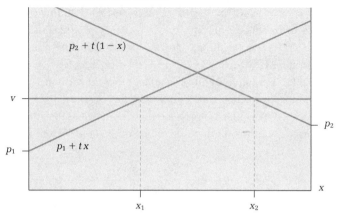

**FIGURE 14.2**
Demand with horizontally-differentiated products

applies to situations wherein sellers offer products which differ according to some characteristic and buyers differ among themselves as to how they value such characteristic.

For example, consider the market for corn flakes and suppose there are two brands which only differ according to sweetness: Brand 1 has no sugar added, whereas Brand 2 has large quantities of sugar added. This is analogous to two sellers at the two ends of a "beach," whereby one end corresponds to minimum sweetness and the other end to maximum sweetness. A consumer's "location" would indicate his or her preference for sweetness. If the consumer is closely located to Brand 1's end of the "beach," then the consumer has a strong preference for no-sugar-added corn flakes. Conversely, a consumer located close to the other end of the "beach" has a sweet tooth. And a consumer located in the middle has a strong preference for corn flakes with some, but not a lot, of sugar added. Finally, the "traveling" or "transportation" cost measures the consumer's aversion to buying something different from his or her optimal degree of sweetness. To summarize: even though we refer to location and transportation costs, the ideas developed in the context of spatial product differentiation can also be applied to differentiation according to some other product characteristic.

Returning to our model, which is known as the **Hotelling model**: the timing (the "rules of the game") are similar to the Bertrand model (cf Section 8.1). Firms simultaneously set prices $p_i$; consumers choose which firm they want to buy from; and finally firms produce and supply the amount demanded, where each unit costs $c$ to produce.

Figure 14.2 illustrates consumer demand. Along the horizontal axis we measure each consumers "address," that is, their preferred product characteristic. Specifically, a consumer of type $x$ has valuation $v$ (the same for all consumers) and must pay a total cost $p_i + t |x - a_i|$, where $p_i$ is firm $i$'s price, $a_i$ firm $i$'s "address" (that is, $a_1 = 0$ and $a_2 = 1$); $|x - a_i|$ is the "distance" between the consumer's preference and the firm's offering; and

$t$ the consumer's "transportation" cost, that is, the drop in utility resulting from one unit of "distance."

Similarly to the case of vertical product differentiation, each consumer chooses the best of three options: not buying from any of the firms, which yields utility zero $u_0 = 0$; or buying from firm $i$ ($i = 1, 2$), which yields utility $v - p_i - t\,|x - a_i|$. As Figure 14.2 suggests, consumers with low values of $x$ (that is, consumers with a relative preference for Firm 1), purchase from Firm 1. In fact, for these consumers (a) $v - p_1 - t\,|x - a_1| > 0$ and (b) $v - p_1 - t\,|x - a_1| > v - p_2 - t\,|x - a_2|$. Similarly, consumers with high values of $x$ (that is, consumers with a relative preference for Firm 2), purchase from Firm 2; and finally, consumers with intermediate values of $x$ don't make any purchase at all.

Similarly to the model of vertical product differentiation, determining the Nash equilibrium of the Hotelling model graphically is not as easy as in the Bertrand case (cf Section 8.1). However, Figure 14.2 shows that, unlike the Bertrand case, a small change in price does not imply a big change in demand. Moreover, it is not sufficient for one firm to price lower than its rival for the firm to capture all market demand.

---

**HORIZONTAL PRODUCT DIFFERENTIATION: FORMAL ANALYSIS.** Suppose $v$ is sufficiently high that a consumer always buys from one of the firms (in terms of Figure 14.2, $x_1 = x_2$). A consumer with address $x$ is indifferent between Firm 1 and Firm 2 if:

$$t x + p_1 = t(1 - x) + p_2$$

Consumers to the left of $x$ buy from Firm 1, whereas those to the right buy from Firm 2. Suppose that consumers are uniformly distributed along the segment $[0,1]$. This implies that Firm 1's demand is simply given by $x$, whereas Firm 2's demand is given by $1 - x$. Solving the above equation with respect to $x$ we get:

$$q_i = \frac{1}{2} + \frac{p_j - p_i}{2t} \tag{14.3}$$

(Check this.) Firm $i$'s profit function is given by:

$$\pi_i = q_i(p_i - c) = \left( \frac{1}{2} + \frac{p_j - p_i}{2t} \right)(p_i - c_i)$$

Taking the derivative with respect to $p_i$ and equating to zero, we get firm $i$'s first-order condition for profit maximization:

$$\left( \frac{1}{2} + \frac{p_j - p_i}{2t} \right) - \frac{1}{2t}(p_i - c) = 0$$

Solving with respect to $p_i$ we get Firm $i$'s best-response mapping:

$$p_i = \tfrac{1}{2}(c_i + t + p_j) \tag{14.4}$$

Suppose that $c_i = c_j$. By symmetry, $p_i = p_j$, and from the above equation:

$$p = c + t \tag{14.5}$$

---

Note that the Bertrand model corresponds to the particular case of the Hotelling model with $t = 0$: when there is no transportation cost, all consumers flock to the seller setting a lower price. More generally, (14.5) suggests that:

> The greater the degree of product differentiation, the greater the degree of market power.

In other words, product differentiation provides a solution to the "Bertrand trap" (cf Section 8.1): in fact, contrary to the prediction of the Bertrand model, price competition does not necessarily lead to pricing at marginal cost level. The latter is only true under the (somewhat extreme) assumptions of homogeneous product, no capacity constraints, and no repeated interaction. In Chapters 8 and 9, we saw that capacity constraints and repeated interaction may imply that firms set prices above marginal cost. We now see that product differentiation is an additional motive for positive equilibrium margins.[h]

Similarly to the case of vertical product differentiation, we can take the analysis one step back to the stage when firms choose their "locations" (that is, the stage of product positioning). Similarly to the case of vertical product differentiation, we can distinguish a direct and a strategic effect of moving one's location to an "address" closer to the center. The direct effect is positive: holding prices fixed, moving closer to the center increases demand and profits. The strategic effect is negative: moving closer to the rival leads the latter to decrease its prices, which in turn decreases a firm's profits.

The precise balance of these effects is likely to depend on each industry's particular circumstances. Consider, for example, retail banking in Europe. Typically, prices (interest rates) are determined at the country level (that is, not at the level of each bank branch). This suggests the strategic effect of moving a branch location is low. As a result, we expect banks to locate their branches close to the center (where demand is higher), even if this implies locating close to other bank branches.[i]

By contrast, suppose that the two ice cream vendors in the one-mile-long beach we considered earlier were to move from the ends of the beach to the center. Since they sell the same product, now that they are located in the same place consumers treat them as the same product; that is, will choose between them solely based on price. As we saw in Section 8.1, this leads to pricing at marginal cost and zero profits. In this setting, we expect competitors to locate far from each other.

> If price competition is very intense, then firms tend to locate far apart (high degree of differentiation). If price competition is not very intense, then firms tend to locate close to each other (low degree of differentiation).

h. However, as we saw in Section 4.3 (monopolistic competition) product differentiation is compatible with zero profits.

i. An additional reason why competitors may locate near each other is that there are demand-side agglomeration economies. I will return to this point in Chapter 16.

Exercise 14.6 considers an application of these principles.

■ **THE MODEL AT WORK: STRATEGIC TRADE POLICY.** In 2005, the US sued the EU before the World Trade Organization (WTO), accusing the Europeans of unlawfully subsidizing Airbus. When making a case of this nature, the plaintiff must argue that there was harm, i.e., that the subsidies by the governments of France, Germany, etc., had a negative impact on Boeing's profitability.

Suppose, for the sake of simplicity, that subsidies to Airbus are given on a per-aircraft basis.[j] Then we can reframe the question as follows: how does Boeing's profit change as Airbus' marginal cost decreases? Figure 14.3 illustrates this case. For simplicity, suppose that Airbus and Boeing (firms $a$ and $b$) compete according to the Hotelling model; that each firm sells one type of plane only; and that initially both firms have the same production cost ($c_a = c_b = c$). It follows that the initial equilibrium is symmetric (point $E_0$ in Figure 14.3), with $p_a^0 = p_b^0$ and $q_a^0 = q_b^0$ (the subscript refers to the firm's identity; the superscript refers to the situation in question, with 0 meaning the initial equilibrium). Now Airbus receives a government subsidy that effectively lowers its marginal cost. The lower a firm's marginal cost, the lower the price it wants to set, everything else equal. In terms of Figure 14.3, this corresponds to a downward shift in Airbus' best-response mapping, from $p_a^{*0}(p_b)$ to $p_a^{*1}(p_b)$.

The shift in Airbus' best-response mapping induces a shift in the equilibrium point, from $E_0$ to $E_1$, with two effects on Boeing: first, reacting to Airbus' more aggressive pricing, Boeing lowers its price as well; and second, to the extent that Boeing lowers its price by less than Airbus ($E_1$ lies below the 45° line), the price difference $p_b - p_a$ increases, which in turn implies a decrease in Boeing's market share. We thus conclude

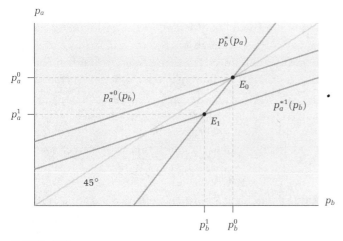

**FIGURE 14.3**
Government subsidies and equilibrium prices

j. In fact, most of the government aid received by Airbus took the form of "launch aid," a sort of insurance mechanism to protect the manufacturer from losses when building a new aircraft. The assumption of per-unit subsidy applies more accurately to the government subsidies received by Boeing.

that Boeing's profit declines as combination of a lower margin (i.e., lower $p_b - c_b$) as well as a lower market share (i.e., lower $q_b$).[k]

---

**THE EFFECT OF GOVERNMENT SUBSIDIES: FORMAL ANALYSIS.** Solving the system (14.4) in the general (asymmetric) case yields:

$$\widehat{p}_i = \tfrac{2}{3} c_i + \tfrac{1}{3} c_j + t$$

(Check this; note that $p = c + t$ is the particular solution when $c_i = c_j$.) Substituting into the profit function and simplifying, we get:

$$\widehat{\pi}_i = \frac{1}{18\,t} \left( 3\,t + c_j - c_i \right)^2$$

Computing the derivative $\partial\,\pi_b / \partial\,c_a$ and *then* substituting $c_a = c_b$, we get:

$$\left. \frac{d\,\widehat{\pi}_b}{d\,c_a} \right|_{c_a\,=\,c_b} = \tfrac{1}{3}$$

In words, for each \$1 of per-unit subsidy that Airbus receives, Boeing's profit declines by \$$\tfrac{1}{3}$. Since Airbus sells $\tfrac{1}{2}$ units, a \$1 of per-unit subsidy implies at total of \$$\tfrac{1}{2}$ in subsidies. If \$$\tfrac{1}{2}$ in subsidies lead to a \$$\tfrac{1}{3}$ decline in profit, we finally conclude that \$1 of subsidies to Airbus implies a \$$\tfrac{2}{3} \approx$ 66 cent loss for Boeing.

---

This Airbus-Boeing case provides an instance of the power of **strategic trade policy**: when oligopoly competitors belong to different countries, import tariffs to foreign competitors or subsidies to domestic competitors may have the effect of increasing the domestic firm's profits at the expense of the foreign firms'.[l]

## 14.3 ADVERTISING AND BRANDING

In Section 14.1, we considered products that are differentiated according to objective, measurable characteristics (house area, car acceleration). By contrast, in this and in the next section we focus on reasons why, from the consumer's perspective, different firms offer different products — even if, "objectively," they are not that different. As the saying goes, "beauty is in the eye of the beholder."

In this section, we focus on advertising, an important component of a firm's strategy in industries such as pharmaceuticals and soft drinks.[m] Some of the topics of interest include the nature and effects of advertising; and its interaction with market competition and market structure.

■ **THE NATURE AND EFFECTS OF ADVERTISING.** Economists classify goods and advertising about goods into different categories. Goods can be search goods or experience goods. A **search good** is one whose features the consumer can ascertain before purchase. For example, the features of a personal computer (microprocessor speed, hard-disk capacity, etc.) can be determined by inspection or by reading the product's literature. An **experience good**, by contrast, is one whose features can only be ascertained upon consumption: no

k. A similar case could be made by Airbus. In fact, within hours of the first WTO case, the EU filed suit against the US claiming harm to Airbus produced by government subsidies to Boeing.

l. In Chapter 8, I consider two other examples in the context of quantity competition (Cournot), namely Exercises 8.13 and 8.14.

m. The pharmaceutical industry is known for its high R&D budgets; but advertising and promotion expenditures are even higher than R&D outlays. To be fair, this depends on how exactly we define advertising and promotion; but it is unquestionable that advertising expenditures play an important role.

matter how much you are told about a given red wine, you won't know how good it is until you smell and taste it.[n]

The distinction between search goods and experience goods leads to a parallel classification of advertising expenditures: **informative advertising** describes the product's existence, its characteristics (e.g., weight, size, speed) and selling terms (e.g., price, financing interest rate); **persuasive advertising**, by contrast, is designed to change consumers' perception about the product's value ("our product tastes better," etc.).[o]

The distinction between information and persuasion is not clear-cut: advertising may be a way of persuading consumers to try an experience good and thus become informed about its qualities. For example, in 1984 Ford Motor Co. financed an advertising campaign consisting of a series of Ford Ranger trucks being thrown out of airplanes or driven off cliffs.[5] The ad carried very little direct information other than announcing the product's existence with an over-the-top campaign. But such "money-burning" strategy may be a way of **signaling** product quality: it's as if the seller's message were, "You should believe us when we tell you this is a high-quality product, one that you should purchase now and continue purchasing in the future; were our product not of high quality, getting you to purchase now would not be worth our while (you would not repeat your purchase); therefore, the mere fact we spent this money should convince you that our product is of high quality."

In practice, most advertising efforts are effective at multiple levels. Take for example eTrade's famous 2000 Super Bowl commercial, featuring a monkey dancing to the tune of "La Cucaracha" and ending with the caption, "Well, we've just wasted two million bucks." Partly this may be a case of signaling as mentioned earlier. Partly it's information about about a new service. Or it may simply be a strategy of running a commercial that is so different from anything else that I and many others still remember it 15 years later.

■ **BRANDING.** The Coca-Cola formula has been one of the world's best-kept secrets since it was first invented by Dr. John Pemberton in 1886. Considering this history, it's unlikely the recipe will be revealed any time soon. But suppose it were: would that make any difference? I suspect it would not: when I drink a can of Coca-Cola I don't simply drink 33ml of a bubbly sweet concoction of darkish color. A can of Coke is much more than a chemical compound: it's a consumption experience. It's a series of memories, of social and psychological associations: it's **branding**.

Examples such as Coca-Cola suggest a different view of advertising: consumers derive utility from a bundle of (a) measurable product characteristics and (b) brand image. In some cases — such as housing or computers — the first component is relatively more important; in other cases — such as soft drinks and fine fragrances — the second component is relatively more important. Advertising expenditures can then be seen as an investment that creates and maintains a stock of goodwill, which we call brand value. Just as building and fixing plants and machines improves a firm's physical capital stock, so TV commercials and other forms of advertising improve a firm's brand; just as the passage of time leads to a decline in the capital stock (through depreciation), so

n. A third category might be that of **credence goods**, when quality cannot be determined even after consumption. Examples include medical and legal services.

o. Exercise 14.8 provides an example of estimating the relative importance of informative and persuasive advertising.

the passage of time leads to a depreciation in brand value (among other things, because consumers forget about the brand).

In Section 14.2, we discussed product positioning in terms of selecting product characteristics. Branding provides an alternative positioning strategy: it defines a series of images and expectations that are "bundled" with a physical product (as in the Coca-Cola example).

Brands may also be associated with an **implicit contract** between buyer and seller. For example, the Hewlett-Packard brand is associated with quality products. In this case, the implicit contract is that HP offers high-quality products; and consumers, expecting to receive high-quality products, pay a high price for what is effectively an experience good (that is, quality can only be observed upon consumption). HP may be tempted to slack off on its effort to provide high-quality products;[p] but branding helps provide the right incentives: were HP not to live up to consumer expectations, it would need to rebuild its brand — or worse still, create a new one.

Branding also helps understand the practice of selling several products under the same name: **umbrella branding** (also known as brand extensions). If brands are bundled with physical products to produce consumer utility, then successful brand extensions should include products that fit. For example, Crest mouthwash and the Häagen Dazs candy bar were judged by consumers as successful hypothetical brand extensions, whereas McDonald's photo processing and Heineken popcorn much less so.[6]

Umbrella branding may also be a way to signal quality. For example, Canon established its reputation as a maker of photographic cameras. In the mid-1970s, it entered into the market for photocopiers. Since what it takes to produce a good camera is similar to what it takes to produce a good photocopier, consumers should expect the quality of a Canon photocopier to be approximately at the level of Canon cameras. In this context, by adding a photocopier to its product portfolio, Canon uses its reputation to profit from the sale of the new product.

■ **ESTIMATING THE VALUE OF ADVERTISING AND BRANDING.** John Wanamaker, one of the pioneers of marketing, once said that, "Half the money I spend on advertising is wasted; the trouble is, I don't know which half." Estimating the effects of advertising is as tricky as estimating consumer demand (cf Section 2.3). The problem is that there are many variables in play; and not all correlations correspond to causal relations. For example, suppose that Mercedes comes out with a fabulous new car model and increases its advertising budget (if you have a great product, you should tell the world about it). That year, we will observe an increase in advertising expenditures as well as an increase in sales. However, most of the sales increase is due to product improvement (causality), not to advertising (mostly correlation).

To put it differently, we must solve the endogeneity problem: in the Mercedes example the change in advertising levels was likely caused by product improvement (that is, the variation was endogenously determined); it follows that the correlation between advertising and sales provides a biased estimate of the effect of advertising on sales (in this case, it would likely overestimate the effect of advertising on sales).

p.  In game-theory terminology, we say there is **moral hazard** on the seller's side.

The solution to this problem is to correlate product sales with variations in advertising levels that are themselves uncorrelated to product-relevant variables. Take for example TV commercials during the Super Bowl, the final game of the US American football season (and the most important TV event of the year). Super Bowl commercials are broadcast nationally, but their local impact depends on local viewership. If the Cleveland Browns are playing in the Super Bowl, then more people watch Super Bowl ads in Cleveland than in the rest of the country. It seems reasonable to assume that this cross-city variation is independent of product characteristics; it thus provides a good setting for estimating the impact of advertising on demand — assuming we also have demand data disaggregated by region.[7] For example, movies advertised during the Super Bowl from 2004–2013 spent an average of $3 million for their ads and saw a 50% increase in opening weekend sales, which corresponds to a rate of return on investment of approximately 3%.

Since brand value results from advertising investment, we may also estimate the impact of brands on demand. In this context, one source of exogenous variation is household migration: it seems reasonable to assume that the decision of moving to a different state is largely independent of the strength of local brands. The identification strategy is then the following: some brands are strong in some cities or states; for example, the Sam Adams beer brand is particularly strong in Boston. We can thus ask the following question: if people who grew up in Boston (and were thus exposed to the Sam Adams brand) move to Denver, do sales of Sam Adams in Denver increase? The answer is that sales do go up, and that the effect is both significant and long-lasting (it is still felt after 40 years or so).[8]

■ **ADVERTISING INTENSITY.** Some industries spend more on advertising than others. For example, in the salt industry, the **advertising-to-revenues ratio** $a/R$ is of the order 0 to .5% ($a$ stands for advertising and $R$ for revenues). For breakfast cereals, by contrast, the ratio falls in the interval 8 to 13%.[9] What determines the advertising intensity of a given firm or industry? It can be shown that a profit-maximizing firm chooses:

$$\frac{a}{R} = \frac{\eta}{-\epsilon} \qquad (14.6)$$

where $\epsilon$ the firm's price elasticity of demand (cf Section 2.2) and:

$$\eta \equiv \frac{dq}{da}\frac{a}{q}$$

is the demand elasticity with respect to advertising expenditures and; that is, $\eta$ measures how much quantity demanded increases (percent wise) when advertising expenditures are increased by 1%. In words, Equation 14.6 states that:

> The advertising to sales ratio is greater the greater the advertising elasticity of demand and the lower the price elasticity of demand (or the greater the price-cost margin).

The last part of the above statement follows from (3.3), the elasticity rule derived in Section 3.2: the optimal price margin (in absolute value) is the inverse of the price elasticity of demand.

---

**ADVERTISING INTENSITY: FORMAL ANALYSIS.** Firm profit is given by:

$$\pi = (p - c)\, q(p, a) - a$$

where $a$ is advertising expenditures and where I note that demand depends on price *and* on advertising expenditures. The first-order condition for an optimal level of $a$ is given by:

$$(p - c)\, \frac{\partial q}{\partial a} = 1$$

Multiplying both sides of the equation by $a/R$, we get:

$$\frac{p - c}{R}\, \frac{\partial q}{\partial a}\, a = \frac{a}{R}$$

Noting that $R = p\, q$ and rearranging terms,

$$\left( \frac{p - c}{p} \right) \left( \frac{\partial q}{\partial a}\, \frac{a}{q} \right) = \frac{a}{R}$$

Finally, equation (14.6) follows from the elasticity rule (3.3).

---

The relation between $a/R$ and the demand elasticities $\eta$ and $\epsilon$ may not be very surprising or particularly illuminating; but it helps answer an important question: how does advertising intensity depend on market structure? At one extreme, as market structure approaches the perfect competition extreme, we expect price elasticity of demand to increase (in absolute value).[q] Based on (14.6), assuming $\eta$ remains approximately constant, we expect advertising intensity to drop to zero; in the perfect-competition limit (commodity markets), firms have no incentive to advertise.

Consider now an increase in the number of competitors from the opposite extreme: monopoly. What effect does this have on the value of $\eta$, the demand elasticity with respect to advertising expenditures? If the primary effect of advertising is to shift market shares across competitors, then we would expect $\eta$ to increase as the number of competitors increases: in the monopoly limit, there is no competition, and thus there is no rival market share to gain by advertising; by contrast, as the number of firms increases, the scope for profitable market-share-stealing advertising increases.

The empirical evidence of many industries suggests an inverse-U shaped relation between market structure and advertising intensity. This seems consistent with the preceding discussion of Equation (14.6): close to the monopoly end of the spectrum, an increase in competition increases firms' incentives to steal market share by means of advertising; close to the perfect competition end of the spectrum, an increase in competition decreases the benefits from advertising, both because margins are lower and because the effect of advertising is primarily to increase rival firms' demand.[r]

■ **ADVERTISING AND PRICE COMPETITION.** How does advertising competition interact with price competition? Consider first the model of horizontal product differentiation presented in Section 14.2. As an illustration, suppose that the product in question is white

q. An alternative way to see this is to recall the elasticity rule (3.3): in equilibrium, a firm's margin is the inverse of the price elasticity of demand. As we approach perfect competition, margins tend to zero and firm-level demand elasticity tends to infinity (in absolute value).

r. If instead of market-share stealing the primary effect of advertising is to increase overall demand, then we have a free-riding problem (cf Section 5.1): advertising increases every firm's demand; and the more firms there are, the more significant the externality is. We would thus expect advertising intensity to decrease as market structure becomes more fragmented. The empirical evidence suggests that, at the monopoly end of market structure, this effect does not outweigh the effect described in the preceding paragraph.

## Box 14.1 Toothpaste wars: why P&G's ad praises archrival colgate[10]

In June 1998, P&G paid for full-page ads in about 100 US newspapers. The ads featured side-by-side comparisons between P&G's Crest MultiCare and Colgate's Total on various toothpaste benefits. Both brands checked on a number of items, such as "helps fight cavities" and "helps brush away plaque." However, when it came to "helps reduce and prevent gingivitis and reduce plaque," only the Colgate Total box was ticked. On the other hand, only Crest's MultiCare checked on "better taste" and "fresher feeling breath."

It is highly unusual for P&G — in fact, for any firm — to cede an advantage to a competitor. P&G asserts that their "policy is to play fair, so our ad did acknowledge the competition's gingivitis claim." However, one can argue that it is in P&G's own interest to act in this way: first, praising the competitor's product makes it more difficult for Colgate to challenge the ad's other claims; and second, one important effect of the ad is to increase the consumers' perception of differences between the two brands, thus softening price competition.

wine; that the only relevant characteristic is sweetness; and that there are two brands: one with minimum sweetness, one with maximum sweetness. If consumers are aware of which brand is which, then in equilibrium firms set prices above marginal cost (and the margin is proportional to the "transportation" cost; that is, the consumer's aversion to a sweetness level different from their favorite level).

Now suppose instead that consumers know that there are two products but do not know which one is which. Although the two wines are objectively different, in the consumers' eyes they are identical. It follows that effectively firms compete as in the Bertrand model, the result being that prices are equal to marginal cost.

In this context, informative advertising — that is, advertising that provides information about product characteristics — softens price competition: the moment consumers perceive the different products as different, firms no longer have the incentive to undercut their rival as when consumers choose solely based on price. An interesting example of this strategy is given by P&G's Crest MultiCare toothpaste advertising campaign; see Box 14.1.

Consider now a different example: it's 3 p.m. on June 6, 2015 when you, an avid Barcelona soccer fan, arrive in Berlin to watch the Champions League final. There is one problem: you still need to buy a ticket; there are two places where you can buy tickets but you don't know how much they are charging; and you only have time to visit one of the ticket stands. In this situation, you might as well select one of the ticket stands at random and pay what you're asked for (up to a limit, say $v$, which is defined by your income and how much of a Barcelona fan you are).

Since last minute fans do not shop, ticket sellers are able to set high prices (perhaps up to $v$) with no fear of losing buyers. Suppose however that ticket sellers advertise their prices at the airport (and there's a penalty for lying, that is, advertising one price and selling for a different price). Then you might as well go and buy the ticket from the cheapest seller. Then we are in a Bertrand-like situation, resulting in prices closer to cost than to buyer valuation.[11]

Empirical evidence from various industries seems consistent with this prediction. As I mentioned before (e.g., Sections 2.3, 9.4, 14.1, and earlier in this section), when it comes to empirical evidence it is important to distinguish correlation from causality. For example, it has been found that prices of eyeglasses are higher in states of the US that forbid price advertising. However, there could be an omitted variable that varies across states and causes both higher prices and the stricter legislation in some states.[12] In this context, a better identification strategy is to examine the **natural experiment** induced by a change in legislation. For example, in 1996 the US Supreme Court overturned a Rhode Island ban on advertising the prices of alcoholic beverages (the 44 Liquormart case). Arguably, the change in legislation came as an exogenous shock to the industry. We can then perform a difference-in-differences analysis to isolate its impact. Using the neighboring state of Massachusetts (where no change in legislation took place) as a control, we ask the question: is there a difference across states in the differences across periods (before and after May 1996) in the prices of alcoholic beverages? The answer is yes, but by a small amount.[13] Specifically, even though prices are lower in states that allow for advertising, the event of allowing for advertising does not seem to imply a significant declines in prices (that is, correlation is not the same as causality). However, following price advertising we do observe a significant shift of customers towards lower-priced stores.

More generally, we conclude that:

> Advertising product characteristics tends to soften price competition. Advertising prices tends to intensify price competition.

The above examples make a series of simplifying assumption. There may be cases when the effect of advertising goes the opposite way. For example, in some countries gas stations are required to post their prices near freeway entrances, so that drivers can be fully informed before deciding where to stop to fill up. The evidence suggests that this practice may have helped gas stations collude on high prices (for a related case, see Box 9.6); so, advertising prices may soften price competition.

## 14.4 CONSUMER BEHAVIOR AND FIRM STRATEGY

In Section 14.3, I showed how advertising may inform consumers about a product's characteristics or indeed change the consumer's perception of a product's characteristics. In this section, I examine additional consumer-related features that may lead to departures from the homogenous-product paradigm.

■ **SEARCH COSTS.** Suppose you decided to buy a new bike: a Schwinn Rocket 7. There are two stores in town that sell this model, but you don't know what prices they charge.

There is no way to find out a seller's price other than actually visiting the store. Visiting a store implies a cost $s$, which we refer to as a **search cost**. Even if the two stores sell exactly the same product, search costs — just like product differentiation — raise the possibility of firms exercising market power.

Specifically, suppose that all consumers value the bike at $v$ and must incur a cost $s$ in order to find a given seller's price. The following is then an equilibrium of the pricing game: (a) both firms charge $v$; (b) each consumer selects one of the stores at random and does not search for a second quote. To check that this is a Nash equilibrium, notice that consumers have no incentive to search: prices are the same in both stores. Firms, in turn, have no incentive to cut prices: consumers do not search, and thus lower prices do not attract more consumers.[14]

Admittedly, this is a rather extreme and simplistic example, but it serves to make the point: if consumers are not informed about prices, then firms are better able to set higher prices without losing customers. In fact, the intuition is the same as in the previous section when we saw that advertising prices tends to intensify price competition.

■ **PRICE DISPERSION.** In the previous model of consumer price search I assumed that all consumers have the same search cost. Consider a slightly more realistic case: some consumers have a search cost $s$, whereas other consumers (shoppers) have no search cost at all. Suppose also that there is a large number of sellers. In this context, the following may be a Nash equilibrium of the pricing game: some firms set a high price and only sell to non-shoppers (that is, consumers with positive search cost); whereas other firms set a low price and sell both to non-shoppers and to shoppers.[15] Low-price sellers have no incentive to increase price as this would imply losing all of the shoppers; and high-price sellers have no incentive to lower price as this would lower the margin without attracting any new shoppers. We thus conclude that heterogeneity of consumer search costs may imply equilibrium **price dispersion**, the situation whereby different firms set different prices for the same product. Exercise 14.7 explores the possibility of equilibria with price dispersion.

■ **SHROUDED ATTRIBUTES AND OBFUSCATION.** As the Internet grew in size, many predicted that e-commerce would bring us into the age of "frictionless" commerce, whereby Bertrand competition would drive the prices of homogenous goods down to marginal cost. The idea is that consumers can easily have access to the prices set by different sellers; and thus choosing the lowest price of a given product on the Internet is an easy task. In other words, search costs should be considerably lower than in the brick-and-mortar world of commerce. However, the evidence suggests that price dispersion in online markets is not very different than offline ones.

Take for example the online segment associated to the price search engine Pricewatch.com: it lists the prices of a large number of small, undifferentiated suppliers of computers and computer parts (as well as other electronics products). Sellers do little or no advertising and receive their customers almost exclusively through the Pricewatch.com search engine. This seems as close to Bertrand competition as one could expect. However, competition patterns are far from those predicted by the Bertrand model. One reason is that sellers engage in **obfuscation** practices, that is, they purposefully make selling terms unclear. At one point in the past, it was not uncommon for firms to announce a super-low price for a certain memory chip, say $1, but then, at the checkout stage, charge a $40 "shipping and handling" fee. Currently Pricewatch.com sets caps on shipping and handling fees, but the page rankings based on price remain less than perfectly clear, making it difficult for consumers to find the actual lowest price. In sum, obfuscation may be interpreted as a seller strategy to increase search costs and thereby soften the degree of price competition.[16]

A related phenomenon is that of **add-on pricing** or **shrouded attributes**: features of a product or of the sales contract that are hidden from a consumer until after purchase takes place. For example, hotels list the price of a one-night stay, but then may also charge for wi-fi access, minibar use, etc.

In some ways, shrouded attributes create a problem similar to the search-cost problem considered earlier: consumers have little incentive to search (all firms charge add-on monopoly prices); and firms have little incentive to lower the price of add-ons (consumers do not search). But now there is a added wrinkle: why don't firms compete in the basic price, which is observed by all consumers? One possible answer is given by adverse selection (cf Section 5.2). Suppose there are two types of shoppers: high value and "cheapskates." As an illustration, suppose that the former are willing to pay $14.99 a night for wi-fi access, whereas the latter are not; moreover, cheapskates are highly sensitive to the base price, whereas high-value consumers are not. In this context, undercutting rivals by offering a lower base price leads to a disproportionate flow of cheapskates, which in turn may lead to lower seller profits (cheapskates tend not to spend on add ons). In sum, add-on pricing may provide an additional mechanism for sellers to soften price competition.[17]

■ **SWITCHING COSTS.** You own a Windows laptop but your Mac OS friends tell you that you should switch. How much will that cost? In addition to the price of a Mac laptop, chances are that additionally you will have to pay for the Mac version of software you were running on your Windows machine — not to mention the cost of learning how to work with a different operating system. The combination of objective and subjective, monetary and non-monetary barriers to change from one brand to another is referred to as a **switching cost**.

The effect of switching costs on product market competition may be divided into two parts. Consider for example the wireless communications market. Due to switching costs, firms may increase prices without losing many of their current customers; we call this the **harvesting effect**. However, when competing for new customers, the expectation of future rents from captive customers leads firms to price more aggressively; we call this the **investment effect**. Which effect dominates? As often is the case in economics the answer is: it depends. If a given industry is dominated by one firm, then the effect of switching costs may be to increase that firm's market power. However, if a given industry is very competitive to begin with — for example, two firms compete head-to-head and hold similar market shares — then the effect of switching costs may be to increase the level of competition.

To recap, we have seen that consumer search costs and switching costs (both of which may be increases as a result of the sellers' strategies) may lead to equilibria with high prices even if, objectively, there isn't much differentiation between sellers. To put it differently,

> When consumers are less than fully rational or perfectly informed, firms may have an opportunity to increase market power.

## 14.5 PUBLIC POLICY

Most chapters of this book conclude with sections devoted to public policy. Typically, the central question is how imperfect competition affects market efficiency; and how government regulation may prevent or remedy the negative effects of market failure. Product differentiation leads to an entirely new area of public policy, namely **consumer protection**. In many ways, competition is the ultimate form of consumer protection; but, as the previous sections suggest, imperfect information about each firm's supply may lead to market power and, more generally, may result in consumer harm. Having said that, neither the diagnosis nor the remedy are clear.

Consider the case of advertising. F. Scott Fitzgerald famously declared that its "constructive contribution to humanity is exactly minus zero," meaning that all that advertising does is to induce **spurious product differentiation**: identical products are perceived by consumers as different. For an economist, this negative verdict is difficult to swallow. First, many times advertising is clearly informative (cf Exercise 14.8). Second, even when advertising falls into the "persuasion" category, a revealed-preference approach to consumption (if you buy $x$ rather than $y$ it's because you prefer $x$ to $y$) would suggest that consumers benefit from the image created by branding (cf Section 14.3). Moreover, the interpretation of advertising as a signal (cf Section 14.3) suggests that seemingly persuasive advertising may actually be informative. Finally, one must consider the interaction between advertising and price competition. For example, if market power is important, then it is likely that equilibrium output falls below optimal output. To the extent that advertising increases consumer demand, advertising may improve allocative efficiency in the output market.[18]

One proposition that economists and policy makers seem to agree on is that advertising should be truthful. Accordingly, an important component of the activity of consumer protection agencies is precisely to enforce truth in advertising. For example, in the US alone, nearly five million consumers are victims of selling schemes of fraudulent weight-loss products; and nearly two million of fraudulent credit card insurance services.

In many cases, judging truth in advertising is not an easy task. For example, online sellers who advertise their price but not their shipping and handling charges may not be lying in the strict sense; but to the extent that shipping and handling charges are orders of magnitude higher than price, their ploy may have an effect that, for all practical purposes, is just like lying: it deceives consumers into believing the seller's total cost is low. The same can be said of add-on pricing policies by hotels, banks, etc. In this context, regulation may be a form of protecting the consumers' interest. For example, online platforms may order sellers by total cost (price plus shipping and handling charges). Another example is given by the Singapore Telecommunications Act of 2000, which requires that hotels price their international phone calls at marginal cost, plus a maximum of 30 Singaporean cents (about 20 cents in US $), thus preventing exploitative add-on pricing by Singaporean hotels.

## SUMMARY

• The greater the degree of product differentiation, the greater the degree of market power. • If price competition is very intense, then firms tend to locate far apart (high degree of differentiation). If price competition is not very intense, then firms tend to locate close to each other (low degree of differentiation). • The advertising to sales ratio is greater the greater the advertising elasticity of demand and the lower the price elasticity of demand (or the greater the price-cost margin). • Advertising product characteristics tends to soften price competition. Advertising prices tends to intensify price competition. • When consumers are less than fully rational or perfectly informed, firms may have an opportunity to increase market power.

## KEY CONCEPTS

• differentiated product • characteristics approach • hedonic prices • vertical product differentiation • direct effect • strategic effect • Hotelling model • strategic trade policy • search good • experience good • credence good • informative advertising • persuasive advertising • signaling • branding • implicit contract • moral hazard • umbrella branding • advertising-to-revenues ratio • natural experiment • search cost • price dispersion • obfuscation • add-on pricing • shrouded attributes • switching cost • harvesting effect • investment effect • consumer protection • spurious product differentiation

## REVIEW AND PRACTICE EXERCISES

■ **14.1. IBM MAINFRAMES.** Empirical evidence suggests that, during the 1970s, a firm with an IBM 1400 was as likely as any other firm to purchase an IBM when making a new purchase, while a firm with an IBM 360 was more likely to purchase an IBM than a firm that did not own an IBM 360. Software for the IBM 1400 could not run on the succeeding generations of IBM models (360, 370, 3000, and 4300), while software for the IBM 360 could run on the 370, 3000, and 4300.[19] How do you interpret these results?

■ **14.2. PRICE DISPERSION.** "Price dispersion is a manifestation — and indeed it is a measure — of ignorance in the market."[20] Do you agree? Compare this explanations with possible alternative explanations for price dispersion.

■ **14.3. UNINFORMATIVE ADVERTISING AND MARKET EFFICIENCY.** Explain how advertising expenditures with no direct informational content can increase market efficiency.

■ **14.4. ADVERTISING AND BRAND SWITCHING.** Empirical evidence suggests that the probability of a household switching to a different brand of breakfast cereal is increasing in the advertising intensity of that brand. However, the effect of advertising is significantly lower for households who have previously tried that brand.[21] What does this suggest about the nature of advertising expenditures (persuasion vs. information)?

■ **14.5. ADVERTISING INTENSITY.** Consider the following industries: pharmaceuticals, cement, perfumes, fast food, compact cars. How would you expect them to be ordered by advertising intensity? Why?

■ **14.6. PRODUCT POSITIONING AND PRICE COMPETITION.** Consider a duopoly where horizontal product differentiation is important. Firms first simultaneously choose their product locations, then simultaneously set prices in an infinite series of periods. Suppose that firms collude in prices in the second stage and anticipate they will do so at the product-positioning stage. In this context, what do you expect the degree of product differentiation to be?[22]

## CHALLENGING EXERCISES

■ **14.7. PRICE COMPETITION WITH SEARCH COSTS.** Twenty-five different stores sell the same product in a given area to a population of 2,000 consumers. Consumers are equally likely to first visit any of the 25 stores. Half of the consumers have no search costs and purchase at the lowest price so long as it is lower than $45. The other half is willing to buy one unit of the product up to a maximum of $70 and must incur a cost of $44 in order to find out about the prices charged by other stores. Each store can sell up to 90 units and has a unit cost of $25.

(a) Show that, in equilibrium, there exist at most two different prices.

(b) Show that, if there exist two different equilibrium prices, then the higher price must be 70.

(c) Show that the following is an equilibrium: five firms set a price of 70 and the remaining 20 firms set a price of 45.

■ **14.8. D EMAND FOR Y OPLAIT YOGURT.** Statistical analysis suggests that the demand for Yoplait 150 yogurt is given by a constant term + 1.85 × advertising exposure − 0.24 × advertising exposure × Number of previous purchases, where "advertising exposure" is the number of 30-second ads for Yoplait 150 observed by each consumer during the week of the shopping trip.[23] How do these results address the debate over persuasion vs. information effects of advertising?

## A PPLIED EXERCISES

■ **14.9. G ASOLINE PRICING.** Collect price data for gasoline sold at different locations around where you live. Use the theoretical framework discussed in this chapter to explain how prices vary by location, additional services offered, population density, etc.

■ **14.10. A DVERTISING CAMPAIGN.** Consider a specific advertising campaign. Based on the discussion in the present chapter, discuss the nature of advertising expenditures (in other words, what theory best explains the motivation and effects of advertising expenditures).

## N OTES

1. The above stylized facts may be found in Ausubel, Lawrence M. (1991), "The Failure of Competition in the Credit Card Market," *American Economic Review* **81**, 50–81, who also suggests additional explanations.

2. Source: Hendel, Ortalo-Magné and Nevo (2009).

3. Hendel, Igal, Aviv Nevo, and François Ortalo-Magné (2009), "The Relative Performance of Real Estate Marketing Platforms: MLS versus FSBOMadison.com," *American Economic Review* **99** (5), 1878–1898.

4. Adapted from Berry, Steven, James Levinsohn, and Ariel Pakes (1995), "Automobile Pries in Market Equilibrium," *Econometrica* **63**, 841–890.

5. See Milgrom, Paul R., and John Roberts (1986), "Price and Advertising Signals of Product Quality," *Journal of Political Economy* **94**, 796–821.

6. David A. Aaker and Kevin Lane Keller (1990), "Consumer Evaluations of Brand Extensions," *Journal of Marketing* **54** (1), 27–41.

7. Hartmann, Wesley R., and Daniel Klapper (2015), "Super Bowl Ads," Stanford and Humbolt Univesities.

8. Bronnenberg, Bart J., Jean-Pierre H. Dubé, and Matthew Gentzkow (2012), "The Evolution of Brand Preferences: Evidence from Consumer Migration," *American Economic Review* **102**, 2472–2508.

9. Source: Sutton, John (1992), *Sunk Costs and Market Structure*, Cambridge, MA: MIT Press.

10. Adapted from *The Wall Street Journal Europe*, June 30, 1998.

11. For a more elaborate argument that price advertising reduces prices, see Butters, Gerard R. (1977), "Equilibrium Distributions of Sales and Advertising Prices," *The Review of Economic Studies* **44**, 465–491.

12. Benham, Lee (1972), "The Effect of Advertising on the Price of Eyeglasses," *Journal of Law and Economics* **15**, 337–352.

13. Milyo, Jeffrey, and Joel Waldfogel (1999), "The Effect of Price Advertising on Prices: Evidence in the Wake of 44 Liquormart," *American Economic Review* **89** (5), 1081–1096.

14. Diamond, Peter (1971), "A Model of Price Adjustment," *Journal of Economic Theory* **3**, 156–168.

15. For a formal derivation of this equilibrium, see Salop, Steven, and Joseph Stiglitz (1976), "Bargains and Ripoffs," *Review of Economic Studies* **44**, 493–510.

16. Ellison, Glenn, and Sara Fisher Ellison (2009), "Search, Obfuscation, and Price Elasticities on the Internet," *Econometrica* **77** (2), 427–452.

17. Ellison, Glenn (2005), "A Model of Add-On Pricing," *The Quarterly Journal of Economics* **120** (2), 585–637.

18. Dixit, Avinash, and Victor Norman (1978), "Advertising and Welfare," *The Bell Journal of Economics* **9**, 1–17.

19. See Greenstein, Shane M. (1993), "Did Installed Base Give an Incumbent Any (Measurable) Advantages in Federal Computer Procurement?," *Rand Journal of Economics* **24**, 19–39.

20. Stigler, George (1961), "The Economics of Information," *Journal of Political Economy* **69**, 213–225.

21. Shum, Matthew (2004), "Does Advertising Overcome Brand Loyalty? Evidence from the Breakfast-Cereals Market," *Journal of Economics and Management Strategy* **13** (2), 241–272.

22. See Friedman, James W., and Jacques-François Thisse (1993), "Partial Collusion Fosters Minimum Product Differentiation," *Rand Journal of Economics* **24**, 631–645.

23. Adapted from Ackerberg, Daniel A. (2001), "Empirically Distinguishing Informative and Prestige Effects of Advertising," *Rand Journal of Economics* **32** (2), 316–333.

# CHAPTER 15

# INNOVATION

Imagine that H. G. Wells' time machine actually works. You are given a $500,000 prize and the option of remaining in current time, 2015, or alternatively traveling to 1815. Were you to decide to move back to 1815, $500,000 would make you a very wealthy person: for example, you would be able to afford a large mansion with many servants. By contrast, $500,000 in 2015 won't get you much of a mansion: at most a very small apartment in London or New York. Does that mean you would be better off by moving the clock back 200 years?

There are many issues involved in the decision of what century to live in. In particular, the set of available goods would normally play an important role. For example, no matter how much money you have in 1815, you won't be able to buy a MP3 player or surf the Internet.

These examples suggest that technical progress — and, more generally, innovation — is an important part of economic development. In Chapter 12, I emphasized the fact that industries change as a result of the entry of new firms and exit of existing ones. In this chapter, by contrast, the emphasis is on the fact that industries change with the introduction of new products and production processes; and on the fact that new products and production processes result to a great extent from firm-level innovation effort.

The economic effect of innovation is usually classified into new products and new production processes. The former is easier to observe and understand: the printing press, the automobile, the smartphone — these and many other new products have changed people's lives radically. But better production processes are also quite important. For example, due to the introduction of the minimill (as well as other factors) the production cost of steel has decreased by about 40% since the 1960s. Finally, many innovations are likely to count both as new products and better production processes; examples include the personal computer and the Internet.

Where do all these wonderful things come from? Partly from firms: Table 15.1 lists the top spenders in research and development (R&D), also indicating the importance of R&D expenditures as a percentage of total sales. At $11.4 billion, Volkswagen's R&D budget is bigger than most if not all universities worldwide. Equally impressive, Intel's investment in R&D exceeds 18% of its revenues. It is also noticeable that the relative importance of R&D expenditures varies considerably across firms and across industries.

From an economics point of view, the values in Table 15.1 suggest a number of interesting questions. Why are R&D expenditures so much higher in some industries than in others? Does industry structure have a significant effect on the extent to which firms innovate? Are today's R&D leaders likely to remain the leaders in the future? More generally, what is the impact of R&D competition on market structure and vice-versa? What role does innovation play in a firm's overall strategy? What is an innovation strategy? How does public policy influence the rate and direction of firms' innovation strategies? These are some of the questions I address in this chapter.

■ **MEASURING INNOVATION.** Einstein said that "not everything that can be counted counts; not everything that counts can be counted." How does this apply to innovation? Can innovation be measured or counted in some meaningful way? Sometimes, there is an obvious dimension over which progress can be measured. Figure 15.1 shows the evolution of computer microprocessor performance over time. The left panel depicts the number of transistors per microprocessor, a measure of technical progress in the design and production of smaller and smaller components. Notice that the vertical axis is measured in logarithms: performance growth over time is so great that it would be difficult to show the values in a linear scale. For example, by 1970 we could fit between $10^3 = 1,000$ and $10^4 = 10,000$ transistors in a microprocessor; by 2015 that number

**TABLE 15.1** The world's 2013 biggest spenders in research and development (in value and as a percentage of sales revenue)[1]

| Firm | $ bn | % | Firm | $ bn | % |
|---|---|---|---|---|---|
| Volkswagen | 11.4 | 4.6 | General Motors | 7.4 | 4.9 |
| Samsung | 10.4 | 5.8 | Google | 6.8 | 13.6 |
| Roche | 10.2 | 21 | Honda | 6.8 | 5.7 |
| Intel | 10.1 | 18.9 | Daimler | 6.6 | 4.5 |
| Microsoft | 9.8 | 13.3 | Sanofi | 6.3 | 14 |
| Toyota | 9.8 | 3.7 | IBM | 6.3 | 6 |
| Novartis | 9.3 | 16.4 | GlaxoSmithKline | 6.3 | 15 |
| Merck | 8.2 | 17.34 | Nokia | 6.1 | 15.7 |
| Pfizer | 7.9 | 13.4 | Panasonic | 6.1 | 6.9 |
| Johnson & Johnson | 7.7 | 11.4 | Sony | 5.7 | 6.9 |

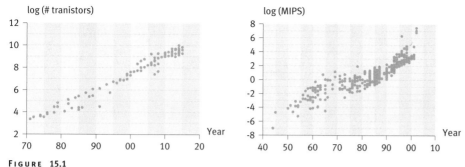

**FIGURE 15.1**
Microprocessor performance over time: number of transistors per microprocessor (left panel) and microprocessor speed (right panel)

is greater than $10^9 = 1,000,000,000$. Similarly impressive numbers are seen in Central Processing Unit (CPU) processing speed (measured in millions of operations per second, or MIPS), shown in the right panel of Figure 15.1.

Alas, for many or most industries no such simple performance measures are available. Moreover, while MIPS is a very objective measure, it is not clear what the *value* of an increase in MIPS is. For these reasons, an alternative way of measuring innovation is to measure the increase in market valuation for the processes, products and services resulting from innovation. Take for example the computed tomography scanner (CTM) industry.[a] Over the 1970s, a number of innovative products and production processes were developed and marketed. By estimating the demand curve for these products (cf Section 2.3) we can also estimate the market value of each innovation; that is, the increase in profits and consumer surplus resulting from the innovation.[2]

---

**VALUE OF INNOVATION.** Suppose that the market demand for a given product is given by $Q = a - p$ (or inverse demand $p = a - Q$), whereas marginal cost is constant at $c$. Let $a_0, c_0, p_0$ be pre-innovation values; and $a_1, c_1, p_1$ the corresponding post-innovation values. The number of firms may be 1 (monopoly) or $n > 1$, in which case we assume that all have the same cost. Then the social value of innovation is given by:

$$\left(\tfrac{1}{2}(a_1 - p_1)^2 + (a_1 - p_1)(p_1 - c_1)\right) - \left(\tfrac{1}{2}(a_0 - p_0)^2 + (a_0 - p_0)(p_0 - c_0)\right) \qquad \textbf{(15.1)}$$

A product-improvement innovation corresponds to $a_1 > a_0$ (higher willingness to pay); a cost-reducing innovation corresponds to $c_1 < c_0$ (lower marginal cost). Exercise 15.3 extends this analysis.

---

Figure 15.2 shows the results of such an exercise. Two time series are plotted: costs and benefits. Costs consist of R&D expenditures in the CTM industry and are measured in the left vertical axis (millions of 1982 US $). Benefits correspond to the

a. A CTM combines a series of X-ray images taken from different angles to produce a 3D image of the scanned object. In medical applications, it allows the user to "see" inside a body.

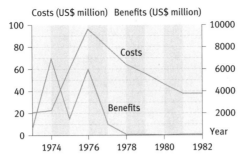

**FIGURE 15.2**
R&D effort and innovation benefits in the computed tomography scanner industry

discounted social value of innovations introduced each year and are measured in the right vertical axis (millions of 1982 US $). The first thing to notice is the enormous difference between costs and benefits: the latter are approximately two orders of magnitude greater than the former (that is, one has to add two zeros for them to be plotted in the same graph): the social benefits from innovation can be very large indeed; the CTM technology, introduced to US hospitals throughout the 1970s, is a case in hand. The second point to notice is that, while beneficial innovations were mostly discovered in the early to mid-1970s, R&D costs remained at a high rate throughout the whole decade and into the 1980s: the relation between inputs and outputs is far from a linear and predictable relationship; uncertainty is part and parcel of the innovation process.

Measuring innovation by market value has its limitations. For example, a new drug that saves millions of lives in poor countries may not have a high market value, but clearly should be considered of enormous social value (see Section 10.4). Moreover, the data requirements for measuring innovation in this way can be quite demanding. For this reason, an alternative solution is to use data on patents: frequently new ideas are patented so as to protect property rights over the innovation in question (cf Section 15.4); a tantalizing possibility is then to count the number of patents as a measure of innovation.

One problem with patent counts is that patent value varies enormously; it is better to weigh the number of patents by some measure of patent value. For example, higher-value patents tend to be cited more often (when filing a patent, applicants must list related patents). Alternatively, one can determine whether each patent in question is renewed: the mere fact that a patent owner renews the patent (at a monetary cost) is a sign that it has monetary value.[3]

Patent data provide an imperfect measure of innovation output. For example, Coca-Cola's famous formula or Google's search algorithm have not been patented: trade secrets provide an alternative path for intellectual property protection. Winston Churchill's famously claimed that "democracy is the worst form of government, except for all the others." All things considered, the same may be said about patents and the measurement of innovation.

# 15.1 MARKET STRUCTURE AND INNOVATION INCENTIVES

In most of the previous chapters, I looked at the causes and consequences of market power. In particular, I examined the consequences of market power in terms of producer's and consumer's surplus. To put it simply, market power implies a loss of allocative and productive efficiency. In this sense, an optimal market structure is one that minimizes the extent of market power: perfect competition (or, absent perfect competition, government regulation that decreases the extent of market power).

When innovation is taken into consideration, allocative and productive efficiency are not the only concerns: which market structure induces the greatest incentives for innovation? Or, to put it somewhat differently: is innovation effort higher in fragmented industries, where each firm is of relatively small size and product market competition is very intense; or, rather, in industries where a few firms command significant market power? One of the great thinkers of the economics of innovation, Joseph Schumpeter, wrote that:

> [Entrepreneurship] replaces today's Pareto optimum with tomorrow's different new thing ... Carrying out innovations is the only function which is fundamental in history.[4]

However, years later he remarked that:

> As soon as we go into the details and inquire into the individual items in which progress was most conspicuous, the trail leads not to the doors of those firms that work under conditions of comparatively free competition but precisely to the doors of the large concerns. ... Perfect competition is not only impossible but inferior, and has no title to being set up as a model of ideal efficiency.[5]

So, which is true: "Schumpeter Mark I," the idea that small entrepreneurs are the main engine of innovation; or "Schumpeter Mark II," the idea that large corporations are responsible for a disproportionate fraction of all innovation?

Had Schumpeter lived for a few decades longer, he would have had the pleasure of confirming his "Schumpeter Mark II" view in examples like AT&T, a monopolist until the 1980s: Bell Labs, AT&T's research branch, were responsible for some of the most important discoveries in the twentieth century, including the transistor and the laser. Table 15.1 suggests that, in today's economy, large firms continue to play a very important role in the overall innovation effort.

However, as we read the biographies of college dropouts such as Bill Gates, Steve Jobs, and Mark Zuckerberg we cannot but appreciate the wisdom of "Schumpeter Mark I" and predict that it's not the large corporation, but the small entrepreneur, working in a garage start-up, who will be responsible for the next big thing.

Empirical evidence from large data sets suggests that the relation between market structure and innovation rates is shaped like an inverted U: innovation rates decline as the industry becomes very close to perfect competition (one end of the inverted U) or very close to monopoly (the other end of the inverted U).[6]

But behind this regularity lies significant variation across industries. Moreover, the one-dimensional characterization of market structure (with monopoly and perfect competition at opposite extremes) hides important characteristics of market structure, of which I stress a few in the next paragraphs.

■ **Creative destruction.** More than perfect competition, "Schumpeter Mark I" corresponds to a world of dynamic competition with some degree of (temporary) market power. Or, to put it the other way around, a form of monopoly that involves some degree of dynamic competition: not competition from currently existing firms, but rather potential competition from new products or production processes that may displace the current monopolist's product or production process. This is, in Schumpeter's words, the process of **creative destruction**. In other words, following Schumpeter, many economists and policy makers subscribe to the view that perfect competition implies efficient resource allocation in a static sense, but that optimality breaks down when one takes dynamic efficiency into consideration. This is not to say that monopoly is the market structure that leads to the highest level of dynamic efficiency. Rather, it implies that the optimal system is one of dynamic competition where, in the short run, there will always be some degree of market power — temporary market power, however.

■ **Dominant firms.** As we look into many innovation-intensive industries, we find that neither monopoly nor perfect competition provide a good characterization. Rather, these industries are characterized by one or two dominant firms that compete with a host of smaller ones. Examples include applications software, smartphones, and online advertising, where dominant firms such as Microsoft, Apple, Google, and Facebook compete with small, highly innovative rivals.

As far as innovation incentives are concerned, is this market structure closer to monopoly, perfect competition or "creative destruction"? Sir Isaac Newton acknowledged that, "if I have seen far, it is by standing on the shoulders of giants." Some commentators claim that, in many high-tech industries, the opposite is true: large, dominant firms benefit from the innovation of smaller start-ups. A very partial list of innovation transfer from start-ups to "giants" includes Google acquiring Applied Semantics (Adsense), Android, and YouTube; Microsoft acquiring Hotmail and Forethought (Powerpoint); Yahoo acquiring Flickr; and Facebook acquiring and Instagram. Is this a good thing?

> In some niches of the software business, Google is casting the same sort of shadow over Silicon Valley that Microsoft once did. "You've got people who don't even feel they can launch a product for fear that Google will get in."[7]

In other words, some view the dominant firm paradigm as that of "giants standing on the shoulders of midgets." However, when it comes to innovation effort by "midgets" (e.g., technology start-ups), it's not clear whether "giants" provide a positive or a negative incentive. Some startups have cashed in billions of dollars when sold to dominant firms. Would they have made the same kind of money if there were no industry "giants"? I return to this issue in the next section when discussing markets for technology.

■ **FIRM SCALE AND SCOPE.** The view that large firms are the main source of R&D and technological progress is primarily based on the observation that large firms have more resources to invest than small firms. But why should size matter? If the gains from innovation for a small firm are very large, why doesn't the firm borrow funds to invest in R&D? The answer is that capital markets are not perfect, especially when it comes to R&D investments. Suppose that a small firm has a great idea but no money to finance it; and a venture capitalist (VC) has money to finance ideas but no ideas. This might seem like a perfect match between supply and demand. The problem is that, in order to convince the VC that the idea is good, the firm needs to reveal it, at the risk of losing the idea without getting the funding.[8] Nondisclosure agreements (NDA) are an attempt to solve this problem, but they seldom work with VCs. By signing an NDA, a VC commits not to disclose or use the information received from the entrepreneur. But many VCs are unwilling to sign such an agreement: they claim they see too many similar ideas every week to have their tongues tied by any single one.[9] And so the problem persists. In fact, this problem is one of the reasons why a large fraction of total R&D investments are self-financed, and indirectly explains why most R&D expenditures originate in large firms. Additional reasons why large firms may be better positioned to perform R&D include economies of scale and economies of scope in performing R&D;[b] and the fact that large firms can more easily spread the risks from large innovation projects.

# 15.2 DIFFUSION OF KNOWLEDGE AND INNOVATIONS

Hybrid corn is one of the greatest agricultural inventions of the twentieth century: the seeds are better at resisting weather and pests, thus allowing farmers to increase yields by an average of 20 %. The first commercial seeds were produced in 1923. However, it took decades for the use of hybrid corn to become generalized. For example, in 1934 less than one-half of 1% of US corn seed was hybrid. By 1944 that percentage had risen to 59%. Nor was the diffusion of hybrid corn uniform in space: the 59% national average (in 1944) masked considerable variation across the country. In the Midwest, the percentage was over 90 %, whereas the South was not reached until years later. Since 1956, with few exceptions virtually all corn planted in the United States has been hybrid corn.

Figure 15.3 shows the penetration rate of hybrid corn in three US states. A common pattern in all three cases is an S-shaped diffusion path: initially, the growth in the number of adopters is rather slow; then it increases very rapidly as penetration rates reach 70 or 80% levels; and then growth rates drop off again. This pattern seems present in many other industries.

In the previous section, I implicitly assumed that, once a firm innovates, its new products are brought to market immediately and adopted by consumers. However, as the hybrid corn example suggests, innovation adoption is far from an instantaneous

b. Regarding economies of scope, one important aspect is that technological advances in one area are frequently used in a different area. A large firm that covers both areas is better positioned to exploit the full benefits from its R&D efforts.

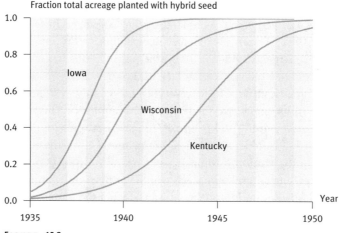

**FIGURE 15.3**
Hybrid corn adoption rate[10]

process. While there are multiple factors that explain the gradual adoption of hybrid corn, adopter heterogeneity seems to have played a central role. All farms are not equal: in particular, they differ in size. If hybrid corn promises a proportional increase in yields and requires the payment of a fixed adoption cost, then larger farms stand to gain more from switching to hybrid corn than smaller ones.[11] As the cost of adopting hybrid corn decreases over time, more and more farms decide that it's time to make the switch, which results in a diffusion path like those in Figure 15.3.

---

**ADOPTER HETEROGENEITY AND DIFFUSION OF INNOVATIONS.** Suppose that the cost of adopting hybrid corn is given by $c_t$. Hybrid corn increases yields by a factor of $\gamma$. For a farm of size $s$ (measured in sales volume), switching to hybrid corn is worthwhile if $\gamma s > c_t$, that is, if the increase in yield is greater than the adoption cost. In other words, all farms of size $s$ greater than the threshold $c_t/\gamma$ adopt hybrid corn. Let $F(s)$ be the cumulative distribution function of $s$, that is, the probability that a given farm's size is lower than $s$. Then the fraction of farms adopting hybrid corn is given by:

$$x_t = 1 - F\left(\frac{c_t}{\gamma}\right) \tag{15.2}$$

If $F(s)$ is a normal (bell-shaped) distribution and if $c_t$ falls over time as a linear function of $t$, then the above equation implies an S-shaped $x_t$ path. Intuitively, when $c_t$ is high, only farms with very large $s$ adopt hybrid corn. Since the normal density function is bell shaped, there are very few such farms, so $x_t$ grows at a slow rate. As the value of $c_t$ decreases to average values, the number of farms crossing the adoption threshold is very large (we are now at the top of the "bell"), so $x_t$ grows at a high rate. Finally, as the value of $c_t$ further decreases, it's now time for the very small farms to adopt hybrid corn. Since there are very few of these, $x_t$ again grows at a slow rate.

---

Now consider a more recent innovation: Gmail. As of June 2012, there were 425 million users, so it's likely you are one of them. You may or may not remember when and why you first created your account, but chances are you heard about Gmail from a colleague, friend, or relative. They probably told you that it works fine and that it's free, whereupon you switched from a previous email provider or added Gmail to your list of email accounts.

In addition to adopter heterogeneity, word-of-mouth communication of this sort can also explain S-shaped diffusion paths. The idea is that, initially, very few people know about Gmail, so the number of "mouths" singing the praises of the new thing is small. Conversely, if most people have adopted Gmail, then there are very few "ears" to hear the praises of Gmail. In both cases, the "word" spreads at a slow pace. By contrast, in the middle section of the diffusion path, many meetings take place where one person knows about Gmail and the other one does not. As a result, we have a diffusion process with slow growth, then fast growth, then slow growth: an S shaped diffusion path.

---

**WORD OF MOUTH AND DIFFUSION OF INNOVATIONS.** Suppose that Gmail is available but very few potential users know about it: at time $t_0$, only a fraction $x_0$ of them. In each period, two email users meet, and one of three things can happen: (a) if one of them has Gmail and the other one does not, then a new user is "converted" to Gmail; (b) if neither of the users who meet know about Gmail, then nothing happens; and (c) if both users already have a Gmail account, then nothing happens.

Let $x_t$ be the fraction of Gmail users at time $t$. It can be shown (Exercise 15.5) that, given the above word-of-mouth process, $x_t$ evolves according to the function:

$$x_t = \frac{1}{1 + \exp\big(-(t-\alpha)\big)} \tag{15.3}$$

where $\alpha = t_0 + \ln(1-x_0) - \ln(x_0)$. Moreover, (15.3) has an S shape very similar to that of (15.2).

---

The above models of innovation diffusion suggest that geography plays a role. In fact, evidence from patent citations confirms that location matters a great deal: for example, citations to US patents are more likely to come from the US, and more likely to come from the same US state as the cited patents; moreover, these effects die out slowly over time.[12] This suggests that knowledge diffuses gradually not only over time but also over space. It also suggests an additional dimension for a firm's innovation strategy: for example, a large pharmaceutical company may benefit from placing labs in different locations so as to gain from local knowledge and technology spillovers.

## 15.3 INNOVATION STRATEGY

Consider the fate of two seemingly equivalent innovative products: Hipstamatic and Instagram.[13] Both began as mobile apps for photo-sharing, video-sharing, and social networking. Basically, you take a picture with your smartphone, apply digital filters to give the image the look of a vintage-camera photo, and then share the final product online with friends. For all the similarities in product design, Hipstamatic and Instagram took very different paths to market. Hipstamatic ("digital photography never looked so analog") was put on sale in the Apple App Store for $1.99. By November 2010, it had sold 1.4 million copies; by January 2012, 4 million. Many app developers would describe this as a success story. By contrast, Instagram — a later comer — was launched in October 2010 as a free app. It rapidly gained popularity: by April 2012, it had more than 100 million active users. That month it was acquired by Facebook for approximately US $1 billion in cash and stock.

The Hipstamatic and Instagram example shows that even very similar ideas may follow very different commercialization strategies. More generally, firms and start-ups must choose their **innovation strategy**.[14] In this section, I consider various factors that influence a firm's innovation strategy, including: the nature of markets for technology; the interplay between market leadership and technology leadership (preemption and replacement effects); the trade-off between risk and return; and the importance of internal organizational.

■ **DEFENSE VERSUS ATTACK.** Imitation is the sincerest form of flattery, so goes the popular saying. If that is the case, then there is a lot of "flattery" in innovative industries: the threat of imitation and rent dissipation is one of the principal challenges facing an innovator. One way to prevent imitation is to follow a strategy of establishing and defending property rights. For example, Microsoft's control over the Windows operating system and many applications built on top of it rests largely on software patents and copyrights.

As an alternative to patenting, a policy of secrecy may do the job as well or even better. In the nineteenth century, several European countries such as Switzerland and Denmark lacked a patent system, but this did not deter many inventors from succeeding: Swiss watch makers, for example, had some of the better inventions (at various world fairs, they would typically dominate the scene). They made sure no one entered their workshops and were very restrictive when hiring apprentices. Watchmakers in other countries attempted to reverse-engineer the Swiss machines, but with no success.[15]

Patents and secrecy have one thing in common: they are strategies for protecting one's intellectual property (IP). But attack may be the best defense: many firms maintain their leadership not so much by protecting their intellectual property as by constantly improving their product offerings and production processes. For example, while Apple owns and enforces its patent portfolio, it may be argued that its business model relies primarily on leading the market with the best combination of quality and innovativeness. Intel, in turn, relies primarily on production efficiency, quickly moving along the microprocessor learning curve. In both cases, success in innovation is more a case of execution than building valuable IP assets.

■ **MARKETS FOR TECHNOLOGY.** Since the 1980s and 1990s we have observed an increasing number of joint ventures, research and development alliances, licensing deals, and other outsourcing arrangements involving firms, universities, and tech start-ups.[16] In other words, we have observed the creation of markets for technology which effectively provide for a "division of labor" between the creation and the deployment of innovation.

The importance of these markets is not uniform across industries. In the biotechnology industry, it is common to observe cooperation between start-up innovators and established firms (innovation for buyout). By contrast, in the electronic industry frequently innovators earn their rents by means of market entry (creative destruction).[17] What makes start-ups take one path or the other? First, a well-functioning market for technology (namely one with well-defined property rights) makes technology transfer a relatively better strategy. Second, if product market entry costs are very high, then technology transfer is again a relatively better strategy. The contrast between biotech and electronics is broadly consistent with this view: software patents are noticeably more vague than biotech patents (a point to which I will return in Section 15.4). Moreover, the costs of bringing a new drug to market are typically higher than the costs of bringing a new electronics product to market.

■ **MARKET LEADERSHIP AND TECHNOLOGY LEADERSHIP.** Consider an industry with technology "leaders" and technology "laggards." Which firms have greater propensity to innovate? Does innovation contribute to the leveling of the field (laggards catching up with leaders), or, on the contrary, is there a force towards **increasing dominance**, whereby leaders tend to solidify their position?

As often is the case in economics, the answer is that "it depends." Consider for example the insulin industry. Advances in biology during the 1970s, in particular the development of "gene-splicing" technology, opened the possibility of producing new medically useful substances. One obvious candidate was insulin, a protein that is used in the treatment and control of diabetes. The US insulin market was then dominated by Eli Lilly & Co. If a new firm were to enter the market with synthetic human insulin, it would be competing against Eli Lilly. As it turned out, it was precisely Eli Lilly that made the greatest effort to secure dominance over the new production process. In May 1996, the pharmaceutical giant convened a conference with experts in recombinant DNA technology to study the possibility of developing the new technology. From then on, Eli Lilly maintained contacts with the various labs working on the project. On August 24, 1978, Genentech finally completed all of the steps required for the synthesis of human insulin (ahead of three other rival labs). One day after Genentech's last experiment, Eli Lilly signed an agreement with the recently formed biotech firm.[18]

Why did Eli Lilly, the technology leader, make a greater effort to innovate (that is, acquire an innovation) than its rivals? Had Pfizer or Merck or another giant pharma bought the synthetic insulin patent, they would need to compete against Eli Lilly. True, synthetic human insulin is vastly superior to animal insulin; nevertheless, the would-be entrant in the insulin industry would not enjoy the same degree of market power that Eli Lilly had before the arrival of synthetic insulin. Now consider Eli Lilly's predicament: the difference between acquiring or not acquiring the synthetic insulin patent is the difference between continuing as a monopolist or becoming a duopolist.

For simplicity, suppose that, had an entrant acquired the patent, Eli Lilly and the entrant would both earn duopoly profits, $\pi^D$. Then the entrant stands to gain $\pi^D$ from acquiring the patent, whereas Eli Lilly stands to lose $\pi^M - \pi^D$ from not acquiring the patent. If $\pi^M > 2\pi^D$ then $\pi^M - \pi^D > \pi^D$, that is, Eli Lilly has more to lose than the rival has to gain. In other words, if total industry profits under duopoly are lower than total industry profits under monopoly ($2\pi^D < \pi^M$), then the monopolist has more to lose from letting go of its position ($\pi^M - \pi^D$) than the entrant has to gain from challenging it ($\pi^D$). This **joint profit effect** (also known as *preemption effect*) implies, in turn, that there is a tendency for the technology leader to maintain its leadership position.

Behavior in the plain-paper copier (PPC) market in the early 1970s illustrates this pattern. Xerox was the leader in the late 1960s: it had invented the plain-paper photocopier and was holding a monopoly position in that market segment. Other firms, most notably IBM, made a significant effort to develop an alternative, or better, technology than Xerox's. However, it was precisely Xerox who invested the most in R&D. See Box 15.1 for details.

But consider now the case of the video game console industry in the late 1980s (see Box 15.2 for details). Nintendo was then the technology and market leader, Sega the laggard. Contrary to the examples considered earlier, in this case it was the laggard who first introduced a new, improved console. Although Nintendo had the possibility of following the same route, the firm decided against it, based on the idea that introducing the better machine would have the effect of eating into their old machine's market share. "The Nintendo philosophy is that we haven't maxed out the 8-bit system yet," said Nintendo. In economics terms, what kept the technology leader from further investment

---

### Box 15.1 Xerox's plain paper copier[19]

One of the great inventions of the 1950s and 1960s was Rank Xerox's technology of electrostatic copying ("xerography"). This technology allowed for copying onto plain paper at a substantially lower cost than photography-based methods. It was also much better in terms of quality than the older technology of "coated paper" copying.

With a view at protecting its near monopoly, Xerox not only patented the process of xerography but also every imaginable feature of its copier technology. As claimed in the suit later filed against it by the SCM Corporation, Xerox maintained a "patent thicket" where some innovations were neither used nor licensed to others. It would appear that the only purpose of these "sleeping patents" was to prevent competitors from inventing a technology similar to Xerox's.

The result was that, when IBM and Litton entered the market in 1972, Xerox sued them under literally hundreds of patents. More than 25% of IBM's R&D budget at the time was devoted to patent counsel, not R&D.

As a result of mounting complaints against Xerox's exclusionary strategy, the Federal Trade Commission eventually ordered Xerox to license its patents to all entrants at nominal cost. Within a few years, prices of plain paper copiers were cut in half. Xerox's market share dropped from 100% in 1972 to less than 50% in 1977.

**BOX 15.2 SEGA VS. NINTENDO**[20]

Video games are a big business. Nintendo, one of the success stories of the 1980s, finished the decade with a market value exceeding Sony's and Nissan's. Nintendo's main product was then an 8-bit machine and a series of games featuring the popular Mario. Sega, although an older firm, was by then a distant second in terms of market share.

Since the late 1980s, Nintendo had been developing a faster, 16-bit machine. Nintendo, however, was not in a hurry to launch the new product: "The Nintendo philosophy is that we haven't maxed out the 8-bit system yet." In fact, by the late 1980s, Nintendo's 8-bit machine was at the peak of its sales. Launching the 16-bit machine might significantly cannibalize the market for the slower system.

Sega did not have to worry about such trade-offs. In October 1988, it introduced its 16-bit Mega Drive home video game system. The advantage of having a more powerful machine is that it allows for better image and sound, as well as the possibility of displaying multilayered images. A better system coupled with aggressive marketing lead Sega to significantly increase its market share during the early 1990s.

Eventually — in September 1991, that is, two years later — Nintendo introduced its own 16-bit machine. A fierce price war ensued, with Nintendo and Sega sharing the market in approximately equal shares.

In the transition from the 8-bit system to the 16-bit system, Nintendo lost its position of near monopoly, having to share the market with Sega. However, it is not clear whether Nintendo could have done better than it did. Although an early launch of the 16-bit system might have protected its market share, it might not have increased the firm's total profits if we include those from sales of 8-bit machines.

was the **replacement effect**, the self-cannibalization that always takes place when a firm introduces a new, improved version of its own product. In this respect, the entrant has nothing to lose, and thus is more likely to innovate.

We can summarize the above results by stating that:

Leading firms have a greater incentive to innovate when the threat of competition by a laggard is high (preemption effect). Otherwise, leading firms have a lower incentive to innovate (replacement effect).

In other words, a technology leader under pressure from entrants will tend to preempt such entry, and in the process reinforce its leadership position. By contrast, a technology leader under little pressure from entrants is more likely to "rest on its laurels" and in the process allow laggards to catch up or even leapfrog.

**PREEMPTION AND REPLACEMENT: FORMAL ANALYSIS.** Consider an industry with a technology leader who must decide how much to invest in innovation. Once that's done, "Nature" decides whether there is a laggard attempting to innovate as well (this happens with probability $\rho$). If there is an active laggard, then the laggard decides how much to invest in innovation.

Innovation proceeds as follows. If only one firm attempts to innovate, then a minimum investment $\alpha$ is required to innovate. If there is more than one firm competing to innovate, then whichever firm invests the most innovates. This can be understood in several ways. One is that there is a patent race and the firm that spends the most reaches a patentable innovation first. Alternatively, we may assume that the innovation already exists and that an auction takes place to decide which firm acquires the innovation.

If the laggard innovates, then laggard and leader both receive market profits $\pi^D$. Otherwise, the leader earns $\pi^M$ and the laggard zero.

As usual, we solve sequential games by looking forward and reasoning backwards (cf Section 7.2). Specifically, the laggard's optimal strategy is as follows: if the leader invests more than $\pi^D$, then drop out; if the leader invests more than $\alpha$ but less than $\pi^D$, then invest a little more than the leader. Finally, if the leader invests less than $\alpha$, then invest $\alpha$.

Moving backward, the leader's optimal strategy is to either invest $\pi^D$, thus inducing the laggard to drop out, or to invest zero. By investing $\pi^D$, the leader guarantees it remains a leader, thus receiving a net payoff of $\pi^M - \pi^D$. By investing zero, the leader expects a payoff of $(1 - \rho)\,\pi^M + \rho\,\pi^D$.

It follows that, (a) if $\rho$ is sufficiently large, then the leader is better off by preempting the laggard's innovation effort and remain a leader if and only if $\pi^M > 2\,\pi^D$; (b) if $\rho$ is sufficiently small, then the leader invests zero and, with probability $\rho$, the rival invests $\alpha$ and innovates. In case (a) the leader preempts the laggard (joint profit effect); in case (b), fear of cannibalization leads the leader not to invest (replacement effect).

■ **ORGANIZATIONAL VS. STRATEGIC CONSIDERATIONS.**[21] The photolithographic alignment industry produces machines that are used by semiconductor manufacturers in the production of DRAMs and other solid-state devices. Over the past decades, the industry has been subject to a fast rate of technical progress. The innovators have been in some cases incumbent firms, in other cases new entrants.

A closer look at the industry reveals some interesting patterns. Although all of the innovations have been gradual from a *market* perspective (i.e., non-innovating incumbents remain active market participants), the same is not true from an *organizational* point of view. Each firm's R&D "production function" consists of a series of capabilities which are best suited for the type of research the firm has conducted in the past. In this organizational sense, some of the innovations in the industry were radical; that is, some of the innovations, if introduced by an incumbent, would imply a significant change in that firm's R&D process and render previous R&D capabilities obsolete. It turns out that all of the radical innovations (in this organizational sense) were introduced by entrants, whereas incumbents mostly introduced gradual innovations (both in the market sense and in the organizational sense). Incumbents did try to invest in more radical innovations, but they were much less successful at this than entrants.

This example suggests a number of observations. First, it suggests that incumbents tend to invest relatively more in gradual innovations, while entrants are the main source of drastic innovations, a prediction that is broadly consistent with the model of **creative destruction**. Second, it shows that there may be a difference between the amount each firm invests in R&D and the actual rate of innovation; in other words, firms may differ in their R&D productivity. Third, and more important, the example suggests that strategic considerations may not be the only driver of R&D and industry structure. In fact, a detailed analysis of the photolithographic alignment industry suggests that **organizational inertia** may be as important or more important than strategic considerations in determining the patterns of R&D investment.

One can find many more examples of incumbent firms that have seen their market position eroded by an innovative entrant. For example, Nokia dominated the smartphone industry until Apple came along; and Netflix overtook Blockbuster in online video-streaming. The reasons for this dynamic turnover are varied, but likely include a combination of investment incentives (as the Nintendo example) and organizational inertia (as in the photolithographic alignment equipment industry).

## 15.4 PUBLIC POLICY

As hinted at the beginning of the chapter, economic growth and welfare result to a great extent from innovation. Not surprisingly, governments are very eager to develop an innovation policy. An obvious way to do so — though not necessarily the most efficient — is to subsidize R&D by firms (and by other institutions, such as universities and research laboratories). In this section, I consider areas of public policy that affect the extent to which firms engage in R&D, including in particular the protection of intellectual property.

■ **INTELLECTUAL PROPERTY (IP) PROTECTION.** The primary purpose of the **patent system** is to reward innovators. However, potentially patents rights may lead to monopoly. As such, patents may imply an efficiency cost: the allocative inefficiency from monopoly pricing. This is the first basic trade-off faced by the policy maker: granting more valuable patents — for example, for a longer period of time — increases innovation incentives, which in the long run results in a higher rate of technical progress. But it may also increase market power, resulting in a lower degree of economic efficiency.[c,d]

In addition to length, there are several dimensions along which patents can be made weaker or stronger. Sections 102 and 103 of the US Patent Code, for example, impose the requirements of **novelty** and **nonobviousness** for a patent application to be accepted. To give a very simplistic example, it would be difficult to obtain a patent on the process of combining tea and ice cubes to produce a refreshing drink (iced tea). In fact, it would be difficult to argue that (a) iced tea is a novel product (after all, it is just tea

c. Exercise 15.6 further expands the discussion of optimal systems for protecting and incentivizing innovation, with a particular focus on the trade-off between length and strength of patent rights.

d. A related instrument for IP protection is copyright. Whereas patents apply to products, processes, substances, and designs, copyrights apply to artistic works and works of authorship, when these are fixed in a tangible medium, such as a book or a computer program. Despite this difference, similar public policy principles apply, including the trade-offs from changing copyright length.

served at a lower temperature) and (b) the production process is not obvious (combining ice with an existing drink is a fairly obvious idea). Aside from extreme examples, there is inevitably room for discretion in determining the extent of the novelty and nonobviousness requirements. Ultimately, it is up to the courts to determine the strength of the protection provided by the system of intellectual property rights. To give an example of actual patent litigation that took place in the 1980s: does a protein produced with recombinant DNA infringe a patent on the same protein produced synthetically?

Innovation is a cumulative process. In this context, one benefit of patents is to make public the state of the art, thus allowing new innovators to build on existing work. However, to the extent that new innovators must pass over the barrier created by the patent they build on, one possible cost is that the patent reduces the incentives for follow-up innovation.

> An optimal patent system balances the benefits from greater innovation incentives against the potential costs of increased market power; and the benefits of disclosing the state of the art against the costs of hindering follow-up innovations.

■ **PATENT THICKETS.** BlackBerry is a smartphone developed by the Canadian firm Research In Motion Limited (RIM). In the early 2000s, RIM sued various companies — including Glenayre Electronics, Good Technology, and Handspring — for patent infringement (mostly patents related to the BlackBerry keyboard). But the opposite was also true: NTP, a Virginia-based patent holding company founded in 1992, sued RIM for violating several of its (NTP's) patents. After a lengthy litigation process, in March 2006 RIM and NTP settled, with RIM paying a lump sum of $612.5 million.

This is not an isolated case: in the 1970s and 1980s, the number of US patent lawsuits hovered around 1,000 per year, but since 1990 it skyrocketed to values as high as 3,000.[22] In some industries, such as telecommunications and computing, the number of patents is so great that it raises a veritable **patent thicket**, a long list of patent rights that those seeking to commercialize a new technology must deal with.[23] The problem is particularly significant when patents are vague (as is frequently the case with software patents), thus creating the danger that new products inadvertently infringe on other patents.

■ **PATENT TROLLS.** As I mentioned earlier, markets for technology establish an efficient "division of labor" between the creation and the implementation of new ideas. Patents play an important role in making these markets possible; thus poorly defined patents lead to poorly performing markets. This may be particularly true in the presence of patent-assertion entities (PAEs), sometimes less politely known as **patent trolls**: these are corporations whose primary assets are patent portfolios and whose primary business model is to generate revenues by licensing and by suing alleged patent infringers. The role played by these entities is rather controversial. On the positive side, PAEs are inter-mediaries that make markets for technology work: they help inventors commercialize their IP. On the negative side, PAEs are responsible for a large share of the enormous increase in patent litigation to which I alluded earlier; and overall this litigation represents a net social loss. Box 15.3 considers one specific example of patent-assertion entities.

■ **PATENT POOLS.** Even if property rights are well defined, licensing markets may lead to inefficient resource allocation. Suppose that producing a new smartphone requires that I license a series of patents. Each patent holder sets a license fee so as to maximize its license revenues. In the process, a negative externality emerges: when an individual patent holder increases its license fee, the smartphone production cost increases; such a cost increase is partly reflected in an increase in the smartphone price, which in turn leads to a drop in demand; and finally to a decrease in the license fees received by other

---

### Box 15.3 Acacia[24]

In 1994 and 1995, two Florida small inventors — Jorge Inga, a surgeon; and Thomas V. Saliga, an engineer — filed two patents related to remotely storing and sharing medical images (patents # 5,321,520 and 5,416,602). In November 2005, the patents were sold to Acacia, the seventh-largest patent-assertion entity in the US (in 2011, it owned 536 patents).

Acacia lost no time in initiating a concerted effort to enforce its newly acquired property rights. It set up a subsidiary, Hospital Systems Corporation; it publicly claimed that its patents covered a very broad scope, including applications software that allow remote users to access image data over the Internet; and in 2007 it launched a lawsuit against major producers of healthcare-related software, including GE, Fujifilm, Siemens, Philips, and McKesson Corp. (later, eight more defendants were added).

The legal proceedings extended for a few years. Eventually, all initial defendants withdrew and signed licensing agreements with Acacia. In the meantime, litigation had a considerable impact on the product market: sales of imaging software by defendants declined from about 1,800 units to about 1,000 units following the onset of litigation. By comparison, rival firms that were not sued by Acacia suffered no drop in sales; nor did the defendants on their related products for which there was no alleged patent infringement.

This drastic drop in sales is likely explained by the drop in incremental innovation by the defendants: no new variations of existing products or new models of imaging software were released during the litigation period. This sudden stop in innovation efforts is likely the result of the chilling effect of litigation, namely the fear of being found guilty of "willful infringement" in the patent suit.

In principle, the above scenario could have taken place with a non-troll patent claimant: Apple, Samsung and many other commercial enterprises also sue for patent infringement. One characteristic that makes corporations like Acacia stand out is that, as a non-practicing entity, their costs of prolonging litigation are likely smaller.

patent holders. As a result, the total license fee is too high and everyone loses in the process. Exercise 15.7 takes a formal approach to this problem, which is reminiscent of the double-marginalization problem considered in Section 13.1.

A **patent pool** may be the solution to this problem. The idea is for the owners of multiple patents to come together and sell their wares in a single package. For example, in the late 1990s various firms were involved in the development of the Digital Video Disk (DVD). Two patent pools were formed (DVD 3C and DVD 6C), both requiring its members to incorporate their new essential patents in the pool. In this way, producers of DVD players had to pay a reasonable, as opposed to an exorbitant, total license fee.

If patent pools solve an externality problem, they may also create their own externality: once a patent pool agreement is signed, the marginal gain from innovating and patenting is shared among all patent pool members, and this is likely to create a free-riding problem. The very first patent pool, the Sewing Machine Combination (1856–1877) illustrates this effect: pool members patented less while the pool was active, and only began to patent more aggressively again after the pool dissolved in 1877.[25] Moreover, there was a divergence of innovation efforts towards inferior technologies that were not covered by the patent pool.[26]

> Poorly defined patents, as well as complex systems of complementary patents, create incentive problems for innovators. Patent pools alleviate some incentive problems but may create additional ones.

■ **Spillovers and R&D agreements.** No man is an island; likewise, no firm performs R&D in isolation: some of the R&D results obtained by individual firms become public knowledge, thus benefiting other firms as well; some other results are leaked out because workers leave the firm to join rival firms, or simply because researchers share their latest achievements at scientific conferences, with little or no concern for the commercial implications of their actions. Whatever the reason may be, patent pools are not the only instance of positive externalities resulting from innovation efforts. Estimates for the US suggest that the gross social rate of return from R&D is about 55%, whereas the private rate of return from R&D is 21%.[27] The latter is still a high rate, but much smaller than the former. At the aggregate level, this gap is estimated to imply a socially optimal level of R&D more than twice as high as the observed level of R&D. In this context, R&D agreements between firms may serve to alleviate the **free-rider problem** associated with public goods.

An additional reason why efficient R&D investment levels may require the cooperation between firms is the sheer size and risk of some R&D projects, like developing a new aircraft, designing a new microchip, or initiating a new line of pharmaceutical research. In these cases, allowing for inter-firm cooperation may be necessary for the research project to be undertaken at all.

The downside is that, as mentioned at the beginning of Chapter 9, whenever firms come together there is always a risk that they will collude in the product market. Even if it starts with a harmless agreement on common R&D investments, soon the exchange may turn into an agreement on pricing or market allocation.

> Interfirm R&D agreements may have the virtue of alleviating the free-rider problem. However, they may also increase the degree of product market collusion.

The latter possibility notwithstanding, public policy towards R&D agreements tends to be far more tolerant than that regarding other inter-firm agreements. As shown in Section 9.5, Paragraph 1 or Article 101 of the Treaty of the European Union prohibits interfirm agreements that distort competition. However, a block exemption was issued in 1984 for agreements pertaining to R&D (Regulation No. 418/85). In the US, the relevant legislation is the National Cooperative Research Act of 1984, which mandates that research agreements, if challenged under US antitrust laws, be judged under a rule of reason (that is, one should investigate whether the alleged restraint of trade was necessary for achieving the ends of the research agreement).

## SUMMARY

• Leading firms have a greater incentive to innovate when the threat of competition by a laggard is high (preemption effect). Otherwise, leading firms have a lower incentive to innovate (replacement effect). • An optimal patent system balances the benefits from greater innovation incentives against the potential costs of increased market power; and the benefits of disclosing the state of the art against the costs of hindering follow-up innovations. • Poorly defined patents, as well as complex systems of complementary patents, create incentive problems for innovators. Patent pools alleviate some incentive problems but may create additional ones. • Interfirm R&D agreements may have the virtue of alleviating the free-rider problem. However, they may also increase the degree of product market collusion.

## KEY CONCEPTS

• creative destruction • innovation strategy • increasing dominance • joint profit effect • replacement effect • creative destruction • organizational inertia • patent system • novelty • nonobviousness • patent thicket • patent troll • patent pool • free-rider problem

## REVIEW AND PRACTICE EXERCISES

■ **15.1. PERFECT COMPETITION AND INNOVATION.** "Perfect competition is not only impossible but inferior, and has no title to being set up as a model of ideal efficiency." Do you agree? Why or why not?

■ **15.2. INNOVATION AND MARKET STRUCTURE.** "R&D competition implies a dynamic system whereby industries tend to become more and more concentrated." Do you agree? Why or why not?

## CHALLENGING EXERCISES

■ **15.3. VALUE OF INNOVATION.** Derive equation (15.1). Assuming that the values of $p_0, p_1$ are set by a profit-maximizing monopolist, show that the value of innovation is greater the greater $a_1$ or the lower $c_1$.

■ **15.4. COST REDUCTION WITH BERTRAND COMPETITION.** Two firms are engaged in Bertrand competition. There are 10,000 people in the population, each of whom is willing to pay at most $10 for at most one unit of the good. Currently, both firms have a constant marginal cost of $5.

(a) What is the equilibrium in this market? What are the firms' profits?

(b) Suppose that one firm can adopt a new technology that lowers its marginal cost to 3. What is the equilibrium now? How much would this firm be willing to pay for this new technology?

(c) Suppose the new technology mentioned in (b) is available to both firms. The cost to a firm of purchasing this technology is 10,000. The game is now played in two stages. First, the firms simultaneously decide whether to adopt the new technology or not. Then, in the second stage, firms set prices simultaneously. Assume that each firm knows whether or not its rival acquired the new technology when choosing its prices. What is (are) the Nash equilibrium (equilibria) of this game?

■ **15.5. WORD-OF-MOUTH DIFFUSION OF INNOVATIONS.** Show that the model of diffusion by word-of-mouth communication implies the adoption path given by (15.3). (Note: this problem is quite challenging, mathematically speaking.)

■ **15.6. STRENGTH AND LENGTH OF PATENT RIGHTS.**[28] Many standardization agreements require that patent holders cross-license their patents on reasonable and non-discriminatory terms (sometimes denoted by the acronyms RAND or FRAND). Suppose consumer demand for a patented innovation is given by $D(p)$. Let $c$ be production cost and $p^M$ monopoly price. Suppose that, if the patent is licensed to a competitor, then firms compete in prices (a la Bertrand), knowing that the second firm's cost includes the per-unit license $f$ to pay the patent holder. Finally, let the patent last for $T$ periods.

(a) Show that, if $f = p^M - c$, then firm profits and consumer welfare are the same with and without patent licensing.

(b) Show that lowering the license fee infinitesimally from $f = p^M - c$ increases consumer welfare without decreasing patent value.

(c) Show that, by decreasing the license fee and increasing patent length, a new patent system can be obtained that provides the same reward to patent holders and makes consumers strictly better off.

(d) What aspects of the innovation reward system may the above analysis miss out (open question)?

■ **15.7. PATENT THICKETS.** Firm X produces a certain smartphone for which market demand is given by $Q = a - p$. Production cost consists of licensing $n$ patents required to produce the gadget. Each patent is owned by a different firm and all license fees $f_i$ are set simultaneously. Given the values of $f_i$ (which we assume are per-unit fees), firm X sets the smartphone price and consumers decide how much to pay.

(a) Show that, in equilibrium, each patent's license fee is given by $f = \frac{a}{n+1}$.

Now suppose that the $n$ patent holders form a pool and jointly set license fees.

(b) Determine the optimal license fees set by the pool.

(c) Show that patent holders, firm $X$ and smartphone buyers are all better off if a patent pool is formed.

## NOTES

1. Source: Strategy and author's calculations.

2. Trajtenberg, Manuel (1989), "The Welfare Analysis of Product Innovations, with an Application to Computed Tomography Scanners," *Journal of Political Economy* **97**, 444–79.

3. Pakes, Ariel (1986), "Patents as Options: Some Estimates of the Value of Holding European Patent Stocks," *Econometrica* **54**, 4755–784.

4. Schumpeter, Joseph (1934), *The Theory of Economic Development*, New York: Harper

5. Schumpeter, Joseph (1942), *Capitalism, Socialism and Democracy*, Cambridge, Mass: Harvard University Press

6. See, for example, Aghion, Philippe, Nick Bloom, Richard Blundell, Rachel Griffith, and Peter Howitt (2005), "Competition and Innovation: An Inverted-U Relationship," *Quarterly Journal of Economics* **120** (2), 701-728.

7. "Microsoft And Google Set to Wage Arms Race," by Steve Lohr and Saul Hansell, *The New York Times*, May 2, 2006.

8. Arrow, Kenneth J (1962), "Economic Welfare and the Allocation of Resources for Invention," in National Bureau of Economic Research, *The Rate and Direction of Inventive Activity*, Princeton: Princeton University Press.

9. *The Wall Street Journal*, November 3, 1999.

10. Griliches, Zvi (1957), "Hybrid Corn: An Exploration of the Economics of Technological Change," *Econometrica* **25**, 501–522. See also Ryan, B., and N. C. Gross (1943), "The Diffusion of Hybrid Seed Corn in Two Iowa Communities," *Rural Sociology* **8**, 15–24

11. For a more complete analysis of the theory of innovation diffusion, see Rogers, E.M. (1962), *The Diffusion of Innovations*, New York: Free Press.

12. Adam B. Jaffe, Manuel Trajtenberg and Rebecca Henderson (1993), "Geographic Localization of Knowledge Spillovers as Evidenced by Patent Citations," *The Quarterly Journal of Economics* **108** (3), 577–598.

13. I thank Joshua Gans for suggesting this example.

14. Gans, Joshua S., and Scott Stern (2003), "The Product Market and the Market for 'Ideas': Commercialization Strategies for Technology Entrepreneurs," *Research Policy* **32** (2), 333–350.

15. Moser, Petra (2005), "How Do Patent Laws Influence Innovation? Evidence from Nineteenth-Century World's Fairs," *American Economic Review* **95** (4), 1214–1236.

16. Arora, Ashish, Andrea Fosfuri, and Alfonso Gambardella (2001), "Markets for Technology and their Implications for Corporate Strategy," *Industrial and Corporate Change* **10** (2), 419-451.

17. Gans, Joshua S., David H. Hsu, and Scott Stern (2002), "When Does Start-Up Innovation Spur the Gale of Creative Destruction?," *RAND Journal of Economics* **33** (4), 571–586.

18. Adapted from Barese, Paul, Adam Brandenbuerger and Vijay Krishna (1992), "The Race to Develop Human Insulin," Harvard Business School Case No. 9-191-121. See also Hall, Stephen S (1987), *Invisible Frontiers: The Race to Synthesize a Human Gene*, New York: Atlantic Monthly Press.

19. Adapted from Bresnahan, Timothy (1985), "Post-Entry Competition in the Plain Paper Copier Market," *American Economic Review* **75**, 15–19.

20. Adapted from Nalebuff, Barry, and Adam Brandemburger (1996), *Co-opetition*, London: Harper Collins Publishers.

21. This subsection is adapted from Henderson, Rebecca (1993), "Underinvestment and Incompetence as Responses to Radical Innovation: Evidence from the Photolithographic Alignment Equipment Industry," *Rand Journal of Economics* **24**, 248–270.

22. Bessen, James, and Michael Meurer, *Patent Failure: How Judges, Bureaucrats, and Lawyers Put Innovators at Risk*, Princeton: Princeton University Press (2008).

23. Shapiro, Carl, "Navigating the Patent Thicket: Cross Licenses, Patent Pools, and Standard Setting," in Jaffe, Lerner and Stern (Eds.), *Innovation Policy and the Economy*, Vol. 1 (2001).

24. Adapted from Tucker, Catherine (2015), "Patent Trolls and Technology Diffusion: The Case of Medical Imaging," Working Paper.

25. Lampe, Ryan, and Petra Moser (2010), "Do Patent Pools Encourage Innovation? Evidence from the Nineteenth-Century Sewing Machine Industry," *The Journal of Economic History* **70** (04), 898–920.

26. Lampe, Ryan, and Petra Moser (2013), "Patent Pools and Innovation in Substitute Technologies: Evidence From the 19th-century Sewing Machine Industry," *RAND Journal of Economics* **44** (4), 757–778.

27. Bloom, Nicholas, Mark Schankerman, and John Van Reenen (2013), "Identifying Technology Spillovers and Product Market Rivalry," *Econometrica* **81** (4), 1347–1393.

28. The following is partly based in Gilbert, Richard, and Carl Shapiro (1990), "Optimal Patent Length and Breath," *Rand Journal of Economics* **21**, 106–112.

# CHAPTER 16

# NETWORKS

For a consumer in the twenty-first, it may be difficult to picture life without telephones (wireless or otherwise). But imagine you live in the 1880s and ask yourself the question: how much would having a telephone be worth? The answer should probably be "not very much," as the number of other telephone owners was then rather small. To take a more recent example, consider electronic mail. Thirty years ago, outside of the military and academic worlds, the benefits of having an email address were not that large, as the number of people with whom one could exchange messages was then rather small. Nowadays, it seems as no one can live without it.

Both of these are examples of **network externalities**: the situation whereby the benefit a consumer derives from owning a product increases when the number of other consumers increases. This is true for both telephones and email. In fact, these two means of communication have one additional aspect in common: both are examples of *direct* network externalities, those that arise when the different buyers form a network of users who communicate with each other.

Direct network externalities are by no means the only relevant instance when consumers care about the number of other consumers. The benefit from buying a Windows-based computer, for example, is greater the greater the number of other buyers of the same operating system: even if a computer user does not directly communicate with others, the fact that there are many of them implies that a great variety of software will be written for the popular operating system. We then say that Windows users benefit from *indirect* network externalities resulting from there being other Windows users.[a]

In this chapter, I look at a number of issues related to competition with network externalities (also referred to as network effects). In Section 16.1, I show that an important implication of network externalities is the possibility of multiple equilibria ("everybody uses Windows because everybody uses Windows," but the opposite would also be

a. Network externalities can also be created by firm pricing. For example, if a cell phone company charges more for calls made to or from outside their network, then a consumer is better off when he or she belongs to a large network, since most of his or her calls will then made within the network, at a lower price. This type of network externalities is known as *tariff-mediated* network externalities.

possible: "nobody uses Windows because nobody uses Windows"). Next I consider various implications of equilibrium multiplicity for the process of adoption of innovations with network effects; this will leads us to concepts such as critical mass, excess inertia, excess momentum, and path dependence. Finally, Sections 16.3 and 16.4 are devoted to firm strategy and public policy, respectively, in the presence of network externalities.

■ **ESTIMATING NETWORK EFFECTS.** Before continuing with the economic analysis of the nature and implications of network effects, it is worth addressing the question of their actual importance in reality. Throughout this book, I have emphasized the difficulty of statistical identification from economics data. The world is full of correlations; some of these correspond to causal effects, most do not. The quest for network effects is no exception; in fact, in some sense estimating direct or indirect network effects is a particularly difficult task.

Suppose that we have time series data on, for example, the number of fax machine users. Suppose moreover that potential adopters estimate network size by finding out the latest published figures (e.g., number of fax machine users in the previous period). We could then estimate an equation of the form $q_t = f(q_{t-1}, p_t, z_t)$, where $p_t$ denotes price and $z_t$ other variables. To the extent that $q_t$ is positively associated to $q_{t-1}$, we might be tempted to conclude network effects are present. The problem with this approach is that there may be unobserved variables (e.g., income) that push $q_t$ and $q_{t-1}$ in the same direction, thus creating a correlation that does not correspond to causality. As much as we try to include these variables in $z_t$, we can never be sure we are not leaving out unobserved sources of correlation (which does not correspond to causality).

Alternatively, we might look for cross-section data. For example, based on data from 110,000 US households in 1997, it is estimated that households are more likely to buy their first home computer in areas where a high fraction of households already own computers. Again, one limitation of this approach is that we may be measuring a correlation, not a causality relation.

A preferred approach is to study what researchers refer to as a "natural experiment." Consider the case the automated clearinghouse (ACH) system used for interbank payments. This system is more efficient that alternative systems, but it requires both payer and payee to acquire the necessary technology. For large US banks, the decision to adopt ACH is taken nationwide; that is, once the technology is adopted, all branches start using it. At the level of small, isolated geographical markets, it seems reasonable to consider the number of nationwide banks using ACH to be an exogenous variable; we can thus look for a causal relation with greater assurance. Specifically, if network effects are important, then we expect small local banks to be more likely to adopt ACH if their neighboring branches do so. The data suggests this is indeed the case: for instance, if a small local bank has an adoption probability of 50%, then an increase of 10 percentage points in the fraction of neighboring banks using ACH raises the small bank's adoption probability by 4.4 percentage points.

## 16.1 CHICKEN AND EGG

Long before Darwin, ancient philosophers such as Aristotle debated the question of whether there was a first chicken or a first egg. The modern-day version of the puzzle is given by social interaction, such as an online network or a night club. The famous American baseball player Yogi Berra, when asked why he no longer went to Ruggeri's (a St. Louis restaurant), is reported to have replied, "Nobody goes there anymore; it's too crowded." Yogism aside, the fact is that many people like going to restaurants precisely because there are other people at the restaurant. The complaint should therefore be, "Nobody wants to go there because it's always empty," or "Everybody wants to go there because it's always full of people."

Before going through the complicated case of demand interdependent systems, consider the simpler case of a "normal" demand curve, as depicted by the thin, straight line in Figure 16.1: a lower price attracts more consumers; and for each price there exists a unique number of consumers who would be willing to purchase. In this case, we are faced with a well-known pricing dilemma: the higher a firm's price, the higher its margin, but the less it sells. This is a non-trivial problem, but nevertheless one that can be solved analytically — which I did, in Section 3.2.

Consider now the case when a consumer's valuation depends on his or her expectation of how many other consumers will make a purchase. If the network externality is sufficiently strong, then the demand curve may look like the thick line in Figure 16.1. From a pricing point of view, the seller is faced with a **chicken-and-egg** problem. Let us continue with the restaurant example. Figure 16.1 implies that, if price is very high — specifically, higher than $\phi$ — then no consumer wants to come to the restaurant. In this sense, the demand curve is like a "normal" demand curve: high prices choke demand

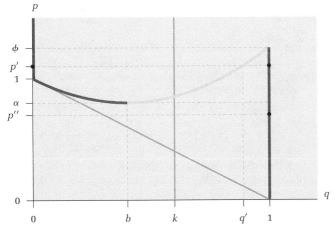

**FIGURE 16.1**
Pricing with network effects

down to zero. By contrast, if price is very low — specifically, lower than $\alpha$ — then all of the potential consumers want to be at the restaurant. Again, this is similar to a "normal" demand curve: for sufficiently low prices, all consumers demand the product. (In this figure, I assume that the maximum demand is given by 1, for example 1 hundred.)

The interesting portion of the demand curve corresponds to the case when price is greater than $\alpha$ but lower than $\phi$. For example, if price is $p'$ then there are at least two possibilities: nobody comes to the restaurant $(q = 0)$ or everybody comes to the restaurant $(q = 1)$.[b] In other words, either "nobody wants to go there because it's always empty" or "everybody wants to go there because it's always full of people."

---

**CHICKEN AND EGG: ANALYTICAL SOLUTION.** Suppose a consumer values the restaurant at $v = u + \phi\, e^2$, where $u$ is is uniformly distributed in $[0,1]$ and $e$ is the consumer's expectation regarding the total number of other restaurant patrons. Notice that if a consumer with $u = u'$ decides to go to the restaurant, then a consumer with $u = u'' > u'$ and the same expectation $e$ also decides to go to the restaurant. Let $u'$ be the lowest value of $u$ among the consumers who go to the restaurant. Then $1 - u'$ consumers go to the restaurant. In equilibrium, consumer expectations must be fulfilled. Therefore, it must be $e = 1 - u'$. Moreover, the consumer with $u = u'$ must be exactly indifferent between going to the restaurant and staying home. Therefore, $u' + \phi\, e^2 = p$, or $u' + \phi\, (1 - u')^2 = p$. Since the value of $q$ corresponds to all consumers with $u > u'$, we have $q = 1 - u'$. Hence, the above equation becomes:

$$p = 1 - q + \phi\, q^2$$

Consider first the case when $\phi = 0$, that is, network externalities are zero. Then the above equation becomes $p = 1 - q$. This is a simple inverse demand curve like the ones we encountered numerous times in previous chapters. In this case, for each value of $p$ there exists one value of $q$ demanded; and the lower $p$ is, the greater $q$ is.

Things get a lot more exciting when $\phi > 0$, especially when $\phi$ is very high. This is the case when people like going to the restaurant primarily because other people go to the restaurant as well. I will next show that a high value of $\phi$ leads to a "chicken-and-egg" problem, where, for a given price level, there exist multiple equilibrium values of the number of restaurant patrons.

First notice that, if $p > 1$, then there exists an equilibrium such that no one goes to the restaurant. In fact, given the expectation that no one goes to the restaurant, the benefit from going to the restaurant is given by $u$; and even the consumer with the highest $u$ $(u = 1)$ would then prefer not to go to the restaurant.

Next notice that, if $p < \phi$, then there exists an equilibrium whereby everyone goes to the restaurant. In fact, if $q = 1$, then the benefit from going to the restaurant is given by $u + \phi$. Even the consumer with the lowest interest in the restaurant $(u = 0)$ would have a utility $\phi$ from going to the restaurant; and this is greater than price.

It follows that, if price falls between 1 and $\phi$ (assuming $\phi > 1$), there exist two equilibria, one where no one goes to the restaurant and one where everyone

b. There is also a third possibility, which I will ignore for the time being.

goes to the restaurant. In fact, as Figure 16.1 shows, even for values of $\phi$ less than 1 but high enough we find two equilibria, one with $q = 1$ and one with $q$ along the downward sloping portion of the demand curve.

---

It makes a big difference which equilibrium is selected: for the restaurant owner, it's the difference between making a lot of money and making no money at all. Which equilibrium plays out in practice depends largely on **consumer expectations**: if consumers expect the restaurant to be empty, then it will be empty; if consumers expect the restaurant to be full, then full it will be. Considering the importance of expectations, these equilibria are frequently referred to as **fulfilled-expectations equilibrium**.

> Network effects may imply multiple demand levels for a given price. Which value takes place depends on consumers' expectations regarding network size.

What if consumers have intermediate expectations? In principle, it would be possible for a point like $(q', p')$ in Figure 16.1 to be an equilibrium: if exactly $q'$ consumers go to the restaurant, and if consumers expect that exactly $q'$ consumers will go to the restaurant, then exactly $q'$ consumers are willing to pay $p'$ or more for the restaurant's services. However, such an equilibrium would be unstable, in the following sense: if expectations were to become ever so slightly more favorable, then more consumers would visit the restaurant, which in turn would shift consumer expectations positively, which in turn would attract more consumers, and so on, until we converge to the equilibrium where everyone wants to go to the restaurant. A similar argument would apply to a negative shock to expectations: if expectations were to become ever so slightly less favorable, then fewer consumers would visit the restaurant, which in turn would shift consumer expectations negatively, which in turn would attract fewer consumers, and so on, until we converge to the equilibrium where no one wants to go to the restaurant.

Whenever there are multiple equilibria, simple economic models like the one I just presented have little to say as to which one is more likely to take place. Frequently, the actual outcome results from additional factors, such as what happened in the recent past. Box 16.1 describes an example where, arguably, the market switched from one equilibrium ("very few traders trade at DTB because very few traders trade at DTB") to another one ("everyone trades at DTB because everyone trades at DTB"). In the next sections, I will present other examples.

Equilibrium multiplicity also gives rise to difficult pricing problems. Suppose that the restaurant in Figure 16.1 is currently setting $p = p'$ and that the restaurant is full. As the figure shows, there are higher values of $p$ such that a full restaurant is still an equilibrium. However, at these price levels a full restaurant is not the only equilibrium: an empty restaurant is also an equilibrium. You can see how a prudent restaurant owner might resist the temptation to increase prices when business is going well: there

**BOX 16.1 THE BATTLE OF THE BUND[1]**

The London International Financial Futures and Options Exchange (LIFFE) was established in 1982 as a member-owned derivatives exchange. In September 1988, future contracts on the Bund (German government bonds) began trading on LIFFE. It was a major success: in little over a year, the Bund was LIFFE's top contract.

Deutsche Terminbörse (DTB), based in Frankfurt, was established in January 1990, and during the same year a Bund contract — essentially identical to the LIFFE contract — began trading. Leading German banks with a stake in DTB signed a gentlemen's agreement whereby they committed to support liquidity on DTB; as a result, by mid-1991 DTB's market share climbed to almost 30%.

One obstacle that DTB faced in attracting non-German traders was to be recognized as an exchange abroad. This effort received a major boost in 1996, when the European Union approved the Investment Services Directive. This new regulation implied that any exchange and investment firm authorized and regulated in one of the European Union countries would be recognized and authorized in all the other countries.

The battle front opened up. LIFFE and DTB intensified their fight on several dimensions, including trading support services, advertising, and pricing (for a while both exchanges waived their fees). DTB's share of the Bund trading, which had remained virtually unchanged at 30% since 1991, gradually increased. Then things moved very fast, and within weeks LIFFE had completely lost the Bund.

One possible story to explain these market dynamics is that traders demand liquidity and low trading costs. Until 1996, DTB had lower costs but LIFFE higher liquidity. As the market share of DTB increased, so did the liquidity it offered. This induced a "snowball" type of dynamics whereby the bigger DTB grew the more attractive it became, eventually leading to the 1997 "tipping point.'

is some potential gain from more expensive entrées, but there is also a large potential loss, namely, that we switch to the empty-restaurant equilibrium.

One additional note regarding the restaurant problem: if capacity happens to be smaller than the number of potential patrons, then the "good" equilibrium implies that some consumers cannot be served, or at least need to line outside waiting for a chance to get in. Again, a prudent restaurant owner might resist the temptation to increase capacity: there is a potential gain but there is also a large potential loss from "rocking the boat." In fact, a line of customers waiting outside may be the best way to persuade consumers that the equilibrium being played is the full-restaurant equilibrium.

# 16.2 INNOVATION ADOPTION WITH NETWORK EFFECTS

In the previous section, I proposed the restaurant problem as an instance of the chicken-and-egg puzzle. For $p = p'$ in Figure 16.1, both $q = 0$ and $q = 1$ are equilibrium numbers of consumers. I showed that, strictly speaking, $q = q'$ is also an equilibrium, albeit an unstable one. In fact, the number $q'$ may be referred to as the **critical mass** of consumers required for a full-restaurant equilibrium to unfold: beginning from $q < q'$ and following the process of adaptive expectations I described earlier (that is, at each moment consumers form their belief of future values of $q$ based on the current value of $q$) we end up with an empty restaurant; whereas, beginning with $q > q'$, we end up with a full restaurant.

The concept of critical mass is particularly important to understand adoption of innovations subject to network effects. In Section 15.2, I proposed two alternative theories to explain the S-shaped diffusion of innovations: one, based on adopter heterogeneity, explains examples such as the diffusion of hybrid corn in the US; another one, based on word-of-mouth effects, seems best fitted to examples such as the diffusion of Google mail throughout the world. The diffusion of innovations with network effects raises additional issues not considered in these models. Consider, for example, the diffusion of fax machines in the US, the path of which is depicted in Figure 16.2. The facsimile technology (fax for short) has been known for many decades. However, until the early 1980s there were virtually no adopters of this communications device. This was partly due to unreliable technology, partly due to confusing communication protocols, and especially due to the high price of fax machines. All of these got better over time. By the early 1990s, most corporations and many households could afford — and did afford — a fax machine. The interesting question is: how did we get from point A to point B?

If network effects are very strong, then, as Figure 16.1 suggests, for intermediate values of $p$ we have three possible equilibria, one of which (the intermediate one) is unstable (as I argued in the previous section). The $\psi(t)$ line in Figure 16.2 depicts the possible equilibrium values of the market penetration of fax machines. This line has a similar shape to the demand curve in Figure 16.1 (notice however that I now measure quantity on the vertical axis, whereas the horizontal axis, to the extent that price decreases over time, measure price in the inverse direction).

From Figure 16.2, we conclude that for $t < t_1$ there is only one equilibrium with low adoption rate; for $t > t_2$ again there is only one equilibrium, this time with a high adoption rate; and for $t_1 < t < t_2$ we can have either a low or a high adoption rate. For example, if $t = t'$, then both $x = x'$ and $x = x''$ and equilibrium levels of adoption. The

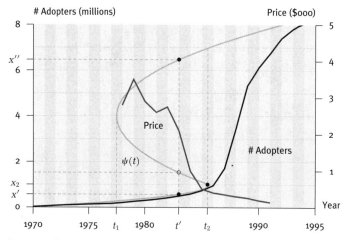

**FIGURE 16.2**
Critical mass in new-technology adoption[2]

overall adoption path depends on how the chicken-and-egg equilibrium multiplicity unfolds.

---

**CRITICAL MASS: FORMAL ANALYSIS.** Suppose that the benefit of adoption is given by $u + \phi(x)$, where $u$ is distributed according to the cumulative distribution function $F(u)$. The cost from adoption, in turn, is given by $p(t)$.

Let $A$ be the total number of potential adopters and $x(t)$ the number of adopters by time $t$. Similarly to the derivation of Figure 16.1, if a user with utility $u'$ adopts, then all users with $u > u'$ and the same beliefs about adoption rates must also adopt.

Specifically, let $u'$ be the "stand-alone" valuation of the user who is just indifferent between adopting and not adopting at time $t$.[c] It follows that:

$$u' + \phi\left(x(t)\right) = p(t)$$
$$x(t) = A\left(1 - F(u')\right)$$

The first equation indicates that user $u'$ is indifferent (benefit equals cost). The second equation indicates that the number of adopters is given by all adopters with $u > u'$. Together, these two equations define the correspondence $\phi$ which gives equilibrium values of $x$ for each $t$.

If $u$ is uniformly distributed, $\phi$ is linear, and $p$ declines linearly over time, then $\psi$ has a shape similar to the demand curve in Figure 16.1 (once we flit it around to account for the fact quantity is now on the vertical axis and price declines from left to right on the horizontal axis). If the distribution of $u$ is smoother than the uniform (e.g., bell-shaped as a normal distribution) and if $\phi$ is sufficiently high, then $\psi$ has a shape similar to what appears in Figure 16.2.

---

c. By stand-alone valuation I mean the part of the user's valuation that is independent of the number of other users.

Suppose that adopters form their beliefs regarding adoption rates based on what they observe at the time adoption decisions are made (or, for practical purposes, the period before). Then the adoption path will proceed along the lower branch of the $\psi$ curve until $t = t_2$ arrives. At this time, the adoption rate "jumps" to the high portion of the $\psi$ curve. In practice, this jump from low to high adoption rates is unlikely to take place instantaneously. Rather, it will look like a very steep S (similarly to the adoption paths in Section 15.2 but for different reasons). In this context, the adoption rate at $t = t_2$ corresponds to the critical mass which I referred to earlier.[d]

■ **EXCESS INERTIA AND EXCESS MOMENTUM.** As I mentioned when discussing Figure 16.2, as far as equilibrium analysis goes, a switch from low to high adoption rates can take place anytime between $t_1$ and $t_2$. In this context, the question may be asked: does equilibrium adoption take place too early or too late (by social welfare standards)? Consider the simultaneous-move game depicted in Figure 16.3. User 1 and User 2 must decide whether to choose an old version or a new version of a given technology. The technology is subject to network effects; specifically, each version is useless unless the other player chooses the same version. If both players choose the old version, then they get positive payoffs $(a_1, a_2)$. If one player chooses $N$ while the other player choose $O$, then the player choosing $N$ receives $-c_i$, whereas the player choosing $O$ receives zero. The idea is that both players already paid the old version's adoption costs but not the new one's, so that choosing $N$ implies an additional cost $c_i$. Finally, if both players choose $N$, then they get $(b_1 - c_1, b_2 - c_2)$.

Suppose that $a_i, b_i, c_i > 0$ and that moreover $b_i - c_i > 0$. Then there are two Nash equilibria: one where both players choose $O$, and one where both players choose $N$. So far, this looks very much like the chicken-and-egg problem we've been considering in this and in the previous section. This time, however, I will compare the equilibrium in terms of player utility.

If $b_i - c_i > a_i$, then we say that the $(N, N)$ equilibrium is Pareto superior to the $(O, O)$ equilibrium; that is, both players prefer the equilibrium where both choose the new version. However, there is no unequivocal game theoretic argument to suggest that the $(N, N)$ equilibrium will play out, or that it is more likely to play out. In fact, suppose that $b_i = 2 c_i$ and that $c_i$ is very large. Then, switching from $O$ to $N$ is like a "lottery"

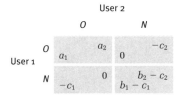

**FIGURE 16.3**
Simultaneous technology adoption decisions

d. For math aficionados: points such as $(t_2, x_2)$ are sometimes called *catastrophe points* of the mapping $\psi$, a reference to the fact that a very small change in $t$ corresponds to a very large change in $x_t$.

whereby player $i$ can either receive $-c_i$ or $+c_i$ (depending on whether the other player chooses $O$ or $N$). By contrast, sticking to $O$ guarantees the player a minimum payoff of zero. You can see how players might prefer to stay put even if the upside from adopting the new technology version is quite high.

Were that to happen, we would have a case of **excess inertia**: although the new-technology equilibrium is Pareto superior, both players stick to the old technology. The switch from AM to FM broadcasting in the late 1940s, which I describe in Box 16.2, provides an example. Most people saw FM as a superior technology. However, fear of getting stranded with a useless (and expensive) FM receiver kept consumers from making the switch, which in turn kept broadcasters from making the switch, which in turn kept manufacturers from making the switch. A similar failure to move to a superior

---

### Box 16.2 AM vs. FM[3]

In 1945, Paul W. Kesten, then Executive Vice President of Columbia Broadcasting Systems, wrote:

> I believe that FM is not merely one aspect of the future of audio broadcasting — but that it contains in itself almost the whole future of audio broadcasting.

In fact, FM was generally viewed as a superior technology to AM. FM eliminates static, has higher fidelity due to the use of wider channels, has a constant effective service area, and allows for closer geographical proximity on the same frequency without interference.

The early optimism notwithstanding, FM did not succeed in supplanting AM during the initial post-war years. In fact, FM's market penetration fell well below expectations. This is especially surprising in light of the fact that, between 1946 and 1948, a large number of broadcasting licenses were issued and a significant number of FM stations went on then air.

Why didn't consumers follow the trend set by broadcasters? One reason is that the US Federal Communications Commission (FCC) shifted the frequencies to be used by FM from those that had been assigned before the war. This created uncertainty on the consumer's side, namely the fear of getting stranded with an obsolete receiver in case the FCC were to change frequencies again. Moreover, the additional cost of an AM/FM receiver was not insignificant (the transistor had yet to be invented). Finally, the FCC policy of allowing "simulcasting" (broadcasting in AM and FM) further reduced the perceived benefit from investing in an FM receiver.

Putting all of these ingredients together, it is not entirely surprising that the industry got stuck to AM. This example of "excess inertia" resulted from a partial chicken-and-egg problem: consumers did not buy FM receivers for fear that other consumers would not adopt and/or the technical features would change in a way that would make their receivers worthless. As a consequence, manufacturers eventually ceased to produce FM receivers and radio stations and for a while reverted back to AM broadcasting.

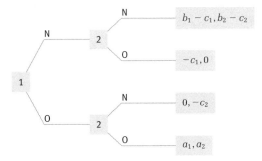

**FIGURE 16.4**
Sequential technology adoption decisions $(a_i, b_i, c_i > 0)$

technology is the quadraphonic sound flop in the 1970s, a case that I describe in greater detail in Box 16.4.

The opposite of excess inertia is — you guessed it — **excess momentum**. Consider the game in Figure 16.4, where I assume that $a_i, b_i, c_i$ are all strictly positive. Player 1 moves first and chooses between an old and a new technology. Upon observing Player 1's choice, Player 2 also chooses between an old and a new technology. Suppose that $b_1$ is greater than, but close to, $a_1$; whereas $b_0$ is greater than, but close to, zero. Then in the subgame perfect Nash equilibrium of this game we observe both players choosing the new technology. In fact, given that Player 1 chooses $N$, Player 2's best choice is $N$ as well, for $b_2 > 0$. Given Player 2's strategy, Player 1's optimal choice is $N$, for $b_1 > a_1$.

Since $b_1 \approx a_1$ and $b_2 \approx 0$, $b_1 + b_2 < a_1 + a_2$. In other words, the equilibrium is "inefficient:" Player 2's loss from the move from $O$ to $N$ is much greater than Player 1's gain. It's a free country, you might say: no one forces Player 2 to choose $N$. Strictly speaking, that is true. However, given strong network effects, Player 2 is, in a sense, forced to go along with Player 1. Player 2 is a victim of a **bandwagon effect**, a common phenomenon when network externalities are strong (the terms **domino effect** or **snowball effect** are also used in this context).

Although the game in Figure 16.4 is rather simple and stylized, the idea is more general: sometimes, preferences are such that society would be better off if no switch to a new technology were to take place, but industry dynamics make the switch inevitable. Software updates are sometimes an example of such excess momentum (the term **forced upgrades** is also used in this context). Many users of Office 95 were quite satisfied with their version of the software. However, when a number of key players adopted Office 97, owners of Office 95 had an incentive to switch to Office 97 for reasons of compatibility. This does not mean that, in the end, these users were made better off. They would probably prefer the initial situation when every user worked with Office 95. However, the new situation (everyone with Office 97) is better than sticking to Office 95 while the rest of the world switches to Office 97. Switching to Office 97 is then the lesser evil, as it were.

> Network externalities may imply *excess inertia*, whereby a new technology is not adopted even though it would be in most people's interest to do so. But network externalities may also imply *excess momentum*, whereby a switch to a new technology occurs even though most people would prefer it not to happen.

■ **PATH DEPENDENCE.**[4]  Standard economics models are a-historical: the equilibrium in a given industry, the value of firms, and so on, are determined by the forces of long-run supply and demand. Yes, there can be other factors that have a transitory effect — a storm, a fad — but sooner or later the forces of supply and demand take the economy back to its equilibrium state. In mathematical terms, we say that the economy is an *ergodic* system: the state of the economy at time $t + k$ does not depend on the state of the economy at time $t$, if $k$ is large enough. In other words, historical events may have an effect, but that effect vanishes as time goes by.

Network externalities provide an interesting challenge to this view of the world. Why did VHS, not Betamax, become the accepted standard for consumer videocassette recorders? Why does Windows, not MacOS, dominate the market for operating systems? More generally, why is English, not Italian, the *lingua franca* of the modern world? In all of these cases, the answer is likely based on the historical process that led to the current equilibrium as opposed to an alternative equilibrium. In other words, there is no clear argument that makes one equilibrium necessarily more compelling than the other one.[e]

To understand the importance of historical events in the development of an industry with network externalities, let us consider a simple model. There are two versions of a new technology, say a videocassette recorder (VCR). The two versions (e.g., Betamax or VHS) are incompatible with each other, so the network externality benefits only accrue to buyers of the same version. The prices of each version are exogenously given; for simplicity, I assume they are the same.

Consumers arrive in the market sequentially; that is, in each period a new consumer must make a decision of which version of the new technology to choose, *A* or *B*. Suppose that each new consumer polls at random three of the past adopters and follows the majority; that is, if three or two of the three previous adopters polled at random chose version x, then the new consumer chooses x as well.

e. Some countries drive on right while others drive on the left. This example, which also features network externalities (if in an extremely dramatic way), suggests that there can be more than one equilibrium.

This situation is depicted on the left panel of Figure 16.5. Three different simulations are shown in dark lines. As can be seen, the market share of a given design converges to either zero or 100%. By contrast, a series of lighter lines in the same panel illustrate the case when there are no network effects: each consumer chooses whatever version he or she prefers, which always gives each version a 50-50 chance of being chosen. By the law of large numbers, each version's market share tends to 50%.

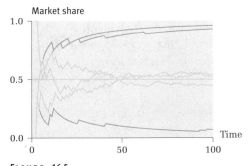

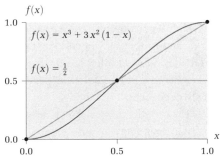

**FIGURE 16.5**
Stochastic dynamics without and with network effects

**STOCHASTIC DYNAMICS: FORMAL ANALYSIS.** Formally, the model I just outlined corresponds to a generalized Polya urn scheme. I keep adding blue or red balls to an urn, one ball at a time. The probability that I add a blue ball is a function $f(x)$ of the fraction $x$ of blue balls currently present in the urn. As the number of balls converges to $\infty$, what happens to the fraction of blue balls in the urn?

The answer is that it depends on the shape of the $f(x)$ function. The right panel of Figure 16.5 plots the functions $f(x)$ corresponding to the two possibilities considered in the left panel. The case when adoption decisions are made independently of previous adopters' decisions corresponds to $f(x) = \frac{1}{2}$, whereas the case when each adopter "polls" three previous adopters corresponds to $f(x) = x^3 + 3x^2(1 - x)$.

It can be shown that, as the number of balls in the urn converges to $\infty$, the fraction of blue balls converges to a **fixed point** of the mapping $f(x)$, that is, a point such that $f(x) = x$.[f] Intuitively, a fixed point is a stable point of the system: a fraction $x$ of the balls are blue, and the likelihood the next ball will be blue is also given by $x$.

If $f(x) = \frac{1}{2}$, then there is only one fixed point: $x = \frac{1}{2}$; it follows that the fraction of blue balls converges to $\frac{1}{2}$. If $f(x) = x^3 + 3x^2(1 - x)$, there are three fixed points: $x = 0, x = \frac{1}{2}$ and $x = 1$. However, for the same reasons that I mentioned in Section 16.1, only $x = 0$ and $x = 1$ are "stable" fixed points; it follows that the fraction of blue balls converges to either 0 or 1.

This model, simple as it is, allows us to derive a number of implications. First, notice that, if network effects are strong (dark lines on the left panel of Figure 16.5), then sooner or later the industry is bound to become locked-in to a given standard.

A second implication is that, in this world, *the best does not always necessarily win.* To understand this, suppose that there are more $A$ fans than there are $B$ fans. In other words, if the sizes of the $A$ and $B$ networks were the same, then more adopters would choose $A$ than $B$. In this context, society would be better off if standard $A$ were chosen. However, it is quite possible that the sequence of events is such that $B$ is the chosen standard.

f. For math aficionados: the fraction of blue balls converges to a fixed point *almost surely*, that is, with probability 1.

This last remark points to a third important characteristic of the model of sequential technology adoption: the eventual outcome, in terms of which design the industry gets locked-in to, will depend on the outcome of a limited, possibly small, number of initial adoptions. In other words, the first consumers' decisions may turn out to be very important *small historical events*. Dynamic processes that have this property are said to be **path dependent**.

The "battle" between Betamax and VHS illustrates several of these points. (See Box 16.3 for a more detailed analysis.) In this industry, the main source of network externalities was that rental store availability of videos for a given format (Betamax,

### Box 16.3 The battle between VHS and Betamax[5]

Sony has a historical reputation of leadership in consumer electronics. It led Japanese producers in the development and marketing of the audiotape recorder and the micro-television, among many other products. The 1974 launch of the Betamax videotape recording system continued Sony's record of technological leadership.

By the mid-1970s, different competing standards of videocassette recording (VCR) were being developed. Its reputation notwithstanding, Sony was aware that it would be unable to set an industry standard by itself. In 1974, seven months before the launch of Betamax, Sony chairman Akio Morita showed his machine to executives from Matsushita, JVC, and RCA, in a effort to get support for the Betamax design. Sony's attitude was that of presenting Betamax as the undisputed standard: "We completed this one, so why don't you follow," he seemed to imply.

Sony's arrogant tone did not go well with its potential partners. When months later Sony invited JVC and Matsushita to inspect the Betamax production facilities, JVC replied that it intended to proceed alone with its VCR development, and so it would be unfair to see any more of Sony's technology. Konosuke Matsushita, in turn, was unhappy he had not been consulted before Sony committed to a design, and decided to withhold his company's participation in Sony's standard. The fact that JVC was (partly) owned by Matsushita also played a role in this decision.

Two years later, JVC introduced the Video Home System (VHS), an incompatible alternative to Sony's Betamax. Sony had the headstart: by the time VHS was introduced, more than 100,000 Betamax machines had already been sold. But the machine JVC introduced in September 1976 was, in some respects, a better product than the Betamax. In particular, its tapes could record two hours, twice as long as the Betamax. In fact, one of the reasons for JVC's refusal to adopt the Betamax standard was precisely the limitation in play time.

Another important difference with respect to Sony is that JVC followed from the start a much more open policy with respect to bringing other firms on board. Says Morita: "We didn't put enough effort into making a family ... The other side, coming later, made a family." By 1984, the VHS group included 40 companies, whereas the Beta group featured only a dozen. A greater "bandwagon" of supporting firms had two effects. First, it gave the VHS standard greater credibility. Second, it induced a faster pace of product improvement at the crucial time when the market was deciding which standard to adopt.

**BOX 16.3 THE BATTLE BETWEEN VHS AND BETAMAX (CONT.)**

Because of its (slight) technological advantage over Betamax, VHS took off at a faster pace than Betamax. By 1980, VHS' share of the installed base was already greater than 50% (see the chart below). In comparison with the installed based in the late 1980s, the numbers in the late 1970s do not amount to much. Thus VHS had the larger share by the late 1970s, but this was a large share of a very small total (less than 10 million adopters).

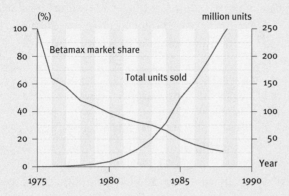

But this advantage proved to be crucial in the 1980s, when sales of VCRs accelerated. In contrast with the 1970s, the consumer in the 1980s used VCRs mainly to watch prerecorded cassettes (mostly movies). This created a snowball effect whereby VHS's initial advantage gradually multiplied, to the point of effectively killing the Betamax standard. As a *Fortune* magazine put it in a 1985 article, "Betamax keeps falling further behind ... As consumers perceive Betamax faltering, they flock in even greater numbers to VHS, worried that those who produce movie cassettes for VCRs might desert Betamax."

In 1988, Sony started production of VHS recorders.

VHS) depended to a great extent on the number of owners of a machine for that format. If there were very few Betamax owners in a given neighborhood, then it was unlikely that a video store would have an interest in stocking tapes recorded in that format. As the model would predict, the industry did indeed get locked-into one of the technologies, VHS. The possibility of an industry getting locked-in to an inferior technology is possibly illustrated by this case: many experts claim that the quality of the Betamax technology was superior to VHS. Finally, the fate of a multibillion dollar industry was decided at a time (late 1970s to early 1980s) when the number of adopters was still relatively small. Their decisions turned out to be important small historical events.

Network externalities may imply multiple potential equilibria, whereby an industry locks into one technology or another. Which technology ends up being chosen depends to a great extent on the actions of early adopters. The eventual winner need not be the superior or most-preferred technology.

## 16.3  FIRM STRATEGY

In Section 16.1, I noted the unstable nature of equilibria when network effects are present: if there are multiple equilibria, switches from good to bad equilibria are always a concern. Consider the example of eBay, whose revenues are collected from listing fees charged to sellers who post their items in the company's website. In 1999, eBay reduced a planned fee increase in response to strong negative reaction from several users. It seems eBay was aware of the danger that a number of its users would "defect" and start selling through rival sites (Amazon.com, Yahoo!, and so on). Such a move might create a "snowball" effect that would end up destroying eBay's competitive advantage of a large installed base of users.[g]

Conversely, a firm whose network is in a "bad" equilibrium (low adoption levels) might use aggressive pricing or other strategies so as to switch to the "good" equilibrium (high adoption levels). Specifically, the owner of a new network might set a low introductory price to get the "snowball" rolling, that is, to get demand past the critical mass and onto the high-adoption equilibrium. The Bell company was one of the first firms to adopt this strategy, shortly after telephones were first introduced in the US in the 1870s. More recently, PayPal actually paid users $10 for opening an account as the online payment network was taking its first steps.

■ **COMPATIBILITY.**  I have mentioned the term **compatibility** several times in this chapter. For example, the reason why Betamex users cared about the number of other Betamax users was that the two designs (Betamax and VHS) were incompatible: Betamax tapes could not be read by VHS machines, and vice-versa. Were the two designs compatible, then a VCR adopter would care about the number of all other VCR adopters, regardless of the particular design.

This example suggests that consumers benefit from compatibility. What about firms? In order to get a better understanding of some of the trade-offs involved in strategic compatibility decisions, let us consider a simple two-stage game. In the first stage, firms decide whether or not to make their technologies compatible. If no agreement is reached, then a "standardization battle" takes place, at the end of which one of the technologies is adopted as a standard. In the second stage, product market competition takes place. If a compatibility agreement was previously reached, then each firms earns duopoly profits $\pi^D$. If no agreement was reached in the previous stage, then whichever firm won the standards battle gets monopoly profits $\pi^M$, whereas the other one gets zero. In which case are firms better off on average: with or without compatibility?

Consider a first possible scenario: the compatibility battle is a battle to attract customers; and in order to do so firms need to spend resources. For example, in the quest to attract customers to its satellite-based digital TV system, in the 1990s UK's BSkyB subsidized customers willing to purchase the decoder required to receive Sky's broadcast signal. Suppose the rules of the game are that the firm that is prepared to spend the most wins the battle. The prize from winning the standards battle is $\pi^M$, the second-stage

g.  At the time, eBay was receiving more than 1.2 million visitors a day, whereas Yahoo! Auctions and Amazon Auctions had only 105,000 and 70,000, respectively.

profit for a standard setter. The standards battle is essentially like an auction: whoever pays the most wins the auction. The result, analogous to Bertrand competition, is that firms will escalate their offers up to the value $\pi^M$. In the end, winning this auction will not produce great satisfaction: the prize $\pi^M$ just compensates the resources spent to get there. Both winner and loser end up with a *net* payoff of zero.[h] No matter how low duopoly profits $\pi^D$ are, firms would be better off if they had reached a compatibility agreement.

Consider now a second possible scenario: the choice of the prevailing standard results from a series of events that firms have no direct control over. For example, consumers happen to like one of the technologies better, start buying it, and the snowball effect described in the previous section does the rest; or, alternatively, a series of government regulations and other policy measures give one of the standards an initial edge which, again, is cemented by self-reinforcing dynamics. For the purpose of the model, suppose that incompatibility implies that each of the technologies is chosen as the industry standard with probability 50%.

What are the equilibrium payoffs now? If firms choose compatibility, then, as before, they end up each getting duopoly profits $\pi^D$. What if they do not agree on making their technologies compatible? Then one of the technologies is chosen as a standard with probability 50% and enjoys monopoly profits $\pi^M$, while the other gets zero. On average, each firm gets 50% $\pi^M$. We conclude that incompatibility is better if and only if 50% $\pi^M$ is greater than $\pi^D$, or simply if $\pi^M > 2\,\pi^D$, a condition that generally holds: it is better to be a monopolist half of the time than a duopolist all of the time.[i] This is especially true if product market competition is very intense, so that $\pi^D$ is much lower than $\pi^M$. In summary, we conclude that:

> If standards competition is very intense, then firms prefer compatibility. If product market competition is very intense, then firms prefer incompatibility.

■ **SPLINTERING.** In my previous description of the compatibility decision, I implicitly assumed that, eventually, one of the two competing designs prevails. This need not be the case. For example, Box 16.4 chronicles the history of the (failed) adoption of quadraphonic sound, where two incompatible standards battled with each other to the point of eliminating the market; that is, instead of selecting one of the competing designs, this standards war ended with two losers, leaving consumers with the (arguably inferior) technology of stereo sound. The main reason for the failure of quadraphonic sound was that consumers became very confused over which standard to choose, thus preferring not to choose any at all.

Some authors refer to this outcome as technology **splintering**.[7] In addition to quadraphonic sound, a possible example is the failed introduction of digital audiotapes. In this case, the two competing technologies were Philips' digital compact cassette and

h. This result is based on the assumption that only the winner pays the bid. This would be the case if the only relevant strategy was the level of adoption subsidies, for example. In practice, an important part of the "bids" are paid regardless of whether the bid is a winning bid. In this case, it is possible that the loser ends up with a negative net payoff.

i. I introduced this condition in Section 15.1, though in a slightly different context.

### BOX 16.4 QUADRAPHONIC SOUND[6]

In the early 1970s, it was the general opinion that the era of stereo sound was coming to an end. Quadraphonic sound — an audio system that records four channels — was considered the next logical development in the industry.

Early studies on quadraphonic sound claimed that up to 80% of the sound perceived by listeners at live concerts is reflected from the walls and ceiling, with the remaining 20% traveling directly from the orchestra to the listener's ears. For this reason, quadraphonic sound allows for a more realistic recreation of the "concert-hall experience" at home.

Two different approaches to quadraphonic sound were developed: the matrix system and the discrete system. The matrix system had the advantage that record production was as simple as the production of stereo records, but suffered from problems in the complete separation of the four channels. The discrete system allowed for a better separation of the four channels, but implied higher production costs and a more complex record player.

In 1971, Columbia Records introduced its quadraphonic system, the SQ, based on the matrix approach. That same year, JVC launched a rival system based on the discreet approach. In January 1972, RCA — Columbia's main rival in record production — announced that it was backing an improved version of JVC's standard. The "quad war" was on.

From the onset, both players were aware there was no room for two incompatible technologies in the market. They were also aware that whichever technology the consumer favored would eventually be adopted. Influencing consumer expectations was therefore an important part of Columbia's and RCA's strategy. This consisted as much of praising the qualities of their own technology as of bashing the rival one. Columbia depicted RCA as a "spoiler" to the establishment of a standard. RCA, in turn, responded that the matrix system was "a Mickey-Mouse approach that only simulates four channels." Columbia countered that its system was already as good as having four separated channels (however, by May, 1973, SQ had already gone through five different generations).

The early market performance of quadraphonic sound was very optimistic. By the beginning of 1974, quad hardware accounted for 25–30% of sales in value, with forecasts as high as 70% by the end of the year. Expert studies predicted that by the end of the 1980s quadraphonic would already had replaced stereo.

This optimism was short-lived, however. Consumers were afraid of getting stranded with the wrong piece of equipment, and the existence of multiple standards confused them. Even though both systems were backward compatible (that is, could play stereo records), matrix and discrete were not compatible with each other (that is, would only get stereo sound from quadraphonic records of a different format). Retailers reflected the customers' uneasiness about quadraphonic, and were thus not keen on pushing the new technology. Beginning in the second half of 1974, disillusionment over quadraphonic sound gradually set in. Despite a final effort by manufacturers to boost sales, stocks of quadraphonic sound equipment continued to pile up.

In 1976, all new products launched in the market were based on stereo. The "quad war" had ended — with no winner.

the Japanese electronics industry's digital audiotape. Both failed to reach any significant degree of market penetration.[j]

Quadraphonic sound and digital audio tapes have one aspect in common: both are new technologies that attempted to replace existing technologies (stereo and analog audiotape, respectively). The fact that consumers had the "easy" option of staying with an inferior but sure technology implied — in both cases — that excess inertia prevailed.[k] In terms of the model above, the existence of a reasonable status quo technology means that the potential costs from a standardization battle are very high — not so much because firms need to spend large amounts of resources (as modeled above) but because the probability that *both* will lose the race is strictly positive.[l]

■ **BACKWARD COMPATIBILITY.**[8] Earlier in this section I discussed the strategic benefits of compatibility of a firm's technology with its rivals'. A related strategic choice is that of compatibility of a firm's technology with previous versions of its technology, a strategy also known as **backward compatibility**. Consider the US handheld video game industry. For a long time, Nintendo was the dominant player, with market shares at or close to 100%. Nintendo's technology evolved over the years: the Game Boy, launched in 1989, gave way to the Game Boy Pocket in 1996, the Game Boy Color in 1998, the Game Boy Advance in 2001, the Game Boy Advance SP in 2003, and the DS in 2004. Some of these product launches were relatively small facelifts (e.g., the Game Boy Advance SP); some marked a new generation in video game technology (e.g., Game Boy Advance).

With the exception of Sony's 2005 introduction of the PlayStation Portable, Nintendo managed to keep competition at bay rather successfully. For example, Nokia's N-Gage, first introduced in 2003, featured a processor that was more than six times faster than the Game Boy Advance SP; but its market share never passed the 1% mark. Although Game Boy was arguably a weaker machine, it was compatible with games

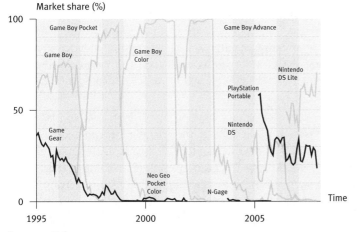

**FIGURE 16.6**

Market shares in the US video game industry, 1985–2008:
Nintendo products (gray lines) and rival products (black lines)

j. I should add that this interpretation of the facts is far from universal. There is a considerable number of authors who believe that the Fundamental Theorem extends to cases when network effects are important: if the market equilibrium is X, then X must be efficient.

k. Compare with the AM vs. FM battle, discussed in Section 16.2, where a similar phenomenon took place.

l. I could then change the model above and assume that, under a scenario of standards competition, the probability that a given firm's standard prevails is $\alpha < 50\%$. If $\alpha$ is sufficiently low, then the same result follows: firms would be better off with compatibility.

developed for older Nintendo machines. As a result, the combination of the Game Boy machine and games was better than the rival's. Other failed challenges to Nintendo's market dominance included Tiger's game.com and SNK's Neo Geo Pocket Color.

In other words, making a new Nintendo platform backwards compatible with Nintendo's previous generation platforms, while preventing rival firms from doing the same, creates a **barrier to entry** (an "applications entry barrier," one might say): backward compatibility increases demand for the new Nintendo platform at the expense of rival platforms.

From Nintendo's point of view, the positive effect of backward compatibility is tempered by a possible negative effect: the incentives for software developers to create new games for the new Nintendo platform are lower, to the extent that users can simply run their existing games.

■ **Two-sided markets and platforms.** The video game example just considered provides a good illustration of a more general phenomenon, namely that of **two-sided markets** or **platforms**. In cases like fax machines, we say there are network effects because the more fax users there are the more users benefit from using fax machines. In the case of video games, it helps to distinguish two different groups: (a) final users and (b) game developers. As in the simple network effects case, we are faced with the potential for a chicken-and-egg situation, but with a twist: consumers are attracted by the abundance of developers and developers are attracted by the abundance of consumers. Specifically, the benefit from owning a gaming platform is a function of hardware quality and, more important, the quality and variety of the games developed for the platform. As to game developers — in particular third-party game developers — their benefit from being associated with a platform is a function of how many users there are: more users means more sales of the games they develop.

From the platform owner's perspective, a good strategy is one that induces the "good" equilibrium, that is, the one that initiates and maintains the "virtuous circle" of users bringing along developers and developers bringing along users. As in the examples of one-sided markets considered earlier, low prices are always a possibility: for example, many game consoles are sold at or below cost (the old razors-and-razor-blades strategy). In platforms, however, a particularly important strategy is providing quality content. For example, many of the apps used by iPhone users were developed by Apple itself, not by third parties.

Within the content-provision strategy, we can find two different variations.[9] If the danger of platform "failure to launch" is significant, then the platform owner may "preempt" content developers by supplying its own content. For example, frequently video game console manufacturers provide first-party games (Microsoft developed Halo for its Xbox 360; Sony developed Gran Turismo for its Playstation 3). If however the platform is safely launched (that is, the danger of a "bad" equilibrium is low), then the platform owner may opt for investments that improve the quality of third-party developers. For example, e-commerce sites provide market information, customer ratings, and search engines that improve buyer and seller experience on their sites.[m]

m. Notice one important difference between these two strategies: in the first case, the platform owner and the developers' effort are substitutes; in the latter case, the platform owner and the sellers' effort levels are complements.

## 16.4 PUBLIC POLICY

Externalities are one of the few instances where economists agree there may be a role for public policy. Does this apply to network externalities as well? If so, what should governments do; that is, how can public policy correct for the externality in question?

Compatibility between different technologies, or **standardization**, implies that the relevant network of consumers is increased, which in turn implies a greater benefit for consumers. In other words, if technology $A$, with $n_A$ users, and technology $B$, with $n_B$ users, become compatible, then an $A$ adopter's value increases from $v(n_A)$ to $v(n_A + n_B)$, where $v(\cdot)$ is the network benefit function. A tantalizing implication is that standardization is a good thing, something that public policy should actively pursue.

Unfortunately, the answer is not so simple. Consider the contrast between Europe and the US in standards setting for second generation mobile telephony. In 1988, the European Parliament established ETSI, the European Telecommunications Standards Institute. Members of ETSI include European telecom operators as well as equipment manufacturers. Although participation in ETSI is voluntary and decisions are not binding, ETSI decisions are normally turned into (binding) European norms by the European Parliament. This process of decision making contributed to a great degree of standardization in European mobile telephony: since the early 1990s, all European countries adhere to the GSM standard, which implies that roaming (using a handset from country A to make calls in country B) was possible across Europe from day one.

No such centralized process exists in the US. As the EU had converged on the GSM common standard, four different standards coexisted in the US market. At an initial stage, this led to an outcome perceived as inferior to Europe, especially because of the limitations it imposed on roaming within the country. However, within a few years each standard's coverage of the US territory was complete or near complete; nowadays, roaming is not an issue in the US (as it was not in Europe from the start). Moreover, within-US standards competition during the 1990s led to sharp reductions in price and to significant technological progress. Arguably, in the end it paid off not to agree on a common standard: when it came to deciding on a standard for third-generation wireless, Europe opted for Qualcomm's CDMA, a technology developed in non-standardized America.[n]

But standardization wars have social costs, too. In the previous section, I mentioned the possibility of technology splintering and eventual demise (e.g., quadraphonic sound). Consider the example of Digital Video Disks (DVDs).[10] In the early 1990s, Sony Corp. and Philips Electronics NV began joint development of a video-on-disk system. Meanwhile, Toshiba Corp. approached the US media conglomerate Time Warner Inc., proposing a rival system. Open warfare started in 1994, with both sides trying to impose their system. Eventually (in December 1995), an agreement was reached on a design, one that drew heavily on the Toshiba-Time Warner design. But in the process, industry squabbling cost producers and consumers a delay of at least 18 months in market introduction. As an IBM manager put it, "competition on a format is not good for the end user or for the companies involved."

n. In addition to innovation, competition also had the benefit of decreasing prices and increasing product variety.

To summarize,

> The benefits from standardization must be weighed against the costs of less competition and product variety.

If deciding whether or not to favor standardization is a difficult question, deciding which technology or standard to favor is an even more difficult one. One interesting — if somewhat extreme — example is driving conventions. For many years, the Swedish norm was to drive on the left. This was considered a sub-optimal equilibrium to the extent that neighbors Norway, Denmark, and Finland all drove on the right. A number of times the issue of switching to the right was discussed and the proposal was either rejected or postponed. Eventually, Sweden did make the switch: Dagen H (day H) was set for September 3, 1967. Before then, it was necessary to reconfigure exit lanes and bus stops; new buses had to be purchased or old ones retrofitted; roads had to be equipped with an extra set of traffic signals and painted lines. On Dagen H itself, all non-essential traffic was banned from 1–6 a.m.. After that, "crazy traffic jams" took place until regular traffic was eventually established.[o]

By many accounts, Dagen H was a fairly costly (and somewhat unpopular) operation; by all accounts, the cost was considerably higher than it would have been had the change taken place decades earlier, as initially proposed. Basically, policy makers are faced with an *information and timing* trade-off: acting too early requires making decisions based on very limited information regarding the relative merits of each standard (is it really worth making the switch?); waiting for too long implies that a switch will be considerably more expensive, as agents will by then have made numerous standard-specific investments (road exits, etc.). What is then the optimal "time window" for government intervention? Is there a window at all?

## SUMMARY

• Network effects may imply multiple demand levels for a given price. Which value takes place depends on consumers' expectations regarding network size. • Network externalities may imply *excess inertia*, whereby a new technology is not adopted even though it would be in most people's interest to do so. But network externalities may also imply *excess momentum*, whereby a switch to a new technology occurs even though most people would prefer it not to happen. • Network externalities may imply multiple potential equilibria, whereby an industry locks into one technology or another. Which technology ends up being chosen depends to a great extent on the actions of early adopters. The eventual winner need not be the superior or most-preferred technology. • If standards competition is very intense, then firms prefer compatibility. If product market competition is very intense, then firms prefer incompatibility. • The benefits from standardization must be weighed against the costs of less competition and product variety.

o.  The number of traffic accidents was actually lower for a few months, perhaps because drivers were trying to be extra careful.

# KEY CONCEPTS

• network externalities • chicken-and-egg • consumer expectations
• fulfilled-expectations equilibrium • critical mass • excess inertia • excess
momentum • bandwagon effect • domino effect • snowball effect • forced upgrades
• path dependent • compatibility • splintering • backward compatibility • barrier
to entry • two-sided markets • platforms • standardization

# REVIEW AND PRACTICE EXERCISES

■ **16.1. B2B.** You have created a business-to-business (B2B) Internet venture directed
at an industry with exactly 50 identical firms. Your services allow these firms to do
business with each other more efficiently as members of your trading network. You plan
to sell access to your service for a price $p$ per member firm. Each firm's benefit from the
service is given by $2n$, where $n$ is the number of other firms joining the B2B network
as a member. So, if 21 firms join your service, each places a value of $2 \times 20$ or 40 on
membership in your network.

Suppose for part (a) that you set the price, $p$, and then firms simultaneously and
independently decide whether or not to join as members.

(a) Show that, for a price greater than zero and lower than 98, there exist exactly
    two Nash equilibria in the simultaneous-move game played by firms deciding
    whether or not to join the network as members.

Suppose for part (b) that you are able to persuade 10 firms to join your network at an
initial stage as "charter members." At a second stage, you set a price for the remaining
40 firms. These 40 firms then simultaneously decide (as in part (a)) whether to join your
network as regular members.

(b) For each price $p$, determine the equilibria of the game played between the
    remaining 40 firms in the second stage.

Finally, consider the same situation as in part (b), but suppose that, when there are multiple Nash equilibria, firms behave conservatively and conjecture that the low-adoption
Nash equilibrium will be played. (Note that, by the definition of Nash equilibrium, this
conjecture is self-fulfilling.)

(c) How much would you be willing to pay (in total to all 10 early adopters) in
    order to persuade the first 10 firms to join the network as charter members?

■ **16.2. SPREADSHEET NETWORK EFFECTS.** Empirical evidence suggests that, between 1986
and 1991, consumers were willing to pay a significant premium for spreadsheets
that were compatible with the Lotus platform, the dominant spreadsheet during that
period.[11] What type of network externalities is this evidence of?

■ **16.3. HOME COMPUTERS.** People are more likely to buy their first home computer in areas where a high fraction of households already own computers or where a large share of their friends and family own computers: a 10% greater penetration in the surrounding city is associated with a 1% higher adoption rate.[12] How can this be explained by network externalities? What alternative explanations are there?

■ **16.4. ATMS.** In the early days of Automated Teller Machines (ATMs), there were very few interbank networks, that is, each bank's network was incompatible with the other banks'. Empirical evidence shows that banks with a larger network of branches adopted ATMs earlier. To what extent can network externalities explain this observation?[13]

■ **16.5. APPLE AND MICROSOFT.** How would you respond to the following quotation:

> Apple Computer, the company that brought you the idiot-friendly Macintosh, is staring at bankruptcy. Meanwhile, the great army of technocrats at Microsoft, which only last year managed to reproduce the look and feel of a 1980's Mac, lumbers on, invincible.
>
> A bad break for Apple? A rare exception to the Darwinian rules in which the best products win the hearts and dollars of consumers?[14]

■ **16.6. EXCESS INERTIA AND EXCESS MOMENTUM.** Explain why the market adoption of a new technology may be too fast or to slow.

■ **16.7. COMPATIBILITY DECISIONS.** Company $A$ has just developed a new technology. Company $B$ approaches Company $A$, stating it has developed its own version of the technology and proposing a compromise that would make the two technologies compatible with each other. What advice would you give Company $A$?

## CHALLENGING EXERCISES

■ **16.8. WIRELESS DEVICE.** You are marketing a new wireless information device (WID). Consumers differ in their willingness to pay for the device. (No one needs more than one.) All consumers value owning a WID more highly, the larger is the total number of consumers using such devices. Denote the expected total number of WID users by $n^e$, which we also can call the "expected size of the WID network."

If all consumers expect the size of the WID network to be $n^e$, and the price of the device is $p$, then the number of users who will want to buy the device (i.e., the total quantity demanded) is given by $n = 100 - p + vn^e$, where $0 < v < 1$. (Note that this is a standard linear relationship between price and unit sales for any given level of expected network size, $n^e$.)

(a) Interpret the parameter $v$. What factors influence $v$?

Suppose that your marginal cost per WID is 20. Suppose also that consumers are quite sophisticated and form accurate expectations about the size of the WID network, for any price $p$ that you might set, so that $n$ must equal $n^e$.

(b) What is the profit-maximizing price of WIDs? How many are sold, and what profits do you earn?

Suppose that you could improve the performance of your WID communications network and thus enhance the network effects, raising $v$ from 1/3 to 1/2.

(c) How much would you pay to develop this enhancement?

■ **16.9. COMPRESS AND SQUEEZE.** Two firms, Compress and Squeeze, offer incompatible software products that encrypt and shrink the size of large data files for safe storage and/or faster transmission. This software category exhibits strong network effects, since users seek to send files to each other, and a file saved in one format cannot be retrieved using the other format. The marginal cost of serving one customer is $40 for either firm.

To keep things simple, suppose that there are only two customers, "Pioneer" and "Follower," and two time periods, "This Year" and "Next Year." As the name suggests, Pioneer moves first, picking one format This Year. Pioneer cannot change her choice once it is made. In contrast, Follower picks Next Year. Follower will be aware of Pioneer's pick when the time comes for Follower to pick. The annual interest rate is 20% for both Compress and Squeeze and Pioneer.

Pioneer regards Compress and Squeeze as equally attractive products. Pioneer values either product at $100 during This Year (before Follower enters the market), and at $100 during Next Year if Follower does not pick the same product. If Follower does pick the same product Next Year, Pioneer's value during Next Year will be $136. (In other words, the network effect is worth $36 to Pioneer.)

Follower has very similar preferences. If Follower picks the same product Next Year as Pioneer did This Year, Follower values that product at $136. Alternatively, if Follower picks a different product Next Year than Pioneer did This Year, the value to Follower of that product will be only $100.

Finally, suppose that Compress and Squeeze simultaneously set prices This Year at which they offer their products to Pioneer. (One could just as well say that they bid for Pioneer's business.) Then Compress and Squeeze simultaneously set prices Next Year at which they will offer their products to Follower.

For simplicity, please assume that Pioneer will pick Compress if Pioneer is just indifferent between Compress and Squeeze, and that Follower will pick the same product as Pioneer if Follower is indifferent between Compress and Squeeze given the values they offer and the prices they charge.

(a) What prices will Compress and Squeeze set Next Year in bidding to win Follower's business if Compress wins Pioneer's business This Year?

(b) What prices will Compress and Squeeze set This Year in bidding to win Pioneer's business?

(c) What product will Pioneer buy, and what product will Follower buy?

(d) What are the resulting payoffs of Compress, Squeeze, Pioneer, and Follower?

(e) Describe in words the advantages of early or late adopters identified in this problem.

(f) How does all of this change if there is rapid technological progress so that costs Next Year are much lower than costs This Year?

(g) How does your analysis change if the (marginal) cost of serving a customer is only $20 rather than $40?

■ **16.10. WALKDVD.** Technological progress (of a sort) has led to the WalkDVD. As the name suggests, this is a miniature DVD player. It is attached to a pair of headphones and special viewing glasses which, together, allow for highly realistic sound and image effects, as well as easy mobility. Three firms, Son, Tosh, and Phil, are planning to launch their WalkDVD players. There are two possible formats to choose from, S and T, and the three competitors have not agreed on which standard to adopt. Son prefers standard S, whereas Tosh prefers standard T. Phil does not have any strong preference other than being compatible with the other firms. Specifically, the payoffs for each player as a function of the standard they adopt and the number of firms that adopt the same standard are given by the table below. For example, the value 200 in the Son row and S2 column means that if Son chooses the S standard and two firms choose the S standard, then Son's payoff is 200.

| Firm | S1 | S2 | S3 | T1 | T2 | T2 |
|------|----|----|----|----|----|----|
| Son  | 100 | 200 | 250 | 40 | 80 | 110 |
| Tosh | 40 | 80 | 110 | 100 | 200 | 250 |
| Phil | 60 | 100 | 120 | 60 | 100 | 120 |

Suppose that all three firms simultaneously choose which standard to adopt.

(a) Show that "all firms choosing S" and "all firms choosing T" are both Nash equilibria of this game.

(b) Determine whether there are any other Nash equilibria in this simultaneous-move game

Son has just acquired a firm that manufactures DVDs for the S format. For all practical purposes, this implies that Son is committed to the S format. It is now up to Tosh and Phil to simultaneously decide which format to choose.

(c) Write down the 2x2 payoff matrix for the game now played by Tosh and Phil. Find the Nash equilibrium of this game.

(d) Do you think Son's move was a good one? How would your answer differ if Phil had a slight preference for the T format (e.g., assume that payoffs for T1, T2, and T3 are 70, 110, and 130, respectively)?

(e) Suppose now that all firms' payoffs are like Phil in the table above. You are Son. If you could choose, would you rather move before Tosh and Phil, or after them? Contrast your answer to what you have learned from the answers to parts (c) and (d).

■ **16.11. AFTER-SALES SERVICE.** Consider the market for a given piece of hardware — a photocopier of brand $x$, for example — that needs after-sale servicing. Suppose that there is free entry into this after-market. Servicing photocopiers implies a fixed cost of $F$ and a marginal cost of $c$ per unit of service provided. Total demand for servicing is given by $D = S(a - p)$, where $p$ is price and $S$ the number of photocopier owners. Finally, suppose that firms in the after-market compete à la Cournot.

(a) Show that consumer surplus (per consumer) in the after-market is given by:

$$U = \frac{1}{2}\left(a - c - \sqrt{\frac{F}{S}}\right)^2$$

an increasing, concave function of $S$. (Hint: apply the results on Cournot competition with free entry derived in Chapter 10. Take into account the fact consumer surplus per consumer is given by $(a - p)^2/2$.)

(b) Relate this result to the discussion of indirect network externalities (at the beginning of the chapter).

## NOTES

1. Cantillon, Estelle, and Pai-Ling Yin (2008), "Competition Between Exchanges: Lessons from the Battle of the Bund," Université Libre de Bruxelles and Stanford University.

2. Data source: GMS Consulting Company and Dataquest. (# adopters after 1990 are estimates).

3. Besen, Stanley M (1992), "AM versus FM: The Battle of the Bands," *Industrial and Corporate Change* **1**, 375–396.

4. Arthur, W Brian (1989), "Competing Technologies, Increasing Returns, and Lock-In by Historical Events," *The Economic Journal* **99**, 116–131.

5. Cusumano, Michael A, Yiorgos Mylonadis, and Richard S Rosenbloom (1992), "Strategic Maneuvering and Mass-Market Dynamic: The Triumph of VHS over Beta," *Business History Review* **66**, 51–94. Nayak, P Ranganath, and John M Ketteringham (1986), *Breakthroughs!*, New York: Rawson Associates; Smith, Lee (1985), "Sony Battles Back," *Fortune*, April 15.

6. Postrel, Steven (1990), "Competing Networks and Proprietary Standards: The Case of Quadraphonic Sound," *Journal of Industrial Economics* **39**, 169–185.

7. Kretschmer, Tobias (2008), "Splintering and Inertia in Network Industries," *Journal of Industrial Economics* **56** (4), 685–706.

8. Claussen, Jörg, Tobias Kretschmer, and Thomas Spengler (2012), "Market Leadership Through Technology — Backward Compatibility in the US Handheld Video Game Industry," CEP Discussion Paper #1124, Centre for Economic Performance, LSE.

9. Hagiu, Andrei, and Daniel Spulber (2013), "First-Party Content and Coordination in Two-Sided Markets," *Management Science* **59** (4), 933–949.

10. Homer, Steve (1998), "Electronics Giants Square Off Over Videodisk Standards," *The Wall Street Journal Europe*, Convergence, Summer.

11. Gandal, Neil (1994), "Hedonic Price Indexes for Spreadsheets and an Empirical Test for Network Externalities," *Rand Journal of Economics* **25**, 160–170.

12. Goolsbee, Austan, and Peter J Klenow (1998), "Evidence on Learning and Network Externalities in the Diffusion of Home Computers," University of Chicago.

13. Saloner, Garth, and Andrea Shepherd (199?), "Adoption of Technologies With Network Effects: An Empirical Examination of the Adoption of Automated Teller Machines," *Rand Journal of Economics* **26**, 479–501.

14. *The New York Times Magazine*, May 5, 1996.

# INDEX